T0364183

The Political Economy of
American Trade Policy

A National Bureau
of Economic Research
Project Report

The Political Economy of American Trade Policy

Edited by   Anne O. Krueger

The University of Chicago Press

Chicago and London

ANNE O. KRUEGER is professor of economics at Stanford University and a research associate of the National Bureau of Economic Research.

The University of Chicago Press, Chicago 60637
The University of Chicago Press, Ltd., London
© 1996 by the National Bureau of Economic Research
All rights reserved. Published 1996
Printed in the United States of America
05 04 03 02 01 00 99 98 97 96   1 2 3 4 5
ISBN: 0-226-45489-4 (cloth)

Library of Congress Cataloging-in-Publication Data

The political economy of American trade policy / edited by Anne O.
    Krueger.
        p.   cm.—(A National Bureau of Economic Research project
    report)
    Includes bibliographical references and index.
    1. United States—Commercial policy—Congresses. 2. Free trade—
United States—Congresses. 3. Protectionism—United States—
Congresses. I. Krueger, Anne O. II. Series.
HF1455.P537 1996
382′.3′0973—dc20   95-21949
                                                                CIP

Relation of the Directors to the
Work and Publications of the
National Bureau of Economic Research

1. The object of the National Bureau of Economic Research is to ascertain and to present to the public important economic facts and their interpretation in a scientific and impartial manner. The board of Directors is charged with the responsibility of ensuring that the work of the National Bureau is carried on in strict conformity with this object.

2. The President of the National Bureau shall submit to the Board of Directors, or to its Executive Committee, for their formal adoption all specific proposals for research to be instituted.

3. No research report shall be published by the National Bureau until the President has sent each member of the Board a notice that a manuscript is recommended for publication and that in the President's opinion it is suitable for publication in accordance with the principles of the National Bureau. Such notification will include an abstract or summary of the manuscript's content and a response form for use by those Directors who desire a copy of the manuscript for review. Each manuscript shall contain a summary drawing attention to the nature and treatment of the problem studied, the character of the data and their utilization in the report, and the main conclusions reached.

4. For each manuscript so submitted, a special committee of the Directors (including Directors Emeriti) shall be appointed by majority agreement of the President and Vice Presidents (or by the Executive Committee in case of inability to decide on the part of the President and Vice Presidents), consisting of three Directors selected as nearly as may be one from each general division of the Board. The names of the special manuscript committee shall be stated to each Director when notice of the proposed publication is submitted to him. It shall be the duty of each member of the special manuscript committee to read the manuscript. If each member of the manuscript committee signifies his approval within thirty days of the transmittal of the manuscript, the report may be published. If at the end of that period any member of the manuscript committee withholds his approval, the President shall then notify each member of the Board, requesting approval or disapproval of publication, and thirty days additional shall be granted for this purpose. The manuscript shall then not be published unless at least a majority of the entire Board who shall have voted on the proposal within the time fixed for the receipt of votes shall have approved.

5. No manuscript may be published, though approved by each member of the special manuscript committee, until forty-five days have elapsed from the transmittal of the report in manuscript form. The interval is allowed for the receipt of any memorandum of dissent or reservation, together with a brief statement of his reasons, that any member may wish to express; and such memorandum of dissent or reservation shall be published with the manuscript if he so desires. Publication does not, however, imply that each member of the Board has read the manuscript, or that either members of the Board in general or the special committee have passed on its validity in every detail.

6. Publications of the National Bureau issued for informational purposes concerning the work of the Bureau and its staff, or issued to inform the public of activities of Bureau staff, and volumes issued as a result of various conferences involving the National Bureau shall contain a specific disclaimer noting that such publication has not passed through the normal review procedures required in this resolution. The Executive Committee of the Board is charged with review of all such publications from time to time to ensure that they do not take on the character of formal research reports of the National Bureau, requiring formal Board approval.

7. Unless otherwise determined by the Board or exempted by the terms of paragraph 6, a copy of this resolution shall be printed in each National Bureau publication.

(Resolution adopted October 25, 1926, as revised through September 30, 1974)

Contents

Acknowledgments

This volume was made possible with the support of many people. Special thanks go to those who gave the benefit of their insights and experience in the Washington meeting of conference participants: William Brock, Anne Brunsdale, Michael Moskow, William Frenzel, and Lloyd Olmer. Martin Feldstein supported the project throughout, contributing in all meetings of participants. Roderick Duncan provided research assistance throughout the project.

The project was financed by a grant from the Ford Foundation. Special thanks go to Seamus O'Clearicain for his support, both in his role as Ford Foundation project officer and in his role as intellectual contributor.

Introduction

Anne O. Krueger

One of the central tenets of economists for the past two centuries has been the proposition that free trade between nations will in most circumstances be highly beneficial, and that any nation which unilaterally adopts a policy of free trade will benefit.[1] Exceptions to the argument for free trade, such as in cases of infant industries and more recently "the new trade theory,"[2] have been recognized, but in most instances, protectionist measures bear little or no relation to those exceptions.

Nonetheless, it has been a source of considerable frustration to most international economists that, in reality, pressure to grant protection to industries often arises in circumstances that appear to bear little resemblance to those cases in which economic analysis suggests it might be warranted on the grounds of national economic interest.

Many economists have therefore turned their attention to attempting to understand the "political economy" of protection, by which is meant the actual

Anne O. Krueger is professor of economics at Stanford University and a research associate of the National Bureau of Economic Research.

1. The recognized exception to this generalization that is relevant for the United States concerns the situation when a country has monopoly power in trade. Even that exception, however, is contingent on the trading partners being unable to retaliate in ways that are sufficiently harmful. There are also arguments that "market failures," such as externalities, might make the adoption of a free trade policy less desirable. Economists' standard answer to that, however, has been to note that the appropriate policy response to these failures is to correct them at their source—e.g., to impose a tax or subsidy to reflect the value of the externality.

2. The "new" trade theory demonstrates that there *may* be circumstances under which an intervention in trade (which might be an export subsidy, an export tax, an import duty, or even an import subsidy) could increase the total economic well-being of a country in circumstances in which the first entrant(s) to an industry become established and receive the economic rents that accrue to first-comers. The basic rationale is that first entrants can achieve sufficient scale of production so that they can simultaneously charge a low enough price to deter other entrants and still have that price significantly above their marginal cost of production.

determinants of which industries receive protection, and of the structure of protection across industries. One line of research has been to develop models of the political process by which protection is determined.

Simultaneously, a number of efforts have been made to estimate empirically the determinants of protection levels (or other trade barriers) for various economic activities. Variables such as the level of employment in the industry, the trend in the industry's employment and profitability, the level of and change in the rate of import penetration, and the geographic concentration of the industry are then used as possible explanatory factors (see Rodrik 1994, 30ff.). In general, almost every variable appeared to have explanatory power in some cases, but no strong systematic pattern has emerged from these analyses.[3]

A large number of questions remain: the assumptions underlying the models of protection determination have not themselves been subject to testing. And, while it has been widely recognized that a variety of factors outside these models may influence protection, little work has been undertaken assessing the relative importance of these factors.

The NBER project on the political economy of American trade policy was designed to try to enrich the understanding of the political economy of trade policy by starting to fill this gap. The intent was to have parallel analytical histories of the process of protection seeking and conferring for a number of American industries. It was hoped that undertaking parallel in-depth analyses of the (economic and political) determinants of protection and its evolution in a number (seven, in the event) of American industries, combined with an examination of the determinants of administered protection across industries, would increase understanding of the processes by which protection and its levels are determined.[4] The expectation was that these analyses of how protection has actually evolved in industries whose circumstances were evidently dissimilar, supplemented by the "cross-section" study of determinants of administered protection, would shed light on the process of protection and its determinants, and perhaps yield richer hypotheses for further analysis.

Questions in the Political Economy of Protection

A starting point for analyzing the political economy of protection must be the basic proposition that, in virtually all circumstances, protection is an economically *inefficient* way of achieving almost any objective. Regardless of whether the objective is the protection of workers in a particular industry or group of industries or the maintenance of productive capacity for national

---

3. See Krueger (1993) for an examination of the structure of U.S. protection and its failure to conform with any of the existing political economy models.
4. "Administered protection" is the term applied to the use of the countervailing duty (against foreign subsidies) and antidumping (against pricing below cost or below sales price in other markets) administrative law by firms seeking relief from import competition.

defense reasons, there are clearly lower-cost ways of achieving those objectives.[5]

A satisfactory theory of the political economy of protection must therefore address the question as to why these lower-cost means are not chosen. However, even prior to that, analysis would need to encompass the determinants of (1) the structure of levels of protection at any particular time (including not only the determinants of why, e.g., apparel is more highly protected than automobiles but also why some industries are not at all protected and why there is much more protection for import-competing industries than for exports); (2) the forms in which protection is granted (quantitative restrictions, export subsidies, tariffs, voluntary export restraints, etc.); (3) changes in the structure of levels and forms of protection over time (which may or may not be the same as items 1 and 2 depending on whether "history matters"), and (4) changes in the overall levels of protection over time.

The first item, the structure of levels, refers to the tariff equivalents of various interventions with trade. It can be thought of as a vector, each component of which represents the extent to which domestic price of a commodity exceeds (or, in the case of an export tax, falls short of) its foreign price (over and above transport costs in the relevant direction) by virtue of interventions with trade. This is the traditional focus of concern of international economists.

In recent years, most theoretical work on the political economy of protection has addressed this issue (see the recent surveys by Hillman 1989 and Rodrik 1994). Models have been developed in which tariffs are determined by the relative strength of interest groups (see Findlay and Wellisz 1982), by the need of politicians to please the general public but also to obtain funds for seeking support or reelection (Magee, Brock, and Young 1989; Grossman and Helpman 1994), and by the median voter (Mayer 1984). A few models have even attempted to address the question as to why (in virtually all countries) interventions with trade are heavily biased against trade rather than in favor of exports (see, e.g., Krueger 1990; Fernandez and Rodrik 1991).

The second question, the determinants of the forms of protection, is also important for understanding. Why do we observe the United States negotiating "voluntary export restraints" with Japan on automobiles, steel, and other products, rather than itself enforcing import quotas (and thus giving the difference between the Japanese price and the U.S. price to Americans, rather than to Japanese producers)? Why did the sugar lobby for years oppose the transformation of sugar import quotas into deficiency payments which would have given sugar producers the same price as they received under the quota system?

---

5. In the case of employment levels, lower-cost ways include subsidization of employment in the industry and adjustment assistance to workers. For national defense purposes, production subsidies for the stipulated level of productive capacity (and sometimes even stockpiling the good in question) can achieve the same objective and simultaneously provide an overall higher level of welfare.

Here, less work has been done, although papers by Hillman (1990) and Feenstra and Lewis (1991) have addressed this issue.

It is quite possible, of course, that the determinants of the structure of protective levels are invariant with respect to time. However, it is also a plausible hypothesis that there are laws of motion with respect to protection, once granted, so that, once protection is accorded an industry, it is easier to obtain a higher level of protection (for a given situation of the industry) at a later date than it would be if there were no preexisting protection. In a sense, protection may be like other "entitlements": something that once received is taken as a given and for which only increments matter politically.

Finally, there are questions as to the determinants of the overall level of protection. Relatively more research has been undertaken on this question (again see Rodrik 1994 for a recent survey). It is widely recognized that U.S. trade policy in the 1950s and 1960s was close in many dimensions to free trade. By the 1980s, policy had shifted further from free trade, and in that sense, the vector of protective rates had changed. A number of hypotheses have been put forth in the literature: clearly, a higher rate of unemployment leads to more pressures for protection across the board (although possibly with differential increases in pressures across industries); likewise, real appreciation of the dollar leads to more difficulties for tradable industries and as such leads to more pressures for protection.

Questions for the NBER Project

Especially for economists, there are many aspects of the political process that are not well understood. While, quite clearly, variables such as industry profitability (or lack thereof), unemployment, and size of industry all matter, there are aspects of the political process that matter as well. The NBER project on the political economy of American trade protection was designed to explore these political phenomena, and their interactions with economic variables. As such, questions arise concerning the role of institutional constraints, lobbies and effective organization, determinants of power and influence, and the factors influencing politicians' decisions.

These are sufficiently unfamiliar ground that it was decided to try to "go to the facts" and examine the level, form, and evolution of protection in several industries, in the expectation that analytical histories and analysis would throw up hypotheses deserving of further exploration in future research.

It was not hoped that analyses of the evolution of protection for individual industries, no matter how well done, would provide definitive evidence in support of a particular theory of protection. However, it was expect that the results would be highly suggestive of new hypotheses and lines of research that may not have emerged from other research approaches.

In the remainder of this introduction, the overall design of the project is briefly explained, including a description of the industries covered in the project. Thereafter, the individual studies are presented. Each such study is an important contribution in its own right to understanding of the political economy of protection and, in addition, provides evidence regarding the more general questions raised above. A final chapter then sets forth the systematic patterns that appear to emerge, as well as the hypotheses and findings that appear to be promising for future research.

Structure of the Project

At the outset, the project was conceived as a new approach to the political economy questions raised above. A brief outline of the results of previous political economy studies, along with the plans for the project, were then sent to potential participants in the project.

On the basis of that paper, an initial meeting of participants was held in the spring of 1993, at which the research agenda was discussed and authors spoke on their plans for research for their industry. It was clear that each author would need to undertake a separate research strategy, depending on the nature of the industry subject to analysis, as well as on the state of existing knowledge. Thus, no central "research design" applicable to all studies was planned. Authors were asked to determine for the activity they were studying what the most meaningful time period for analysis would be: as can be seen in the individual studies, it varies greatly from one study to another, ranging all the way from Orden's focus on the relatively short period during which the North American Free Trade Agreement was subject to negotiation and congressional debate to Finger and Harrison's coverage of the evolution of the Multi-Fiber Arrangement from the 1950s to the 1990s.

Authors were asked to provide an analytical history of the determinants of protection—both its form and its height—and then to consider how and why protection changed over time. They were asked, among other things, to examine who supported and who opposed protection, who gained and who lost. Readers will find matrices of winners and losers mapped against initial supporters, initial opponents, and those who were inactive. As can be seen in each of the following chapters, what the authors have come up with is rich in insights as to the phenomena that enter into decisions regarding forms and levels of intervention with trade.

Because focus on the politics of trade-related decisions is relatively new, a consensus emerged at the spring 1993 meeting that it would be very useful to hold a session for discussion with people who had held key policy-making roles in the trade policy process. People who had recently been or were in key roles in the trade community were then invited to come and talk with, and field questions from, the authors regarding the particulars of protection and also more general issues. A two-day session was then arranged in Washington in early July, in which the "witnesses" spoke informally with participants in the project. The people who gave some of their valuable time to the project in that

connection included the Honorable William Brock, former U.S. trade representative; Commissioner Anne Brunsdale of the International Trade Commission;
the Honorable William Frenzel, former congressman and member of the House
Ways and Means Committee; Michael Moskow, former deputy U.S. trade representative; and Lloyd Olmer, former under secretary of commerce and international trade.

All of these persons were invited, and some were able also to participate
in the February 1994 conference described below (and their contributions as
discussants are reproduced in what follows). All of the individual industry
studies, as well as the hypotheses raised in the final chapter, were greatly en-
riched by the contribution of these individuals, to whom the quality of the
volume owes much.

Once authors had completed their studies, a conference was held in February
1993, in which the papers were presented and discussed.[6] In light of those
discussions, papers were revised and constitute the next eight chapters of this
volume.[7]

Industries Covered in the Project

Choice of industries to be included was dictated by several considerations.
First, it was desirable that there be a variety of industries, with different situa-
tions. Second, it seemed important to include industries that had sought different forms of protection. Third, it was thought that the mix of industries covered
should include at least one industry with each of the following characteristics:
an industry with high political visibility, a relatively obscure industry, at least
one producer of final goods for the consumer market, and at least one that
produces producer goods. Fourth, it was essential to locate first-rate researchers knowledgeable about the industries in question who could provide their
"human capital" to the project.

Given the constraints on the total number of studies and these three considerations, it was finally decided that there should be seven industry studies and
one study of process (administered protection). Among the seven industry
studies, two should focus on various aspects of agricultural protection, and five
on industrial. Among the industries, it was desirable to include an older industry long subject to protection (textiles and apparel), a newer high-tech industry
(semiconductors), industries in which voluntary export restraints (VERs) had

6. At that conference, there was a panel discussion among those of the policymakers who were
able to attend, which was also invaluable. Although an effort was made to record that discussion
in a format appropriate for reproduction in this volume, it was, regrettably, unsuccessful. For most
authors, it was one of the highlights of the conference.

7. After the chapters included in this volume were completed, the authors prepared shorter
versions, which were presented at a conference held in Washington in September 1994, in order
to provide the policymakers and analysts there with an overview of the project results.

been negotiated (automobiles and steel), and a small industry (lumber). A brief overview of each of these industries may help the reader in approaching the individual studies. A final study was sought to analyze how one mechanism for protection—administered protection through antidumping and countervailing duties—actually operates. Since this protection is provided under a quasi-legal process, it appeared important to examine the extent to which even these processes are influenced by political and economic factors.

Steel and automobiles, by contrast, are industries in which U.S. firms held dominant positions worldwide until at least the early 1970s. Since that time, both industries have lost their preeminent positions, imports have increased, and both have sought protection. Both are highly visible industries but neither is "labor intensive," and both are reasonably geographically concentrated. Protection for automobiles came in the form of "voluntary export restraints" on imports from Japan for a period of time in the early and mid-1980s—there had been pressures earlier, and yet it was not until then that VERs were adopted, and they were later abandoned. Douglas Nelson traces the protection for automobiles under the VER agreed to by Japan in the early 1980s until the abandonment of VERs several years later. In the case of automobiles, it was apparently the fear that congressional action would result in even more restrictive and protective arrangements for automobiles that led the U.S. administration to accept a VER arrangement.

Michael Moore undertook the steel study. Protection for steel under VERs and other administrative arrangements was accorded for much of the 1970s and 1980s after the industry filed a large number of complaints alleging unfair trade practices on the part of foreign producers. These pending cases were then used as a bargaining instrument in negotiating export restraints with foreign governments. By the end of the 1980s, however, the steel industry's ability to achieve protection through this means was greatly diminished.

The semiconductor industry, by contrast, is much smaller and is also a "new" industry. It is certainly not labor intensive, and it is reasonably geographically concentrated. In his study, Douglas Irwin traces the initial development of the industry in the 1960s and 1970s. American firms were world leaders and initially dominated the industry, but by the late 1970s, the preeminence of these firms was being challenged by successful Japanese entry into the market. Starting in the early 1980s, the industry sought protection, which it finally achieved—at least in part—in the Semiconductor Agreement of 1986, and subsequent agreements, negotiated with Japan. The political economy of that agreement is interesting in many regards, not the least of which is Irwin's account of the extent to which the industry's goals (and, at one point, the goals of a single firm) became the U.S. government's negotiating position. The semiconductor industry is also interesting because of the important third-country effects that impaired the ability of the United States to deal bilaterally on a trade issue. Not only did the Europeans protest the U.S.-negotiated deal under which Japanese firms were not to export below prices set in the agreement, but the higher prices which followed the agreement were clearly a factor in supporting Korean entry into the semiconductor industry.

Interestingly, these three industries were protected through bilateral arrangements made between U.S. and foreign governments. As can be seen in the individual studies, the U.S. administration (and the foreign government) was frequently reluctant to enter into such protective arrangements but did so in the belief that failure to undertake these measures would spur administered protection or congressional action that might be even more protective of the industry.

Textiles and apparel represent an industry whose fortunes have been declining since the early part of the twentieth century, and in which pressures for protection have been intense since the mid-1950s. Many parts of the industry are relatively labor intensive, and it is geographically widespread, although its political power is based in the South. Protection began in the mid-1950s, when the United States negotiated a Short Term Arrangement covering cotton products with Japan (on the rationale that because of agricultural policies in the United States, Japanese producers could obtain needed cotton from the United States more cheaply than could U.S. producers), but then went to longer-term agreements at first covering cotton products only and then extending to other products and other countries. European countries also began protecting their textiles and apparel, and finally, in an effort to bring some discipline to bear on these bilateral quantitative restrictions, protection has been granted the industry under the Multi-Fiber Arrangement (MFA), an increasingly complex set of quantitative restrictions on imports negotiated by individual product category under an umbrella arrangement concluded under the auspices of the General Agreement on Tariffs and Trade.[8] Michael Finger and Ann Harrison explore the ways in which the industry sought, and received, protection and how it became modified over time. In the case of the MFA, Finger and Harrison report estimates that protection for textiles and apparel accounted for more than 80 percent of the entire economic cost of U.S. protection as of the late 1980s.

The U.S. lumber industry represents yet another situation. As Joseph Kalt points out, the industry is relatively small and geographically concentrated. It certainly does not have the visibility of textiles and apparel, automobiles, steel, or even semiconductors. Nonetheless, since the early 1980s, the U.S. lumber industry has also sought protection against Canadian imports through the administered protection process. In the eyes of many U.S. trading partners and economists, administered protection under U.S. trade laws has become the "protectionist weapon of choice." As such, inclusion of an industry whose primary approach to the protection process was through the use of "fair trade laws" seemed highly desirable in the project.

8. Under the Uruguay Round agreement, the MFA is to be phased out over a 12-year period.

There are two industry studies which focus on agriculture, where the mechanisms and instruments used for protection are quite different than those for American industry. Bruce Gardner's study focuses on wheat, and the emergence of the Export Enhancement Program (EEP) under which wheat farmers pressured for subsidies to be given for U.S. exports of wheat. Wheat has long been a major grain crop in the midwestern part of the United States, is grown by relatively numerous producers, and is a crop in which the United States is generally believed to have considerable comparative advantage. Facing declining exports due to appreciation of the dollar, European subsidies, and unsustainable domestic price supports, an EEP was implemented for wheat, under which American wheat farmers in effect received "protection" for their exports during the 1980s. It was started when farm incomes had been badly hit by a combination of factors including the disinflation of the early 1980s and the real appreciation of the U.S. dollar. Once in place, EEP was extended despite the disappearance of the initial circumstances which had resulted in the pressure for its enactment.

The other agricultural study, by David Orden, examines the roles and fortunes of various agricultural groups in the negotiations leading up to the North American Free Trade Agreement (NAFTA). Agriculture comprises many diverse sectors: some sectors—such as wheat—are exporters and will benefit from reduced protection at home and abroad; other sectors—such as sugar—are protected from import competition. In the negotiations, these interests competed within the broader framework of other aspects of the NAFTA. Some agricultural export producers were considerably more effective than others at gaining access to the Mexican market. Likewise, the effectiveness of import-competing sectors at delaying or reducing the rate at which trade with Mexico would be freed from restraints varied. Orden's analysis of who was influential, and why, sheds further light on the determinants of protection.

The final study focuses on administered protection seen from a different perspective. Critics of U.S. administered protection have suggested that the process not only provides protection in cases where dumping or subsidies do occur but even gives U.S. producers protection in that the processes are biased against foreign importers and the threat of being hit with an antidumping or subsidies suit is itself a deterrent to foreign importers. Staiger and Wolak study this phenomenon, with findings that are important in their own right and simultaneously provide insight from yet another angle into the understanding of the overall political economy of protection. As can be seen from their results, despite the legal constraints on the process of protection, it would appear that factors other than the criteria laid down by law influence the outcome of these deliberations.

Each of these studies alone is of interest. But, together, they also shed additional light on the political economy of U.S. trade policies. The final chapter therefore summarizes some of the important findings and questions that arise from analysis of the individual studies.

References

Feenstra, R. C., and Lewis, T. R. 1991. Distributing the gains from trade with incomplete information. *Economics and Politics* 3 (1): 21–40.

Fernandez, R., and Rodrik, Dani. 1991. Resistance to reform: Status-quo bias in the presence of individual-specific uncertainty. *American Economic Review* 81 (5): 1146–55.

Findlay, Ronald, and Wellisz, Stanislaw. 1982. Endogenous tariffs, the political economy of trade restrictions, and welfare. In *Import competition and response,* ed. Jagdish N. Bhagwati. Chicago: University of Chicago Press.

Grossman, Gene, and Helpman, Elhanan. 1994. Protection for sale. *American Economic Review* 84 (4): 833–50.

Hillman, Ayre. 1989. *The political economy of protection.* Chur, Switzerland: Harwood.

———. 1990. Protectionist policy as the regulation of international industry. *Public Choice* 67: 101–10.

Krueger, Anne O. 1990. Asymmetries in policy between exportables and import-competing goods. In *The political economy of international trade,* ed. Ronald W. Jones and Anne O. Krueger. Cambridge: Blackwell.

———. 1993. The political economy of U.S. protection in theory and in practice. In *Trade, welfare and economic policies,* ed. Horst Herberg and Ngo Van Long, 215–36. Ann Arbor: University of Michigan Press.

Magee, Steven, William A. Brock, and Leslie Young. 1989. *Black hole tariffs and endogenous policy theory.* Cambridge: Cambridge University Press.

Mayer, T. 1984. Endogenous tariff formation. *American Economic Review* 74 (5): 970–85.

Rodrik, Dani. 1994. What does the political economy literature on trade policy (not) tell us that we ought to know? NBER Working Paper no. 4870. Cambridge, Mass.: National Bureau of Economic Research, September.

1   Trade Politics and the Semiconductor Industry

Douglas A. Irwin

1.1   Introduction

On March 27, 1987, President Ronald Reagan announced that prohibitive (100 percent) tariffs would be imposed on $300 million worth of imports from Japan. This unilateral retaliatory action—the largest and the first such action against this U.S. ally in the postwar period—arose from the Reagan administration's determination that Japan had violated a 1986 bilateral agreement on international trade in semiconductors. More than any single event, this action dramatized the seriousness with which the U.S. government viewed the semiconductor agreement, which in turn reflected how important the government regarded the interests of U.S. semiconductor producers.

Indeed, the very existence of a semiconductor trade agreement was testimony to the U.S. industry's success in getting the government to act on its behalf in its dispute with Japan. Few industries ever receive the sustained, high-level attention needed to result in the negotiation of a governmental agreement on trade in just one sector. Such a sectoral agreement is attractive from the perspective of virtually any import-competing industry because it virtually guarantees the institutionalization of trade policy for that industry. In the case of semiconductors, getting such special treatment in the first place was more difficult than perpetuating it: once the agreement was on paper, the policy debate within the U.S. government was essentially over. The government, including those agencies that may have originally opposed the

Douglas A. Irwin is associate professor of business economics at the Graduate School of Business of the University of Chicago. He served on the staff of the Council of Economic Advisers during 1986–87.

The Lynde and Harry Bradley Foundation provided financial support for this work through a grant to the Center for the Study of the Economy and the State at the University of Chicago. The author is greatly indebted to Steve Husted and Tom Dorsey for invaluable discussions and generous assistance. He thanks Peter Klenow and Anne Krueger for helpful comments.

agreement, then had a direct stake in its enforcement, lest the credibility of such foreign commitments be undermined. Once the agreement was in place, it required monitoring and at some point renewal or renegotiation. This provided a natural rationale for ongoing contacts between the industry and the government, providing the industry with easy access to key policymakers and allowing close industry-government ties to develop.

The semiconductor industry's success on these dimensions did not prevent the 1986 accord with Japan from arguably representing the most controversial U.S. trade policy action of that decade. In this agreement, the government of Japan agreed to end the "dumping" of semiconductors in the United States and in other markets and to help secure 20 percent of the Japanese semiconductor market for foreign producers within five years. The antidumping provisions—resulting in part from the extraordinary self-initiation of an antidumping action by the U.S. government against Japan—later proved to be in partial violation of the General Agreement of Tariffs and Trade (GATT) and drew the ire of prominent high-technology semiconductor-using industries, particularly computer systems manufacturers. Computer producers formed a countervailing interest group to oppose these provisions and eventually forced them to be dropped in the 1991 renegotiation of the agreement.

The 20 percent market share provision—an exceptional request from the standpoint of traditional U.S. trade policy—was the negotiated solution to the problem of market access in Japan based on circumstantial evidence that the market was closed to foreign semiconductor producers.[1] This provision proved successful in that foreign producers achieved a 20.2 percent market share in Japan in the fourth quarter of 1992, although the share fluctuated subsequently. But by concentrating on specific, quantitative "results" and "outcomes" rather than the principle of market access, the provision provoked sharp debate: it was either heralded as a positive, concrete step toward gaining greater sales in Japan ("making the cash registers ring," as it was commonly put) or scorned as a step toward cartelized "managed trade" and export protectionism via government-fixed market shares. Despite this controversy, the provision has survived as a part of U.S. trade policy toward semiconductors, having been supported and perpetuated by three different U.S. trade representatives (USTRs—Clayton Yeutter, Carla Hills, and Mickey Kantor) serving under three different presidential administrations, the most recent of which promised to expand the concept of import targets with Japan to other sectors. (See table 1.1 for a chronology of the trade dispute.)

This chapter examines how the U.S. semiconductor industry became the beneficiary of this unprecedented sectoral trade agreement by analyzing the

1. The theory of commercial policy now includes this new instrument of trade policy in its analysis: Jagdish Bhagwati has dubbed such market share targets as "voluntary import expansions" (VIEs), the import counterpart to voluntary export restraints (VERs). See the analysis and critique of import targets in Irwin (1994).

Table 1.1	Chronology of the U.S.-Japan Semiconductor Trade Dispute
1977	Semicondutor Industry Association (SIA) formed
1981–82	Cyclical downturn in the semiconductor industry
	Japan achieves domination of the DRAM market
	SIA first approaches U.S. government about trade relief
1982–83	U.S.-Japan High Technology Working Group negotiations
1985	Cyclical downturn in the semiconductor industry
	U.S.-Japan agree to eliminate tariffs on semiconductors
	SIA files section 301 petition alleging import barriers in Japan
	Micron files antidumping petition on 65K DRAMs
	President Reagan delivers "fair trade" speech; USTR begins self-initiating section 301 cases
	Intel, AMD, and National Semiconductor file antidumping petition on EPROMs
	Commerce Department initiates antidumping investigation on 256K + DRAMs
1986	ITC issues affirmative "material injury" final ruling in 64K DRAM case
	U.S.-Japan reach a semiconductor trade agreement, preventing dumping and improving market access in Japan
1987	U.S. retaliates against Japan for noncompliance with the agreement
1988	DRAM prices soar in the United States as computer demand recovers
1989	Computer Systems Policy Project (CSPP) founded by semiconductor users IBM, Tandem, and Hewlett-Packard to oppose the agreement
1991	U.S.-Japan renegotiate 1986 agreement, removing antidumping provisions and formalizing 20 percent market share target
1992	Foreign share of Japan's semiconductor market breaks 20 percent in the fourth quarter

political and economic forces leading up to the 1986 accord and shaping subsequent events. The primary purpose is to understand how various groups—firms in the U.S. semiconductor industry, agencies within the U.S. government, and domestic semiconductor-using industries—interacted in the political realm in the determination of policy. To this end, I shall address how the economic structure of the industry and the legal framework of U.S. trade institutions shaped the opportunities of and the constraints on the industry and policymakers, and hence helped determine the observed outcomes. Particular attention will be devoted to how the political process functioned in the semiconductor case, with its unusual amalgamation of antidumping and market-opening actions which have been both celebrated and vilified. Furthermore, much of the interesting politics and negotiations behind U.S. semiconductor trade policy was not between the industry and the government as monolithic actors, but between factions *within* the industry and *within* the government. Although such maneuverings are often hidden from the public record, I shall attempt to shed some light on the consensus-building process within the industry and the government that ultimately led to the 1986 agreement and the willingness of the Reagan administration to impose high tariffs against a large foreign ally.

1.2   Organization of the U.S. Semiconductor Industry

Semiconductors are a key microelectronic component used in a multitude of goods ranging from televisions and microwave ovens, aircraft and automobiles, computers and calculators, to telephones and watches. The origins of the semiconductor industry date from 1947 when Bell Labs developed the first transistor and from 1959 with the invention of the integrated circuit. Integrated circuits, in which increasing numbers (at first hundreds, then thousands, and now millions) of transistors are etched onto a thin wafer of silicon, quickly became the building block of the industry. Propelled by the demands for such circuits by the military and space programs, which generated sizeable revenues to be plowed back into research and development (R&D) expenditures, the U.S. semiconductor industry grew rapidly in the 1960s. Rapid growth and technological change continued in the 1970s and 1980s with the proliferation of commercial applications for semiconductors, particularly in computers, telecommunications, and consumer electronics.[2]

The rapid growth experienced by the U.S. industry is illustrated in table 1.2, which indicates that the nominal value of shipments grew at a 15.7 percent average annual rate from 1975 to 1991, an average that masks negligible growth in 1981–82 and 1989–90 and a 17.5 percent contraction in 1984–86.[3] By contrast, overall industrial production in manufacturing increased only by an average 4.5 percent annually over the same period. Competition among semiconductor producers is marked by rapid technological change and continual product innovation driven by the devotion of substantial resources to R&D. In 1989, for example, the U.S. electronic components industry spent 8.3 percent of net sales on R&D, compared with 3.1 percent for U.S. industry overall.[4] These R&D investment expenditures reflect firms anticipating production in the next generation of semiconductors and result in relatively short product life cycles.

Semiconductors are often divided into three broad product categories, discrete devices (basic transistors), optoelectronic devices (light-sensitive chips), and—by far the largest category—integrated circuits. Integrated circuits accounted for over 80 percent of U.S. semiconductor consumption in 1985 and include several different types of products, including logic chips (for arithmetic and decision-making functions), microprocessors (the central processing

2. As demand shifted away from military applications toward new consumer electronics (often produced outside of the United States), foreign firms began to enter the market and the position of U.S. semiconductor producers began to erode gradually in the 1970s. Military demands accounted for roughly half of U.S. semiconductor shipments in the early 1960s but dropped to 10 percent by 1981.

3. The undeflated average growth rate severely understates real output growth because semiconductor prices have experienced secular declines. See fig. 1.1.

4. Electronic components (SIC 367) is a broader industry aggregate than semiconductors (SIC 3674). When federal funds are included, the industry spent 9.3 percent of net sales (National Science Foundation, *Research and Development in Industry, 1989,* NSF 92–307 [Washington, D.C.: Government Printing Office, 1992], Detailed Tables, 77).

Table 1.2   **Selected Economic Indicators of the U.S. Semiconductor Industry**

Year	Value of Shipments (billion $)	Total Employees	Production Workers	Payroll per Employee ($)	New Capital Expenditures (million $)	Exports (billion $)	Imports (billion $)
1975	3.277	96,700	52,400	12,414	282.9	n.a.	n.a.
1976	4.474	102,500	57,900	13,377	362.3	n.a.	n.a.
1977	5.323	114,000	63,500	14,044	409.0	n.a.	n.a.
1978	6.435	130,800	73,600	14,517	636.9	1.785	1.661
1979	8.267	142,900	81,100	15,741	850.5	2.521	2.351
1980	10.501	160,700	87,300	18,268	1,595.8	3.347	3.157
1981	11.702	169,500	84,900	20,088	1,493.1	3.873	3.189
1982	12.430	166,500	81,300	22,732	1,723.8	4.579	3.434
1983	14.339	169,300	84,100	25,322	1,831.6	5.589	4.171
1984	19.135	192,300	96,100	27,124	2,817.6	7.846	5.531
1985	16.487	190,400	91,800	26,346	2,831.7	5.596	4.411
1986	15.785	172,900	79,200	28,728	2,220.2	5.939	5.054
1987	19.795	184,600	87,400	29,766	1,920.8	7.783	6.559
1988	22.597	179,400	86,500	32,884	2,680.9	10.963	9.035
1989	25.708	184,000	90,500	34,316	3,132.0	12.329	12.745
1990	25.977	181,800	87,700	35,382	3,439.3	12.169	13.324
1991	29.668	175,000	86,200	37,090	2,945.0	13.083	14.348

Source: U.S. Department of Commerce, Bureau of the Census, *Annual Survey of Manufacturers* (Washington, D.C.: Government Printing Office, various years).

Note: Data are for SIC code 3674, semiconductors and related devices. Export and import figures are from unpublished census data on U.S. trade by SIC code. They are affected, however, by the off-shore assembly provisions of the U.S tariff code and by the substantial trade in components.

unit in computers), and various application-specific integrated circuits (configured for particular user needs). Even within these categories semiconductors perform quite different functions and are generally imperfect substitutes for one another, with specific devices often filling small market niches. Amid this product variety, technological progress tends to be incremental, and specific product generations are not clearly defined.

Much of the intense international competition and consequent trade dispute in the 1980s, however, centered on a unique set of digital integrated circuits—memory chips—which are primarily used in computers to store and retrieve data in various forms.[5] Memory chips accounted for 18 percent of all U.S. semiconductor purchases in 1985. DRAMs, the largest volume of all semiconductor products, constituted 7 percent of the total market and EPROMs another 3 percent (see Federal Interagency Staff Working Group 1987, 5). Within the several categories of memory chips, the market approximates perfect competi-

5. Random-access memories (RAMs) temporarily store data or information; dynamic random-access memories (DRAMs) are designed to store large amounts of data, while static random-access memories (SRAMs) are faster but hold less information. Read-only memories (ROMs) store data more permanently than RAMs; erasable programmable read-only memories (EPROMs) allow data programs to be easily erased and reprogrammed.

tion: DRAMs, for instance, are a standardized product and are almost perfectly interchangeable regardless of which firm produces them. In addition to product homogeneity, DRAMs are marked by well-defined generations that give rise to distinct product cycles. In 1970, the 1K RAM chip (capable of storing 1,024 bits of information) was introduced. This was followed by the 4K chip in 1973, 16K in 1976, 64K in 1979, 256K in 1982, 1M in 1985, 4M in 1989, and 16M in 1991. A key industry transition occurs when the cost per bit becomes equivalent for adjacent generations of chips. For example, in 1978 price per bit equivalency was achieved between 4K and 16K chips, accelerating the demise of 4K demand, and hence the value of investments specific to the production of 4K chips, and the assent of 16K demand. Firms unprepared for such transitions could see their sales evaporate in the space of months.

Such rapid product cycles imply that firms have a relatively short period in which to earn sufficient profits to recover their generation-specific R&D and capital investments. The riskiness of having a relatively short horizon in which to recover the earlier R&D and up-front capital expenditures is compounded by low marginal costs of production (the actual material and labor costs of manufacturing semiconductors are quite small), which leads to the temptation during periods of weak demand to undercut the price of rivals and thereby undermine industry profitability. Both the large fixed costs (in the form of R&D and capital expenditures) and learning by doing imply that only a few firms can survive in the memory chip segment of the industry.[6] Continuous innovations in high technologies offset this tendency and allow small start-up or spin-off firms to enter the semiconductor market and possibly experience rapid growth (though the failure rate is high).

These distinctive aspects of the semiconductor industry give most firms an interest in obtaining certain government policies to reduce risks in the sector: more favorable tax treatment for R&D, relaxed antitrust restrictions on joint research ventures, greater patent protection for chip designs and innovations, and so forth. These common interests were behind the formation of an industry association in 1977. Perhaps the strongest impetus for an industry group, however, arose from the entry of Japanese semiconductor producers in the late 1970s. This new competition shocked the U.S. industry and provided a common external threat that motivated the start of concerted political action. Before discussing Japanese competition in more detail in the next section, some additional economic features of the U.S. semiconductor industry that bear upon its entry into the political market require analysis.

In *The Logic of Collective Action* (1971), Mancur Olson pointed to economic size and concentration (both geographic and economic) as key determi-

---

6. Firm-specific learning by doing, wherein past production experience provides valuable information that allows firms to reduce their cost of production, generates dynamic economies of scale in that firms that have large (cumulative) output should have cost advantages over other producers. For a recent evaluation of learning by doing in the semiconductor industry, see Irwin and Klenow (1994).

nants of whether firms could successfully organize for cooperative political action. Even though current U.S. trade laws enable individual firms to seek import relief even in the absence of industry collective action, these factors remain influential in the political market and are worth describing in the context of the semiconductor industry. In 1989, the value of U.S. semiconductor industry shipments was $25.7 billion and total U.S. employment was 184,000 (roughly 1.3 percent of total manufacturing employment). Compared with the two manufacturing sectors most notable in receiving U.S. trade protection— the textile and apparel industry with shipments of $130 billion and employment of 1,671,000, and the motor vehicle industry with shipments of $149 billion and direct employment of 250,000—semiconductors may seem small. Yet the steel industry—with shipments of $63 billion and employment of 256,000—is only twice as large as the semiconductor industry, which is certainly larger than, say, the shipbuilding industry (with $9.6 billion in shipments and employment of 119,000).[7] While the semiconductor industry is a relatively small part of the economy as a whole, it is not (unlike the products it produces) minuscule by standard measures. Furthermore, the industry has often been thought to take on an economic importance larger than such numbers would indicate, owing to its "strategic" position in the high-technology sector with "critical" downstream linkages to the computer and defense industries (to borrow the rhetoric of such industry groups as the National Advisory Committee on Semiconductors).

What the industry lacks in sheer economic size is compensated by a fair degree of concentration in a few parts of the United States. According to the 1987 Census of Manufactures, about a third of U.S. semiconductor employment was located in California, with Arizona, Texas, and New York accounting for another third. Particularly because of its concentration in "Silicon Valley," part of northern California around San Jose, the industry has been able to capture the attention and services of California's congressional representatives. During the 1980s, Republican Senator Pete Wilson and Democratic Senator Alan Cranston both strongly championed the cause of U.S. industry, sponsoring congressional actions to assist the industry and to pressure the executive branch to act upon the interests of the industry.

Geographic concentration is matched by some degree of economic concentration. Firms in the industry range from the enormous—such as International Business Machines (IBM), by far the largest semiconductor producer in the world in the mid-1980s—to the minuscule—such as tiny Micron Technology, which specialized exclusively in DRAMs. In 1989, IBM employed about 383,000 people and had $41,586 million in revenues, generating net income of $3,758 million (9.0 percent of revenue). An unknown fraction of its re-

---

7. These figures are taken from U.S. Department of Commerce *U.S. Industrial Outlook, 1992* (Washington, D.C.: Government Printing Office, 1992). The data are for semiconductors and related devices (SIC 3674), textile mill (SIC 22) and apparel and other textile products (SIC 23), motor vehicles and car bodies (SIC 3711), and steel mill products (SIC 3312, -15, -16, -17).

sources are devoted to semiconductors, but IBM was reputed to have semiconductor output nearly 25 percent greater than the next largest competitor, Nippon Electric Corporation (NEC), in the mid-1980s. By contrast, Micron had 3,000 employees in 1989 with a net income of $106 million on sales of $446 million (23.8 percent of revenue).[8] Despite this gross mismatch in terms of overall size (Micron's sales were only two-tenths of 1 percent of IBM's), both firms proved equally pivotal in determining U.S. trade policy in semiconductors.

Between these extremes lie a handful of prominent midsized firms that constitute the core of the U.S. semiconductor industry. Five key firms (1989 data) are Texas Instruments (TI), with 70,000 employees and a net income of $291.7 million on revenues of $6,521.9 million (4.5 percent of revenue); Motorola, with 104,000 employees and a net income of $498 million on net sales of $9,620 million (5.2 percent); Advanced Micro Devices (AMD) with 13,072 employees and a net income of $46.1 million on sales of $1,604.6 million (2.9 percent); National Semiconductor with 32,200 employees and suffering a net loss of $23.2 million on net sales of $1,647.9 million ($-1.4$ percent); and Intel with 22,000 employees and a net income of $391.0 million on sales of $3,126.8 million (12.5 percent). The 1991 market share rankings of these firms in the North American semiconductor market (including captive production) were 9.8 percent for Intel, 9.3 percent for Motorola, 5.1 percent for TI, and 3.8 percent for National Semiconductor.[9]

The political economy of the industry's trade policy efforts, however, hinges more on structural features of these firms—particularly the distinction between captive and merchant firms—than on firm size or profitability. Captive producers—such as IBM, American Telephone and Telegraph (AT&T), Hewlett-Packard, and Control Data—are vertically integrated and manufacture semiconductors mainly for internal consumption, that is, for use in downstream goods and services that they produce and sell themselves. These firms rarely, if ever, supply their semiconductors to other producers.[10] Primarily because of IBM's position as the world's largest semiconductor producer, captives account for a substantial share of U.S. output, but they may have little impact on semiconductor prices and trade because most of their transactions take place within the firm.[11] Yet captives are generally unable to produce the entire range of semiconductors for their own use, and they are often large purchasers

8. These 1989 data, as well as those in the next paragraph, are taken from *Moody's Industrial Manual, 1991.*

9. U.S. International Trade Commission (USITC 1993b, 7).

10. After deregulation, AT&T briefly sold DRAMs on the open market. IBM reportedly feared the antitrust implications of entering the DRAM market, as well as the awkward position of supplying a key input to its competitors in the computer market. In 1992, however, IBM began selling its DRAMs on the merchant market.

11. Captives accounted for 15.8 percent of the North American semiconductor market in 1991, 11.2 percentage points of which was IBM (USITC 1993b, 7).

of semiconductors, particularly IBM, which is frequently a major consumer to the industry as a whole.

Merchant firms, by contrast, produce semiconductors for sale to other firms. Motorola is the largest U.S. merchant firm that, along with TI, is diversified and produces semiconductors for its own products—telecommunications equipment in the case of Motorola, calculators and defense electronics in the case of TI. Motorola and TI also have production facilities in Japan and export to the United States. Other firms, including Intel, AMD, National Semiconductor, and Micron, are smaller, less diversified, and more purely merchants in that all production is sold to other semiconductor-using firms. These companies also differ in size and in the range of products they produce.

The divide among firms as captives or merchants plays a key role in the political economy of the industry. Merchant firms potentially reap a substantial gain from diminishing import competition and maintaining high prices for semiconductors; captive producers are likely to be net purchasers of semiconductors and desire low input prices. These sharply diverging and conflicting interests within the industry have plagued its efforts at unified political action, and each group has had to make partial accommodation with the other in the collective industry association.

The international nature of semiconductor production also influences the types of trade policies the industry has sought. In an effort to reduce costs, the U.S. semiconductor industry by the early 1970s began to move labor-intensive assembly operations overseas, particularly to Southeast Asia. Off-shore assembly was encouraged by sections of the U.S. tariff code under which only foreign value added is taxed upon the reimportation of designated goods. It may not be uncommon, for example, for a semiconductor to be designed in the United States, fabricated in Japan, assembled in Malaysia, and distributed for sale in Europe. Unlike industries traditionally seeking protection against import competition, that is, domestic producers whose assets are generally fixed in the United States (such as textiles and steel) and whose rivals are based abroad and export to the United States, the international character of semiconductor production and assembly implies that import protection via nondiscriminatory tariffs or quotas are not desirable to the industry since many U.S. firms are the importers. In fact, as will be discussed below, the U.S. industry (i.e., management) spearheaded a successful effort to eliminate most tariffs on semiconductor products in both the United States and Japan in 1985. The fundamental challenge facing U.S. firms was not excessive imports to be remedied through higher tariffs, but competition from non-U.S. producers regardless of the location of their production.

While industry concentration and location relate to the costs and benefits of collectively organizing for political activity, the theory of international trade points to the economic interests of various factors of production, such as labor and capital owners, in shaping the configuration of trade policy lobbying. As

Mussa (1974) and others describe, these economic interests depend on the intensity with which the factors are used in a given sector of production and their specificity to that sector. Economic theory suggests that the more specific and immobile are labor and capital in a given sector of employment, the more their fate is tied to the fortunes of that sector and the more likely they are to seek policies favoring that sector.

Unlike many import-competing sectors in which organized labor plays a major role in the industry's political action, semiconductor workers did not directly participate in the quest for government relief from Japanese competition. That average weekly wages in the semiconductor industry, which averaged $614 in 1987, were roughly 24 percent above the average for manufacturing overall might suggest that labor should be concerned that an industry contraction would place this premium in jeopardy.[12] Yet the apparent lack of political activism among semiconductor workers can be explained by evidence that many of them have skills useful in various related industries, thereby ensuring their mobility across the high-technology sector. Ong and Mar (1992) calculated how a sample of semiconductor workers laid off in 1985—a year in which half the workforce was furloughed (either temporarily or permanently) and industry employment in northern California fell by 14 percent—were faring two years later based on data from California's unemployment insurance program. They found that workers reemployed by other semiconductor or high-technology firms earned comparable wages to those rehired by their original semiconductor employer, suggesting the presence of sector-specific rather than industry- or firm-specific human capital.[13] If such labor is mobile across the high-technology sector, workers do not have a particularly strong stake in the fate of semiconductor firms per se as long as other high-technology sectors are performing well. That labor was largely silent in the semiconductor trade dispute does not mean that its interests were neglected by politicians: labor's political action committee (the International Brotherhood of Electronic Workers [IBEW] Committee on Political Education) channeled $1.6 million to political candidates in 1985–86 and over $2.2 million in 1987–88, according to the Federal Election Commission.[14]

Thus, in the many congressional hearings held on policy toward the semiconductor industry in the 1980s, testimony was taken almost exclusively from corporate executives and industry officials, not labor representatives. The stance of management, the principal capital owners in the industry (merchant firms were not uncommonly still controlled by their founders), hinged primar-

12. U.S. Department of Labor, *Employment and Wages, Annual Averages for 1987* (Washington, D.C.: Government Printing Office, 1988). These figures are unadjusted for skill differences.

13. In their sample, 57 percent of workers were rehired, 16 percent became reemployed in other semiconductor or high-technology firms, and 27 percent found employment in other sectors. Workers reemployed in non–high-technology sectors, however, suffered earnings losses of 27–36 percent relative to rehired workers.

14. This does not include contributions by several IBEW local union political action committees (PACs).

ily on whether the firm was a merchant or captive producer of semiconductors. Captive producers, most importantly IBM, were cautious about initiating any trade dispute with Japan. Not only did IBM's substantial investments in Japan provide a rationale to avoid trade friction, but as a net purchaser of semiconductors it had little interest in policies that might result in higher semiconductor prices. TI was similarly cautious about acting against Japan: with a long-standing direct investment stake in Japan (it was the first U.S. firm to produce semiconductors in Japan), TI did not wish to jeopardize its economic or political ties there, nor would it welcome trade restraints that might prevent it from importing into the United States production from its Japanese facilities.

Executives from merchant producers were the most vociferous proponents of policies that would diminish Japanese competition and raise the price of their output. Politically active Motorola often took an aggressive stance against its Japanese rivals, filing antidumping complaints against Japanese exports of pagers and cellular phones during the 1980s, for example. Micron, which was not well diversified and only produced chips for sale on the open market, strongly supported import protection against Japanese competition and pushed for decisive actions against the "dumping" of semiconductors in the United States. Larger merchant firms such as Intel, AMD, and National Semiconductor were also concerned about competition from Japan and wanted intellectual property protection to prevent foreign firms from copying chip designs.

In 1977, several merchant producers banded together to form the Semiconductor Industry Association (SIA) to promote common interests.[15] The SIA was founded by five industry leaders (all but one were either chairmen or chief executive officers)—W. Jerry Sanders III (AMD), Robert Noyce (Intel), Wilfred J. Corrigan (Fairchild), Charles Sporck (National Semiconductor), and John Welty (Motorola). Each of these firms competed fiercely with one another on certain dimensions—suing each other over alleged patent violations, for example, or even conducting espionage against one another—but they could agree on several common policy objectives, such as obtaining greater patent protection for chip designs, improving the tax treatment of R&D investment, and heightening political awareness of the emerging Japanese competition.

Despite entering the policy arena as political novices, the SIA did not find a particularly hostile audience in Washington for any of these objectives, especially in Congress. But because the few firms that the SIA comprised lacked the stature needed to give the organization visibility and political weight in Washington, specific accomplishments in the form of legislation or policy action were initially absent. To redress this weakness, the SIA broadened its membership in 1982 to include vertically integrated captive producers, such as IBM, Hewlett-Packard, Digital Equipment Corporation (DEC), and AT&T. Beyond adding to the political standing of the SIA, this move had a more important impact on its lobbying activities. The inclusion of the captive producers

---

15. See Mundo (1992) for a general discussion of the SIA's organization and objectives.

exerted a moderating influence on the SIA trade policy stance because it forced the merchants to consult with the captives in order to arrive at an industry consensus on policy positions.[16] Four large merchant producers also formed PACs with which to provide campaign contributions to national political candidates. The disbursements of these PACs appear to be related to the trade dispute with Japan: payments totaled $354,318 at the peak of the dispute in 1985–86, 40 percent higher than in 1983–84 and 17 percent higher than in 1987–88 after trade tensions had simmered down.[17]

Several characteristics distinguish the SIA from most other industry interest groups. The industry association remains an extremely small institution: in 1992, the entire SIA staff consisted of just 13 people, seven professionals and six office personnel. The firms that the SIA comprises sought to prevent the organization from becoming a large, independent, staff-driven entity that would pursue objectives increasingly divorced from the industry that it was intended to represent. The SIA's primary function is to provide a forum for industry leaders to reach a consensus on issues of joint concern and to oversee any political action based on whatever consensus emerged. The main forum for determining the industry's views on trade policy is the SIA's Public Policy Committee, consisting of representatives from several (but not all) member firms.[18] In carrying out that consensus, the SIA coordinates the industry's political strategy but must (by virtue of its size) rely heavily on the work done by individual companies. Thus, it is the individual companies that constitute the SIA that are mainly engaged in political action, rather than the association as an independent entity. The SIA staff rarely testify before Congress, for example, but work with member companies to enlist or designate the upper management of a given firm to testify on behalf of the association.

The SIA was also deliberately located in San Jose, California, not in Washington, D.C., to ensure close contact with industry. However, many members of the SIA—such as Motorola, IBM, TI, and Intel, for example—maintain their own Washington offices to monitor policy developments of interest. These offices primarily support the political activities of the firms, but they also work on SIA initiatives. Consequently, there was little need for the SIA to maintain an office in Washington, because the work of the industry association fell heavily on member firms that already had offices there. The SIA had an additional resource in Washington: the services of the law firm Dewey Ballantine. By subcontracting part of its policy activity to Dewey Ballantine, the SIA avoided the overhead costs of maintaining staff in Washington, as well as gain-

16. By 1992, the SIA had 32 regular members, although not all are equally politically active.

17. These data are from the Federal Election Commission. The semiconductor PACs include the National Semiconductor Corporation Employees PAC, the Intel PAC, the Motorola Employees Good Government Committee, and the Constructive Citizenship Committee of Texas Instruments. Many of the contributions went to California congressmen.

18. The SIA has other committees on, for example, industry statistics, occupational health, environment, and communications.

ing the counsel of politically astute Washington insiders, including the well-connected trade lawyer Alan Wolff. Such contracting reduced the start-up costs of political action, and the SIA reportedly spent only about $1 million per year on Washington activities during the mid-1980s.

Yoffe (1988) points to other factors of the SIA's organization and strategy that allowed it to advance its political agenda in Washington successfully after 1982. In contrast to many large industry associations in which the primary workload falls to the staff level, the lobbying activity by the semiconductor industry was distinguished by a high degree of personal involvement by chief executive officers and upper management. Robert Noyce, a co-inventor of the integrated circuit and chairman at Intel, reportedly spent 20 percent of his time in Washington during the early 1980s. Such high-level involvement commanded respect among politicians and gave semiconductor producers access to policymakers at higher levels of government than the ordinary staff of any industry association could normally achieve. Extensive internal debates within the SIA before seeking specific policy actions allowed a consensus to emerge among members on a common approach to a given issue of collective interest. This consensus added to the credibility of the industry association, which targeted its efforts at friendly institutions within the government (often Capitol Hill, the Commerce Department, and the Office of the USTR).

Producer interests seeking protectionist policies sometimes face the countervailing force of downstream users of that particular good. For a period of time, the SIA did not face or was able to defuse potential opposition to its proposals. Computer manufacturers are the most important domestic users of memory chips, and it is precisely from this group that one would expect potential opposition to proposals that would raise semiconductor prices. Semiconductors constituted 6.4 percent of the value of output in the electronic computing equipment industry in 1982, a share that rose to 15.0 percent in 1986.[19] With shipments of $59.8 billion and total employment of 263,000 in 1989, the computer industry (narrowly construed) was also slightly larger than the semiconductor industry.[20] Semiconductors also constituted 6.7 percent of the value of output in the telephone and telegraph equipment industry, 8.3 percent in the radio and television communications equipment industry, and 5.0 percent in the home entertainment equipment industry in 1986. These semiconductor consumers were broadly organized in the American Electronics Association (AEA), a large group that included many SIA members and one that supported the SIA's complaint about the lack of market access in Japan. With the rise in DRAM prices subsequent to the 1986 agreement, the AEA proved too unwieldy and diverse to organize opposition to the accord, and computer

---

19. Calculated from input-output tapes of the U.S. Department of Commerce, Bureau of Economic Analysis.

20. From U.S. Department of Commerce, *U.S. Industrial Outlook, 1992* (Washington, D.C.: Government Printing Office, 1992), for computers and peripherals (SIC 3571, -2, -5, -7).

manufacturers formed a splinter group to counter the SIA's influence on U.S. semiconductor trade policy.

Individual Japanese producers, their industry association (the EIAJ—Electronics Industry Association of Japan), and the government of Japan were the only other major groups engaged in political action during the semiconductor trade dispute. Japanese firms hired legal counsel in the United States to defend them at various administrative hearings (related to both the antidumping and section 301 actions) and hired specialists in public relations and policy monitoring. According to the Department of Justice, all Japanese firms and the EIAJ spent $3.8 million in 1985–87 on semiconductor trade-related political action, the bulk of this expense in 1986. Roughly $1.1 million over these three years was devoted, mainly by the EIAJ, to countering the section 301 action. This suggests that lobbying expenditures by the SIA and Japanese producers were roughly comparable on this particular issue.[21]

1.3 Semiconductor Competition from Japan

Japan's emergence as a major producer of semiconductors beginning in the late 1970s manifested itself in a dramatic increase in its share of the world semiconductor market. At the end of the 1970s, U.S. firms accounted for over 60 percent of the world market and Japanese firms less than 30 percent; by mid-1985, the market shares of the two countries were about equal at 45 percent, after which time the Japanese took the lead. This success was most spectacular in the DRAM market, arguably the natural class of semiconductors in which a Japanese entrant could achieve dominance given the relatively straightforward design technology and high degree of quality control required in large-volume DRAM production. In the worldwide DRAM market, the United States and Japan traded places: the U.S. share plummeted from 70 percent in 1978 to 20 percent in 1986, while the Japanese share jumped from under 30 percent to peak at 75 percent in that same period.[22]

The rapid expansion of Japanese production did not vastly increase Japan's import penetration in the United States. Figures in Tyson (1992, 129) indicate that Japan's share of total U.S. semiconductor consumption rose from 7.5 per-

21. Office of the Attorney General, *Administration of Foreign Agents Registration Act* (Washington, D.C., various issues). I am indebted to Steve Husted for providing these data to me. Yoffe (1988, 89) cites no source for the claim that Japanese firms spent $30–$50 million opposing the trade petitions of SIA members in the mid-1980s. The $1 million annual figure of SIA does not include the costs borne by private firms in their Washington lobbying effort, particularly in pursuing separate antidumping actions, nor PAC contributions. The figure for Japanese firms is also inflated partly due to the redundancy of a half-dozen or so Japanese firms seeking separate legal counsel in the United States (owing to potential conflicts of interests among the attorneys) rather than coordinating their activities as a group like U.S. firms.

22. After making initial inroads in the 16K DRAM market, Japanese producers shocked U.S. producers with the rapid introduction of the 64K chip in 1978. Japanese firms accounted for about two-thirds of the 64K DRAM market from 1979 to 1986 and achieved over 80 percent of the smaller but burgeoning market for 256K DRAMs from 1982 to 1986. See Tyson (1992, 106ff.).

cent in 1982 to 12.3 percent in 1984, before dropping back to 9.8 percent in 1986. The U.S. share of the Japanese semiconductor market exceeded Japan's share of the U.S. market until the mid-1980s and was roughly comparable for a few years thereafter. But 70 percent of Japanese semiconductor exports to the United States were DRAMs, where they accounted for about 20 percent of the U.S. DRAM market in the mid-1980s. Japan's share of the U.S. market was not fully indicative of the force of the new competition in DRAMs because, in an integrated world market, Japanese producers could only capture market share abroad by forcing the market price downward everywhere.

The rise of Japan's semiconductor industry was driven by the rapid expansion in demand for transistors from the domestic consumer electronics industry. The different basis for the growth of the American and Japanese semiconductor industries reflected the considerable differences in end-use demand for semiconductors in the two markets: in Japan, consumer electronics provided 47 percent of semiconductor demand (the comparable figure in the United States being 8 percent), while data processing constituted 44 percent of U.S. demand in 1984. The different structure of final demand also led to a different way of meeting that demand in Japan. Whereas the U.S. industry was composed primarily of independent merchant producers of modest size, the major Japanese semiconductor producers were also the major semiconductor consumers (i.e., the electronics firms). According to Okimoto (1987, 394), the 10 largest firms accounting for 80 percent of Japan's semiconductor production also accounted for 50 percent of Japan's total consumption. A few large, quasi–vertically integrated producers—such as NEC, Toshiba, Hitachi, Fujitsu, Mitsubishi, Matsushita, Sharp, Sony, Sanyo, and Oki Electric—dominated Japan's industry and ensured a high degree of captive production, ranging from 75 percent for Sanyo, to 55 percent for Matsushita, 50 percent for Fujitsu, and down to about 20 percent for NEC, Hitachi, Mitsubishi, and Toshiba in the mid-1980s. These firms also tended to specialize in the production of certain types of semiconductors and trade these devices with one another based on long-term contracts or long-standing ties to one another.

Japan overtook the United States in overall semiconductor production by making substantial investments in production capacity. Indeed, throughout the late 1970s and early 1980s, the U.S. industry failed to keep pace with the investment rates of Japanese firms. According to the Organisation for Economic Co-operation and Development (OECD 1992, 147), Japanese firms devoted roughly an average of 28 percent of their sales to capital spending during 1978–85, while the comparable figure for U.S. firms was 16 percent. Such large investments were facilitated by a structural feature of Japanese industry that perhaps constituted its most decisive advantage over U.S. producers. Japanese firms are often affiliated with a large bank that can play a role in corporate governance through equity ownership and corporate board participation (such activities are illegal in the United States). Such bank ties not only gave Japanese semiconductor firms easier access to capital but allowed them to weather industry downturns much better than their U.S. counterparts. Hoshi, Kashyap, and Scharfstein (1990) find evidence that Japanese firms with bank ties produce and invest more in periods of financial distress (cash flow disruptions) than firms without such bank connections. Thus, large and diversified Japanese firms with deep financial resources to undertake investments and sustain losses were pitted against undiversified, midsized merchant firms in the United States.

Indeed, continued production and investment by Japanese firms in the face of slack demand baffled and infuriated U.S. producers, who would scale back both activities in industry recessions. In the aftermath of the industry downturn in 1974–75, a period in which foreign competition was not yet a serious concern, U.S. semiconductor firms were cautious about investing in additional production capacity. Consequently, there was a shortfall in U.S. capacity when semiconductor demand surged in 1977—even IBM entered the merchant market as a purchaser of DRAMs. Then when price per bit equivalency between 4K and 16K DRAMs was achieved in 1978, new Japanese producers aiming to enter the 16K market were able to satisfy the world demand that U.S. producers could not meet. Japan seized 40 percent of the 16K DRAM market by 1979. This situation repeated itself in the next recession of 1981–82. Demand again slackened just as U.S. firms had caught up and became well established in the 16K market. Japanese firms continued to invest and shifted production up to 64K chips, capturing 70 percent of that market by the end of 1981.

The Japanese government also played a modest role in fostering domestic production of memory chips as a by-product of its effort to promote the domestic computer industry. The Ministry of International Trade and Industry (MITI) sponsored the Very Large Scale Integration (VLSI) program of 1976–79, which directed $200 million in funds over four years, as well as interest-free loans, to several major manufacturers of semiconductors, such as Fujitsu, Hitachi, Mitsubishi, NEC, and Toshiba. These firms formed cooperative laboratories for the joint development of basic semiconductor technology (manufacturing technology and circuitry design), although not product development. In comparison with similar programs in the United States (albeit skewed toward defense-related and not basic research), formal Japanese support for its semiconductor industry was modest at best. But the perception that the programs constituted "unfair industry targeting" by MITI was fully exploited by the U.S. semiconductor producers and generated sympathy for their pleas in Washington.

Aside from the different financial and economic structure of the Japanese semiconductor industry, U.S. firms faced several additional obstacles beyond their control. The SIA attributed the investment difficulties of member firms to the high cost of capital in the United States in the early and mid-1980s compared with Japan. The industry's problems were exacerbated by the substantial appreciation of the U.S. dollar on foreign exchange markets in the early 1980s, which harmed U.S. exports of low-margin DRAMs and provided a favorable boost to the Japanese industry. The U.S. industry also left itself exposed to the potential entry of foreign rivals in several ways. The industry was unprepared for a change in process technology away from the standard N-channel metal oxide semiconductor (NMOS) to the complementary metal oxide semiconductor (CMOS) favored by Japan. Compounding these technical problems were questions about the quality of U.S. semiconductors. In a widely publicized paper presented at an industry conference in 1981, a representative from Hewlett-Packard presented evidence that the firm experienced many fewer defects on 16K chips from Japanese producers than from U.S. producers. This U.S. producers heatedly denied, but the perception (and later acknowledged reality) of a quality gap allowed long-term supply contracts to shift to Japanese firms.[23]

All of these factors contributed to an exodus of U.S. firms from the DRAM market: while there were 15 U.S. producers of the 4K chip, 12 of the 16K chip, and at one time 10 producers of the 64K chip, all except two merchants were driven from the market. Most firms simply abandoned DRAM production and concentrated on other product lines, but one firm (Mostek) went bankrupt.

With the onslaught of Japanese competition, two issues framed the U.S. industry's complaints: "dumping" and market access. The dumping complaints arose from the periodic sharp price declines that were a feature of the industry recessions. As Baldwin (1994) points out, the semiconductor market is one in which price rather than output adjusts in response to demand fluctuations; even in the industry recession of 1985, for example, output continued to grow rapidly while prices fell steeply. This is a consequence of the underlying economic structure of the industry: low marginal costs of production induce firms, even in periods of soft demand, to cut margins and maintain production at high levels to generate additional revenue.[24] Such industry recessions had occurred in the absence of foreign competition (as in 1974–75), but the rapid buildup of production capacity by Japanese firms (and their willingness to continue production and investment in the face of an adverse cash flow situation, due to the bank ties discussed above) exacerbated the concomitant price collapses when demand was slack. This contributed to the steep declines in world prices in 1981 and 1985, illustrated in figure 1.1, of which the U.S. industry was a casualty. Despite the U.S. industry's complaint that such "dumping" was "predatory" and "unfair," price declines of this sort clearly do not require predatory intent or unfair competition when high production and inventory levels confront a negative demand shock.[25]

The U.S. industry also complained about the lack of access to Japan's mar-

---

23. This is recounted in Okimoto, Sugano, and Weinstein (1984).

24. Marginal costs are so low that it may not pay to reduce output and thereby sacrifice revenues that might pay off fixed costs or be invested in the next generation of semiconductors. Learning-by-doing effects, wherein cumulative experience helps improve yields and reduce costs, provide firms with an additional incentive to keep output high even when demand is slack.

25. Dick (1991) and Flamm (1993a) analyze the issue of semiconductor dumping.

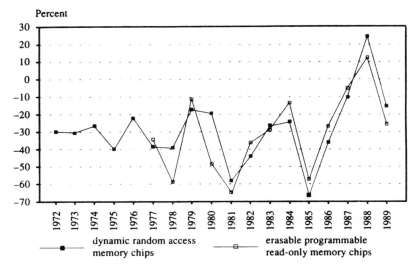

Percent

Fig. 1.1   Fisher-ideal price indexes, 1972–89
Source: Flamm (1993b, 273).

ket. Prior to 1975, imports of semiconductors into Japan were restricted by formal quotas and prior-approval requirements, and foreign investment was so strictly regulated as to be essentially forbidden. These restrictions were liberalized in 1975, after which few formal governmental trade barriers remained in place. Yet the U.S. share of the Japanese market scarcely budged after 1975. Supported by evidence that was necessarily anecdotal, the SIA claimed that informal nontariff barriers lingered in Japan after 1975 and that MITI used active countermeasures to undermine the liberalization. One explanation for the failure of the formal liberalization to alter the U.S. share was the structure of the Japanese industry. Not only was the structure of final demand different, but U.S. merchants encountered difficulties in selling to captive producers and overcoming long-term relationships between Japanese firms.[26]

26. As Okimoto (1989, 103ff., emphasis added) points out:

The difficulties of breaking into the organizational nexus are particularly frustrating for foreign producers of high-tech intermediate goods, because the enclosed and long-term nature of relations between buyers and sellers alters the character of spot-market, arms-distant transactions. . . . Instead of meeting all their needs on the merchant market, Japanese computer companies make their own semiconductors and sell what they do not use. Captive, in-house production thus imposes limits on the expansion of foreign shares in Japan's semiconductor market. . . . Japanese industrial organization emphasizes the importance of extramarket factors, especially the strong preference for stable predictable, long-term business relationships based on mutual obligation and trust. This has had the effect of raising the barriers to entry from the outside, whether by foreign manufacturers or by nonmainstream Japanese producers. *Such nontariff barriers, deeply embedded in the structure of the industrial economy, are not directly connected to Japanese industrial policy.* But their existence, whether by design or by accident, serves basically the same function as formal measures of home market protection—only more effectively, because they do not diminish the vigor of market competition between domestic producers.

The SIA sought to blame both the dumping and market access problems on the Japanese government, enabling them to invoke the politically attractive rhetoric of "fair trade" and to argue that the playing field of international competition was skewed. This was precisely the interpretation in *The Effect of Government Targeting on World Semiconductor Competition,* published by the SIA in 1983, which set out to "describe the decade or more of coordinated effort by the Japanese government to put the Japanese producers in a dominant world-wide position in key product lines."

According to the SIA, Japanese government support took three forms. First, the government provided direct and indirect financial assistance to the domestic industry. The SIA claimed that anywhere from $507 million to $2 billion was directed to Japan's semiconductor industry during 1976–82 in government funds, as well as tax breaks and other advantages. These promotion policies supposedly provided a "favorable environment" that gave firms a willingness to invest even during a recession. By reducing risks, this led to capacity-building races and, with a downturn in domestic demand, export "avalanches." Second, the government formed a research cartel within the domestic industry to pool R&D resources and promote large firms. The government's aim was to "organize and channel the collective resources of Japan's largest electronic firms" to achieve domination of the world market. In addition, the government telecommunications monopoly transferred at little cost to NEC, Fujitsu, and Hitachi the design and manufacture technology of 256K DRAMs. Third, the government protected the domestic market for its semiconductor firms by condoning and reinforcing "buy Japan" policies among its major producers and consumers. According to the SIA, the government undertook active countermeasures to undermine the liberalization in 1970s and 1980s. By securing the home market for domestic producers, Japanese firms benefited from the cost reductions associated with production experience, thereby assisting in their penetration of the world market.

There are two noteworthy elements to this key SIA document. First, it does not explicitly accuse Japanese firms of dumping. The report argues that overcapacity led to aggressive pricing by Japanese firms, driving prices lower than they otherwise would be. But the report, in effect, concedes that because Japanese costs of production were not known, no dumping complaint could be made. This is significant: while many individual U.S. semiconductor producers accused Japan of dumping from the late 1970s, throughout the entire trade dispute the SIA itself never filed an antidumping petition. The captive producers in the SIA prevented the group from taking a strong position on the dumping issue until the 1986 accord, when the merchant firms reasserted themselves in determining SIA positions.

Second, the document pins the blame for the lack of U.S. market access squarely on the Japanese government, not on the behavior of private firms or the structure of the Japanese market. This reflects the SIA's preparation for a section 301 action against Japan. Section 301 of the Trade Act of 1974 provided a remedy for foreign unfair trade practices, but at this time had only been used to attack government policies (unlike the antidumping laws, which relate to the prices charged by private firms). If the R&D and capital investments were made solely by shrewd private firms in Japan without government support, the sense of unfairness, and hence the claim to government assistance, would have been lost.

To remedy the situation, the SIA called for the U.S. government to "announce as U.S. policy that foreign industrial targeting practices will not be allowed to undermine U.S. technological and economic leadership in this critical industrial sector." In addition, the "U.S. government must identify, analyze, and counter the distorting effects of foreign industrial targeting practices" by monitoring foreign developments such as predatory export drives and market barriers, promising to enforce U.S. trade laws as necessary. This is as close as the SIA came in this document to advocating antidumping duties. However, one recommendation stands out: "U.S. firms must receive real, not 'cosmetic' market access, reflected in significantly greater participation by U.S. firms in the Japanese market. This will require an affirmative action program to normalize competition in Japan. The Japanese government should establish necessary programs to see that this result is achieved" (SIA 1983, 6).

Thus, the report reflected the divisions within the SIA—no consensus on whether antidumping measures were appropriate, but stronger sentiment that the Japanese market must be "opened up" in such a way that "the cash registers ring." But the U.S. government lacked effective policy instruments to suspend the R&D or investment policies of another country or to recast the vertical links or organizational structure of private foreign firms. Hence, the legal requirements of U.S. trade policy forced the SIA to address only the trade-related symptoms of its problem, namely, the exports of semiconductors from Japan (through antidumping measures) and imports of semiconductors by Japan (through section 301).

1.4   Early Industry Pressure, 1977–84

The demands by U.S. semiconductor producers for trade relief are strongly associated with the industry recessions of 1974–75, 1981–82, and 1985–86; in intervening periods of high demand, the attention of industry executives was diverted from pressing the government for actions on their behalf. The industry recession of 1974–75, predating large-scale production by Japanese firms, was not marked by significant foreign competition, and hence there was no significant pressure to limit imports or take other trade-related actions.[27] Yet Japan's entry into the semiconductor market helped trigger the formation of the SIA

27. In 1971, Sprague Electric Company, of North Adams, Mass., petitioned the U.S. Tariff Commission for adjustment assistance under section 301 of the Trade Expansion Act of 1962. Sprague complained about imports of capacitors, transistors, and integrated circuits, but the commission determined that imports as a result of concessions granted under trade agreements were not a cause of serious injury.

in 1977. But until the industry was actually harmed, there was little the government was prepared to do. "After a transcoastal pilgrimage to Washington to inform Robert Strauss, the U.S. Trade Representative during the Carter Administration, that 'the Japanese are coming,'" writes Flamm (1993b, 256 n. 13), "semiconductor executives were reportedly dismayed to get a 'so?' reaction from Strauss." The SIA prompted a Senate subcommittee of the Committee on Banking, Housing, and Urban Development to request a report from the International Trade Commission (ITC) on the competitive position of the U.S. industry just as Japanese firms were making inroads in the 16K DRAM market in 1978. Issued in late 1979, the ITC report concluded that the U.S. industry could maintain its lead despite trade barriers abroad and foreign government support for their industry.

Steeply falling prices for semiconductors during the industry recession of 1981, along with the early Japanese capture of 70 percent of the market for 64K DRAMs, triggered a more concerted political response by the U.S. industry. "It was at this juncture in the fall of 1981," recalls Clyde Prestowitz (1988, 148), then deputy assistant secretary for international economic policy in the Department of Commerce, "that representatives of the U.S. semiconductor industry began making regular trips to Washington," among them Robert Noyce of Intel, Charles Sporck of National Semiconductor, and W. Jerry Sanders III of AMD. According to Prestowitz (1988, 149–50), who championed the industry's cause within the government:

> These representatives of the semiconductor industry visited the departments of Commerce, State, and Treasury as well as the U.S. Trade Representative and members of Congress. They asked not for protection but for an end to the Japanese dumping, for the same opportunity to sell in Japan as the Japanese had in the United States, and for an end to Japanese copying of new chip designs. They got a reception as cool as the autumn weather in Washington. The lawyers, academic economists, and career bureaucrats who filled many key government positions shared a suspicion of business as protectionist and opposed to consumer interests. . . . Lionel Olmer and I, who represented the Commerce Department in these meetings with industry, disagreed, however, with the majority of other officials.

This cool reception can be traced to several things. First, the newly installed Reagan administration had an ideological or, perhaps more accurately, rhetorical commitment to free trade and limiting government intervention in the economy. The initial reaction of most Reagan officials to any industry complaining about foreign competition was likely to be one of skepticism. Many officials believed that this was the first time that these insulated U.S. producers had to confront the rude shock of foreign competition and that a healthy dose of such competition was no cause for alarm. Second, the U.S. semiconductor industry was hardly on its deathbed. While sales of the U.S. merchant semiconductor firms fell 7.1 percent in 1981, they had risen almost 30 percent in each of the preceding three years. According to SIA statistics, the merchant industry was still profitable: after three years in which pretax income as a percentage of sales was roughly 12 percent, this measure slipped to 4.7 percent in 1982 before registering a slight loss of −1.4 percent in 1983.

Furthermore, in the absence of a formal complaint under U.S. trade law, it was unclear what specific action the industry wanted the government to undertake. Motorola seriously considered filing an antidumping petition on 64K DRAMs in early 1982 but failed to do so to avoid antagonizing Hitachi, a Japanese partner, and for lack of industry support: IBM, as a new member of the SIA, strongly opposed such a move, and ultimately the SIA took no formal action. Instead, Motorola requested that the Commerce Department informally monitor Japanese prices. This request put government officials in an awkward situation because they could not really act without a formal complaint—"our only tools were bluff and persuasion," lamented Prestowitz (1988, 150), who attributed the lack of a formal complaint from Motorola to the cost and length of time such an action would take rather than to divisions within the industry. At any rate, Lionel Olmer, who as under secretary for international trade was responsible for administering the antidumping laws, warned MITI that the Commerce Department was inclined to monitor Japanese chip prices in the United States. This led to an interesting instance of government agencies working at cross-purposes: the mild threat appeared to "work" in that MITI informed Japanese firms of this possibility and exports to the U.S. were reduced, but just months later the Department of Justice launched an antitrust investigation into reports of Japanese collusion to raise prices in U.S. market![28]

The idea of a section 301 action was also broached in 1982. However, USTR William Brock advised the SIA against filing a petition because the case appeared weak. While the Japanese had captured a large share of the DRAM market, the U.S. share of the world semiconductor market was still roughly twice Japan's share and the industry appeared to be in reasonable financial health as well. Thus, the semiconductor industry was viewed as fundamentally sound and Japanese competition healthy for the industry. In this context, Brock reported the administration consensus that a section 301 action would not be viewed favorably.

Yet in the midst of the sharpest U.S. recession in the postwar period with widespread fears of "deindustrialization," concerns about the fate of this "sunrise" industry could not be dismissed entirely by the administration. The entrepreneurial mystique surrounding Silicon Valley high-technology industries had bipartisan appeal in Congress, which demanded the administration at least appear to be doing something about high-technology trade with Japan. Consequently, Brock formed a U.S.-Japan High Technology Working Group to relieve trade-related tensions, although the working group's negotiations with

28. Flamm (1993b, 262) reports that "the Japanese semiconductor industry openly acknowledged that these reductions in exports were spurred by MITI guidance." Nothing came of the antitrust investigation.

Japan did not have a precise goal and were not viewed as a top priority within the U.S. government. Prestowitz (1988, 153–54) complained that

> we had to operate within the bounds of a consensus obtained from the various agencies on the U.S. negotiating team that included members of the Office of the U.S. Trade Representative, the Council of Economic Advisers, the National Security Council, the Office of Management and Budget, and the departments of State, Labor, Treasury, Commerce, and Defense. The consensus was that, while it was appropriate to request better market access, asking for a specific market share or sales volume would violate free-trade doctrine and hence be unacceptable. Similarly, with regard to dumping, collecting data on the volume of shipments was acceptable—but not on prices, because in view of the Justice Department that might violate antitrust laws on price fixing. . . . Thus, before even talking to the Japanese, we limited ourselves to asking simply for a more open market, whose meaning we did not define, and a system of gathering statistics on semiconductor shipments. Moreover, the consensus, strongly influenced by the State Department and the National Security Council, would not allow—even as a tactic—the suggestion of any retaliation if Japan did not respond favorably for fear that the overall relationship between the two countries might be harmed.

Discussions with Japan began in June 1982 and led to an accord in November, which in Prestowitz's (1988, 155) opinion was more a "monument to clever drafting than anything else." Besides stating broad principles, an agreement was reached to reduce both country's tariffs and to collect Japanese semiconductor shipment data (but not price information), allowing the Commerce Department to better monitor the market.

The agreement did nothing to change the underlying, fundamental determinants of supply or demand in the semiconductor market. Hence, "within three months, further threats of congressional action along with the possibility of private unfair-trade suits drove the U.S. delegation to a second round of negotiations, one focusing entirely on market access," Prestowitz (1988, 155) writes. The recommendations (it cannot really be called an agreement) that emerged from the working group in November 1983 called for complete tariff elimination in the United States and Japan, better data collection, a removal of investment barriers, and greater market access for U.S. firms. On market access, the text stated that "the Government of Japan should encourage Japanese semiconductor users to enlarge opportunities for U.S.-based suppliers so that long-term relationships could evolve with Japanese companies." But, according to Prestowitz (1988, 156), a key part of the negotiations "was the confidential chairman's note from Kodama [the MITI negotiator] to Murphy and me [the U.S. negotiators], in which Kodama said that MITI would 'encourage' (a euphemism for 'give guidance to') the major Japanese chip users to buy more U.S. chips and to develop long-term relationships with U.S. suppliers." This proved to be too weak a version of the "affirmative action" the industry requested because, with no fundamental change in the organizational structure of the Japanese semiconductor industry, this moral suasion would be ineffective.

The 1983 negotiations marked the end of the first round of U.S.-Japan discussions over semiconductors. The round ended not because of success in resolving any of the underlying grievances of the U.S. semiconductor industry, but because the industry entered a period of surging demand from mid-1983. Distracted by the business of filling orders and making new investments, industry executives took the heat off the government.

Despite accomplishing little to resolve its trade dispute with Japan, the SIA did achieve several legislative and administrative goals during the pronounced industry expansion of 1983–84. First, the SIA succeeded in its desire to eliminate tariffs on final and unfinished semiconductors in the United States and Japan. As late as 1978, the United States maintained a 6 percent tariff on imported semiconductors, while Japan had a 12 percent tariff. In 1982, as a result of the first U.S.-Japan Working Group talks, both countries set their tariff at 4.2 percent. The Trade and Tariff Act of 1984 authorized the president to negotiate even lower tariffs on semiconductors. In February 1985, USTR Brock and the foreign minister of Japan exchanged letters that eliminated most tariffs on semiconductors.

Although major U.S. semiconductor firms already benefited from the offshore assembly provisions of the U.S. tariff code, the SIA wanted the additional assurance that its members could ship semiconductor components into and out of the United States and Japan at no tariff charge.[29] According to the SIA, this action would benefit U.S. producers more than Japanese exporters because 75 percent of U.S. imports were shipped by U.S. firms. Tariff elimination, it argued, would save U.S. firms roughly $100 million per year, which could be plowed back into R&D expenditures, as well as increase access to the Japanese market. The SIA further maintained that abolishing the duty would not result in shifting production abroad because the tariff was too small to influence plant location decisions. In addition, the SIA viewed a U.S.-Japan agreement to abolish semiconductor tariffs as establishing the principle of free trade, as well as a step toward securing greater governmental concern about reducing the alleged import barriers in Japan. The AEA and the Computer and Business Equipment Manufacturers Association (CBEMA), representing important semiconductor-using industries, also supported the proposed tariff elimination.

The tariff elimination was opposed by one small U.S. merchant producer, Micron Technology, whose production focused on memory chips, precisely the device most subject to Japanese import competition. Micron contended that the move would increase Japan's penetration of the U.S. market without changing the ability of U.S. firms to sell in Japan. Micron also wanted to delay elimi-

29. This and the next paragraph draw on USITC (1985).

nating the semiconductor tariff until the European Community and Korea also reduced their trade restrictions. Despite the European Community's 17 percent tariff and Korea's 30 percent tariff on semiconductors (at the time), both countries would be eligible for duty-free shipments of semiconductors to the United States as the tariff abolition would apply on a most-favored-nation basis.

The IBEW also opposed tariff reduction on the grounds that U.S. producers would shift production to foreign assembly plants as a result. They maintained that, because U.S. exports to Japan were so small and Japanese exports to the U.S. were so large, tariff elimination would give Japanese firms a financial boon five times the amount of U.S. firms. Japan, they argued, could reinvest these funds in R&D and further undermine the domestic industry.

Given their failure to obtain a sympathetic hearing from the administration about possibly filing a section 301 petition, a second SIA objective was to broaden the scope of governmental practices that could be actionable under the statute. Section 301 provided for government action against "unreasonable, unjustifiable, and discriminatory" foreign trade practices, but these key words were left undefined and gave open-ended discretion to the government in deciding to accept a petition. The Trade and Tariff Act of 1984 amended section 301 by mandating that the definition of unreasonable "includes, but is not limited to, any act, policy, or practice which denies fair and equitable market opportunities." [30] The scope of section 301 was thereby broadened to include just the sorts of activities that the SIA was seeking to attack in Japan.

Finally, Congress enacted SIA-supported legislation on intellectual property rights and R&D in 1984. The National Cooperative Research Act relaxed the antitrust treatment of joint R&D ventures and the Semiconductor Chip Protection Act of 1984 prohibited the unauthorized copying of chip designs.

1.5   Petitions, Procedures, and Negotiations, 1985–86

The 1983–84 boom ended with yet another industry recession in 1985. Compared with other downturns, this industry recession was extremely severe and was particularly concentrated on the memory chip market. While overall semiconductor sales slumped about 20 percent in 1985, the DRAM market contracted by about 60 percent. The root cause was a brief slowdown in the computer market: after increasing by a factor of five between 1981 and 1984, domestic shipments of microcomputers actually fell 8 percent in 1985, as depicted in figure 1.2. With chip shipments and inventories remaining relatively

---

30. This was further strengthened (along lines desired by the SIA) in the Omnibus Trade and Competitiveness Act of 1988 to include the denial of "fair and equitable market opportunities, including the toleration by a foreign government of systematic anticompetitive activities by private firms or among private firms in the foreign country that have the effect of restricting, on a basis that is inconsistent with commercial considerations, access of United States goods to purchasing by such firms."

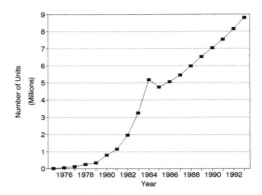

Fig. 1.2   U.S. domestic output of microcomputers
Source: Computer Business Equipment Manufacturers Association, *Information Technology Industry Databook, 1960–2002* (Washington, D.C., 1992), 94.

high, prices collapsed in the face of slumping demand. The price of a 64K DRAM fell from roughly $3.00 in the first quarter of 1984 to $0.75 by the middle of 1985; the price of 256K DRAMs fell from $31.00 to $3.00 over the same time period. Rapid price declines were always expected in the semiconductor industry because of learning by doing, but not so sharply in such a short period of time (see fig. 1.1).

As a result, merchant semiconductor firms racked up unprecedented losses: pretax income as a percentage of sales fell from over 14 percent in 1984 to almost −10 percent in 1985. Capacity utilization among the merchant firms dropped from over 70 percent in 1984 to under 45 percent in 1985, according to SIA statistics. Merchant semiconductor employment fell nearly 20 percent (about 55,000 workers) in the first three quarters of 1985. The 1985 industry recession pushed virtually every U.S. producer out of the DRAM market— Mostek went bankrupt, and AMD, Intel, Motorola, and National Semiconductor abandoned DRAM production to concentrate on other semiconductor product lines. Only TI and Micron remained in the merchant DRAM market, although IBM and AT&T continued captive production. Imports were not a direct cause of the recession: Japanese import penetration actually fell in the two years after 1984, and three-quarters of the fall in revenues of U.S.-based semiconductor companies in 1985 was due to declining overall demand, only a quarter due to lost market share, according to calculations in Federal Interagency Staff Working Group (1987, 10). Indeed, Japanese firms experienced similar losses and layoffs as world demand had slumped in an integrated world market.

Just as the industry recession of 1981–82 spawned industry efforts at political action, the 1985 recession precipitated a similar response. As Prestowitz (1988, 159) dramatically put it, "With survival at stake in the spring and summer of 1985, executives of the U.S. companies and their industry associations descended on Washington."[31] However, this descent received a much warmer welcome than had been the case in 1982. Then the industry was just one of many U.S. industries reeling from recession and appealing for help. Although the dollar was just peaking on foreign exchange markets, the U.S. economy was in its third year of expansion in 1985, and fewer industries were facing the dire straits of the semiconductor industry. Therefore, competition among industries for the attention of policymakers was less intense. In 1982, the industry was split on filing an antidumping petition and faced resistance on any section 301 action; in 1985, it pursued (and the government largely welcomed) both courses of action.

The industry's timing was propitious for a related reason: unlike 1982, the appreciation of the U.S. dollar on foreign exchange markets and the accompanying lurch into a large trade deficit served to focus the Reagan administration's attention on international economic policy. The Economic Policy Council, the cabinet-level group chaired by Secretary of Treasury James Baker and responsible for formulating the administration's economic policy, met frequently during this period amid complaints about the gaping U.S. trade deficit from industries highly exposed to international trade. The administration responded by formulating a two-pronged policy of containment: an exchange rate policy aimed at reducing the foreign exchange value of the dollar, and market-opening initiatives aimed at diverting protectionist "pressure by focussing on measures to open up the Japanese market rather than closing the U.S. market."[32] After a strong "fair trade" speech by President Reagan outlining this new approach in September 1985, the USTR for the first time began to self-initiate section 301 cases.[33] The principal audience for this "tough" trade policy was Congress: the administration desperately sought to avoid a congressional trade bill that would force the president to impose sanctions (like the Gephardt amendment) against countries having a trade surplus with the United States.[34] With this political backdrop, a high-profile industry in search of a market-opening initiative against Japan was far more likely than in previous years to achieve a sympathetic hearing from the administration.

For its part, the semiconductor industry was so shaken by economic condi-

31. Needless to say, the executives do not descend on Washington when times are good, and the financial losses of U.S. firms were real in 1984–85. Yet U.S. firms maintained large market shares in many categories of semiconductors besides DRAMs and were not being driven from all markets.

32. Niskanen (1988, 152). William Niskanen was the acting chairman of the Council of Economic Advisers during 1984–85.

33. The first three cases of what Jagdish Bhagwati has called "aggressive unilateralism" concerned Brazil's informatics policies, Japan's tobacco restrictions, and Korea's insurance regulations. With the U.S. government acting on its own in self-initiated cases, the likelihood of retaliation is greater if no progress is made in reducing foreign trade barriers. The more symbolic Market-Oriented Sector-Specific (MOSS) talks with Japan also began, which aimed at increasing Japanese purchases of telecommunications, pharmaceutical, forest products, and other items.

34. For a discussion of the political environment of trade policy in the mid-1980s, see Destler (1992).

tions in early 1985 that the question was not whether to take action, but what particular form the action should take within the constraints and remedies specified under U.S. trade law. Filing a petition under U.S. trade law would constitute a formal request for a specific government remedy and would end the informal, ad hoc, and sporadic bilateral negotiations that had done little to alter the industry's position vis-à-vis Japan. The advantage of filing under U.S. trade law was that by initiating a specific process, pressure would be placed on the Japanese to change their actions or face retaliation. This drove the industry once again toward a section 301 action. Other trade statutes were less attractive because their main remedy was simply the imposition of higher tariffs on semiconductors. While individual merchant firms might desire higher tariffs on Japanese imports, captive producers ensured that the industry as a whole would not favor the imposition of tariffs that it had sought to eliminate in the first place. This made objectionable to the SIA applying either for escape clause protection under section 201 of the Trade Act of 1974 (which, in addition, had a special ITC injury test, leaving no assurance that tariff protection would even be forthcoming) or for antidumping duties under section 731 of the Tariff Act of 1930 (more easily obtained because of a more lax injury standard). Just because the SIA was deadlocked on the antidumping issue, of course, did not constrain individual firms either inside or outside the association from proposing such remedies.

Unlike most industries seeking assistance, the semiconductor industry had important links to the defense industry and therefore had a special appeal—national security—that enabled the industry to seek invocation of section 232 of the Trade Expansion Act of 1962. This statute permits the president, upon the recommendation of the Department of Commerce, to take remedial action against imports that threaten to impair national security. The semiconductor industry's active friends in the Commerce Department, combined with the view that semiconductors were a "strategic" component of U.S. defense, might have arranged this course of action.[35] But the remedies would not be substantially different than those obtained under the antidumping or escape clause laws, and market access in Japan was not a clear national security issue.

Even though this option was never seriously considered, one might suspect that the Reagan administration would have supported the semiconductor industry's pleas on national security grounds. Somewhat surprisingly, the foreign policy and national security agencies were divided in the semiconductor dispute. In the mid-1980s, the Central Intelligence Agency expressed its concern over U.S. dependence on foreign semiconductor products, a view strongly supported in a 1987 report by the Defense Science Board, an industry advisory group. But the Department of Defense was neutral in the semiconductor dispute, not only because it usually played a minor role in trade policy issues

35. There is no ITC injury test under this statute, and Congress cannot override the president's decision.

overall but because another faction within the Pentagon supported inexpensive sourcing of microelectronic components from Japan, in their mind a key strategic ally with whom continued good relations were vital.[36] The National Security Council supported this position, and its opposition to any trade action against Japan deprived the industry of a potentially influential supporter and meant that administration support for the industry on "national security" grounds was unlikely. Curiously enough, USTR Yeutter took the national security argument seriously and sometimes argued that position against the National Security Advisor in cabinet-level meetings.

In any event, section 301 and antidumping petitions were soon filed. Unlike the indecision of 1981–82, the actual filing of complaints triggered an administrative timetable at the end of which loomed the possible imposition of large retaliatory or antidumping duties.

1.5.1   Market Access and Section 301

The case for filing a section 301 petition first had to be made within the SIA. This action—involving substantial legal resources and personnel time (both on the SIA staff and in individual firms)—was financed by a special assessment above regular SIA membership dues to meet the estimated $900,000 cost. A draft version of the petition supported by Intel and AMD called for import restraints on Japanese semiconductors should the negotiations on market access fail. IBM and other larger purchasers balked at this proposal, and to prevent the captive firms from opposing the petition altogether, the final version eliminated this demand.

On June 14, 1985, the SIA filed a petition with the Office of the USTR under section 301 of the Trade Act of 1974. The general thrust of the SIA's complaint about market access in Japan was no different from what it had been in the early 1980s, only the context (the Reagan administration's view of market opening), the law (section 301 as amended in 1984), and the USTR (Clayton Yeutter had replaced William Brock) had changed. The petition focused on four aspects of Japan's semiconductor policy. First, the petition provided circumstantial evidence of market barriers in Japan. In 1984, the U.S. semiconductor industry accounted for over 83 percent of sales in the U.S. market, 55 percent in the European market, 47 percent in the other (Asian) markets, but only 11 percent in the Japanese market. The U.S. share of the Japanese market, they noted, remained fixed near 10 percent for a decade despite the formal liberalization of the Japanese market in 1975. Second, the SIA argued that structural barriers in the Japanese market, such as "buy Japan" attitudes and reciprocal trading or tie-in relationships among firms, were an impediment to U.S. entry. Third, the Japanese government condoned anticompetitive practices and undertook countermeasures such as administrative guidance and VLSI

---

36. The Pentagon has often been liberal on trade issues, reflecting the export-oriented stance of many defense contractors.

subsidies to undermine the 1975 liberalization. Finally, by reducing investment risks and adding to capacity, these government policies promoted the dumping of semiconductors by Japanese firms.

These actions, concluded the SIA, violated U.S. trade agreements with Japan (article XI of the GATT on the transparency of trade barriers, and the 1983 bilateral agreement on greater U.S. participation in the Japanese semiconductor market), denied U.S. firms "fair and equitable market opportunities," and therefore were "unreasonable" under the meaning of section 301. The SIA requested relief in the form of an "equivalence of market participation" in the Japanese market and an end to "dumping." Therefore, the SIA encouraged USTR to get the Japanese government to stimulate greater purchases of U.S. semiconductors, to develop a price-cost framework to prevent dumping, and to initiate an investigation of antimonopoly law violations. If no settlement was reached, the SIA recommended sanctions against Japan to achieve these objectives as long as the sanctions would not deny domestic semiconductor consumers access to adequate volumes of these goods.

The procedures governing USTR's handling of section 301 cases are quite different from administered protection cases considered by the Commerce Department and the ITC. Once a section 301 petition has been formally filed, USTR (in consultation with other agencies) has 45 days to accept or reject the petition. During this period, USTR and key agencies within the administration must be persuaded that the case is legitimate. Although section 301 cases are handled principally by USTR, they are constrained to the extent that they had to solicit (if not heed) advice from other agencies.[37] More substantively, Lande and Van Grasstek (1986, 42) note that "whereas Commerce and the USITC are intended to deal with cases solely on their objective merits as defined by the relevant statutes, the USTR's task is more subjective. It must not only investigate the petitioner's allegations, and determine whether a legal right of the United States has been violated, but also must be prepared to devise and pursue a negotiated solution with a foreign government. The USTR both adjudicates and advocates these cases."

Consequently, "the USTR exercises greater legal and political judgment when it accepts a petition under section 301" than the Commerce Department does in antidumping and countervailing duties investigations. In fact, "the USTR has complete discretion to accept or reject petitions" and can reject a petition "if, in its judgment, the case might lead to unwanted political complications for the United States." Acceptance of a petition is treated as a serious matter because, once it is accepted and the United States begins to negotiate,

37. As Prestowitz (1988, 424) notes: "The trade representative coordinates by chairing a series of interdepartmental committees, culminating in a cabinet-level committee that passes recommendations to the president. The concern for ensuring that all possible interests are considered in making any trade policy means that virtually every agency of the government sits on these committees. This procedure puts strong emphasis on consensus. Unanimity is not required, but major efforts are made to accommodate dissenting agencies."

the government becomes an interested party and its credibility is at stake. The government must be persuaded that a real trade barrier exists and that a settlement is feasible.

Thus, once the section 301 request had been filed, the SIA's job had just begun. Now the administration had to be convinced not only that the case had merits, but that the U.S. could obtain a settlement with Japan that would not seriously affect diplomatic relations between the two countries. "Because Japan is both friend and ally, and because the problem with Japan arose from a set of interrelated policies carried out over many years rather than from a specific trade action," Prestowitz (1988, 160) points out, "there was great reluctance in Washington, particularly at the Department of State and the National Security Council, to brand Japan an unfair trader." The SIA sought to persuade all agencies in the administration, particularly those that might oppose the petition, such as the traditionally skeptical Office of Management and Budget (OMB) and Council of Economic Advisers (CEA), about the merits of its case.

How as the section 301 petition initially received within the Reagan administration? From Prestowitz's (1988, 159–60) perspective at the Commerce Department, "While Commerce and the Trade Representative's office were sympathetic, other departments such as State, Treasury, the National Security Council, and even Defense argued that Japan had opened its market by removing formal tariffs and quotas in 1975. They dismissed the countermeasures to the liberalization as merely a matter of Japanese government exhortation to its industry with no concrete significance and again blamed the problems of the U.S. industry on poor management which had not taken the long-term view and had not really tried to get into the Japanese market." This statement somewhat overstates the hostility to the petition. Prior to the filing of a petition, the industry consults the administration on the advisability of taking formal action. Unless there is positive feedback, a petition is unlikely to be filed, as happened in 1982. The SIA's petition was attractive in many respects: it was in line with the administration's emerging stress on opening foreign markets, did not directly advocate closing the U.S. market, and would help mollify congressional critics who wanted a tougher Japan policy. Personal contacts also appear to have secured the petition a sympathetic hearing at USTR. In 1985, William Brock (who had rejected a section 301 in 1982) had been replaced as USTR by Clayton Yeutter. The SIA main counsel, Alan Wolff of Dewey Ballantine, had worked with both Yeutter and his deputy, Michael Smith, at USTR in the Ford administration.[38] Such high-level contacts in USTR ensured that the SIA's petition would receive serious consideration.

Yet Prestowitz's recollection also captures some of the skepticism in the administration. Any petition, particularly a controversial one guaranteed to

---

38. Wolff was general counsel at USTR during 1975–77. Yeutter was deputy special trade representative at USTR during 1975–77. Smith was chief of the Textile and Fiber Division at the State Department during 1973–75, chief textile negotiator at USTR during 1975–79, and deputy special representative for trade negotiations at USTR during 1979–81.

generate a major confrontation with Japan, would encounter a fair degree of caution and even opposition within the administration. But his recollection does not do justice to the troublesome problems with the petition. First, what were the "unfair" and "discriminatory" government trade barriers that were actionable under section 301? The SIA pointed to past government policies, but no current practices, inhibiting imports. Aside from vague and amorphous claims about the policies and attitudes of the Japanese government and firms, the SIA resorted to identifying the structure of the Japanese market as a barrier to trade. They merely observed that the largest semiconductor producers were also major consumers, that captive production was large (25 percent of total consumption), and that producers engaged in reciprocal trading. By SIA's numbers, foreign firms already had nearly 20 percent of the Japanese market if captive production was excluded from "the market" as it was in the United States.

As for the widely distributed SIA pie charts showing country shares in regional markets, an alternative hypothesis was consistent with no Japanese unfair practices: U.S. producers dominated the U.S. market, Japanese producers dominated the Japanese market, and U.S. producers essentially split European and other markets with other producers, holding a slightly higher share in Europe owing to long-standing direct investments in Europe behind the tariff barrier that kept out Japanese imports. The strongest statement the SIA could muster was that "these trade [market share] figures, coupled with Japan's protectionist heritage in microelectronics, *strongly suggests* that market barriers still exist in Japan."[39] To economists at OMB, CEA, Justice, and elsewhere, no compelling, persuasive evidence of market barriers existed: defunct government policies, vertical integration (like IBM and AT&T), and long-term relationships hardly seemed to constitute actionable unfair trade practices. To wit, Japanese access to the U.S. market in the early 1980s may have been hindered by a discriminatory distribution system.[40]

These economists also pointed out that U.S. semiconductor firms were the beneficiaries of just as much government support as Japanese semiconductor producers. In 1986, U.S. government financial support for semiconductor R&D outstripped Japan's support by a factor of 10, although U.S. support tended to be not commercial, but defense related.[41] The SIA wanted "equal market access," but the U.S. market share in Japan was comparable to the Japanese market share in the United States. Furthermore, the current industry reces-

39. SIA and Dewey Ballantine, *Japanese Market Barriers in Microelectronics,* Memorandum in Support of a Petition Pursuant to Section 301 of the Trade Act of 1974, as amended, June 14, 1984 (Washington, D.C., 1985), 2. Emphasis added.
40. U.S. semiconductor firms contained Japanese access to the U.S. market by terminating contracts with distributors who agreed to carry Japanese products. Japanese semiconductor firms had only one nationwide distributor in the United States (Marshall Industries) because of the "unspoken ban on Japanese franchises" and the "dictum that large houses will not take on the Japanese so long as they are supported by domestic suppliers" (see *Electronic News,* December 9, 1985, S28).
41. Federal Interagency Staff Working Group (1987, 31).

sion was worldwide, with no import surge in the United States and with Japanese firms experiencing financial losses and layoffs as well. If the SIA's case appeared weak to government economists, the remedies proposed by the SIA appeared worse. They feared that any governmental agreement would result in a worldwide cartel with the government fixing prices and arranging market shares by fiat. The SIA was requesting an unprecedented package: a promise by the Japanese government to force its firms to raise its prices, not just in the United States but in *all* markets, as well as agree to a market share performance target for market access. Left unclear was precisely the Japanese government's obligation and mechanism by which those ends would be achieved. Although the SIA never filed a dumping complaint, the section 301 petition also touched on the sensitive issue of antidumping remedies, raising questions about the appropriateness of this avenue of relief.

In its persuasion effort, the SIA tried to ensure that there were no obvious domestic opponents to the petition by coopting potential opposition. No one could seriously object to the principle of market access, but the mention of antidumping measures in the petition raised some alarms. The AEA was the one organization containing major semiconductor users and might object to policies that increased the price of semiconductors. Many members of the AEA were sympathetic to anything that resembled market opening in Japan, a precedent that many of its members would have liked to see established and emulated for their own industry. These semiconductor users could not foresee any possible resolution of a section 301 case that could harm its interests. The SIA shrewdly consulted with the AEA before and after filing the petition, and in the end the AEA wrote a letter to USTR supporting the petition. However, semiconductor equipment manufacturers publicly opposed the petition because they would be hurt by efforts to reduce Japanese production investments, but they appear not to have engaged in lobbying efforts.[42]

The SIA also hired a public relations firm to elicit media coverage and organized a support group of 20 congressmen from both political parties to spearhead activities on Capitol Hill. They put pressure on the administration to support the SIA's petition, often writing letters to or holding meetings with administration officials, or organizing votes on nonbinding resolutions. Perhaps the most important congressional service to the SIA was providing access to key administration officials. Senator Alan Cranston of California set up meetings for SIA representatives with Secretary of State George Shultz. At one meeting, recounted by Coleman (1987), Secretary Shultz was apparently impressed with SIA charts depicting the low U.S. market share in Japan compared to other markets and was evidently persuaded of the merits of their case.

---

42. As an official of the Semiconductor Equipment Manufacturing Institute stated, "I can tell you that American semiconductor production equipment firms are being kept alive today only from Japanese orders. We have 'zero' orders from U.S. semiconductor manufacturers. If it weren't for the Japanese manufacturing expansion, many U.S. equipment firms would be out of business" (*Electronic News,* June 24, 1985, 62).

The State Department's traditional defense of Japan was muted in this particular case, an achievement that could not have happened without converting the secretary. This in turn may not have happened had not a senator insisted on a meeting with one of the busiest administration officials.

By contrast, the scope for Japanese lobbying while the petition was being considered was actually quite limited. Recognizing that congressional support would never be forthcoming in the current environment, the Japanese government concentrated their diplomatic efforts on the foreign policy establishment, such as the State Department and National Security Council, to forestall the section 301 action. The EIAJ and the SIA kept the international trade lawyers busy by filing counterbriefs to each other's briefs. The EIAJ argued that U.S. firms were successful in the Japanese market, that Japanese market structure did not prevent U.S. participation, and that the section 301 case was not actionable because no current government practice was identified. The EIAJ strenuously objected to giving the SIA a "guaranteed" market share in Japan.

In the end, the pressures to move forward with a significant market-opening initiative against Japan triumphed. Less than a month after the filing of the SIA petition, USTR initiated the semiconductor case and requested consultations with the government of Japan.

1.5.2 Antidumping

The opposition of the captive producers to higher tariffs on semiconductors prevented the SIA from ever filing an antidumping complaint. This did not, of course, prevent any individual member from filing on its own, although there would be pressure not to break ranks from the SIA consensus. But the antidumping issue was forced by a small semiconductor firm that was (at the time) not even a member of the SIA—Micron Technology of Boise, Idaho. On June 24, 1985, Micron filed an antidumping complaint against four principal Japanese exporters of 64K DRAMs—NEC, Hitachi, Mitsubishi, and Oki—alleging that these firms had been dumping DRAMs in the U.S. market. Furthermore, Micron contended that the home market sales of the Japanese producers were below their costs of production so that the foreign market value (the "fair" U.S. sales price) had to be based on constructed value (i.e., a U.S. government-imputed cost of production).

How could Micron argue that it represented the industry with the SIA actively in place? If the relevant market for determining legal standing is judged to be 64K DRAMs alone, then all U.S. merchant producers except Micron and TI had abandoned DRAM production by the end of 1985. While the SIA remained formally neutral in the antidumping process, AMD, Mostek, Motorola, National Semiconductor, TI, and Intel all indicated their support for the petition during the ITC investigation. (Motorola, TI, and Intel even sent representatives to testify before an ITC hearing.) The participation of TI, the only other remaining producer of DRAMs, is somewhat surprising. TI did not cosponsor the petition for fear of jeopardizing ties in Japan, where it produced semiconductors and had long-standing direct investments. Both AT&T and IBM as captive producers took no position on the petition, and silence is generally viewed as support.

Merchant members of the SIA soon broke ranks: on September 30, 1985, Intel, AMD, and National Semiconductor filed for antidumping action against imports of EPROMs from Japan, aimed primarily at Hitachi, Mitsubishi, and Fujitsu. Notably absent from this list once again was TI, the largest U.S. producer of EPROMs. Like Micron, these producers claimed that Japanese home prices were below their costs of production so that the foreign market value had to be determined by means of constructed value.

Then Prestowitz (1988, 161) at the Commerce Department stepped in. "Since shock treatment was needed in order to get some negotiating leverage, I recommended that the U.S. government do what it had the legal authority to do but never had done before: start its own dumping case on 256K RAM chips without waiting for private industry to file a suit, and thus move the government from the position of intermediary to one of advocate."[43] Secretary of Commerce Malcolm Baldrige agreed, and the proposal went to a cabinet-level trade task force, which—after contentious discussions—did not oppose it. In December 1985, the Commerce Department self-initiated an antidumping case on 256K and future generations of DRAMs.

The scope for Japanese lobbying in such administrative trade cases is severely limited. The antidumping process is one in which the provision of information can be important but is not susceptible to much influence as a result of foreign pressure. Each of the "defendants"—NEC, Hitachi, Fujitsu, Mitsubishi, Toshiba, and Oki—hired separate legal counsel in the United States to defend their cases before the Commerce Department and the ITC. But once the petitions had been filed and the formal antidumping administrative process was underway, there were great incentives for the Japanese to settle the dispute with the petitioners directly rather than to see the antidumping process through in the hopes of vindication: the Commerce Department virtually always finds dumping, often at high margins, although there is some uncertainty about whether the ITC will find final injury. Faced with the likely prospect that antidumping duties will be imposed, the antidumping process affords an opportunity for the domestic industry and their foreign competitors to arrive at some mutually agreeable solution, such as a VER. The strict timetable of the antidumping process—cases must be resolved within roughly 280 days—provides a fixed deadline for such negotiations.

As the semiconductor antidumping petitions ground through the administrative trade bureaucracy toward the inevitable conclusion, the pressure steadily built on Japan. In August 1986, the ITC issued a preliminary determination in

---

43. The Commerce Department acquired statutory authority over the antidumping laws in 1979. The Treasury Department had initiated several cases on its own related to the trigger-pricing mechanism covering steel products.

the 64K DRAM case affirming that there was a reasonable indication of material injury to the domestic industry by means of imports. In December, the Commerce Department announced its preliminary determination that Japanese firms were pricing at less than fair value. But by this time, the negotiations had begun.

1.6   The Semiconductor Trade Agreement of 1986

After many preliminary discussions in late 1985, negotiations between MITI (and the EIAJ) and USTR (and the SIA) to settle both the antidumping and the market access questions began in earnest in early 1986. The deadline imposed by the section 301 statute for the negotiations was July 1, although this was later extended to July 31, which was also when the final antidumping determinations were due from the Commerce Department. Since no party (with the possible exception of Micron) had an interest in seeing the antidumping duties imposed, this date became the fixed endpoint to the negotiations, which, of course, lasted until the last moment with an agreement finally being reached shortly before midnight on July 30.[44]

The objectives of the parties can be briefly described as follows. MITI and the EIAJ wanted an agreement that would end both the section 301 and antidumping cases without making specific promises to guarantee market access or prevent third-country dumping. These were precisely the issues that the SIA viewed as essential parts of any agreement: an end to dumping on a worldwide basis and "real" market access in Japan. Any agreement that just prevented dumping in the United States would be inadequate; this would not only make the United States a "high-price island" of semiconductors to the detriment of domestic user industries but (more directly in the SIA's interest) would harm the sales of U.S. firms in third markets as Japan shifted its sales elsewhere. The SIA also required not just better opportunities for sales in Japan, but the actual realization of sales ("the cash registers must ring," as it was put at the time) to be assessed by a quantitative appraisal of market access. On the basis of studies it had commissioned, the SIA believed it would have at least 24–40 percent of the Japanese market under "free" conditions and wanted the agreement to stipulate some explicit target share.

For its part, USTR essentially wanted any agreement that satisfied the SIA. Although only government officials could be present at and participate in the formal negotiations, held in the Winder Building (which houses USTR, on 17th Street across from the Old Executive Office Building in Washington), SIA representatives were often in an adjacent room, available for close consultations during the negotiations and ready to advise USTR about what was accept-

---

44. The principal negotiators with final responsibility for the agreement were Clayton Yeutter, the USTR, and Michio Watanabe, the minister of MITI. Their deputies (Michael Smith and Makato Kuroda) and staff handled most of the detailed negotiations.

able and what was not.[45] The principal location of the negotiations in Washington is also not insignificant as the USTR negotiators thereby benefited from the services of the U.S. intelligence community, which appear to have played a role at more than one juncture in this dispute.

The sticking points of the negotiations were, as expected, third-country dumping and market access. In early 1986, MITI offered to institute an export price floor or related VER on shipments to the United States. The industry and therefore the administration rejected this offer because it would still permit dumping in third markets. On market access, MITI also approached members of the SIA and reportedly offered to guarantee 20 percent of the purchases of Japan's five largest users of chips to U.S. suppliers by 1990. The SIA rejected this offer as disingenuous because it would only raise the U.S. market share in Japan 4 percentage points to about 13 percent.[46]

Meanwhile, the antidumping cases were slowly grinding their way through the trade bureaucracy. In January 1986, the ITC ruled without dissent in the 256K+ DRAM case that there was a "reasonable indication" the domestic industry was materially injured. In March, the Commerce Department announced preliminary dumping margins on EPROMs and 256K and higher DRAMs. Reported with the Commerce Department's usual precision, the margins were astounding, ranging from 21.7 to 188.0 percent for EPROMs and from 19.8 to 108.72 percent (for a weighted average of 39.68 percent) for 256K and 1M DRAMs. Upon the announcement of preliminary margins, importers had to post bond, meaning the duties went temporarily into effect. At the end of April, the Commerce Department issued its final dumping determination in the 64K DRAM case against four major Japanese firms, with a weighted average 20.75 percent dumping margin (ranging from 11.87 to 35.34 percent). It must be made clear what these determinations implied—that Japanese prices in the United States (foreign market values) were below the constructed cost figures of what prices "should have been" in Japan. It is by no means evident that Japanese firms were pricing below average costs and therefore losing money on sales to the United States. To the contrary, according to the Commerce Department's report, the one Japanese firm that provided verifiable profit data for the first six months of 1985 on 64K DRAM sales earned a profit that exceeded the 8 percent statutory minimum, and this profit was imputed to others in determining the foreign market value of Japanese exports.[47]

45. The USTR, Clayton Yeutter, speaking at an SIA dinner in September 1986, remarked: "With so many familiar faces in the audience, I feel particularly at home here this evening. We joked in Washington that many of you were becoming permanent fixtures at USTR during the innumerable days (and nights) of semiconductor talks with the Japanese" (Ambassador Clayton Yeutter, United States Trade Representative, Remarks at Semiconductor Industry Association Annual Forecast Dinner, September 23, 1986, Santa Clara, Calif.).
46. MITI sometimes communicated directly with specific members of the SIA rather than the U.S. government or the industry association itself, possibly in an effort to divide the industry.
47. *Federal Register,* April 29, 1986, 15946; also USITC (1986c, a-11).

At the end of May, the ITC voted 4–2 in the final determination in the 64K DRAM case that the domestic industry was materially injured, the affirmative citing the poor financial condition of domestic producers as well as the sharp decline in market prices. This outcome presaged a similar finding in the 256K+ DRAM case and thus made it absolutely clear that, barring an agreement, the antidumping duties would remain in effect with the Commerce Department's final determination. Two dissenting commissioners, however, argued that the industry was experiencing a normal cyclical downturn with no evidence of injury by means of imports. Commissioner Anne Brunsdale pointed to two striking facts. First, import penetration of Japanese DRAMs had actually fallen sharply: the ratio of imports from Japan to apparent U.S. consumption dropped to 13.5 percent in 1985, from 23.6 percent in 1984 and 29.3 percent in 1983. Second, ITC data indicated that the 64K DRAM had been quite profitable for the industry: gross profits by U.S. and Japanese firms amounted to $165 million over 1983–85 with an average margin of nearly 18 percent (the particularly large margins in 1983 and 1984, reaching 33.2 percent in 1984, compensated for deep losses in 1985).[48] The final Commerce Department determinations on EPROMs were due on July 30, and on 256K+ DRAMs on August 1, with the final ITC rulings in these cases slated for September.

The large preliminary antidumping findings and the first material injury decision strengthened the bargaining position of U.S. negotiators even further: Japan had to settle the case to avoid the automatic and nonnegotiable imposition of these duties, as well as possible section 301 sanctions. Congress reinforced the leverage of U.S. negotiators: in May, the House of Representatives voted 408–5 to recommend that the administration take some action (i.e., retaliate) under section 301 if it could not secure a market access agreement with Japan. The Japanese also confronted a broad administration consensus that some type of semiconductor trade agreement was needed. In late June, Deputy USTR Michael Smith informed the Japanese that the cabinet was prepared to retaliate if no agreement was reached. This apparently was a bluff, but a highly credible bluff nonetheless.[49]

In the end, Japan largely capitulated and acceded to most of the U.S. negotiator's (i.e., industry's) demands. While USTR did quite well in securing what the SIA wanted, the EIAJ felt abandoned by MITI, which may account for its later reluctance to adhere to MITI's guidelines enforcing the agreement. However, the agreement was plagued by two problems regarding third-country dumping and market access that soon brought the governments into renewed conflict with one another: (1) the considerable ambiguity as to the exact obliga-

---

48. USITC (1986c, 48, 53).
49. According to Prestowitz (1988, 171), "In fact, no one will ever know whether the cabinet would actually have voted against the Japanese. To some extent Smith's move was a ploy to scare them." Prestowitz also notes that "the critical change had been at the State Department, which for years had acted to protect Japan from its critics."

tions of the government of Japan and (2) the inexact timetable for achieving the objectives of the agreement.

Under the agreement, Japan agreed to take actions that would end dumping in the United States. The antidumping provisions of the arrangement hinged on a suspension agreement between the Department of Commerce and the individual Japanese firms in which Japanese exporters agreed to report data on all U.S. sales and on actual and anticipated costs of production. Based on this information, the Commerce Department would determine company-specific price floors (foreign market values, or FMVs) each quarter and provide this information to the Japanese firms.[50] In monitoring prices and costs of shipments to the U.S. market, the agreement stipulated that "the Government of Japan will take appropriate actions . . . to prevent exports at prices less than company-specific fair value." The agreement primarily concerned DRAMs and EPROMs, but the United States reserved the right to add or drop semiconductor products from the list.

Despite the U.S. understanding that Japan was obligated to prevent dumping in third-country markets, the agreement makes no explicit statement of the government's responsibility for taking action to prevent such dumping. In a separate section of the agreement on third markets, the text merely reads: "Both Governments recognize the need to prevent dumping. . . . In order to prevent dumping, the Government of Japan will monitor, as appropriate, costs and export prices on the products exported by Japanese semiconductor firms from Japan." There is no mention of the government of Japan taking "appropriate actions," and MITI later denied responsibility for preventing third-country dumping, although the phrase "in order to prevent dumping" implies some measure of responsibility.

On the issue of market access, how did U.S. negotiators handle the SIA's demand for specific targets for increasing sales in Japan? In 1985, in the midst of congressional pressure over the surging trade deficit, the administration had considered but rejected a proposal that Japan import a specified quantity of U.S. manufactured goods.[51] Even if the notion of import targets had been circulating within the administration for congressional consumption, market opening under section 301 usually took the form of removing a formal government trade barrier, such as a quota or some form of nonnational treatment, and then allowing the market to operate without interference. There was still great resistance to specifying an exact import market share because it smacked of man-

---

50. The purpose of company-specific FMVs was to avoid a fixed export price floor and allow low-cost producers the freedom to cut prices.

51. According to Niskanen (1988, 152), "In preparation for the Reagan-Nakasone meeting in January 1985, a paper prepared by [Beryl] Sprinkel [then undersecretary for monetary affairs at the Department of Treasury, and later chairman of the CEA] proposed that the United States insist that the Japanese set quantitative targets to increase manufactured imports; this proposal was broadly supported, against my lonely opposition, through four cabinet council meetings until the intervention of [Secretary of State] Shultz and [Secretary of Defense] Weinberger reminded the president of our larger interests in Japan."

aged trade and raised questions of how Japan could implement such targets. Prestowitz (as an advocate of targets) provides one perspective on this point:

> It's not that we don't try to force the Japanese to make the commitments; it's more that we ourselves are loathe to spell out just what the commitment should be. To some extent, the Japanese outnegotiate us, but they do so because we handicap ourselves. We never allow our negotiators to negotiate for an explicit share. In this negotiation of semiconductors, our negotiators could never actually ask for 20 percent. And the reason was not because the Japanese didn't let them; the reason was because our own trade policy, our own thinking about economics, prevents us from asking for a market share. We think it's contradictory to the free-market principles that we uphold. So we never allow our negotiators to ask for anything concrete. And so they were always in a position where they ask for market access. The Japanese say, "You have market access." And our negotiators say, "Yeah, but we never sell anything." The Japanese say, "Well, how much do you want?" And the Americans can never respond to that. They often have to say we want significantly more. The Japanese say, "That's fine. How much more?" And Americans say, "Buh-buh-buh-buh-buhhh." The Japanese say, "How about . . ." and they name a number. Then you get into winking and nodding across the table. (Quoted in Warshofsky 1989, 167–68)

The official text of the 1986 agreement supports this view, simply stating that "the Government of Japan will impress upon the Japanese producers and users of semiconductors the need to aggressively take advantage of increased market access opportunities in Japan for foreign-based firms which will improve their actual sales performance. . . . Both Governments agree that the expected improvement in access should be gradual and steady over the period of this Arrangement." This language is little different from the 1983 High Technology Agreement in which MITI agreed to encourage Japanese firms to buy U.S. semiconductors.

Contra Prestowitz, however, a "number" was discussed at various levels in the government from the start of the negotiations because that was the specific remedy proposed by the SIA. Yet final authority to request a specific number (a highly sensitive and controversial issue) is appropriately limited to cabinet-level officials, specifically the USTR, rather than lower-level bureaucrats. In this case, USTR Yeutter explicitly asked for 20 percent in a Tokyo meeting with Minister Watanabe on May 28, 1986. A now infamous, secret side-letter to the final agreement, reproduced in the appendix, explicitly mentions the 20 percent market share. However, the language of the secret side-letter is vague, reading simply that "the Government of Japan recognizes the U.S. semiconductor industry's expectation" that sales will rise to "slightly above 20 percent" in five years and that "the Government of Japan considers that this can be realized." This language surely is ambiguous as to whether it constitutes a binding governmental commitment, and this later proved to be a source of dispute. Although its contents were widely known at the time (the side-letter was partially published in the *Financial Times* prior to the conclusion of the agreement), the letter remained officially secret—and in fact was withheld by USTR from other government agencies.[52] This secrecy allowed both sides to deny that they had carved up markets in a "managed trade" agreement, but the effect of the secrecy was asymmetric: Japan denied there was any explicit commitment about guaranteeing a market share, while the United States held Japan accountable for such a commitment though it could not produce the text in public to support its position.

With the agreement in place, Japan confronted the next critical issue: how was it to be enforced? What policy measures and instruments did they have at their disposal, beyond mere exhortation, to guarantee that Japanese firms did not dump in the world market and bought the requisite amount of foreign-made chips? Implementation—quite mistakenly—was not viewed as a major concern for U.S. negotiators, but it was a real problem for Japan precisely because it was now committed to certain actions in a governmental agreement and under threat of sanction if the terms of the agreement were violated. Having made a commitment, Japan now faced the burden of making the agreement work. The U.S. government now expected Japan to adhere to the agreement, illustrating how the semiconductor industry had turned its grievance into the government's affair.

To prevent dumping, the Japanese government (specifically, MITI) did the only thing it knew how to do—reduce the quantity of semiconductors exported in an effort to raise export prices sufficiently. MITI essentially imposed an "antidumping VER"—an export restraint designed to meet a price target rather than a quantitative target, and therefore inherently more difficult to administer. MITI issued supply and demand forecasts to provide targeted production levels and induce firms to trim output. MITI had no statutory authority to force any firm to comply in reducing output, but bureaucratic delays in approval of export licenses—also tightened to prevent dumping—could unexpectedly arise for recalcitrant firms. These guidelines and regulations were at first easily evaded, and MITI's initial efforts to prevent dumping were not fully successful and semiconductors leaked out of Japan into third markets. TI-Japan was reportedly one of the least cooperative firms in cutting output and adhering to its FMV for sales to the United States.

The agreement's first problem materialized even before the official signing of the agreement on September 2, 1986.[53] In August, the Commerce Department issued the first quarterly FMVs, and because the minimum prices were based on old production data, by late September the U.S. price of a 256K DRAM had almost doubled. Semiconductor users in the AEA were shocked. They regarded the high antidumping margins announced during the course of

---

52. This secrecy bred deep suspicion in other executive agencies of USTR and Commerce, particularly as the market access commitment became one of the grounds for retaliation.

53. The SIA supported a public signing of the agreement in the Rose Garden of the White House to underscore the gravity of the commitments undertaken.

the negotiations as a bargaining tool and (perhaps naively) never actually believed that they would be implemented. The AEA complained that members might have to move production of computers and other electronics goods overseas to avoid high U.S. semiconductor prices. The CBEMA wrote to the commerce secretary requesting a change in the methodology for setting FMVs. The SIA sought to sooth these concerns by bringing better data to the Commerce Department, and prices were brought down when the next quarter's FMVs were issued.

The second problem concerned the issue of third-country dumping. In late October, the SIA complained to USTR that such dumping was continuing and proposed retaliation for Japan's noncompliance with the agreement. After consultations with USTR, MITI issued a directive urging dumping to cease. Yet MITI continued to have difficulty in getting Japanese firms to comply with the request and prices continued to be depressed in third markets. A striking differential in semiconductor prices arose across international markets, and colorful stories surfaced of arbitragers purchasing chips in Asia, flying them to Canada or Mexico, and then smuggling them across the U.S. border. The trunk of a passenger vehicle supposedly accommodates approximately 25,000 chips, meaning a price difference of $2 or so per chip can save a firm upward of $40,000 in one car!

The third problem arose in early October when the European Community strenuously objected to the semiconductor accord and filed a complaint before the GATT. The European Community argued that the third-market provisions set "arbitrary [price] increases" for European semiconductor consumers and the market access provisions afforded U.S. firms "privileged access" to the Japanese market. A GATT panel ruled in 1988 that monitoring of export prices on third-market sales by Japan violated article XI of the GATT (on governmental quantitative restrictions), although the market access provisions of the agreement were not found to violate most-favored-nation treatment. As a result, Japan announced that it would desist from monitoring sales in third countries. In 1989, the European Community and Japan concluded their own semiconductor agreement that set minimum export prices on sales in Europe. The European Community remained suspicious that the market share target discriminated against European semiconductor producers. In 1992, the European Electronic Components Manufacturers Association demanded their own market share target of 5 percent in Japan.[54]

As for the market access provisions of the 1986 agreement, the SIA directed attention to the quarter-by-quarter movement in the foreign share of the Japanese semiconductor market. Foreign producers held 8.5 percent of Japan's market in the second quarter of 1986, just prior to the agreement, and the share

---

54. In setting this target, the association noted that Europe's estimated world market share outside of Europe and Japan was roughly 5 percent, while its share in Japan was less than 1 percent. European producers believed they had been excluded from trade missions sponsored by the SIA and the EIAJ (see *Electronic News*, December 14, 1992, 23).

was constant at 8.6 percent in the second half of that year. The SIA deemed this as evidence of Japan's noncompliance. Although this share rose to 9.0 percent in the first quarter of 1987, this was not known until well after preparations had begun for retaliation.

By early 1987, MITI's export controls on sales to the United States succeeded in preventing dumping, but the SIA renewed its complaints about the continuation of third-country dumping and about the lack of movement in its market share in Japan. MITI had insufficient power to force Japanese producers to purchase foreign chips in the space of a few months but tried to boost DRAM prices by issuing recommendations (administrative guidance) in February to reduce output by 10 percent. From MITI's perspective, such a production cutback would not only assist in enforcing the agreement but would be a step toward an antirecession cartel to coordinate production and investment decisions for the industry's benefit.

At least one merchant producer (Micron) argued that a 10 percent reduction was insufficient. But the SIA blasted the move, accusing MITI of trying to create "artificial shortages" and increasing government interference in the market.[55] This baffling criticism—that the SIA did not want Japan to sell less, they just wanted them to charge a higher price—ignored the fact that the production cuts were a natural outcome of the agreement. As Prestowitz (1988, 166–67) observed, requiring the Japanese government to drive up prices in the United States and in third markets "amounted to getting the Japanese government to force its companies to make a profit and even to impose controls to avoid excess production—in short, a government-led cartel. For the free-traders of the United States to be asking Japan to cartelize its industry was the supreme irony. Yet it was logical. . . . It was subsequently criticized for doing so, but it had little choice."

After having devoted so much time to securing an agreement with Japan, the administration was concerned—even after less than six months of operation—that Japan was not adhering to the agreement: "dumping" continued in third countries and market access had not "measurably" improved.[56] Fears of a loss of credibility with Capitol Hill (if not with Japan), which could trigger a backlash against another "failed" trade agreement with Japan, meant that even executive agencies opposed to the agreement felt it necessary to adopt strong measures to ensure its implementation. By the end of January 1987, the administration gave Japan 60 days to demonstrate that it was enforcing the agreement. On March 19, 1987, the Senate passed by 93–0 a nonbinding reso-

55. Andrew Procassini, president of the SIA, stated that "rather than requiring Japanese semiconductor producers to price devices at or above cost, as the agreement requires, MITI is trying to drive up prices artificially by creating shortages through production controls" (*Electronic News*, September 14, 1987, 1).

56. Japanese officials, of course, denied the existence of third-country dumping. The Central Intelligence Agency lured Japanese sales agents of Oki Electric into DRAM transactions at less than FMVs in Hong Kong in March 1987. Invoices were then presented to Japanese negotiators by USTR officials.

lution, introduced by Senator Pete Wilson (R-Calif.), calling on the administration to force compliance with the trade agreement, although it fell short of explicitly calling for retaliation. By that time the administration had already made preparations to impose retaliatory tariffs. Eight days later the White House announced its intent to retaliate against Japan.

On April 17, 1987, President Reagan imposed 100 percent tariffs on $300 million worth of laptop computers, desktop computers, televisions, and power tools imported from Japan. According to administration calculations, $135 million of the retaliation was for the injury suffered by domestic firms from continued third-country dumping, and $165 million for lack of progress in increasing the foreign market share.[57] The sanctions were crafted to hit the exports of the principal Japanese semiconductor producers—such as NEC, Toshiba, Hitachi, and Matsushita—but not entail significant consumer losses by virtue of close substitutes (except laptops) from domestic and other foreign producers. The retaliation ranks among the most dramatic events of postwar U.S. trade policy. Japan was stunned, but the move played directly into MITI's hands and enhanced its power; indeed, there were reports that some in MITI were secretly pleased about the retaliation because it proved to Japanese firms that they should follow MITI's directives.

The third-country dumping sanctions were gradually eased for diplomatic reasons as well as the gradually increasing effect MITI's controls had on external prices of Japanese semiconductors. In June, $51 million in sanctions were lifted before the annual G-7 summit for partial compliance with the third-country dumping provisions. In November, the administration found Japan in full compliance and the remaining $84 million in tariffs were removed. The $165 million in market access sanctions remained intact until the signing of the 1991 semiconductor accord.

1.7   Toward the 1991 Revision

The U.S. retaliation convinced Japanese firms to fall in line and follow MITI's directives more closely. By the end of its first year of operation, the semiconductor agreement succeeded in ending Japanese "dumping" in the United States and, by and large, in third markets. To adhere to the antidumping terms of the agreement, the Japanese government restricted export volume in order to meet the price targets, the functional equivalent of a VER.

As is usually the case with other VERs with Japan, the beneficiaries included Japanese semiconductor firms. The MITI-induced production cutbacks provided a substitute for cooperative industry behavior and raised the price of DRAMs on sales abroad, generating an enormous windfall for Japanese producers. According to market analysts reported in Flamm (1989, 21), profits

---

57. There was much discussion within the administration on the precise dollar amount of retaliation. The Commerce Department had floated an early figure of $1 billion.

on 1M DRAM sales for Japanese producers amounted to $1.2 billion in 1988 alone. As with other VERs, these implicit quota rents could be plowed back into R&D, capital spending, and product upgrading. Japanese firms also opened new semiconductor fabrication lines in the United States to avoid the FMVs. Other foreign beneficiaries included foreign producers not covered by the VER, particularly in South Korea where higher worldwide DRAM prices accelerated the entry of Samsung, Goldstar, and Hyundai.

The U.S. semiconductor industry was a partial beneficiary of the antidumping provisions of the 1986 accord. Even prior to the agreement, Hughes, Lenway, and Rayburn (1993) found significant positive abnormal stock returns to U.S. merchant semiconductor producers on several key announcement dates in 1986 and 1987. In the DRAM market, the main beneficiaries were limited to only two merchant firms—TI (which was reluctant to initiate any aggressive trade policies against Japan) and Micron (which ranked among the smallest of U.S. producers). According to market analysts reported in Tyson (1992, 116–17), DRAM sales accounted for as much as 60 percent of TI's profits in 1988, and Micron's sales rose by a factor of six between 1986 and 1988. The employment effects of the agreement were probably small: TI and Micron had a total DRAM-related employment of approximately 13,000, and a back-of-the-envelope calculation by Denzau (1988) suggests that for each job retained in DRAMs, another was lost in downstream computer manufacturing.[58]

For all the concern about the importance of DRAMs, however, there was no reentry of U.S. producers into the market in the aftermath of the agreement. In August 1986, Motorola agreed to buy prefabricated semiconductor dies from Toshiba, assemble the semiconductors in Malaysia, and ship them to the United States to avoid the FMVs. In June 1989, several firms—AMD, Hewlett-Packard, DEC, Intel, LSI Logic, and National Semiconductor—contributed $50,000 each to finance U.S. Memories, a consortium to establish domestic DRAM production. These firms committed themselves to buy output from U.S. Memories equivalent to half of their equity in percentage points (a firm owning 5 percent of U.S. Memories, e.g., was obligated to purchase 2.5 percent of the consortium's output). Despite even IBM's support, U.S. Memories was stillborn and collapsed in January 1990 owing to insufficient financial support and an unwillingness of other major buyers, such as Apple Computer and Sun Microsystems, to commit to future purchases. Yet beginning in 1988, the industry received extensive financial support ($100 million per year for five years) from the Department of Defense for Sematech (SEmiconductor MAnufacturing TECHnology), a industry-led process R&D consortium.

The clear losers from the semiconductor agreement were the larger and far more numerous semiconductor users, particularly computer manufacturers de-

---

58. Further back-of-the-envelope calculations by Hufbauer and Elliott (1994, 106–10) suggest increased domestic semiconductor employment of about 2,300 workers, increased producer surplus of $260 million, increased foreign producer surplus of $835 million, and reduced consumer surplus of $1.2 billion.

pendent on DRAMs. Despite numerous complaints among users and even isolated instances of outright antagonism toward the accord—Tektronix wanted to revoke the agreement completely—opposition to the 1986 agreement failed to crystalize before 1988. As figure 1.1 illustrates, DRAM prices (which usually fell sharply after introduction) shot up dramatically in 1988. The price of 256K DRAMs jumped from about $2.20 at the end of 1986 to $3.50 by the end of 1988—although long-term supply prices in Japan were largely unchanged. The price bubble mainly reflected a surge in demand for DRAMs from another rapid expansion in the computer industry as well as the MITI-induced production cutback, which now had affected capacity investment decisions.

There were also indications that Japanese producers were cooperating in a de facto market-sharing cartel. Flamm (1993b, 280) notes that "before the Semiconductor Trade Arrangement of 1986, episodes of successfully coordinated restraint on exports or output by Japanese producers seem to have occurred only after bureaucrats and politicians responded to trade friction." But even as MITI's intervention in the DRAM market became less pronounced from 1989, DRAM prices in the United States remained substantially above estimates of the FMVs. There is evidence that trade restrictions became, in Krishna's (1989) term, a "facilitating practice," that is, facilitated tacit collusion between Japanese exporters.[59] As a result of production controls, Japanese firms had to ration output to U.S. consumers, and this possibly fostered coordination and collusion. U.S. firms criticized Japanese producers for denying them adequate volume of semiconductors and hinted that it was a deliberate attempt at retribution. Japanese firms more likely allocated their production to firms with whom they had long-standing ties and avoided selling "too much" in the United States.[60] No such bubble appeared in the price of EPROMs, which were also subject to the FMVs. Intel, AMD, TI, National Semiconductor, and other U.S. producers never exited the EPROM market, and the much lower Japanese share of this market meant their power to produce a substantial price rise was much less.

The price bubble for 256K DRAMs in 1988 proved so costly to semiconductor users that it heralded the end of the SIA's monopoly position as USTR's adviser on U.S. semiconductor trade policy. Three CEOs of major computer systems firms—John Akers (IBM), James Treybig (Tandem), and John Young

---

59. Evidence on Japanese collusion is considered in Tyson (1992) and Flamm (1993b).

60. As Okimoto (1987, 389–90) points out, just as purchasers of semiconductors rely on other ties besides price, "from the supplier's standpoint, too, organizational factors can overwhelm narrowly defined market forces. During periods of economic upturn, for example, when supply fails to keep pace with demand, Japanese companies are not inclined to sell on a neutral, first-come, first-served basis. Rather, they are apt to allocate limited stocks of semiconductor components according to an implicit hierarchy of customers. Loyal, long-standing customers get priority over companies that buy sporadically on a spot market basis. Vendors and end-users alike operate within the framework of long-term, reciprocal relations, which constrain free entry into, and exit from, market transactions and which change the calculus of commercial transactions."

(Hewlett-Packard)—formed the Computer Systems Policy Project (CSPP) in early 1989 as a forum for policy discussions and coordination in this segment of the electronics industry. These executives believed that the interests of the computer industry were not being met either by the AEA (owing to its size and inclusion of semiconductor firms) or the CBEMA (owing to the membership of Japanese firms).[61] The CSPP was designed explicitly to function as a counterpart to the SIA: it was to facilitate and coordinate the industry's positions on public policy at the CEO level, with only a small staff to manage the activities of individual companies. In May 1989, these three firms invited (at an entry fee of $50,000) other firms—including AT&T, Apple Computer, Compaq Computer, Control Data, Cray Research, DEC, NCR, Prime Computer, Sun Microsystems, Tektronix, and Unisys—to join the CSPP.[62] The overarching objective of the CSPP was to develop policy recommendations relating to the competitive position of the computer manufacturers, although in the invitational letter to other firms the CSPP founders wrote that "issues relating to the U.S.-Japan semiconductor agreement" were the group's "first project" and noted that without collective political action the government "may well adopt policies counterproductive, and in some cases inimical, to the interests of our companies."[63]

Opposition among semiconductor consumers, of course, first materialized in the weeks after the initial FMVs had been issued. But this opposition remained ineffective for nearly two years because it lacked organization. The CSPP succeeded in advancing its agenda for precisely the same reasons the SIA had succeeded—CEOs were directly involved, sympathetic political audiences were targeted, and proposals carried an industry consensus. And the CSPP began its organizational life by directly opposing the SIA on several issues. John Young, the CEO of Hewlett-Packard, wrote to Senator John Heinz (R-Pa.) that the "tone" of a Senate resolution in mid-1989 on Japan's noncompliance with the 1986 agreement would "set back rather than advance" the interests of computer manufacturers.

The newly invigorated opposition to the accord was the first of a series of setbacks for the SIA in 1989. The Bush administration's new USTR, Carla Hills, criticized the 20 percent figure in the semiconductor agreement as "managed trade" and announced a dedication to "process not results" in trade policy. Hills later clarified that she would enforce the provisions of the semiconductor agreement, but her devotion to the accord was brought into question, and the SIA did not view her as an ally. Some in the semiconductor industry argued

61. As early as July 1988, Tandem argued before the AEA's executive board that there was an "urgent need" to request "significant modifications" to the 1986 semiconductor agreement to curb its "adverse impact" on downstream semiconductor users. This proposal was essentially ignored. (See *Inside U.S. Trade,* August 19, 1988, 13–14.)

62. The charter members of the CSPP were Apple Computer, Unisys Corporation, Compaq Corporation, Cray Research, Hewlett-Packard, IBM, NCR, Sun Microsystems, and Tandem. At the end of 1993, membership also included AT&T, Control Data, Data General, and DEC.

63. *Inside U.S. Trade,* June 16, 1989, 3.

that the perception that Hills took the heat off Japan stalled further progress in market access, quantitatively measured; the foreign market share stood at 13.6 percent in the third quarter of 1989 and, after rising slightly, fell back to 13.4 percent in the first quarter of 1991.

Other setbacks for the SIA arose when the 20 percent market share target appeared beyond reach for the deadline of the end of 1991. The SIA pressured the Bush administration to have Japan cited as a priority country, under the new "Super 301" provision of the Omnibus Trade and Competitiveness Act of 1988, for its failure to abide by the 1986 agreement. The EIAJ declared that such a designation would jeopardize cooperation between the two groups and threatened to propose Japan's withdrawal from the agreement. Then the CSPP and the CBEMA both directly opposed the SIA's bid in letters to USTR Hills. While supportive of policies to promote greater market access, the CSPP thought that a "priority" designation was "unnecessary and unwise" and bluntly stated that the "CSPP does not believe that the Semiconductor Arrangement should be extended." The CBEMA also attacked the notion of import targets, suggesting that an approach focusing specifically on excluded products "would be far more productive than continually reiterating the dated approach of a 20 percent market share, which was arbitrary at its inception in 1986, and remains so today."[64]

As a result of this coalition of semiconductor consumers, trade negotiators at USTR no longer faced a single voice—the SIA's—on what should determine U.S. semiconductor trade policy. With the expiration of the accord on the horizon, USTR could not possibly negotiate a satisfactory agreement in the face of sharply conflicting domestic interests. Rather than mediate between the producers and users, USTR instructed the SIA and the CSPP to resolve their differences over trade policy themselves. Whereas the SIA wanted the status quo, the CSPP wanted the agreement scrapped, or at least the antidumping provision of the agreement that kept U.S. semiconductor prices high. The CSPP was basically indifferent toward the market access provision, so long as sanction for noncompliance did not impinge on its interests.

After lengthy negotiations, the SIA and the CSPP announced in October 1990 a joint proposal concerning the shape of a renegotiated agreement. They declared the antidumping provisions of the 1986 agreement a "success" and maintained that the Commerce Department should no longer collect costs or price data or issue FMVs for DRAMs and EPROMs. (However, a "fast track" for new antidumping complaints would be maintained.) They also agreed that "market access results should be measured by quantifiable indicators of progress" and that the 20 percent market share should be attained by the end of 1992, an extension of one year.

64. The CBEMA also argued that priority designation was "inappropriate" because the 1986 agreement already was an "adequate mechanism for pursuing the market access goal for semiconductors" (*Inside U.S. Trade,* April 20, 1990, 8–10).

The cooperative front formed by the two groups was important to the SIA. The joint statement avoided the embarrassment of a larger, downstream high-technology industry vocally opposing renegotiation of the semiconductor agreement and was in its tradition of defusing potential opponents. This compromise also eased the burden on USTR of renegotiating the 1986 agreement prior to its expiry in mid-1991. Although Japan first denied the need for a new agreement, they were soon brought to the bargaining table. With the antidumping provisions no longer a key issue, the main discussions centered on whether the market access provisions should move from the now not-so-secret side-letter into the agreement's text. Japan resisted but agreed, in exchange for the removal of the remaining $165 million in sanctions. The final (five-year) agreement was reached on June 4, 1991, and the text on this provision read: "The Government of Japan recognizes that the U.S. semiconductor industry expects that the foreign market share will grow to more than 20 percent of the Japanese market by the end of 1992 and considers that this can be realized. The Government of Japan welcomes the realization of this expectation. The two governments agree that the above statements constitute neither a guarantee, a ceiling, nor a floor on the foreign market share."

The comparative ease of the 1991 negotiations demonstrated how institutionalized the semiconductor agreement had become. Unlike the serious conflicts during the 1986 negotiations, both the United States and Japan had grown accustomed to the arrangements by 1991. Cooperative interaction between the SIA and the EIAJ and their members had expanded immensely since 1986. The Deputy USTR S. Linn Williams flatly stated that the accord was "a much more businesslike agreement than its predecessor." When asked what was different between the October joint SIA-CSPP proposals and the final agreement, Williams remarked, "I would characterize most of these differences as questions of technical matters, not policy."

In awaiting the end of 1992, the only decision left to the SIA was whether to recommend retaliation if the market share target was not reached. In March 1992, the SIA released a report entitled "Headed towards Crisis" that argued that the trade agreement was "at the threshold of failure" and urged "immediate and decisive action" by all parties to ensure compliance. Contrary to virtually all expectations and propelled by weakness in the Japanese economy, the foreign (merchant) market share in Japan reached 20.2 percent in the fourth quarter of 1992. How was the market share target achieved? Even prior to the 1986 agreement, certain (nonintegrated) Japanese firms (such as Sony) purchased over 20 percent of their semiconductors from U.S. firms. MITI pressure on other purchasers (by conducting surveys of the purchasing plans of firms) and a greater presence in Japan by U.S. firms probably accounted for the gradual increase in U.S. market share. Two other hypotheses—that the composition of Japanese demand shifted toward products the United States was better at producing, or U.S. technological advance in certain rapidly growing product lines, such as Intel's 486 microprocessors, account for the larger U.S. share—are largely unsupported by disaggregated evidence on sales in Japan, according to figures presented in Bergsten and Noland (1993, 136).

How would the SIA react if the 20 percent market share were maintained? The SIA (1990, 33) once argued that "after a 20 percent level had been achieved, [the] foreign share would float to an appropriate level based on competitive merit and without further government targets. . . . [The target was] a threshold from which market forces would then take over and operate." Shortly after the 20.2 percent figures was released, a spokesman for TI stated that the industry "would be happier with less government involvement" in overseeing market access since they were becoming "part of the *keiretsu*."[65] The SIA quickly disavowed abandonment of market share targets, however, and some industry sources indicated that perhaps the market share target should be increased. After the market share dropped to nearly 18 percent in mid-1993, however, USTR Kantor requested "emergency" consultations with Japan to discuss the market access targets.[66]

The beginning of 1993 brought the SIA better news when an administration sympathetic to high-technology industries and market share targets with Japan took office.[67] Yet, as keenly illustrated in a virtual repeat of the semiconductor trade dispute in 1992–93, with South Korea as the defendant, the Clinton administration's embrace of import targets stumbled on the political realities of trade policy determination. In April 1992, Micron filed an antidumping petition alleging "less than fair value" imports of 1M and higher DRAMs from Korea. In October, the Commerce Department announced preliminary dumping margins (based on petitioner information) against Samsung (87.40 percent), Goldstar (52.41 percent), and Hyundai (5.99 percent). Faced with stiff antidumping duties, the Korean industry and government proposed in January 1993 a bilateral semiconductor trade agreement fashioned on the earlier one with Japan. In exchange for a suspension of the antidumping case, the Korean industry promised to monitor prices of export sales to the United States. The Korean government offered to sign an agreement in which it would commit itself to (as a draft stated) "demonstrable and measurable results in terms of increasing sales in Korea of U.S. semiconductors and semiconductor equipment." The government also promised to reduce or eliminate the Korean tariff

65. *Wall Street Journal,* June 7, 1993, A3.
66. One MITI official was quoted as saying, "The more the U.S. side overemphasizes this decline in the market share, the more we are convinced that we will never again negotiate a semiconductor-type arrangement" (*Wall Street Journal,* December 28, 1993, A3).
67. In early March, after less than two months in office, both the USTR (Mickey Kantor) and the Secretary of Commerce (Ronald Brown) of the Clinton administration had traveled to California to address the SIA. Kantor promised to be "vigilant" in monitoring the agreement, while Brown embraced the 1986 and 1991 accords as fine examples of results-oriented agreements, which he promised the administration would expand to other sectors. In addition, Laura D'Andrea Tyson, who had extensive personal contacts in the semiconductor industry and known policy positions sympathetic to the industry, was named chair of the CEA.

Irwin, Douglas A., and Peter J. Klenow. 1994. Learning-by-doing spillovers in the semiconductor industry. *Journal of Political Economy* 102 (December): 1200–27.

Krishna, Kala. 1989. Trade restrictions as facilitating practices. *Journal of International Economics* 26 (May): 251–70.

Lande, Stephen L., and Craig Van Grasstek. 1986. *The Trade and Tariff Act of 1984: Trade policy in the Reagan administration.* Lexington, Mass.: Lexington Books.

Mundo, Philip A. 1992. *Interest groups: Cases and characteristics.* Chicago: Nelson-Hall.

Mussa, Michael. 1974. Tariffs and the distribution of income: The importance of factor specificity, substitutability, and intensity in the short and long run. *Journal of Political Economy* 82 (November/December): 1191–1204.

Niskanen, William A. 1988. *Reaganomics: An insider's account of the policies and the people.* New York: Oxford University Press.

Okimoto, Daniel I. 1987. Outsider trading: Coping with Japanese industrial organization. *Journal of Japanese Studies* 13 (Summer): 383–414.

———. 1989. *Between MITI and the market: Japanese industrial policy for high technology.* Stanford, Calif.: Stanford University Press.

Okimoto, Daniel I., Takuo Sugano, and Franklin B. Weinstein, eds. 1984. *The competitive edge: The semiconductor industry in the U.S. and Japan.* Stanford, Calif.: Stanford University Press.

Olson, Mancur. 1971. *The logic of collective action.* Cambridge: Harvard University Press.

Ong, Paul M., and Don Mar. 1992. Post-layoff earnings among semiconductor workers. *Industrial and Labor Relations Review* 45 (January): 366–79.

OECD (Organisation for Economic Co-operation and Development). 1992. *Globalisation of industrial activities, four case studies: Auto parts, chemicals, construction, and semiconductors.* Paris: Organisation for Economic Co-operation and Development.

Prestowitz, Clyde V., Jr. 1988. *Trading places: How we are giving our future to Japan and how to reclaim it.* New York: Basic Books.

Recommendations of the U.S.-Japan Work Group on High Technology Industries—Semiconductors. 1983. November 2. (Available from Office of the U.S. Trade Representative, Washington, D.C.).

SIA (Semiconductor Industry Association). 1983. *The effect of government targeting on world semiconductor competition.* Cupertino, Calif.: Semiconductor Industry Association.

———. 1990. *Four years of experience under the U.S.-Japan Semiconductor Agreement: "A deal is a deal."* Cupertino, Calif.: Semiconductor Industry Association, November.

Tyson, Laura D'Andrea. 1992. *Who's bashing whom?: Trade conflict in high-technology industries.* Washington, D.C.: Institute for International Economics.

USITC (U.S. International Trade Commission). 1979. Competitive factors influencing world trade in integrated circuits. USITC Publication no. 1013. Washington, D.C.: U.S. International Trade Commission, November.

———. 1985. Probable economic effect of providing duty-free treatment for U.S. imports of certain high-tech products. USITC Publication no. 1705. Washington, D.C.: U.S. International Trade Commission, June.

———. 1986a. Dynamic random access memory semiconductors of 256 kilobits and above from Japan (731-TA-300, Preliminary). USITC Publication no. 1803. Washington, D.C.: U.S. International Trade Commission, January.

———. 1986b. Erasable programmable read only memories from Japan (731-TA-288, Final). USITC Publication no. 1927. Washington, D.C.: U.S. International Trade Commission, December.

———. 1986c. 64K Dynamic random access memory components from Japan (731-TA-270, Final). USITC Publication no. 1862. Washington, D.C.: U.S. International Trade Commission, June.

———. 1993a. DRAMs of one megabit and above from the Republic of Korea (71-TA-556, Final). USITC Publication no. 2629. Washington, D.C.: U.S. International Trade Commission, May.

———. 1993b. Industry and trade summary: Semiconductors. USITC Publication no. 2708. Washington, D.C.: U.S. International Trade Commission, December.

Warshofsky, Fred. 1989. *The chip war.* New York: Scribners.

Yoffe, David B. 1988. How an industry builds political advantage. *Harvard Business Review* 66 (May–June): 82–89.

Comment   Andrew R. Dick

Douglas Irwin has constructed a detailed case study of semiconductor trade policy starting in the late 1970s, when the industry first received sustained attention from policymakers and among trade theorists. His analysis has three primary strengths. First, rather than confining attention narrowly to policy outcomes, Irwin analyzes how industry characteristics and U.S. trade institutions also shaped the negotiating *process* in market access and antidumping disputes. Second, Irwin appropriately emphasizes the semiconductor industry's efforts to build a political consensus both within its ranks and within U.S. trade agencies. As he points out, it is incorrect to regard the industry and the government as monolithic actors in the semiconductor dispute. Finally, Irwin addresses the three questions that George Stigler required in any study of economic regulation: (1) What determines the timing of protection? (business cycles and import penetration trends), (2) What determines the level of protection? (the political costs of and returns to industry lobbying), and (3) What determines the form of protection? (the industry's risk and cost characteristics).

Irwin's chronology of the semiconductor trade dispute is comprehensive and carefully documented. Accordingly, my comments focus not on the facts of the case study but instead on their interpretation and the conclusions that can be drawn. First, I believe that the semiconductor industry proved less adept at exploiting its political capital than Irwin suggests. Despite its designation as a "strategic" industry, its adoption as a focal point in U.S.-Japanese trade negotiations, and the absence of effective downstream opposition, the industry failed to earn a politically sustainable level of administered protection. Second, Irwin correctly notes that countervailing pressures limiting semiconductor protection came largely from *within* the industry, rather than from Japanese competitors or major semiconductor purchasers. He stresses the opposing pricing objectives of integrated and nonintegrated semiconductor firms as the primary factor limiting industry influence. Another influential factor deserves equal attention,

Andrew R. Dick is assistant professor of economics at the University of California, Los Angeles.

however: the extensive scale of international cross-ownership in semiconductor production, which erodes the policy distinction between American and Japanese firms. Third, while Irwin does not emphasize them, his case study offers insights into ongoing policy debates over "rules" versus "outcomes" approaches to trade negotiations and bilateralism versus multilateralism.

How Successful Was Semiconductor Lobbying?

Irwin argues that the "semiconductor industry received all it asked for from the government" (section 1.8) and notes that "few industries ever realize the sustained, high-level attention needed to result in the negotiation of a governmental agreement on trade in just one sector" as semiconductor producers received (section 1.1). The industry's policy achievements include (1) convincing the International Trade Commission and Department of Commerce to levy antidumping duties on Japanese DRAMs, (2) persuading the U.S. Trade Representative (USTR) to press for greater access to Japanese markets under section 301, and (3) setting the terms for negotiations in 1986 and 1991 to regulate Japanese pricing and import practices. While these achievements proved largely unsuccessful in revitalizing the U.S. industry, the consensus view is that when the semiconductor industry spoke, U.S. trade agencies listened.

While not denying that the semiconductor industry received unprecedented and prolonged attention in Washington, I believe that the industry proved to be less successful at exploiting its political capital than Irwin (and most other researchers) have concluded. By this I do not mean simply that protection turned out to be ineffective empirically for the reasons that Robert Baldwin (1982) has noted, but rather that the industry failed to earn a politically sustainable level of administered protection. Consider the 1986 agreement, which was intended to curb Japanese "dumping" in U.S. and third-country markets.[1] Irwin notes that even before the agreement was officially signed in November 1986, it began to unravel in response to domestic and foreign political pressures. Major semiconductor purchasers successfully challenged the Department of Commerce's fair-market-value (FMV) methodology for setting minimum Japanese import prices. Downstream opposition also forced the agreement's antidumping provisions to be dropped when its terms were renegotiated in 1991. Furthermore, the agreement's requirement that Japan regulate its third-country pricing proved unenforceable in light of the intransigence of the Ministry of International Trade and Industry and European objections. In sum, the twin pillars of the agreement's pricing provisions—FMV pricing in the United States and curbing third-country dumping—were soon undermined by political (rather than purely economic) forces in the United States, Japan, and Europe.

---

1. Contrary to the Department of Commerce's affirmative findings of dumping in its investigations of Japanese DRAM and EPROM pricing, there is little economic evidence of below-cost sales by Japanese producers. For an analysis of the dumping cases, see Dick (1991).

Why Would We Expect Successful Semiconductor Lobbying?

Semiconductor firms entered the 1980s with three important political advantages that raised the stakes for both the industry and U.S. policymakers. Viewed in isolation, these advantages guaranteed that the industry would receive unparalleled attention in Washington.

First, as Irwin notes, events in the semiconductor industry were driven in large measure by macro-level rather than industry-level pressures. Japan's trade surplus with the United States was growing steadily, and the trend was particularly acute in the computer and computer components sectors. The semiconductor industry seemed to mirror what was "wrong" in general: an industry that the United States had dominated in research and sales since its postwar inception was struggling to compete against Japanese producers buoyed by government subsidies and perceived unfair trade practices. It was in this environment that the semiconductor industry was adopted as the cause célèbre for those seeking to turn up the pressure on U.S.-Japan trade relations in general. Heeding the semiconductor industry's predictions of its imminent demise was the equivalent of drawing a line in the sand for U.S. policymakers.

Second, semiconductors had been designated a "strategic" industry. The defense establishment, which had underwritten much of the industry's basic research and acted as a major demand source since its infancy, has long regarded a secure domestic supply of semiconductors (and semiconductor producers) as essential to military preparedness. The strategic trade policy literature, which began in the early 1980s and quickly received attention in policy circles, also stressed the semiconductor industry's steep learning curve, large up-front research investments, short product cycles, and downstream linkages.[2] That literature has shown how government policies can interact with such strategic industry characteristics to allow firms to make credible commitments to preempt rivals' investments. When trade policy acquires a strategic value, the economic return to intervention grows and the industry's potential base of political support expands.

Third, the Semiconductor Industry Association (SIA) was fortunate in that semiconductor purchasers mounted only disorganized and ineffective opposition. The American Electronics Association (AEA), representing manufacturers of computer systems and communications equipment, had diverse interests and even included several semiconductor producers. While computer manufacturers ultimately split from the AEA to form a splinter lobby group, Irwin notes that the SIA retained "its monopoly position as the USTR's advisor on semiconductor trade policy" until early 1989. By then, semiconductor trade policy had been institutionalized and the debate shifted away from whether to protect the industry and toward how to enforce the agreements already negotiated with Japan.

---

2. A 1984 conference in Washington, D.C., exposed many policymakers to the basic concepts of strategic trade policy and was later published in Krugman (1986).

Why Did Semiconductor Lobbying Fall Short of Expectations?

Given these three political advantages, why was the semiconductor industry less than completely successful in its lobbying activities? Irwin suggests, and I agree, that the SIA's heterogeneous membership forced it to temper its lobbying objectives. After an initially unsuccessful effort to press its case in Congress, the SIA was forced to expand its membership from just merchant firms (which sold on the open market, and thus favored higher prices) to include also vertically integrated firms (which produced largely for internal use, and thus sought to avoid price increases). Broadening its membership raised the SIA's political visibility and potential clout but also forced the association to moderate its lobbying position. Opposition by integrated firms, for example, forced the SIA to abandon plans to file an escape clause petition for import relief or to seek antidumping duties under the more lenient section 731 of the Tariff Act of 1930.

Another influence dampening semiconductor lobbying that merits greater attention than it receives stems from the extensive scale of international cross-ownership in semiconductor production. American and Japanese semiconductor firms have extensive cross-ownership in the form of direct equity stakes, research joint ventures, technology-licensing agreements, and second-sourcing of production. During negotiations leading to the 1986 industry agreement, for example, U.S. semiconductor firms had a total of 52 research, technology, and production agreements with their Japanese competitors (Haklisch 1986, 57). Elsewhere, I have shown how even much lower levels of cross-ownership can substantially dampen strategic policy incentives (Dick 1993). Cross-ownership not only directly lowers the economic and political return from protection but also raises the domestic industry's lobbying costs by introducing heterogeneous interests into the political coalition. In the semiconductor industry, this heterogeneity severely constrained SIA lobbying. For example, while firms without extensive Japanese ties such as Motorola and Micron aggressively lobbied for industry protection, their demands were muted by firms such as Intel which had numerous second-sourcing and technology-sharing agreements with Japanese competitors (Haklisch 1986; United Nations Center on Transnational Corporations 1986).

Drawing Conclusions from the Semiconductor Dispute

While he does not highlight them, Irwin's case offers insights into two ongoing policy debates: "rules" versus "outcomes" and bilateralism versus multilateralism. The USTR's adoption of numerical targets for American firms' Japanese market penetration mirrors the broader shift away from developing overall trading rules or principles in favor of mandating specific market outcomes. Setting market share targets gives the appearance of adding flexibility and objectivity to dispute resolution. The semiconductor agreements illustrate why both appearances are deceptive. When the U.S. share of the Japanese market fell modestly below the 20 percent target in late 1993, the USTR reacted by seeking emergency consultations with Japan. The SIA also hardened its position, contending that failure to maintain the arbitrary 20 percent quota placed the agreement "at the threshold of failure." [3]

Market share targets ultimately proved to be unsustainable, however, not because of their rigidity but because they lacked any economic foundation. Throughout the trade dispute, the SIA failed to offer persuasive evidence of market barriers to its exports. The SIA sought "equal market access," yet as Irwin notes, the U.S. share of the Japanese semiconductor market actually *exceeded* Japan's share of U.S. chip consumption up until the mid-1980s and remained roughly comparable for a few years later. And while the SIA pointed to "unfair trading practices" to explain its stagnant Japanese market share, those practices—vertical integration, long-term relationships among producers, and exclusive distributorships—were equally commonplace in the U.S. industry. The SIA's success in pressing allegations of market barriers, absent empirical evidence, illustrates how an outcomes-based approach is susceptible to self-interested industry pressures.

The semiconductor case study also illustrates the pitfalls of bilateral dispute resolution when international markets are highly integrated. The USTR recognized that any agreement with Japan which merely prohibited dumping in the U.S. market would make the United States a high-price island and, by diverting Japanese exports to Europe, would reduce American semiconductor exports. Instead of seeking a multilateral agreement, however, the United States demanded that Japan raise prices in *all* export markets. Japan's inability (or unwillingness) to curb third-country dumping naturally led to smuggling of chips from lower-price Asian markets into the United States. The European Community also objected to being made a silent partner in the U.S.-Japan Semiconductor Agreement and ultimately persuaded a General Agreement on Tariffs and Trade panel that monitoring Japanese export prices on third-country sales violated article XI. To protect its own faltering semiconductor industry, the European Community eventually opted for a bilateral trade strategy that mirrored failed U.S. policies: initiating antidumping proceedings against Japanese DRAM and EPROM producers and signing a pricing agreement with Japan in 1989 (Schlesinger 1989). Europe's bilateral approach proved equally unworkable and spawned secondary trade disputes with the United States. Extensive integration in the semiconductor market required a multilateral pricing or production agreement rather than a market-by-market response.

References

Baldwin, Robert E. 1982. The inefficacy of trade policy. Princeton Essays in International Finance, no. 150. Princeton University.

3. In one sense, the SIA demonstrated considerable flexibility toward the market share target. After the 20 percent quota was met in the fourth quarter of 1992, several semiconductor firms disavowed their earlier position that market forces should resume guiding trade flows and instead recommended raising the target.

Dick, Andrew R. 1991. Learning by doing and dumping in the semiconductor industry. *Journal of Law and Economics* 34:133–59.

———. 1993. Strategic trade policy and welfare: The empirical consequences of cross-ownership. *Journal of International Economics* 35:227–49.

Haklisch, Carmela S. 1986. *Technical alliances in the semiconductor industry.* New York: Center for Science and Technology Policy.

Krugman, Paul. 1986. *Strategic trade policy and the new international economics.* Cambridge: MIT Press.

Schlesinger, Jacob M. 1989. Japan chip makers reach agreement with EC on prices. *Wall Street Journal,* August 21, A6.

United Nations Center on Transnational Corporations. 1986. *Transnational corporations in the international semiconductor industry.* New York: United Nations.

2   Steel Protection in the 1980s: The Waning Influence of Big Steel?

Michael O. Moore

2.1   Introduction

Over the last three decades, giant vertically integrated companies such as U.S. Steel, LTV, and Bethlehem and their union counterpart, the United Steelworkers of America (USW), have faced extreme economic difficulty. Total steel sector employment has fallen from 512,000 in 1974 to only 140,000 in 1992 and many of these so-called integrated firms have filed for bankruptcy, permanently closed mills, or severely curtailed production. These changes have caused enormous disruptions, especially in traditional steel-making regions of the Midwest.

The integrated industry and its allies have argued that unfair foreign competition is the principal source of the industry's economic decline. This argument has been bolstered by the widely acknowledged presence of pervasive foreign government steel subsidies, in both the industrialized and developing worlds. These subsidies, combined with a structural slowdown in world steel demand, have contributed to worldwide overcapacity in steel that persists in 1994. Foreign firms, the steel industry has argued consistently, have dealt with this overcapacity by "dumping" excess production into the United States.

The U.S. industry has attempted to secure government intervention to overcome the alleged injury caused by these foreign practices. Congress has passed certain limited provisions designed to help the industry, but large-scale domestic intervention has not been forthcoming. Instead, the industry has focused

Michael O. Moore is associate professor of economics and international affairs at the Elliott School of International Affairs at George Washington University.

The author thanks Bill Lane, Cameron Griffith, Jack Sheehan, and Laird Patterson for their help on this project. Special thanks go to Art Stern for his help compiling statistics on steel imports and to Jeff Alexander and Dana Stryk for their invaluable research assistance. The author also acknowledges the insightful comments of both Jim Markusen and Mike Moskow. The views expressed herein are strictly the author's.

most its efforts on arguing for an aggressive unilateral U.S. steel trade policy to counter international economic pressures. In pursuing this trade policy goal, the integrated industry has used nearly every available path to limit the flow of imported steel products into the United States. These avenues have included pressuring Congress for direct legislative relief, lobbying the executive branch for multilateral steel agreements (MSAs), and, most important, filing literally hundreds of petitions under the trade remedy laws. The steel industry's use of the antidumping (AD) and countervailing duty (CVD) laws has been particularly successful, given the extent of foreign subsidies.

Many outside observers do not dispute the existence of foreign subsidies but question their overriding importance. Instead, they point to other origins of the U.S. steel sector's crisis. Crandall (1981) and Adams and Mueller (1986) assert that self-inflicted ills and increased domestic competition are the main source of the integrated steel industry's difficulties. Specific problems cited have included slowness to adopt new technologies (such as continuous casting and basic-oxygen furnaces), overly generous labor contracts (such as the Experimental Negotiating Agreement of the 1970s), and outdated management techniques. Intensified domestic competition has emerged from the expanding importance of domestic minimills and the growing number of integrated competitors. Finally, falling steel demand has caused further deterioration in the domestic industry's economic fortunes.

The integrated industry has generally won these public policy debates. Over the years, a "steel triangle" comprising steelworkers, integrated steel firms, and steel-community congressional representatives has consistently dominated steel import policy. The result has been three decades replete with import restrictions of various kinds (see table 2.1), though with mixed results in permanently aiding the sector's competitiveness. Principal protectionist episodes have included the 1969 voluntary restraint agreement (VRA), the trigger price mechanism (TPM) in the Carter administration, and a series of VRAs negotiated in the 1980s. Thus, the steel industry has managed to obtain import restrictions from Democratic and Republican administrations, in peace and in wartime, and in years of both a growing and a contracting economy.

A common aspect of these episodes has been that the integrated steel sector has secured intervention outside the normal administrative protection (AP) procedures of U.S. trade law. The standard steel industry approach is to use, or threaten to use, the relatively nondiscretionary AD and CVD processes as a lever to obtain an agreement providing some degree of U.S. price stability. First, integrated steel producers (often with close cooperation of the USW) file massive petitions under U.S. trade remedy laws, especially AD and CVD petitions. Such petitions have particular appeal for the steel industry because foreign practices have made successful litigation likely. An additional attraction for the steel sector is that these rules-based procedures include no presidential discretion whatsoever. Parallel to the trade remedy cases, congressional supporters of the steel industry propose quota legislation inconsistent

Table 2.1   **Chronology of Steel Trade Events**

1969	Negotiation of VRAs with European Community and Japan (scheduled to last until 1974)
1977	Inauguration of TPM for all steel imports
January 1982	Dozens of AD and CVD petitions filed against EC countries
October 1982	Negotiation of VRA with European Community (scheduled to last through December 1985)
January 1984	Escape clause petition filed by Bethlehem Steel and USW
July 1984	ITC rules affirmatively in the escape clause petition in five of nine product categories (affirmative: sheet and strip, plate, structural shapes, wire and wire products, and semifinished steel; negative: pipe and tube, bar, rod, and rails)
September 1984	Negotiation of VRAs on all nine steel products in escape clause petition; market share for participating nations of 18.4 percent (set to end in September 1989)
November 1988	Candidate Bush promises to continue VRA
July 1989	President Bush announces Steel Liberalization Program: (a) 2.5 years VRA extension, (b) 1 percent annual increase for countries willing to stop unfair practices (up to 20.9 percent by March 1992), and (c) negotiations for MSA begun to remove "trade-distorting" steel practices
April 1992	Termination of VRA; breakdown of MSA over allowable ("green light") subsidies
June 1992	AD and CVD petitions filed against flat-rolled products
July 1993	ITC rules affirmatively only on a subset of steel industry petitions

with the General Agreement on Tariffs and Trade (GATT). Before the quasi-judicial AP process can grind to completion and prior to final votes on the legislation, the executive branch will urge the steel industry to accept a negotiated settlement with foreign exporters, usually a VRA. This sequence was repeated with slight variation in 1969, 1977, 1982, and 1984. In essence, the rules-based AP procedures have been utilized as a credible threat to force political settlements of steel disputes.

This impressive string of protectionist victories has led many observers to use the steel industry as perhaps the prime example, along with textiles, of a U.S. manufacturing industry whose political clout is so extensive that it can "always" obtain protection. "Big Steel," composed of about a half-dozen vertically integrated producers and the USW, seemed always capable of profoundly influencing steel trade policy.

Perhaps the most impressive of these trade policy victories came in 1984. The industry was finally able to obtain one of its important long-term trade policy goals—comprehensive quotas on steel imports, administered on a country- and product-specific basis. In addition, this decidedly nonmarket outcome was wrested from the free-market–oriented Reagan administration.

Despite the success in securing the global 1984 VRA, evidence will be presented below that this managed trade agreement represents the high point of the integrated steel sector's ability to influence trade policy. This is clear from two separate outcomes. The first is the battle over the VRA extension in 1989.

While the VRA was formally extended for two and a half years, the results were hardly what the steel industry wanted. Specifically, the steel industry did not obtain a five-year extension of the VRA as requested, did not obtain a tightening of the quota, and, in the event, the VRA was not binding neither on a product or country basis for the vast majority of the extension. The second piece of evidence of falling political clout is the failure to obtain meaningful protection after the VRA expired in April 1992. The steel industry secured neither an extension of the VRA (a goal of the USW) nor an international consensus on steel policy through a multilateral steel agreement (a goal of both steel producers and the USW). The industry instead was forced to litigate AD and CVD cases to final outcomes. Since this is largely an impartial process and devoid of obvious means to apply outside pressure, the industry's choice of pursuing a nonpolitical route to its final conclusion also reflects the integrated steel sector's self-perception of reduced political clout. In the end, even the AP cases were highly unsatisfactory. Contrary to industry expectations, the AP route was only partially successful in 1993 in securing permanent high duties on foreign steel. Indeed, at the end of 1993, the domestic steel industry has less steel protection than at any time since 1977.

This reduced political influence reflects the radically changed nature of the domestic U.S. steel industry. A number of factors stand out.

First, no longer does a small group of mammoth steel companies dominate the domestic market. The fragmentation of the domestic industry has eroded one of the most important traditional political advantages of the industry, namely, a cohesive coalition with shared interests.

The most important example of this fragmentation is the growing importance of "minimills." Minimills, a relatively new market form, are small, innovative steel companies that use the latest technologies and frequently use incentive-based labor compensation schemes with a nonunionized workforce. These minimills have been less likely to support specific protection-seeking efforts by the integrated firms, especially since they generally produce a different product line than the integrated firms. Thus, minimill and integrated mill interests only partially coincide. A further complication for the integrated sector's position is that the CEO of the most successful U.S. minimill (Nucor) is a passionate and very vocal free trader.

The industrial structure of the U.S. industry has been changed further by so-called reconstituted mills. These mills have arisen out of integrated firms selling off parts of their operations in order to lower costs. Many of these plants have continued to operate, thereby creating further competition for the integrated firms. Finally, a number of foreign steel firms, especially Japanese, have purchased a part or controlling share in integrated firms. Examples include NKK's purchase of a controlling interest in National Steel and Kawasaki Steel's joint ownership of Armco's carbon steel division (U.S. International Trade Commission [USITC] 1989a).

The restructured U.S. industry is also increasingly competitive internationally, which further weakens the argument that the industry deserves special import protection. In the 1980s, integrated firms modernized facilities and the USW negotiated wage concessions. In addition, the declining value of the dollar in the second half of the decade contributed to the U.S. industry's improved international position.

While the downsized industry has improved its competitive position, the declining number of steelworkers has weakened the political base of the steel sector in Congress. Many traditional steel-producing cities such as Pittsburgh no longer host major integrated steel plants, each of which formerly employed thousands of workers. This both reduces the absolute number of steel industry voters and lessens the number of congressional districts where steel is an important economic factor.

The other factor is the growing importance of organized steel-user groups lobbying against steel protection. This occurred most prominently in 1989 when the integrated industry faced organized *domestic* opposition in the form of the Coalition of American Steel-Using Manufacturers (CASUM), an industrial steel-user group that argued against the extension of the VRA. They argued that the VRA program threatened more American jobs than it protected and foreign producers received extra profits in the quota-protected market. These arguments seem to have been effective, not only on their own merits, but also because the politically weakened integrated steel sector was less able to dominate the steel import policy discussions.

The goal of this paper is to document this waning political influence of Big Steel. The paper will concentrate on the carbon steel subsector since this is by far the largest segment of the domestic steel industry. However, many of the same issues are present in the specialty and stainless steel sectors.

The remainder of this paper is organized in the following way. Section 2.2 will briefly discuss the technical aspects of the industry that will prove vital for later discussion. Section 2.3 will outline a basic political economy framework used in the analysis. This will include a discussion of the various options available to the industry for protection and the relative advantages and disadvantages of each. A short history of the steel trade policy and the economic conditions of the steel sector up to 1982 is presented in section 2.4. Section 2.5 provides a detailed look at the genesis of the 1984 VRA, the battle over the 1989 extension, the refusal of the Bush administration to extend the VRA in 1992, and the outcome of the AD and CVD cases in the summer of 1993. Conclusions are provided in section 2.6.

2.2   Technology and Market Structure of the U.S. Steel Industry

The market structure of the industry has played a particularly important role in the integrated steel sector's effectiveness in influencing import policy. Most important, economies of scale and geographical concentration have resulted in the traditional political cohesion of the steel industry actors. Thus, we turn first to the basic economic relationships in the industry before discussing the political economy of the steel industry. We will see later that the changing market structure of the industry in the 1970s and 1980s has been a critical aspect of the industry's declining political power.

Crude steel is produced by combining iron ore and carbon as well as other constituent elements through a number of different processes. Using traditional methods, coke (a processed form of coal produced in coke ovens) is combined in a blast furnace to produce molten pig iron. Pig iron is then transferred to a furnace where other materials are added which results in crude steel. The molten crude steel is then cast into ingots, which are rolled into blooms, billets, and slabs. These intermediate products are reheated and rolled into final products such as sheet, bars, and plate. The defining feature of an "integrated" mill is that all of these steps take place at one location.

Integrated steel making has undergone relatively few major changes in the past 40 years. The two most important innovations have been the basic-oxygen furnace (BOF), which is more efficient than open-hearth furnaces (OHF), and continuous casting, which eliminates the reheating of ingots and intermediate rolling (Gold et al. 1984).

The nature of the modern integrated steel-making process, which requires coke ovens, blast furnaces, BOFs, as well as casting and rolling facilities, creates important scale economies. The minimum efficient scale of a new integrated plant is about 7 million tons of capacity per year, which represents about 7 percent of total U.S. steel consumption (Barnett and Crandall 1993). Lumpy investment and high start-up costs of a new integrated mill obviously act as important impediments to entry by new integrated firms.

High fixed costs also acted as a deterrent to entry in other ways. Specifically, integrated firms have strong incentives to maintain high capacity utilization in order to keep average costs low. In periods of weak demand, established firms therefore will have an incentive to price below average *total* costs, to the extreme disadvantage of new entrants. The pressure to compete aggressively on price has been a persistent problem of large-scale steel operations for over a century. Consequently, steel firms all over the world have responded to this tendency to price below total costs by implementing various methods to maintain price stability. Cartel arrangements, at both the domestic and international levels, have been especially important.[1]

Another important feature of integrated production has been its geographic concentration. Approximately 54 percent of U.S. steel capacity was located in Pennsylvania, Ohio, and Indiana in 1965 (American Iron and Steel Institute [AISI], 1969). This pattern was repeated in the United Kingdom (e.g., Manchester) and in continental Europe (e.g., the Ruhr valley). The reasons for this

---

1. U.S. Steel, for example, used to act as a price leader and residual supplier so that prices would not fall in times of low demand. See Adams and Mueller (1986) for details. For a discussion about international cartel arrangements, especially before World War II, see Gillingham (1991).

Table 2.2   U.S. Steel Industry in the Domestic Economy (million tons unless
                  otherwise noted)

Year	Steel Imports	Import Market Share (%)	Total Steel Production	Apparent Final Steel Consumption	Steel Sector Employment (thousands)	Real Domestic Steel Sales (billion 1982–84 $)	Steel/GDP[a]
1960	3.3	4.7	99.2	71.5	572	48.0	0.036
1964	6.4	7.3	127.1	87.9	555	52.9	0.038
1968	17.9	16.7	131.4	107.6	552	53.4	0.038
1974	13.4	15.9	145.7	119.6	512	77.5	0.037
1977	19.3	17.8	125.3	108.4	452	65.5	0.031
1981	18.9	19.8	120.8	105.4	391	47.4	0.027
1982	16.6	21.8	74.5	76.3	289	29.2	0.020
1984	26.2	26.4	92.5	98.9	236	28.9	0.024
1989	17.3	17.9	97.9	102.7	169	25.4	0.021
1990	17.1	17.5	98.9	97.5	164	23.4	0.020
1991	15.8	17.9	87.9	88.3	146	19.7	0.018
1992	17.1	18.0	92.9	95	140	18.9	0.018

Sources: AISI (varous issues); *Economic Report of the President* (1993).
[a]Steel/GDP = steel consumption (million tons)/GDP (billion 1987 $).

concentration were twofold. First, the high costs of transporting iron and coal meant that steel facilities clustered in areas with easy access to these raw materials. Second, high transportation costs of the finished product made competitive pricing outside a limited geographical area difficult.

International trading patterns in steel were affected by transportation costs as well. Transoceanic shipping costs were critical impediments to imported steel's becoming a threat to the U.S. steel industry for many decades. However, as these costs fell in the 1960s and war-ravaged industrial economies rebuilt, imports into the United States began to rise. As table 2.2 shows, imports, which in 1960 reached only 3.3 million tons or 4.7 percent of the U.S. market, soared to 17.9 million tons by 1968 and a 16.7 percent domestic market share.

Despite the growing importance of foreign steel sources, the large traditional steel producers continued their domination of the domestic market for many years. Table 2.3 indicates that in 1979 the eight largest integrated steel makers still controlled nearly two-thirds of the domestic market. However, technological changes and the low price of scrap steel encouraged the rise of minimills in the 1970s. Their emergence would remake the internal market structure of the U.S. steel industry.

Minimills are relatively simple operations, especially in comparison to an integrated steelworks. A standard minimill consists of an electric-arc furnace (EAF), a continuous caster, and a rolling mill. Minimills do not produce raw steel but instead melt steel scrap using high-temperature EAFs. The molten steel is cast and then rolled to produce final steel products in similar fashion to an integrated mill. However, because minimills have only recently emerged,

Table 2.3   Estimated Market Share of U.S. Participants

Type	1979			1991		
	Number of Firms	Shipments	Share (%)	Number of Firms	Shipments	Share (%)
Major integrated mills	8	73.4	64	5	30.3	34
Reconstituted mills	0	0	0	15	22.4	25
Other traditional mills	20	17.7	15	6	3.5	4
Minimills	48	8.2	7	52	21.3	24
Specialty steel mills	10	1.0	1	9	1.5	2
Domestic total		100.3	87		79	89
Imports		17.5	15		15.7	18
Exports		2.8	2		6.5	7
Total market		115	100		88.2	100

Source: World Steel Dynamics (1992).
Note: Shipments in million tons.

they use efficient continuous casters almost exclusively, in stark contrast to most older integrated works that continue to produce ingots.[2]

Because minimills do not actually make steel but instead recycle scrap, they do not need expensive coke ovens and blast furnaces and have no incentive to locate near iron or coal supplies. The minimum efficient scale for an EAF is therefore much smaller than for a BOF, which lowers capital costs significantly. In fact, few minimill operations have a capacity exceeding 1 million tons per year.

The minimills have differed from their integrated competitors in other important ways. Since nearness to iron and coal supplies is irrelevant to minimills, they are free to position themselves near the end market, undercutting the integrated mills further by reducing transportation costs. This means that minimills are relatively unconcentrated geographically. This fact, combined with small workforces, implies that no community relies on a minimill as a prime source of large-scale regional employment, in sharp contrast to the integrated sector.

Minimills have also adopted new labor and management techniques. Flexible work rules and incentive-based pay for both their nonunion and union workforces have reduced unit labor costs and increased productivity. Minimill labor costs are lower also because their relatively young workforces result in much lower health and pension costs than their integrated rivals that still struggle with the "legacy" costs of retired production workers (especially after the massive layoffs of the 1980s). The low capital costs also allow the minimills to build plants with relatively short lifespans, thereby allowing for more timely introduction of new technologies (Barnett and Crandall 1986, 20).

The success of the minimills in the U.S. market has been remarkable. Table

---

2. For a comparison of minimill and integrated mill production techniques, see Hogan (1987).

2.3 indicates that, according to one estimate, minimills were shipping 8.2 million tons of steel in 1979. This represented 7 percent of the U.S. domestic market. By 1991, minimill shipments had risen to 21.3 million tons and 24 percent of the market. This increased market share came almost exclusively at the expense of the integrated sector. Major and minor integrated firms represented 79 percent of the market in 1979 but fell to 63 percent in 1991. Imports, on the other hand, grew from only 15 percent to 18 percent of the U.S. market.

Profit rates for the minimill sector have also been very impressive. Minimills have operated more profitably than the integrated sector in every year for which disaggregated data are available. In addition, the industrywide figures indicate that, while the integrated firms lost money in 1985, 1986, and 1991, minimills were posting net gains in each year. This general pattern was also true in the early 1980s, when minimills were more profitable than integrated mills in head-to-head competition in individual product categories (USITC 1984).

Minimills have traditionally been "niche" producers. They have focused their efforts on "long" products such as wire, rod, and bars. The cost advantage of the minimills has led to near domination of these product lines. For example, estimates in table 2.4 indicate that the minimill share of domestic wire rod shipments will grow from 86 percent in 1990 to 100 percent by 2000.

Despite these important cost advantages, significant constraints have precluded the minimills from repeating this success in other product lines. The most important constraint is the use of scrap as a feedstock. This leads to more impurities in the final product than in steel produced by integrated mills. This lower quality of output has dramatically reduced the use of minimill steel in flat-rolled products destined for home appliances and automobile bodies. Consequently, integrated firms have continued to dominate the domestic shipments of these high value-added "flat" products.

Unfortunately for the integrated mills, recent technological advances mean

Table 2.4   **Estimated Minimill Share of Domestic Production[a]** (by product category)

Category	1980	1985	1990	2000
Semifinished slab	0	0	5	20
Long products				
Wire rods	45	80	86	100
Merchant bars	37	60	65	85
Rails	0	0	0	100
Flat products				
Plate	15	20	25	45
Hot-rolled sheet	0	0	2	35
Cold-rolled sheet	0	0	1.5	15
Electrogalvanized	0	0	0	0

Source: Donald Barnett/Economic Associates Inc.

[a]Minimill figures include some independent firms that do not use EAFS.

that minimills may soon be able to compete effectively in flat-rolled products as well. Some minimills have begun to experiment with the use of directly reduced iron and iron carbide as feedstocks, both of which reduce reliance on scrap and significantly increase the quality of EAF output. New techniques such as thin-slab casting will also increase the ability of minimills to produce sheet and plate competitively. For example, Nucor inaugurated a 1 million ton sheet mill using thin-slab casters in 1989 and followed with another sheet mill in Hickman, Arkansas, that will produce 2 million tons per year by the end of 1994 (*Financial Times,* July 8, 1993).[3] Many analysts see continued strong performance of the minimills in the flat-rolled market. Minimill operators themselves predicted in 1993 that up to 45 percent of the flat-rolled market would be provided by EAF minimill operations by 2001 (*Iron Age* 1993).

In summary, the internal market structure of the U.S. steel sector has undergone substantial evolution over the last two decades. Minimills have created enormous pressure on the integrated mills and have almost completely driven the major firms out of the long-product markets. The traditional integrated firms having increasingly retreated into flat products. Continued technological progress may mean that the integrated sector will soon be forced to compete with minimills in this end of the market as well.

The rise of the minimill, in essence, has created a steel sector much more in line with economists' vision of a competitive market. The dramatic drop in entry and exit costs means that the U.S. steel sector now hosts many more competitors. Economies of scale have also become much less important. As we will see in sections 2.4 and 2.5 below, this changing domestic market structure has begun to have a significant influence on the integrated mills' ability to shape steel trade policy.

2.3   The Political Economy of Integrated Steel Lobbying

2.3.1   General Political Economy Framework

An agent's influence over public policy depends largely on its ability to consolidate and apply political pressure, the strength of potential opposition, and the available policy options under a nation's institutional and legal structures.

An intervention-seeking agent would prefer a policy so narrowly defined that only that agent receives it. In the case of a firm, this might be a firm-specific tax break or subsidy. This would clearly result in higher returns relative to all of the firm's competitors. However, since only one firm receives the intervention's advantages, the obvious difficulty with this strategy is that the firm

---

3. With the expansion of the Hickman and Crawfordsville plants, Nucor will become the third largest steel firm in the United States, after U.S. Steel and Bethlehem.

must rely exclusively on its own political muscle to secure the benefit. Very few agents will have enough influence to accomplish this alone.

Usually, agents are forced instead to form multimember coalitions.[4] The most obvious advantages of such coalitions are that lobbying costs can be shared and large numbers of coalition members translate into significant ballot-box clout in a majority-vote–based democracy.

There are, however, certain important disadvantages of large coalitions. First, the coalition must identify others with common interests. The larger the number of possible coalition members, the more costly are efforts to identify and organize them. Many coalition members also create monitoring burdens— each individual member will have an incentive to shirk on lobbying efforts but still retain the benefits of the coalition's lobbying. The possibility of free ridership makes lobbying a less attractive option since the net benefits of the lobbying efforts will be less the fewer the numbers of effort-contributing individuals.

The coalition's success also depends on its cohesiveness and permanence. Do the members cooperate on a permanent basis or do they constantly shift alliances? The more often that the members act in concert, the more likely that each member can develop a reputation and be able to exclude shirkers. In addition, permanent alliances have the political advantage that they are more predictable to vote-seeking politicians who need not try to predict the coalition's strength or policy position. The political strength and positions of a newly formed or ad hoc coalition, on the other hand, are much more difficult to predict. It will be difficult both to gauge the new group's political muscle and whether the coalition will remain intact after the immediate policy issue is resolved.

One solution to these transaction costs is to create permanent institutions that represent the affected members' interests. Examples include trade associations for industry groups and a union for workers. Payment of dues to the association will help overcome free-rider problems. In addition, members only need organize the association once; subsequently, it will act as the coalition's representative so that individual members need not reassemble on each issue to reach decisions.

A particularly important source of coalition cohesion is immobility of factors in an industry.[5] Factor immobility means that all industry participants (labor, management, stockholders, etc.) will find that their economic interests are

---

4. For the classic treatment of lobbying in multimember coalitions, see Olson (1971).

5. A factor may be incapable of moving to another industry if the factor has some industry-specific attributes. In the case of capital, the machinery may be specialized so that it is useless in other production processes. Similarly, a worker may have developed human capital that cannot be easily transferred to another sector. Factors also may be immobile out of choice—if a factor is gaining rents (i.e., payment above the next best opportunity), that factor may be highly resistant to moving to another, lower-paying, industry.

closely tied to the industry's economic health. If the price of the output rises, incomes for all immobile factors in the industry will rise as well. If the price falls or the price of intermediate inputs rises, the factors suffer a real income loss.

Another way to think usefully about this immobile-factors model is in simple partial equilibrium terms. An increase in the price of an imported product will result in an increase in "producer surplus," or payments to those employed in the import-competing industry. The price increase also means that domestic consumers of the product will pay more for the product and suffer a loss in "consumer surplus." The lasting impact of this price increase on the consumer will depend in part on the characteristics of the product. If the product is a final consumption good, then the consumer may be forced to bear much of the price increase. The effects are more subtle for a protected intermediate input. In particular, if the consuming industry can pass along the increased input costs to its own final consumers, then intermediate input protection will be less damaging. The consuming industry will consequently be unlikely to lobby against the import protection. If instead the consuming industry is a price taker in its market, it will be forced to absorb the cost increases and will be more likely to resist protection. An example of such an industry would be one that competes on a world market as a price taker.

An industry with immobile factors also has a number of distinct advantages when confronting the transaction costs of coalition building identified above. Specifically, coalitions based on fixed factors have low organizing costs since potential coalition partners are easily identifiable. In addition, specific factors are familiar to each other since they are "permanently" in the same industry and deal with each other on many policy and economic issues (e.g., collective bargaining). The familiarity translates into established reputations. These permanently intertwined interests mean that coalition members are less likely to take different positions on other issues facing the industry as a whole. They will have strong economic incentives to ensure that the industry's economic pie is as large as possible.[6]

The consequences of immobile factors for lobbying effort should be clear. The more immobile the factors, the more likely that those factors will have strong incentives to protect the economic interests of the industry as a whole. In addition, the more closely associated the factor is with the industry, the more likely the benefits to lobbying for the industry will outweigh the transaction costs of lobbying. If, on the other hand, factors are mobile, their economic interests will generally not be identifiable with a particular industry. Conse-

---

6. This cooperation clearly need not extend to intraindustry issues such as arguments over labor contracts, profit sharing, etc. In other words, the fixed factors are likely to be extremely quarrelsome when trying to divide up any benefits that they have won through their cooperation on helping the industry as a whole.

quently, they would be less likely to expend any resources lobbying on the industry's behalf.[7]

The presence of immobile factors not only provides political strength by encouraging the growth of a coalition. It also provides clear signals to politicians seeking to represent their constituents' interests. The reason is that the degree of mobility will help determine whether factors in an industry will speak with "one voice." Immobile factors will generally have an economic incentive to do so, which will help an elected representative avoid choosing to support one constituent group over another.[8]

2.3.2   Application to the Integrated Steel Sector

The highly effective coalition that has developed over the last few decades to limit steel imports has attributes consistent with the successful lobbying characteristics described above. The outstanding feature of the effort has been the stability of the alliance between integrated steel firms and the steelworkers' union. The most important sources of the steel coalition's integrity have been the relatively small number of actors in the group and the immobility of the factors employed in the integrated industry. These two elements have allowed the industry to consistently overcome the transaction costs of organizing an coalition to fight for import barriers.

As outlined in section 2.2 above, the basic economics of the integrated steel sector has contributed greatly to the small number of actors in the traditional industry. As late as 1979, eight producers controlled nearly two-thirds of the domestic market. In addition, the integrated firms had a tradition of cooperating on cartel pricing schemes and had a well-functioning, established trade association in the AISI. The steel sector also was highly unionized through a single union representative, the USW. The existence of these two institutions means that organization costs for lobbying efforts could be kept reasonably low and also significantly reduced the likelihood of free riders within the integrated sector. The actors in the AISI and USW were also quite familiar to one another, either through the trade association, collective bargaining arrangements, or cooperation on other steel-related public policy issues. The combination of familiarity among the steel sector actors and their relatively small number translated into an effective lobbying coalition.

The immobility of steel industry inputs also enhances coalition building in favor of protection. Capital is highly specialized in the steel industry and generally very long lived. The relatively unskilled nature of steelworker tasks and higher than normal compensation for the manufacturing sector mean that eco-

---

7. An intermediate case where some factors are mobile and others immobile can be found in Mussa (1974). For an extension of this framework to a model with voting behavior in a formal political economy framework, see Mayer (1984).

8. A former trade official with the U.S. government has indicated in an interview that an industry is especially persuasive when labor and management cooperate on trade issues.

nomic rents can be substantial for steelworkers. Steel industry wages have consistently been much higher than average manufacturing wages. This suggests that steelworkers have strong incentives to resist transfer to other occupations. This immobility provides further incentives for steelworkers and capital owners to work together to obtain protection. It also leads to stability of the relationships, which in turn helps the AISI and USW work together effectively.

Labor-management cohesion has also helped the integrated steel sector attract congressional support that is highly effective. This support is decidedly nonpartisan and organized along geographical lines. Prominent industry allies have included both Democrats (e.g., Representative Murtha of Pennsylvania and Senator Rockefeller of West Virginia) and Republicans (e.g., Representative Schulze and Senator Heinz, both of Pennsylvania). The tendency to have strong political support from district- and state-based politicians has been further strengthened by the traditional industry's geographic concentration. The large number of workers concentrated in a few districts and states with many electoral votes leads to substantial political leverage, not only in Congress, but potentially in presidential elections as well.

The traditional inability of domestic steel-*using* industries to organize effectively stands in stark contrast to the integrated sector. Their weaknesses are mirror images of Big Steel's strengths. Most important, the costs of steel protection are widely dispersed across user industries. While protection can raise the costs of steel significantly, steel generally represents only a modest portion of most industries' total input costs. Further impediments include large organizing costs arising out of the large number of firms that use steel as an input. This raises the likelihood of free riding, which further discourages coalition building. Finally, steel users do not have a set of common interests other than steel around which to organize.[9] Consequently, any effort to fight steel protection is almost necessarily ad hoc. This combination of factors means that a coalition against steel protection is unlikely to form and, if it does coalesce, is highly unstable. Finally, the geographical dispersion of steel-using industries has meant that there are few congressional districts where steel users are as important economically as a full-scale integrated steelworks might be. This creates less direct congressional support for steel-using industries in their fight against protection.

2.3.3 Choosing the Avenue to Protection

The steel industry, as any other U.S. import-competing industry, must choose among a host of options when pursuing government intervention. A particular option will be considered only if its benefits, weighted by the probability of success, outweigh the costs of seeking government help. If a number

---

9. In a 1978 steel trade conference, a representative of a major steel-consuming firm noted that "to represent adequately the viewpoints of a wide range of [steel-using] industries is manifestly impossible" (Williams 1978, 90).

of choices are individually potentially profitable, the industry must then choose the option or combination of options that maximizes expected profits.[10]

The choices available to an integrated steel firm seeking government intervention can be divided into two distinct categories, each with its own advantages and disadvantages. These options include assistance to the integrated sector as a whole and assistance to the entire domestic steel industry.[11]

The former option is clearly the more attractive. A strategy directed narrowly at the integrated sector not only will help the integrated sector compete with imports but also will not benefit the minimill sector. Examples of such intervention include changing the relative regulatory environment (e.g., relaxing pollution requirements for the BOFs used by the integrated firms but maintaining them for EAFs used by minimills), changing the relative price of intermediate inputs (e.g., raising the price of electricity, which will hurt minimills), or changing the relative labor costs (e.g., by reducing the legacy costs of retired production workers, a problem much more severe for the more mature integrated sector than for minimills with their younger workforces). Unfortunately for the integrated firms, most of these efforts to obtain direct benefits have had only limited success.[12]

The integrated firms have been much more successful in obtaining import barriers. Import restrictions, however, have the major drawback that all domestic import-competing firms in the protected industry are equally benefited, whether or not they have contributed to the lobbying effort to secure the restrictions.[13] In the steel industry context, this means that minimills have an incentive to free ride on the efforts of the integrated sector.[14] Even if the integrated producers can narrow the protection to flat-rolled products, where they dominate, the increase in profits will provide further incentive for minimills to solve the technological barriers blocking their entrance into these product lines.

Has the integrated steel industry irrationally pursued free-rider–producing import barriers that help their strongest competitors, domestic minimills? The answer would seem to be "no." While the *benefits* of interventions directed solely at the integrated sector are larger than those from protection, one must also consider other factors when comparing the two paths. In particular, import protection in the United States has two major advantages: (1) the cost of pursuing protection, especially administered protection, is low relative to lobbying

10. See Moore and Suranovic (1992) for an analysis of the welfare implications of an industry choosing between multiple paths to protection.

11. A third option, firm-specific interventions, are the most advantageous to an individual steel producer. As discussed above, these are so difficult to obtain that we ignore them here.

12. Examples of domestic interventions that have helped the integrated sector relative to the minimill sector include "safe harbor" tax deductions in the 1981 Reagan tax plan, transitional "carryback" rules in the 1986 Tax Reform Act, and limited research and development subsidies for integrated steel making. For details, see U.S. Congress, Congressional Budget Office (1987).

13. For a discussion about the free-rider problem of tariffs and lobbying, see Rodrik (1986).

14. See Lenway and Schuler (1991) for an empirical analysis of integrated vs. minimill lobbying activities for import restrictions.

for subsidies and (2) the probability of obtaining protection is much higher than receiving direct government subsidies.

Lobbying costs in the AP process are relatively low mainly because they involve permanent government institutions whose procedures are standardized and transparent. The domestic industry need only file a petition and assemble supporting materials for an import remedy case and let the government incur the balance of the costs. While these AP transaction costs can be quite substantial (and have run into millions of dollars for the steel industry), the costs are known with relative certainty before the effort is begun.

Lobbying for direct intervention, on the other hand, potentially involves much more extensive effort and cost. Most important, domestic intervention requires the passage of separate legislation or convincing the executive branch to reinterpret existing law. Constructing a legislative majority to pass new legislation requires extensive effort and also may open the intervention-seeking industry to the charge that it is receiving special favors. Subsidies are especially problematic since they involve a direct transfer from domestic taxpayers to the industry. Reinterpretation of existing law is perhaps less difficult, but the industry still must have considerable political muscle to convince the executive branch and/or the bureaucracy to change existing regulatory practices. Lobbying for direct relief can also be open ended; no one can know how many resources are necessary to persuade legislators to pass a new law or to convince administrators to change existing procedures.

Another important advantage of import barriers is that protection seekers can characterize the argument as a choice between helping domestic citizens or foreigners. Protection seekers will argue that opponents are abandoning domestic interests in favor of foreign suppliers. Vote-seeking domestic politicians will likely ignore the effects on foreign suppliers' welfare and will concentrate solely on the "benefits" of protection unless domestic consumers can organize effectively. This dynamic changes considerably if the debate concerns a purely domestic intervention. In this case, the arguments are necessarily about internal domestic distribution of income. A subsidy to one industry means that taxpayers must pay and the industry gets special benefits not offered to other sectors. This implies that the political debate will be among competing domestic constituencies, which raises considerably the political costs of supporting one industry.

Consequently, there are strong incentives for the steel industry to pursue a trade-related remedy. The most important trade options include: (1) an unfair trade remedy petition, (2) an escape clause petition, and (3) a VRA.[15]

Two types of unfair trade remedies are available for an import-competing firm. The first is the AD process wherein a domestic firm accuses a foreign

15. Other possible remedies include relief under section 406 (Market Disruption from State Trading Countries), section 301 (Unfair Foreign Trade Practices), and section 232 (National Security Import Restrictions).

firm of either selling in the U.S. market below fully allocated cost (i.e., average total costs) or selling in the U.S. below the price charged in the exporter's home market. The second remedy is the CVD process. In these petitions, the domestic firms allege that a foreign government has provided a grant or subsidy that was intended specifically to increase exports.

Each AD and CVD petition is product and country specific. If two slightly different steel products are allegedly dumped by five separate countries, 10 separate petitions are filed, each of which in principle is adjudicated independently and may receive a separate dumping or subsidy margin.

Under U.S. procedures, the Department of Commerce (DOC) determines the dumping or subsidy margin while the U.S. International Trade Commission (ITC) rules whether the domestic industry is "materially" injured by "reason of" the unfair trade imports. Since 1980, both agencies are also subject to strict statutory deadlines for completion of their investigations.

The AD and CVD procedures progress in a staggered fashion. The ITC first issues a preliminary material injury decision. If the ITC decision is affirmative, the DOC calculates a preliminary dumping or subsidy margin. If the DOC rules affirmatively at its preliminary stage, imports must pay a bond equal to the estimated dumping or subsidy margin. This bond is adjusted in a final DOC determination and becomes a definitive duty only if the ITC rules in a final decision that the dumped or subsidized imports are causing "material" injury. In addition, once the duty is in place, the duty has no specific expiration date. In fact, a number of U.S. AD duties have been in place for over 20 years.

These procedures offer a number of distinct advantages to intervention-seeking firms. For example, the interests of consumers of the imported good are entirely absent from the unfair trade process. The responsible agencies look only at unfair trade margins and injury—no account is made for the costs of imposing retaliatory duties. In addition, the process is relatively automatic and free from overt political considerations; if the DOC and ITC rule affirmatively at a final stage, the final estimated duty is imposed without *any* direct involvement of either the president or any other elected official. This process is, by design, supposed to be a rules-based, nondiscretionary procedure that is immune to political influence. There is considerable evidence that the ITC decision process in particular is remarkably impervious to outside pressures.[16] Finally, the chances of receiving a positive dumping or subsidy margin from the DOC are quite high because of a number of arguably biased procedures.[17]

The AD and CVD processes also offer specific benefits to the integrated

16. There have been a number of empirical studies that have examined whether political pressure can influence ITC decisions. Most authors have found that the ITC basically uses economic criteria consistent with the law in voting on material injury (see, e.g., Devault 1993; Anderson 1993). Moore (1992) also finds such economic factors are preeminent but finds weak evidence that Senate oversight committees may affect the ITC's decisions. Devault and Anderson, using more recent data, find no such evidence.

17. Over the 1980s, over 90 percent of all petitions resulted in a positive margin at the preliminary and/or final stage. This is at least in part a reflection of upwardly biased procedures used by

steel industry. Perhaps most important, there is general recognition that there has been widespread government intervention in steel markets.[18] While there is considerable dispute about the actual effects of these subsidies on the U.S. steel industry, their existence makes positive subsidy margin calculations by the DOC quite likely. In addition, positive AD duties are also highly probable since, as discussed in section 2.2, integrated firms with high fixed costs will often sell below average total costs in recessions.

The steel industry also can use the product- and industry-specific nature of the AD and CVD processes to its advantage. By nature, steel output is highly differentiated. Steel products contain varying levels of alloys and can be heat-treated, cold- or hot-rolled, carbon or stainless. The differentiated nature of the products, combined with the large number of countries that export to the United States, means that the steel industry may choose to file a large number of petitions simultaneously.

Another important advantage of using the AD and CVD processes is the rhetorical high ground that they afford. Since both involve allegations of "un-fair" foreign trade practices, industry representatives and their political allies can claim that the industry does not seek protection but instead only consideration of legitimate grievances. Allegations of unfair trading practices can also help blunt complaints that intervention is being awarded to a noncompetitive industry.

There are, however, certain major disadvantages to the unfair trade remedy procedures. Perhaps most important, the unfair trade remedies may offer only limited protection since only a subset of countries may finally be "convicted." This leaves open the possibility of supply diversion from unfettered exporters. The second disadvantage, at least for a politically powerful industry, is that the bureaucratic nature of the process limits direct lobbying. In addition, the product- and country-specific nature of the petitions means that substantial legal costs are necessary since separate cases must be litigated.

The second major option for import restrictions is an escape clause petition. In an escape clause case, the ITC determines whether imports have been a substantial cause of serious, as opposed to material, injury. If the ITC rules affirmatively, it makes recommendations to the president about temporary protection. The president then must decide within a specific time period whether to accept, modify, or reject the ITC's recommendation. If protection is forthcoming, then across-the-board restrictions are imposed on *all* countries' exports of the affected product. Since there is no allegation of unfair trade, the exporting country in principle is offered compensation in the form of lowered

---

the DOC in calculating the margins. See the contributions in Boltuck and Litan (1991) for a thorough discussion of these procedures.

18. These actions include a steel-led development strategy in many developing countries (e.g., Brazil) and extensive EC attempts to rationalize the steel industry through subsidies, guaranteed loans, input subsidies, guaranteed minimum prices, and production quotas (Howell, Noellert, and Wolfe 1988).

tariffs on other products. If the United States offers no compensation, the GATT recognizes the right of the exporting nation to raise tariffs on U.S. exports in retaliation.

As with the AD and CVD processes, the escape clause offers both advantages and disadvantages to an intervention-seeking industry. The two most important advantages are: (1) the protection is comprehensive and (2) no unfair trade practices need be proved. In addition, the legal costs are potentially lower since only one determination must be made for the entire industry and not for individual products and exporters.

There are, however, important potential drawbacks. First, the industry faces a higher injury standard at the ITC than with unfair trade cases (serious as opposed to material injury). Second, and more important, the president has final discretion about the implemented policy. The president can reject the ITC recommendation for any reason deemed important to the national interest, including foreign policy concerns or national economic interests. This discretion also allows the president to weigh consumer interests in the decision. Third, the protection-seeking industry will benefit, but potentially only at the clear expense of another domestic industry because if the president offers protection under the escape clause, he must offer compensation by lowering other import barriers or face increased duties on another U.S. industry's exports. Either way, another U.S. industry must "pay" for the protection. This will increase the political cost to the president of accepting an affirmative ITC decision and make protection less likely to be granted.

Finally, an industry seeking trade protection can try to engineer a settlement completely outside of the normal U.S. trade policy framework. The most important example of this for an import-competing industry has come to be VRAs. Under such a quantitative restriction, foreign exporters agree to limit their exports to the United States, usually in exchange for the domestic industry refraining from filing trade remedy petitions. The foreign firms receive guaranteed access to the protected market and hence will receive higher profit margins.

A VRA has a number of attributes advantageous to a protection-seeking firm. Most important, the VRA is a quota and thus leads to highly predictable ceilings on foreign competition. VRAs are also not subject to GATT rules so that issues of MFN treatment of imports, compensation for raising GATT-bound tariffs, and injury determinations are all irrelevant. In addition, foreigners will often cooperate in negotiating a VRA since compensation in the form of quota rents is transferred to foreign firms.

A VRA's major disadvantage to the integrated steel sector is that it, like all comprehensive import restrictions, will aid free-riding domestic firms. In addition, unless the VRA is implemented on a narrowly defined product basis, foreign firms will have an incentive to upgrade to higher value-added steel products. Finally, unless *all* foreign suppliers are included, a VRA may simply lead to supply diversion to other non-VRA countries.

2.3.4   Determination of the Intervention Level

The determination of the final intervention level depends on two factors. The first is what intervention is being considered, and the second is the relative political strengths of the opponents and proponents of the intervention.

If U.S. unfair trade procedures are the basis of the intervention, the level of protection is determined exclusively by the dumping or subsidy margin. This leaves little or no room for discretion or political lobbying over the precise duty.

There is substantially more discretion under the escape clause and under a VRA. The president explicitly considers factors other than injury to the import-competing industry in an escape clause petition. The president may also modify the ITC's recommendation in any way he deems appropriate. Similarly, since a VRA is negotiated, the level of protection is necessarily a political decision. Since both the escape clause and a VRA allow political actors to play a role, unlike an unfair trade case, the final intervention level will depend on the relative strengths of opponents and proponents of protection. One would expect therefore that politically powerful industries would seek to obtain protection through either a VRA or escape clause. Politically weak industries would opt instead for AD and CVD procedures.[19]

2.4   Steel Trade Policy prior to 1982

The U.S. integrated steel industry reached the height of its power in the immediate postwar period. During the 1940s and 1950s, the industry invested in new and larger-scale OHF capacity to keep up with wartime demand and the postwar consumer boom. This investment solidified the large integrated firms' lead over both smaller domestic mills and foreign firms in Europe and Japan still struggling with war-ravaged plant and equipment. The industry was therefore able to maintain healthy profits, keep imports low, and be the world's leading steel exporter.

This period of Big Steel economic dominance was accompanied by a highly antagonistic relationship between the U.S. government and the steel firms. The large integrated firms, especially U.S. Steel, were frequently accused of operating a domestic cartel and were targets of antitrust rhetoric, if not action. Specific complaints emerged from the Kefauver Committee in Congress, which claimed that "steel prices since 1947 have moved steadily and regularly in one direction, upward," even in the midst of a recession (Adams and Mueller 1986). The highly charged atmosphere perhaps reached its peak during the Korean War when President Truman unsuccessfully attempted to nationalize

---

19. Finger, Hall, and Nelson (1982) have distinguished these two as the "political track" and the "technical track" to protection.

the steel industry in 1952. Confrontations continued in 1962 when President Kennedy challenged steel company executives over price increases. Nonetheless, the integrated firms' ability to dominate the domestic market was largely untouched until the mid-1960s.

The seeds of the destruction of the oligopolistic control over the U.S. steel market were sown at the end of the 1950s. In particular, significant steel imports began in 1959 when a 116-day strike severely reduced the domestic availability of steel. Domestic steel-using firms, especially in the automobile industry, were forced to look for the first time to foreign suppliers as an important source of steel. Soon afterward, the United States became a permanent net importer of steel.

As the 1960s wore on, high prices and high demand in the United States caused import market share to surge from 7.3 percent in 1964 to 16.7 percent in 1968. This increase was partly the result of new and efficient foreign production facilities. New European and Japanese capacity, for example, utilized recently developed BOFs, which were significantly more efficient than the plant introduced in the United States a mere 15 years earlier. An overvalued dollar and low wage rates, especially in Japan, were other important factors in the declining competitiveness of U.S. steel. Finally, foreign exports were also encouraged by government support, most notably in Japan. The Japanese government singled out the steel industry as particularly important in its drive to industrialize the nation (see Howell et al. 1988 for details).

The reaction of integrated producers and the USW to the new competitors was to call for import restrictions. During the late days of the Johnson presidency, the administration gave in to the pressure and negotiated in 1969 the first of many VRAs with the European Community and Japan. In exchange, the U.S. steel producers agreed not to pursue administered protection and furthermore argued that they would use the protection to modernize their plants to compete more effectively with imports.

These agreements, however, provided only limited comprehensive import protection. While the VRAs restricted both the European Community and Japan to an overall import level of 5.8 million tons of steel annually, the agreements did not specify the product mix. Consequently, exporters were free to upgrade to higher value-added products, especially from carbon steel to specialty steels. In addition, other countries moved in to replace the displaced Japanese and European steel exports since the quotas were not global. The VRAs remained in force through 1974, when rising steel demand abroad reduced steel exports to the United States.

This reduction in import pressure was soon followed by the 1974–75 worldwide recession. Most of world's steel firms interpreted the recession as a normal cyclical downturn and continued to install new plant. Japanese gross steelmaking capacity expanded from 138 million metric tons in 1974 to 157 million metric tons in 1979. The European Community followed similar trends and increased steel-making capacity from 178 million to 203 million metric tons in 1979. U.S. steel capacity, on the other hand, remained essentially flat during this period (World Steel Dynamics 1994).

It is clear ex post that the recession of 1974 was also accompanied by a structural shift in world steel demand. Thus, the decisions to continue to add new capacity resulted in vast world overcapacity in steel. Figure 2.1 shows how production capacity in the Western world continued to increase after 1974 even as production fell off strongly from the trend line of the pre-1974 period.

Continued substantial intervention by many nations' governments exacerbated this overcapacity. After the onset of the crisis in 1974, Western European nations with significant public ownership of steel firms (especially France, Belgium, the United Kingdom, and Italy) provided subsidies to slow plant closures. Other EC nations with privately owned firms, especially Germany and the Netherlands, were bitterly opposed to this direct state aid. After an initial attempt to reconcile these differences under the first Davignon Plan, the situation deteriorated sufficiently in 1980 when some nations seriously considered intra-EC barriers in steel, previously unthinkable in the "Common Market." The European Commission subsequently proclaimed a "manifest crisis" and enforced mandatory production quotas and, later, mandatory minimum prices for all steel products. The commission also closely monitored and approved

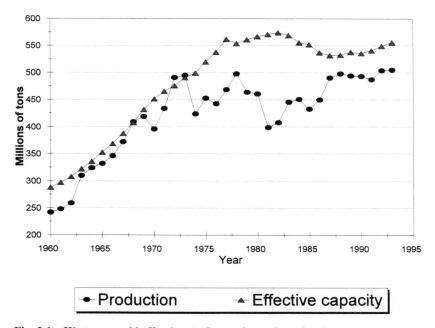

Fig. 2.1   Western world effective steel capacity and production
Source: World Steel Dynamics (1994).

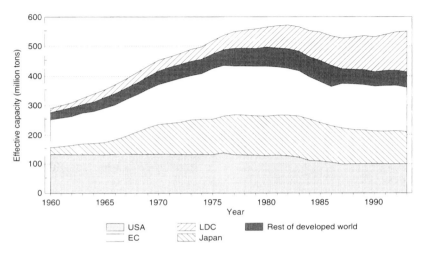

Fig. 2.2   Distribution of western world steel capacity
Source: World Steel Dynamics (1994).

firm investment decisions and endorsed certain state aid to help relieve the crisis situation (Tsoukalis and Schwartz 1985). Nevertheless, significant differences in steel sector subsidies remained among the EC nations. As we will see, U.S. firms used the differential rates of intervention and the threat of near chaos in the European steel sector to its clear advantage in 1982 when they filed for protection under the AD and CVD laws.

After the mid-1970s, other countries provided subsidies for new capacity rather than for covering operating losses as in Europe. Governments in the developing world were especially aggressive in adding to new capacity. Notable examples include the efforts in Brazil and in South Korea.[20] Figure 2.2 illustrates how the steel capacity in the developing world grew rapidly in the period. The increase in capacity was especially important during the 1980s but began in the 1970s, both as part of import substitution programs as well as export promotion programs to earn foreign exchange after the oil shock of 1974.

The structural change in steel demand is also evident within the internal U.S. market. In table 2.2 we see that steel use as a percentage of real GDP rose continually until 1974. Subsequently, steel consumption has stabilized at or near 100 million tons per year even while the U.S. economy has continued to grow. This reflects both the growth in the service economy, for which steel is a negligible input, as well as the growing use of substitute materials such as plastics and aluminum.

---

20. A complete catalog of developing country steel practices is beyond the scope of this paper. The interested reader should see Howell et al. (1988).

The U.S. industry's responded to the post-1974 crisis with renewed pressure for import relief. Steel imports began to rise significantly in 1977, with imports rising to an unprecedented 17.8 percent. Japanese and EC exports were most prominent in this renewed international pressure. Subsequently, a number of U.S. firms began to close plants and others announced large worker layoffs.

The political allies of the integrated sector organized in response to the economic pressure. Most notably, representatives from steel-producing communities formed the Congressional Steel Caucus to press the steel industry's case through legislative action. In essence, the steel caucus acted as a clearinghouse for lobbying efforts by the various fixed factors (labor, producer, and steel-dependent local communities) associated with the integrated steel industry.

Members of the steel caucus drew up legislation calling for strict import quotas. The Carter administration, fearing that executive branch passivity would result in a major trade policy fiasco, urged the industry to file dumping cases under the revised AD rules in the 1974 Trade Act rather than push for a legislated quota (Crandall 1981). The industry followed this advice.

There was every reason to believe that the cases would end affirmatively since the European Community in particular was clearly subsidizing its industry. The Carter administration therefore worked to fashion a compromise that would relieve the political pressure to provide special quotas but would prevent final AD duties. The end result was the inauguration of the TPM. This plan created a minimum U.S. import price based on the production costs of Japanese steel firms (widely recognized as the world's low-cost suppliers) plus a "fair" profit margin of 8 percent. Any steel entering the U.S. market below this minimum price would trigger the self-initiation of an AD petition by the administration. In exchange, U.S. firms agreed to withdraw all AD and CVD petitions and refrain from filing new cases.

The integrated sector agreed to the plan for a number of reasons. One particularly attractive aspect of the plan for the integrated sector was that the TPM applied to all imports. Thus, the TPM discouraged trade diversion to other sources, unlike the 1969 VRA. Second, the industry could avoid further litigation costs of pursuing the AP cases. Finally, the plan explicitly provided import price stability. This in turn limited price competition among domestic rivals and helped maintain a cartellike discipline.

The system provided a number of important benefits to some foreign firms as well. All exporters would be in a much better position to judge what was "acceptable" price competition in the United States. This would help them avoid AD petitions. In addition, the program also guaranteed high-cost European firms significant profits in the United States since the TPM created a price floor based on the lowest-cost producer.

Like the 1969 VRA, the TPM is most notable because the industry was able to obtain a result outside normal U.S. trade law processes. The steel industry, with the strong threat of congressional action and a credible threat of AD procedures, secured minimum prices for imported steel and helped domestic firms maintain capacity utilization and profit levels higher than under unfettered competition.

2.5   The Quest for Comprehensive Quotas

2.5.1   Tactical Use of the AD Process: 1982 VRA with the European Community

The TPM created some breathing room for the American integrated sector. Overall import market share fell from 21.1 percent in 1978 to 15.5 percent in 1981 and net operating profits reached $1.6 billion in 1981.

Nevertheless, the integrated steel sector in the United States began the 1980s with major long-term economic problems. In 1981, the U.S. steel sector use of outdated OHFs remained at 36.5 percent of its operations. In contrast, Japanese and EC firms used this decades-old process in only 4.1 and 26 percent of their plants, respectively. Use of modern continuous casting techniques followed similar patterns: 20.3 percent in the United States versus 70.7 percent in Japan and 44.9 percent in the European Community (International Iron and Steel Institute 1991).

Labor costs were also an important problem for U.S. firms. Average unit labor costs for U.S. steel firms in 1979 were $162.7 per ton, while Japanese rates averaged around $49.8 and Thyssen of Germany averaged $111.1 per ton (World Steel Dynamics 1990). Labor productivity was also low in the United States (217.3 tons per employee) when compared to Japan (474.2 tons per employee) and South Korea (448.7 tons per employee).

Contributing factors to the high labor costs included outdated physical capital, rigid work rules, and wages that had risen under the Experimental Negotiating Agreement of 1974. This labor arrangement guaranteed a 3 percent nominal increase in pay plus a full cost-of-living adjustment in return for an agreement not to strike. As table 2.5 shows, steel sector nominal labor compensation in 1980 was $17.5 per hour, or nearly double the average manufacturing compensation of $9.9 per hour. Ironically, this labor arrangement, which was an important contributor to decreased international competitiveness through high labor costs, was instituted as a means to cope with import competition. Specifically, steel producers believed that the threat of strikes in the late 1960s and early 1970s had caused steel-using industries to sign contracts with importers to protect themselves from supply disruptions. The industry consequently felt that a labor contract that prevented strikes would limit imports and thus was worth the added labor costs (Williams 1978).

The industry was therefore ill equipped to cope with a major downturn and a renewal of intense international competition. The onset of the deep recession in 1981–82 was thus nearly catastrophic for the U.S. industry. Table 2.6 shows that total steel sector capacity utilization fell from 78 percent in 1981 to 48

Table 2.5   Production Worker Compensation

| | All Steel Firms | | | All Manufacturing | | |
Year	Nominal Compensation[a]	Real Compensation[b]	Productivity Index[c]	Nominal Compensation[a]	Real Compensation[b]	Productivity Index[c]
1980	17.5	21.2	100.0	9.9	12.1	100.0
1981	19.0	20.9	108.8	10.8	11.9	102.3
1982	22.7	23.5	88.3	11.6	12.0	104.9
1983	21.1	21.2	113.8	12.1	12.1	110.3
1984	20.3	19.5	127.7	12.5	12.0	116.3
1985	21.4	19.9	135.5	13.0	12.0	121.5
1986	22.0	20.0	137.9	13.2	12.1	126.1
1987	22.6	19.9	148.1	13.4	11.8	130.8
1988	23.6	19.9	163.1	13.9	11.7	134.3
1989	23.5	18.9	158.5	14.3	11.5	138.0
1990	24.3	18.6	163.8	14.8	11.3	141.6

Source: USITC, "Annual Survey Concerning Competitive Conditions in the Steel Industry and Industry Efforts to Adjust and Modernize" (Washington, D.C., various years).
[a]Compensation figures (given in dollars per hour) include both direct and indirect payments.
[b]Real compensation based on CPI-U (1982–84 = 100).
[c]Productivity index given as output per hour.

percent in 1982.[21] Even as sales and capacity utilization dropped, average costs rose so that operating profits for all steel firms fell to a loss of $3.4 *billion* in 1982. As table 2.2 shows, total steel sector employment dropped sharply from 391,000 in 1981 to 289,000 in 1982, or nearly 25 percent. Import market share rose from 19.8 percent of the market in 1981 to 21.8 percent in 1982, thereby exceeding 20 percent of the U.S. market for the first time in the twentieth century. However, it is important to note that this overall increase in import share reflected mainly a precipitous drop in domestic consumption since the absolute level of all imports *fell* from 18.9 to 16.6 million tons in the same period.

Despite the overall drop in volume, imports of European steel into the United States did increase substantially. For example, the volume of U.S. imports of EC hot-rolled carbon steel plate, hot-rolled sheet and strip, and cold-rolled sheet and strip rose 20, 25, and 41 percent, respectively from 1980 to 1981 (USITC 1982). The rise in European exports reflected the fact that Europe was also in the midst of a severe recession and, unlike the United States, had continued to add steel capacity through the late 1970s. European firms tried to maintain high capacity utilization to keep costs down. Since the Davignon Plan effectively limited intra-Europe sales, many firms aggressively exported to the United States.

The integrated industry therefore pointed to Europe, and especially the ef-

21. Capacity utilization in Japan and the European Community fell less sharply to 62 and 57 percent, respectively (World Steel Dynamics 1994).

Table 2.6   **Profit Rates and Capacity Utilization**

Year	Entire Steel Sector		Integrated Sector		Minimill Sector		All Manufacturing	
	Profit Rate[a]	Capacity Utilization	Profit Rate[a]	Capacity Utilization	Profit Rate[a]	Capacity Utilization	Profit Rate[a]	Capacity Utilization
1980	1.8	73	n.a.[b]	87	n.a.[b]	90	7.6	80
1981	3.8	78	n.a.	79	n.a.	78	7.4	79
1982	−12.0	48	n.a.	48	n.a.	50	5.3	73
1983	−9.1	56	n.a.	56	n.a.	57	6.3	75
1984	−0.6	68	n.a.	69	n.a.	67	7.1	80
1985[c]	−1.7	66	−2.9	68	3.1	64	5.9	80
1986	0.2	64	−1.2	64	5.1	65	5.8	79
1987	5.3	80	4.5	84	7.9	74	7.3	81
1988	8.7	89	8.1	96	9.6	79	8.3	84
1989	7.1	85	6.5	90	7.5	76	6.9	84
1990	4.8	85	2.9	88	7.1	80	5.7	82
1991	−0.3[d]	74	−4.6	78	4.2	68	3.6	78

Sources: For steel industry data, USITC, "Annual Survey Concerning Competitive Conditions in the Steel Industry and Industry Efforts to Adjust and Modernize" (Washington, D.C., various years); for integrated and minimill capacity utilization, WEFA Group, "Steel Market Outlook, 4th Quarter 1992" (Philadelphia, 1993); for manufacturing sector data, Council of Economic Advisors, *Economic Indicators* (Washington, D.C.: Government Printing Office, various issues).

[a]Operating profits divided by net sales.

[b]Dissaggregated series for minimill and integrated sectors unavailable prior to 1985.

[c]For 1985 onward, steel industry profits are the average for the last six months of the current year and first six months of the next. This was the reporting method for the ITC annual steel reports (1991–92).

[d]Author estimate.

fects of government subsidies, as the main source of its difficulties. They also argued that the TPM was failing to protect the industry from the effects of these foreign subsidies. The combination of these three factors induced U.S. producers to force the end of the TPM. On January 11, 1982, Bethlehem Steel, U.S. Steel, Republic Steel, Inland Steel, Jones and Laughlin Steel, National Steel, and Cyclops Steel filed 61 CVD and 33 AD duty petitions against eight countries of the European Community, as well as Brazil and Romania.

The cases' sheer complexity nearly brought the administrative process to a halt as the responsible agencies struggled under the statutory deadlines recently introduced in the 1979 trade act. Indeed, many observers thought that the industry's strategy was to overload the AP system and force a negotiated quota.

The cases reached their first important juncture when the ITC ruled affirmatively in 20 of the CVD cases and 18 of the AD petitions. However, these numbers understate the rulings' overall impact since a significant number of the petitions were lost in the CVD process but won as AD cases. The varied outcomes also had important subtle impact. For example, the ITC determined that imports of hot-rolled plate from France, Italy, and Luxembourg had not caused material injury but ruled affirmatively on plate from Belgium, the United Kingdom, and West Germany. The petitioners alleged that these "guilty" exporters dumped steel by margins of 6.8, 100, and 78.9 percent, respectively. The widely varying allegations reflected in part the variable treatment afforded different European firms by their respective governments. The potential variation among different countries' plate exports meant that EC plate exports might have received radically different treatment when entering into the United States, ranging from no extra duties on French plate exports to 100 percent duties on U.K. exports.

Most observers believed that the DOC was highly likely to make affirmative final decisions on dumping and subsidies. The rapid increase in EC exports, huge domestic financial losses, and massive steelworker layoffs also made an affirmative ITC material injury decision quite probable. This likelihood of affirmative decisions meant that highly divergent duties on EC exports were forthcoming. This created an extraordinarily favorable negotiating position for the domestic industry. A closed U.S. market for a subset of European exporters combined with a barrier-free EC market would have meant massive trade diversion within Europe. Thus, the Europeans faced the real possibility that their steel industry would be thrown into the same chaos that they had so narrowly avoided in 1977 and in 1980 (Tsoukalis and Schwartz 1985). The Europeans had every reason to negotiate with the United States.

The Reagan administration also wanted to avoid the open-ended and prohibitive duties on many European steel exports if the ITC voted affirmatively at the final AP stage. If AD and CVD duties were imposed, the president would lose discretion in steel policy with the European Community, one of the United States' major political and military allies. Complicating matters was a concurrent dispute with the European Community over a natural gas pipeline from the Soviet Union to Western Europe. Reagan administration officials believed that punitive duties on steel exports would make talks over this issue even more problematic and impede cooperation on what the administration saw as a critical security policy issue. These factors induced the administration to enter negotiations with the European Community for a new VRA.

The agreement, finally reached in October 1982, limited EC exports to 5.5 percent of the U.S. market. In return, the U.S. firms dropped their unfair trade petitions and agreed to refrain from filing new cases until the agreement expired in January 1986. The agreement provided benefits that they had originally expected from the TPM. In particular, the VRA both allowed U.S. firms to avoid further AP litigation costs and provided protection against all EC imports rather than only a subgroup, thereby avoiding supply diversion. The industry's disappointment with the details of the TPM administration were solved by the reliance on numerical targets rather than on a bureaucratically administered price-based system.

The U.S. firms' motivation for filing unfair trade remedy petitions rather than using other options such as the escape clause is quite clear. First, there was no question that some European firms had been subsidized by their governments. Consequently, affirmative dumping and subsidy decisions by the DOC were highly probable. This in turn provided the steel sector with enormous leverage since the dumping and subsidy margins would vary widely among the EC nations. The possibility of highly divergent, and perhaps permanent, AD and CVD duties that varied across countries exploited EC fears about a renewed steel industry collapse within Europe. Second, the lower injury standard under AD and CVD rules meant that the probability of an affirmative decision at the ITC was higher than with an escape clause serious injury determination. This was of major concern to the industry, given the ITC's 1980 negative decision on an automobile escape clause case. Finally, the highly technical and nonpolitical nature of these cases and the lack of a presidential role in AD and CVD processes created a credible threat to secure high duties. This was particularly important since the industry doubted whether President Reagan would impose significant tariffs under the escape clause process.

2.5.2   Comprehensive Quotas at Long Last: 1984

Despite the VRA victory, the respite for the integrated industry was short lived. The noncomprehensive nature of the agreement led quickly to supply diversion, so that other imports rapidly filled the void created by the fall in EC exports. Imports from all sources rose slightly from 16.6 million tons in 1982 to 17.1 million in 1983.

The domestic firms' position was weakened not only by supply diversion. As figure 2.3 shows, the steel sector was strongly affected by the start of the dollar's spectacular rise in value. This reduced sharply the landed price of foreign steel into the United States and helped cause import volume to rise by almost 52 percent from 1983 to 1984.

Integrated firms, severely disappointed by an import share still exceeding 20 percent despite the VRA, began once again to prepare trade cases. Two efforts were initiated. One, spearheaded by U.S. Steel, resulted in dozens of new AD and CVD cases involving non-EC countries. The second strategy was initiated in January 1984 when Bethlehem Steel and the USW filed an escape clause petition on behalf of the entire carbon (and alloy) steel industry. Both efforts seemed to have a negotiated global VRA as an objective, but the tactics to reach that goal were quite different.

U.S. Steel and its allies wanted to pursue a strategy similar to the one utilized against European imports in 1982. They believed that the case for unfair foreign practices was so clear that very high and potentially open-ended duties could be placed on foreign exporters. In addition, many of the exporting nations named in the new round of petitions were developing countries in which steel sector government intervention was even more extensive than in Europe. A further advantage of the AD and CVD processes from the steel industry's perspective was the continued exclusion of President Reagan from any role.

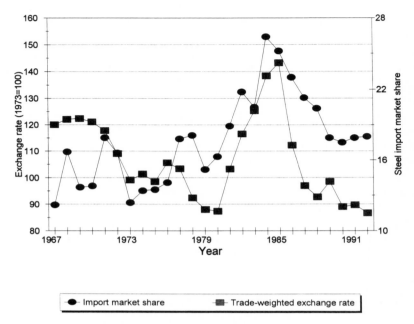

Fig. 2.3   Steel import market share and trade-weighted exchange rate
Sources: AISI (various issues); Federal Reserve Board.

Bethlehem and the USW, on the other hand, had come to believe that unfair trade remedies, used or threatened by the industry for over 10 years, had yielded at best only partial protection. Consequently, this alliance of an integrated firm and steelworker union opted to push finally for a comprehensive import barrier program, but one that might last for only five years under the escape clause mechanism.

The first important hurdle in the escape clause case was to win an affirmative decision at the ITC. The two most critical issues at the ITC was the definition of the "domestic industry" and whether imports were a substantial cause of serious injury. If the ITC's ruling was affirmative, the decision would then be on President Reagan's desk in September 1984, less than two months before the presidential election.

Even as the ITC considered this escape clause petition, the integrated firms, the USW, and their congressional allies proposed legislation imposing an across-the-board 15 percent quota on imported steel, an import share last seen in 1976. A revised bill also included a provision requiring the industry to reinvest all net cash flow from steel operations back into the steel industry. This was a direct concession to the USW since union leaders feared that protection-induced profits would be used to diversify out of steel as U.S. Steel had with the purchase of Marathon Oil.

The title of the quota bill, The Fair Trade in Steel Act of 1984, attests to the importance of trying to reach the rhetorical high ground. The focus, proponents of H.R. 5081 insisted, was not protection but redress of legitimate grievances against foreigners. For example, Representative John Murtha (D-Pa.) said that there may be room for argument about "academic assertions" that the industry had offered overgenerous labor contracts and had modernized slowly but "there is absolutely no room for argument regarding the predatory pricing and trade practices being implemented by foreign steel producers in their zeal to acquire the commanding share of the domestic steel market in the world's largest free market—the United States" (U.S. Congress, House 1984, 7).

Congressional skeptics of the legislative effort insisted that the industry should use the extant trade remedy apparatus rather than obtain a special quota. Sam Gibbons (D-Fla.) also noted that factors other than unfair foreign competition were at the heart of the integrated sector's problems: "Imports of steel for 1974 were about 16 million tons and imports in 1983 were still only about 17 million tons. . . . What has happened is that, one, the domestic steel market has shrunk as less steel is being used and, two, minimills have entered the market" (U.S. Congress, House 1984, 51).

Representatives of the steelworkers, steel producers, and steel-based communities were highly visible in the legislative hearings. Not surprisingly, all argued strongly in favor of the quota bill. Much of the focus was on foreign subsidies, global overcapacity, and the wrenching effects on steel communities as the industry restructured.[22]

Opposition to the bill came mainly from administration representatives (including Commerce Secretary Malcom Baldrige and Special Trade Representative William Brock), academic opponents, and a number of representatives of steel importers. Some important industrial consumers of steel did testify against the quota bill, including officials from Caterpillar, Inc. However, domestic steel-using industries apparently were prepared to do little more than offer token testimony in opposition; according to both steel-user and steel industry representatives, extensive outside lobbying activity by users was extremely limited. In private conversations, a user-industry representative acknowledged that the massive steel sector employment losses, combined with the foreign subsidies, created little room for effective opposition to steel protection.

Perhaps the most fascinating congressional testimony offered in opposition to the import restrictions came from Kenneth Iverson, CEO of Nucor Corporation, the most successful minimill firm in the United States.[23] Iverson spoke

22. See, e.g., testimony by John Sheehan of the USW, David Roderick of U.S. Steel, and Mayor Richard Caliguiri of Pittsburgh, a leader of Local Officials for Fair Trade (U.S. Congress, House 1984).

23. Other minimill firms were more sympathetic to the quota legislation. See, e.g., the testimony by James Collins, president of the Steel Manufacturers Association (SMA), a minimill trade group (U.S. Congress, House 1989).

out strongly against any trade protection and asserted that "we believe that tariff or nontariff trade barriers will delay modernization of our steel industry, [and] will cost the consumer billions of dollars." He argued that the government could instead offer assistance in retraining programs and various special tax credits directed specifically at the integrated sector (U.S. Congress, House 1984, 288–89).

In July, the ITC rendered its decision on the escape clause petition. The commission ruled that only five of the nine constituent steel "industries" were eligible for import relief. To relieve the injury, the ITC recommended that the president impose a combination of tariffs and quotas on imports for the seriously injured industries producing steel sheet and strip, plate, structural shapes, wire and wire products, and semifinished steel. The protection would be phased out over the next five years. The ITC, however, found that the industries producing pipe and tube, bar, rod, and rails were injured for other reasons more important than import competition.

The ITC's decision was a mixed outcome for the industry and reflected the rising importance of the minimills in the United States. In particular, the commissioners argued that intraindustry competition (i.e., domestic minimills) was a more important source of injury than foreign competition for the four product categories denied relief. Indeed, the ITC pointed out that minimills had consistently undersold both imported and integrated mills and had still remained profitable for the previous three years (USITC 1984, 47–54).

President Reagan once again was faced with a dilemma over steel trade policy. The law required the president to accept, reject, or modify the ITC's recommendations by September 1984. If he followed the ITC plan and provided protection for only the five ITC-approved petitions, the steel industry was likely to press forward with the other unfair trade petitions. Accepting the ITC's escape clause suggestions would also mean foreigners could retaliate against U.S. exports if compensation was not forthcoming. If the president rejected import relief altogether, the industry still could rely on AD and CVD cases in which the president played no role whatsoever. Total rejection of relief might also lead to passage of the quota legislation which Reagan would be forced to veto right before the election.

There was intense disagreement among administration advisers about the proper action. Some counseled that Reagan should hold fast to his free trade principles. Others, especially political advisers, counseled that some action was necessary since rejection of all relief would lead to potentially significant consequences in the 1984 elections.[24]

In the end, the Reagan administration formally rejected the ITC recommendations but announced simultaneously a program to deal with steel imports. The heart of the plan, scheduled to expire in 1989, was a comprehensive steel

---

24. See Niskanen (1988) and Walters (1988) for further discussion about these intra-administration disagreements.

quota encompassing *all* of the industries in the section 201 petition, *including* the four products for which the ITC had recommended no relief. The VRA would apply to countries "whose exports to the United States had increased significantly in the previous years" (49 *Federal Register* 36813). This would include all major suppliers to the United States, including the European Community, Brazil, South Korea, Japan, and others. (See table 2.8 for a list of included exporters.)

The VRA was designed to limit imported finished steel products from the covered countries to 18.4 percent of the domestic market (adjusted annually) and a specific quota of 1.7 million tons for semifinished steel. A critical new aspect of the program was that the administration agreed to administer the quota on a product- and country-specific basis. This would help alleviate product upgrading and supply diversion, both of which had been major industry complaints with the 1969 VRA with the European Community and Japan and the 1982 VRA with the European Community. Finally, the program incorporated an aspect of the congressional quota bill that required the domestic industry to reinvest all net cash flow from their steel operations back into their steel plants.

The 1984 VRA program was a major political victory for the integrated sector. The industry secured its most important long-term trade goal, namely, a comprehensive quota covering nearly all products and all exporting countries. The industry certainly would have preferred the 15 percent quota embodied in the legislation, but it did obtain an import share in line with that of the late 1970s. The USW also could claim an important triumph since the industry was *required* to reinvest steel sector profits back into steel operations and provide some funds for worker retraining.

The integrated industry was able to win this victory through brilliant use of the multiple paths of protection in the United States. The industry simultaneously pursued legislative action, relief under the escape clause, and the imposition of AD and CVD duties. The threat of the AD and CVD duties was perhaps most significant since they confronted the administration with the reemergence of near-prohibitive duties that could be imposed without any executive branch input.

The timing of the lobbying effort also served to maximize political pressure on the Reagan administration in an election year. The escape clause petition in particular was structured so that the president would have to reach a decision only eight weeks before the election.[25] If the 1984 presidential election had proved to be a close one, the electoral votes of major steel-producing states such as Pennsylvania and Ohio could have been decisive.

The program was clearly an unusually protectionist regime. Not only did the administration approve a comprehensive protection scheme for the steel

---

25. Representatives from both the USW and a major steel firm both deny, however, that presidential election considerations played any role in the timing of the escape clause petition.

industry, it did so by negotiating VRAs rather than imposing a tariff under the escape clause. Most economists consider such quantitative restrictions clearly inferior to the imposition of tariffs since they transfer potential tariff revenue to foreign exporters in terms of quota rents.[26] Second, the administration offered protection far beyond what was required under U.S. trade law since four of the products included in the VRA program were ruled ineligible for relief by the ITC. The administration also instituted a managed trade program since specific numerical targets were included for countries and products. Finally, the mandated reinvestment of net cash flow back into steel operations contrasted starkly with the administration's general predilection to allow markets to determine capital allocation.

Why did the "free market" Reagan administration offer such sweeping and broad-based protection? This acquiescence to steel industry and steel union demands clearly was not a result of an ideological predisposition for protection and intervention. The answer must be that the steel industry had enough political clout to force an outcome acceptable to them.[27]

Nonetheless, the VRA program provided distinct political advantages for the administration over other possible outcomes. President Reagan could assert that, as with the automobile agreement with Japan, he was not imposing tariffs but negotiating an agreement. This would allow him to score political points with steel sector voters while retaining his free trade rhetoric. A negotiated agreement also insured that the administration would retain some control over steel trade policy decisions. This was particularly important given the sensitive nature of steel issues within the European Community. Such discretion would have been impossible if final AD and CVD duties had been imposed. The use of a VRA also enabled the administration to control the timing of protection offered the steel industry. Unlike AD and CVD measures, which have no precise expiration date, the VRA expired in October 1989, fully 11 months *after* the 1988 presidential election. This would help limit the ability of the steel industry to reinject steel trade policy into presidential politics.

In summary, the 1984 VRA demonstrated the significant political power of the U.S. integrated steel industry.[28] Industry producers, union leaders, and congressional representatives of steel-producing communities worked hand in hand to secure a highly interventionist trade policy outcome from the Reagan

26. Moore and Suranovic (1993) have shown that VRAs may welfare-dominate tariffs when GATT-consistent compensatory tariff reductions or retaliation are included.

27. It is also interesting to note that the copper industry, a less politically powerful industry, also won an escape clause case at the ITC at about the same time. President Reagan refused to provide protection in this case.

28. Another example of steel industry clout was the appointment of Eugene Frank to the ITC in 1981. Frank was strongly backed for the position by Pennsylvania Senator John Heinz and had long and close ties with the steel industry. Prior to his appointment, he organized regional Committees for Fair Trade. Frank's nomination was strongly opposed by foreign steel producers who asserted that he was "clearly biased" (*Wall Street Journal*, July 15, 1981). Commissioner Frank has had the most protectionist voting record in commission history and voted affirmatively in all material injury decisions on which he cast a vote.

administration. They pursued a multifaceted approach that exploited the highly cohesive nature of the steel industry coalition, the lack of organized opposition by steel-using industries, and the AP procedures available to them. Subsequent steel policy outcomes in the 1980s and early 1990s would not be nearly as favorable to Big Steel.

2.5.3   The VRA Renewal Campaign: 1989

Economic Performance of the Steel Industry: 1984–88

The economic condition of the U.S. steel industry improved dramatically after the introduction of the global VRAs in October 1984. Table 2.6 shows that capacity utilization for the domestic industry rose from 68 percent in 1984 to 89 percent in 1988. Operating profits increased from a *loss* of $186 million in 1984 to a gain of over $3.5 billion in 1988. Not only did the steel industry's performance improve relative to its own position in 1984, it also performed better relative to the U.S. manufacturing sector as a whole. Specifically, in 1988 steel sector capacity utilization and profit rates finally exceeded the overall manufacturing average. This represented a dramatic improvement over the disastrous performance of the early 1980s.

A number of factors contributed to this improvement in economic performance. The reduction in import competition was one factor. Total imports from all sources fell from a historic high of 26.4 percent (26 million tons) in 1984 to only 20.4 percent (21 million tons) in 1988. However, the VRA program was not the sole contributor to the reduced imports. Most important, the U.S. industry's international competitiveness greatly improved, some of which was a consequence of integrated sector restructuring and other purely exogenous factors.

Perhaps the most important source of improvement was the moderation of labor costs during this period. The USW, for example, offered concessions in labor negotiations totaling $4.5 billion as well as flexibility on work rules (Williams 1988). As table 2.5 shows, these efforts resulted in important gains in unit labor costs. Productivity rose by 27.5 percent from 1984 to 1988, while real steelworker compensation rose by only 2 percent. In contrast, productivity for the entire U.S. manufacturing rose about 21 percent, while real compensation wages actually fell by approximately 2 percent. Thus, labor costs corrected for productivity seemed to moderate in the steel sector, in contrast to the steelworkers' poor productivity growth and guaranteed wage increases in the 1970s.

The integrated producers also continued their intensive rationalization and modernization efforts. Rationalization efforts included U.S. Steel's abandonment of five integrated plants and National Steel's sale of its Weirton, West Virginia, plant to its employees in 1984 (Hogan 1987). Technological backwardness vis-à-vis foreign producers lessened as modernization expanded the use of continuous casting in the United States from 39.6 percent of production in 1984 to 61.3 percent in 1988. The use of outdated OHFs also fell from 9 percent to just over 5 percent over the same period. However, the use of BOFs remained essentially unchanged over the period and reflected a continuing need for modernization (International Iron and Steel Institute 1991).

Perhaps the most important exogenous factors were the substantial weakening of the dollar after 1985 and strong worldwide economic growth. Figure 2.3 shows that after the dollar's depreciation in 1985, steel import market share fell substantially in the United States. Steel consumption patterns also contributed to a reduction of exports to the United States. In particular, while U.S. consumption remained essentially unchanged from 1984 to 1988, steel demand rose by 37 percent in the European Community, 16.2 percent in Japan, and 20 percent in the developing world (International Iron and Steel Institute 1991). Thus, exchange rate changes and strong price pressures abroad both created powerful incentives for foreign steel firms to exploit non-U.S. markets.

Another critical aspect of the improved overall economic statistics of the U.S. steel industry was the continued strong performance of domestic minimills. As table 2.6 indicates, minimills' capacity utilization and profits were consistently higher than the integrated sector. Since the market share of minimills was growing throughout the 1980s, the minimills' economic experience helped bring up the average performance of the sector. Persisting minimill pressure also contributed to continuing competitive pressures on the integrated mills, even if import pressures had subsided somewhat.

All of these indicators of improved economic performance became important factors as decisions about renewal of the VRA program approached in 1988.

Steel Policy and Presidential Politics in 1988: Déjà Vu All Over Again

One of the supposed key political advantages to the VRA program announced in 1984 was that it would extend beyond the next presidential campaign into 1989. This, the Reagan administration hoped, would prevent the steel industry from using the presidential election to affect steel trade policy. Indeed, as the presidential campaign wore on, it appeared that steel import policy would play only a minor role in the election. Governor Michael Dukakis, the Democratic party nominee, did come out in favor of a VRA renewal but never made it an important part of his election campaign.

However, in the late summer and early fall, Republican presidential candidate George Bush was significantly behind in the polls. As part of the general effort to coordinate a come-from-behind victory and to help solidify political support among blue-collar workers in the steel region, the Bush campaign agreed to support a VRA extension. Industry and campaign representatives negotiated for some time in the early fall to have Bush appear at a steel facility where he would announce support for an extension. Though this appearance never materialized, the Republican campaign arranged instead for the vice president to outline his support for a continued special steel program in a letter to Senator John Heinz, a Republican from Pennsylvania and an ardent supporter of the steel industry in particular and of aggressive U.S. trade policy in general.

In the letter dated November 4, 1988, Bush stated that "one of the significant successes of the Reagan Administration has been the President's Steel Program. . . . A comprehensive VRA program has proven to be more effective in offsetting unfair trade practices than trying to counter these practices on a case-by-case basis. . . . One of the key trade policy goals of a Bush Administration will be to achieve an international consensus on eliminating [dumping and subsidizing of steel], and, pending that, I can assure you of my intention to continue the voluntary restraint program after September 30, 1989." The vice-president, however, did not outline any specifics about the timing and details of his proposed program.

This letter, written just as George Bush was about to win an overwhelming election victory, reflected the steel industry's continued image as a powerful political presence. However, the industry's inability to nail down specific promises about the nature of the VRA extension was to haunt it later in 1989.

Soon after inauguration, posturing began over the extension's exact details. In previous public discussions, integrated steel producers and their allies dominated the field. In essence, these early steel trade arguments revolved only around the benefits of steel protection and the presence of foreign government intervention. Little regard for the effects on domestic steel consumers was evident in decisions. This was to change in a profound way during this period. Most important, steel-user interests were to play a much more prominent role in the public discussions and in the final outline of the policies.

Big Steel versus CASUM

One of the first public indications of the increased importance of the VRA's user effects appeared in February 1989. The House Ways and Means Trade Subcommittee requested that the ITC conduct an investigation into the costs of the VRAs to steel-*using* industries. The ITC was instructed to consider the VRA's effects on the exports, imports, and prices of steel-using industries and to poll these industries concerning their positions on the VRA's renewal.

In the report, the commission estimated that the VRAs had increased the weighted average of domestic and imported steel prices by 0.6 percent in 1985 and 1.6 percent in 1986. The estimates of price increase rose to 1.4 percent in 1987 and fell to 0.2 percent in 1988. The commission also calculated that the steel restraints reduced U.S. exports of steel-using industries by over $1.7 billion dollars in 1985–88. The ITC study also noted that strong demand for certain types of steel and the weakened dollar were important causes of separate upward pressure on prices (USITC 1989b).

This report is a highly unusual document. The views and interests of *protection seekers* are totally absent since the report was commissioned as a purely investigative study and not part of an AD, CVD, or escape clause petition. The focus, therefore, was on the costs rather than the benefits of protection. The commissioning of this report, however, was only a hint of how user interests were to play a near-dominating role in the 1989 VRA extension debate.

As 1989 wore on, the usual array of actors lined up in favor of the VRA extension (see table 2.7). Steel-producing community representatives in the bipartisan Congressional Steel Caucus, the integrated firms' trade association (AISI), and the steelworkers' union (USW) reassembled the coalition that had been so successful five years earlier. The SMA, the minimill trade association, also strongly supported the extension in congressional testimony, but the major players continued to be members of the integrated steel sector. The main goals of the steel industry and its allies were to push for a five-year extension of the existing program, but with the inclusion of nonparticipating nations (Canada and Sweden) into the extended VRA.

The proponents of a continuation and enlargement of the program argued that the improved economic performance of the industry noted above was "proof" that the VRA had been the most successful steel trade policy program in U.S. history. The industry, they argued, was now competitive but still needed five more years to complete the modernization program. Without a full five-year extension, modernization plans might be disrupted. Allegheny-Ludlum, for example, asserted that a $5 billion dollar expansion would be abandoned if the VRA were not extended. They also used the results of ITC steel-user

Table 2.7   Policy Positions and Economic Stakes on 1989 VRA Extension

Economic Consequences of VRA Extension	Policy Position		
	Support	Neutral	Oppose
Benefited	AISI (association of integrated producers) USW (steelworker union) SMA (association of minimill producers)		Nucor Corp. (minimill producer)
Unaffected	Congressional Steel Caucus (Congress members from steel-producing districts and states)		
Hurt	Coalition for a Competitive America: Steel Users for VRAs (steel-user group organized by AISI) Chrysler Corp. (steel-using automobile producer)	General Motors Ford Motor Co.	CASUM (steel-user group) Caterpillar, Inc. (heavy equipment manufacturer and exporter) PMA (small businesses processing steel for intermediate input use)

Sources: Policy position based on testimony before Congress (U.S. Congress, House 1989). Positions of other individual steel-user industries can be found in USITC (1989b).

investigation to argue that price increases due to the VRAs had been small, especially compared to the effects of the depreciating dollar. The industry also asserted that VRAs were the only "viable trade policy in view of the continuing lack of access to foreign markets, unfair trading practices of foreign countries and structural world overcapacity in steelmaking" (AISI 1989, 1). The industry also argued that if the VRA were not extended, they would be forced to rely on AD and CVD petitions. In appearance after appearance, the industry raised the specter that these unfair trade remedies would be even more disruptive than a VRA since the margins would be very high and vary greatly across countries and products (AISI 1989, 17).

While these arguments may have had a familiar ring, the actions of steel-user groups in this period were radically different from earlier steel trade debates. Most important, a lobbying coalition of users successfully overcame transaction and organizational costs to mount a campaign against the renewal. This ad hoc lobbying organization, CASUM, was headed by Caterpillar, Inc., a manufacturer of earth-moving equipment and a major U.S. steel-using exporter, and the Precision Metalforming Association (PMA), a trade association of small businesses that process raw steel for industrial manufacturers, especially for the automobile industry.

CASUM's position was that the president should terminate the VRA program. Their highly public campaign focused on four major points. The first was that steel-using firms provided much more employment than steel-producing firms. Furthermore, they argued that the VRAs harmed U.S. export competitiveness of manufactured goods since they were important steel users. Foreign competitors, CASUM insisted, had access to lower world prices of steel and consequently could charge lower prices than U.S. exporters.

The second argument was that the steel quotas had increased prices and led to spot shortages, especially for firms using modern inventory management techniques ("just in time" delivery). The spot shortages were exacerbated by the "short supply" provisions under which quotas were supposed to be relaxed if a domestic firm could show that a particular steel product was unavailable domestically. In addition, the steel *user* bore the burden of proof in showing that such conditions existed. Other complaints by CASUM included a provision that limited the amount of short-supply steel that could be granted a specific country and a nontransparent application process that could take many weeks.

Third, CASUM argued that the steel industry should rely, like virtually all other domestic industries, on the established AP procedures to address its trade complaints. If unfair competition was occurring, then AD and CVD petitions should be adjudicated to their final conclusions.

Finally, CASUM pointed to the high profits in 1988 and improving domestic steel industry competitiveness as evidence that the domestic industry did not deserve special help.

The overall strategy of CASUM was to turn the debate away from the actions of foreign firms and governments and away from an argument about free trade versus protection. Instead, CASUM tried to direct the discussion toward the VRA's effects on U.S. manufacturing interests, especially exporters and small businesses. This was a highly effective tactic since both have broad political support. CASUM also appealed indirectly to protectionist elements in Congress by emphasizing that VRAs rewarded unfair traders through the transfer of quota rents. In conjunction with this strategy of stressing how the VRA hurt U.S. domestic manufacturing interests, CASUM steadfastly refused any cooperation from foreign steel companies and U.S. steel importers, the traditional major opponents of steel import barriers. The coalition also made a concerted effort to identify steel-using firms in the districts of Congress members who had supported the steel industry in the past. This helped provide constituent counterbalance to the votes of the steel-producing industry.

CASUM's efforts caught the pro-VRA coalition almost totally off guard. In response, steel industry lobbyists hurriedly organized a user-industry group (named Coalition for a Competitive America: Steel Users for VRAs) as a counterweight to CASUM. The most prominent large steel user in this group was Chrysler Corporation, an automobile company and a major steel user. This position reflects the trade activist philosophy of Lee Iaccoca, a frequent critic of liberal U.S. trade policy. However, although Chrysler did lend its name to the effort, its public participation was limited. For example, Chrysler representatives did not appear before congressional committees in favor of the VRA extension.

Another indication of integrated steel firms' concerns about CASUM was an AISI-published refutation (*VRAs and the Steel Consumer*) of an earlier Caterpillar position paper on the effects of the VRA. The AISI strongly rejected Caterpillar's claims that the VRAs had hurt U.S. export competitiveness or that the steel industry had gained sufficient strength to prosper without special relief. The USW also argued forcefully against CASUM, both in press releases and in testimony before Congress.

The most important aspect of the fight between CASUM and VRA supporters was that Big Steel was forced to enter into a domestic debate with other U.S. industries about the domestic costs of the program. This radically changed the nature of the debate since it removed the discussion from simply making a case about unfair foreign practices and the social costs of massive steel employee layoffs. In addition, the fact that a major U.S. exporting firm (Caterpillar) was complaining of the VRA's effects helped sway opinions among politicians who view imports as "bad" because they destroy jobs and view exports as "good" because they create jobs.

The VRA Extension and Its Aftermath

In the final analysis, the VRA was continued as candidate George Bush had promised. The new program, entitled the Steel Trade Liberalization Program, granted a two-and-a-half year extension but at the same time set a final and permanent expiration date. After the expiration date, the steel industry would be required to rely on normal trade remedy procedures for any import restrictions. The administration also promised to begin multilateral steel trade negotiations aimed at eliminating the underlying reasons for trade frictions, most importantly foreign subsidies and worldwide steel overcapacity.

The program was a far cry from that requested by the integrated industry. Perhaps the most disappointing provision was the two-and-a-half rather than five-year extension. The Bush administration also allowed for a 1 percent *increase* per year in the quota for countries willing to begin eliminating trade-distorting steel sector practices. The short-supply provisions for products unavailable in the United States, a major sore point for CASUM members, were also substantially liberalized. The program instituted a fast-track 15-day procedure for obtaining steel under short supply when the product was either not produced domestically or when domestic capacity utilization for that product exceeded 90 percent. In addition, the burden of proof in this application process shifted to domestic steel producers, away from steel consumers. These changes reduced the ability of domestic steel suppliers to raise prices in the face of tight supplies on subcategories of steel. Finally, President Bush added no new countries to the VRA program as requested by the steel industry.

In short, the 1989 VRA extension was a major disappointment for the integrated industry and a major victory for the steel-using industries. This is evident from the press reports at the time. The *Far Eastern Economic Review* (August 10, 1989), for example, observed that the outcome "is a demonstration of the new lobbying power of the steel users, especially Caterpillar." *Iron Age* (September 1989, 62), the most important steel trade magazine in the United States, reported that Milton Deaner, president of the AISI, viewed the Bush plan as naive and left the industry too vulnerable to unfair trade practices. The magazine also noted that Caterpillar was elated by its prospects under that the new VRA.

If the VRA extension was so disappointing to the integrated sector, why did the steel firms and USW not reject the VRA extension and pursue AD and CVD cases as they had in previous years? Most important, the industry would have had a difficult time winning an AD or CVD petition. Even if the industry could have showed that dumping and subsidization were taking place, proving material injury would have been highly uncertain given the industry's healthy financial position. Thus, a less-than-ideal VRA was more appealing than undertaking the major expense of a massive and likely unsuccessful AD and CVD campaign.

The disappointing results of the 1989 extension may have been an unexpected consequence of the industry's acceptance of VRAs in 1984. In the purely technical AP process, DOC and ITC administrators cannot consider user effects. The industry consequently would have probably secured affirmative material injury decisions in 1982 and 1984 and received definitive duties. Instead, steel producers agreed to the VRAs in order to obtain comprehensive protection. As it turned out, the ultimate problem with this strategy was that it allowed the user groups to reenter the policy debate when the VRAs were up for renewal. This was complicated by the fact that the industry's fragmentation and improved economic performance undercut its political position in favor of import protection.

It is, however, unclear exactly *why* the Bush administration proposed a steel program so unfavorable to the steel industry. It is possible that the greatly improved economic performance of the industry in 1988 convinced the administration that a highly restrictive VRA was unnecessary. It is also possible that the lobbying campaign by CASUM, nearly unprecedented in U.S. trade policy history, swayed opinions in the White House and on Capitol Hill. CASUM's campaign more likely simply provided political cover for the administration to follow its free trade instincts. In any case, the administration was sufficiently unafraid of the political clout of the integrated steel sector to propose and implement a trade policy highly unsatisfactory to Big Steel.

An intriguing aspect of the 1989 VRA extension was the timing of its final expiration. President Bush's two-and-a-half year extension meant that the program would expire about eight months before the 1992 presidential election. Some participants recall that this date was simply "splitting the difference" between the five years requested by the industry and an immediate termination. Regardless of the motivation, this timetable meant that the integrated steel sector would have a chance to use its leverage in a presidential campaign in 1992 just as it had in 1984.

The actual experience of the VRA in the post-1989 period strongly suggests that, not only was the program less than what the integrated firms wanted, the quotas may have had very little effect at all on the domestic steel market. In particular, the quotas were not filled on a country or product basis for most of the post-1987 period.

Table 2.8 shows that the quotas were binding or nearly binding for most of the first two years. However, beginning in 1988, the overall quota fill rate fell from 79 percent to a low of 54 percent in the last three months of the VRA in 1992. In addition, subsequent to the extension in October 1989, no country filled its overall quota, and in only one instance (Finland in the October–December 1990 period) did imports reach over 90 percent of the quota limits. This pattern is also repeated for individual product categories. Table 2.9 shows that after 1988, the quotas were binding or near binding only in some specialty products—alloy tool steel, tin plate, and stainless steel plate and sheet.

The nonbinding quotas suggest that the integrated industry achieved very little in the way of protection in the 1989 VRA extension. The industry may have enjoyed some benefits through an upper bound on foreign competition; this may have helped investor confidence in integrated firms and eased some

Table 2.8   **Percentage of VRA Filled (by country)**

Country	10/84–12/85	1986	1987	1988	1/89–9/89	10/89–12/90	1/91–3/92
Australia	95	97	94	95	84	85	81
Austria	n.a.	101	77	54	44	64	46
Brazil	97	96	105	92	85	87	59
Czechoslovakia	100	88	99	75	62	38	45
East Germany	99	99	95	88	47	39	14
EC (12)[a]	101	102	96	83	68	75	60
Finland	99	103	97	85	68	94	75
Hungary	46	68	98	98	93	77	25
Japan	108	95	88	72	63	69	56
South Korea	103	103	99	77	59	72	42
Mexico	77	98	87	82	65	64	37
China	n.a.	n.a.	92	90	75	83	53
Poland	111	86	100	94	87	54	41
Romania	101	96	91	82	61	60	28
Trinidad and Tobago	n.a.	n.a.	123	88	92	59	64
Venezuela	90	89	94	65	87	68	40
Yugoslavia	134	89	108	69	41	68	49
Total	102	99	94	79	67	73	54

Sources: USITC (various issues); U.S. Department of Commerce, Office of Agreements Compliance.

[a]Includes Spain and Portugal, both of which were not part of the original VRA agreement.

financing efforts, but it is highly unlikely that the industry effectively limited import competition during this period.[29]

The domestic industry continued to evolve after the VRA extension. In particular, minimills recommenced their strong surge forward vis-à-vis domestic integrated firms *and* imports. A measure of strong minimill international competitiveness is that quotas on traditional minimill long products were filled at an even lower rate than other VRA categories. Table 2.9 shows that in the final period of the VRA, imports of bars, wire products, and structurals reached only 38, 68, and 23 percent of allowable imports, respectively. But perhaps the strongest indicator of future minimill strength was the already-mentioned inauguration by Nucor of its Crawfordsville sheet mill, which began production of flat-rolled products using horizontal thin-slab casting techniques in 1989.

The other major aspect of the Bush administration's steel policy was the multilateral steel negotiations, conducted parallel to the VRA program. The Bush administration hoped that a MSA would eliminate the underlying problems that had bedeviled steel trade for 20 years, especially global overcapacity,

---

29. However, Helpman and Krugman (1989) have argued that there is a theoretical possibility that nonbinding quotas can lead to price increases in an imperfectly competitive market.

Table 2.9   Percentage of VRA Filled (by product)

Product	1986	1987	1988	1/89–9/89	10/89–12/90[a]	1/91–3/92[b]
Flat-rolled	107	95	81	71	81	68
Plate	105	100	89	72	80	62
Semifinished	95	100	87	77	51	71
Alloy tool steel	105	91	96	95	86	76
Stainless bar and rod	87	89	92	78	83	79
Other stainless and specialty products	82	94	81	94	72	62
Oil country tubular goods	86	86	70	63	92	88
Other pipe and tubes	111	99	86	58	82	62
Wire rod and wire products	95	87	81	73	68	68
Bars	82	79	79	52	55	38
Structurals	92	92	88	55	41	23
Other steel products	72	78	62	56	33	49
Flat-rolled (disaggregated)						
Hot-rolled sheet and strip	104	96	82	72	94	84
Cold-rolled sheet and strip	101	93	77	71	86	78
Blackplate	102	112	93	61	82	58
Electrical sheet and strip	113	96	97	94	93	97
Stainless plate	98	93	86	100	100	97
Stainless sheet and strip	98	94	93	98	90	84
Tin plate	107	96	96	97	96	78
Tin-free steel	104	96	93	98	94	68
Electrogalvanized	102	99	80	37	68	48

Source: U.S. Department of Commerce, Office of Import Compliance.

Note: Product-level data prior to 1986 is no longer available from DOC.

[a]Excludes Australia, Brazil, China, Finland, Mexico, Trinidad, and Venezuela. DOC data is no longer available.

[b]Excludes Trinidad and Tobago. DOC data is no longer available.

tariff and nontariff barriers, and trade-distorting practices such as dumping and subsidies. The entire industry, including the USW, the AISI, and the SMA, strongly supported this effort. Indeed, a multilateral solution to steel problems had long been the principal long-term public policy goal of all members of the domestic steel industry.

The major stumbling blocks of the MSA centered on familiar issues—foreign steel subsidies and U.S. AD and CVD procedures. The U.S. integrated industry's position was known as "MSA plus." The industry wanted an outright ban on *all* subsidies to steel firms, including those for research and development, environmental technologies, and regional development subsidies. The industry also insisted that any agreement not affect U.S. steel firms' or the USW's access to AD and CVD procedures.

As the April 1992 demise of the VRA program approached, the interested actors in the steel industry developed positions about what policy should be adopted afterward. The Bush administration held fast to the position that all quantitative restrictions *permanently* end on April 1. Surprisingly little support emerged in the steel industry for another extension of the VRA program. Only the USW, Bethlehem Steel, and the specialty steel sector publicly supported an extension. The balance of the integrated industry, extremely disappointed with its experience with the VRA after 1988, expressed no public interest whatsoever in an extension.[30] Instead, these steel firms announced repeatedly that they would file another round of AD and CVD petitions, but this time they vowed to pursue them to final decisions. The industry, in other words, threatened that it would try to obtain the definitive AD and CVD duties that would provide significant and lasting protection.

The decision of the industry to forgo any public lobbying for a VRA is probably the best indicator of the diminished clout of the steel industry. As mentioned earlier, a politically strong industry is more likely to pursue an escape clause or a VRA. Both avenues are characterized by considerable presidential discretion so that political muscle can be brought to bear on the final decision. A politically weak industry, on the other hand, is more likely to exploit the "technical" track to protection and will use the AD and CVD processes in which political clout is almost entirely irrelevant.

The steel users also were largely absent from the discussions at this stage. This reflects two factors. The coalition brought together in 1989 to form CASUM was inherently unstable. The interests of the members intersected essentially only on steel import policy. The group had no reason to continue extensive cooperation on other public policy issues once a steel policy was in place in 1989. In addition, a major argument of CASUM was that the steel industry should not lobby for VRAs but instead use the normal trade remedy apparatus. If the industry was intent on filing AD and CVD cases, Caterpillar and other CASUM members could not credibly complain.

In the event, the VRA program expired on April 1, 1992, and the multilateral steel negotiations ended with no agreement. As promised, the Bush administration refused to take special action, and also as promised, the steel industry filed over 80 AD and CVD petitions in the summer of 1992. These petitions, as did many rounds of AP petitions before, involved the United States' major trading partners, including Mexico, Canada, Japan, and the European Community.

The superficial parallels to the situation in 1984 are striking. Once again a free-trade–oriented Republican president faced reelection while a torrent of steel industry AP petitions wound through the bureaucracy. Further complicating the political calculus, Bush faced both a weak economy and a much more formidable opponent in Clinton than Reagan had faced with Mondale in 1984. Many veteran industry observers fully expected that the administration would reach an accommodation with the steel industry before the AP process worked

---

30. The integrated firms' *private* position insistence is somewhat in dispute. A staff member insists that the firms had no interest in an extension. However, an official at the Trade Representative's office insists that the industry was in favor of extension until December 1991 when it became clear that they would not obtain it from the Bush administration.

to a conclusion.[31] The implicit assumption, of course, was that high final AD duties were near certain and that the administration would be unwilling to allow them to be imposed. These expectations for a negotiated outcome grew even stronger as the polls continued to show President Bush lagging behind Governor Clinton. A negotiated outcome was even more likely if the political clout of the industry had remained undiminished, given the tight presidential election.

If the steel industry wanted to use the AP petitions to inject steel policy into the 1992 presidential campaign and pressure President Bush, they failed utterly. President Bush held firm to his pledge not to extend any special deals to the industry despite rising doubts about his chances for reelection. The fact that George Bush never again tried to appeal to the steel sector is emblematic of the industry's decreased political importance in American presidential elections.

With the election of Bill Clinton, a politically powerful integrated steel industry might have used the opportunity to force steel import policy into policy avenues with political discretion and away from the AP process. Instead, the industry pressed the AP petitions.[32] Provisional AD and CVD duties were placed on most of the products covered in the petitions in January 1993 immediately after the Clinton administration took office.

These preliminary duties meant that foreign firms were required to post a bond equal to the estimated margins, so that imported steel prices rose at once. This in turn allowed the integrated firms, by far the most important domestic producers of flat-rolled products, to raise prices significantly on their domestic sales, a goal that had eluded them since slow economic growth began in 1990. The firms were able to credibly raise the prices, even though the duties were only provisional, since market participants fully expected that the duties would become permanent.

The AD process reached its next important juncture in June 1993 when the DOC announced average final duties of 36 percent on flat-rolled products. As expected in AD and CVD cases, individual product and country duties were highly divergent and ranged from under 2 percent to 109 percent. These final estimates pleased steel industry representatives since many were sharply higher than the January 1993 preliminary duties.

The cases then proceeded to the ITC for a final ruling on material injury. The presumption of most observers was that the industry would win at this final stage. However, on July 27, 1993, the ITC ruled affirmatively on 32 cases and negatively on 41 petitions, which translated into about roughly half of the imports in value terms.

---

31. E.g., see the comments of long-time steel editor George McManus in *Iron Age* (May 1992).
32. After the petitions were filed, a number of foreign suppliers expressed serious interest in a negotiated settlement. E.g., firms and governments from Argentina, Australia, Austria, Brazil, Finland, Germany, Mexico, Poland, Sweden, and New Zealand all submitted proposals to the DOC in May 1993 for "suspension agreements" whereby the firms would agree to raise their prices to preempt duties. The DOC did not seriously consider the proposals.

Carbon steel plate received by far the most comprehensive protection—only France, Italy, and Korea escaped with no definitive final duties. Over 71 percent of plate imports were covered by final definitive duties which ranged from 1.4 to 109 percent. Similarly, 83 percent of corrosion-resistant steel imports were faced with affirmative duties. In contrast, all petitions involving hot-rolled products and all but three of the cold-rolled petitions (representing 34 percent of imports) were dismissed.

While the commission recognized that the industry was suffering injury in the period under review, the majority of the ITC's members concluded that dumped and subsidized imports were not important causes of domestic problems in much of the industry. Instead, the majority of the ITC reasoned that price competition among domestic firms was the main source of difficulty and pointed out that imports were sold at prices that were often *higher* than domestic sources (USITC 1993). The ITC's argument closely echoes that of the 1984 serious injury determination. In that earlier decision, the ITC had also ruled that domestic competition was the main cause of injury in the four minimill-dominated sectors. These two ITC decisions, in other words, reflected a growing recognition that a newly fragmented and highly competitive U.S. steel market makes oligopolistic price discipline very difficult to maintain.

The outcomes took most observers almost entirely by surprise and were highly disappointing to the industry. The best indicator of the shock was the fall of major steel firm stock prices. For example, U.S. Steel, Bethlehem, and National Steel stock prices fell 13, 21, and 27 percent, respectively, on July 22.

In sum, the spotty protection (final high duties placed on some countries' products and all provisional duties removed on others) meant that the integrated industry could count on very little significant comprehensive protection from these cases. The duties' lasting effect will depend in large part on whether countries not covered by final duties will step in to replace the displaced imports. If they do so, the domestic price effects of the duties may be minimal.

For the first time in about 25 years, steel had clearly and publicly lost a major trade policy debate. The industry's most important trump card, the threat of final and near-prohibitive duties obtained through the nondiscretionary AD and CVD process, had been played, and little had come of it. The industry was able to raise prices and garner significant short-term increases in profits during the period of provisional duties, but the strategy did not lead to permanent comprehensive protection.[33]

---

33. Some observers have noted that the industry still was a net beneficiary of the trade litigation. In particular, the temporary price increases made possible by the prospect of final duties more than paid for the legal fees associated with the cases, according to Gary Horlick, a noted trade lawyer in Washington (Cato Institute conference on foreign steel, November 1993). This strategy may not work in the future, however. The use of AD and CVD petitions may no longer be such a credible threat in the future, so that domestic buyers may be much more reluctant to accept price increases when only provisional duties are in place.

It is difficult, however, to assess the precise political implications of the results of these cases. As repeatedly emphasized in this paper, the AD and CVD process are largely apolitical. Consequently, the disappointing results of the cases do not directly imply that the industry has less political power than in previous years. Nonetheless, the cases would likely have never reached the final ITC decision stage if the industry were still a dominant political force.

The inability to force a comprehensive political solution to the cases is perhaps even more striking given that a Democrat was once again president. One might have expected that President Clinton would have made every effort to reach out to help the integrated steel industry and, by implication, the USW. Instead, it appears that the Clinton administration, like the Republican administration before it, is not inclined to pursue a policy of import restrictions to help Big Steel.[34]

2.6 Conclusion

The U.S. integrated steel industry has long enjoyed unusual success influencing import policy. Steel producers and the steelworkers' union have managed to gain special trade regimes in 1969, 1977, 1982, 1984, and 1989. The most important sources of this political strength have been the cohesiveness of the coalition in favor of import restraints, the number of potential voters in the steel sector, and the legal and rhetorical advantage gained by massive foreign government intervention.

The cohesiveness of industry players when lobbying for protection and the relative disorganization of domestic interests harmed by steel barriers have been particularly important. The main source of the coalition's cohesiveness has been a small number of major integrated producers that traditionally have dominated the industry. This market structure arose out of the scale economies of traditional steel operations where fixed costs acted as a barrier to entry for new domestic rivals. The large scale of operations also created a highly geographically concentrated production pattern. Consequently, thousands of workers were consolidated in a relatively small number of production sites. This translated into a highly powerful political presence in a limited number of states and congressional districts. This market structure is in sharp contrast to domestic steel users who are widely dispersed geographically and must overcome significant transaction cost to organize an effective counterweight to the integrated sector.

---

34. Another indication of the integrated industry's reduced clout is reported by the *Financial Times*. On October 6, 1993, interested parties were invited to the White House to discuss their positions on a proposed new MSA. Not only did the U.S. trade representative meet first with a group of steel users about the proposal, when steel producers were invited in, the traditional integrated producers were joined by Kenneth Iverson of Nucor, a committed and aggressive free trader. The presence of both steel users and Iverson is a clear indication that the integrated steel producers no longer speak with complete authority on steel issues in U.S. policy-making circles.

The sheer number of steel sector employees also contributed to the political strength of the steel industry. Over half a million Americans were employed in the steel sector in 1974. This voting power was further increased by the geographical concentration in states with large electoral votes (Pennsylvania, Ohio, and Indiana), which gave the steel sector unusual clout in presidential elections.

Finally, extensive foreign government steel sector intervention (in Japan during the 1960s and in Europe and the developing world in the 1970s and 1980s) provided the U.S. industry with major political leverage. Most important, government intervention meant that steel firms could credibly threaten foreign firms with legal action under U.S. trade provisions. The nondiscretionary nature of the U.S. unfair trade process meant that the president would be faced with the prospect of bureaucratically imposed high duties on foreign allies if special deals were not negotiated. The integrated sector also gained major rhetorical advantages from the foreign practices since it diverted attention away from domestic shortcomings, including slowness to adopt modern technologies and high labor costs.

Despite past success and strength, there is evidence that this influence may have finally begun to wane. The unsatisfactory 1989 extension of the VRA program and the inability to obtain significant import restraints in 1993 both point to lessened, though still formidable, clout. The weakened political position of the integrated sector also allowed domestic steel-using industries to play a more prominent role in import policy. Most important, steel users organized an ad hoc coalition during the fight a VRA extension in 1989. The presence of domestic manufacturers (especially exporters) arguing against import barriers acted as an important counterweight to protectionist arguments from the integrated sector. In the event, the VRAs were relaxed and became largely nonbinding for the last two years of the program. While this one-issue user coalition may be inherently unstable over an extended period, it did provide an important impetus for a liberalized steel trade policy.

The reasons for the integrated steel sector's drop in political clout are linked directly to the fundamentally changed market structure of the U.S. steel sector. First, political power has waned simply because of the drop in steel sector employment to only 140,000 in 1992. The much smaller workforce means that fewer politicians have an interest in attracting steelworker votes. Second, the industry is radically different from 20 years ago. Large integrated firms are less and less dominant domestically but at the same time are more competitive internationally. The improvement in competitiveness is largely due to rising labor productivity, increasing use of modern steel production techniques such as continuous casting, and a significantly weakened dollar. This improved economic competitiveness paradoxically has contributed to a weakened political position for the industry since it undercuts the argument that the steel industry is in need of special import policy.

But perhaps the most important change has been the growing importance of minimills in the U.S. economy. Technological advances have lowered the minimum efficient scale of steel-making operations in a number of product categories. This has allowed minimills to push the integrated mills entirely out of certain product lines and threaten them in the remaining high-end steel products. These changes mean that even if the integrated steel firms can successfully litigate unfair trade cases, these large firms will continue to be under intense competitive pressures from domestic minimills.

Steel industry strategies to secure government intervention will change dramatically in the future as the industry continues to restructure. Steel firms, including many minimills, will likely use unfair trade petitions as long as significant government steel sector intervention continues abroad. From the integrated sector's viewpoint, this strategy is less and less attractive. Such import barriers raise profits to all domestic steel firms and simply accelerate the onslaught of the more efficient minimills. In the future, this will be true even in flat-rolled products that have been the last market sector dominated by integrated producers. The integrated mills will consequently have strong incentives to direct their lobbying efforts to improve their position vis-à-vis the minimills rather than try to erect import barriers.

Hints of a possible change in strategy have begun to appear. Certainly the most important recent example is the strong effort to obtain government relief on health and pension costs of early retirees in the steel industry. Early versions of President Clinton's health care reform would lead to an important reduction in these legacy costs. This would be one of the most important ways to immediately help the integrated sector compete with the minimills, whose relatively young workforces present no such massive burden. The integrated firms also obtained an exemption from President Clinton's proposed BTU tax for the use of coke as a feedstock. If Congress had implemented this tax, the integrated industry's exemption would have helped it compete with the minimills.

Direct lobbying struggles with the minimills, however, will be much more problematic than with importers. Most important, since minimills are domestic firms, they will have domestic allies. The integrated sector will therefore face a struggle with other domestic interests rather than lobby for protection from "unfair" foreign competition. Further, the minimills are often portrayed as classic American success stories—small, innovative entrepreneurs fighting the lumbering, bureaucratic steel behemoths. This gives them a rhetorical advantage in lobbying struggles with the traditional steel mills.

As the minimills grow in importance, we will also likely see a growth in their political strength. If the minimills continue their technological advances, we might even see a growing impatience with a lack of export opportunities abroad. In fact, it is conceivable that in the not too distant future, the most politically powerful steel firms in the United States might focus their lobbying, not on barriers on imported steel, but instead on a reduction in protection abroad.

In short, political lobbying and government lobbying in the steel industry will likely continue well into the future. The political muscle of the industry will remain formidable. Nevertheless, steel sector lobbying will likely take on a very different form than in the past. The days of integrated producers and the steelworkers' union consistently forcing special trade deals on reluctant administrations are almost assuredly gone forever.

References

Adams, Walter, and Hans Mueller. 1986. The steel industry. In *The structure of American industry,* 7th ed., ed. Walter Adams. New York: Macmillan.
AISI (American Iron and Steel Institute). 1989. *VRAs and the steel consumer.* Washington, D.C.: American Iron and Steel Institute.
———. Various issues. *Annual statistical report.* Washington, D.C.: American Iron and Steel Institute.
Anderson, Keith B. 1993. Agency discretion or statutory direction: Decision-making at the U.S. International Trade Commission. *Journal of Law and Economics* 36(2): 915–35.
Barnett, Donald F., and Robert W. Crandall. 1986. *Up from the ashes: The rise of the steel minimill in the United States.* Washington, D.C.: Brookings Institution.
———. 1993. Steel: Decline and renewal. In *Industry studies,* ed. Larry L. Deutsch. Englewood Cliffs, N.J.: Prentice-Hall.
Boltuck, Richard, and Robert Litan, eds. 1991. *Down in the dumps: Administration of the unfair trade laws.* Washington, D.C.: Brookings Institution.
Crandall, Robert W. 1981. *The U.S. steel industry in recurrent crises: Policy options in a competitive world.* Washington, D.C.: Brookings Institution.
Devault, James. 1993. Economics and the International Trade Commission. *Southern Economic Journal* 60(2): 463–78.
Economic report of the president. 1993. Washington, D.C.: Government Printing Office.
Finger, J. Michael, Keith Hall, and Douglas Nelson. 1982. The political economy of administered protection. *American Economic Review* 72: 452–66.
Gillingham, John. 1991. *Coal, steel, and the rebirth of Europe, 1945–1955: The Germans and French from Ruhr conflict to economic community.* Cambridge: Cambridge University Press.
Gold, Bela, William Pierce, Gerhard Rosegger, and Mark Perlman. 1984. *Technological progress and industrial leadership: The growth of the U.S. steel industry 1990–1970.* Lexington, Mass.: Heath.
Helpman, Elhanan, and Paul R. Krugman. 1989. *Trade policy and market structure.* Cambridge: MIT Press.
Hogan, William T. 1987. *Minimills and integrated mills: A comparison of steel making in the United States.* Lexington, Mass.: Lexington Books.
Howell, Thomas R., William A. Noellert, and Alan W. Wolfe. 1988. *Steel and the state: Government intervention and steel's structural crisis.* Boulder, Colo.: Westview.
International Iron and Steel Institute. 1991. *Steel statistical yearbook.* Brussels: International Iron and Steel Institute.
Iron Age. 1993. Confronting cultural change. April.
Lenway, Stefanie, and Douglas A. Schuler. 1991. Corporate political involvement in trade protection. In *Empirical studies of commercial policy,* ed. Robert Baldwin. Chicago: University of Chicago Press.

Mayer, Wolfgang. 1984. Endogenous tariff formation. *American Economic Review* 74 (5): 970–85.

Moore, Michael O. 1992. Rules or politics?: An empirical analysis of ITC antidumping decision. *Economic Inquiry* 30 (3): 449–66.

Moore, Michael O., and Steven M. Suranovic. 1992. Lobbying vs. administered protection: Endogenous industry choice and national welfare. *Journal of International Economics* 32: 289–303.

———. 1993. A welfare comparison between VERs and tariffs under the GATT. *Canadian Journal of Economics* 26(2): 447–56.

Mussa, Michael. 1974. Tariffs and the distribution of income: The importance of factor specificity, substitutability and intensity in the short and long run. *Journal of Political Economy* 82: 1191–1203.

Niskanen, William A. 1988. *Reaganomics: An insider's account of the policies and the people.* New York: Oxford University Press.

Olson, Mancur. 1971. *The logic of collective action.* Cambridge: Harvard University Press.

Rodrik, Dani. 1986. Tariffs, subsidies and welfare with endogenous policy. *Journal of International Economics* 21 (3): 285–99.

Tsoukalis, Loukas, and Robert Strauss. 1985. Crisis and adjustment in European steel: Beyond laisser faire. *Journal of Common Market Studies* 23 (3): 207–28.

U.S. Congress. Congressional Budget Office. 1987. *How federal policies affect the steel industry.* Washington, D.C.: Government Printing Office.

U.S. Congress. House. Ways and Means Committee. 1984. *Problems of the U.S. steel industry.* Serial 98–93. Washington, D.C.: Government Printing Office.

———. 1989. *Steel Import Stabilization Extension Act.* Serial 101–30. Washington, D.C.: Government Printing Office.

USITC (U.S. International Trade Commission). 1982. Certain steel products from Belgium, Brazil, France, Italy, Luxembourg, the Netherlands, Romania, the United Kingdom, and West Germany. USITC Publication no. 1211. Washington, D.C.: U.S. International Trade Commission.

———. 1984. Carbon and certain alloy steel products. USITC Publication no. 1553. Washington, D.C.: U.S. International Trade Commission.

———. 1989a. Annual survey concerning competitive conditions in the steel industry and industry efforts to adjust and modernize. USITC Publication no. 2226. Washington, D.C.: U.S. International Trade Commission.

———. 1989b. The effects of the steel voluntary restraint agreements on U.S. steel-consuming industries. USITC Publication no. 2182. Washington, D.C.: U.S. International Trade Commission.

———. 1993. Certain flat-rolled carbon steel products from Argentina, Australia, Austria, Belgium, Brazil, Canada, Finland, France, Germany, Italy, Japan, Korea, Mexico, the Netherlands, New Zealand, Poland, Romania, Spain, Sweden, and the United Kingdom. USITC Publication no. 2664. Washington, D.C.: U.S. International Trade Commission.

———. Various issues. Monthly Report on the Status of Steel Industry. Washington, D.C.: U.S. International Trade Commission.

Walters, Robert. 1988. *U.S. negotiations of voluntary restraint agreements in steel, 1984: Domestic sources of international economic diplomacy.* Washington, D.C.: Pew Charitable Trusts.

Williams, Harold, ed. 1978. *Free trade, fair trade, and protection: The case of steel.* Kent, Ohio: Kent State University Press.

Williams, Lynn. 1988. Basic steel industry conference—1988 Policy statement. Washington, D.C.: United Steelworkers of America. Mimeograph.

World Steel Dynamics. 1990. Core report NN. New York: Paine-Webber.
————. 1992. Battle of the minis, part II. New York: Paine-Webber.
————. 1994. Core report VV. New York: Paine-Webber.

Comment   William C. Lane

By selecting the subject of steel protection in the 1980s, Michael Moore has chosen one of the most interesting examples of the political economy. While it is unlikely this subject will ever find its way into a made-for-TV movie, the plot does have a certain Shakespearean appeal.

Imagine: The curtain opens with the king (U.S. steel industry) at the height of his power. He has just won a long sought after prize (comprehensive import protection). But as events would have it, the prize is a mixed blessing. The king discovers that his chief competitors (minimills and foreign steel companies) are also benefiting from his prize. Even more disturbing is the realization that possession of the prize is fostering great unrest among his countrymen (customers). In fact, his countrymen are so upset that they form an army (Coalition of American Steel-Using Manufacturers) and challenge the king's authority. After a heated battle, the curtain falls, with the king's power diminished, the prize lost, and the king's competitors stronger than ever.

Whether this drama qualifies as comedy or tragedy is uncertain, but it does serve to illustrate what happened to the U.S. steel industry during the 1980s. In 1984, the political influence of the U.S. steel industry was at a new high. By convincing the U.S. government to impose steel quotas on imports from 19 countries and the European Community, Big Steel had won the type of comprehensive import protection that it had long sought. All that remained was to extend the quota coverage to include the few missing countries (Canada and Sweden) and take steps to ensure the quota program does not expire.

The duration of the new trade regime was initially set at five years. But most trade practitioners believed convincing Congress to extend the program for another five years would be relatively easy. After all, the steel industry's political clout was well established. Besides, the protectionist tool being sought— voluntary restraint agreements (VRAs)—was an unfamiliar concept which largely escaped public scrutiny. Finally, foreign countries had a big incentive to support the new VRA program because VRAs not only exempted participating countries from U.S. trade laws but rewarded them with a share of the "quota rent."

William C. Lane is international governmental affairs manager for Caterpillar, Inc. During 1988–89, he played a prominent role in organizing and directing the 320-member steel consumer group Coalition of American Steel-Using Manufacturers (CASUM).

In spite of these factors favoring renewal, the 1988–89 VRA debate had a most unexpected outcome. After a bruising political fight with a newly formed coalition of U.S. steel consumers, the steel industry was only able to win an abbreviated VRA extension that was, in many ways, little more than a placebo.

How did the politics of protectionism change so quickly? Did market forces overwhelm the steel industry's hold on Washington? Or was it the growth of new, more-efficient minimills that upset the political balance? What about steel users? After being on the political sideline for 30 years, why did they suddenly feel compelled to aggressively challenge the steel industry's call for more protection?

Moore's paper does an excellent job of answering these questions by examining the economic and political dynamics that eventually invalidated the steel industry's claim for industry-specific protection. He provides a thorough history of U.S. steel programs since the 1960s. His analyses of trade flows, production output, and capacity levels allow for a complete understanding of the effectiveness of the various protectionist schemes employed since 1969. He also avoids the common pitfall of viewing the steel industry from only the integrated mills' point of view; the rise of minimills and resurrection of reconstituted mills are important elements of his paper.

What sets Moore's paper apart from other studies of the steel industry, however, is his in-depth understanding of the events that changed the "politics of protectionism." Quota-induced shortages in 1987 and 1988 forced steel users from the political sidelines. Once that happened, the political battlefield that the steel industry had learned to master changed dramatically. No longer could Congress view protection for the steel industry as a domestic versus foreign issue. With steel users engaged in the debate, Congress was in the uncomfortable position of having to favor one U.S. industry over another. In many ways, the 1988–89 VRA debate was more a fight about U.S. competitiveness than about the evils of protectionism.

The compromise that emerged in 1989 reflected this new political reality. New steel quotas were extended for two and a half years not five. The new VRA program provided a user-friendly short-supply mechanism. Most important, the new quotas were so large that they had little or no impact on international commerce.

The price the steel industry paid for this illusion of protection was significant. In exchange for new VRAs, the steel industry had to agree to exempt foreign steel producers from U.S. trade laws. In other words, the industry had to give up all of its leverage to discipline foreign subsidies and unfair pricing.

Subsequent actions by the steel industry further confirmed the extent to which the steel industry lost its bid for special protection. When VRAs finally expired in March 1992, Big Steel abandoned all efforts to win industry-specific protection from Congress. Instead, the steel industry made good on its long-standing threat to file scores of AD and CVD trade cases.

Surprisingly, few in government or industry objected to this new development. After all, Big Steel was availing itself of the same trade rules that apply to any other industry. The U.S. response was merely to evaluate the cases and render the appropriate decisions. Rather than creating havoc on the international trading system as some steel industry executives predicted, the cases were handled in stride. Of the 84 trade cases filed, the steel industry won 32. This outcome served to confirm the view that normal trade remedies did in fact work for the steel industry. Since then there has been no serious suggestion that the U.S. steel industry needs or deserves industry-specific protection.

While the paper was comprehensive, a few issues deserve more attention from Moore.

1. Why didn't consumers of other protected industries (i.e., textiles, autos, and sugar) challenge protection as aggressively as steel users did in 1988–89? What was unique about steel during this period?

2. Why did the steel industry accept such a lopsided compromise in 1989? Wouldn't the threat of a massive filing of trade cases dampen imports far more than a 30-month extension of nonbinding quotas?

3. Did the 1988–89 steel debate discredit VRAs as a trade policy tool? Prior to 1989, VRAs were ballyhooed as a managed trade tool that really worked. After the VRA debate, this "gray area" trade remedy was rarely proposed. In 1993 the General Agreement on Tariffs and Trade even disallowed VRAs from being used as a part of a safeguard action.

While Moore's paper will not become a Shakespearean classic, it is an important contribution to the study of the political economy and how it affects trade policy. It should be required reading for any serious student of business and government.

Comment   James R. Markusen

The steel industry is certainly an excellent choice for a case study of the political economy of trade policy. It is an industry that has had significant difficulties in many countries over the last several decades, been a focus of an industrial strategy in others, and been a source of considerable political debate in many more countries than just the United States. Next to agriculture, steel was perhaps the most distressed, regulated, and/or subsidized industry in many countries during the decades of the 1960s through the 1980s. Indeed, in many respects an international focus for the paper might have been preferable. I believe that the exclusive U.S.-centric focus of the paper leads to shortcomings, as I

James R. Markusen is professor of economics and chairman of the Department of Economics at the University of Colorado, Boulder, and a research associate of the National Bureau of Economic Research.

will suggest. While there are many fine aspects to this paper, my comments will focus on what I regard as the two difficulties.

Moore gives us a rather stark view of the U.S. steel industry in the three decades of the 1960s through 1980s. He characterizes the industry as using outdated technology and management techniques and awarding overly generous labor contracts. Minor reference is made to the nature of world steel markets, foreign subsidies, foreign development strategies, and a badly overvalued U.S. dollar in the early 1980s. The U.S. steel industry is portrayed as a rent seeker, resistant to structural change and modernization.

It may well be true that the U.S. industry suffered from self-inflicted ills. It may also be true that it engaged in aggressive rent-seeking behavior and resisted structural change. I have few problems with these notions. However, economic theory does lead us to expect efficient firms, and so it would be good to have a convincing explanation, not just an assertion of industry inefficiency. But this is likely beyond the scope of the paper.

Based on my limited knowledge of the industry, I am concerned with the author's neglect of the role of the worldwide steel industry's problems and foreign government steel programs. I believe that the paper presents a distorted view of the situation and possibly arrives at incorrect conclusions.

I am sorry that I have not had time to go back and review the history of the industry, but my general recollections of the 1960s through 1980s are as follows. First, the world steel industry was characterized by tremendous excess capacity. Indeed, there were significant additions to capacity in some countries as governments, as in Brazil, targeted the steel industry as part of a development strategy. Many countries (particularly European) were heavily subsidizing production and capital expenditures for modernization and expansion. Government ownership allowed huge losses to be passed on to taxpayers (e.g., British Steel). In these respects, the steel industry is quite different from some of the other industries analyzed at this conference, such as automobiles.

In general, it seems that during the 1960s through 1980s, there was in fact very substantial subsidization occurring outside the United States and, I am sure, substantial dumping into the U.S. market by foreign firms desperate for any sales at or above marginal cost. Subsidized sales and dumping really were occurring and were not simply figments of the U.S. industry's public relations campaign.

We could take the view of many economists that we should welcome foreign subsidies, thank them for selling to us below costs, and not worry about the domestic industry and its workers. Or we could take the present author's approach, *implicitly* dismiss the relevance of foreign subsidies, and conclude only on the basis of the poor performance of the domestic industry that protection is unjustified.

But I think that those economists' arguments are really beside the point. If foreign governments are subsidizing and if foreign firms are dumping, then it is perfectly appropriate for U.S. firms to seek relief under trade remedy laws.

This is proper and legal under U.S. laws and General Agreement on Tariffs and Trade (GATT) rules. If economists do not like antidumping (AD) and countervailing duty (CVD) laws, perhaps our criticism should be directed at them and not always at the firms which avail themselves of these legal options.

The author sees a moribund industry facing "efficient foreign producers," obtaining relief through political manipulation. There is considerable innuendo to the effect that such relief is undeserved. Yet the author himself seems uncertain about this at several points. He states on several occasions that the International Trade Commission (ITC) processes on AD and CVD are relatively apolitical. During the period, the ITC found in favor of the industry on a great many occasions. It appears that the ITC found something that is being missed here. Clearly, not all of the foreign producers were efficient.

The author states that "the steel industry, in other words, has obtained special trade policy treatment unavailable to nearly all other domestic industries." First of all, that is almost certainly not true (depending on the meaning of "nearly all other")—agriculture, textiles, clothing, shoes, autos, shipping, and even petroleum in the 1950s and 1960s come to mind. Second, the author needs to deal seriously with the possibility that there was something going on in the world that justified relief under U.S. and GATT law, if not under economic theory.

This brings me to my second main point. Since relief for the industry was unjustified on any legal or economic grounds in the author's mind, he attempts to explain the industry success in seeking relief up to 1989 in terms of a traditional lobbying model. In part, high concentration and unionization are characteristics that win protection in such a worldview.

This model has great appeal to economists. My problem here is that it almost always performs poorly in empirical tests. Measures of lobbying power such as concentration and unionization are not good explainers of protection in the United States. Industries that are in trouble are the ones that tend to receive protection. Let me refer to some results from the work of Daniel Trefler, including a recent paper (Trefler 1993).

Trefler finds that special interest models of trade policy perform only moderately well in empirical tests. By several criteria, concentration and number of firm variables are not economically important. In fact, he finds that none of the lobbying cost variables are important.

Trefler notes in his work that special interest lobbying models cannot explain the high levels of protection in industries such as textiles, clothing, lumber, and leather. These industries are neither highly concentrated nor unionized, employ less-skilled labor, face high rates of unemployment, and operate under decreasing returns. Trefler sees the explanation more in terms of a public interest group approach, or what I would term a "conservative social welfare function," to use Max Corden's term. The public opposes protection unless it helps workers in distressed industries and redistributes income to the lower-paid, less-skilled workers. Unemployed, low-paid workers are recipients of protection.

Trefler arrives at several conclusions which are consistent with results that I have seen elsewhere: (1) Concentration and other lobbying variables are economically unimportant; scale is important but negatively related to protection. (2) Unionization is negatively related to protection, although the sign switches to positive if textiles are omitted. (3) High protection is found in industries with significant import penetration, semiskilled workers, and high unemployment rates.

I would like to offer an alternative explanation, consistent with the same facts Moore presents for the steel industry. First, the steel industry, although inefficient with overpaid workers, was subject to competition from heavily subsidized foreign firms. Significant dumping was occurring by firms with huge losses and excess capacity. For part of the period (particularly the early 1980s), the U.S. dollar was badly overvalued.

Second, subsidies and dumping were deemed to exist and to be causing injury by the ITC (though not the only cause of the industry's troubles) and relief was granted on many AD and CVD cases.

Third, comprehensive quotas were introduced, not because of the great political clout of the industry, but because they were much preferred to the tangled web of duties that would otherwise be legitimately won through AD and CVD cases.

Fourth, protection was withdrawn in the 1990s, not because the industry lost the clout (that it may never have had), but simply because protection was no longer justified. This change was partly due to the rationalization of the U.S. industry, partly due to reduced capacity and subsidization in Europe and elsewhere, and partly to the stronger depreciation of the U.S. real exchange rate after 1985. The withdrawal of protection, like its institution, is consistent with a public interest or conservative social welfare function theory of trade policy.

Reference

Trefler, Daniel. 1993. Trade liberalization and the theory of endogenous protection: An econometric study of U.S. import policy. *Journal of Political Economy* 101:138–60.

Comment   Michael H. Moskow

Moore's main argument is that the change in the domestic structure of the U.S. steel industry has led to significantly reduced political influence by large integrated producers. Industry fragmentation has developed because of the growth

Michael H. Moskow is president of the Federal Reserve Bank of Chicago. Prior to this he was professor of strategy and international management at the J. L. Kellogg Graduate School of Management at Northwestern University. He is a member of the board of directors of the National Bureau of Economic Research. During the Bush administration he was deputy U.S. trade representative.

of minimills, reconstituted mills, and foreign ownership or joint venturing with U.S. firms. Whereas, historically, a small number of large integrated producers executed considerable influence on U.S. policymakers, Moore believes that the above structural changes and resulting fragmentation have caused a major reduction in the integrated producers' political power.

Although Moore provides considerable support for his main thesis, he does not address the underlying reason that U.S. integrated steel producers have sought protection from the federal government. Is it primarily because there is worldwide excess capacity in steel caused by extensive government subsidies in other countries or is it because of inefficiencies particular to the U.S. producer? Since U.S. government policy has been based on the assumption that foreign government subsidies and excess capacity is the problem, Moore could provide an extremely useful service by analyzing this issue and providing his views. My personal view is that subsidies are the underlying problem, but I would welcome a thorough analysis of this issue. While serving as deputy U.S. trade representative in the Bush administration, one of my major responsibilities was to negotiate a multilateral steel agreement (MSA) covering over 30 countries. The main purpose of the agreement from the U.S. standpoint was to eliminate or significantly reduce foreign government subsidies (mostly from European countries) to their steel producers. In return, duties on steel would be reduced to zero, thus increasing access of foreign producers to the U.S. market. New dispute resolution procedures were drafted that would have resolved rapidly any claimed violations of the MSA through a process culminating in binding arbitration.

We made it clear to our trading partners that President Bush would not extend the voluntary restraint agreement (VRA) on steel that was scheduled to expire on March 31, 1992. The parties made strenuous but unsuccessful efforts to reach agreement on the MSA before the March 31 deadline.

Some uncertainty persisted among other countries and within the steel industry as to whether President Bush would let the VRAs expire if negotiations on the MSA were unsuccessful. The speculation was fueled by Bush's decision to extend for two years on a phase-out basis the VRA for the machine tool industry that expired on December 31, 1991. Nevertheless, no discussion of extending the steel VRA ever took place within the Bush administration, and only the stainless steel producers attempted to convince the administration and Congress to extend their VRA.

The two key unsolved issues in the MSA negotiations were the level of permitted subsidies and the process for "consultations" on antidumping cases. We had narrowed the areas for permitted subsidies significantly but were never able to bridge the gap. The antidumping consultation issue was particularly difficult because, in my view, it masked an underlying philosophical difference between the United States and other countries. The MSA did not change the U.S. antidumping laws, but other countries seem to believe that consultations on individual cases could somehow significantly reduce the number of steel cases filed or flowing through the full process for handling cases. There were no objections to the U.S. trade representative's hearing other countries' views on individual cases, but this could not in any way interfere with the legislated process that the Department of Commerce and International Trade Commission (ITC) followed in deciding these cases. If this was the extent of "consultations," then what benefit would this be to other countries?

Another important issue in negotiations was the phase-out of existing subsidies, particularly in reference to what were called "countries in transition." While we wanted to encourage Eastern European countries to continue shifting from socialistic to market economies, we had to find ways to temporarily ease the impact of removing their steel subsidies. Another example was Brazil, which was attempting to privatize its steel industry but needed a transition period of continued protection to avoid massive dislocations. VRAs or some form of temporary quota for these countries in transition was part of the negotiations.

Following the break-off of negotiations in March 1992, the U.S. integrated steel producers filed 84 countervailing duty and antidumping cases that were subsequently largely decided against the steel producers by the ITC. The producers are currently appealing the ITC decisions. Strong attempts were again made to agree on an MSA in late 1993 as part of the Uruguay Round GATT negotiations. The round includes the elimination of steel tariffs, which was part of the MSA, but negotiations on the key provisions of the MSA reducing subsidies in the steel industry were again unsuccessful.

3 The Political Economy of U.S. Automobile Protection

Douglas R. Nelson

Americans tend to view the automobile as *the* archetypal American product. Not only does auto production loom large economically, but the automobile itself bears a unique social relationship to the national self-image.[1] Thus it is not surprising that, as the auto industry has followed the textile and steel industries into a trade-related adjustment crisis, the domestic and international political economy of that crisis has taken on extraordinary significance.[2] While there are some signs that the U.S. auto industry has recently improved its competitive position, at the time this project was begun the industry had just withdrawn from a very publicly "leaked" intention to file a major antidumping suit against all imports of automobiles from Japan. This suggests that an evaluation of the current state of the auto industry and its relationship to the industrial/trade policy process in the United States is a matter of considerable importance. Such an evaluation is pursued here.

The main argument of this paper is that competition by Japanese auto producers in the U.S. market constituted a fundamental threat to the regime regu-

Douglas R. Nelson is associate professor of economics at Tulane University.

A large number of people have generously helped in the preparation of this paper. Michael Hagy and Keith Hall at the U.S. International Trade Commission were very helpful in providing data on the auto industry. Dave Richardson provided not only data but also much good advice. Anne Brunsdale, Richard Cooper, Anne Krueger, and conference participants made many useful comments. Mursaleena Islam provided excellent research assistance. Any failures of fact, judgment, and good taste, sadly, remain the author's.

1. The industry is a major consumer of steel, plastics, rubber, and machine tools, and it accounts (directly and indirectly) for something on the order of one in six people employed in the economy. A convenient short discussion of the economics of the auto industry is given by Adams and Brock (1986). For interesting discussions of the more general social role of the automobile and its production see Rothschild (1973) and Flink (1988).

2. Note that this sentence does not imply a causal relationship between the textile and steel crises, only a family resemblance. In fact, however, the politics and economics of the steel and auto industries are closely related. As will be suggested below, one of the goals of this project is to consider this relationship in more detail than it has heretofore received.

lating relations among the major auto producers (GM, Ford, and Chrysler) and between those producers and the United Auto Workers (UAW).[3] Where the U.S. government played only a modest role in the historical development of this regime over most of the auto industry's history, the existence of a foreign threat ultimately required government participation in its reconstitution. By emphasizing the threat of Japanese competition to the sectoral regime, the political economic perspective of this paper helps explain the centrality of trade policy to the auto industry's political agenda during the late 1970s and 1980s when there is considerable evidence that a number of other factors were considerably more important in accounting for the industry's economic problems.

The first step in the analysis is an examination of the political process through which the U.S. auto industry pursued and ultimately received protection from Japanese competition. This is presented in section 3.1. In the next two sections we evaluate the economic basis of the industry's aggressive pursuit of protection, examining research on the competitiveness of the industry (section 3.2) and on the effects of protection on industry performance (section 3.3). On the basis of the research reviewed in sections 3.2 and 3.3 it is not at all obvious that trade protection was the most effective policy response to the industry's economic problems. The remainder of the paper argues that the industry's political strategy reflects a response to a crisis in the political economic regime regulating relations among the major interests in the U.S. auto industry. To make this argument, section 3.4 develops the notion of a sectoral regime and applies it to the auto industry. Section 3.5 develops the argument further, suggesting that conditions in the industry constituted a regime crisis and reexamines the industry's pursuit of aggressive trade policy toward Japanese producers in this context. Section 3.6 illustrates the usefulness of this perspective by examining the politics of North American integration from the perspective of the auto industry. Section 3.7 concludes.

3.1   The Politics of Protection in the Auto Industry

Prior to the mid-1970s, trade policy had not been a priority on the auto industry's political agenda. During the mid- and late 1960s the U.S. auto industry actively pursued access to the Japanese market, seeking both lower tariffs and liberalization of the Japanese investment regime. While these auto industry issues added somewhat to relations already strained over textile quotas, steel exports, and Okinawa, they were not significant political priorities to either the U.S. government or the auto industry. The industry was far more concerned

---

3. The concept of a regime, which is discussed in detail in section 3.4, refers to the institutions, rules, and norms that regulate relations among the members of the regime. We are interested here in the sectoral regime regulating relations among producers of automobiles—especially the firms, labor, and the U.S. government. In addition, as we will see in our discussion of the politics of the integration of the U.S.-Canadian auto market, independent producers of intermediate goods for the auto industry have occasionally been significant participants in the politics of auto trade policy.

with achieving relief from environmental and safety regulations. Beginning in the mid-1970s, however, trade policy activism became a much more prominent part of the industry's political agenda. In this section, we focus on the development of the main plank in that agenda, the attempt to regulate Japanese competition in the U.S. market through both short-term protection (via the escape clause/voluntary export restraint [VER] mechanism) and through legislation on rules of domestic access that bring Japanese producers more explicitly into the regime (domestic content).

The UAW was the first major player to actively pursue protection. Although the UAW continued to support the liberalization program through the 1970s, the sharp increases in auto imports in 1974 led the union to publicly suggest the introduction of quotas. By mid-1975 the UAW was supporting a congressional request (to the Treasury Department at this time) for a dumping investigation of auto exports from seven countries.[4] There was a strong negative reaction by European trading partners, who suggested that such an action could threaten the Tokyo Round negotiations, which was a foreign policy priority of the Nixon administration (though by 1975 the administration was presided over by Gerald Ford). In addition, the Council on Wage and Price Stability stated that not only was there no evidence of dumping but imports provided a moderating influence on U.S. prices and the International Trade Commission (ITC) investigation should be ended. In 1976, the Treasury Department decision (supported by the UAW) was that even though dumping existed in some cases, it would halt its investigation and seek a negotiated solution with the foreign companies. In addition, the Labor Department ruled that workers in auto plants were eligible for adjustment assistance, even though the import share of apparent consumption had fallen and shipments by U.S. producers had rebounded strongly in 1976 (38 percent increase in value of shipments from 1975 to 1976).

Despite industry statements in early 1977 that the increased competitiveness of U.S. product offerings would hold imports to no more than 15 percent of the U.S. market, by April the import share stood at 20 percent with Japanese imports sharply up. By the end of the year the UAW was once again calling for import restrictions unless the Japanese invested in U.S. production. This demand continued to figure prominently in the public statements of the industry (and especially labor) in 1978 and was made an explicit part of government

---

4. This may well have been part of a UAW strategy to encourage Japanese investment in the United States. At least from the mid-1970s, the UAW had suggested to Japanese auto producers that investment in the United States was in Japanese producers' best interest. In 1975 Leonard Woodcock publicly argued for such investment, and in 1977 UAW vice president Pat Greathouse made a widely reported visit to Japan to lobby as well (Halberstam 1986). While neither of these interventions was successful, U.S. investment by Japanese firms continued to be a major part of UAW political strategy. The claim that such investment was necessary to avert growing protectionist sentiment in the United States always figured prominently in the UAW's public statements. The call for quotas coming from a union with a strong free trade tradition is, thus, probably best seen as part of a strategy of encouraging local investment in the United States.

policy when the U.S. trade representative (USTR) pressured Toyota and Datsun to manufacture autos in the United States. The situation deteriorated further in 1979 with further devaluation of the dollar, higher oil prices, and worldwide inflation. The U.S. majors announced plans to invest billions of dollars in overseas production facilities (e.g., $10–$13 billion by GM). By the end of the year, imports had a 22 percent market share, industry production had fallen to a million units below pre–oil shock levels, and more than 200,000 people in the industry were unemployed. Also by the end of the year, the industry became increasingly vocal in demanding some form of trade-related relief.

Perhaps the most prominent auto-related event in 1979 was the near bankruptcy of the weakest of the Big Three, Chrysler, and the negotiation of a $1.5 billion loan guarantee from the government as part of a package to assist in the restructuring of the firm.[5] Chrysler had pursued an aggressive international expansion during the 1960s, running into deep financial trouble as early as 1970 when it lost $27 million in the first quarter. When the first oil price shock hit, Chrysler began selling off its recently acquired international assets and closing some domestic factories. In 1978 Chrysler lost nearly $205 million and owed more than $1 billion. When the first half of 1979 proved even worse than 1978, Chrysler's creditors became increasingly unwilling to extend further loans. The Carter administration did not strongly support the idea of organizing a financial rescue. The Treasury Department in particular was concerned about the precedent that would be set by such an action. On the other hand, the UAW, the Michigan congressional delegation, and Detroit Mayor Coleman Young were actively mobilizing popular and congressional support for a bailout. Reich (1985) reports only weak opposition, primarily from the unusual coalition of the National Association of Manufacturers, Ralph Nader's Congress Watch, and the National Taxpayers Union. Recognizing that 1980 was an election year, the administration agreed to extend large loan guarantees as part of a major reorganization. The plan involved substantial concessions from the UAW and the firm's creditors and the replacement of John Riccardo by Lee Iacocca. Even with the new money, Chrysler continued to have problems with demand for its new K-cars and ended the year with losses in excess of $1 billion with problems continuing into 1980. The need for further financial assistance led to more concessions by labor and lenders in 1981, and by 1982 Chrysler's sales and profitability were improving. However, in 1979 and 1980 the sight of one of the Big Three negotiating with the government for assistance to avoid bankruptcy was a graphic illustration of the plight of the industry.

By early 1980 many members of Congress had recognized that auto industry distress had widespread appeal as a political issue. That a core industrial sector

---

5. See Reich (1985) and Reich and Donahue (1985) for an interesting account of the Chrysler loan in the context of a more general discussion of industrial policy in the United States. The details of this paragraph are drawn from Reich (1985, 318–25).

long dominated by U.S. firms was "threatened" by Japanese competition crystalized public concern with the nation's economic performance and the role of "unfair" foreign competition in that performance. These public concerns made the auto issue a focus of a much wider range of political activity than even an industry as economically significant as the auto industry would normally expect to generate. Furthermore, trade policy had become less "controllable" in Congress. Specifically, as a result of congressional reforms primarily induced by Watergate, the influence of the House Committee on Ways and Means was substantially reduced.[6] Unfortunately, from the perspective of trade policy, this structure had been an essential institutional support of the liberal orientation of U.S. trade policy in the postwar era. Trade policy, because of the connection to tariff policy (a revenue measure), had historically been controlled by Ways and Means, and Ways and Means, at least under Democrats, had been controlled by supporters of the trade liberalization program.[7] The post-Watergate reforms reduced congressional control of trade policy and reduced the influence of Liberals on trade policy at precisely the moment when deteriorating economic conditions and increased international competition implied greater trade policy demands from well-organized industrial and labor groups.[8] As we will see, committed executive leadership by the Carter administration resisted protectionist demands, as well as successfully completing the Tokyo Round. However, uninterest in trade policy during the Reagan and, to a lesser extent, the Bush administration resulted in greater congressional control, greater protection and protectionism, and minimal advance in trade liberalization. Thus the threat of direct legislation became more potent with the collapse of the committee system in the early 1970s.

In March 1980 the Trade Subcommittee of the House Committee on Ways and Means began hearings on the auto industry in which representatives of the UAW and Ford strongly argued for import restriction. On the other hand, the Carter administration, represented by USTR Reuben Askew, testified that such

---

6. One of the consequences of the Watergate scandal was the election of a freshman class of strongly reform-oriented representatives, and one of their primary targets was the committee system and the central role of the House Committee on Ways and Means in that system. Under Democratic control of the House, Ways and Means exercised control over committee appointments because the Democratic membership of Ways and Means was constituted as the Democrat Committee on Committees. Given the importance of committee assignments to reelection prospects, this gave Ways and Means a powerful tool for ensuring passage of key legislation. This kind of control, and the virtually authoritarian control by the chair of the committee (Wilbur Mills), made Mills, Ways and Means, and the committee system a natural target for a freshman class committed to improving democratic responsiveness. It is probably not irrelevant that a group of freshman found the central role of seniority to be a problematic element of the system. The reformers, with the unintentional help of Wilbur Mills, succeeded in reducing the power of Ways and Means, and of the chair within Ways and Means.

7. During most of the postwar period there were two litmus tests for Democratic membership on Ways and Means—support of the trade agreements program and support of the oil depletion allowance.

8. Throughout this paper I capitalize "Liberal" to refer to liberalism in the traditional sense of support for minimal regulation of economic activity.

restrictions would undermine the effect of the market forcing U.S. firms to become more competitive, would undermine access to fuel-efficient automobiles when energy conservation was a key administration goal, and would, through increased prices, undermine the administration's goal of reducing inflation. Hearings on the state of the auto industry were also initiated by several other committees in the House and the Senate. Under increasing pressure from the auto industry and Congress, the Carter administration introduced a package of measures intended to provide economic support to the industry short of trade protection. These measures, involving both regulatory relief (especially from emission standards) and the provision of loan guarantees to auto dealers, were clearly intended to preempt protectionist pressure.

However, Ford and the UAW remained convinced that trade action was necessary, and in June and August 1980 they filed escape clause cases with the ITC. Chrysler was not a major participant in this action because it had already received assistance in the form of the loan guarantee and it did not want to oppose the administration on this issue. GM was unwilling to support the petition at least in part because part of its strategy for responding to competition in small cars was to import small cars under its nameplate from Japan. Following standard procedure, the ITC initiated both internal studies and public hearings to determine whether imports of cars and light trucks were a "substantial cause" (understood to mean that no other cause was more important) of the problems experienced by the industry. To rather general surprise, the ITC (on a 3–2 vote) announced in November 1980 their determination that imports were not a substantial cause of the industry's problems. Specifically, the commission determined that general macroeconomic recession was a more important cause, and that the demand shift toward smaller, more fuel-efficient cars was at least as important as increased import competition. As a result of these findings, the ITC recommended that the executive take no action against Japanese auto imports.

One of the most interesting parts of this story begins with the election of Ronald Reagan to the presidency. The new president was the closest thing to a doctrinaire Liberal the United States has seen in the postwar era. Adding to the strength of the victory, the Senate also passed into Republican hands and, while Democratic control of the House continued, the size of the Reagan victory led to a particularly prolonged and broad honeymoon. Furthermore, the Reagan government explicitly interpreted its victory as a mandate for a Liberal economic program of deregulation and reduction of government participation in the economy. Nonetheless, four months after entering the White House the Reagan administration announced a three-year VER program for autos. Part of the explanation for this surprising outcome derives from structural conditions that would have affected, say, a second-term Carter administration, but part of the explanation is administration and president specific.

The structural conditions that would have affected any administration can be sorted into two broad categories: public sentiment and institutional bias.

With respect to the former, it is clear that the public responds strongly to the perception of substantial economic distress experienced by a significant group of people. Furthermore, there is considerable research suggesting that people vote on the basis of such perception.[9] When it is also perceived that the source of the distress is "unfair" trading practices by a foreign firm, the pressure for political action can become virtually irresistable. In the case of the auto industry, the existence of distress was unquestionable: low or negative profits (fig. 3.1), large drops in share of world output (fig. 3.2), substantial surplus capacity (fig. 3.3), rapidly dropping employment (fig. 3.4) and output (fig. 3.5), and increasing inventories. All tell a story of an industry in distress. These statistics were widely reported in the press and usually accompanied by human interest stories of the implications for autoworkers, their families, and their communities. The simultaneous large jumps in the market share of Japanese producers (fig. 3.6) led many people to conclude that there was a causal connection between the imports and the distress. When we add the widely held notion that the Japanese government and industry cooperate to increase exports ("Japan, Inc."), it is easy to see how increased Japanese market share could be seen as unfairly gained. The ITC's determination that trade, whether fair or unfair, was not a substantial cause of distress was irrelevant to large numbers of U.S. citizens whether employed in the auto sector or not.

In the context of widely perceived trade-related distress, the pressure for direct action on the "political track" began.[10] For a political entrepreneur with presidential ambitions, trade (and auto trade in particular) appeared to be a viable, national issue for the first time in nearly 50 years. In February 1981, the new chairman of the Senate Finance Committee's Subcommittee on Foreign Trade, John Danforth, and the ranking minority member, Lloyd Bentsen, introduced legislation to impose a three-year quantitative restriction on automobiles that would roll back the level of Japanese imports to the 1978–79 average. By May, the bill had attracted 21 cosponsors. Nelson (1989b) documents in detail, for the case of the 1981 auto VER, the existence of systematic bias in favor of protection seekers from the way that the law of administered protection structures the politics of protection. In particular, that paper isolates three main sources of protectionist bias: definition of the issue, determination of standing, and order of participation. The most significant of these is the definition of the issue: the politics are defined in terms of trade, and unfair

---

9. Considerable theoretical research suggests that neither voting nor other forms of political action are generally supported by individual pursuit of strictly self-regarding, materialist interests. Similarly, there is a substantial body of empirical research, based on both survey research and econometric evaluation of outcomes, that strongly supports the notion that elections are determined by "sociotropic voting," i.e., voting based on evaluations of performance that extend well beyond material self-interest (Kinder and Kiewiet 1979, 1981; Weatherford 1983; Lewis-Beck 1988).

10. This discussion of the "political track" is drawn primarily from Nelson (1989b). That paper also develops in more detail the notion of a political track and a technical track for trade policy outcomes.

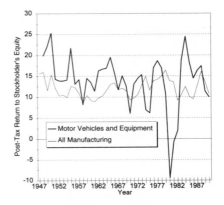

Fig. 3.1   After-tax return to shareholders' equity
Sources: U.S. Department of Commerce, *Historical Statistics of the United States* (Washington, D.C., various years); U.S. Department of Commerce, *Statistical Abstract of the United States* (Washington, D.C., various years).

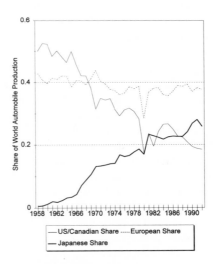

Fig. 3.2   Shares of world auto production
Sources: USITC (1985c); USITC, "The U.S. Automobile Industry: Monthly Report on Selected Economic Indicators" (Washington, D.C., February of various years).

trade at that. Although after careful study and public hearings the ITC clearly came to contrary conclusions, the issue before Congress and the public was framed in terms of international competition and the industry's need to have protection from that competition. Directly related to this is the issue of standing: who has a "right" to participate in the process. While the ITC and the congressional hearings were open, there are strong norms against participation

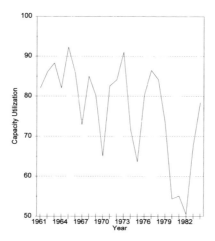

Fig. 3.3   Capacity utilization
Source: Fuss and Waverman (1992).

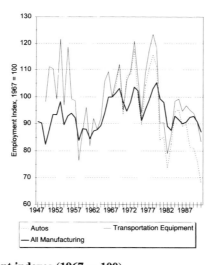

Fig. 3.4   Employment indexes (1967 = 100)
Sources: U.S. Department of Commerce, *Historical Statistics of the United States* (Washington, D.C., various years); U.S. Department of Commerce, *Business Statistics, 1963–1991* (Washington, D.C., 1992).

unless one's interests are directly at stake. Thus, for example, dealers of Japanese autos did testify against trade restrictions, but such testimony is often discounted because the dealers are in some sense foreign agents. Industries that are indirectly affected, for example, through general equilibrium effects, simply do not have standing. This is particularly true if the testimony is from

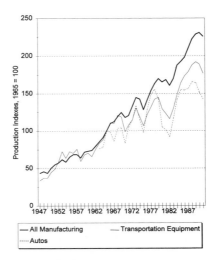

Fig. 3.5   Production indexes (1965 = 100)

Sources: U.S. Department of Commerce, *Historical Statistics of the United States* (Washington, D.C., various years); U.S. Department of Commerce, *Business Statistics, 1963–1991* (Washington, D.C., 1992).

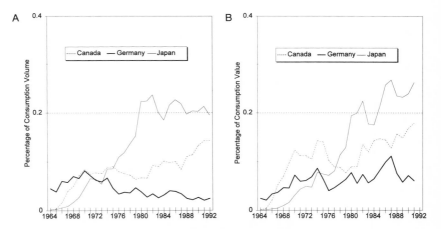

Fig. 3.6   Ratio of imports to apparent consumption by country of origin— Canada, Germany, and Japan: (A) volume and (B) value

Sources: USITC (1985c); USITC, "The U.S. Automobile Industry: Monthly Report on Selected Economic Indicators" (Washington, D.C., February of various years).

exporters, who, by definition, are perceived to be doing well. Consumer interests, for the usual collective action reasons, are not generally well represented in the process. Finally, the protection seeker has a significant first-mover advantage. Not only did the auto industry choose the specific form of administered protection from which to start, but it controlled the timing and form of the public debate over the auto industry. Taken together, these advantages, along with the public sentiment favoring the industry, suggest that any executive would have been under considerable pressure to accommodate the auto industry.

Nonetheless, it is still worthwhile to compare the Carter and Reagan responses to auto industry pressure. Both the international and domestic policy commitments of these administrations differed considerably. With respect to international politics, while trade policy was a strong priority in Carter administration foreign policy, the Reagan administration was overwhelmingly focused on anti-Communism. Thus, although there was no shortage of free trade rhetoric, as Niskanen (1988) and others argue there was no coherent trade policy and no leadership on trade. As a result, trade policy developed in response to initiatives from domestic economic interests, from Congress, and from trading partners.[11] In the absence of strong leadership from the White House, Congress became increasingly assertive on the trade issue, legislating on a wide variety of trade issues—both extensions of administered protection as well as expansion to new, aggressive market access legislation (Super 301). As with international politics, with respect to domestic politics President Carter was himself committed to trade liberalization and the resistance of protection. As a result, the administration was relatively consistent in its statements on trade and in its efforts to resist protection. Under President Reagan, the administration was split between a small group committed to free trade (Regan, Weidenbaum, Stockman, and Shultz) and a larger, ultimately more influential group committed to the traditional Republican strategy of giving business what it wants (Lewis, Baldrige, Brock, and Meese).[12] In addition, Baker appears to have supported auto import restraints because of a concern that without them Congress would legislate restraints, and that a veto would sap congressional goodwill necessary to carry the tax reform that was the central priority of the administration (Interview). The combination of lack of leadership with a strong probusiness bias led to an inconsistent overall policy with a protectionist bias reflecting both the probusiness orientation and the congressional pressure. The result on automobiles was not a fluke; again quoting Niskanen (1988,

11. Although the Uruguay Round did start during the Reagan administration (the Punta del Este meeting was in September 1986), it was not the result of a U.S. effort and was only closed with sustained effort by the Clinton administration. This may be unduly harsh on the Bush administration, which certainly did pursue a stronger General Agreement on Tariffs and Trade (GATT) policy than the Reagan administration.

12. In addition to the useful discussion in Niskanen (1988, 139–41), see also the colorful account in Stockman (1986, 154–58).

137), "In response to domestic political pressure, the administration imposed more new restraints on trade than any administration since Hoover." Thus, while the economic and political circumstances were such as to encourage protectionist outcomes from any administration, the transition from Carter to Reagan resulted in a more protectionist, not a less protectionist, trade policy.

The uneasy relationship between the official ideology of the Reagan administration and its extensive trade activism led to difficult international relations. In the case of the auto industry, the attempt to protect the public perception of a commitment to Liberal trading relations while providing significant protection to the industry led, first, to a preference for a "voluntary" export restraint and, then, to an attempt to retain the appearance of complete independence from the process of determining the level of the restraint.[13] From fairly early on in the political process, the Japanese Ministry of International Trade and Industry (MITI) and the Japanese auto industry were supportive of some degree of export restraint. The problem was the unwillingness of the U.S. government to publicly bargain over and then commit to a specific level of restraint. The practical problem for the Japanese industry was a very real concern that such a restraint without explicit executive commitment could lead to antitrust prosecution. This produced an embarrassing period of nonnegotiation in which the Japanese government regularly asserted its willingness to restrict trade if the United States would give it some idea of the level of restriction that would be acceptable, while the U.S. government asserted that if the Japanese wanted to restrict exports it would probably be a good thing (although the administration was always committed to free trade). This culminated, in late March 1981, in a trip to Tokyo by USTR Brock that was explicitly *not* about the auto issue but at the end of which the Japanese government announced that it would voluntarily restrict its exports to 1.68 million units (a reduction of 7.7 percent from the previous period) during the first year of a three-year agreement, with some unspecified growth in the next two years. In the event, given the continued poor performance of the U.S. industry, the Japanese government agreed to retain the limit at the original level in all three years.

In fact, as research reviewed in sections 3.2 and 3.3 suggests, given the depressed conditions in the U.S. auto industry, the VER was not binding in its first two years. However, in 1983 and 1984, with a rebound in domestic demand, the VER resulted in sharply increased prices and profits for U.S. firms. In fact, news reports of large executive bonuses in 1984 led to a considerable amount of dissatisfaction with the VER. Nonetheless, although some in the administration argued that the restraint should be allowed to lapse, the fact that 1984 was an election year provided sufficient support for the proponents of

13. According to Stockman (1986, 157), Edwin Meese deserves credit for the strategy of encouraging the Japanese to voluntarily restrain auto exports without any official negotiations: "Under the Meese formulation our hands would be clean; the Japanese would do the dirty work themselves. It was another case of not knowing the difference between campaigning and governing."

continuing the agreement in place for another year. The result was that the agreement was extended to March 1985 with the quota expanded to 1.85 million units.[14] With another year of high profits in 1985, the administration decided to let the agreement lapse. However, given rent transfers to Japanese producers on the order of $2 billion (Hufbauer, Berliner, and Elliott 1986) as a result of the auto VER, it is not surprising that the Japanese government announced that it would be willing to continue the restriction in the interest of maintaining orderly markets in the United States.

The implementation of a protectionist policy against Japanese auto producers was at best, from the perspective of the key members of the auto regime, only part of the strategy of socializing the Japanese firms in the norms of that regime. The other key element involved an attempt to force the Japanese firms to engage in local production with substantial local value added. As we will see below, well before its adoption of trade protectionism the UAW had attempted to encourage U.S. production by Japanese auto firms. Given the political economic conditions described in this section, the UAW decided to make a major push for domestic-content legislation. In early December, 1981 Representative R. Ottinger (D-N.Y.) introduced the Fair Practices for Automotive Product Act (H.R. 5133). The terms of this legislation (table 3.1) would have required Toyota, Nissan, Honda, Toyo Kogyo, Mitsubishi, and Isuzu, as well as Volkswagen (VW), to engage in substantial local production to retain their current levels of sales. Of these, only VW could conceivably have met these requirements. As with the politics of the VER, Ford and Chrysler supported the UAW on domestic content, while GM was strongly opposed.

This legislation provides an excellent illustration of the breakdown of Ways and Means control over the trade issue that was described above. Representative Ottinger was the chair of the Energy Conservation and Power Subcommittee of the House Energy and Commerce Committee, and it was the Subcommittee on Commerce, Transportation, and Tourism of that committee that held the initial hearing on Ottinger's bill. The bill was passed by the Energy and Commerce Committee, then under the chairmanship of John Dingell (D-Mich.). Although the bill was referred to Ways and Means, Dingell arranged that his committee could override a negative report from Ways and Means.[15] The chair of Ways and Means, Sam Gibbons (D-Fla.), was strongly opposed to the bill and tried to stall it by holding lengthy hearings, but Ways and Means' capacity to manage legislation had declined. As a result, even though Ways and Means was strongly opposed to the measure, the House passed the legislation by a large margin (215–188). It was recognized at the time that this was bad legislation and could probably not have been passed over a veto. Thus, given

14. It is interesting to note that GM lobbied strongly for an increase in the quantity limit to permit it to increase imports of Isuzu and Suzuki automobiles for sale under GM nameplates. On the other hand, Chrysler lobbied strongly for continuing the restrictions at their original levels.

15. I.e., Ways and Means was given only sequential referral. Kabashima and Sato (1986) provide a compact summary of the politics of domestic-content legislation in 1982.

Table 3.1   Summary of Terms under the Fair Practices in Automotive
                Product Act

Number of Vehicles Sold	Required Minimum Percentage to Be Produced Locally		
	1983	1984	1985+
Less than 100,000	0.0	0.0	0.0
100,000–149,999	8.3	16.7	25.0
150,000–199,999	16.7	33.3	50.0
200,000–499,999	25.0	50.0	75.0
500,000 and more	30.0	60.0	90.0

Source: Coughlin (1985).

the public popularity of trade action on auto imports from Japan, representatives were fairly safe to engage in public position taking for electoral reasons. However, systematic econometric research suggests that these votes were completely consistent with a public pressure model and that less dramatic domestic-content rules might well survive.[16] Although the legislation ultimately died in the Republican-controlled Senate, a clear signal had been sent, and over the next several years the Japanese auto producers began or expanded U.S. production.

Given the expressed trade policy goals of the more active auto industry participants in the trade policy process (Ford and the UAW), one would have to conclude that the industry was quite successful in achieving those goals: quantitative restrictions were imposed on Japanese firms and the threat of content legislation appears to have been taken as, at least, plausible. The next questions relate to the economic consequences of that success. In the next section we address the preliminary issue of the competitiveness of the U.S. industry, following which we examine the consequences of the VER.

3.2   Competitiveness of the U.S. Automobile Industry

Given the deterioration of market shares of U.S. producers in the late 1970s, it is hardly surprising that a number of studies have attempted to identify the foundations of that deterioration. In this section we will consider analyses based on relative costs of inputs (especially labor), technical efficiency, and managerial efficiency (especially labor-management relations). However, before considering analyses of declining competitiveness based on conditions within the auto industry, it is useful to briefly consider the argument that the apparent decline in competitiveness was primarily a function of macroeconomic disequilibrium of one kind or another.

16. The voting in this legislation has been extensively studied; see Coughlin (1985), Kabashima and Sato (1986), McArthur and Marks (1988), and Marks and McArthur (1989).

At the broadest level, it is interesting to note that all three postwar surges in import share in U.S. apparent consumption coincide with macroeconomic contractions. The link between recession and the declining fortunes of the U.S. auto industry, more generally the highly cyclical nature of auto sales, is straightforward and often commented upon.[17] With respect to the third import surge (1979–80), the ITC noted, in rejecting the industry's appeal for relief under the escape clause, that this period was characterized by "rapid increases in the cost of credit, increasing unemployment, declines in real spendable earnings, large cutbacks in consumer spending, and deteriorating consumer confidence in the economy and in future earning power" (U.S. International Trade Commission [USITC] 1980, A-67–68). Since a substantial part of auto demand in the United States is replacement demand and thus can be put off more or less indefinitely, recession results in postponement of purchases.[18] At the same time, recession also resulted in substitution toward less expensive, small cars—the market segment most penetrated by imports. When one recalls that this was a period of sharply increased gasoline prices, which also induces substitution toward small cars, the increasing Japanese sales is readily understood. That is, the problems faced by the U.S. industry had more to do with the state of the macroeconomy than with international competition.

In addition to the effects of depressed macroeconomic conditions and increased gasoline prices, recent work has also emphasized the importance of disequilibrium exchange rates for the trade balance and, through the effect on competitiveness, on demand for protection.[19] The early and mid-1980s saw an exceptionally sharp appreciation of the dollar, peaking in early 1985 and then dropping sharply (see fig. 3.7). Under the best of circumstances, such a dramatic appreciation of the dollar would have created serious problems for import-competing firms. For an industry already beginning to experience recession combined with surging imports, rapid appreciation of the dollar was extremely bad news.[20] Eichengreen's (1988) analysis shows employment in the motor vehicle industry to be strongly responsive to the exchange rate, as well as to energy prices and business cycle effects. Specifically, he estimates that

17. These macroeconomic factors are given particular significance by the fact that the ITC's 1980 rejection of the auto industry's escape clause petition was based on the conclusion by a majority of the commissioners that macroeconomic disequilibrium was a more significant cause of industry distress than increased foreign competition.

18. For systematic treatments of auto demand that explicitly take into account the ability of consumers to delay purchases, see Smith (1975) and Westin (1975).

19. For characteristic general discussions of the link between disequilibrium exchange rates and protection, see Bergsten and Williamson (1983), Corden (1984), Dornbusch and Frankel (1987), McKinnon (1987), and the papers in Marston (1988). In the context of the Michigan CGE model, Deardorff and Stern (1986, chap 5) find the transportation equipment industry to be among the sectors most strongly responsive to exchange rate changes. This paper is not the place to discuss the causes of exchange rate disequilibrium in the 1980s, but see Obstfeld (1985), Feldstein (1986), and Branson (1988) for useful discussions.

20. Papers by Citrin (1985) and Clifton (1985) document the responsiveness of auto exports to changes in the exchange rate.

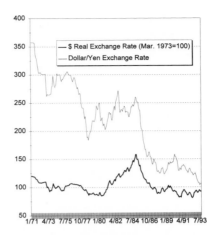

Fig. 3.7   Yen/dollar and average dollar exchange rates
Source: International Monetary Fund, *International Financial Statistics* (Washington, D.C., various years).

"the real appreciation of the dollar between the second half of the 1970s and the first half of the 1980s . . . reduced employment in motor vehicles . . . by nearly 10 percent" (1988, 330). Furthermore, in the early 1990s the major depreciations of the dollar against the yen in 1985–88 and in the early 1990s appear to have substantially improved the competitiveness of U.S.-produced autos relative to Japanese-produced autos. The second of these episodes appears to have encouraged the major Japanese producers to shift output to their U.S. facilities. However, Richardson (1988) provides a careful analysis of a number of measures of the exchange rate in the early and mid-1980s with particular reference to the auto industry and its competitiveness, concluding that exchange rate changes were a considerably less significant source of the industry's competitiveness problems than deteriorating cost competitiveness. To which we now turn.

The simplest approach to the analysis of cost competitiveness pursues a Ricardian strategy of focusing only on labor costs and labor productivity to generate a measure of unit labor costs. If this measure rises relative to that for manufacturing as a whole by more than the same measure for another country, one can conclude that the industry has shifted down the chain of comparative advantage. Kreinin (1982, 1984) presents the data in tables 3.2 and 3.3 for this purpose. For the United States, unit labor costs in the auto industry rise relative to the manufacturing average, while in Japan the unit labor costs track the manufacturing average fairly closely, suggesting a deterioration in U.S. comparative advantage in autos relative to Japan. It is interesting to compare the sources of this change. In the United States the majority of this divergence is accounted for by wages rising relative to the manufacturing average while productivity increased in line with the manufacturing average. Interestingly,

Table 3.2 **Unit Labor Costs in the U.S. Motor Vehicle Industry**

Year	Compensation		Output per Worker		Unit Labor Cost	
	Motor Vehicles	All Manufacturing	Motor Vehicles	All Manufacturing	Motor Vehicles	All Manufacturing
1967	100	100	100	100	100	100
1968	107	107	106	104	101	103
1969	113	115	105	105	108	109
1970	122	122	103	105	119	117
1971	139	130	117	112	119	117
1972	148	137	120	117	123	117
1973	159	147	122	123	130	119
1974	178	162	121	121	148	135
1975	200	182	128	124	156	147
1976	218	196	134	129	162	151
1977	243	212	143	133	170	160
1978	265	230	142	134	187	172
1979	284	252	139	135	205	187
1980	314	279	139	135	227	207

Source: Kreinin (1982).

Table 3.3 **Unit Labor Costs in the Japanese Motor Vehicle Industry**

Year	Compensation		Output per Worker		Unit Labor Cost	
	Motor Vehicles	All Manufacturing	Motor Vehicles	All Manufacturing	Motor Vehicles	All Manufacturing
1965	100	100	100	100	100	100
1966	111	110	110	110	101	100
1967	126	124	130	126	96	98
1968	146	144	154	142	95	101
1969	172	171	170	164	101	104
1970	204	203	185	185	110	110
1971	233	235	202	193	115	122
1972	272	271	234	212	116	128
1973	346	333	269	237	129	141
1974	448	438	251	246	178	178
1975	530	513	276	256	192	200
1976	599	550	315	280	190	196
1977	656	606	284	305	231	199
1978	723	644	259	326	279	198
1979	776	693	326	352	238	197
1980	832	755	419	374	199	200

Source: Kreinin (1982).

wages in Japan diverge from the manufacturing average by about the same proportion as in the United States, while increasing relative productivity allows the Japanese auto industry to improve its unit labor costs relative to the manufacturing average by a small amount.

A number of studies have attempted to incorporate a greater variety of cost components at the expense of the general equilibrium framework developed in Kreinin's Ricardian analysis. Specifically, in the late 1970s and early 1980s a number of studies attempted to evaluate the competitive prospects of the auto industry via fairly simple ad hoc accounting exercises. The two most prominent studies at the time examine relative costs in 1981, at the onset of the trade adjustment crisis: Abernathy, Harbour, and Henn (1981, hereafter AHH; also Abernathy, Clark, and Kantrow 1983, hereafter ACK) and Flynn (1984).[21] They conclude that Japanese producers in 1981 had a labor cost advantage in the $1100–$1400 range and a materials cost advantage in the $600–$800 range. AHH also argue that these differentials do not result from more capital-intensive production because the Japanese apply less capital per unit of output than do U.S. firms. Taking into account both transportation and marketing costs in the United States, ACK conclude that the Japanese had a $1200–$1500 cost advantage over U.S. producers in 1981.[22] Flynn's analysis is similar to that of AHH/ACK, though there is more detail on the composition of labor costs. Ultimately, Flynn concludes that Japanese producers possess a $1432 labor cost differential and a $1498 landed cost advantage. Cole and Yakushiji (1984) review a number of other estimates of the Japanese cost advantage, concluding that the landed cost advantage for a subcompact auto is $1468.[23]

Alternative approaches using more sophisticated approaches based on production theory estimated cost advantages of similar orders of magnitude.[24] The most sophisticated of the studies of relative cost is by Fuss and Waverman (1992, hereafter FW).[25] FW are particularly concerned to incorporate short-run

21. AHH construct firm-level data for Ford, GM, Toyo Kogyo, and Nissan on labor and materials costs as well as a variety of other manufacturing and nonmanufacturing (including transportation) costs in producing a comparable (small) car.

22. AHH arrive at the slightly larger $1650 as their estimate. Gomez-Ibanez and Harrison (1982) argue that the AHH/ACK estimates are based on a number of ad hoc assumptions that serve to artificially inflate their estimates of Japanese cost advantage. Simply adjusting for these factors, Gomez-Ibanez and Harrison conclude that the 1981 Japanese landed cost advantage was more on the order of $800–$1000. Fuss and Waverman (1992) make similar adjustments, in particular drawing on a U.S. Federal Trade Commission (1984) study that showed double-counting by AHH in their determination of U.S. costs, concluding that the landed cost advantage for the Japanese was in the range $554–$896 in 1979 and $986–$1315 in 1981.

23. Given the Kennedy Round tariff rate of 3.5 percent on motor vehicles and the then recently negotiated Tokyo Round rate of 2.5 percent, this landed cost advantage was judged considerable.

24. The first of these, Winston and Associates (1987), estimated landed cost advantages for Japanese firms ranging from $2098 in 1970 to $1301 in 1982.

25. In addition to providing a sophisticated analysis of cost competitiveness in the auto industry, FW are admirably clear on all stages of the research program leading to their conclusions: formal model, data construction, and estimation. One can learn much about how to do practical, industry-level analysis from reading this book.

market disequilibrium, in terms of excess capacity and disequilibrium exchange rates, and technical change as fundamental elements of their analysis. With respect to capacity, FW argue that the auto industry is characterized by product-specific manufacturing facilities. If tastes shift substantially, as we have argued they did during the 1970s, significant variation in capacity utilization can occur, affecting measured efficiency.[26] Given the massive dislocations the auto industry faced in the late 1970s and early 1980s, explicitly incorporating short-run disequilibrium would seem to be a major advance. FW find a very large cost disadvantage of U.S. firms (35 percent) in 1980 but find that this does not reflect equilibrium cost disadvantage but primarily the effects of short-term disequilibrium. FW's results thus provide further support for the proposition that the industry's economic problems were not primarily trade related.[27]

3.3 Economic Consequences of Automobile Trade Policy

The standard approach to evaluating the welfare effects of protection involves estimation of a simple, partial equilibrium model usually under the assumption of perfect competition. However, as we will see below in more detail, the auto industry is far removed from the state of perfect competition in both product and factor markets. In addition to the fact that the industry is large enough to have sizeable general equilibrium effects, the industry is characterized by both product differentiation and small numbers competition. As a result, in the decade or so since the auto VER was introduced there has been a substantial amount of research on its welfare effects, using a wide variety of methodologies and assumptions about the market.

The standard approach to evaluating the welfare effects of the VER involves a straightforward extension of the textbook partial equilibrium analysis of triangles and rectangles. The basic strategy involves taking observed price and quantity data as equilibrium values and using explicit assumptions about functional forms and estimates of elasticities of demand and supply. Since there is some evidence that consumers view U.S. and Japanese autos as distinct products, virtually all of these studies develop distinct demand and supply relations for each, under explicit assumptions about cross-elasticities of demand. Tarr

---

26. Bresnahan and Ramey (1993) explicitly study the effect of changes in demand across auto size segments on capacity utilization, presenting results which strongly confirm the existence of effects of the sort conjectured by FW.

27. It is interesting to note that materials price increases are the major source of increased costs in all countries and improvement in technical efficiency is the major source of cost reduction for all countries except Canada, whose producers derive particularly strong benefits from improvements in capacity utilization. FW are able to show that, while a substantial element of the U.S. disadvantage vis-à-vis Japan in the 1978–80 period (as well as virtually all of the improvement in 1980–84) was a function of underutilization of capacity, the Japanese industry steadily improved its long-run equilibrium technical efficiency vis-à-vis the United States. Specifically, this study estimates that, over the 1970–84 period, while the Japanese rate of growth in total factor productivity was about 3 percent per year, the rate for the North American industry was only about 1 percent.

and Morkre (1984) present a particularly clear exposition of this methodology.[28] Under a variety of assumptions on elasticities and cross-elasticities, as well as on the initial state of demand, these studies yield consumer costs from $1 billion to nearly $6 billion, consumer costs per job saved ranging from $95,000 to $220,000, and increases in domestic profit rent transfers to Japanese firms both on the order of $2 billion.[29] The estimates for the years immediately following the imposition of the VER are consistently lower than those for later years. This is a result of the continuing recession in the industry.

In all of the previous studies the relations between firms were assumed to be competitive, or at least nonstrategic. We have already referred to a number of studies suggesting that this assumption is of doubtful validity. Furthermore, recent research on the relationship between exchange rate changes and the do-

28. In addition to Tarr and Morkre, studies by Hufbauer et al. (1986, 1993), Willig and Dutz (1987), and Gomez-Ibanez, Leone, and O'Connell (1983) apply this methodology to the auto case.

An alternative approach involves the use of historical data from the unrestrained period to predict unrestrained values of relevant data for the period under restraint. The ITC's report on the VER (USITC 1985b) uses this strategy in conjunction with market assumptions of the sort described above to derive estimates of employment and consumer costs for both a weak-demand year (1981) and a strong-demand year (1984). Crandall (1984) presents one of the first analyses of this sort along with a number of other attempts to develop estimates of the orders of magnitude of effects associated with the VER. These results are broadly consistent with the other studies, yielding considerably lower costs in the low-demand year than the Tarr and Morkre estimates and very similar estimates for 1984 to those of Hufbauer et al.

Following important theoretical papers by Falvey (1979) and Rodriguez (1979), and empirical work by Feenstra (1984, 1985, 1988a), a number of papers have incorporated quality upgrading. The basic insight of the Falvey and Rodriguez analyses is that if quantities are restrained, foreign producers will maximize the return per unit exported by shipping higher-quality units, which sell for higher prices. This is the "quality upgrading" effect of a quantitative restriction. In terms of welfare analysis, since some fraction of the higher price is a function of higher quality, analyses that do not incorporate these effects will tend to overestimate the welfare costs of the VER. Since Feenstra concludes that two-thirds of the price increase is compensated by an increase in quality, the welfare costs are considerably lower than other estimates. Dinopoulos and Kreinin (1988) provide an interesting extension of the Feenstra analysis by incorporating substitution toward unrestrained European producers as well as toward U.S.-produced autos. Because their analysis finds considerable quality-adjusted price increases by European producers, their estimate of rent transfers is considerably greater than Feenstra's.

The final basic research strategy, based on a partial equilibrium/competitive framework, involves explicit specification of a set of behavioral relations on prerestraint data and the comparison of the predicted results for the restrained period with the observed results. Collyns and Dunaway (1987) provide a particularly clear presentation of this approach, with particular attention to quality upgrading and nonrestrained foreign suppliers. Their analysis provides estimates that range from $1.65 billion for a low-demand year to $6.6 billion for a high-demand year. Bryan and Humpage (1984) argue that inventory adjustment is an essential element of auto industry adjustment to shocks, and therefore, in addition to quality adjustment effects, they develop and estimate a model that treats such adjustments explicitly. As a result of inventory adjustments, the employment effects in their model are much smaller than those found in other models. Thus the consumer cost per job saved is nearly seven times larger than the next largest estimate. Winston and Associates (1987) pursue a similar strategy, using predicted and realized prices based on Crandall (1987) and a sophisticated model of auto demand incorporating general macroeconomic conditions and used cars as well as differentiated new car offerings. They conclude that in 1984 auto employment was reduced by nearly 32,000 and consumer welfare costs were $14 billion.

29. See case M-22 (automobiles) in Hufbauer et al. (1986) for a convenient survey of the input data that have appeared in the literature.

mestic currency price of foreign automobiles suggests that, especially Japanese, firms are able to adjust foreign currency prices to retain market shares.[30] This suggests the importance of evaluating the sensitivity of computational analyses of the economic effects of trade policy in the auto sector to strategic behavior. Dixit (1988) provided the starting point for this important work. As with competitive partial equilibrium analyses like Tarr and Morkre (1984), Dixit takes observed price and quantity data to be equilibrium outcomes and uses the assumed structure of the market to calibrate a computational model that can then be used to perform policy experiments.[31] Dixit adopts a clever strategy of using the conjectural variation term to evaluate the competitiveness of the auto market in 1979 (a high-demand year) and 1980 (a low-demand year). Dixit's primary conclusion, for our purposes, is that although welfare-improving trade policy is possible, the gains are generally small. However, Dixit also explicitly evaluates the interesting case in which, as a result of union bargaining, there is a substantial rent component in the auto wage. Since this creates an additional source of gain from expanding output, the gains from trade activism are considerably greater. Further work by Krishna et al. (1989) and Fuss, Murphy, and Waverman (1992) make it clear that the results of this sort of analysis are highly sensitive to the assumptions made about the strategic structure, as well as to those made about the economic structure. As with Feenstra's research on quality upgrading, these papers suggest that the estimates of cost of protection based on competitive market conditions should also be treated with caution.

The final major extension of work on the welfare costs of protection to the auto industry involves moving beyond the partial equilibrium framework applied in all the previous studies to a general equilibrium framework. De Melo and Tarr (1992, chap. 1) argue that this is an essential task because the partial equilibrium analysis produces systematic overestimates of the costs of protection because they do not take into account the trade balance constraint and thus the effect of changes in the real exchange rate. Furthermore, in the general equilibrium context, agent welfare is affected by both price and wage effects. Nonetheless, even in the base case involving constant returns to scale and competitive behavior the de Melo and Tarr estimates of welfare costs exceed those in the partial equilibrium studies, primarily because their estimates of the rent transfer to foreigners are considerably larger than those in the earlier studies. Next, the authors examine a variety of alternative factor market assumptions. Their most interesting finding here is that, when there is an endogenous wage premium, the imposition of a quantitative restriction in automobiles raises the premium (i.e., increases the distortion), undermining the employment-creating

---

30. This "pricing to market" behavior is inconsistent with competitive market conditions. For studies of such behavior that explicitly consider the auto industry, see Feenstra (1989), Ohno (1989), Marston (1990), Knetter (1989, 1992, 1993), and Gagnon and Knetter (1992).

31. Krishna, Hogan, and Swagel (1989) provide a particularly clear exposition and extension of this methodology for the oligopoly case.

effects and, unlike the case in Dixit and Krishna et al., increasing costs of protection (see also de Melo and Tarr 1993).

Two major results stand out from the considerable body of research on the costs of the VER program for the auto industry. First, protection is quite costly. In Hufbauer et al.'s evaluation of special protection, only textiles and steel have higher total consumer costs. Second, in addition to the substantial magnitudes of these estimates, the other important regularity in research on the costs of the VER is the relatively low costs in the first two years of the VER resulting from continued recession in the industry. However, the recovery of demand resulted in much greater transfers from consumers to both U.S. and Japanese firms.

All of the research reported above is essentially static in nature. None of these papers address the more difficult question of the effect of protection on the long-term competitiveness of the U.S. auto industry. One of the problems in carrying out such an analysis is, of course, determining the time horizon over which to make the relevant evaluations. We have already seen, for example, that the direct effects of protection vary over time, primarily as a function of general macroeconomic conditions. We can, however, informally consider trends in three essential correlates of competitiveness: wages and labor productivity, investment, and quality. With respect to wages, the industry experienced a short-term gain in the immediate aftermath of the VER by extracting substantial wage concessions from the UAW. Ford and GM, in particular, negotiated wage reductions in 1982 in exchange for limited profit sharing. The effect of these arrangements shows up in figure 3.8 as a sharp drop in the rate of increase of labor costs in 1983 and in figure 3.9 as a drop in the wage differential between autoworkers and the manufacturing average. Figure 3.8 also shows a considerable increase in the rate of improvement of productivity of labor. However, as figure 3.3 (following the logic of FW) clearly suggests, much of this increase in productivity is due to substantially improved capacity utilization. With the protection in place, and the recovery of profits shown in figure 3.1, the UAW was able to negotiate quite generous wage increases in the 1984 agreements with Ford and GM. Again, these show up clearly in figures 3.8 and 3.9. Given our previous conclusion that the jump in profits reflects primarily increased rent extraction from U.S. consumers, this suggests that the postwar pattern of rent sharing between labor and capital in the auto industry continued more or less unchanged. Thus it would be difficult to conclude that the industry gained much in terms of its relations with labor from either import competition or the subsequent protection.

To a considerable extent the senescent industry argument for protection relies on the protected industry using the period of protection to make fundamental adjustments in the organization of production to improve its competitiveness. It is certainly the case that all three U.S. majors have attempted to make both physical and organizational changes in response to competition from Japanese firms. As figure 3.10 suggests, the industry did undertake considerable

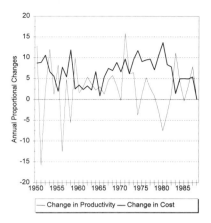

Fig. 3.8   Labor productivity and costs
Source: U.S. Department of Commerce, Multifactor Productivity Project.

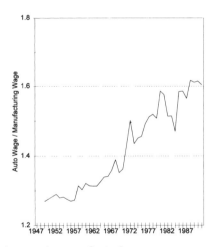

Fig. 3.9   Ratio of auto wage to manufacturing wage
Source: U.S. Department of Commerce, *Annual Survey of Manufactures* (Washington, D.C., various years).

new capital spending in the immediate post-VER period and again in the early 1990s. In addition to the investments needed to develop and produce new products to meet the demand for smaller, more fuel-efficient cars, the industry invested extensively in new production technologies (e.g., industrial robots). Where the former investments seem to have been successful, at least for Ford and Chrysler, journalistic accounts suggest that the latter were not. In addition to physical investment, the U.S. majors have experimented with new forms of

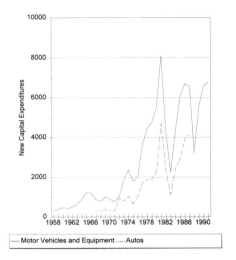

Fig. 3.10   Annual investment
Source: U.S. Department of Commerce, *Annual Survey of Manufactures* (Washington, D.C., various years).

relations with both labor and suppliers that emphasize greater flexibility. To this point, the record is mixed, with both striking success and striking failure at the plant level, but no discernible overall pattern.[32]

The final dimension related to long-run competitiveness relates to quality and the perception thereof. At least as important as the industry's product-mix problems was the deterioration in quality and the widespread perception of the U.S. majors as suppliers of high-priced, low-quality automobiles. Table 3.4, based on frequency of repair data from *Consumer Reports,* suggests considerable improvement in quality by Chrysler in the late 1980s and early 1990s, while Ford and GM show no clear trend. While there has been some deterioration of overall Japanese quality, the most striking fact revealed by table 3.4 is the continuing gap in quality between U.S. and Japanese producers of automobiles. Perhaps most important, there does not appear to be any obvious relationship between quality and the VER.

One's overall evaluation of the long-run effect of U.S. trade activism with respect to the auto industry also depends on how one evaluates the increased investment in the United States by the major Japanese producers. Journalistic reports suggest that, without the VER and the threat of domestic-content protection, Japanese firms would have been unlikely to invest in the United

32. Turner (1991) reviews existing research on the attempts to reorganize production in the U.S. auto industry and develops additional plant-level research from the perspective of the union. A more systematic study by Katz, Kochan, and Keefe (1987) was unable to find strong statistical relations between measures of production organization and productivity.

Table 3.4   **Frequency of Repair for U.S. and Japanese Firms**

Year	AMC/Chrysler	Ford	GM	Japan
1975	3.8	2.8	2.9	2.3
1976	4.1	2.8	2.9	2.4
1977	4.3	2.9	3.0	2.0
1978	4.0	3.3	3.1	1.7
1979	3.4	3.5	3.5	1.4
1980	3.3	3.2	3.5	1.7
1981	3.6	3.0	4.2	1.7
1982	3.5	3.0	4.2	1.5
1983	3.9	3.0	4.2	1.3
1984	4.2	3.5	4.0	1.3
1985	3.9	3.7	4.1	1.3
1986	3.7	3.4	3.9	1.6
1987	3.6	3.6	4.0	1.7
1988	3.6	3.7	4.0	1.4
1989	3.4	3.8	4.2	1.6
1990	3.4	3.8	4.0	1.6
1991	3.7	3.9	4.3	1.9

Note: Every April from 1972 to 1992 *Consumer Reports* published an overall frequency-of-repair index ("trouble index") evaluating autos on a scale: 1—much better than average; 2—better than average; 3—average; 4—worse than average; and 5—much worse than average. The data reported in this table are average values for each U.S. major and for all Japanese firms taken together. Note that these averages are not weighted by sales and no attempt has been made to isolate product lines that are directly competitive.

States.[33] In the event, however, the combination of a major realignment in exchange rates and the nonunionization of their production facilities would seem to have increased the competitiveness of Japanese firms and made it harder to affect them through trade policy in the future.

Overall, there is no question but that the VER resulted in a substantial increase in industry profits once the U.S. economy recovered from recession and auto demand increased.[34] However, it also appears that those profits primarily reflect increased rent extraction from U.S. consumers. More important, Ford and possibly Chrysler appear to have made substantial adjustments over the period of the mid- and late 1980s that have increased their competitiveness vis-à-vis their Japanese competitors. It seems reasonable to conclude that the U.S. industry is somewhat smaller, somewhat more flexible, and somewhat more efficient. One must, however, be careful in evaluating the relationship between international competition, protection, and this improved competitiveness. With or without trade protection these firms would have made the adjustments in

33. See Halberstam (1986). Bhagwati, Dinopoulos, and Wong, in various combinations, have developed the logic of quid pro quo investment in some detail. See Bhagwati et al. (1992). It is interesting to note that their primary example is the auto industry.

34. However, as examination of fig. 3.1 suggests, this recovery was relatively short lived. Overall industry profits drop sharply in the late 1980s.

output mix, production facilities, and organization of production. It is Japanese competition not U.S. protection that accounts for the improvements in performance by the major U.S. auto producers. The Chrysler experience is particularly informative when compared to the VER. In the former case, the publicness of the transfer and the emphasis on the responsibility of the Chrysler Corporation and the UAW for the problems of the firm and the solution to those problems created strong incentives to improve performance. With the VER, the implication that the problem was, probably unfair, competition from abroad created poor incentives to improve performance. Whereas the Chrysler loan was repaid ahead of schedule, the VER, originally intended as a three-year measure, dragged on for nearly a decade.

Table 3.5 provides a very rough summary of this discussion. The participants are entered in the table roughly in order of their degree of support for trade activism with respect to Japanese auto producers (i.e., support for both the VER and domestic-content legislation): the UAW and Ford were the most active supporters, with Chrysler holding back during the early period because of the loan guarantee and the Carter administration's opposition to auto protection; GM opposed protection, but not very actively; and the Japanese producers, and the dealers, opposed protection strongly. Although the consumer interest was not well represented (except perhaps by the dealers), they are included in the table to remind us that they are the source of most of the gains realized by the other participants. Because the restraint was not binding in the immediate post-VER period, only the UAW experienced any effect. As a result of the general economic conditions the UAW made significant concessions during this period. The other agents in the auto industry experienced essentially no gains as a result of the VER. In the medium term, as the economy recovered and the VER became binding on Japanese firms, all of the active agents gained, while the inactive consumers lost. The evaluation of the long run depends on two factors: how one evaluates the use that was made by the U.S. firms of the period during which the VER was binding and how one evaluates the effect of increased Japanese investment in the United States. We have argued above that the former effect appears to be small and positive to zero, while the latter effect

Table 3.5   **Summary Table for Political Economic Analysis**

	Time Horizon		
Participant	Short	Medium	Long
UAW	−	+	−
Ford	0	+	0/−
Chrysler	0	+	0/−
GM	0	+	0/−
Japanese	0	+	+
Consumers	0	−	+

is primarily negative. The entries in the last two cells in the third column reflect primarily the effect of a more competitive domestic market.

3.4   Sectoral Regimes: Structure and Crisis

The notion of a sectoral regime is central to this paper's analysis. An economic sector is defined in terms of a set of products that are understood by the firms and households that make up the economy to constitute a distinct group.[35] That is, the sector's outputs are close substitutes in consumption and the firm's understand themselves to be in competition with one another. While this may prove difficult to apply in general, the application to passenger autos should not prove particularly problematic (though, as the minivan case suggests, the boundaries are always contested terrain). A regime is the set of formal and informal institutions, rules, and norms that regulate the relations between the participants in the regime.[36] In modern (i.e., "welfare state") capitalism, sectoral regimes are expected to support efficient contracting subject to provision of satisfactory levels of political economic order and equity. Since sectoral regimes are ultimately constituted by the behavior of the participants in the regime, when the regime fails to provide satisfactory performance with respect to efficiency, order, and equity, firms and households will engage in behavior which violates regime norms simultaneously with attempts to transform the regime. We refer to such a situation as a sectoral crisis.

A sectoral crisis can emerge for many reasons.[37] The overall cultural and/or political system in which the sectoral regime is embedded can experience a crisis, undermining the performance of an otherwise perfectly stable sectoral regime. Thus the "blue-collar blues" of the late 1960s and early 1970s that were widely held to have affected labor-management relations, and labor performance more generally, in the auto industry were clearly part of the larger social crisis affecting the United States as a whole in that period. Nonetheless, this situation led to early struggles between the firms and labor in the auto industry to reestablish the terms of their relationship. Alternatively, crisis can emerge as a result of the normal operation of the regime. It is conceivable, for example, that Ford could increase its market share vis-à-vis GM to the point at which GM's leadership was not sustainable but Ford was unable to assert equivalent leadership. The collapse of price leadership could result in extensive competition reducing profits and undermining relations with the UAW and suppliers. Again, this would be a sectoral crisis. The sort of crisis with which

---

35. The idea of a sector used here is motivated by Harrison White's (1981a, 1981b) important work on the social structure of markets.

36. The systematic study of such regimes is a central concern of economic sociology extending at least to Max Weber. For a recent focus on sectoral regimes in the U.S. economy, see Campbell, Hollingsworth, and Lindberg (1991).

37. Nelson (1986, part 1) develops a theory of sectoral crisis, based on Habermas (1973), consistent with the discussion here.

we are concerned in this paper, however, derives primarily from external shock(s) not easily accommodated by the existing regime. The combination of Ralph Nader, OPEC, and Japan produced a situation in the late 1970s and early 1980s that the auto regime appeared unable to accommodate. In the next section we briefly review the conditions that led to a crisis in the auto regime. Before that, however, we introduce the primary actors in the precrisis regime: the U.S. major auto producers, the UAW, and the U.S. government.

It is convenient to think of the basic units of analysis in the political economy as households and firms. Households own portfolios of factors of production (e.g., labor, human capital, and capital) that generate a flow of income from which they consume and invest. In addition to their preferences over the goods available for consumption and investment, households also make evaluations of the overall performance of the economy in terms that are not in general strictly self-interested. These latter evaluations form the basis of household political activity, which takes the form of voting and making relatively small contributions to political entrepreneurs (see n. 9 on sociotropic voting). Firms hire factors of production from households and intermediate goods from other firms to produce outputs which are, in turn, sold to other firms and/or households. Whereas households are generally small with respect to both the economy and the political system, firms are not generally small.[38] Furthermore, while firms do not vote, they do engage in political action, often on a large scale, through direct lobbying and by making relatively large contributions to political entrepreneurs. Thus, while households and firms interact directly in the economy, they rarely engage in direct political conflict or cooperation. Finally, unlike households, firm political activity is taken to be motivated strictly by direct, material self-interest.

Household political activity has not played much of a role in the political economy of trade policy for the auto industry. We have just argued that the primary form of household political activity is either voting or relatively passive support of political entrepreneurs. Because, until very recently, trade policy has not been an electoral issue of any significance, this has meant that households have had no direct effect on its determination. Of course, household preferences may well have an indirect effect on trade policy outcomes via their effect on overall macroeconomic performance.[39] Given the uneven distribution of production across electoral districts (except for that of the president), the optimal policy for a politician certainly need not be free trade, even if he or she is genuinely interested in maximizing some notion of aggregate

38. While one can imagine this statement eliciting objections in general, when the actors in question are GM, Ford, Chrysler, and the UAW it must surely be unproblematic.

39. Note that each household will have four elected representatives: one House member, two senators, and one president. It is important to recognize, with reference to research on sociotropic voting, that the community with reference to which a household makes its political economic evaluation need bear no relationship to any of the relevant electoral districts.

constituent welfare.[40] Thus, even with the shift of that production away from the eastern north central states, a state like Michigan with a large share of total auto output and a large share of auto production in state output could well have a positive optimal tariff for shifting welfare from the rest of the country to Michigan. If we take politicians to pursue some mix of social welfare maximization and election-related venality, and the auto industry to generally prefer a tariff greater than the welfare optimal tariff, politicians will be cross-pressured on the tariff. Because the auto industry is so large, and so tied up in the American self-image, these indirect effects are not insignificant.

We will, however, focus primarily on direct political action. In particular, we will focus on the direct political action of the primary, organized participants in the auto regime: the firms, labor, and the state.

3.4.1   U.S. Firms, the Auto Regime, and Trade

The most significant actors in the political economy of auto trade policy are unquestionably the U.S. majors: GM, Ford, and Chrysler. These are three of the largest firms in the U.S. economy, engaged in complex production and distribution relations that extend into all 50 states. A key issue in political economic analysis relates to how such firms organize their competitive relations. On the one hand, the main properties of passenger autos as a product and the technology for producing and marketing them is relatively standardized. Given the small number of firms, this should permit some form of implicitly collusive behavior. On the other hand, these three firms have very different production structures and very different relations to the world economy. For example, GM historically has outsourced 10–15 percent of its component inputs, Ford 40–50 percent, and Chrysler has varied widely in its degree of vertical integration (Hunker 1983, 31). Perhaps more important, in 1980, 10 percent of Chrysler sales, 22 percent of GM sales, and 45 percent of Ford sales were outside the United States; and while Ford actively pursues a strategy of global integration, GM's strategy involves local integration for sale in national and regional markets.[41]

Although GM was created from a number of smaller firms under du Pont financial leadership, as U.S. Steel was created with Morgan financial leadership, all three majors retained a strongly entrepreneurial orientation. It is certainly true that the considerable entry costs and GM's dominant position in the post–World War II market, until the large increases in Japanese market share in the early 1970s, served to make the auto industry, along with steel, the textbook

40. This statement makes no claim with respect to the existence of a coherent measure of aggregate welfare, nor with respect to the existence of instruments appropriate to achieve it. All it says is that a politician seeking to do the best for his or her district could determine that a positive tariff on some industry, or industries, would be better than free trade. The theory of optimal tariffs and strategic trade policy are simply attempts to capture this type of logic.

41. By way of comparison, in 1980, Toyota, Nissan, Honda, Mitsubishi, VW, Peugeot-Citroen, and Renault all sold in the neighborhood of 60 percent outside their home market, with Honda selling nearly 70 percent.

example of a tight oligopoly. Casual evidence of high profits (see fig. 3.1) and downward-inflexible prices are supported by numerous systematic studies suggesting implicitly collusive or leader-follower pricing behavior.[42] Nonetheless, GM never exercised the hegemonic domination over the auto industry that U.S. Steel exercised over the steel industry. Extensive competition for market share through styling changes, intensive advertising, and extensive dealer networks characterized the industry throughout the postwar era. Thus it is not surprising that, although the auto industry is collectively represented by the Motor Vehicle Manufacturers' Association (MVMA), each of these firms engages in extensive independent political activity.[43] By contrast, the integrated steel producers, with a slightly larger number of major producers, have pursued a much more coordinated and aggressive political agenda on the trade issue. In addition to the greater similarity in production and organizational structure among major integrated steel producers (compared to the auto majors), the steel industry has not had the tradition of corporate independence that has obtained in the auto industry from its founding to this day.

Until recently, U.S. auto producers have been economically confident of their ability to compete in any market. Their domestic political activity was focused primarily on resisting government attempts to regulate safety, emissions, and fuel economy. Prior to the late 1970s, trade policy was not a political priority of any of the auto majors. The industry's entrepreneurial tradition led it to generally support the trade liberalization program, and its success in turning back the import surge of the late 1950s without government intervention made it uninterested in the administered protection mechanisms. To the extent that it did pursue a trade policy agenda, the auto industry focused on support of liberalization in general and on access to closed foreign markets in particular. In fact, during the late 1960s and early 1970s one of the most contentious ongoing issues between the U.S. and Japanese governments was the desire, especially by Ford and Chrysler, to invest in Japan for local production.[44] However, as Japanese exports to the U.S. market surged in the late 1970s and could not be controlled by captive imports and new small car offerings, the industry began increasingly to seek protection. However, recall from section 3.1 that there was an important split in the industry: GM, confident of its long-run capacity to compete in the United States and intending to rely on imports of small cars from Japan in the short run, was not a supporter of protection; Ford, whose short-run small-car strategy depended primarily on Europe, was a strong proponent of protection. Chrysler was not active in this period because

42. Adams and Brock (1986) is a useful source for the more casual evidence of imperfect competition in the auto industry. For more systematic studies of the pricing behavior that explicitly tests collusive and/or leader-follower models, see Boyle and Hogarty (1975), Bresnahan (1981, 1987), Kwoka (1984), and Berndt, Friedlander, and Chiang (1990).

43. Actually, the MVMA no longer exists. In 1992, the name was changed to the American Auto Manufacturers' Association when the Japanese producers were expelled from the MVMA.

44. See Duncan (1973) for a convenient journalistic treatment of the attempts by U.S. auto firms to gain access to the Japanese market.

it had already received government intervention in the form of a government-backed loan, but it was to become one of the stalwarts of the protectionist cause.

Auto industry trade policy activism illustrates an important aspect of the political economy of protection in the United States: intersectoral reciprocal noninterference. Auto firms are major consumers of steel, glass, synthetic rubber, electronics, machine tools, and textiles, all of which are heavily involved in the politics of protection on their own accounts, and all of whom have received extensive protection. Nonetheless, the U.S. auto majors, prior to the onset of their own trade-related problems, never actively opposed protection to these key upstream sectors. Part of the difficulty is that there is no institutional point of access for antiprotection, except at the point of legislating the rules of administered protection. At least as important, however, is the widely held norm that firms experiencing competitiveness problems have a right to protection, and firms not experiencing such problems have no right to oppose that protection. That is, even though auto industry performance was affected by protection to a wide range of its inputs, neither the auto majors nor the MVMA violated the norm against interfering with that protection.

3.4.2   U.S. Labor, the Auto Regime, and Trade

The second major participant in the auto regime is organized labor—the UAW. In the early years of the twentieth century, the auto industry pursued an aggressively antiunion strategy, but the combination of the Depression and the Roosevelt administration led, through the efforts of the UAW, to industry acceptance of union organization. During World War II, the relationship between the firms and the UAW was closely regulated by the National War Labor Board, but when the war ended, a brief, though intense, struggle ensued over the shape of the labor relations component of the auto regime. For the purposes of this paper, the three aspects of labor relations in the postwar era identified by Katz (1985) are particularly significant. *Wage rules,* involving an annual improvement factor (intended to increase wages along with improvements in productivity) and cost of living adjustments (COLAs), led to steady increases in the wages and benefits paid to autoworkers and a wage differential between autoworkers and the average private sector production worker that held very steady at around 30 percent until the late 1960s. That is, as in the steel industry, the auto producers sought to insure stability in the industry by sharing the oligopolistic rents with labor. This premium led firms to use large-scale layoffs as a strategy for dealing with the highly cyclical demand that characterizes the auto industry (fig. 3.11 compares percentage changes in employment in manufacturing, motor vehicles, and autos).[45] However, the inflationary experience of the 1970s led to an explosion in auto industry wages that, along with increasing

---

45. It is interesting to note, in fig. 3.2, that the auto industry employment follows the same cycles as does manufacturing as a whole, but, as is noted in the text, with considerably greater volatility.

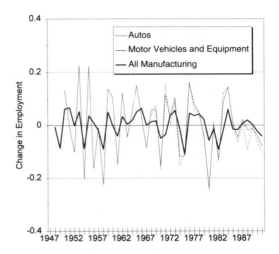

Fig. 3.11   Change in employment
Source: U.S. Department of Commerce, *Survey of Current Business* (Washington, D.C., various years).

import competition, rendered this element of the labor relations subregime unstable. Katz refers to the standardization of contracts across firms and across production facilities within firms as *connective bargaining.* This second aspect of labor relations in the auto industry, implemented through pattern bargaining, creates a highly hierarchical structure with national corporate leaders and national union leaders setting terms for the industry as a whole. The third key attribute of labor relations in the auto industry was *job control unionism:* that is, the channeling of union efforts to control the production process into detailed and legalistic efforts to define and regulate access to particular jobs. Not only did this render the production process inflexible from the perspective of management, but it also tended to alienate workers from the production process. Like the relationship between firms described above, the labor relations subsystem of the auto regime was both functional and stable as long as all major participants in the market were covered by the regime.[46]

Unlike the auto majors, the UAW (initially CIO-Auto Workers) was an active proponent of the trade liberalization program within the union movement, in the Democratic party, and in Washington from the end of World War II until the late 1960s.[47] This support was primarily related to the concern that a post-

46. See Katz (1985, chap. 2) for a useful discussion of the ways in which this system of labor relations served the interests of both labor and management in the postwar period prior to the shocks of the 1970s and early 1980s.
47. See Leiter (1961) and Donahue (1992) for general discussions of the politics of trade and protection within the U.S. union movement. In particular, both stress the strong support by CIO

war depression would lead to major reverses for the union movement and a belief that liberal trading relations would support continued output growth through export growth. The UAW, which left the AFL-CIO in 1967, was a consistent supporter of the trade liberalization program into the 1970s. For example, when the AFL-CIO strongly supported the Burke-Hartke legislation (1973), Leonard Woodcock spoke strongly against it. However, by 1980 the UAW joined Ford in filing the escape clause suit for protection against Japanese imports, and in the hearings on the 1988 Omnibus Trade and Competitiveness Act, Owen Bieber was one of the most strident opponents of the trade liberalization program and one of the strongest proponents of an aggressive trade policy.

Just as internationalization of auto competition undermined the relations among firms in the regime, the labor relations system was also threatened. Japanese competition affected U.S. labor relations in at least three important ways. First, considerable evidence suggested that relatively low labor costs were a significant part of the Japanese firms' competitive advantage. This led to a number of attempts by the U.S. firms to reduce labor costs. For example, GM attempted a "southern strategy" of shifting production facilities to states with a weak union tradition in the 1960s and 1970s, but the UAW was able to respond, maintaining virtually 100 percent organization of production workers in Big Three production facilities. More successfully, given the lower degree of success of the UAW in the auto parts industry, all three firms have spun off facilities engaged in parts production. The data in table 3.6 are fairly suggestive in this regard: the wage differential between production workers in auto production and in manufacturing has increased, but the share of production worker wages in value added in the final production of autos (SIC 3711) has fallen, as has the share of final motor vehicle production in total auto production (SIC 3711+3714). Second, it has been widely argued that the Japanese auto producers have developed a new management/production technology ("lean production") that produces higher-quality autos at lower costs.[48] Attempts by U.S. firms to implement mixes of team production, flexible machine tools, and robots in final assembly have met with considerable resistance from the UAW in many plants, and even when such programs have been implemented, many have been less than successful (Turner 1991, chap. 1; Keller 1993). Nonetheless, the evidence of Japanese success with less restrictive labor regimes has created additional tension in the structure of the auto regime. Third, the local production of autos by Japanese firms in the United States has raised both of these issues in even more striking ways as, at least to date, these firms have been successful at resisting union organization of their production

---

unions of the trade liberalization program, and Donahue stresses the leadership role of the CIO-Auto Workers.

48. The standard reference on this argument is the best-seller from MIT's International Motor Vehicle Program, *The Machine That Changed the World: The Story of Lean Production* (Womack, Jones, and Roos 1991).

Table 3.6   Employment Data for Auto Industry

Year	Auto Employment (thousands)	Auto Wage ($ per hour)	Auto Wage Bill/ Value Added (%)	Auto/ Manufacturing Employment	Auto/ Manufacturing Wage
1967	262.3	4.00	28.54	1.83	1.42
1968	272.4	4.29	27.53	1.88	1.43
1969	293.4	4.47	28.13	1.99	1.40
1970	245.3	4.82	31.25	1.75	1.44
1971	283.0	5.36	26.30	2.09	1.50
1972	284.0	5.79	28.90	2.02	1.52
1973	309.1	6.23	29.98	2.08	1.52
1974	262.2	6.93	32.89	1.79	1.57
1975	235.1	7.62	32.61	1.80	1.58
1976	273.8	8.45	29.87	2.01	1.62
1977	289.9	9.23	30.58	2.05	1.62
1978	303.5	10.12	31.03	2.06	1.64
1979	292.0	10.99	31.31	1.94	1.64
1980	220.6	12.63	39.08	1.55	1.74
1981	223.4	13.94	38.46	1.59	1.75
1982	193.5	14.45	34.04	1.52	1.70
1983	216.5	14.75	29.12	1.73	1.67
1984	247.6	14.46	29.49	1.86	1.57
1985	249.7	16.70	31.09	1.91	1.75
1986	233.8	17.22	25.93	1.82	1.77
1987	235.5	17.33	22.68	1.82	1.75
1988	213.6	18.68	21.06	1.62	1.83
1989	212.5	19.40	18.22	1.60	1.85
1990	200.0	20.31	20.55	1.54	1.88
1991	178.5	21.32	17.37	1.43	1.91

Source: U.S. Department of Commerce, Survey of Current Business (Washington, D.C.: Government Printing Office, various years), for SIC 3711 (motor vehicles and car bodies).

facilities, and they have begun to implement labor and supplier management strategies more like those found in Japan than like those found in the United States.

3.4.3   The U.S. Government, the Auto Regime, and Trade

The final major participant in the auto regime is the state. Although the U.S. government is not involved in direct corporatist arrangements of the sort that characterize auto regimes in, say, Germany and Japan, it remains a major participant.[49] Most obviously, the state stands behind any legally constituted ele-

49. Although the Japanese industry has been notable for its independence from MITI, relative to other sectors of Japanese industry, it is also the case that MITI has been heavily involved in the promotion of the industry and in attempts to restructure the industry. A useful short discussion can be found in Cusumano (1985, Introduction). The close relations between industry and the state, with a subordinate labor movement, have led Pempel and Tsunekawa (1979) to refer to Japanese corporatism as "corporatism without labor." The German case is more classically corporatist:

ments of the regime—for example, labor law. Similarly, it has been argued that American antitrust law (especially the Sherman Antitrust Act) that outlaws collusion but permits extensive vertical and horizontal integration has encouraged the creation of large, integrated firms in the United States (Bork 1978; Lamoreaux 1985).[50] Labor and antitrust law were not particular problems for the auto industry in the postwar period, and the industry did benefit from extensive road building and low gasoline taxes. As a result, given its size and significance, the auto industry has had a surprisingly small and relatively cooperative relationship with the state. This can be contrasted with the stormy relationship between the steel industry and the state. As consumerism and environmentalism became significant political forces, both of which focused significant parts of their political efforts on the auto industry, however, this relaxed relationship began to break down.

The trade policy goals of the U.S. government are harder to characterize. Prior to 1980 it would not be unreasonable to characterize the preferences of the U.S. executive as strongly Liberal. That is, the executive has aggressively pursued extensions of the trade agreements program and the GATT while opposing extensions of both legislated and administered protection.[51] While some of this may be attributable to the president's national constituency, it is more significant that, for the president, trade policy has been primarily a foreign policy issue and, because the preeminent foreign policy goal has been containment of Communism, the extension and protection (against protectionists) of the multilateral trading system has been seen as a key instrument in the pursuit of that goal. On the other hand, for Congress trade policy is primarily a domestic political issue. However, as long as the executive was able to attach trade policy to foreign policy the trade agreements program was relatively safe and

---

strong, centralized owners' associations face a strong, centralized union. The national government has rarely intervened in the auto industry, though state governments have been quite active and the "big three" banks (Commerzbank, Deutsche Bank, and Dresdner Bank) have also played a major role. Zysman (1983) presents an extensive discussion of the role of banks in policy making. See Hart (1992) for a useful discussion of industrial policies for the auto industry in the United States, Japan, France, United Kingdom, and Germany.

50. It is interesting to note that virtually all of the antitrust actions against auto firms have involved noncore activities of the firms. Thus, the 1953 suit against GM and the 1964 suit against Chrysler involved attempts to acquire the Euclid Motor Machine Company and Mack Truck, respectively; while the 1961 suit against Ford involved Electric Auto-Lite Company. Similarly, the Justice Department pursued GM over its putatively anticompetitive practices with respect to its financing arm (GMAC) from 1939 until the consent decree in 1952. Probably the most famous case, *United States v. General Motors* (1966), involved an attempt by a group of dealers to get GM to stop selling to a discount outlet. Compared with the steel industry, and given the concentration in the auto sector, the U.S. government's relationship to the auto industry in the post–World War II period appears benign.

51. There is some significant partisan variance. With the notable exception of Nixon, and possibly Bush, Republican presidents in the post–World War II period have continued the prewar pattern of greater protectionism (as revealed in commitment to the trade agreements program, accommodation of protectionist pressure, and voting record of appointees to the ITC) than Democratic presidents.

congressional protectionism could be controlled through a combination of presidential leadership and Democratic control of trade policy–relevant institutions.[52] However, as argued in section 3.1, executive leadership and congressional institutions broke down, for unrelated reasons, at the same time that protectionist pressure was increasing. As a result, Congress played a much more significant role in defining the trade policy preferences of the U.S. government.

3.4.4   Other Participants and Regime Environment

Of course, given the size and complex nature of auto production, there are many other participants in the auto regime. Upstream and downstream firms that are linked to auto production are certainly significant players in many aspects of the auto regime, though rarely with respect to trade policy. Similarly, local communities and governments in major auto-producing areas are often involved in the regime, but at least to this point, they have not been extensively mobilized on the trade issue the way the steel industry has mobilized the grass roots in its interests. What makes the auto industry interesting from the point of view of the NBER project is the entry into the regime of a new player that was not socialized to the regime and could not be informally regulated by the leader-follower structure or the union, or formally regulated by the U.S. government: the Japanese auto producers. The linkage of the U.S. market to the world market shattered every aspect of the postwar regime, creating a crisis with which the industry is still struggling.

To understand the significance of the Japanese threat to the auto regime, it is important to understand the global organization of that regime as well as the domestic organization. For a variety of reasons, both economic and political, markets for autos prior to the mid-1960s were primarily national (or at most regional). The interaction of taste and policy was essential here. As a result of government policies toward development of roadway systems, auto taxation, and petroleum taxation, consumers demanded very different automobiles in different countries. In the United States, extensive road building and low taxation of automobiles and petroleum led to demand for large, powerful, comfortable automobiles, with no particular demand for fuel efficiency. Europe and Japan, with less extensive road systems and much higher taxes led to demand for smaller, more fuel-efficient, more agile automobiles. Many of the European producers emphasized niche marketing, either for luxury automobiles (Daimler-Benz) or popular automobiles (VW); in Japan the auto producers emphasized the development of products for a growing market with a relatively low household income. In addition, with the exception of the United States, auto markets developed behind relatively high barriers to imports.[53]

52. Nelson (1989a) discusses the link between foreign policy and trade liberalization in more detail, while Nelson (1989c) discusses the role of congressional institutions and executive leadership.
53. The U.S. market had considerable natural protection because of the very different type of automobiles demanded by U.S. consumers.

As a result primarily of the existence of the Big Three U.S. producers, national governments outside the United States pursued two sorts of policy toward their national auto market. On the one hand, the governments of Canada, Britain, and Germany permitted extensive direct investment (primarily by Ford and GM); while, on the other hand, the governments of Japan and France attempted to restrict their markets to national producers.[54] Policies of the former type resulted in entry by U.S. majors and their participation in essentially oligopolistic regimes. Not surprisingly from a competitive standpoint, but interestingly given the difficulty the U.S. majors had in developing small cars in the North American market, in the United Kingdom and Germany the U.S. majors produced small cars of the sort demanded in those markets. As Quinn (1988) points out, these European auto markets were not particularly profitable for national or multinational firms because the relatively small national markets did not allow production at efficient scales. Nonetheless, the key firms in the industry (GM and Ford) were unwilling to surrender any open market to the other. The expectation was that growth in national income would lead to a rapidly expanding demand for automobiles, the exclusion from which could result in competitive disadvantages later.

In France and Italy, the policy of reserving the national market for nationally owned firms was associated with macroeconomic goals related to employment creation and balance of payments, as well as national prestige. As a result, the governments' goals were consistent with the maintenance of a stable, noncompetitive market. The result was relatively inefficient industries focused on the national and regional markets. In the Japanese case, while the government succeeded in reserving the national market for nationally owned firms, it did not succeed in its attempt to regulate entry by such firms. The result was a highly competitive auto industry that, from early in its postwar history, recognized the necessity of exporting to achieve the efficient scales of production necessary to compete in the national market. This strong export orientation, emerging from a highly competitive national market, was an essentially new element in the global auto regime. The first national auto regime to experience the adjustment crisis associated with export-oriented national producers was the most open national market, the United States.

3.5   Trade Adjustment Crisis in the U.S. Automobile Industry

The 1970s were a watershed for the auto industry. As we have just seen, from the end of World War II through the 1960s, the U.S. auto market was dominated by three firms in a classic tight oligopoly, with a shrinking fringe of small competitors (see fig. 3.12).[55] Over the course of the 1970s this structure, and the political economic system of which it was a part, unraveled com-

---

54. See Hart (1992) for a comparison of state policies in the auto (as well as steel and semiconductor) sector.
55. See White (1971) for a detailed analysis of the U.S. auto industry in this period.

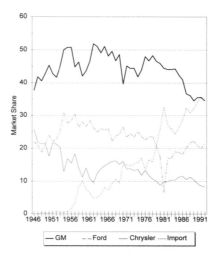

Fig. 3.12   Market shares—GM, Ford, Chrysler, and import
Sources: Ward's and *Automotive News.*

pletely. The attempt by the major actors in that political economic system to reestablish a profitable and stable political economic order is what we refer to as an adjustment crisis.[56] This section presents a brief review of the recent economic history of the auto industry and the evidence of sectoral crisis.

Much of the history of the U.S. auto industry can be told in the context of a product life cycle framework adjusted for large economies of scale in production, distribution, and marketing.[57] The early history of the industry was characterized by a large number of essentially craft producers selling to an unstable, specialist market. Henry Ford's recognition of the gains from standardization and large-scale production resulted in rapid growth in Ford Motor's market share. However, as the market expanded, Alfred Sloan was able to expand General Motors' market share dramatically, and surpass Ford as the industry leader in market share and profitability, by offering a wide array of products. Given the large minimum efficient scales in virtually all aspects of auto production (e.g., engine, transmission, frame, and body production and final assembly), growth of the market was essential to GM's strategy.[58] As figure

56. Note that we are using the expression "political economic system" to refer to the structurally local system anchored on the U.S. auto industry. That this system is part of a national and global political economic system is undeniable but essentially beyond the scope of this paper. Thus, as we will discuss in greater detail below, the primary actors in this system are the major auto producers (home and foreign), the UAW, and the relevant parts of the executive and legislative branches of government. Other actors include foreign governments, state and local communities and governmental organizations, and upstream and downstream industries related to the auto industry.

57. The notion of a product life cycle was originally developed by Vernon (1966) and Hufbauer (1966) and has since become standard fare in textbooks in international economics and marketing.

58. White (1971) argues that, in addition to the economies of scale in production and marketing, the risks associated with introducing new products in the auto industry mean that it is no longer possible to sustain a competitive position in this market with a single product line.

Fig. 3.13   Ratio of imports to apparent consumption and ratio of exports to U.S. shipments
Sources: USITC (1985c); USITC, "The U.S. Automobile Industry: Monthly Report on Selected Economic Indicators" (Washington, D.C., February of various years).

3.12 illustrates, the logic of scale worked itself out in the mature postwar U.S. market, with small U.S. producers being driven from the market. Perhaps most striking of all, the smallest of the Big Three, Chrysler, was saved from bankruptcy only through the exceptional agency of a government guaranteed loan.

As the demand for automobiles in the rest of the world rose over the middle years of the twentieth century, the U.S. industry served this developing market with both exports from the U.S. and local production. However, since the exports and imports constituted a tiny proportion of U.S. output (see fig. 3.13) and the foreign production was run essentially independently of the home market, the industry's relationship to the world market had little impact on its structure and dynamics in the United States. Furthermore, prior to the 1970s, the U.S. major producers seemed oblivious to the implications of the final part of the product life cycle: the emergence of global competition as the product and its production technology becomes standardized.

Prior to the mid-1980s, the story of international competition in the U.S. market is a story about small cars.[59] In the early postwar period, the U.S. majors consciously chose to not enter the small-car market.[60] Figure 3.14 from Abernathy et al. (1983, 53) clearly shows the basic economics of this decision: whereas small cars cost only slightly less than large cars to make, the price

59. White (1971, chap. 11) provides an excellent short treatment of the small-car market in the United States, on which the discussion presented here depends heavily.

60. In fact, both GM and Ford announced in 1945 that they would introduce small cars to serve what appeared to be a considerable market. Both firms began to design the cars and arrange for their production, and both canceled the projects in mid-1946.

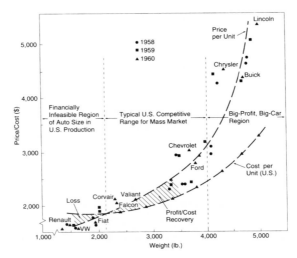

Fig. 3.14   Ratio of price to cost of production by size of car
Source: Abernathy et al. (1983).

differential was considerable. Furthermore, the U.S. majors believed that the demand for automotive transportation was sufficiently inelastic that most consumers with a preference for small cars would still buy large cars if small cars were not available. In addition, White (1971) argues that concern with the stability of the oligopoly encouraged the majors to stay out of the market. The concern was based on the fear that, while the small-car market might support one firm, if all three majors entered the market it would not be profitable for any of them. Since there was no legal way to share the profits if only one firm entered the small-car market, they cooperated by jointly staying out of the market.[61] The first response to the decision by the majors not to produce small

61. Knickerbocker (1973) develops this type of argument at greater length for the case of entry into small national markets. Specifically, he develops an entry concentration index to measure clustering (in time) of direct investments in a given national market and shows that low values of the index (i.e., low amounts of competitive entry) characterize both competitive and tight oligopolistic market structures, while high values of the index are characteristic of loose oligopolies. The notion is that an oligopoly with a small number of members is able to collude more effectively, while loose oligopolies are unable to do so, resulting in inefficient (from the industry's perspective) entry. As White (1971) argues, the decision by Ford and GM not to enter the market is evidence of, at least implicit, collusion within a tight oligopoly.

With respect to the Knickerbocker argument, the behavior of the U.S. majors with respect to small cars can usefully be compared to their behavior with respect to entry in foreign markets. The existence of a stable sectoral regime regulating the U.S. market clearly did not extend to regulation of foreign competition—U.S. firms made direct investments in a number of small to medium-sized markets that, at least at the time of entry, did not obviously support minimum efficient scale production (e.g., Canada, Mexico, and even the initial entry into European markets). The existence of nonregime firms and a nonparticipant state seems to have made it impossible to extend the U.S. regime to foreign markets.

cars was an attempt by U.S. independents, in the early and mid-1950s, to serve that market niche. However, none of the independents were able to offer their small cars at prices competitive with the low-price full-size models of the majors, and none (except Rambler, which was importing its small car from England) was still in the small-car market in 1955.

The effective response to the oligopolistic caution of the U.S. industry came from foreign (primarily European) producers. From less than 1 percent of apparent consumption through the mid-1950s, imports surged to over 9 percent in 1958 and to over 10 percent in 1959. The initial reaction by GM and Ford was to import small cars from their subsidiaries in Germany (Opel and Taunus) and England (Vauxhall and Ford). A more substantial response came in 1959 with the introduction of domestically produced small cars (e.g., Falcon, Corvair, and Valiant), which, while substantially reducing sales of captive imports and taking some sales from full-size cars, successfully reduced the market share of foreign cars to 6.4 percent in 1960 and 4.9 percent in 1961. With imports no longer a threat, the U.S. industry began to increase the size and weight of their "small" cars (Kwoka 1984). Thus, although imports had been held around 5–6 percent of the market in the early 1960s, 1966 saw an import share of nearly 10 percent and a steady rate of growth of imports to a 24 percent share in 1970. Again the U.S. majors responded first with captive imports and then with small cars of their own (Vega, Pinto, and Gremlin), but this time the environment was different.

Perhaps the most significant difference was the fact that foreign suppliers had by this point established marketing networks and solid reputations in the small-car market segment. Thus, even with locally produced small cars, the U.S. majors were unable to drive the import share below 20 percent.[62] Foreign producers, now including the Japanese, had replaced small independent firms focused on niche production for the U.S. market as the competitive "fringe" in the U.S. market. These foreign firms, and especially the Japanese with their strong export orientation, were not part of the U.S. auto regime: GM did not dominate the small-car segment (even in the United States) and was not globally organized to compete with the Japanese firms in a way that would permit enforcement of the U.S. pricing regime. Perhaps more important, the Japanese were not part of the labor relations subsystem of the auto regime, which in the late 1960s was undergoing significant strain. In the context of rapid inflation, the COLA clauses were generating large increases in wages at a time when poor labor relations were contributing to low productivity.[63] As the studies of

62. It should be noted that this 20 percent is a bit deceptive. During the late 1960s the largest source of "foreign" cars was Canada, and the growth in Canadian imports was a function of the rationalization of North American production by the U.S. majors as a result of the U.S.-Canada Automotive Products Trade Agreement. However, substantial increases in Japanese market share in the late 1960s and early 1970s were a cause of some concern.

63. Rothschild (1973) provides an excellent contemporary account of the pressures on the auto regime in the early 1970s. The account of labor relations at GM's Lordstown plant is particularly striking. It is also interesting to note that the Japanese do not figure prominently as competitors

competitiveness reviewed above suggest, the labor cost differential between U.S. and Japanese producers was a considerable source of competitive advantage for the Japanese. Thus, given the strains already existing in the labor relations system, it is easy to understand the profound impact of Japanese competition on that system. When the first oil price shock hit in October 1973, inducing a substantial demand shift toward the smaller cars in which foreign producers had established themselves as market leaders, the foundation was laid for another upward jump in foreign market share.[64]

In addition to changed competitive and demand conditions, U.S. firms also faced a changed regulatory environment. In the early and mid-1970s, at precisely the time that the industry was struggling to redesign old product lines and come up with new ones to compete with the foreign competition in the expanding small-car market, the federal government imposed strict emission control standards under the Clean Air Act of 1970 and binding corporate average fuel economy (CAFE) standards under the Energy Policy and Conservation Act of 1975. The most detailed study of the consequences of federal motor vehicle regulation, Crandall et al. (1986), concludes that, of these regulatory interventions, the emission control regulation had the most deleterious effect on the industry's competitiveness vis-à-vis foreign producers and that this effect was most severe precisely at the time when the industry was seeking to make a transition in its product offerings. Specifically, there were particularly severe quality problems in the 1974 model year producing changed expectations with respect to the quality of U.S. small cars in the future—expectations that the U.S. industry succeeded in meeting. Thus, when the second oil shock reinforced the shift to small cars in the late 1970s the jump in foreign market share was both greater and more permanent than that in the early 1970s—from a fairly stable 25 percent share in apparent consumption in the mid-1970s, the foreign share jumped to 28 percent in 1979 and 35 percent in 1980.

From the perspective of political economic analysis, it is important to understand that these regulatory shocks were independent of the changes in international competitive conditions. That is, while it is important to understand the negative consequences of auto regulation for the international competitiveness of the industry, it is also important to recognize that the form and magnitude of that regulation emerged from a political process in which the industry played a significant role—first of neglect and then of poorly considered political action. Well before imports became a problem for the American auto majors the consumer movement had begun to focus on the auto industry. One of the most famous documents of early consumerism is Ralph Nader's (1965) *Unsafe at Any Speed,* which criticized not only the quality of the product but the entire

---

for the U.S. market. Rather the primary concern, relative to the Japanese, seems to be the inability of the U.S. firms to compete beyond the increasingly saturated U.S. market.

64. Numerous studies establish a strong causal connection between the price of gasoline and the demand for small cars: Blomqvist and Haessel (1978), Carlson (1978), and Irvine (1983).

auto regime. The auto industry's attempt to smear Nader backfired badly, rendering their political attempt to short-circuit consumerist legislation considerably more difficult. That is, while the consumerist movement (and more generally the populist mentality of the 1960s) was exogenous to the auto regime, the response by the firms unquestionably worsened the situation. To a significant extent, the industry bears considerable responsibility for the hostile political economic environment in the context of which the initial import shock of the 1970s occurred.

Thus, the U.S. auto regime was collapsing. The product market oligopoly and the labor relations regime that relied on it were under pressure from international competition and from domestic populist sources. The government appeared to be increasingly hostile. By the mid-1970s the U.S. auto industry, along with the overall economy, was moving into a deep recession. Profits fell from around 20 percent (after-tax profit to stockholders' equity) for GM and Ford in 1978 to -4 percent for GM and -18 percent for Ford in 1980.[65] Similarly, employment in the motor vehicle industry fell from 925,000 to 714,000 employees. The industry needed a political instrument with which to reconstruct political economic order. "Unfair" Japanese competition was ideal. Japanese exporters were rapidly increasing sales to the U.S. market (see figs. 3.15A and 3.15B). From 8.5 million units sold in 1978, the U.S. industry sold 5.8 million in 1980. Over the same period, when most other foreign producers experienced little in the way of gains in the U.S. market, Japanese auto producers increased their shipments to the United States from 1.5 million to nearly 2 million units. Even though, as we have seen, foreign competition was not the most significant of the industry's problems, trade policy was politically ideal. The focus on foreign competition directed political attention away from problems of the industry's own making while simultaneously emphasizing the need for more flexibility from the government on domestic regulatory issues and from labor on both compensation and work rules. The emphasis on unfairness encouraged wider support in both government and civil society. Finally, protection was expected to have the effect of disciplining Japanese firms to participate in the U.S. regime, with the additional benefit of tariff-induced transfers from consumers to producers. In this situation, it is hardly surprising that the industry sought protection from Japanese competition.

Labor's support for protection is less understandable in the broader political economic context developed in this section. Other things being equal, labor could expect to share in the increased rents accruing to the industry, whether transferred from U.S. consumers or Japanese producers. Furthermore, the increased protection was expected to increase the share of Japanese sales in the U.S. market sourced from local production facilities—long a priority of

65. Average profit rates for manufacturing as a whole, for comparison purposes, were 15 percent in 1978 and 14 percent in 1980. Comparable numbers are not available for Chrysler which was already in a government bailout program. These figures, as well as those in the text, are reported in Adams and Brock (1986).

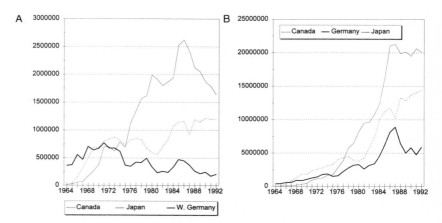

Fig. 3.15   Import volumes (A) and values (B) by country of origin—Canada, Japan, and West Germany
Sources: USITC (1985c); USITC, "The U.S. Automobile Industry: Monthly Report on Selected Economic Indicators" (Washington, D.C., February of various years).

the UAW under the assumption that such facilities would be organized by the union. However, both of these expectations relied on the more basic assumption that the auto regime would continue to function more or less as it had prior to the late 1960s. But we have seen that this assumption was, to a considerable extent, falsified by later events. The industry used Japanese competition as a justification for extracting concessions from labor that reduced its share of rents in the short run and weakened its bargaining position in the long run. At the same time, many of the new Japanese facilities were not unionized, further reducing UAW influence on the auto regime. Finally, the political focus on trade protection seems to have weakened labor's long-standing drive to increase plant and industry regulation by government.[66] Nonetheless, given the UAW's strong support for protection after a long history of active opposition, we must conclude that their evaluation of the benefits (in terms of increased rents and industry expansion) exceeded their evaluation of the possible costs.

The discussion of this section provides some insight into why the auto regime crisis beginning in the late 1970s came to be defined politically as a trade adjustment crisis in the face of compelling economic evidence that international competition was not the primary source of the industry's problems. While Japanese auto producers may not have constituted a fundamental threat to the existence of U.S. auto producers, they did constitute a fundamental threat to the political economic regime that regulated relations in the auto sector of the U.S. economy. In addition to responding directly to the most serious threat

66. Labor's attempts to increase the government's presence in the workplace can be understood, in part, as an attempt to shift the balance of power in capital-labor bargaining. See Noble (1986) for an extremely useful discussion of the politics of OSHA.

to the auto regime, defining the crisis in that regime as a trade adjustment crisis had the added benefit to the firms of justifying an attempt to reconstitute the labor-management system of the regime that had preceded the trade shock by at least a decade and of making labor an ally in the politics of adjustment. The next section provides a further illustration of this logic by considering the extension of the auto regime on a continental scale.[67]

3.6   Regulating the Japanese in the North American Market: APTA, CUFTA, and NAFTA

The story of the auto industry's role in North American integration is interesting in its own right, as well as with respect to the light it sheds on the issue of adjustment to crisis in the auto regime induced by Japanese competition. In the heat of the recent politics of the North American Free Trade Agreement (NAFTA), the rhetoric on all sides of the issue often lost sight of the facts that many U.S. industries (including the auto industry) were already operating on a continental scale and that international political frameworks for such integration were already in place for auto trade from 1965 under the Automotive Products Trade Agreement (APTA) and for trade and investment more generally from 1988 under the Canada-U.S. Free Trade Agreement (CUFTA).[68] APTA, and the politics related to APTA through the 1970s, resulted from political economic strain on the periphery of the auto regime, but with the entry of the Japanese into the North American market the key participants in the regime became active participants in the politics of CUFTA and NAFTA.

For all of the usual reasons (from national pride, to employment, to balance of payments/foreign exchange preservation) the Canadian and Mexican governments have both adopted import substitution policies with respect to both final auto assembly and the production of original equipment ("parts"). In both countries these policies were implemented with high tariffs and high domestic-content requirements. Furthermore, in both cases the governments were concerned to develop a local parts industry because of high value added in first-tier supply.[69] Thus, for example, prior to 1962 the Canadian government levied a 17.5 percent tariff on finished automobiles and parts but suspended the tariff on parts if the part was not produced in Canada and 60 percent of the factory cost of the final product was produced in Canada. Certain key parts (e.g., engines, automatic transmissions, brake linings, and piston facings) faced a tariff of 25 percent whether or not the content provision was met. Since both markets

---

67. We will focus on the U.S.-Canada case because there is a longer history of active political economic involvement by the industry and because it is more interesting from the regime-theoretic perspective adopted in this paper.

68. Implementing legislation for CUFTA was passed in late 1988 with a 10-year phase-in period. Thus, the full effects of the CUFTA regime are not to be felt until 1998. It is, of course, true that these agreements apply only to trade and investment between the U.S. and Canada.

69. "First-tier supply" refers to the assembly of components into major subassemblies that are then combined to produce the completed automobile.

were perceived by producers to be potentially lucrative in the future, all three U.S. majors had established themselves in both Canada and Mexico (with AMC also investing in Canada). The result in both markets was the same, straightforward extension of the oligopolistic regime with inefficient production (due to levels of output at below efficient scale) sold at high prices yielding relatively high profits. All major participants in the regime found this a satisfactory arrangement: the firms protected the stability of the oligopoly at satisfactory levels of profit; the unions and parts-producing firms were not forced to compete across national boundaries; the governments of Canada and Mexico had national auto industries at no apparent cost to the U.S. government.[70]

As a result of increased competition from European (especially British) auto producers in the 1950s the Canadian government became increasingly concerned with the competitiveness of the Canadian auto industry: "Automobile and parts production being an important source of income and employment, and the national car having become in many people's eyes a sign of industrial adulthood and a fetish of national identity, the difficulties of the Canadian automotive industry naturally elicited a variety of schemes for improving the situation" (Johnson 1963, 212). It was clear at the time that the essential problem was that Canadian producers were producing virtually the same range of products as they did in the United States at inefficiently small scales.[71] At the same time, the Canadian auto unions were lobbying aggressively for a government response that would protect employment in the industry. As a result, the Canadian government sought to improve the efficiency (and thus competitiveness) of Canadian auto production while increasing the level of production and employment in the auto sector.[72] To pursue these goals, the Canadian government opted for a scheme in which parts imports would be permitted as long as the producer (1) increased its exports by an amount equal to the value of the imports and (2) increased the input of other Canadian parts to maintain the 60

70. Of course, the losers were the Canadian and Mexican consumers who paid a substantial premium on automobiles for the questionable benefit of having a national auto industry.

71. Using White's (1971) estimate that minimum efficient scale (m.e.s.) for an assembly plant producing a single model was about 200,000 units per year and that a firm would want to produce at least two models, FW use the fact that in 1961 five firms were producing 327,000 autos to conclude that "the total output of the Canadian assembly industry in 1961 was less than White's estimate of m.e.s. for a single firm, and less than White's estimated m.e.s. for two plants" (172).

72. The explicit commitment to protection of the industry was justified on the grounds that since government policy had now created the conditions for extensive employment in the auto sector, it would be "socially irresponsible to adopt any policy which might lead to its drastic contraction" (Royal Commission on the Automotive Industry 1961, 48). This justification led Harry Johnson to comment: "Some day, someone should write an essay on the concept of responsibility in Canadian public life; suffice it to remark here that the implied doctrine that no mistakes should ever be admitted, and no errors ever corrected, if anyone might be hurt thereby is an exceedingly poor basis for intelligent policy-making, especially in an allegedly free-enterprise economy, and a perfect recipe for the preservation and augmentation of wasteful inefficiency and the strangulation of economic growth" (Johnson 1963, 213). Wonnacott (1965) offers a somewhat kinder evaluation of the Bladen plan and of the policy actually adopted.

percent domestic content. Initially (1962) this scheme was applied only to imports of engines and transmissions (both subject to 25 percent duty), but in 1963 the scheme was extended to encompass all imports of autos and parts.

While this policy had the intended effect of permitting Canadian firms to rationalize production while expanding employment and output, its effect on the North American auto regime was not so positive. Because final assembly firms "paid" for their increased imports by exporting to the United States, the segregation of national markets was broken down, and with it the universal acceptance of the regime by active participants. The arrangement continued to be acceptable to the final assembly firms, which were now able to arrange production somewhat more efficiently. Similarly, the arrangement met the Canadian UAW's concern that any policy to increase competitiveness should not result in economic losses to its membership, and it did not affect the core membership of the U.S. UAW. However, a number of U.S. parts suppliers experienced increased competition from Canadian parts producers as the North American majors substituted Canadian parts in U.S. production to "pay" for the export of U.S.-produced engines and transmissions. As a result, U.S. parts producers began to complain to congressional representatives, and in April 1964, Modine Manufacturing (a producer of radiators) filed a countervailing duty suit with the Treasury Department alleging that the Canadian rebate scheme constituted an export subsidy.[73] An affirmative finding would have put the U.S. government on a collision course with the Canadian government because the countervailing duty would have offset the Canadian scheme, undermining their auto policy.[74] Although the U.S. major producers all supported the Canadian policy and the U.S. government (with the possible exception of the Commerce Department) hoped to avoid levying duties, most experts were of the opinion that Modine's suit would be successful. In the context of the Kennedy Round of negotiations, the executive would have found it difficult to veto the recommendation for countervailing duties. While the Canadian government did not want to withdraw its auto policy and could not politically afford to be seen to knuckle under to U.S. pressure, it obviously wanted to avoid a trade war.

Thus, under a deadline imposed by the countervailing duty process, the U.S. and Canadian governments negotiated the APTA. The agreement that was finally negotiated was not a free trade agreement, but an asymmetric arrangement that essentially allowed the Canadian government to pursue its policy of rationalization and expansion of the Canadian auto industry without threat of U.S.-administered protection. Specifically, the United States agreed to permit duty-free access of Canadian-produced autos and parts if they met a 50 percent

73. Recall that, at this time, it was not necessary to prove injury to have a countervailing duty imposed.

74. See Keeley (1983) for a detailed description of the politics of both the duty remission scheme and the APTA.

North American content requirement.[75] On the other hand, for duty-free access to Canada, automakers were required to (1) maintain the same ratio of Canadian-produced autos to Canadian sales as prior to APTA (and specifically not less than 75 percent) and (2) maintain the level of domestic content that obtained in 1964. In addition, the Canadian government sought agreement to a 6 percent annual increase in Canadian output. However, the U.S. government found such a proposal unacceptable as part of an official agreement. As a result, the Canadian government negotiated side-agreements in the form of letters of agreement with the major producers that they would (1) increase Canadian value added by at least 60 percent of any growth in Canadian sales and (2) increase Canadian valued added by an additional C$260 million above the 1964 level, and above that necessary to meet the growth agreement, by 1968.

Keohane and Nye (1977, 207) report a comment by an American official to the effect that, "We knew about the Canadian plan to blackjack the companies, but we expected them to be better bargainers." But, of course, this misses the point. The firms were perfectly satisfied with this arrangement. The problem was not the firms, but the conflicting expectations of the U.S. and Canadian governments.[76] The U.S. government saw the Canadian safeguards as a temporary expedient intended to ease the transition to genuine U.S.-Canadian free trade in automotive products, while the Canadian government saw the safeguards as a permanent part of a market-sharing agreement that was itself part of industrial policy for the auto industry. Although the U.S. government regularly expressed dissatisfaction with Canada's unwillingness to phase out the safeguards, there was no pressure from the industry and so the safeguards stayed in place.

Under APTA the U.S. majors were, in fact, able to rationalize Canadian production. The number of different models produced in Canada and, more important, the number of models produced in each Canadian factory, were dramatically reduced.[77] It took the shock of Japanese entry into the North American market, and especially Japanese foreign direct investment, to produce active lobbying by the major auto producers and the U.S. UAW. We have already seen that U.S. protection, along with equivalent protection in Canada, led to decisions by the major Japanese producers to invest in the North American

75. Recall that we are using "parts" to refer to inputs for original equipment, not replacement parts. The latter were excluded from the arrangement completely because it proved impossible to find a formula that was satisfactory to U.S. and Canadian parts producers simultaneously.

76. In addition to Keeley (1983), see Wonnacott (1987) for a useful discussion of the conflicting expectations of the U.S. and Canadian governments with respect to APTA.

77. FW argue that, while there were efficiency gains from North American liberalization of auto trade, much of the expansion of Canadian auto production would have occurred in any case as a result of a growing market, a falling Canadian dollar, and relatively low costs of capital, labor, and inputs. However, FW's analysis does not take into account the fortuitous, for the Canadian industry, decision to specialize Canadian production facilities in new, small cars that were to be an essential part of the U.S. industry's response to Japanese imports. In any event, the core participants in the North American auto regime continued to be satisfied with its functioning.

market. The attempt to regulate such investment in a manner consistent with oligopolistic control of the North American market encouraged the auto producers to become politically active on an issue that would pit the U.S. UAW against the Canadian autoworkers' union (ultimately resulting in secession by the Canadian autoworkers and the formation of a new Canadian Auto Workers [CAW] union) and the U.S. government against the Canadian government.[78] Where the unions and the governments were primarily concerned with maximizing national shares of any new production or employment, the auto firms wanted to socialize the Japanese firms into the ways of the local oligopoly . . . as junior partners. As a result, where the main issue for the national unions and governments related to Canadian attempts to use the duty rebate scheme to encourage Japanese investment in Canada, the firms were more interested in defining the domestic-content rules and rules of origin to their advantage.

Where the Canadian duty rebate program of the early 1960s elicited objections only from the periphery of the auto regime (parts manufacturers), when Canada reintroduced rebates of duties on imports from Japan in exchange for Japanese exports *to the United States,* in 1984–85, during a period of auto regime crisis, the response by the U.S. UAW and the U.S. government was immediate. Although, as Wonnacott (1987) points out, the countervailing duty channel was no longer available since it was not clear that the U.S. industry could show injury under the new title VII regulations, the U.S. government sought to change the auto regulations through the negotiations on the broader CUFTA. The primary goals of U.S. negotiators, with respect to autos, were to construct a system with more symmetrical obligations for Canada and the United States, and to move toward regional free trade in autos. In addition, the U.S. majors and the UAW lobbied for stronger controls on Japanese firms producing in the North American market. The United States was successful with respect to all three goals.[79] CUFTA calls for duty-free trade between the United States and Canada in autos and parts following a 10-year phase-in. Because the tariffs created the barrier that made the duty remission an effective policy, the move to free trade in automotive products essentially accomplishes both of the first two goals. That is, U.S. auto and parts producers could theoretically shut down Canadian operations and serve the Canadian market duty free from the United States as long as they met CUFTA rules of origin. The only remaining reason to retain APTA producer status would be to be able to import third-country automotive products into Canada duty free. With respect to the last goal, after a phase-in period, CUFTA prohibits the introduction of new duty waivers and the granting of APTA producer status to any firm that did not

---

78. See Yates (1993) for a useful discussion of the labor politics of North American auto integration.

79. See Johnson (1993) for a detailed discussion of the effects of CUFTA on the rules regulating U.S.-Canadian auto trade. The ITC's report on rules-of-origin issues in NAFTA (USITC 1991) provides a convenient short discussion of these issues with a detailed discussion of rules of origin.

already have such status.[80] Thus, unlike U.S. majors that retain APTA producer status, Honda, Toyota, and Hyundai will be unable to import autos and parts into Canada from third countries (i.e., Japan and Korea) duty free, even if they meet domestic-content standards (all three have production facilities in Canada). Thus, without the duty waiver, to the extent that these firms source a considerable share of inputs from third countries, they will be at a competitive disadvantage vis-à-vis the North American majors. At the same time, producers that meet North American content requirements will have duty-free access to the entire North American market. Thus, third-country producers can serve the Canadian market duty free from the United States without meeting APTA safeguard conditions.

While CUFTA will be replaced by NAFTA, the latter essentially extends the main details of CUFTA to include Mexico. Some of the details of the transition have involved minor revision (e.g., the date for ending export-related duty drawbacks is pushed forward to 1996). The major change is that NAFTA rules of origin are more stringent than those in CUFTA, thus increasing somewhat the cost of non–North American firms in competition with North American firms.

While it is extremely unlikely that Canadian, or Mexican, production of autos and parts will be completely shut down, the conditions that led to booming Canadian auto sector production and employment in the 1980s are unlikely to continue.

3.7 Conclusions: The Future of the North American Auto Industry

We have seen that during the 1970s the auto industry, unable to respond to increased competition from Japanese firms, turned increasingly to the government for assistance. In addition to regulatory relief and a variety of lesser subsidies, the industry succeeded in convincing the government to provide direct restraint on Japanese imports. As a result of continuing recession, and thus low demand for autos, the trade restraints were not binding in the first two years of the program; however, the recovery of the economy led to surging demand, employment, and output. In addition, the industry was able to raise prices without fear of competition from the restrained Japanese producers. The result was historically unprecedented levels of profit, and equally unprecedented levels of executive compensation. At least in part as a consequence of this strategy of exploiting the protected market, when imports squeezed Big Three profits in 1985 and then when the market turned down again in 1986, the reservoirs of public sympathy were considerably lower.[81] Unfortunately for protectionists,

80. Export-based duty remission must end by January 1, 1994, and production-based duty remission by January 1, 1996.
81. Some have argued that the industry's reduced influence in the late 1980s and early 1990s results from the reduced size of the industry—both in financial and employment terms. While the industry certainly did shrink through the 1980s, it remains one of the largest and most concentrated

Japanese import quantities also turned down sharply in 1987 (see fig. 3.12), and although the Japanese government announced continuing observance of a 2.3 million unit VER in 1988 and 1989, this was not even close to binding.[82]

Through the mid- and late 1980s the Japanese increasingly served the North American market from North American production facilities. As a result, whereas the Japanese exported only 1.73 million automobiles and light trucks to the United States in 1991, their North American facilities sold 1.3 million units. Furthermore, this period also saw substantial increases in North American investment by Japanese parts producers. Thus, when sharp drops in sales in 1990 and 1991 led to sharp reductions in employment and large losses at GM and Chrysler, simple trade restrictions would accomplish neither the short-term goal of protection nor the longer-term goal of imposing regime discipline on foreign competition. The Bush administration, facing what appeared to be only modest reelection pressure, offered a scheme based on marginal adjustments in antitrust and trade enforcement. Specifically, the Justice Department announced that it intended to enforce U.S. antitrust laws against the U.S. operations of Japanese firms, with particular reference to the relationship between auto assemblers and their parts suppliers. In addition, the U.S. Customs Bureau ruled that autos produced by Honda in Canada did not contain sufficient domestic content to enter the United States duty free.[83] In the context of the NAFTA, negotiations on rules-of-origin issues for the auto industry, this was a fairly clear signal of protectionist intent. At the same time, the Treasury Department suggested changing the tariff on minivans from 2.5 to 25 percent. However, the industry and the UAW pushed for stronger restrictions in Congress. Representatives Gephardt (D-Mo.) and Levin (D-Mich.) proposed restricting Japanese firms' sales to 3.8 million vehicles, including local production with local content less than 50 percent. Senator Baucus (D-Mont.) proposed even stronger legislation, restricting sales to 3.6 million units with a 70 percent local-content requirement.

The essential point, however, is that unlike the period of the late 1970s and early 1980s, the public debate involved considerably more criticism of the U.S. firms, their management, and the UAW (Stokes 1992). High wage premiums for UAW workers and large executive pay increases combined with a continuing large quality differential between the products of Japanese and American auto firms tended to undercut public support for trade activism. When market conditions and the performance of U.S. firms improved in 1993, a widely

---

in the U.S. economy. Similarly, while UAW membership has declined dramatically, it remains a major force, with concentrations of influence in more or less the same places as it had in the late 1970s. The existence of sizable Japanese producers in the United States must have some influence, but their foreign ownership continues to create serious problems in projecting the influence that would normally be a correlate of their economic significance.

82. It is interesting to note, though, that whereas import quantity turned sharply downward in 1987, import values merely stabilized.

83. See Palmeter (1992) for a useful discussion of the details of this bizarre case.

leaked plan by Ford and the UAW to file antidumping charges against Japanese exporters was never advanced, and although Harold Poling and Owen Bieber suggested that the ITC self-initiate such an investigation, the issue has not been pursued.[84]

Ford, Chrysler, and, probably, GM emerged from the political economic crisis of the late 1970s and 1980s more competitive and more international. Relations with parts suppliers, the UAW, and dealers are still being worked out but appear to be moving toward new foundations that will permit both greater competitiveness and improved long-run relations. Along with substantial exchange rate adjustments, these changes have allowed the U.S. majors to increase market share and profitability of the North American market. This will undoubtedly lead many to conclude that the trade policy activism of the 1980s was a success. But such a conclusion is based on no more than the fallacy of post hoc, ergo propter hoc. It seems to me that there are two broad lessons of the auto experience in the 1980s. First, competition improves performance. It was the sustained competition from efficient, export-oriented Japanese firms that produced the changes in the U.S. auto producers that are being celebrated in the specialist auto media and the popular press today. There is not a shred of evidence that the innovations in organization, product, and process that define the new auto industry would have occurred without that competition. Second, trade policy was not essential to improved performance. The primary effect of trade activism, during the brief period in the mid-1980s when it was binding, was to transfer rents from consumers to foreign and domestic firms.

Also of interest are two political economic lessons. First, short of autarky, trade policy is not able to enforce a domestic sectoral regime. One of the striking things about the story told in this paper is that, while the auto industry got more or less what it wanted from the state, it was the U.S. industry, not the Japanese industry, that did the adjusting. Competition in the auto industry is now global competition. Given international sourcing strategies, multinational investment, joint ventures, and captive imports, even the meaning of a "national" industry has become unclear. The U.S. auto industry's attempt to resist this reality ultimately failed.[85] That is, the protection may have delayed the adjustment by a matter of five or six years, at considerable cost to the consumer, but the result is a global auto regime. The continued viability of GM, Ford, and Chrysler depends on their ability to adjust to this new reality and to participate in the creation of a political economic regime that does not rely on the policy actions of a single national government, even one as powerful as the United States.[86]

---

84. See *Inside U.S. Trade,* February 26, 1993, for a report of the comments by Poling and Bieber.
85. The attempts by the European industry and by Canadian labor to avoid this logic seem increasingly desperate, though both continue to fight the valiant fight.
86. Note that I am not arguing that government intervention has no effect. Quite to the contrary. We have seen in this paper that the effects can be considerable. The point is that, in the context of large changes in a complex industrial regime, it is virtually impossible to predict consequences even if control of such a regime were possible.

The second political economic lesson is that only strong, consistent executive leadership can protect Liberal trading relations. The auto case illustrates clearly that rhetorical commitment to free trade is far from sufficient. Without strong leadership, local interests dominate the process of making trade policy. This has always been true. One of the triumphs of the New Deal was the institutionalization in the executive and legislative branches of a commitment to trade liberalization. The breakdown of these institutions in Congress makes executive leadership all the more important. One of the failures of the Reagan administration, especially by comparison to the Carter administration, was the lack of leadership on trade. The result of this lack of a systematic trade agenda, as Niskanen (1989) cogently argues, was sequential response to crises and the institutionalization for the first time in the postwar era of fair trade as the practical core of administration trade policy. The irony of recent trade policy is that, whereas the Democrats and Republicans in Congress switched from their traditional positions on the trade issue, with the exception of Richard Nixon (and possibly George Bush), Democratic presidents have continued to show greater commitment to trade Liberalism than Republican presidents.[87] Industries will continue to seek transfers via the trade policy process and will continue to claim unfairness as part of their strategy. As the case of the Carter administration shows, only the commitment of real political resources, as well as rhetorical commitment, can substitute for the institutions that disappeared in the 1970s.

References

Abernathy, W. 1983. *The competitive status of the U.S. auto industry.* Washington, D.C.: National Academy Press.

Abernathy, W., K. Clark, and A. Kantrow. 1983. *Industrial renaissance: Producing a competitive future for America.* New York: Basic Books. (ACK)

Abernathy, W., J. Harbour, and J. Henn. 1981. *Productivity and comparative cost advantage: Some estimates for major automotive producers.* Report to the Transportation Systems Center, Department of Transportation. Cambridge, Mass. (AHH)

Adams, W., and J. Brock. 1986. The automobile industry. In *The structure of American industry,* ed. W. Adams, 126–71. New York: Macmillan.

Bergsten, C. F., and J. Williamson. 1983. Exchange rates and trade policy. In *Trade policy in the 1980s,* ed. W. Cline, 99–120. Washington, D.C.: Institute for International Economics.

Berndt, E., A. Friedlander, and J. Chiang. 1990. Interdependent pricing and markup

---

87. Because he did not serve a second term, the comparison may be a bit unfair to George Bush. While he did not show the commitment of a Johnson or a Carter, Bush did actively promote the GATT process, named consistently more Liberal members to the ITC than the Republican norm, and appeared committed to resisting demands for administered protection. On the other hand, the Tokyo trip is so extreme an example of traditional Republican trade behavior as to cause one to wonder about the trade policy content of the second term. Should Clinton prove to have more in common with the Democratic party in Congress than with the executive tradition, history may date the transition with Nixon and look on the Carter–Reagan period as the anomaly.

behavior: An empirical analysis of GM, Ford and Chrysler. NBER Working Paper no. 3396. Cambridge, Mass.: National Bureau of Economic Research.

Berry, S., J. Levinsohn, and A. Pakes. 1993. Automobile prices and market equilibrium, part I and II. NBER Working Paper no. 4264. Cambridge, Mass.: National Bureau of Economic Research.

Bhagwati, Jagdish, Elias Dinopoulos, and Kar-yiu Wong. 1992. Quid pro quo foreign investment. *American Economic Review* 82 (2): 186–90.

Blomqvist, A., and W. Haessel. 1978. Small cars, large cars, and the price of gasoline. *Canadian Journal of Economics* 11 (3): 470–89.

Bork, Robert. 1978. *The antitrust paradox: A policy at war with itself.* New York: Basic.

Boyle, S., and T. Hogarty. 1975. Pricing behavior in the American automobile industry, 1957–1971. *Journal of Industrial Economics* 24 (2): 81–95.

Branson, W. 1988. Sources of misalignment in the 1980s. In *Misalignment of exchange rates,* ed. Richard Marston, 9–31. Chicago: University of Chicago Press.

Bresnahan, T. 1981. Departures from marginal cost pricing in the American automobile industry. *Journal of Econometrics* 17:201–27.

———. 1987. Competition and collusion in the American automobile oligopoly: The 1955 price war. *Journal of Industrial Economics* 35:437–55.

Bresnahan, T., and V. Ramey. 1993. Segment shifts and capacity utilization in the U.S. automobile industry. *American Economic Review* 83 (2): 213–18.

Bryan, M., and O. Humpage. 1984. Voluntary export restraints: The cost of building walls. *Economic Review* (Federal Reserve Bank of Cleveland) Summer: 17–37.

Campbell, J., J. R. Hollingsworth, and L. Lindberg, eds. 1991. *Governance of the American economy.* Cambridge: Cambridge University Press.

Carlson, R. 1978. Seemingly unrelated regression and the demand for automobiles of different sizes, 1965–1975: A disaggregate approach. *Journal of Business* 51 (2): 243–62.

Citrin, D. 1985. Exchange rate changes and exports of selected Japanese industries. *IMF Staff Papers* 32 (3): 404–29.

Clifton, E. 1985. Real exchange rates, import penetration, and protectionism in industrial countries. *IMF Staff Papers* 32 (3): 513–36.

Cole, R., and T. Yakushiji. 1984. *The American and Japanese industries in transition: Report of the Joint U.S.-Japan Automotive Study.* Ann Arbor: Center for Japanese Studies, University of Michigan.

Collyns, C., and S. Dunaway. 1987. The cost of trade restraints: The case of Japanese automobile exports to the U.S. *IMF Staff Papers* 34 (1): 150–75.

Corden, W. M. 1984. *The revival of protectionism.* New York: Group of 30.

Coughlin, C. 1985. Domestic content legislation: House voting and the economic theory of regulation. *Economic Inquiry* 23:437–48.

Crandall, R. 1984. Import quotas and the auto industry: The costs of protection. *Brookings Review* 2 (4): 8–16.

———. 1987. The effects of U.S. trade protection for autos and steel. *Brookings Papers on Economic Activity,* no. 1: 271–88.

Crandall, R., H. Gruenspecht, T. Keeler, and L. Lave. 1986. *Regulating the automobile.* Washington, D.C.: Brookings Institution.

Cusumano, Michael. 1985. *The Japanese automobile industry: Technology and management at Nissan and Toyota.* Boston: Harvard University Press.

Deardorff, A., and R. Stern. 1986. *The Michigan model of world protection and trade.* Cambridge: MIT Press.

de Melo, J., and D. Tarr. 1992. *A general equilibrium analysis of U.S. foreign trade policy.* Cambridge: MIT Press.

———. 1993. Industrial policy in the presence of wage distortions: The case of the U.S. auto and steel industries. *International Economic Review* 34 (4): 833–51.

Dinopoulos, E., and M. Kreinin. 1988. Effects of the U.S.-Japan auto VER on European prices and on U.S. welfare. *Review of Economics and Statistics* 70 (3): 484–91.

Dixit, A. 1988. Optimal trade and industrial policy for the U.S. automobile industry. In *Empirical Research in International Trade*, ed. R. Feenstra, 141–69. Cambridge: MIT Press.

Donahue, P. 1992. "Free trade" unions and the state: Trade liberalization's endorsement by the AFL-CIO, 1943–1962. *Research in Political Economy* 13:1–73.

Dornbusch, R., and J. Frankel. 1987. Macroeconomics and protection. In *U.S. trade policies in a changing world economy*, ed. R. Stern, 77–130. Cambridge: MIT Press.

Duncan, W. 1973. *U.S.-Japan automobile diplomacy: A study in economic confrontation*. Cambridge, Mass.: Ballinger.

Eichengreen, B. 1988. International competition in the products of U.S. basic industries. In *The United States in the world economy*, ed. M. Feldstein, 279–353. Chicago: University of Chicago Press.

Falvey, R. 1979. The composition of trade within import-restricted product categories. *Journal of Political Economy* 87 (5): 1105–14.

Feenstra, R. 1984. Voluntary export restraint in U.S. autos, 1980–81: Quality, employment and welfare effects. In *The structure and evolution of recent U.S. trade policies*, ed. R. Baldwin and A. Krueger, 35–65. Chicago: University of Chicago Press.

———. 1985. Automobile prices and protection: The U.S.-Japan trade restraint. *Journal of Policy Modeling* 7 (1): 49–68.

———. 1988a. Gains from trade in differentiated products: Japanese compact trucks. In *Empirical methods for international trade*, ed. R. Feenstra, 120–39. Cambridge: MIT Press.

———. 1988b. Quality change under trade restraints in Japanese autos. *Quarterly Journal of Economics* 103 (1): 131–46.

———. 1989. Symmetric pass-through of tariffs and exchange rates under imperfect competition: An empirical test. *Journal of International Economics* 27 (1/2): 25–45.

Feldstein, M. 1986. The budget deficit and the dollar. In *NBER Macroeconomics Annual—1986*, ed. S. Fischer. Cambridge: MIT Press.

Flink, J. J. 1988. *The automobile age*. Cambridge: MIT Press.

Flynn, M. 1984. Estimating comparative compensation costs and their contribution to the manufacturing cost differences. Working Paper Series, no. 21. Center for Japanese Studies, University of Michigan.

Fuss, M., S. Murphy, and L. Waverman. 1992. The state of North American and Japanese motor vehicle industries: A partially calibrated model to examine the impacts of trade policy changes. NBER Working Paper no. 4225. Cambridge, Mass.: National Bureau of Economic Research.

Fuss, M., and L. Waverman. 1992. *Costs and productivity in automobile production: The challenge of Japanese efficiency*. New York: Cambridge University Press. (FW)

Gagnon, J., and M. Knetter. 1992. Markup adjustment and exchange rate fluctuations: Evidence from panel data on automobile exports. NBER Working Paper no. 4123. Cambridge, Mass.: National Bureau of Economic Research.

Gomez-Ibanez, J., and D. Harrison. 1982. Imports and the future of the U.S. auto industry. *American Economic Review* 73 (3): 319–23.

Gomez-Ibanez, J., R. Leone, and S. O'Connell. 1983. Restraining auto imports: Does anyone win? *Journal of Policy Analysis and Management* 2:196–218.

Habermas, Jürgen. 1973. *Legitimation crisis*. Boston: Beacon.

Halberstam, D. 1986. *The reckoning*. New York: Morrow.

Hart, J. 1992. *Rival capitalists: International competitiveness in the United States, Japan, and Western Europe*. Ithaca, N.Y.: Cornell University Press.

Hufbauer, G. C. 1966. *Synthetic materials and the theory of international trade*. Cambridge: Harvard University Press.

Hufbauer, G. C., D. Berliner, and K. Elliott. 1986. *Trade protection in the United States.* Washington, D.C.: Institute for International Economics.

———. 1993. *Trade protection in the United States,* 2d ed. Washington, D.C.: Institute for International Economics.

Hunker, J. A. 1983. *Structural change in the U.S. automobile industry.* Lexington, Mass.: Heath.

Irvine, F. 1983. Demand equations for individual new car models estimated using transactions prices, with implications for regulatory issues. *Southern Economic Journal* 49:764–82.

Johnson, H. G. 1963. The Bladen Plan for increased protection of the Canadian automotive industry. *Canadian Journal of Economics and Political Science* 29 (2): 212–38.

Johnson, J. 1993. The effect of the Canada-U.S. Free Trade Agreement on the auto pact. In *Driving continentally: National policies and the North American auto industry,* ed. M. A. Molot, 255–83. Ottawa: Carleton University Press.

Kabashima, I., and H. Sato. 1986. Local content and congressional politics: Interest group theory and foreign policy implications. *International Studies Quarterly* 30 (2): 295–324.

Kaplan, Daniel. 1986. Automobiles. In *Has trade protection revitalized domestic industries?* by D. Kaplan, chap. 5. Washington, D.C.: Congressional Budget Office.

Katz, H. 1985. *Shifting gears: Changing labor relations in the U.S. automobile industry.* Cambridge: MIT Press.

Katz, H., T. Kochan, and J. Keefe. 1987. Industrial relations and productivity in the U.S. automobile industry. *Brookings Papers on Economic Activity,* no. 3: 685–727.

Keeley, J. 1983. Cast in concrete for all time? The negotiation of the auto pact. *Canadian Journal of Political Science* 16 (2): 281–98.

Keller, M. 1993. *Collision: GM, Toyota, Volkswagen and the race to own the 21st century.* New York: Currency Doubleday.

Keohane, R., and J. Nye. 1977. *Power and interdependence.* Boston: Little, Brown.

Kinder, D., and D. R. Kiewiet. 1979. Economic discontent and political behavior: The role of personal grievances and collective economic judgements in congressional voting. *American Journal of Political Science* 23 (3): 495–527.

———. 1981. Sociotropic politics: The American case. *British Journal of Politics* 11:129–61.

Knetter, M. 1989. Price discrimination by U.S. and German exporters. *American Economic Review* 79 (1): 198–210.

———. 1992. Multinationals and pricing to market behavior. In *Multinationals in the new Europe and global trade,* ed. M. Klein and P. J. J. Welfens, 65–87. Berlin: Springer.

———. 1993. International comparisons of pricing to market behavior. *American Economic Review* 83 (3): 473–86.

Knickerbocker, F. 1973. *Oligopolistic reaction and multinational enterprise.* Cambridge: Graduate School of Business Administration, Harvard University.

Kreinin, M. 1982. U.S. comparative advantage in motor vehicles and steel. In *Michigan fiscal and economic structure,* ed. H. Brazer and D. Laren. Ann Arbor: University of Michigan Press.

———. 1984. Wage competitiveness in the U.S. auto and steel industries. *Contemporary Policy Issues* 4 (1): 39–50.

Krishna, K., K. Hogan, and P. Swagel. 1989. The non-optimality of optimal trade policies: The U.S. automobile industry revisited, 1979–1985. NBER Working Paper no. 3118. Cambridge, Mass.: National Bureau of Economic Research.

Kwoka, J. 1984. Market power and market change in the U.S. automobile industry. *Journal of Industrial Economics* 32 (4): 509–22.

Lamoreaux, Naomi. 1985. *The great merger wave in American business.* New York: Cambridge University Press.

Leiter, R. 1961. Organized labor and the tariff. *Southern Economic Journal* 28 (1): 55–65.

Lewis-Beck, M. 1988. Economics and the American voter: Past, present, future. *Political Behavior* 10 (1): 5–21.

Marks, S., and J. McArthur. 1989. Empirical analyses of the determinants of protection: A survey and some new results. In *International trade policies: Gains from exchange between economics and political science,* ed. J. Odell and T. Willett, 105–39. Ann Arbor: University of Michigan Press.

Marston, Richard, ed. 1988. *Misalignment of exchange rates.* Chicago: University of Chicago Press.

———. 1990. Pricing to market in Japanese manufacturing. *Journal of International Economics* 29 (3/4): 217–36.

McArthur, J., and S. Marks. 1988. Constituent interest vs. legislator ideology: The role of political opportunity cost. *Economic Inquiry* 26: 461–70.

McKinnon, R. 1987. Protectionism and the misaligned dollar: The case for monetary coordination. In *The new protectionist threat to world welfare,* ed. D. Salvatore, 367–88. Amsterdam: North-Holland.

Molot, M. A., ed. 1993. *Driving continentally: National policies and the North American auto industry.* Ottawa: Carleton University Press.

Nelson, D. 1986. Social choice in the tropics. Part I: Aggregation of political preferences. Part II: State production of political output. Washington, D.C.: World Bank (MADIA Project). Manuscript.

———. 1989a. Domestic political preconditions of U.S. trade policy: Liberal structure and protectionist dynamics. *Journal of Public Policy* 9 (1): 83–108.

———. 1989b. On the high track to protection: The U.S. automobile industry, 1979–1981. In *Pacific dynamics,* ed. S. Haggard and C. Moon, 97–128. Boulder, Colo.: Westview.

———. 1989c. The political economy of trade policy. *Economics and Politics* 1 (3): 301–14.

Niskanen, W. 1988. *Reaganomics: An insider's account of the policies and the people.* New York: Oxford University Press.

Noble, Charles. 1986. *Liberalism at work: The rise and fall of OSHA.* Philadelphia: Temple University Press.

Obstfeld, M. 1985. Floating exchange rates: Experience and prospects. *Brookings Papers on Economic Activity,* no. 2: 369–450.

Ohno, K. 1989. Export pricing behavior of manufacturing: A U.S.-Japan comparison. *IMF Staff Papers* 36 (3): 550–79.

Palmeter, N. D. 1992. The Honda decision: Rules of origin turned upside down. *Free Trade Observer,* no. 32A: 513–23.

Pempel, T. J., and K. Tsunekawa. 1979. Corporatism without labour: The Japanese anomaly. In *Trends toward corporatist intermediation,* ed. P. Schmitter and G. Lehmbruch. Beverly Hills, Calif.: Sage.

Quinn, D. P. 1988. *Restructuring the auto industry: A study of firms and states in modern capitalism.* New York: Columbia University Press.

Reich, R. 1985. Bailout: A comparative study in law and industrial structure. *Yale Journal on Regulation* 2 (2): 163–224.

Reich, R., and J. Donahue. 1985. *New deals: The Chrysler revival and the American system.* New York: Basic.

Richardson, J. D. 1988. Exchange rates and U.S. auto competitiveness. In *Misalignment of exchange rates,* ed. Richard Marston, 215–40. Chicago: University of Chicago Press.

Rodriguez, C. A. 1979. The quality of imports and the differential welfare effects of tariffs, quotas, and quality control as protective devices. *Canadian Journal of Economics* 12 (3): 439–49.

Rothschild, E. 1973. *Paradise lost: The decline of the auto-industrial age.* New York: Random House.

Royal Commission on the Automotive Industry. 1961. Report (The Bladen report). Ottawa: The Queen's Printer.

Smith, R. P. 1975. *Consumer demand for cars in the USA.* Cambridge: Cambridge University Press.

Stockman, D. 1986. *The triumph of politics: How the Reagan revolution failed.* New York: Harper & Row.

Stokes, B. 1992. Protection—for a price. *National Journal,* April 4, 794–99.

Tarr, D., and M. Morkre. 1984. *Aggregate costs to the U.S. of tariffs and quotas on imports.* Washington, D.C.: Federal Trade Commission.

Turner, L. 1991. *Democracy at work: Changing world markets and the future of labor unions.* Ithaca, N.Y.: Cornell University Press.

U.S. Congress. House. Committee on Ways and Means. Subcommittee on Trade. 1980. *World auto trade: Current trends and structural problems.* Serial no. 96–78. Washington, D.C.: Government Printing Office.

U.S. Federal Trade Commission. 1984. *Report of the Bureaus of Competition and Economics concerning the General Motors/Toyota joint venture,* 3 vols. Washington, D.C.: U.S. Federal Trade Commission.

USITC (U.S. International Trade Commission). 1980. Certain motor vehicles and certain chassis and bodies therefor: Report to the president on investigation TA-201-44 under section 201 of the Trade Act of 1974. USITC Publication no. 1110. Washington, D.C.: U.S. International Trade Commission.

———. 1985a. The internationalization of the automobile industry and its effects on the U.S. auto industry. USITC Publication no. 1712. Washington, D.C.: U.S. International Trade Commission.

———. 1985b. A review of recent developments in the U.S. automobile industry including an assessment of the Japanese voluntary restraint agreement. USITC Publication no. 1648. Washington, D.C.: U.S. International Trade Commission.

———. 1985c. The U.S. automobile industry: U.S. factory sales, imports, exports, apparent consumption, suggested retail prices, and trade balances for selected countries in motor vehicles, 1964–1984. USITC Publication no. 1762. Washington, D.C.: U.S. International Trade Commission.

———. 1986. U.S. trade related employment, 1978–1984. USITC Publication no. 1855. Washington, D.C.: U.S. International Trade Commission.

———. 1991. Rules of origin issues related to NAFTA and the North American automotive industry. USITC Publication no. 2460. Washington, D.C.: U.S. International Trade Commission.

Vernon, R. 1966. International investment and international trade in the product cycle. *Quarterly Journal of Economics* 80 (2): 190–207.

Weatherford, S. 1983. Economic voting and the "symbolic politics" argument: A reinterpretation and synthesis. *American Political Science Review* 77 (1): 158–74.

Westin, R. B. 1975. Empirical implications of infrequent purchase behavior in a stock adjustment model. *American Economic Review* 65 (3): 384–96.

White, H. 1981a. Production markets as induced role structures. In *Sociological methodology—1981,* ed. S. Leinhardt, 1–57. San Francisco: Jossey Bass.

—————. 1981b. Where do markets come from? *American Journal of Sociology* 87 (3): 517–47.

White, L. 1971. *The automobile industry since 1945.* Cambridge: Harvard University Press.

—————. 1982. The automobile industry. In *The structure of American industry,* ed. W. Adams, 136–90. New York: Macmillan.

Willig, R., and M. Dutz. 1987. US—Japanese VER: A case study from a competition policy perspective. In *The costs of restricting imports,* 30–69. Paris: Organisation for Economic Co-operation and Development.

Winham, G., and I. Kabashima. 1982. The politics of U.S.-Japanese auto trade. In *Coping with U.S.-Japanese economic conflicts,* ed. I. M. Destler and H. Sato, 73–119. Lexington, Mass.: Heath.

Winston, C., and Associates. 1987. *Blind intersection? Policy and the U.S. automobile industry.* Washington, D.C.: Brookings Institution.

Womack, J., D. Jones, and D. Roos. 1990. *The machine that changed the world.* New York: Harper-Collins.

Wonnacott, P. 1965. Canadian automotive protection: Content provisions, the Bladen plan, and recent tariff changes. *Canadian Journal of Economics and Political Science* 31 (1): 98–116.

—————. 1987. *U.S. and Canadian auto policies in a changing world environment.* Toronto and Washington, D.C.: Canadian-American Committee.

Wonnacott, P., and R. Wonnacott. 1967. The Automotive Agreement of 1965. *Canadian Journal of Economics and Political Science* 32 (2): 269–84.

Yates, C. 1993. Public policy and Canadian and American auto workers: Divergent fortunes. In *Driving continentally: National policies and the North American auto industry,* ed. M. A. Molot, 209–29. Ottawa: Carleton University Press.

Zysman, J. 1983. *Governments, markets and growth.* Ithaca, N.Y.: Cornell University Press.

Comment   Anne E. Brunsdale and Randi Boorstein

In this paper, Douglas Nelson provides a tremendous synthesis of information and an excellent and thorough review of papers having to do with international auto trade.

We agree with the author's main conclusion (1) that trade policy was not successful in achieving the long-run political goal of disciplining Japanese competition and (2) that it was competition, not trade policy, that spurred the U.S. industry to improve quality and lower costs. However, these points are not supported well by the literature survey. Rather, the conclusion seems almost tangential. The paper would benefit from a more focused approach that allows the conclusion to flow from the material. The second major conclusion, that strong and consistent executive leadership is needed to protect liberal trade, is

Anne E. Brunsdale is former chairman of the U.S. International Trade Commission. Randi Boorstein, currently an economist at the Federal Trade Commission, formerly was senior economics advisor to Anne E. Brunsdale at the U.S. International Trade Commission.

also true. However, we challenge the generalization that Democrats are more likely than Republicans to be "free trade" executives (section 3.7).

1. Nelson's point that protection did not work can be viewed from different perspectives. For example, the protection was not tough enough. Clearly, there is some combination of trade policy and foreign investment restrictions that could have ensured high profits to the U.S. industry as long as they remained in effect. However, the U.S. government was unwilling to impose those kinds of high costs on U.S. consumers or to grant such special treatment to the Big Three. The government was also unwilling to classify Japanese transplants as outside the U.S. auto industry, showing that its auto policy was more sensitive to the jobs issue than to the profit issue.

2. While the paper touches on the quality-upgrading literature (i.e., Feenstra), it does not mention the positive effect U.S. restrictions had on Japanese firms and their ability to move into the mainstream in the eyes of U.S. consumers. In the early 1980s it became very clear to consumers that Japanese cars were of higher quality and more reliable than most U.S. cars. That, coupled with the executive bonuses mentioned in the paper, made it difficult for politicians to make a convincing case against Japanese auto imports. Too many American consumers were choosing Japanese cars. The auto market is very different from a commodity market, such as steel, where the ultimate consumer does not have the same kind of visible preferences.

At some point, when it became clear that the Japanese auto industry was doing a better job than the U.S. industry, the emphasis of the Big Three and protectionist politicians shifted to accusing Japanese of blocking U.S. imports into Japan. That was needed to provide some foundation for U.S. protection.

3. The welfare analysis section (section 3.3) could be beefed up and discussed more fully. As policymakers confronted with different conclusions by highly respected economists, we would like very much to know whether one approach, and which one, is more reliable than the others. Another, more picky point is that the section on comparative advantage comparing costs (tables 3.2 and 3.3) concludes that unit labor cost in U.S. autos versus U.S. manufacturing is higher than that same ratio for Japan. However, the numbers seem very unreliable for such a conclusion. If one looks at 1978 rather than 1980, the unit labor cost in Japanese autos looks comparatively high.

4. The political economy conclusions are a bit simplistic, although it is clear that politicians do not maximize social welfare functions, as defined in theoretical terms. Economists looking at overall welfare always assume some costless redistribution scheme that can leave the protected industry as well off as it would be with protection and leave everyone else better off. In reality, of course, the redistribution does not happen: protection is not usually replaced with another less costly alternative. Therefore, politicians support their constituents; for example, Michigan politicians support the auto industry. Politicians are willing to trade protection of one industry for protection of another (textiles

for autos, or perhaps for other local legislation). Thus politicians in all protected sectors help each other.

Economists, assuming they believe that trade protection is injurious, may be less influential than they could otherwise be because so much effort is concentrated on finding exceptions where trade policy can help a country's welfare to improve. For example, the whole Krugman strategic trade debate was picked up by the popular press and by special interest groups looking for trade protection. While interesting from a theoretical point of view, the concentration on exceptions to the rule may actually confuse the debate for policymakers.

5. We disagree with Nelson's conclusion that administrated protection (section 201 and title VII) plays a fundamental role in supporting the liberalization process. Particularly in recent years, dumping cases and dumping regimes have proliferated. They are a very dangerous form of protection because once the rules are spelled out and once a set of commissioners is in place, there is no check on their use.

- Duties tend to be very high, and there is no sunset provision on those duties.
- Specific countries can be targeted (e.g., China and Japan) so that there is no global outcry over their use.
- In the case of Eastern Europe and the former Soviet Union, the threat of dumping is likely to lead to restrictive agreements such as the uranium and aluminum agreements. Why? Because these industries are likely to sell their products below cost (as defined by the Department of Commerce) during their transition to fully operational market economies.
- With respect to autos, the Big Three have difficulty prevailing in an antidumping suit because Japanese transplants are treated as part of the U.S. auto industry, and U.S. automakers' production in Canada is not. Also, the Big Three have been making money in recent years. The minivans case, although resulting in a negative determination, did lead to price increases in Japanese minivans.

6. As the author discusses, big business and unions were not pushing for protection for most of the postwar era. Then energy shocks, combined with the rise in the value of the dollar, created unprecedented pressure to protect certain U.S. industries. While one can fault the Reagan and Bush administrations for certain trade policy actions, they certainly cannot be blamed for the Multi-Fiber Arrangement or for steel restrictions that had been in place for many years. Moreover, Bush deserves most of the credit for the North American Free Trade Agreement (NAFTA), for keeping the Congress at bay, for holding Super 301 initiatives to a minimum, and for appointing some free trade commissioners. (One should keep in mind that all commissioners must be approved by Congress. Congress would not approve Baldwin in the 1980s.)

In addition, it may be harder for a Republican than for a Democrat to keep the Democratic Congress in line for free trade initiatives. It is likely that Democratic opposition to NAFTA would have been stronger if Bush had been making the proposal.

Comment   Richard N. Cooper

Nelson has written a fine paper, blending traditional economic analysis, political analysis, and analysis of regime stability and stress. I learned much and have little to add. It should be read by trade policy officials. It is useful to repeat two of Nelson's conclusions, buried in the middle of the paper, in summing up the troubled period of the last two decades for the automobile industry: "It seems reasonable to conclude that the U.S. industry is somewhat smaller, somewhat more flexible, and somewhat more efficient. . . . *It is Japanese competition, not U.S. protection, that accounts for the improvements in performance by the major U.S. auto producers*" (emphasis added). This is an important lesson for policymakers and the auto industry in Europe, where Japan has been persuaded to restrain its auto exports, and for policymakers and other industries in the United States. Protection through Japanese voluntary export restraint (VER) on automobiles to the United States, begun for two years in 1981 and finally allowed to lapse only in 1993 (lesson: treat with extreme skepticism the term "temporary" as applied to import restrictions), served mainly to permit both Japanese and American firms to extract higher profits from American consumers and to provide a framework within which Japanese firms could establish themselves as reliable producers of upscale automobiles in the United States, not to increase employment in the auto industry.

The American automobile industry for years largely ignored the signals it was getting from American consumers, particularly those along both coasts of the country, far from Detroit. Through their purchasing behavior, consumers started signaling in the mid-1950s that they wanted a smaller, more economical car, suitable for congested urban traffic and parking. Growing sales of the homely Volkswagen Beetle was the main manifestation. The American majors did not respond with their "compacts" until imports finally reached 10 percent of total sales. I purchased one of the responses, a 1961 Ford Falcon stationwagon. Six years later that model had been lengthened by well over a foot. I currently own a 1973 Plymouth Valiant, a fine car produced by Chrysler as a "compact," that is, its response to import competition in the early 1970s. In 1994 it is the largest car in my neighborhood. The majors were determined to sell large cars—perhaps, as Nelson suggests, because they made much higher profit per unit on large cars and because they deemed U.S. demand for autos to be price inelastic, thus greatly underestimating the move by Americans to two- and even three-car households, with the supplementary cars often being small, and imported.

One of the rationales for limiting imports was to protect employment in an important U.S. industry. The VER clearly failed in this regard. Although U.S. auto production reached the level of its previous 1978 peak again in 1985, and greatly exceeded it in 1988–89, employment continued to decline from 1985

Richard N. Cooper is the Boas Professor of International Economics at Harvard University. Formerly he was under secretary of state for economic affairs.

on, after a brief recovery from the 1982 recession. By 1989 it was only 1.6 percent of U.S. employment in all manufacturing, compared with 2.1 percent in 1978. Part of the reason is the continuing rise in the wages of autoworkers compared with the average wage in all manufacturing, from 64 percent higher in 1978 to 88 percent higher in 1990. But part of the reason is that the auto majors chose to use protection from Japanese imports to raise their prices rather than to increase their share of sales in the domestic market. That is, they chose to forgo increases in production that the VER would have permitted in the mid-1980s. That was not a surprising result to theorists of trade policy.

Import competition under tariffs breaks any monopoly power that domestic producers may have. But quantitative restrictions on imports restore that power and permit domestic producers to raise prices to the point at which marginal costs equal downward-sloping marginal revenue by restricting production below what it otherwise might be. The domestic producers' room for pricing maneuver is increased even if the quantitative restrictions do not bind. Thus the auto firms gained not only at the expense of American consumers, but also, during this period, at the expense of autoworkers laid off or not rehired. They also unwisely permitted the Japanese firms to raise their prices higher than otherwise, thus raising the profits and investment of Japanese firms, to upgrade their product quality, and to establish brand loyalties among American consumers for upscale Japanese automobiles. In short, the American majors may have profited in the short run of several years in the 1980s at the expense of long-run market share, production, employment, and profits.

Nelson's already long paper would have been more complete if it had also looked at the political economy of the VER in Japan. As Nelson notes in passing, Japan's automobile industry was not under close control by the Ministry of International Trade and Industry (MITI), but that was not for lack of several attempts by MITI to bring autos under its wing. Ironically, U.S. protectionist pressure brought final success to MITI. If Japan was to limit exports of automobiles to the United States to 1.68 million per year (later 1.85 million, then 2.3 million, and down to 1.65 million in 1992–93), some mechanism had to be found for allocating the limit among the six or more contending Japanese firms and for policing it. That role fell to MITI. As usual with quantitative restrictions, the bulk of the allocation went to the firms that were already well established in the U.S. market, the newer and more rapidly growing firms bore the brunt of the restriction, and potential new entrants were frozen out. That may have suited the larger Japanese firms, who were the major beneficiaries of the price increases permitted by the VER. But the key point is that it brought an independent and highly competitive industry under MITI control for a decade, greatly enhanced profits in the established Japanese auto firms, and reduced competition in the U.S. market not only between U.S. and Japanese firms but also among Japanese firms.

The U.S. automobile firms and U.S. policymakers should be asking themselves: was the "breathing spell" worth it?

4   The MFA Paradox: More Protection and More Trade?

J. Michael Finger and Ann Harrison

4.1   Introduction

The U.S. Constitution gives Congress the authority to regulate commerce with foreign nations. Yet, since the Smoot-Hawley Tariff of 1930, Congress has been reluctant to impose protection directly, choosing instead to delegate that authority to the executive branch. Yet Congress has never given the executive unlimited authority to regulate trade; instead, it has allowed the executive branch to take specific actions under well-defined circumstances.

Given Congress' preference for indirect protection, special interests seeking protection must either (1) nudge Congress to legislate conditions which would justify protection and/or (2) convince the executive that economic conditions satisfy previously legislated criteria for protection. Because administered protection often gives the executive considerable discretion, an industry seeking protection must not only convince the executive that the industry meets the criteria set by Congress but that the industry is also "deserving" of protection. The action of the executive is thus as much a political act as is passage by Congress of laws that establish administered protection.[1]

J. Michael Finger is a lead economist of the International Trade Division of the International Economics Department at the World Bank. Ann Harrison is assistant professor of economics and finance at Columbia University and a faculty research fellow of the National Bureau of Economic Research.

1. We use the word "political" to describe a decision in which the deciding agent has the authority to determine the criteria by which the decision will be made. The U.S. Constitution gives Congress the authority to regulate foreign commerce but does not specify criteria that Congress must take into account in deciding if or to what degree foreign commerce will be regulated. Congress' decisions are therefore by our definition political decisions. In contrast, there are also "technical" decisions. A technical decision is one in which the criteria are exogenously specified: the deciding agent is charged only to decide if these criteria are met. Antidumping cases exemplify technical decisions. In such cases, detailed law and administrative regulations specify the relevant criteria and the executive has no discretion to put these criteria aside—its authority to take action (impose an antidumping order) is directly tied to its determination as to whether or not the specified criteria are met.

In the post–World War II era, the U.S. textile industry achieved a degree of protection unparalleled in the rest of the manufacturing sector. Its success is evident from the fact that it was the only industry for which the U.S. government negotiated a multilateral arrangement for quotas within the framework of the General Agreement on Tariffs and Trade (GATT). But the international arrangements that were negotiated did not establish limits on U.S. imports; those limits were imposed through administrative actions. The authority of the executive to take these actions rested on the legislation passed by the U.S. Congress, not on international agreements such as the Multi-Fiber Arrangement (MFA). Thus protection for the textile industry was administered protection, not directly legislated protection.

Our focus in this paper is on the administrative dimensions of protection. Our contention is that the game played within these administrative mechanisms was different from the game played in the high-level politics of protection. Those interests that opposed protection had a significant influence on which sectors within textiles and garments received protection, as well as on the degree of protection.

We emphasize the administrative dimension for two reasons: (1) the more visible conflict between nations over the international agreements to restrict textile and apparel trade have been extensively and skillfully studied, and (2) overlooking the administrative dimension of how protection was put in place leads one to overlook one of the most powerful actors in the story—the state itself. In determining the scope and magnitude of protection to U.S. textile and garment interests, the U.S. government was much more than a neutral intermediary. It was one of the most influential players in the game.

We begin our analysis with a review in section 4.2 of political economy models of protection. We go on to apply these models to analyze (1) how the textile and apparel industries won the creation of the MFA system of protection (sections 4.3 to 4.5) and (2) how, within this system, quotas were determined on individual products imported from different countries (sections 4.6 and 4.7). In the final section we evaluate the most important influences on protection in the textile and garment industries.

4.2   Political Economy Models of Protection

Theoretical models on the political economy of protection (see, e.g., discussions by Baldwin 1985 and Trefler 1993) provide a useful starting point for our analysis.

4.2.1   Effective Organization

Many theories emphasize that in a representative democracy, where there are costs to participation as well as information costs, those who gain most from protection will organize into political pressure groups. Success, in turn, will depend on the relative ability of different groups to overcome the free-rider problem. Although only some voters or business groups provide resources to support lobbying, all the members of a particular sector are likely to gain. This suggests that—other factors constant—sectors with fewer numbers of workers and more concentrated production structures will lobby more effectively for protection. Activities with fewer and larger producing units and protected from entry by significant barriers to entry would be expected to be more effective in winning protection.

4.2.2   Value of the Political Payoff

Other theories, such as the "adding machine" model formulated by Caves (1976), focus instead on the behavior of politicians who seek to maximize their election prospects. The adding machine model suggests that protection increases with the number of employees in an industry. Empirically, this suggests that protection rises with the number of voters who earn their living in the sector, that is, with the size of its workforce. The adding machine model and the special interest model described above imply opposite relations between the size of a sector's workforce and its political influence.

Other theories bring out qualitative dimensions of the results of political action. Some focus on the likelihood that more disadvantaged sectors of the population are more likely to receive protection. Baldwin (1985) reviews what he describes as the "adjustment assistance" model and the "equity concern" model. In the first case, the government seeks to minimize short-run labor adjustment costs and protects sectors which are having the most difficulty adjusting. This suggests that low-growth sectors are more likely to be protected. In altruism or equity concern models, politicians want low-income workers (i.e., those with lower wage rates) to be protected from trade policy changes. Caves also suggests that protection is more likely in sectors with many, smaller plants. Another consideration that will condition the value to a politician of political action to protect a particular sector is the importance to the politician's constituency of that sector. Action in favor of a sector that provides a large share of constituent jobs is more likely than action in favor of one that provides a smaller share.

The altruism models discussed above suggest that factors other than the immediate self-interest of the decision makers influence the degree of protection a sector will receive.[2] The following paragraphs summarize other models that likewise take into account influences other than the immediate economic interests of the sector in question.

4.2.3   Power and Influence of the Exporting Countries

The relationship between the United States and the exporting country might also influence a decision to protect or not to protect a particular sector. (See,

---

2. These models are grouped as they are because they point to characteristics of the sector itself as determinants of the degree of protection a sector will receive.

e.g., Helleiner 1977 for a lengthier discussion of such considerations.) In the context of a bargaining framework, the United States is most likely to impose trade restraints on countries whose retaliation would be less costly to the United States. One implication is that the United States would be more likely to protect products where the majority of imports are received from small countries or countries that import little from the United States.[3] More general foreign policy considerations point to historically established relationships and the strategic interests of the United States, for example, the location of U.S. military bases.

The attraction of the U.S. government in recent years to policy instruments such as "Super 301" suggest that the perceived commercial fairness of the exporting countries might also be a determinant of which U.S. sectors are protected. For example, the perception that Japan has evaded its GATT responsibilities and has maintained high trade barriers in Japan is likely to lead to restrictive U.S. actions against Japanese exports, despite the fact that Japan is a large country and receives a large volume of U.S. exports.

On the other hand, equity concerns could apply as well, particularly if such concerns overlap with U.S. strategic interests. Special programs for U.S. allies, such as the Caribbean Basin Initiative, have been introduced to allow poorer countries access to the U.S. market that their bargaining power or strategic worth would not predict.

4.2.4 Power of the State

With administered protection, the outcome on protection is likely to be different from a direct vote, special interest model. Congress creates administered protection mechanisms because these mechanisms insulate the state from special interests.[4] Particularly in the early years of administered protection, the executive enjoyed considerable discretion even when the criteria for protection were met. This discretionary authority allowed a considerable discrepancy between constituent pressures and the resulting protection. The Reciprocal Trade Agreements Act (RTAA) of 1934 was a particularly important change in the mechanics of protection. The discretion granted the executive in other mechanisms could frustrate constituent pressures for increased protection. The RTAA

---

3. The recent debate over extending China's textile quotas for export to the U.S. market provides an excellent illustration of the bargaining model. The U.S. government stated that it was only willing to grant China more generous quota levels in textiles and apparel in exchange for increased access to the Chinese market.

4. That the power to make individual decisions on protection rests with the state does not suggest that state enjoyed autocratic power. Administered protection mechanisms are created through a democratic process. They have been described by I. M. Destler as providing protection for Congress from constituents, but there is no suggestion in this that constituents were somehow duped. Administered protection could likewise be described as providing protection for constituents from constituents—from the prisoner's dilemma of any individual sector being better off with protection, but all being collectively worse off if all receive protection.

served not only to thwart industry-specific pressures for protection but to create momentum for reducing protection.

4.3 The 1930s: Protection

The Smoot-Hawley Tariff was passed in 1930. The reaction of other countries to the Smoot-Hawley Act, combined with the worldwide economic depression, made it politically impossible that Congress would vote additional protection. But there remained administrative mechanisms through which such action might be encouraged. Section 336 of the Smoot-Hawley Act provided one such avenue, the trade section of the National Industrial Recovery Act provided another. Passage in 1934 of the RTAA provided a means by which the president could negotiate down U.S. tariff rates, but its provisions could not be used to gain an increase in protection.

4.3.1 The NIRA and Protection

One administrative avenue to protection was provided by the National Industrial Recovery Act (NIRA), passed in June 1933. This act provided for companies in an industry to negotiate and maintain, under government supervision, codes of fair competition. In addition to their provisions for maintaining product prices, the codes set up specific standards to improve labor conditions, specifically (1) setting an industry minimum wage, one substantially above the prevailing market rate, (2) limiting hours of work per week, and (3) improving working conditions. The NIRA code established in the textile industry included the elimination of child labor, defined as employment of persons under 16 years of age.

Section 3(e) of the NIRA recognized the necessity of preventing foreign competition from rendering these codes ineffective. Section 3(e) provided that the Tariff Commission, when directed by the president to do so, would investigate the conditions of competition resulting from increasing imports. If the commission found that imports were interfering with the operation of a code, the commission was to recommend to the president the import restraint—either a quota or an additional import fee—that would eliminate the effects of imports on operation of the code.

The NIRA had a short history: the U.S. Supreme Court decision in the Schechter Poultry Case of May 27, 1935, rendered it practically inoperative. After that date the Tariff Commission suspended work on all section 3(e) cases under way and never opened another case.[5]

The investigations the Tariff Commission undertook under section 3(e) of

---

5. When the Schechter case decision was returned, the Tariff Commission had under way section 3(e) investigations on horse and mule shoes and on bleached cotton cloth. The president had directed an investigation on cotton and linen netting, but the Tariff Commission had not begun to work on it.

Table 4.1   **Tariff Commission Investigations under Section 3(e) of the National Industrial Recovery Act, and Outcomes**

Article	Policy Outcome
Wood-cased lead pencils	Affirmative. VER with Japan.
Quicksilver	The Tariff Commission found no section 3(e) grounds for relief.
Wool felt hat bodies	The Tariff Commission found no section 3(e) grounds for relief.
Matches	Affirmative. Congress imposed an additional excise tax on the type of matches imported.
Cotton chenille rugs	Affirmative. An import fee (in addition to existing customs duties) was imposed. Also, VER with Japan.
Hit-and-miss-rag rugs	Affirmative. VER with Japan.
Imitation oriental rugs	Affirmative. An import fee (in addition to existing customs duties) was imposed.
Other rugs	Affirmative. An import fee (in addition to existing customs duties) was imposed. Also, VER with Japan.
Red cedar shingles	Affirmative. VER with Canada.
Braided hat bodies in part of synthetic textile	The Tariff Commission found no section 3(e) grounds for relief.

Source: U.S. Tariff Commission, *Annual Report* (Washington, D.C.: Government Printing Office, 1933, 1934, 1935).

the NIRA are listed in table 4.1. Of the 10 completed investigations, seven led to import controls, including five voluntary export restraints (VERs). Of the five VERs, four were with Japan.

Each of the investigations involving Japan displayed two common characteristics: (1) there was large difference between the price of imports from Japan versus imports from other sources, and (2) Japan had quickly become the dominant supplier of imports of the article, often the dominant supplier of the article in the U.S. market. In the lead pencils case, for example, imports had been coming primarily from Germany and Czechoslovakia. In 1933, Japan became the main source, supplying 70 percent of U.S. imports. Japanese prices far undercut the other exporters: Japan, $0.23 per gross; Germany, $4 per gross; and Czechoslovakia, $3 per gross (U.S. International Trade Commission [USITC] 1934, 42). The cotton chenille rugs investigation found that Japan's share of the U.S. market had gone from 12 percent of domestic consumption in 1931 to 80 percent by December 1933. From the beginning to the end of 1933, U.S. domestic production on a monthly basis fell by 85 percent (USITC 1934, 45).

Each of the cases involving Japanese exports ended with a VER. The four rugs cases displayed a pattern of outcome that would become standard for textile products: import duties to control imports from Europe, VERs to control imports from Japan. Of the four rugs investigations, for example, only the investigation of imitation oriental rugs did not lead to a VER, but this type of rug was imported almost entirely from Europe: France, Belgium, and Italy (USITC 1934, 48).

Resolution of most of the NIRA section 3(e) complaints by negotiating VERs was not an unusual outcome.[6] Indeed, the Tariff Commission itself, in its 1934 *Annual Report* pointed out that negotiation of a VER was in the 1930s a common form of import relief (USITC 1934, 4).

4.3.2   Section 336

Section 336 of the Smoot-Hawley Act established a mechanism for administrative adjustment of tariff rates. In a section 336 case, the U.S. Tariff Commission would conduct an investigation to determine the cost of producing a product in the United States and in exporting countries. Based on that information, the Tariff Commission would then recommend to the president the rate change that would "equalize competition," that is, a tariff rate that would make the foreign cost plus the tariff equal to the domestic cost.

Section 336 allowed for applications for tariff reductions as well as for increases. As table 4.2 shows, one-third of requests for investigations were for investigations to support reductions of tariffs.[7] Investigations could begin in several ways: by the Tariff Commission's own motion, by order of the president, by request of either house of Congress, or by request of an interested party.[8]

The Tariff Commission's response to these requests reflects both the reluctance of the executive to increase U.S. tariff rates and the deference it paid to Congress on such matters. All of the 82 requests for "investigation" without specification whether the objective was an increase or a reduction of a tariff rate were requested by Senate resolution, and all of them led to initiation of investigations.[9] But of the requests for tariff increases, 85 percent were dismissed by the Tariff Commission without initiation of an investigation. The reluctance of the executive to increase protection is also reflected in the outcomes of the investigations that were undertaken. Almost half the time (as table 4.3 reports), the Tariff Commission recommended no change of the tariff. In all, the commission initiated section 336 investigations on 101 products, and only 29 of these led to tariff increases. An almost equal number, 25, produced a tariff reduction.

When the RTAA was passed in 1934, negotiations between the United States and exporting countries became an alternative means for reducing tariffs. A 1935 tabulation by the U.S. Tariff Commission lists over 400 reductions of the

6. One outcome of the investigation of red cedar shingles imported from Canada was that the Canadian industry adopted a code of fair practice similar to the one in place in the U.S. lumber industry. Restraint of exports to the United States became a part of that Canadian code.

7. Most of these were submitted by U.S. importers, but some were from foreign exporters.

8. The Tariff Commission had almost limitless discretion to determine whether a request from an interested party justified initiation of an investigation.

9. One investigation was by the Tariff Commission's own motion, all others were by request of interested parties.

Table 4.2   **Applications for Section 336 Investigations, 1931–41**

Type of Application	Number[a]	Percentage of Total
Total applications received	357	100
Action requested		
Tariff increase	145	41
Tariff reduction	121	34
Investigation	82	23
Adjustment[b]	7	2
Shift to American selling price	2	c

Source: Tabulated from U.S. Tariff Commission, *Annual Report* (Washington, D.C.: Government Printing Office, 1931–41).

[a]Numbers given are the numbers of tariff lines covered by applications. The total number of applications received, strictly speaking was 297. The Tariff Commission *Annual Reports,* however, provide information on the nature of requests and outcomes only by tariff line.

[b]These requests were for shifts from specific to ad valorem rates, the reverse shift, or for changes in a compound rate that would move the ad valorem component in one direction and the specific component in the other.

[c]Less than 0.5 percent.

Table 4.3   **Outcomes of Section 336 Cases, 1931–41**

Product Category	Outcome[a]			Total	Percentage of All Cases
	Increase[b]	Decrease	No Change[c]		
Textiles	3	2	2	7	7
Apparel	3	1	1	5	5
Chemicals, oils, paints	0	2	4	6	6
Earths, earthenware, glassware	1	2	5	8	8
Metals, metal manufactures	7	2	7	16	16
Wood, wood manufactures	1	2	2	5	5
Sugar, molasses, manufactures thereof	0	2	0	2	2
Agricultural products	9	5	16	30	30
Miscellaneous manufactures	5	7	10	22	22
Total	29	25	47	101	100

Source: U.S. Tariff Commission, *Annual Report* (Washington, D.C.: Government Printing Office, 1931–41).

[a]Numbers of outcomes, by tariff line affected.

[b]Includes shifts to American selling price valuation on one agricultural product and on one item included in miscellaneous manufactures.

[c]In some of the investigations we have placed in this category, the Tariff Commission determined that the present tariff equalized foreign and domestic costs and the president issued a formal proclamation of no change. In others, the Tariff Commission determined that the domestic product and the imported product in question were not comparable, and hence that section 336 did not apply. In these instances there was no presidential proclamation. The tabulation reported here includes one change (on a chemical product) in which the ad valorem component was increased and the specific component reduced.

U.S. tariff through reciprocal negotiations. With the availability of this means for tariff reductions and the demonstrated reluctance of the executive to increase protection through section 336 actions, section 336 was used less and less. The Tariff Commission reports no applications for section 336 investigations after 1941.

4.3.3   Use of These Mechanisms by the Textile and Apparel Industry

At the time the NIRA was struck down by the Supreme Court, the Tariff Commission was conducting a section 3(e) investigation on cotton cloth. This investigation was suspended but soon came back in another guise. The sequence of events that led to a voluntary restraint agreement was as follows:

March 1935: The Senate directed the Tariff Commission to investigate under section 336.

April 1935: The Tariff Commission investigation began.

October 1935: Negotiation of a VER began between the U.S. and Japanese governments. The U.S. State Department requested that the Tariff Commission delay submitting its report.

April 1936: Under industry pressure, the Tariff Commission sent its report to the president, recommending a tariff increase. The State Department recommended that the president delay action.

May 1936: The president proclaimed a tariff increase of 42 percent.

August 1936: Private direct negotiations replaced government-to-government negotiations.

January 1937: The Japanese cotton industry agreed to quotas for 1937 and 1938, later extended to cover 1939 and 1940.

The agreement struck between the U.S. and Japanese industries was quite detailed. Besides specifying export limits, the agreement specified how to measure exports and how to handle transshipment from third countries to the United States. The memorandum of understanding between the industries also established a joint committee of representatives from each country's industry; the function of the committee would be to deal with whatever administrative difficulties might arise and to act as a negotiating committee in establishing subsequent arrangements between the two industries with regard to future limitations or other means of control (Bauge 1987, 63).

The quotas were only 64 percent filled over the four years they were in effect. Bauge (1987, 66ff.) explains that the U.S. industry had been willing to accept a large quota to pin down the Japanese in the future. Also, in 1937, Japan declared war on China. The war took an increased share of Japanese output, and Japanese resources were allocated to other industries more directly supportive of the war.

Similar sequences of events led to VERs with Japan on cotton hosiery and on velveteen and corduroy. In the agreement on velveteen and corduroy, the U.S. industry agreed to refrain from requesting the Tariff Commission to publish and send to the president its report, provided the Japanese exports remained within the agreed quota.[10]

4.3.4 Lessons from the 1930s

Although the U.S. textile industry during the 1930s was heavily protected, its protection was about average relative to other U.S. industries. The U.S. textile industry came into the decade with protection about equal to the average for all U.S. industries, and it was no more successful than other industries in the 1930s at gaining increased protection.

The administration of President Franklin Roosevelt initially assigned the tariff to a domestic policy role, but a secondary one: the tariff was to be used to defend the domestic economic policies set out in the NIRA and the Agricultural Adjustment Act (AAA). After passage of the RTAA, import protection became increasingly a foreign policy concern of the executive. One consequence was that the executive's interest shifted toward reductions, not increases, in the tariff. As trade policy became more a foreign policy concern, the executive turned increasingly to VERs when pressed to restrict imports. Negotiations were the traditional means of conducting foreign policy; hence it was only logical that the executive should increasingly use this means for limiting U.S. imports.

Both the tying of the tariff to specific domestic policies and its later use as a foreign policy tool demonstrates the power of the state to isolate trade policy from immediate constituent pressures. This is the primary lesson of the 1930s import policy experience.

4.4 The 1950s: From Ordinary Protection to Exceptional Treatment

From 1950 to 1962, merchandise imports of textiles and apparel accounted for about 3 percent of U.S. consumption, declining from 6 percent at the end of the 1930s and 10 percent in the 1920s. In apparel, figure 4.1 (below) shows that imports took a smaller share of U.S. consumption than of other industrial goods. Clearly, high import volumes *on average* were not the primary determinant of protection in the industry. Yet increases in imports tended to be concentrated in specific product lines, which consolidated the opposition. Imports of cotton manufactures surged between 1939 and 1958, increasing from 3.4 percent of domestic production in 1939 to 22 percent in 1958. The import share of cotton goods continued to escalate after 1958, climbing to 36 percent. These import surges prompted inflammatory statements against Japanese exports and an occasional congressional bill to impose quotas or other sorts of limits (Bauge 1987, 95).

---

10. A detail of this agreement was that cotton velveteen or velvet ribbons would be excluded from the categories under restraint. This exclusion was not pressed for by the Japanese, but rather by a Tariff Commission determination that the U.S.-made and the imported variants of the products were not comparable and hence that section 336 provided no authority for a tariff increase.

4.4.1   Congressional Politics of Trade Policy

There was little chance that such bills would gain approval. The lessons of the Smoot-Hawley Tariff were fresh in mind, and Congress was reluctant to encourage direct action. Congress had created several administrative routes to protection, discussed below. Through each of these, a specific administrative finding gave the president authority to restrict imports but left him with the discretionary authority not to do so. There was evolving the political system that I. M. Destler (1992) has called "protection for Congress," in which a representative under pressure to protect imports could direct a constituent to the appropriate administrative mechanism.

Although the executive's administration of these mechanisms was designed to provide minimal protection, such mechanisms sheltered Congress against the wrath of special interests who pressured members for import relief. The 1950s were generally prosperous times during which the United States enjoyed substantial trade surpluses. Pointing a protection-seeking industry into a maze of administrative procedures bought time. By the time the industry eventually emerged from the end of the maze without a prize, business had improved and it pressed its case no further. Besides, the system satisfied the American sense of fairness. It provided a place to complain where officials listened, investigated, and held hearings. One had one's day in court. To complain further would be un-American, and maybe even pro-Communist, if the closing of the U.S. market tipped a country to the Soviet side in the Cold War.

GATT solidified the reciprocal trade agreements approach as the general approach to tariff setting, further minimizing the likelihood that Congress would return to direct tariff making. This further assured that the "ordinary" process of tariff making or a direct congressional vote of special protection would be difficult avenues to protection. There were, however, other mechanisms available.

4.4.2   Presidential Politics of Trade Policy: Trade Policy as Foreign Policy

There was even less chance that a protectionist bill would avoid a presidential veto. While the Congress perceived trade policy as a means for helping local industry, the executive branch of the U.S. government saw trade policy as an important instrument of foreign policy.[11] The ideas that dominated executive branch thinking are revealed in the following two statements from Cordell Hull, the first secretary of state to President Franklin Roosevelt and the father of the RTAA:

---

11. The difference at the time between presidential and congressional trade politics is illustrated by the birth and death of the proposal to create the International Trade Organization (ITO). The proposal to create such an organization and the first draft of a charter came from the U.S. government, the executive branch. The ITO failed to be established in large part because the U.S. Congress refused to approve it.

I felt that all nations should be urged to make their chief rallying point the establishment of a state of world order under law, so as to maintain conditions of permanent peace. (Hull 1948, 173)

The other statement expresses in a more casual way the role trade could play in establishing peace:

When I was a boy on the farm in Tennessee, we had two neighbors—I'll call them Jenkins and Jones—who were enemies of each other. For many years there had been bad feelings between them—I don't know why—and when they met on the road or in town or at church, they stared at each other coldly and didn't speak.

Then one of Jenkins' mules went lame in the spring just when Jenkins needed him most for plowing. At the same time Jones ran short of corn for his hogs. Now it so happened that Jones was through with his own plowing and had a mule to spare, and Jenkins had a bin filled with corn. A friendly third party brought the two men together, and Jones let Jenkins use his mule in exchange for corn for the hogs.

As a result, it wasn't long before the two old enemies were the best of friends. A common-sense trade and ordinary neighborliness had made them aware of their economic need of each other and brought them peace. (Hull 1948, 364)

In addition to the Wilsonian idea of international rule of law and the populist idea that trading made good neighbors, the executive's instinct to trade policy was also conditioned by two decades of process, two decades in which the executive had been in an almost continuous negotiation with its trading partners over trade restrictions. Not just principle but conditioned reflex pushed the executive away from unilateral action on trade restrictions.

4.4.3   Textile Industry Strategy

The textile industry's strategy was the obvious one: to maintain pressure on all political fronts and at the same time to use all administrative remedies available.

On the political front, through the 1950s the textile industry was active at public hearings concerning the U.S. government's intentions to cut tariffs. These included not only hearings on proposed negotiating authority but also the hearings the trade agreements required on the products on which it might negotiate tariff reductions, for example, "peril point" hearings. In 1955, the industry placed special focus on opposing the Eisenhower administration's trade bill that asked for the tariff-cutting authority that eventually allowed U.S. participation in the Dillon Round of GATT negotiations.

4.4.4   Trade Remedies and VERs

The activity of the industry created considerable concern in Japan. The Japanese feared that the textile industry would either win special protection from the U.S. Congress or succeed in limiting the authority that Congress would grant the president to negotiate a general reduction of U.S. import restrictions.

In August 1955 the Textile Export Council of Japan established a committee of government and industry members to develop a solution for the situation in the United States. This committee sent a team to Washington where it met with U.S. industry officials. The U.S. industry team reported to the U.S. State Department that the Japanese were willing to negotiate a settlement, but the State Department replied that they would vigorously oppose quotas, even negotiated quotas. The U.S. industry, however, carried their case to the White House and President Eisenhower asked his chief of staff, Sherman Adams, to meet with the Japanese. As a result of these negotiations, the Japanese industry-government textile committee announced in December 1955 that they intended to restrict their 1956 exports to the United States of cotton cloth and of cotton blouses (Brandis 1982, 9).

The U.S. industry took steps to assure that these limits would be put in place but at the same time viewed the arrangement as inadequate. The arrangement covered too few products, and it covered only Japan. The industry also preferred a restraint system that did not depend on the Japanese government or industry for enforcement, that is, in which the U.S. administration would have the legal authority to enforce the limits at the U.S. border.

In this regard, the industry achieved an important victory when it won (in May 1956) the addition of section 204 to the Agriculture Act of 1956. Section 204 authorized the president to negotiate with foreign governments to limit the export to the United States of agricultural *or textile* products, and to carry out such an agreement by limiting the entry of such products into the United States. Several companies also petitioned the Tariff Commission for "escape clause" investigations.

But the industry was learning that creating the legal authority for the president to limit imports of textiles is one thing, inducing him to use that authority is another. While these administrative mechanisms provided additional tribunes to which the industry could present its case for protection, none of the petitions led directly to import relief. The behavior of the U.S. government and Japanese industry provides some insight into the politics of the matter.

Section 22, added to the AAA on August 24, 1935, authorizes the president to impose import fees or quotas to restrict imports of agricultural commodities *or the products thereof* if those imports render or tend to render ineffective or materially interfere with U.S. agricultural programs. The section, by design, was similar in scope and purpose to section 3(e) of the NIRA.[12]

---

12. According to Cordell Hull, President Franklin Roosevelt saw the AAA and the NIRA as the centerpieces of his economic policy and, derivatively, sections 22 and 3(e) as the centerpieces of his trade policy—at least of the economics of his trade policy. Thus Hull (1948, 353) writes:

> The President, still pursuing the theory of retaining full discretionary authority to fix tariff rates at any height deemed necessary for the successful operation of the AAA and NIRA, was slow to embrace my liberal trade proposal. . . .
> Gradually, however, the forces favoring high tariffs, together with a number of the President's economic advisors connected with the NIRA and AAA, increasingly urged him to abandon the idea of tariff reductions in order that our Government might, if necessary, impose restrictions on imports to enable NIRA and AAA to function successfully.

The first attempt by the textile industry to use section 22 occurred in 1939. President Roosevelt however directed the Tariff Commission to undertake *separate* investigations of raw cotton and of cotton textile products. Price support programs under the AAA had moved U.S. fiber prices above world prices and had attracted substantial foreign sales. At the same time, the domestic price of cotton being higher than the world price put textile manufacturers at a disadvantage vis-à-vis foreign manufacturers.

In 1939, within four weeks of the president's directive to the Tariff Commission, the commission had reported in the affirmative on cotton fiber, and the president ordered a tight quota on imports. But the commission delayed for more than two years its investigation of imports of cotton manufactures and eventually terminated the investigation when World War II disrupted foreign supply and revived domestic demand.

In 1955, the Eisenhower administration exploited the fact that there were no deadlines for the various steps in the section 22 process and left the matter tied up in the secretary of agriculture's preliminary investigation. Continued pressure however from the industry and its congressional delegation eventually won a meeting with the secretary of commerce plus the relevant assistant secretaries of state, commerce, and agriculture. In this meeting the government offered a three-point program: (1) urge third countries to import more from Japan; (2) impose a fee equalizing the internal and the world prices of cotton on all textile exports; and (3) exchange formal diplomatic notes with Japan, officially taking note of Japan's VERs.

The industry continued to press for legislative action and came within a 43–45 Senate vote of attaching to a foreign aid bill an amendment mandating textile import quotas.

All the while, government-to-government negotiations continued with Japan. These resulted, in January 1957, in the Japanese government announcing a comprehensive plan to control textile exports to the United States (Brandis 1982, 26).

Throughout the negotiations with Japan, the executive avoided the activation of section 22's authority to restrict imports. Though the textile industry had petitioned in 1955 for section 22 action, when the restraint agreement was concluded in 1957 the secretary of agriculture still had not completed his preliminary investigation. As in 1939, the administration was reluctant to take steps that would provide it explicit legal authority to restrict textile imports.[13]

Hull's description of how he won President Franklin Roosevelt's support for the RTAA suggests that President Roosevelt saw its value entirely in its foreign policy dimensions: that he saw its economic dimensions as costs, not as benefits.

13. No restriction was the administration's preferred outcome, negotiated restrictions its fallback position. The following statement by Secretary of State John Foster Dulles is characteristic of the liberal, foreign policy view of trade policy that dominated administration thinking: "The United States does not have a single import quota on manufactured products, and to restrict trade at a time when the free world must depend on the expansion of trade for so much of its strength would

The Japanese industry and government seemed to share that concern. Bauge (1987, 129) points out that soon after the Tariff Commission initiated an investigation of injury from imports of a product, for example, cotton gingham, the Japanese government announced exports limits on the product. While the escape clause allowed the president discretion not to act even when the Tariff Commission returned an affirmative injury finding and recommended import relief, it did not give the president discretion to prevent a Tariff Commission investigation. An interested party could petition the commission directly, and the commission had no authority to turn down a valid petition.

4.4.5   Hong Kong Holds Out

As the industry was convincing the executive to arrange a VER with Japan, Hong Kong was becoming a significant exporter. Hong Kong in 1961 supplied almost 35 percent of U.S. imports of cotton textiles in 1961, up from less than half of 1 percent in 1956. But Hong Kong proved more difficult than Japan to push into a voluntary agreement.[14] As a foreign policy matter, Hong Kong was important to the United States as a capitalist example and as a post for gathering information on China. And Hong Kong was a colony of the United Kingdom, thereby enjoying the benefits of the special relationship that existed in the post–World War II years between the United States and the United Kingdom.

Furthermore, Hong Kong had earlier agreed to limit its textile exports to the United Kingdom and had learned several hard lessons from that experience. With Hong Kong exports restrained, India's and Pakistan's exports to the United Kingdom began to grow. And as soon as Hong Kong had agreed to restraints on exports to the United Kingdom, France, Germany, and Switzerland had begun to press for similar restraints, including restraints on Hong Kong exports to France's colonies and former colonies in Africa. The United Kingdom had promised to support Hong Kong in resisting such expansion of the restraints to other countries but had not proved vigorous in doing so.

Furthermore, Hong Kong had fewer economic alternatives than Japan. Indeed, the Ministry of International Trade and Industry (MITI) at the time was counseling the Japanese textile industry to move from cotton textiles to synthetics. Hong Kong, on the other hand, had to find some way for a rapidly increasing population to earn a living, as continuing numbers crossed the border from China. Providing a job, particularly in the clothing industry, required minimal investment and demanded minimal skill.

There were pressures within Hong Kong that favored negotiation of export limits. Aggarwal (1985, 68ff.) points to the problem that small Hong Kong exporters were creating for larger companies. Just as Japan was seeing its sales

severely weaken the United States and the free world" (Quoted by Bauge 1987, 128; from U.S. Department of State, *Department of State Bulletin* 31 no. 861 [December 26, 1955]: 105).

  Dulles added that he would prefer to see domestic industry protected by voluntary action of the exporting nations.

  14. The following discussion draws considerably from Aggarwal (1985).

of cotton manufactures displaced by Hong Kong sales, large Hong Kong manufacturers were aggressively courting buyers who came to Hong Kong. Aggarwal quotes the *Far Eastern Economic Review* calling for the Hong Kong government to step in to control exports to the United States unless the small manufacturers would "agree to temper their ambition" (Aggarwal 1985, 69).

A second factor that pushed toward Hong Kong accepting limits was a suggestion by President Eisenhower that the U.S. government would, as a quid pro quo, support U.S. private investment in Hong Kong.

Hong Kong, in December 1959, offered to limit for three years its exports of five categories of garments but asked for growth allowances of 10–15 percent and for provision to carry forward any quota not used in a year. The U.S. industry refused to accept, and imports from Hong Kong were not controlled until the Short Term Arrangement had been signed and the U.S. Congress had delegated to the president the power to enforce limits at the U.S. border.

4.4.6   How the Executive Frustrated the Use of Trade Remedies

The industry attempted again in 1959 and in 1961 to use section 22. In June 1959 the National Cotton Council and the American Textile Manufacturers Institute (ATMI) filed with the secretary of agriculture a section 22 petition that asked for quotas on cotton textile and apparel imports. President Eisenhower took advantage of administrative regulations that had been issued by President Roosevelt in 1937.[15] He directed the Tariff Commission to investigate but severely limited the scope of the commission's investigation. He directed the commission to investigate if it were necessary, in order to prevent cotton textile imports from interfering with the cotton export program, to impose a fee on imported cotton textiles equal to the amount of the subsidy on raw cotton exports (Brandis 1982, 14).

Thus, President Eisenhower's directive to the Tariff Commission frustrated the industry's petition. It eliminated quotas as a possible form of relief. More critically, it focused the investigation on how textile imports affected the cotton export program rather the cotton price support program.

In June 1960, the commission ruled 4–2 that textile imports were not interfering with the cotton export program.

In 1961, after President Eisenhower had retired and John F. Kennedy was president, the industry filed a similar petition. It met the same fate. The Tariff Commission, proceeding within a presidential specification that was in sub-

---

15. The administrative regulations to implement section 22 provided for a preliminary investigation by the secretary of agriculture, who then makes his recommendations to the president. The president, in turn, would direct either that no further action be taken, or that the Tariff Commission make a full investigation. The regulations also provided that the secretary of agriculture would prescribe the manner in which requests for action under the section should be submitted by interested parties. Because the directive to the Tariff Commission would come from the president, and because the secretary of agriculture served at the pleasure of the president, the regulations gave to the president the authority to define the terms of the investigation.

stance the same as what President Eisenhower had delivered in the 1959 case, again ruled 4–2 that textile imports were not interfering with the cotton export program (Brandis 1982, 15).

At about the same time the ATMI asked for quotas on imports of cotton, synthetic fiber, silk, and wool products under the national security provisions of the Trade Agreements Act. The ATMI pressed the matter on occasion through the 1960s, but the executive took advantage of the absence of a time limit on such investigations and never announced a decision.

4.5   The 1960s: Protection Made Multilateral

The textile industry, by the beginning of the 1960s, felt that it was being squeezed between U.S. agricultural policy and U.S. foreign policy. The U.S. agricultural programs maintained fiber prices in the United States above world levels; to export at least a part of surplus production, the government paid a subsidy on exports. The export subsidy the U.S. government paid was particularly onerous since it gave foreign competitors access to U.S. cotton at a price below what the U.S. industry had to pay.

At the same time, the executive branch of the U.S. government viewed trade policy primarily as foreign policy. The executive resisted the industry's attempts to gain legislated restrictions, and it exploited loopholes in administered protection to frustrate the industry's attempts to use that protection. The executive worked not just to avoid using the authority these administrative mechanisms conferred to restrict textile imports, it worked to avoid that authority being conferred.

For the industry, the main lesson of the 1950s was that the executive, even when the legal authority to restrict textile imports was available, would be reluctant to do so. And though industry-to-industry contacts with the Japanese indicated a willingness on the part of Japan to restrain imports, the U.S. State Department appeared to the industry to be openly hostile to negotiating such restrictions. The industry's strategy thus became more directly a political one, a strategy that looked for opportunities to bring the power of the industry to bear on national elections.[16]

As to the mechanics of restricting imports, the strategy of the industry was still to press for import quotas.[17] Quotas were the preferred instrument because the industry concluded that they had little chance in the existing political climate of winning tariffs sufficiently high to make up the difference between their costs and those of Japan and Hong Kong.[18]

The eventual focus on the VER as the standard policy instrument was less a

16. From conversations with textile industry association spokespersons.
17. The South Carolina legislature in 1955 passed a law requiring each business that sold Japanese textiles to post a sign in its front window announcing that it sold Japanese goods. While quotas were the industry's preferred instrument, they were not the only instrument it would use.
18. From conversations with textile industry association officials.

matter of strategy than an accommodation to the circumstances the industry itself faced. Negotiation was an important part of the ethos of trade policy. Unilateral action violated the Wilsonian principle of international rule of law and the populist idea that cooperation made for good neighbors. It also brought back memories of the beggar-thy-neighbor policies of the 1930s.[19]

The idea of negotiating a multilateral agreement to legitimize and regulate these restrictions was likewise an accommodation rather than a strategy. In all then, the path from the first VERs with Japan on cotton textiles to the MFA was less a grand design than a sequence of steps that were guided, one at a time, by circumstance.

4.5.1   President Kennedy and the First Multilateral Agreements[20]

To win the presidency, John Kennedy focused on New England, the traditional Democratic party strongholds, the northern industrial states, and the South. A promise of protection for the textile industry would help in the South and in New England: it would be particularly important in the South, where Kennedy's Catholicism was a significant liability. And polls indicated a close race with Republican candidate Richard M. Nixon.

Kennedy's pledge to make a solution to the cotton textile import problem a top priority of his administration won the support of several Southern leaders, including Luther Hodges, a textile executive and former governor of North Carolina, Governor Ernest Hollings of South Carolina, and Governor Terry Sanford of North Carolina. The cotton textile industry evaluated John Kennedy's promise of support as more concrete than Richard Nixon's, and many members of the industry worked actively to support Kennedy's election.[21]

By the fall of 1961, the Trade Expansion Act (TEA) had become an important part both of President John F. Kennedy's foreign policy and economic agenda. As it had been to other postwar presidents, to President Kennedy and to his allies in the government, commercial diplomacy was first of all a tool of foreign policy. Through a new round of GATT negotiations the president could build a relationship with the increasingly successful European Common Market and thereby renew the strategic alliance between the United States and Western Europe. He could also take the lead on special measures to help devel-

19. In addition, the VER is consistent with the "property rights" implicit in the GATT. The basic element in the GATT is an exchange of concessions, an exchange between countries of the right to access to each other's market. If a country wants to take back some of the access it has thus "sold"—impose a new import restriction—it owes compensation to the trading parties that "own" that concession. If compensation is not made, trading parties have the right to retaliate, i.e., take back an equal amount of the market access that they had "paid" to the offending country. GATT provides separate processes to decide offense, compensation, and retaliation. A VER considers all of the rights in one negotiation and thus provides for efficient trade-offs. This view is elaborated in Finger (1984).

20. This section draws extensively from Zeiler (1992).

21. Textile industry association officials told us that the two Eisenhower elections had not been close enough for them to extract significant commitments from either side.

oping countries, bringing them on board of his aggressive Cold War policy. Kennedy hoped that the TEA would boost U.S. export competitiveness thereby helping to slake the U.S. payments imbalance and the gold drain. The act also took on some of the burden to stimulate the domestic economy: it became something of a panacea for present problems and future circumstances, foreign and domestic.

But President Kennedy was also a New Dealer: he felt it was the government's job to cure economic distress. Before he became president he had supported import restrictions of particular interest to New England industries, among them textiles and fish processors. The rhetoric Kennedy had used to explain his position on trade was the usual. He attacked imports as the result of "cutthroat competition" from foreigners; he disagreed with "unjustifiable protection" but felt that "a tariff to equalize competition is necessary."

President Kennedy sought no common denominator between what he saw as the benefits and the risks of negotiating down U.S. protection. Striking a balance was not a philosophical process, it was a political one. To explain how President Kennedy went about putting together the votes needed to pass the act, Zeiler quotes a Kennedy associate: "You want the votes, you give the guy the post-office." In the Boston school of politics in which John F. Kennedy was trained, this was how philosophical differences were reconciled.

The textile industry, particularly the cotton textile industry, had been pressing forward on several fronts to gain import protection and other forms of government support. To win their support for the TEA, President Kennedy in May 1961 offered a seven-point program that included: action to eliminate or offset the raw cotton price differential; assurance that careful consideration would be given to a textile industry application for protection under the escape clause or the national security provisions of trade law; and direction to the State Department to convene a conference of textile-importing and exporting countries to develop an international agreement governing textile trade.[22]

Zeiler reports (1992, 86) that by March 1962, President Kennedy had implemented or had made commitments that would soon implement all seven points. The highlights of Kennedy's actions (see also table 4.4 for a chronology of events) were the following:

July 1961: The Short Term Arrangement (STA) on Cotton Textiles was signed.

February 1962: The Long Term Arrangement (LTA) on Cotton Textiles was signed.

April 1962: President Kennedy embargoed eight categories of cotton textiles from Japan.

June 1962: Congress passed and President Kennedy signed a bill giving the

---

22. These three, according to Brandis (1982, 19), were the points of major interest to the industry.

Table 4.4   **Chronology of International Events**

July 1961	The Short Term Arrangement (STA) is agreed.
February 1962	The Long Term Arrangement (LTA) is agreed, to commence October 1, 1962, to last for five years.
1963–64	The United States tries and fails to secure an international agreement on wool products.
June 1965	The United States tries and fails to negotiate restraints on Japanese exports of wool products.
June 1966	The United Kingdom implements a global quota scheme in violation of the LTA—the LTA providing only for product-specific restraints.
April 1967	Agreement is reached to extend the LTA for three years.
October 1970	Agreement is reached to extend the LTA for three years. It was later extended three months more, to fill the gap until the MFA came into effect.
1969–71	United States negotiates VERs with Asian suppliers on wool and man-made fibers.
December 1973	The MFA is agreed, to commence January 1, 1974, and to last for four years.
July–December 1977	The European Economic Community and the United States negotiate bilateral agreements with developing countries prior to agreeing to extension of the MFA.
December 1977	The MFA is extended for four years.
December 1981	The MFA is extended for four years and seven months.
July 1986	The MFA is renewed for five years. The Reagan administration, under pressure from increased imports resulting from dollar appreciation, negotiates tough quotas.
July 1991	The MFA is extended pending outcome of the Uruguay Round negotiations.
December 1993	The Uruguay Round draft final act provides for a 10-year phase-out of all MFA and other quotas on textiles.

president authority to limit imports from nonsigners to a multilateral agreement.[23]

The textile industry kept its part of the bargain. As Zeiler (1992, 86) reports their reaction: "[Kennedy] earned an acknowledgment from the journal *Textile World* that [he] had 'gone to bat for the industry.' The National Cotton Council announced its support for the Trade Expansion Act because of the 'exceptional treatment' given by Kennedy to the textile import problem. Victory was definitely his, however, when the American Cotton Manufacturers Institute thanked him on March 31, 1962, for his 'unprecedented degree of thoughtful consideration and constructive action for textiles.' The ACMI then endorsed the Trade Expansion Act."

In June 1962 Congress passed the TEA of 1962. Two-thirds of Congressman

23. The two-price cotton problem was not resolved until April 1964 when President Lyndon B. Johnson signed a bill that established a payment-in-kind program that made cotton available to manufacturers inside the United States at the world price.

Carl Vinson's (D-Ga.) Textile Conference Group voted for the bill and against critical amendments that would have substituted a bill that offered considerably restricted negotiating authority to the president. Eighty-two of 105 House Southern Democrats voted for the act, and in the Senate, 19 of 20 Southerners.[24]

4.5.2 Provisions of the LTA

The STA provided for one-year restrictions of imports of cotton products and for further international negotiations to develop a long-term solution. Before it expired, the LTA had been agreed (see table 4.4).

The main operative provision of the LTA was article 3. That article provided that whenever imports of a particular product caused or threatened market disruption, the importing country could request the exporting country to restrict its exports. While the arrangement specified that the request for restraint be accompanied by a "detailed factual statement of the reasons for the request," it implicitly left to the importing country the authority to determine when "disruption" was present or threatened.

Annex B specified that the minimum level to which exports could be restrained was the level of actual imports for the 12-month period ending three months before the restraint went into effect. If the restraint was in effect for more than one year, the restraint level should be increased by at least 5 percent each year. Market disruption did not have to be demonstrated again for renewal.

Article 3 also provided that if 60 days after an importing country had requested an exporting country to restrain, no agreement to do so had been reached, the importing country could take unilateral action, subject to annex B's statement of minimum levels.

Article 4 specified that the arrangement "shall not prevent the application of mutually acceptable arrangements on other terms not inconsistent with the basic objectives of this arrangement."

The 1984 GATT textile study (1984, 73) points out that bilateral agreements negotiated under article 4 eventually became the form of application of the arrangement preferred both by the United States and by exporting countries. Article 3 agreements had to be renewed each 12 months, longer-term agreements were administratively convenient for the United States and provided exporters greater long-range security (Aggarwal 1985, 91).

Several factors contributed to other countries acquiescing to U.S. pressure

---

24. Textile restrictions were not the only deal President Kennedy made for the TEA. Senator Robert S. Kerr of Oklahoma led the congressional delegation that represented the oil producers. The price to lift Kerr's opposition to the TEA was the Arkansas River Bill—federal money to make the Arkansas River navigable into Oklahoma. "You know, Bob, I never really understood the Arkansas River bill before today," President Kennedy remarked as he accepted the deal (Zeiler 1992, 114).

President Kennedy was criticized by members of his own party for the mercenary way in which he put together the votes needed to pass the TEA.

for a multilateral agreement to limit textile exports. Not the least of these, of course, was the power of U.S. pressure at the time. Japan, for its part, had not yet gained the economic strength that allowed it to hold out for several years against the expansion of the agreement to wool and man-made fibers. In 1962, Japan still had a trade deficit with the United States.

Many European countries had retained their post–World War II quotas on Japanese textiles when Japan acceded to the GATT. Japan viewed a multilateral agreement as possibly improving its access to European markets. Also, the Japanese and U.S. cotton textile industries had been in close contact in the 1930s and had reestablished that contact in the 1950s. The Japanese industry had considered generous the quotas it had negotiated previously with the United States. Many European countries had imposed similar quotas on developing country exports, in many cases declaring them under the balance-of-payments provision (article XII) of the GATT. When GATT regulations on use of balance-of-payments provisions by developed countries were tightened in 1958, these European countries were left looking for GATT cover for restrictions they were reluctant to remove (Aggarwal 1985, 73).

As to the exporting countries, U.S. pressure was probably the most important factor. It is possible that exporting countries viewed a multilateral agreement as an instrument the U.S. government might use to resist rather than to advance the proposals of the U.S. industry. A similar argument had been applied in generic terms to the GATT, and the U.S. government had displayed a reluctance to use the authority to restrict textile imports that U.S. law provided. In addition, there was fear of an individual exporting country getting left out in the country-by-country bargaining that seemed to be the real alternative to a multilateral agreement. Hong Kong, after agreeing to limit its exports to the United Kingdom, had lost to India and Pakistan some of its share of the U.K. import market.

A final factor is that the exporting countries may have underestimated the authority over textile imports that the combination of a multilateral agreement and domestic law, particularly section 204 of the Agriculture Act, would provide. Section 204 (passed in May 1956) authorized the president to negotiate with foreign governments to limit the export to the United States of agricultural *or textile* products, and to carry out such an agreement by limiting the entry of such products into the United States. The LTA thus activated the president's "204" authority in place, and President Kennedy quickly imposed limits on several categories of imports from Hong Kong. By the end of 1963, the United States had in place restrictions against 17 countries (Keesing and Wolf 1980, 38).

4.5.3   Evolution and Expansion into the MFA

Richard Nixon, running for the presidency in 1968 against Hubert Humphrey, had learned from the 1960 lesson of the power of the textile industry. He thus pledged in his campaign to negotiate an international agreement that would include wool and man-made fiber products. Japan by this time was in a stronger position, and experience with the STA and LTA had taught exporting countries what they could expect from an international agreement.

The provisions of the MFA reflected a shift of power toward the exporting countries. The hortatory statement of the agreement's intentions is more detailed and more extensive about the expansion of exports of developing countries. The agreement also urges importing countries who restrict imports to pursue policies to promote adjustment. Article 3, as did the parallel article in the STA, provides for an importing country to seek from an exporting country an agreement to limit its exports, it also provides that the importing country may take unilateral action if agreement is not reached within 60 days. Annual limits, whether agreed or unilateral, were to be based on the 12 months ending two months before. If a limit was extended, the minimum growth rate was 6 percent.

There were two significant differences between the MFA and the LTA:

1. The MFA did not provide for "mutually acceptable arrangements on other terms;" that is, there was no end-around the limits the arrangement put on allowable quotas.

2. MFA created a multilateral surveillance institution, the Textiles Surveillance Body (TSB), to supervise the functioning of the arrangement. Participants were required to report safeguard actions to the TSB, which reviews their conformity with the provisions of the arrangement. The TSB is also the forum for dispute settlement.

The extensions of the MFA through 1986 tended to shift the balance toward tighter import restrictions. In 1977, at the urging of the European Economic Community, a provision was added to allow "jointly agreed reasonable departures" from the limits of the agreement. This provision shifted greater power to the individual countries negotiating the bilateral agreements under the MFA, away from a multilateral solution. In negotiating bilateral agreements, industrial countries were much less likely to care about opening up new markets and much more concerned about protecting their industries from additional imports. Aggarwal (1985) argues that the combination of the 1977 provision and the important role of bilateral agreements in implementing the provisions of the MFA exacerbated the trend toward more protection.

In the rest of this paper, we focus on the scope and impact of the protection received under the MFA. While the protection the U.S. textile industry received was substantial, it was, to some degree, leaky. Although the U.S. government was forced to establish the legal statements of the multilateral arrangements and their implementation in domestic law—principally in section 204, as amended, of the Agriculture Act—considerable effort was applied within the government to limit the application of those legal instruments.

4.6   Protection, but Not Complete Protection

While the protection won by the industry was substantial, policymakers remained uneasy with the extent of trade restrictions in textiles. Officials who were chosen to lead the negotiations were often aggressively protrade; implementation of the agreements has often been lax. The ultimate test is provided by the impact of these restrictions on imports, domestic production, and the overall health of the industry. Textile imports as a percentage of U.S. consumption are now four times higher than they were in 1960; apparel imports are seven times higher. The industry never completely overcame the executive branch's reluctance to provide protection and the trading community's inventiveness at finding ways to evade the mechanisms of restriction.

4.6.1   Negotiation and Implementation of the Textile Agreements

One early example of the reluctance to embrace managed trade in textiles is provided by President Kennedy's candidate for negotiating the multilateral restraint agreement. Kennedy gave the position to George Ball, then under secretary of state for economic affairs.[25] Ball was a leading internationalist in the U.S. government and a leading spokesperson for the foreign policy view of trade policy. In the first year of the Kennedy administration he had been the State Department official responsible for the administration of U.S. foreign aid, and he had led the reorganization of this administration into the Agency for International Development. He also had the lead within the Kennedy administration on the TEA.

While we have located no public statement by Ball that reveals his opinion of the textile negotiations that he led, his feelings on textile restraints are revealed by a later statement regarding textile negotiations during the Nixon administration: "If our relations with Europe have suffered from neglect and presumptuousness, interspersed with occasional pettiness . . . the Nixon Administration was reckless to the point of irresponsibility when it weakened the alliance ties that bound Japan to the West. The primal cause of the deterioration of relations was a tradesman's argument over the export of Japanese textiles to the United States" (Ball 1976, 175).

After President Kennedy assigned Ball to negotiate a textile agreement, Ball visited several national capitals to line up support. According to the ATMI, Ball's briefing to them on his findings included the following points:
- The State Department is opposed to United States control of textile product imports.
- It intends to seek agreement only on cotton textiles.
- It proposes to use the 1960 level of imports as the base.

---

25. A textile executive who was then active in industry politics told us that Ball was "embarrassed" by this assignment.

- It plans for the agreement to provide for increases of 5 percent (quoted by Brandis 1982, 20; from the ATMI report to its membership).

Senator Pastore and Congressman Vinson organized a group of 39 senators and 124 representatives to protest the State Department position directly to President Kennedy (Brandis 1982, 21), but the draft arrangement the U.S. delegation took to the negotiations contained these terms, and these terms are the ones in the agreed arrangement.

To oversee the textile program President Kennedy created the Cabinet Textile Advisory Committee and a lower level committee now named the Committee for Implementation of the Textile Agreements (CITA). These committees include representatives of the Departments of Commerce, State, Labor, and Treasury, and the Office of the Trade Representative. The day-to-day process of implementing the agreements goes somewhat as follows.[26]

The MFA provides for restraint of imports that cause "market disruption." When the textile industry feels that market disruption is occurring in a particular product category, they make the facts known to CITA.

CITA meets usually at the level of deputy assistant secretary (senior civil service), with the Commerce Department representative chairing. The CITA presents its own "disruption statement," on which the industry often comments. That comment often includes the provision of more-current data on the state of the domestic industry: output, prices, employment, and so forth. Sometimes an industry association surveys U.S. companies to obtain up-to-date information, then submits these data as a comment on the CITA's disruption statement.

The basic factual inputs into the disruption report are quantities and unit values of imports that have an adverse impact on the U.S. industry. These data are buttressed with data on domestic production, employment, capacity utilization, and so forth. Sometimes other relevant information is provided, such as a decision by a U.S. producer to cancel an investment or expansion plan.

In the end, industry officials insist, there is a loose relation between the disruption statement and the quota that is set. Although the decision on *whether* to impose a quota appears to be significantly influenced by industry recommendations, industry representatives argue that quota *levels* are often set at levels which are much higher than they requested. Under MFA rules, the United States may set an initial quota on a new product, but the United States must then enter into negotiations with the exporting country to agree a final quota level. While the Commerce Department administrators are usually sympathetic to the industry's position, the final quota level must be negotiated by the trade representative with the exporting country and must win the approval of the interagency committee. This committee includes two "general interest" departments, State and Treasury. Often the final level is more than twice the

---

26. The following four paragraphs are based on interviews with industry association officials.

level of the initial quota, and even the initial quota is larger than the limit actually needed to stop market disruption.

From the industry's perspective, there are some who feel that the restraint agreements have not been rigorously enforced. The ATMI evaluated that in the 12 months the STA was in force, imports were one-third higher than if the minimums the agreement allowed had been achieved. The same evaluation concluded that "while President Johnson successfully pushed through legislation abolishing the two-price system, his administration was much weaker in carrying out the textile import quota system" (Brandis 1982, 27ff.).

In 1984, when imports surged as the dollar appreciated, the ATMI testified that through the first 10 months of 1984, of the imports of uncontrolled products that were causing market disruption and eligible for a "call" under the MFA, only one-third had in fact been called. A call is a notification to an exporting country that its exports of a particular product are causing market disruption, and that a preliminary quota will be imposed.

Another way to soften enforcement of limits is through the various dimensions of customs enforcement, for example, lax policing of transshipment of Chinese textiles through countries not under restraint or unable to fill their quotas from their own production. A recent agreement between the United States and China involved allegations that transshipment of Chinese textiles to the United States exceeded $2 billion per year. Since China's textile exports to the United States under the MFA were $4.68 billion in 1993, this suggests that transshipments could raise export levels to 150 percent of actual quotas (*Financial Times* 1994).

4.6.2   Impact of Protection on the Health of the Industry

The changing economic situation of the textile and apparel sectors is described in appendix table 4A.1. In 1960, apparel and textile employment together accounted for 13.4 percent of total manufacturing employment. That share declined moderately over a 20-year period: by 1985, the textile and apparel industries combined still accounted for 10 percent of total employment in manufacturing. Although union membership in most sectors has rapidly declined, the share of unionization in textiles and apparel remained almost constant, declining slightly between 1960 and 1980.

As a share of total manufacturing output, textile and apparel production fell from slightly over 7 percent of total output in 1960 to 4.4 percent of total manufacturing output in 1985. Despite the nearly 50 percent fall in manufacturing share, relative wages remained fairly stable and capital's share in value added increased. Wages in the textile industry were on average 65 percent of average wages in the rest of manufacturing, a figure which remained stable until 1985. In apparel, where the inroads made by import competition were steeper, relative wages fell from 56 percent of average manufacturing wages in 1960 to 50 percent of average manufacturing wages in 1985.

Capital's share in value added, which we define as value added less labor costs, divided by the value of shipments, actually rose in both sectors. This value, which is labeled "profits" in table 4A.1, rose from 18 to 20 percent in textiles and from 17 to 27 percent in apparel between 1960 and 1985. One interpretation of the relatively stable wages and capital share during this 25-year period is that both labor and capital benefited from protectionist measures.

There is no question that the protection won by the industry was substantial. Cline (1990, 191) estimates that quotas as of 1986 provided the equivalent of a 28 percent tariff on textiles and a 53 percent tariff on apparel. Other industries on average enjoy tariffs of no more than 5 percent. Without this protection, according to Cline, there would be about 21,000 fewer jobs in textiles and 214,000 fewer in apparel production in the United States.

The extent to which protection in the textile industry actually restricted imports is documented in figures 4.1 and 4.2. As indicated in figure 4.1, import penetration in the textile sector appears to have considerably slowed under protection. In comparison to other industries, import penetration increased at a much slower rate. In the 1980s, however, import penetration rapidly increased. Figure 4.2 documents the changes in import penetration in the apparel sector. Although protection also appears to have dampened the upward trend in imports in the 1970s, increases in import penetration were much more dramatic than in textiles. In the 1980s, import penetration in apparel surged, growing at a more rapid pace than in other industries. Between 1960 and 1985, while

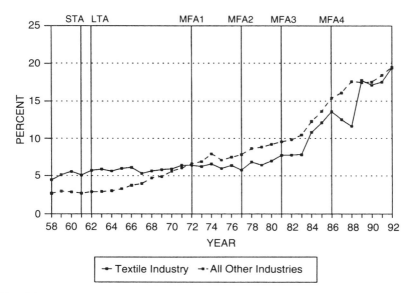

Fig. 4.1   Import penetration in U.S. textile industry, 1958–92 (comparison with all other U.S. industry)
Source: Abowd (1991).
Note: "Other" excludes both textiles and apparel.

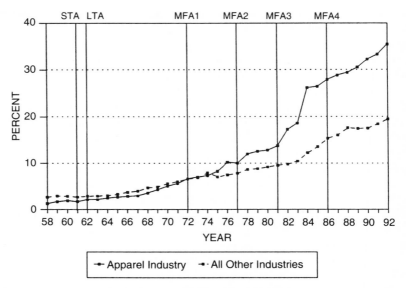

Fig. 4.2   Import penetration in U.S. apparel industry, 1958–92 (comparison with all other U.S. industry)
Source: Abowd (1991).
Note: "Other" excludes both textiles and apparel.

import penetration increased from 5.5 to 12.1 percent in textiles, imports surged from 1.9 to 26.4 percent in apparel (table 4.A.1). In both sectors, exports generally remained low, increasingly only around 1980 with the devaluation of the dollar in the late 1970s.

The story presented in figures 4.1 and 4.2 and table 4A.1 is supported by the evidence in table 4.5, which is taken from Cline (1990). Table 4.5 presents changes in import volumes (not import penetration). The evidence does seem to suggest that the MFA slowed down import growth, particularly in the textile industry. After the MFA was introduced, growth rates in imports of textiles and apparel both fell. In textiles, growth rates became negative, and only recovered in the early 1980s. Table 4.5 also documents the significant increases in imports during the first half of the 1980s. Cline attributes these increases to the overvaluation of the dollar and recovery from the recession.

The evidence suggests that textile imports kept pace with the rest of U.S. industry, while apparel imports surged ahead. The dramatic increases in apparel imports during the 1980s and early 1990s, as well as the more moderate increases in textile imports, is particularly illustrative of the leaky protection which has characterized the MFA. According to Cline, textile and apparel imports rose by 100 percent in real terms between 1983 and 1986. How could such an increase occur under a regime which was committed to import growth rates of no more than 6 percent annually? Evidently, quota allocations were

Table 4.5   **Annual Growth Rates of Real U.S. Imports of Textiles and Apparel**[a]
                   (percent)

Sector and Year	SYE[b]	Deflator	Deflator
Textiles			
1961–72	16.1[c]	5.9	4.2
1972–77	−9.1	−4.9	−9.3
1977–81	−2.1	4.3	0.4
1981–86	−21.9	12.7	12.6
Apparel			
1961–72	18.3[c]	13.8	14.8
1972–77	2.9	11.1	6.7
1977–81	4.7	6.8	1.9
1981–86	12.9	16.4	17.4

Source: Cline (1990, 170).
[a]Calculated from log-linear regressions for each period.
[b]Square-yard equivalents.
[c]Figures are for 1964–72.

sufficiently flexible and underutilized (see table 4.6) to allow the sudden increase. Nor, according to the Congressional Budget Office, could these increases be accounted for by imports from unrestricted sources (see Cline 1990).

Although import protection saved thousands of jobs in textiles and apparel, it did not prevent significant downsizing of employment. Although as a share of total manufacturing employment, textiles and apparel only declined moderately, figures 4.3 and 4.4 document the significant downsizing of employment in the textile and apparel industries between 1958 and 1986. Downsizing was more significant in the textile than in the apparel industry. Between 1958 and 1986, employment in textiles shrank by 30 percent. In apparel, which faced even steeper import competition, employment declines only totaled 20 percent. By 1986, total employment in the two industries had shrunk to between 70 and 80 percent of their 1958 levels.

The textile industry was more successful in downsizing its labor force, in part due to technological advances in the industry which encouraged mechanization. However, productivity performance in both sectors has not been particularly impressive. Figure 4.5 shows the trends in output per worker for the textile, apparel, and other manufacturing sectors. Although the textile industry performed relatively better than apparel, both sectors lagged in productivity increases compared to the rest of manufacturing. The divergence between the rest of manufacturing and these two sectors appears to begin in the early 1970s, when the MFA was put in place.

Using the NBER trade database, we also computed measures of total factor productivity growth (TFPG) for textiles, apparel, and the rest of manufacturing. The trends in TFPG are reported in table 4.6. TFPG was calculated by

Table 4.6   **Total Factor Productivity Growth in Textiles, Apparel, and the Rest of the Manufacturing Sector**

Sector	1959–72	1973–86
Textiles	1.3	0.6
Apparel	0.6	0.5
Other manufacturing	1.2	1.4

subtracting growth in labor (number of workers), material inputs, and capital stock from output growth. Labor and material inputs were weighted by their shares in output.

The trends in TFPG are similar to the trends in labor productivity. Prior to 1973, productivity growth in textiles was slightly higher than the manufacturing average. Productivity increases in apparel, on the other hand, were significantly behind, averaging a 0.6 percent increase per year in comparison with 1.2 percent for the rest of manufacturing. During the 1973–86 period, the gap widened even further. While TFPG averaged 1.4 percent for the rest of manufacturing, productivity growth for textiles slipped to 0.6 percent and for apparel to 0.5 percent. The net evidence seems to suggest that, at least in the apparel industry, protection did not serve as a vehicle for a productivity turn-

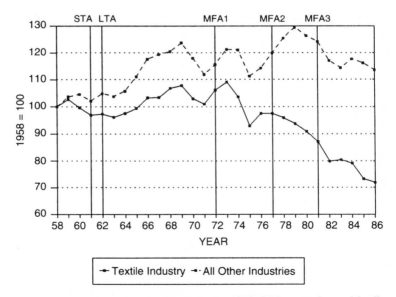

Fig. 4.3   Employment in U.S. textile industry, 1958–86 (comparison with all other U.S. industry)
Source: Abowd (1991).
Note: "Other" excludes both textiles and apparel.

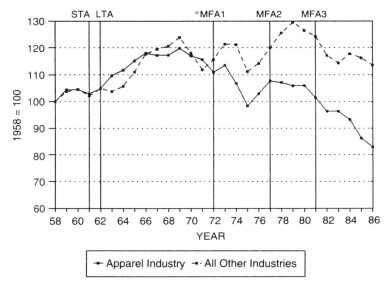

Fig. 4.4   Employment in U.S. apparel industry, 1958–86 (comparison with all other U.S. industry)

Source: Abowd (1991).

Note: "Other" excludes both textiles and apparel.

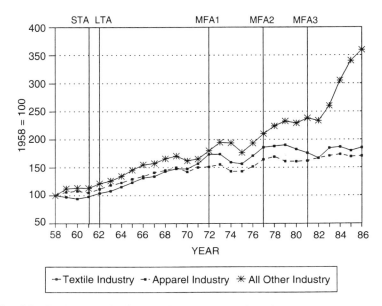

Fig. 4.5   Real value of shipments/employment, 1958–86

Source: Abowd (1991).

around. The textile industry, while it performed slightly better than the industry average during the 1960s and early 1970s, lagged behind after 1973.

The evidence presented above suggests that the protection granted to the industry, while substantial, was not enough to prevent significant increases in import competition. The MFA led to a decline in the growth rate of textile and apparel imports during the 1970s, but this decline was followed by a surge in the early 1980s when the dollar's appreciation was combined with an economic recovery. The surge in imports during the 1980s provides persuasive evidence that MFA protection was certainly not complete. Additional evidence is provided by U.S. administration efforts to implement protective legislation in less restrictive ways.

4.7   Quantifying the Determinants of MFA Protection, 1981–89

Despite the vast literature on protection in the U.S. textile industry, few studies attempt to quantify the determinants of protection within the industry. Most empirical studies, such as the comprehensive study by Cline (1990) and the recent volume edited by Hamilton (1990), focus on either measuring welfare costs of protection or evaluating its impact on industry profits, productivity, and trade. Cline (1990), for example, estimates that the cost of textile and apparel protection (in 1986) amounted to between $20.3 billion and $40 billion annually. This translates to a cost per household of between $240 and $500 annually, in 1986 dollars.

One area that has been almost entirely neglected is how U.S. policymakers allocate import quotas across exporting countries. One exception is Dean (1993), who evaluates MFA quota allocations across large and small exporting countries. Dean (1993) models the determinants of quota allocations as a function of country size, export volumes, and export growth. She finds that the size of the exporter was a critical determinant of restraint under the MFA1. In contrast, under MFA2 and MFA3 she finds a strong bias toward restraining very small sellers and those whose exports grew rapidly. Benedict (1993) examines the allocation of VERs for a different industry—the steel sector in the United States. He also finds that large countries and countries with rapid export growth were more likely to be targeted.

The political economy literature suggests that many other factors are important in determining quotas, such as the health of the import-competing sector, employment and wage trends, exchange rate movements, and the importance of foreign markets as a destination for U.S. exports. The analysis below provides a comprehensive examination of which of these factors were the most important in determining the allocation of textile and apparel quotas. Our analysis also differs from previous research by examining the entire 1980s, a period when quotas expanded at a rapid pace. Finally, we also analyze the factors which determined the *size* of the allocated quotas—an issue which has been entirely ignored. These quota allocations represented a significant fraction of total export earnings for many developing countries. Understanding the determination of quotas is consequently of practical importance.

4.7.1 Empirical Framework

The analytical models described in section 4.2, combined with the administrative criteria for quota allocations outlined in section 4.6, suggest a relationship between the variables listed in table 4.7 and quota determination in the United States. For each variable, table 4.7 indicates whether it serves as an MFA criterion for market disruption or whether it acts as a proxy for factors likely to be important in determining protection from theoretical models of endogenous protection. The last two columns in table 4.7 indicate whether the expected relationship between quotas and each of the variables is likely to be positive or negative.

There are two columns of expected signs, one relating to the question, On which products imported from which countries is it more likely that there will be a quota? In this framework, we are simply trying to identify whether a quota will be imposed (i.e., the answer is either yes or no). The second column refers to the question, On which products imported from which countries is the import quota likely to be larger? A larger quota, of course, is a less restrictive one; hence the signs in the last column are the reverse of the signs in the first column.

The expected sign is the one predicted by the model *best* proxied by the variable. In reality, the distinction between the various models may be somewhat blurred. For example, we list employment (number of workers) as a proxy for the adding machine model, which suggests that the number of employees (i.e., voters) will be positively correlated with the likelihood of a sector winning protection. But a large number of people working in a sector may present organizational problems, and hence the political organization models would suggest a negative correlation between number of workers and the likelihood of winning protection. However, we consider the latter a secondary fit between proxy and model and have not listed it in the table. As to proxies for organizational problems, we consider the number of plants a better indicator of organizational problems than the number of workers. Within a plant, lines of communication to workers are already established; hence the organizational challenge between plants will be more severe than between workers in a plant.

Our principal hypothesis is that the process of imposing MFA-sanctioned quotas is not limited to taking into account only the criteria that the MFA specifies as justifying such quotas. We have placed at the top of the list of explanatory variables those that are specified by the MFA as the criteria that justify an import quota. If there were no room for discretion in MFA administration, then these and only these variables would contribute significantly to the explanation of actual quota allocations.

The second group of variables listed in table 4.7 are indirect proxies for pressure from import competition. The higher the capital/labor ratio of a sector

Table 4.7   **Explanatory Variables: Their Relations with Alternative Models of Protection**

		Expected Sign	
Variable	Model Represented	Yes-No Quota	Size of Quota
Change in U.S. production	Market disruption; MFA criterion	−	+
Change in employment	Market disruption; MFA criterion	−	+
Change in import penetration	Market disruption; MFA criterion	+	−
Import penetration	Market disruption; MFA criterion	+	−
Change in capital stock	Market disruption; MFA criterion	−	+
Profits	Market disruption; MFA criterion	−	+
Capital/labor ratio	U.S. comparative advantage; lesser pressure from imports	−	+
Exchange rate	Expensive foreign currency lessens pressure from imports	−	+
Wages	Equity concern; the poor are deserving	−	+
Employment	Political payoff; number of votes	+	−
Number of plants	Political organization; free riding from large numbers	−	+
Plant size (employees per plant)	Political organization; resources available for organization	+	−
	Political organization, barriers to entry limit free riding	+	−
Change in U.S. exports	Value of market to U.S. exporters	−	+
GDP growth in quota country	Equity concern; the poor are deserving	+	−

the stronger should be U.S. comparative advantage and the lower the likelihood that the sector will experience a degree of import competition sufficient to cause it to ask for quota protection. The exchange rate, measuring the dollar cost of the exporting country's currency should have a similar impact, though over time rather than across sectors.

In the lower part of the table we have listed the various political influences brought out by the models of protection reviewed in section 4.2. Some of these reflect domestic influences such as the number of votes at stake or the ease with which the sector can organize or can control free riding. Others reflect international considerations such as the value of the market to U.S. exporters.

4.7.2   Specifications

To quantify the determinants of textile and garment quotas during the 1980s, we analyze two different dependent variables. We begin by examining the decision to impose a quota, using data which covers both protected and unprotected products and countries. We then examine the determination of quota levels, using a Tobit specification. We describe these two approaches in more detail below.

We begin by addressing the following economic problem: what determines whether a quota will be imposed on a particular country or product? For a particular product i in country j and time t, a quota is either imposed ($Y_{ijt} = 1$) or not ($Y_{ijt} = 0$). Whether a quota is imposed is a function of both country- and product-specific attributes, denoted by the vector x. This problem could be rephrased as follows:

(1) $$Y^*_{ijt} = B'x_{ijt} + u_{ijt}.$$

We assume that u has a logistic distribution. Y^* is not observed; what we do observe is the following:

$Y = 1$ if $Y^* > 0$ (i.e., a nonzero quota is imposed);

$Y = 0$ otherwise (no quotas).

This problem is a standard logit problem which can be easily solved using conventional maximum likelihood estimation. We include the following variables in the vector x as determinants of the probability of protection: (1) wages$_{i,t-1}$ (MFA product category i at time $t - 1$), (2) total number of employees$_{i,t-1}$, (3) total number of plants$_{i,t-1}$, (4) average plant size$_{i,t-1}$, defined as employees$_{i,t-1}$/plants$_{i,t-1}$, (5) change in U.S. production$_{i,t-1}$, (6) change in import penetration$_{i,t-1}$, (7) import penetration$_{i,t-1}$, (8) percentage change in U.S. exports to country j at time t, (9) GDP growth$_{jt}$ for trading partner j at time t, (10) U.S. bilateral (nominal) exchange rate with country j at time t, (11) change in capital stock$_{i,t-1}$, (12) profits$_{i,t-1}$, and (13) the capital/labor ratio in sector i at time $t - 1$.

All variables except profits, capital/labor ratio, GDP growth, import penetration, and U.S. production are measured in logarithms. Wages are defined as average compensation per worker, deflated by the consumer price index. To avoid endogeneity problems, all variables except exchange rate, GDP growth, and change in U.S. exports are measured at time $t - 1$ for a quota imposed in period t. The change in import penetration is defined as import penetration at time $t - 1$ less import penetration at time $t - 2$. Changes in U.S. production and capital stock are defined as differences of lagged values as well.

A second approach is not just to focus on *whether* a sector received quota protection (yes or no) but to analyze what determines the relative magnitudes of quotas across different sectors. Since quotas were imposed for only 20 percent of the 20,000 observations in the sample, the resulting function is likely to be highly nonlinear. Although ordinary least squares estimation would lead to biased estimates, Tobit estimation can be used to address the censoring problem. The data is censored in the sense that we do not observe the quota level for a large share of the sample. However, unlike standard censoring problems, in which the dependent variable is generally censored from below (typically at zero), in this case the censoring occurs from above—absence of a quota should be represented not by a 0 value, but by a number large enough that it has no restrictive effect. For a product on which no quota is imposed, the quota's magnitude might be approximated by an arbitrarily large quota, greater than or equal to an upper limit denoted by U. Then, equation (1) can be rewritten as follows:

$$Y^*_{ijt} = Bx_{ijt} + u_{ijt};$$

(2) $\quad\quad Y = Y^* \quad \text{if } Y^* < U \text{ (a quota is imposed)};$

$\quad\quad\quad\quad Y = U \quad \text{if } Y^* \geq U \text{ (no quota imposed)}.$

The quota level, measured by the value of the latent variable Y^*, is only observed if a quota is imposed. If no quota is imposed, we interpret the quota as having an infinite magnitude, and we model the infinite quota as a quota which is censored at an upper limit U. In the estimation, we specify U to be equal to the maximum quota level observed during the sample period. We also experimented with alternative values for U, but these did not affect the results and consequently are not reported. The Tobit model with censoring from above can be estimated using standard maximum likelihood techniques.

4.7.3 Data

The database, which covers the period 1981–89,[27] was created by merging information from a number of different sources. Data on quota levels and imports at the level of each MFA category was collected by the International Economics Department at the World Bank, based on the Expired Restraints of the Performance Report prepared by the U.S. Department of Commerce. A more detailed description of the World Bank MFA data is provided by Erzan, Goto, and Holmes (1990). Information on quota levels is available annually, at the level of the individual country exporting to the United States and the individual MFA product category. All quota levels are defined in physical quantities, such as dozens of dresses or square yards of cotton cloth. Rather than attempt to use conversion factors which provide crude ways to aggregate across different units of measurement, we used the original quantities. However, to avoid nonsensical comparisons between different physical units, we included

---

27. This time period was chosen because a previous World Bank project had prepared a database on U.S. quotas that covered those years. The cost of acquiring and cleaning up additional information prevented our extending these data back or forward.

type dummies for each of the eight different quantity measures included in the database.[28]

MFA quotas and shipments were merged with Bureau of Labor Statistics data on numbers of establishments, wage bill, and total employment. Wages, employment, and establishments are recorded annually, at the four-digit Standard Industrial Classification (SIC). To merge the two sets of data, we created a concordance between the SIC and the MFA categories. Since there were fewer than 100 SIC codes for textiles and apparel (SIC categories 22 and 23) but several hundred MFA categories, this required sometimes using the same SIC code for several different MFA categories. Real wages were computed by dividing the wage bill by the number of employees then deflating by the consumer price index.

Information on U.S. production and total U.S. imports, in physical units and by MFA category, is collected by the Textile Division of the U.S. Department of Commerce. The import data aggregates over all imports into the United States. Using this data, import penetration was calculated as the share of imports in domestic consumption, defined as the sum of imports and domestic production. Although it would have been preferable to subtract U.S. exports in calculating import penetration, this information was not available by MFA category.

The import penetration and production data was directly merged by MFA category with the database on quotas and shipments. Source-country GDP (in real levels), GDP growth rates, U.S. total exports to each MFA exporter, and exchange rates were all taken from World Bank sources. The exchange rate, in dollars per unit of foreign currency, was converted to an index using 1981 as a base year.

Data on U.S. capital stock for the four-digit SIC categories that include textiles and apparel was taken from the NBER trade data file. Details on construction of the capital variable is provided by Abowd (1991). Using variables from the NBER trade files, we constructed a profits variable using the following definition:

(3) Profits = (Value added − Payroll)/(Value of shipments).

The profits variable could also be regarded as the capital share in the value of output, or the return to capital normalized by the value of output. One problem with such a measure is that it is likely to be higher in sectors with greater capital intensity. To the extent that the capital stock or some other measure of capital intensity is included in the regression, however, this problem is less severe. Other shortcomings of this profit measure, which has been frequently used in the empirical industrial organization literature, are discussed in Schmalensee (1986). Since the capital stock variable is only available in the NBER

---

28. Physical quantities are reported in the following different units: dozens, square meters, square yards, kilograms, dozen pairs, pieces, pounds, and square feet.

trade files until 1986, we will present results with and without the capital and profit variables.

There are at least two potentially important sample selection issues which arise in assembling this data set. The first is that the database generally excludes most industrial countries, with the exception of Japan and Canada. Consequently, the sample of countries is incomplete. For a complete analysis, we would need to include all exporters to the United States, including industrial country sources such as Italy. This is an ongoing project for future work. In the meantime, however, it is possible that the results are subject to sample selection bias. For example, if only the poorer countries are included in the sample, then it is likely that the coefficient on real GDP presents inconsistent estimates of the relationship between exporter wealth and U.S. protection.

A second source of selection bias is the sample's restriction by data availability. In particular, only those observations are included which have nonmissing information on wages, employment, U.S. production, and total U.S. imports. If the Department of Commerce is more likely to have nonmissing data for products with high import or production volumes, this could also lead to selection bias.

4.7.4   Empirical Results

Table 4.8 provides an overview of the trends in MFA quota coverage during the 1980s. For each country in the database, we computed average quota utilization for 1981, 1985, and 1989 by dividing actual shipments (in physical units) by quota allocations. The fourth column reports the average growth rate in quota allocations by country, averaging over all product categories for each country. The last column reports the magnitude of U.S. exports to each country in 1989.

In the first three columns, a missing value indicates that no quotas were imposed on the exporting country. It is evident from table 4.8 that the coverage of the MFA, in terms of affected countries, increased significantly in the 1980s. In 1981, only 22 countries had ceilings imposed on their exports of textiles and garments; by 1989, the number of quota-constrained countries—which totaled 38 in all—had nearly doubled.

The extent to which these quotas were actually binding is the topic of another paper. However, it is clear from table 4.8 that several major textile exporters attained levels very close to the quota ceiling. On average, China, Taiwan, and Hong Kong filled their quotas by over 80 percent across all MFA categories. India increased its average utilization rate from 20 percent in 1981 to 73 percent in 1989; Mexico increased from 26 to 63 percent.

Despite the significant increase in quota coverage during the 1980s, however, quota ceilings were also significantly relaxed. The fourth column in table 4.8 shows that, on average, import quotas increased by almost 6 percent annually. In other words, although coverage increased, imports into the United States were also allowed to rise at a moderate rate, as mandated by the terms

Table 4.8   **MFA Quotas in the 1980s for the United States: An Overview**

Country	Quota Utilization by Year (%)			Growth in Quota Allocation 1981–1989	Total U.S. Exports 1989 (millions)
	1981	1985	1989		
Costa Rica	100	78	66	4.2	880
China	91	75	82	10.2	5,807
Taiwan	87	83	70	3.4	11,323
Hong Kong	85	82	79	2.2	6,304
Sri Lanka	85	52	–	10.0	143
Malaysia	83	77	53	16.0	2,875
Korea	82	86	74	1.0	13,478
Dominican Republic	81	71	–	13.2	1,646
Pakistan	55	54	43	1.6	1,136
Japan	49	81	27	−1.6	44,584
Haiti	39	39	36	7.0	474
Philippines	29	37	70	3.0	2,206
Mexico	26	30	63	2.6	24,969
Brazil	22	56	45	4.8	4,799
India	20	73	73	4.6	2,463
Macao	20	24	29	−0.6	11
Singapore	20	21	29	2.0	7,353
Thailand	16	75	78	11.6	2,292
Romania	13	13	8	−3.4	156
Colombia	11	15	26	−10.2	1,916
Poland	9	7	9	−2.2	414
Yugoslavia	0	66	46	12.4	501
Turkey	–	91	–	83.4	2,004
Egypt	–	77	31	1.8	2,610
Guam	–	75	60	2.6	2
Indonesia	–	74	87	11.4	1,256
Hungary	–	63	55	8.4	122
Uruguay	–	45	–	15.6	133
Mauritius	–	45	59	10.0	12
Peru	–	35	41	−2.2	690
Pacific Islands	–	34	–	4.8	–
Guatemala	–	14	95	5.8	662
Maldives	–	11	–	0.4	3
Panama	–	5	1	−9.2	729
Bangladesh	–	–	84	17.4	282
United Arab Emirates	–	–	79	35.8	1,240
El Salvador	–	–	66	−39.6	521
East Germany	–	–	60	0.0	94
Jamaica	–	–	37	18.8	1,009
Burma	–	–	35	5.8	5
Northern Marianas	–	–	32	5.8	–
Nepal	–	–	28	3.8	9
Canada	–	–	21	–	78,266
Trinidad and Tobago	–	–	1	12.4	562
Average across all countries	47	52	49	5.7	–

of the MFA. In some cases the increase in quota allocations exceeded 10 percent per year (such as in China, Malaysia, Dominican Republic, Thailand, Turkey, Indonesia, Uruguay, Bangladesh, Jamaica, and Trinidad and Tobago). The combination of increasing quota coverage and increasing access to U.S. markets is a key characteristic of the MFA, which has sought to both increase access by developing countries to industrial countries and yet ensure an orderly process which would minimize "market disruption" in industrial country markets. There are some notable exceptions, however. Quota allocations to two of the largest exporters—Taiwan and Hong Kong—increased by less than 4 percent; allocations to Japan actually declined by almost 2 percent annually.

In table 4.9, we compare the means for wages, employment, and all the other independent variables for the quota-constrained and unconstrained MFA categories. Although these comparisons fail to control for other factors, they do provide a general indication of differences in economic conditions across protected and unprotected sectors.

A series of t-tests were used to test the hypothesis that the means are equal across protected and unprotected products. A high t-value indicates a rejection of the hypothesis that means are equal across the two groups. Column (3) in table 4.9 shows that the means are statistically different for wages, capital stock, number of plants, average plant size, import penetration, GDP growth in the exporting country, and capital/labor ratio.

The results suggest that wages are lower in protected categories, confirming the predictions of both theoretical models and anecdotal reports on protection in the U.S. textile industry. As pointed out earlier, however, this could simply reflect the United States' greater comparative advantage in high-wage sectors. The results also point to a higher number of plants, smaller plant sizes, and greater import penetration (in levels) in protected sectors. Using either the capital stock or the capital/labor ratio as a measure of capital intensity, we find that no-quota sectors are significantly more capital intensive. Finally, the results show that quota-constrained countries exhibit higher GDP growth rates.

The "Yes-No" Model

The logit results from estimating the probability of imposing a quota as a function of the x-vector of independent variables are presented in table 4.10. All specifications include annual dummies, but the coefficients on the year effects are not reported in the table. Since capital and profit variables are only available until 1986, columns (1) and (2) report the results from excluding these two variables, which nearly doubles the sample size. Columns (3)–(6) report the results from using two different measures for capital: changes in capital stock and capital/labor ratio. Each of these three basic specifications is reported with and without the inclusion of average plant size. Since plant size is defined in terms of two other variables (number of employees divided by number of plants) we exclude it from some of the specifications to control for potential collinearity problems.

Table 4.9   *t*-Tests of Differences across Protected and Unprotected MFA
Categories, 1981–89

Variable	No Quotas (1)	Quotas (2)	*t*-Value for *t*-Test of Means (3)
Change in U.S. production	−0.02	−0.01	1.67
	(.32)	(.30)	
Change in employment			
Change in import penetration	0.015	0.015	0.41
	(.06)	(.06)	
Import penetration	0.32	0.35	7.88*
	(.23)	(.22)	
Change in capital stock	−0.004	−0.004	0.37
	(.027)	(.027)	
Profits	0.25	0.26	0.88
	(.05)	(.04)	
Capital/labor ratio	0.0067	0.0064	2.81*
	(.006)	(.006)	
Exchange rate	3.87	3.85	1.05
	(1.32)	(1.28)	
Wages	9.50	9.49	10.25*
	(.16)	(.16)	
Employment	11.14	11.15	0.26
	(.79)	(.83)	
Number of plants	6.16	6.22	3.78*
	(.98)	(1.05)	
Plant size	4.55	4.49	6.14*
	(.59)	(.62)	
Change in U.S. exports	0.033	0.028	0.89
	(.37)	(.29)	
GDP growth in quota country	3.20	4.15	13.49*
	(4.93)	(4.80)	

Note: Numbers in parentheses are standard errors. All variables except profits, capital/labor ratio, GDP growth, import penetration (levels and differences), and U.S. production are measured in logarithms. All variables except exchange rate, GDP growth, and change in U.S. exports are measured at time $t-1$ for a quota imposed in period t.

*Rejection of equal means across protected and unprotected categories at the 1 percent level.

The coefficients on the independent variables are generally robust across the six different specifications, and the resulting signs and significance levels are consistent with our hypothesis that the MFA criteria are significant determinants of protection, but not the only determinants. As indicated by the stated MFA criteria for protection, high levels of import penetration in the previous year increase the likelihood of a quota. Likewise, lower levels of net investment (change in capital stock) increase the likelihood of protection, as do lower levels of profits.

It was a small surprise to find that changes in U.S. production have no explanatory power in the regression. The capital/labor ratio, which we interpret

Table 4.10   Logit Model of the Decision to Impose a Quota

Variable	(1)	(2)	(3)	(4)	(5)	(6)
Change in U.S. production (−)	0.06	0.06	0.14	0.13	0.20	0.19
	(.07)	(.07)	(.12)	(.12)	(.12)	(.12)
Change in employment	−1.49*	−1.59*	−1.40*	−1.85*	−1.76*	−2.08*
	(.35)	(.33)	(.50)	(.46)	(.48)	(.45)
Change in import penetration (+)	−0.72	−0.72	−0.31	−0.37	−0.12	−0.16
	(.40)	(.40)	(.55)	(.55)	(.55)	(.55)
Import penetration (+)	0.43*	0.42*	0.46*	0.43*	0.47*	0.45*
	(.08)	(.08)	(.10)	(.10)	(.10)	(.10)
Change in capital stock (−)			−3.63*	−3.44*		
			(1.06)	(1.05)		
Profits (−)			−1.28*	−0.94*	−0.26	0.05
			(.56)	(.54)	(.59)	(.56)
Capital/labor ratio (−)					10.00	12.01
					(6.44)	(6.33)

Exchange rate (−)	−0.03*	−0.08*	−0.08*	−0.08*	−0.08*
	(.01)	(.02)	(.02)	(.02)	(.02)
Wages (−)	−0.07	−0.80*	−0.53*	−0.74*	−0.59*
	(.13)	(.22)	(.19)	(.25)	(.23)
Employment (+)	−0.17*	−0.26*	−0.03	−0.26*	−0.09*
	(.08)	(.11)	(.05)	(.11)	(.06)
Number of plants (−)	0.19*	0.32*	0.12*	0.28*	0.14*
	(.07)	(.09)	(.04)	(.09)	(.05)
Plant size (+)	0.08	0.23*		0.18*	
	(.07)	(.10)		(.10)	
Change in U.S. exports (−)	0.00	−0.42*	−0.42*	−0.42*	−0.42*
	(.05)	(.09)	(.09)	(.09)	(.09)
GDP growth in quota country (+)	0.06*	0.06	0.06	0.06	0.06
	(.00)	(.00)	(.00)	(.00)	(.00)
N	20,609	12,961	12,961	12,961	12,961

Note: Numbers in parentheses are standard errors. All equations include annual time dummies. Constant terms not reported. All variables except profits, capital/labor ratio, GDP growth, import penetration (levels and differences), and U.S. production are measured in logarithms. All variables except exchange rate, GDP growth, and change in U.S. exports are measured at time $t-1$ for a quota imposed in period t.

*Significant at the 5 percent level.

as an indicator of U.S. comparative advantage, also is insignificant. We had hypothesized that the higher the capital/labor ratio of a sector the stronger should be U.S. comparative advantage and the lesser the likelihood that the sector will experience a degree of import competition sufficient to cause it to ask for quota protection. The exchange rate, measuring the dollar cost of the exporting country's currency should have a similar impact, though over time rather than across sectors. The exchange rate is significant, but the capital/labor ratio is not.

The political variables that are significant reflect both the equity concern and the political organization models of protection. Sectors with lower wage rates tend more often to be protected, likewise for sectors with relatively large plants. Large plant size represents both a barrier to possible entry and a likelihood that managerial organization is sufficiently large to permit some managerial resources to be made available for political action. These results suggest that textile producers who are numerous and relatively large (in terms of total employment) are most effective in lobbying for protection.

Some of the correlations we found were not expected, for example, a negative correlation between the size of the workforce and the probability of protection. Perhaps the explanation is that sectors with fewer workers are better able to organize and overcome the free-rider problem. The ATMI may also take employment into account in making recommendations for protection, perhaps interpreting a low level of employment as a sign of industry problems. This interpretation might also account for the negative relationship between employment and protection.

The impact of international commercial politics is reflected in the negative correlation between the likelihood of a quota and the growth of U.S. exports to the exporting country. In addition, quotas were more likely to be imposed against countries with higher levels of GDP and against countries whose levels of imports from the United States were large. These variables both reflect foreign export capacity, and in this sense the signs of the correlations make sense. But they are the best indicators we have of the capacity to retaliate, so our results, taken at face value, indicate that a foreign carrot (rapid growth of imports from the United States) does influence U.S. decision makers, but a foreign stick (the threat of retaliation) does not. This is at variance with anecdotal evidence that suggests that China has been effective in defending its export interests by threatening to stop its purchases of U.S. agricultural goods.

Another possible explanation is that, to the extent that richer countries are systematically excluded from the data sample, the coefficient on the level of GDP is upward. Thus, if the sample also included industrial country trade partners of the United States, that is, countries not subject to quota constraints under the MFA, we might have found that higher levels of GDP are associated with lower protection. If more powerful countries (as measured by the level of GDP) are less likely to be the target of U.S. protectionism, then this suggests an inverted U-shape between exporter GDP and U.S. protectionism. Very poor countries and very rich countries are less likely to be quota constrained than middle-income developing countries.[29]

The "Size of the Quota" Model

The logit results show the impact of various factors on the probability of a quota. The Tobit estimates, presented in table 4.11, examine the impact of these same factors on the *size* of the quota. The extent to which the estimates in table 4.10 and table 4.11 are consistent will depend on whether the process which generates whether or not to impose a quota also determines the size of the quota. Let us assume that the two decisions are generated in the same way. Since a larger quota allocation reflects a less restrictive trade policy, then the sign on the coefficients in table 4.10 should be reversed in table 4.11. For example, if higher wages were negatively associated with the probability of a quota in the logit results, then higher wages should be positively associated with bigger quotas (less restrictive trade policies) in the Tobit estimates.

The dependent variable in the Tobit estimates in table 4.11 is the logarithm of the quota allocation, which is specified in physical units. Product dummies are included to account for the fact that not all MFA categories are measured in the same units. The coefficients on wages, employment, number of plants, plant size, GDP, U.S. exports, and exchange rate—which are all measured in logarithms—can be interpreted as elasticities. In column (1), a 1 percent increase in wages leads to a 5.4 percent increase in the level of the quota, which indicates looser quotas (i.e., less protection) in products where U.S. workers earn higher wages.

The results from the Tobit specification ("size of quota" model) are consistent with the logit estimates ("yes-no" model). The same MFA variables and political variables are significant in the two specifications, while their signs—as hypothesized—are reversed from one model to the other. The Tobit results point to a strong relationship between quota size and the indicators of market disruption sanctioned by the MFA. The coefficient on change in employment,

---

29. Omitted product- and country-specific effects that are unobserved and remain constant over time are a possible source of bias in the estimates presented in table 4.10. In a linear regression framework, these unobserved effects could be accounted for by introducing product and country dummies, or by taking deviations from product-country means. In a logit framework, the problem is considerably more complicated. However, Chamberlain (1980) proposed an approach which allows these so-called fixed effects to be taken into account using conventional estimation methods. In the two-period case, consistent estimates can be obtained by only keeping those cases where quota coverage switched from 0 to 1 (or vice versa) over time. The resulting pairs of (0,1) and (1,0) observations are then estimated as a function of the x variables differenced over the two periods.

We applied this approach to the 1983–89 and 1983–86 periods to examine the robustness of our original specification. Since the resulting point estimates were either comparable to the results in table 4.10 or statistically insignificant, they are not reported here. A large share of the estimates, although consistent with table 4.10, were statistically insignificant. One possible reason for this is that the cross-section variation in the sample is much greater than the time-series variation, which is used to identify the fixed effect model.

Table 4.11 Tobit Specification of the Distribution of Quota Allocations across Textile and Garment Exporters to the United States: Dependent Variable = log (Quota)

Variable	(1)	(2)	(3)	(4)	(5)	(6)
Change in U.S. production (+)	-0.16	-0.16	-0.62	-0.53	-0.53	-0.45
	(.35)	(.35)	(.63)	(.62)	(.63)	(.62)
Change in employment (+)	4.48*	4.77*	5.70*	7.35*	6.77*	8.86*
	(1.74)	(1.69)	(2.52)	(2.37)	(2.43)	(2.28)
Change in import penetration (−)	2.99	3.01	0.58	0.95	0.52	0.91
	(1.98)	(1.98)	(2.77)	(2.76)	(2.76)	(2.75)
Import penetration (−)	-2.13*	-2.08*	-2.06*	-1.92*	-1.83*	-1.70*
	(.44)	(.43)	(.55)	(.54)	(.55)	(.55)
Change in capital stock (+)			11.22*	11.20*		
			(5.67)	(5.67)		
Profits (+)			-5.60	-6.23	-3.98	-5.36
			(4.02)	(4.01)	(3.99)	(3.95)
Capital/labor ratio (+)					145.29*	126.90
					(44.71)	(43.97)

	(1)	(2)	(3)	(4)	(5)	(6)
Exchange rate (+)	0.20*	0.20*	0.50*	0.49*	0.49*	0.49*
	(.06)	(.06)	(.12)	(.12)	(.12)	(.12)
Wages (+)	5.37*	5.18*	9.44*	8.30*	6.33*	5.26*
	(1.07)	(1.03)	(1.54)	(1.41)	(1.74)	(1.68)
Employment (−)	1.67*	1.44*	2.51*	1.59*	2.63*	1.46*
	(.41)	(.23)	(.57)	(.30)	(.57)	(.30)
Number of plants (+)	−1.40	−1.20*	−2.41*	−1.63*	−2.38*	−1.39*
	(.35)	(.18)	(.47)	(.23)	(.47)	(.24)
Plant size (−)	−0.24		−0.94		−1.21*	
	(.35)		(.49)		(.50)	
Change in U.S. exports (+)	0.10	0.10	2.36*	2.36*	2.36*	2.36*
	(.26)	(.26)	(.46)	(.46)	(.46)	(.46)
GDP growth in quota country (−)	−0.24*	−0.24*	−0.25*	−0.25*	−0.25*	−0.25*
	(.02)	(.02)	(.02)	(.02)	(.02)	(.02)
N	20,633	20,633	12,985	12,985	12,985	12,985

Note: Numbers in parentheses are standard errors. All equations include annual time dummies and unit dummies (for type of quota). Constant terms not reported. All variables except profits, capital/labor ratio, GDP growth, import penetration (levels and differences), and U.S. production are measured in logarithms. All variables except exchange rate, GDP growth, and change in U.S. exports are measured at time $t-1$ for a quota imposed in period t.

*Significant at the 5 percent level.

which varies from 4.5 to 8.9, suggests that if the rate of growth of employment increased from 0 to 1 percentage point annually, import quotas would expand between 4.5 and 8.9 percent. The coefficient on capital stock, which is 11.2, implies that if the growth rate of the capital stock were to increase from 0 to 1 percentage point annually, import quotas would expand by 11.2 percent. A 1 percentage point increase in import penetration (which varies between 0 and 1) leads to a reduction in import quotas by between 1.8 and 2.1 percent. This is a very large effect: if import penetration increased from 0 to 10 percent of domestic consumption, this would imply a contraction in quota levels of 20 percent.

The impact of several of the political variables is also significant. A 1 percent increase in wages leads to a 5 to 9 percent increase in the level of the quota. This suggests that the equity concern factor is important—more protection is granted when U.S. workers earn lower wages.

The size of the workforce, number of plants, and plant size have smaller effects. A 1 percent increase in employment leads to between 1.4 and 2.6 percent increase in the size of the quota, suggesting a negative relationship between size of the workforce and probability of protection. Higher numbers of plants and larger plant sizes are both associated with more restrictive quotas: a 1 percent increase in the number of plants decreases the size of the quota by 1.2 to 2.4 percent. A 1 percent increase in plant size reduces the size of the quota allocation between 0.2 and 1.2 percent.

Consistent with the earlier results, richer countries and countries with high GDP growth rates are subject to more-restrictive quotas. Countries which increase GDP growth rates by 1 percentage point can expect a 24 percent contraction in export quotas. As in table 4.10, the results point to a negative relationship between the growth in U.S. exports and quota protection. The point estimates indicate that a 1 percentage point increase in U.S. exports to an MFA exporter leads to an expansion in its quota allocation (on average) of between 0.1 and 2.4 percent.

4.7.5   Lessons

Based on our analysis of the pattern of quota coverage under the MFA during the 1980s, we can draw the following lessons:

1. The coverage of the MFA expanded significantly during the 1980s. Despite the increased quota coverage, however, the protection received by the industry was porous. Quota utilization rates were, on average, considerably below 100 percent. Quota allocations, which grew at slightly below 6 percent annually in real terms, grew at an even faster pace for some of the major exporters, such as China. Although there is strong evidence that increased import penetration led to expanded quota coverage and more restrictive quotas, quota allocations were also adjusted upward to account for growing import volumes.

2. The determinants of protection *within* the industry are likely to be quite different from the determinants of protection across different industries. These

differences can be traced to the political process itself. The power to draw votes was an important factor in gathering national support for the passage of the STA, LTA, and MFA. This suggests that the industry's large share of manufacturing employment in the 1950s and 1960s was a major factor in contributing to the industry's success in winning protection. Within the industry, however, it appears that textile and apparel producers who represented a smaller share of the labor force—as proxied by the total number of employees—were better able to win protection.

3. In general, textile and apparel producers with the following characteristics were more likely to win protection: fewer employees, more plants, lower wages, lower profits, falling investment, higher import penetration, and larger plant sizes.

4. *Among countries against which quotas are imposed,* richer countries and countries with higher growth rates were more likely to have quota restraints imposed on their exports. Since our sample excludes most of the industrial countries, the results suggest that the richest developing country suppliers (such as Hong Kong and Taiwan) had almost no negotiating power. Countries not included in our sample—the industrial countries, except Japan—are absent because they are powerful enough to avoid having their exports of textiles and clothing subjected to MFA quotas. The countries with enough political power to avoid protection were excluded from the sample—the majority of the industrial countries. This suggests an inverted-U curve between U.S. protectionism and level of exporter GDP: the richest and poorest countries escape protection. Among the middle-income developing countries, the most successful exporters (measured in terms of levels or growth rates of GDP) were punished with higher quotas.

5. Countries that bought increasing volumes of U.S. exports were also less likely to face greater protection.

4.8 Evaluation

We are now in a position to evaluate several basic questions relating to the protection that the textile industry has received:

1. What range of mechanisms was available to the industry, and why did the industry use one or several of these more effectively than others?

2. Was the economic and political organization of the industry a significant factor?

3. What was the nature of opposition to the industry's pressure for protection, and how did it influence the degree or form of protection that the industry received?

4. What factors influenced the pattern of quotas across textile and apparel products and MFA suppliers?

The key to the industry's political power in the 1950s and 1960s, when it gained and institutionalized a significantly higher degree of protection than any other industry, was that it was the leading industry in the South, and the South enjoyed disproportionate power in the U.S. Congress. In the northern states (see Bauer, Pool, and Dexter 1972), the textile industry was on the decline, and although the traditional protectionist stance was maintained, it was mostly passive. Despite a few representatives who strongly supported protection for textiles, most northern representatives focused on securing funds for "regional development" and on attracting diversified industries to the region.[30]

The South drew its power in Congress from the intersection of the seniority of Southern senators and representatives and the power that seniority enjoyed in the committee systems of the House and Senate. In the 87th Congress (1961–62), Southern Democrats held the chairs of 11 of 18 standing committees in the Senate and 13 of 21 standing committees of the House. Their influence over agricultural legislation (which they used to put domestic legal teeth into the international textile agreements) was particularly strong. In the House, Southern Democrats held the chair of the Agriculture Committee and provided, in addition, the eight senior members of the committee. They chaired 12 of 14 standing subcommittees on agriculture. In the Senate, a Southern Democrat chaired the Agriculture Committee, five of six senior members were Southern Democrats, and Southern Democrats held the chairs of the four standing subcommittees on agriculture.[31] Table 4.12 shows that in the 1950s the textile and apparel industries accounted for a significant share of manufacturing jobs in all the Southern states—over half of the manufacturing jobs in several of them.

The political power of Southern textile interests, combined with a lack of opposition from other industries, meant that the executive branch was forced to make important concessions to the textile and apparel industries. These concessions were made in spite of the fact that the executive perceived foreign policy interests as best served by a policy of free trade. By the 1990s, however, the balance of power had shifted away from the textile and apparel interests.

In 1994, the U.S. government signed the Uruguay Round agreement, which provides that all textile and apparel quotas be eliminated within 10 years. Yet this loss by the industry does not reflect any realization by the U.S. voting public or even the U.S. government that protecting textile and apparel products came at a significant cost to U.S. consumers. Rather, it reflects two unrelated factors. First, changes in congressional rules and Southern voting patterns diminished the Southern delegation's influence. Second, support for U.S. textile and apparel producers weakened as Asian countries that are major textile exporters gained importance as markets for U.S. exports. Textile-exporting countries such as China are now valued as markets for services and technology-

---

30. Bauer et al. (1972, 306) point out that "in 1946, the industry (woolen-worsted industry) employed 28000 in Textiletown, but . . . late in 1953, most of the mills had moved South, and textile employment ran to only 6000 or 7000 persons. Furthermore, at least half of this employment was threatened by the prospect of some of the remaining mills closing."

31. Tabulated from Congressional Quarterly, Inc. (1961, 1962).

Table 4.12   **Employment in the Textile and Apparel Industries as a Percentage of Total Manufacturing Employment, by State, 1963**

State	Textiles	Apparel	Textiles and Apparel
Alabama	14	13	27
Georgia	27	15	42
North Carolina	42	9	51
South Carolina	50	14	64
Tennessee	18	16	34
Mississippi	4	24	28
Virginia	12	10	22
Florida	1	15	16
Rhode Island	21	3	24
Connecticut	3	4	7
Massachusetts	6	9	15
New Jersey	3	9	13
New York	3	16	20
Pennsylvania	5	12	17

Source: U.S. Bureau of the Census, *Census of Manufacturing, 1963. Vol. 3, Area Statistics* (Washington, D.C.: Government Printing Office, 1966), table 6.

based products. Consequently, the mercantilist interests of the U.S. textile and apparel industry were traded for those of other U.S. producers.

4.8.1   Mechanisms

The most direct way to achieve protection is to petition for legislative action that grants protection—a tariff increase or a quota voted explicitly by Congress. The textile industry had considerable influence in Congress, but Congress was reluctant to take up directly protectionist legislation. Part of the explanation for this reluctance was the memory of the Smoot-Hawley Tariff. Another part was the considerable sympathy in Congress for the liberal foreign policy view of U.S. trade policy—a view that dominated and is most associated with executive branch thinking. Congress thus was a willing co-conspirator with the executive in the evolution of a system of indirect and administered protection that infrequently provided protection, though it did provide representatives and senators a degree of political protection from protection-seeking constituents. And finally, protection voted directly by Congress would have little chance of avoiding a presidential veto.[32]

The threat of legislated protection for the industry was frequently used to push executive use of the authority that the existing trade remedies process provided. Beginning as early as the 1950s, the threat of congressional action

32. A presidential veto might have been avoided by attaching an amendment providing protection for the textile industry to a bill the president would not want to lose. But the industry was not able to achieve this, e.g., in 1955 losing by two votes in an attempt to add to the foreign aid bill an amendment that would have imposed quotas on textile imports.

provided leverage with the Japanese industry and government in the negotiation of VERs.

4.8.2   Administered Protection

The textile industry used the administrative mechanisms that were available, filing both escape clause and section 22 (of the AAA) cases. These avenues could be used to provide the executive with the authority to restrict imports, but they did not mandate that the executive use that authority. Having failed in the 1950s to force the executive to use the authority that existing administrative protection mechanisms provided, the industry made minimal effort to use its influence to have Congress eliminate the discretion these mechanisms allowed the executive. That would be a strategy developed later, in the late 1970s and the 1980s, and principally by other industries.

Eventually the industry was successful in forcing the creation of an administrative mechanism specifically for its benefit. The mechanism was internationally sanctioned by the MFA and its predecessor cotton agreements, but its legal base was the authority that domestic law gave the president to restrict U.S. imports of textiles and clothing. But, while this special purpose mechanism did provide protection for the industry, it did not isolate the determination of how much protection from the political influences that worked against such protection.

4.8.3   Voluntary Export Restraints

The VER was an instrument that accommodated the various influences that came together to shape protection. Pressure for protection from the textile industry was, of course, one of these influences, but there were counterpressures as well. In the 1930s, after the Smoot-Hawley Tariff was enacted and other countries had retaliated, governments were wary of triggering further retaliation. Negotiation with the exporting country was the usual response to domestic pressure for increased protection. The success of the reciprocal trade agreements program and the creation under U.S. leadership of the GATT intensified the U.S. executive's focus on negotiation as the way to establish trade policy. Along with these changes came an increased reluctance to limit U.S. imports, even through negotiations. Under pressure, however, the executive would turn to the VER. It minimized harm to the "relationship" that existed between the United States and the exporting country.[33]

---

33. The quotation above from George Ball is an example of the routine use of the phrase "the relationship" in State Department conceptions of international policy. One of the authors of this paper, Finger, remembers interagency discussions in the 1970s over the various proposals for a New International Economic Order, e.g., commodity agreements and tariff preferences for developing countries, in which State Department arguments stressed that U.S. support for such proposals was important to maintaining "the relationship" between the United States and developing countries. In a discussion of the proposed international tin agreement, Finger suggested that the

4.8.4 Organization

The existence of the ATMI certainly facilitated the presentation of the industry's case for protection. But the existence of such an organization was not unique to the textile industry, and the tightness of the organization seems more likely the result of the means through which the industry gained protection than an exogenous determinant of that protection.

Many U.S. industry organizations trace their beginnings to the way in which the U.S. government mobilized industry for World War I. Later, the National Recovery Act spurred another round of organization, to implement President Franklin Roosevelt's policies to pull the U.S. economy out of the 1930s depression. At the same time, the Japanese government had sponsored a reorganization of Japanese industries. Thus industry organizations similar to those that existed in the United States and in Japan existed in many industries.

The ATMI was, in the 1950s, the American Cotton Manufacturers Institute (ACMI). The particular association between cotton manufacture and the strength of the Southern congressional delegation led to the cotton manufacturers being the first segment of the industry to win protection. Later, the association of wool manufacturers was merged into the ACMI, which became the ATMI. The manufacture of products from man-made fibers was developed on the whole by companies that began in cotton textile manufacture.

A feature of the textile industry that may have contributed to its political success was that the industry includes a number of very large companies plus a large number of relatively small ones. The presence of large companies meant that among them political organization was relatively easy—among them, the free-rider problem was minimal. In addition, the large number of small companies contributes a large roll of dues-paying members and the basis for wide public sympathy. The size distribution of firms in the industry may enable it to take advantage of both the adding machine and the pressure group routes to protection.

4.8.5 Adaptation

Adaptation to circumstances and to opportunities was an important element in the industry's gaining import protection. The use of VERs as the major instrument, as explained above, was an adaptation rather than an exogenous strategy of the industry. Likewise, the idea of international negotiations to sanction textile agreements was not an explicit strategy of the industry, but when the Kennedy administration undertook such negotiations as the means of providing protection that would do the least damage to its foreign policy, the industry

---

tin agreement would mean the United States would pay more for tin and asked for a list of the economic benefits the United States might be able to extract from tin-exporting countries through the relationship that U.S. support for the tin agreement would establish. The question was never answered; indeed, it was treated as if it were too vulgar to warrant answering.

quietly and skillfully secured passage of legislation that would give the authority to enforce such agreements to the U.S. government—removing dependence on the exporting country for enforcement.

Another indication of successful adaptation involved the treatment of the European Community. The industry in the 1960s wanted quotas on imports from Europe as well as on imports from Asia. But the politics of reaching international agreement eventually shifted the U.S. industry to treat European producers as allies rather than as competitors. Also, the strongly pro-Europe foreign policy position of the U.S. government in the 1960s and 1970s made the U.S. executive branch a less than enthusiastic colleague in restraining European exports. The accommodation that evolved was to leave the tariff on textiles relatively high while controlling Asian exports with quotas. The tariff was sufficient to provide relief from European producers, whose costs were significantly higher than those of Asian producers.

4.8.6   Opposition

Domestic opposition to the industry's pressure for protection came primarily from within the U.S. government—the executive's unwillingness to take action against imports. The executive could count on support from U.S. heavy industry and from large U.S. banks when it sought authority to negotiate at the GATT to reduce U.S. protection, but U.S. business provided no direct opposition to textile industry petitions for protection. The auto industry, for example, would support President Kennedy's TEA but it would not testify at an escape clause or section 22 investigation that restrictions on textile exports would increase its costs and thereby endanger jobs in the auto industry.

Bauer et al. (1972, 218) note that a reluctance to directly oppose another business' petition for government assistance was a part of U.S. business ethics in the 1950s and 1960s. Schattschneider (1935, 144) likewise noted that in testimony before the congressional committees that wrote the Smoot-Hawley Tariff, companies whose costs would be increased by a tariff increase requested by another company would oppose that company's request. They would ask for a compensating increase in their own request.

The success of the textile industry in securing legislation to implement with controls at the U.S. border international agreements such as the LTA and the MFA can be ascribed to the lack of direct opposition to textile industry protection. This lack of opposition was due in part to the skill and the power of the Southern congressional delegation. Because this delegation controlled important agricultural committees, it could use agricultural legislation as a vehicle to pass *implementing legislation* for the agreements the executive was negotiating. For example, in 1962, as the STA was being negotiated, the industry gained passage of an amendment to section 204 of the Agriculture Act. Section 204, before the amendment, gave the president power to negotiate limits on exports to the United States of agricultural products and of textiles and to enforce with U.S. import restrictions such agreements. The amendment gave the president power to limit imports from countries *not party* to the agreement (Curtis and Vastine 1971, 167). Congressman Thomas Curtis, a strong supporter of the liberal trade program usually identified with the executive, complained that the amendment had been passed after less than one hour's debate and had been seen before that only by the industry and by the administration that was committed to providing protection for the industry. Curtis also pointed out that this back-room action took place at the very time Congress was holding public hearings on the TEA (Curtis and Vastine 1971, 167).

Consumer groups in opposition to the textile industry's protection were not active until the 1980s, when the renewals of the MFA became political events. Before, consumer groups were weaker and focused primarily on regulation of health, safety, and product standards. Furthermore, the AFL-CIO, which was opposed to trade liberalization, was an important funding source.[34]

While foreign governments were minimally active in opposing creation of the STA and the LTA, by the 1970s, when the first MFA was negotiated, they became perhaps the major source of direct opposition to U.S. textile protection.

4.8.7 MFA Quota Allocations

Although the coverage of the MFA expanded significantly during the 1980s, the protection was leaky. Quota utilization rates were, on average, considerably below 100 percent. Quota allocations, which grew at slightly below 6 percent annually in real terms, grew at an even faster pace for some of the major exporters, such as China. Although there is strong evidence that increased import penetration led to expanded quota coverage and more restrictive quotas, quota allocations were also adjusted upward to account for growing import volumes.

Domestic politics had a lot to do with how quotas were set. In general, textile and apparel producers with the following characteristics were more likely to win protection: fewer employees, more plants, lower wages, lower profits, falling investment, higher import penetration, and larger plant sizes.

The MFA and the predecessor international cotton agreements, by establishing "market disruption" as a legitimate reason for restricting imports, had the effect of sanctioning such domestic considerations, but, of course, only for the textile and apparel industries.

We also found that while the MFA effectively legitimized market disruption as a reason for protection, it did not succeed in isolating market disruption as the *only* determinant. Other influences have a role in quota determination, and some of these influences—particularly international political influences—tend toward looser restrictions. Countries that increased their demand for total U.S. exports are rewarded with larger quotas. Furthermore, the industrial countries (except Japan) avoided the U.S. MFA, but poorer developing countries are less likely to have quota restraints imposed on their exports than richer ones. This

---

34. From conversations with textile industry association officials.

suggests an inverted-U curve between U.S. protectionism and level of exporter GDP: the richest and poorest countries escape protection. Among the middle-income developing countries, the most successful exporters (measured in terms of levels or growth rates of GDP) were punished with higher quotas.

4.8.8 Summing Up

All told, the major factors underlying the success of the textile industry in winning protection were: (1) the political power of the industry, based on its close association with the Southern congressional delegation; (2) the relatively weak influence over U.S. policy of the Asian countries against which export restraints were directed; and (3) the success of the industry in adjusting its demands on the form of protection that it wanted to the possibilities allowed by the international politics of the day.

Appendix

Table 4A.1   Statistics for the Textile and Apparel Industries, 1960–85

Year	Employment (thousands)	Value of Output (million 1972 $)	Import Penetration (%)	Export Share (%)	Relative Wages[a]	Profits[b]	Unionization (%)
			Textiles				
1960	895	15,194	5.5	3.4	0.65	0.18	17.3
1965	893	19,911	6.0	2.6	0.67	0.19	17.5
1970	924	23,861	5.9	2.4	0.71	0.19	17.5
1975	835	25,304	6.0	4.9	0.66	0.18	17.4
1980	817	29,477	7.0	6.9	0.66	0.21	15.4
1985	658	29,076	12.1	3.6	0.64	0.20	–
			Apparel				
1960	1,288	19,801	1.9	1.3	0.56	0.17	36.5
1965	1,420	23,787	2.7	1.0	0.56	0.20	36.5
1970	1,441	26,102	5.1	1.0	0.57	0.23	36.4
1975	1,214	26,288	8.3	1.9	0.54	0.23	35.6
1980	1,307	29,527	12.9	3.5	0.50	0.26	31.5
1985	1,064	31,138	26.4	1.8	0.50	0.27	–

[a]Relative wages are defined as average wages in the sector divided by average wages in the rest of manufacturing.

[b]Profits defined as (value-added-remuneration to labor)/value of shipments.

References

Abowd, John M. 1991. Appendix: The NBER immigration, trade and labor markets data files. In *Immigration, trade, and the labor market,* ed. John M. Abowd and Richard Freeman. Chicago: University of Chicago Press.

Aggarwal, Vinod K. 1985. *Liberal protectionism: The international politics of organized textile trade.* Berkeley and Los Angeles: University of California Press.
Baldwin, Robert E. 1985. *The political economy of U.S. import policy.* Cambridge: MIT Press.
Ball, George W. 1976. *Diplomacy for a crowded world.* Boston: Little, Brown.
Bauer, Raymond A., Ithiel de Sola Pool, and Lewis Anthony Dexter. 1972. *American business and public policy: The politics of foreign trade,* 2d ed. Chicago: Aldine-Atherton.
Bauge, Kenneth L. 1987. *Voluntary export restriction as a foreign commercial policy with special reference to Japanese cotton textiles, 1930–1962.* New York and London: Garland.
Benedict, J. G. 1993. VERs: A historical, political-economic-theoretical and empirical analysis. Ph.D. dissertation, Columbia University.
Brandis, R. Buford. 1982. *The making of textile trade policy 1935–1981.* Washington, D.C.: American Textile Manufacturers Institute.
Caves, R. E. 1976. Economic models of political choice: Canada's tariff structure. *Journal of Economics* 9:278–300.
Chamberlain, G. 1980. Analysis of covariance with qualitative data. *Review of Economic Studies* 47:225–38.
Cline, William R. 1990. *The future of world trade in textiles and apparel,* rev. ed. Washington, D.C.: Institute for International Economics.
Congressional Quarterly, Inc. 1961, 1962. *Congressional Quarterly almanac,* vols. 17 and 18. Washington, D.C.: Congressional Quarterly, Inc.
Curtis, Thomas B., and John Robert Vastine, Jr. 1971. *The Kennedy Round and the future of American trade.* New York: Praeger.
Dean, J. 1993. Market disruption and the incidence of voluntary export restraints under the Multifibre Arrangement. Johns Hopkins University. Manuscript.
Destler, I. M. 1992. *American trade politics,* 2d ed. Washington, D.C.: Institute for International Economics with the Twentieth Century Fund.
Erzan, R., J. Goto, and P. Holmes. 1990. Effects of the Multi-Fibre Arrangement on developing countries' trade: Empirical investigation. In *Textiles trade and the developing countries: Eliminating the Multi-Fibre Arrangement in the 1990s,* ed. Carl B. Hamilton. Washington, D.C.: World Bank.
Financial Times. 1994. Last minute deal freezes U.S. textile imports from China. January 18, 1.
Finger, J. Michael. 1984. The political economy of trade policy. *Cato Journal* 3, no. 3 (Winter): 743–50.
GATT (General Agreement on Tariffs and Trade). 1984. *Textiles and clothing in the world economy.* Geneva: General Agreement on Tariffs and Trade, July.
Hamilton, Carl B., ed. 1990. *Textiles trade and the developing countries: Eliminating the Multi-Fibre Arrangement in the 1990s.* Washington, D.C.: World Bank.
Helleiner, G. K. 1977. The political economy of Canada's tariff structure: An alternative model. *Canadian Journal of Economics* 10, no. 2 (May): 318–29.
Hull, Cordell. 1948. *The memoirs of Cordell Hull.* New York: Macmillan.
Keesing, Donald B., and Martin Wolf. 1980. *Textile quotas against developing countries.* London: Trade Policy Research Centre.
Schattschneider, E. E. 1935. *Politics, pressures and the tariff.* New York: Prentice-Hall.
Schmalensee, R. 1986. Inter-industry studies of structure and performance. In *Handbook of Industrial Organization,* ed. R. Schmalensee and R. Willig. Amsterdam: North-Holland
Trefler, Daniel. 1993. Trade liberalization and the theory of endogenous protection: An econometric study of U.S. import policy. *Journal of Political Economy* 101 (1): 138–60.

USITC (U.S. International Trade Commission). 1934. *Annual report.* Washington, D.C.: U.S. International Trade Commission.
Zeiler, Thomas W. 1992. *American trade and power in the 1960s.* New York: Columbia University Press.

Comment   Robert E. Baldwin

It is a pleasure to read a paper that presents a general survey of how protection in the textile and apparel sectors has evolved over time. There have been numerous papers analyzing particular aspects of protection in these sectors or particular periods of protection, but few with as broad a historical perspective as this one.

A major task of any paper on textile and apparel protection is to explain how and why these sectors have obtained such high levels of protection. As the authors' data indicate, in the 1950s and the 1960s when quantitative import restrictions in these sectors became significant, the level of import penetration in textiles was only around 6 percent and in apparel only about 3 percent. How does one explain why many other industries with much higher import penetration levels did not also receive significant protection at this time?

One explanation offered by the authors is that senators and representatives from southern states enjoyed special influence in Congress because of their long tenure and the practice of choosing committee chairs on the basis of seniority. Most would agree that this must have been an important part of the explanation. However, one should ask why the increased protection did not come earlier, since members from southern states had this special power long before the 1950s and 1960s. One should also consider whether the decline in the power of southern members of Congress as a result of congressional reforms in the 1970s and 1980s made it more difficult for the textile and apparel sectors to gain protection.

Wasn't one of the factors accounting for textile and apparel protection in the 1950s and 1960s the significant rise in textile and apparel employment in the South during these years as these industries moved out of New England? The resulting increase in the size of the bloc of votes represented by these industries then made it worthwhile for southern legislators to exercise their special congressional power.

Another point made by the authors is that the executive branch treated trade policy as foreign policy during this period and, therefore, was reluctant to grant import protection for fear of undermining its foreign policy goals. In my view, this is a key factor not only in explaining the difficulty in gaining protection in the 1940s and 1950s, but in explaining why it became much easier for indus-

Robert E. Baldwin is Hilldale Professor of Economics at the University of Wisconsin-Madison and a research associate of the National Bureau of Economic Research.

tries to receive protection in the 1960s and later. By the 1960s, Europe and Japan had restored production to their prewar levels, and there was less force to the argument that we needed a liberal trade policy to help other countries become economically strong in order to resist Communist expansion. Consequently, the foreign policy implications of trade policy were much less important for the United States by the 1960s.

In analyzing protection in the textile and apparel sectors, the authors mention, but do not discuss, that the quotas established under the Multi-Fiber Arrangement will be phased out over a 10-year period under the Uruguay Round agreements. How do we explain this significant shift in policy in view of the fact that, as they point out, tough quotas were imposed in these sectors as late as 1986? It would be helpful, incidentally, if the authors presented a table indicating just how average levels of protection changed in textiles and apparel over recent years.

Picking up on a theme that the authors stress in the early part of their paper, one factor that may help account for the Uruguay Round agreement in textiles and apparel is the shift in the economic power of the developing countries. As the authors point out, the political and economic weakness of these nations in the 1960s and 1970s helps explain the high levels of protection imposed in these years. However, by the late 1980s and early 1990s, international power relationships had changed significantly. In response to the rapidly expanding market opportunities in the developing countries, the United States and other developed countries established as major Uruguay Round negotiating objectives the opening of developing country markets for services, the elimination of their trade-related investment measures, and the strengthening of their enforcement of intellectual property rights. Since the developing countries believed (rightly in my view) that responding favorably to these negotiating goals would lead to severe adjustment problems, they insisted on balancing concessions from the developed countries. In particular, they pressed for liberalization in the textile and apparel sectors since they clearly have a comparative advantage in producing these products. Thus, it seems likely that negotiators from the United States and other developed countries were willing to accept liberalization in the textile and apparel sectors in exchange for acceptance by the developing countries of liberalization of their services trade, elimination of trade-related investment measures, and stricter enforcement of intellectual property rights.

Next let me turn to the empirical analysis in the Finger-Harrison paper. One very interesting point they make is that a private trade association, the American Textile Manufacturers Institute, plays a major role in allocating quotas across countries and across products. Indeed, they found evidence that most of the industry's recommendations are accepted by the government committee making the final decisions. This suggests that they may want to consider how a political economy model in which a private industry makes the decisions differs from one in which the government makes the final trade decisions.

I suspect that notions of fairness and equity play an even greater role in such a model than in a political economy model in which the government makes the trade policy decisions. They do, in fact, find that these concepts seem to be important in decisions on textile and apparel protection. For example, they find that quotas are more likely in textile and apparel product lines in which wages are low, import penetration levels are high, production is very labor intensive, and the size of plants is small. All of these factors can be interpreted as reflecting fairness and equity concerns. Incidentally, in all of this analysis, I think it is important to separate textiles and apparel. They are quite different in terms of such factors as labor intensiveness, skill levels, and size of plant.

One regression result that is somewhat puzzling to the authors is the increased likelihood of quotas being imposed the higher a country's GDP and the greater its exports to the United States. A bargaining power view of the political economy process would lead one to expect a negative correlation. However, causality runs in both directions between these variables. Countries such as Hong Kong and Taiwan were able to achieve high levels of GDP through high exports of textiles and apparel. In the process of raising their income levels through outward-looking policies, the textile and apparel markets of developed countries were disrupted, and their governments imposed quantitative import controls on textiles and apparel. So perhaps it is not surprising to observe a positive association between high GDP levels and highly restrictive quotas.

Comment   I. M. Destler

I find the Finger-Harrison analysis basically on the mark:
- In its rich political history, though this fades away sometime in the Johnson administration;
- In its characterization of the outcome—comprehensive but leaky protection;
- In its characterization of the *form* of textile protection—nonstatutory VERs, with Congress not even ratifying the multilateral and bilateral textile agreements;
- In its conclusions about the structure of interests that brought about this level of protection—a concentration of a few large companies that are natural leaders with a large number of small firms that are natural followers.

I would extend this characterization to the congressional support for textile protection as well: concentration in the Carolinas and Georgia, from which leadership typically comes (Strom Thurmond, Ernest Hollings, and Ed Jenkins), with smaller firms scattered in New York, California, and numerous

I. M. Destler is professor in the School of Public Affairs of the University of Maryland and visiting fellow at the Institute for International Economics.

other states, resulting in numerous legislators whose constituencies incline them toward support.

There are at least two anomalies that the authors do not address:

• Their basic argument attributes textile protection to the structure of the industry and its *congressional* power base, but its two big breakthroughs—the LTA and the MFA—followed directly from successes in *presidential* politics, from winning promises from John F. Kennedy in 1960 and Richard M. Nixon in 1968.

• The main protection was achieved *before* the big import surge of the 1980s, and the industry was unable to win major new increments in protection in the wake of that surge. So in addition to the intersectoral comparisons suggested by Robert Baldwin and Jagdish Bhagwati, an intertemporal comparison would be useful.

My major problem with the paper, however, is that the two parts do not really mesh. The historical analysis stops in the late 1960s, at least 12 years before the period of the quantitative analysis of specific quotas and levels. Thus the paper omits a lot that is important for its own sake and that could inform the hypothesis testing.

It omits the Nixon interlude in textile policy, which was the polar opposite of the nuanced, foreign policy sensitive, balanced effort under Kennedy.[1] Initially in charge was not the multifaceted George Ball but the monotonic (if not monomaniacal) Maurice Stans. Low politics came to dominate high politics, as the return of Okinawa to Japan was conditioned on Prime Minister Eisaku Sato pledging a textile quota agreement. When he proved unable to deliver, this precipitated arguably the most serious crisis in U.S.-Japan relations from World War II to the present, and it brought Congress closer to enactment of broad statutory protection than it has come from Smoot-Hawley to the present.

The paper also misses the statutory politics of 1985–90, with Congress passing (and Presidents Ronald Reagan and George Bush vetoing) no less than three separate quota bills that the House then failed to override by margins of 8, 11, and 10 votes, respectively. In missing this, it also misses the modest but relevant impact of the apparel retailers, who mobilized against this legislation.

Another development since the 1960s has been the growing divergence in the experiences of the textile and the apparel producers, with the former proving much the more competitive. With this divergence of experience came divergence in their political positions, with the textile mill interests represented by the American Textile Manufacturers Institute (ATMI) (always the political heart of the coalition) increasingly acting in ways that do not serve their apparel brethren. The "triple transformation" test which they extracted on NAFTA is a case in point: it makes sure that any clothing imported from Mexico under NAFTA contains North American fiber and cloth, but it leaves apparel firms competing head to head with Mexican counterparts. The ATMI posture on the

---

1. For more than many readers may want to know, see Destler, Fukui, and Sato (1979).

General Agreement on Tariffs and Trade is similar, seeking to trade off removal of textile import barriers in Third World countries for its reluctant acquiescence to phase-out of the Multi-Fiber Arrangement (MFA).

And finally, the Finger-Harrison paper does not complete the story of what became the basic formula for industry success and does not discuss its (still puzzling to me) departure from this formula after 1985.

The basic approach, which the paper describes in its treatment of the 1950s and 1960s, was to eschew serious efforts at achieving statutory protection but threaten to block broader trade liberalization measures unless the demands of the textile industry were met by other means. The reigning administration was thus invited to buy the industry's silence, and sometimes even support, on major new multilateral trade rounds.

This was done in the Kennedy Round, as the paper nicely documents, where the Short Term Arrangement/Long Term Arrangement initiated in 1961 cleared the way for the Trade Expansion Act of 1962.

This was done under Nixon and Gerald Ford, when the multifiber agreements with Japan and the East Asian newly industrialized countries in 1971 and the MFA of 1973 put the textile issue aside again, allowing passage of the Trade Act of 1974.

The same device was sprung, suddenly, on Jimmy Carter and Robert Strauss in the fall of 1978, when the textile industry blocked completion of the Tokyo Round by getting the Senate—and then the House—to pass bills retracting all U.S. concessions on textile tariffs. This forced Strauss to negotiate new protection for the industry—in this case a tightening of current quota arrangements with major East Asian suppliers.

A slightly different variant arose in 1983, when the textile industry threatened broad U.S.-China trade relations by submitting a countervailing duty case attacking China's dual exchange rate system as a countervailable subsidy. Rather than risk a possibly disruptive outcome by allowing the case to run its course, the Reagan administration struck a deal: it tightened the screws a bit more on East Asian suppliers, and the ATMI withdrew its suit.

This strategy made possible a mixed, not especially friendly, but positive-sum relationship between industry leaders and administration trade liberalizers. The latter always felt that the industry demanded too much and got too much but that nevertheless bargains could be struck and the liberalizers' top priority could proceed. The question, then, is why the industry abandoned this strategy in the latter part of the 1980s, pursuing instead the will-o'-the-wisp of statutory textile quotas.

When the "Jenkins Bill" mandating global, statutory quotas was introduced in the spring of 1985, it seemed to some a continuation of the old strategy. And in fact, after President Reagan vetoed the bill that fall, industry supporters cleverly got the override vote postponed until summer 1986, so the "threat" would press the administration to toughen its stance in the MFA renewal negotiations. But thereafter, perhaps misled by the seeming closeness of the override vote (eight votes short of the two-thirds required), and perhaps encouraged by several Democratic victories when the industry targeted Republican Senate and House candidates in the southeastern states that November, the industry made quota legislation its overriding objective.

There was comprehensive trade legislation coming down the track once again in 1987 and 1988. But this time the industry did not seek to block such legislation, or to use the threat of blockage to bargain for new special protection. Indeed, all it asked of congressional leaders was that they promise House and Senate votes on the Jenkins Bill *after* the omnibus legislation went through! It was already fall 1988 when the Senate completed action, and the operative question among Democrats was not whether the bill could be enacted, but whether to let it die in conference (as Ways and Means Chairman Dan Rostenkowski wanted) or to force the president to veto it so that Democrats could use that fact against Republicans in November. Then, after that House override vote predictably failed, the industry pushed the bill through Congress a *third* time in 1990, with virtually identical results. An industry once astute at using Congress to gain its ends was now being *used by Congress,* as members were free to cast symbolic votes for textile protection that they knew (happily, in many cases) would have no impact.

Why? The best reason this observer has heard is that the ATMI staff in Washington—which understood the political game rather well—was overruled by stubborn and willful mill executives, Roger Milliken in particular. This would be an all-too-human explanation of why, in an environment exceptionally favorable for protectionist action, the textile industry failed to deploy the substantial congressional forces it had as leverage for a negotiated outcome.

An alternative explanation might be that this was an industry past its political prime, which sensed that and decided to make one last roll of the dice—in fact, three last rolls—to try to lock in a stronger, statutory regime of protection before its reduced power became evident in the broader trade community. In any case, the industry was less effective in securing new protection in the 1980s, when import growth was fiercest, than it had been in the 1960s and 1970s. A current sign of its limited power—and of the textile-apparel split— is the fact that the industry did not mount a strong campaign against congressional approval of the Uruguay Round agreements phasing out the MFA. So steel may not be the only large U.S. industry whose political capacity to obtain protection has waned.

Reference

Destler, I. M., Haruhiro Fukui, and Hideo Sato. 1979. *The textile wrangle: Conflict in Japanese-American relations, 1969–71.* Ithaca, N.Y.: Cornell University Press.

5   Precedent and Legal Argument in U.S. Trade Policy: Do They Matter to the Political Economy of the Lumber Dispute?

Joseph P. Kalt

5.1   Introduction: Applying Rational Political Economy to the U.S.-Canada Lumber Dispute

Efforts by interested parties to secure trade protection are frequently carried out in the United States through the quasi-judicial regulatory framework of countervailing duty (CVD) law, as administered by the Department of Commerce (DOC). This framework structures at least the form and content of the arguments for and against requested CVD protection. At the same time, however, interested parties have other venues through which to make their case—Congress, the White House, political channels within the DOC, and other potentially involved agencies. Parties who participate in the department's litigation process often confess to perceptions that the process is a charade, that the hearings and filings before the department's International Trade Administration (ITA) and International Trade Commission (ITC) have no influence on the ultimate policy outcomes. Instead, it is averred, the policy outcomes are driven by interest group politics, leaving the litigatory apparatus to serve merely as beside-the-fact "packaging" for decisions made elsewhere and through different, "purely political" processes. If this portrayal is true, the nation pays a high cost for packaging.

This study tries to get at the questions of whether and how the quasi-judicial regulatory process by which CVD law is administered affects the success or

Joseph P. Kalt is the Ford Foundation Professor of International Political Economy and academic dean for research at the John F. Kennedy School of Government of Harvard University.

The author has served as an economic consultant to the governments of Canada and British Columbia in the "Lumber III" trade dispute and has benefited greatly from access to the documentary record in that proceeding. He has also benefited from the helpful comments of the participants in the conference on the political economy of trade protection, especially Frank Wolak and Anne Krueger, and the workshop in law and economics at the University of Chicago. Any errors or omissions are solely the author's, as are the views set forth in this study.

failure of parties petitioning for protection. The research posits two primary, and one subsidiary, theories of the role that institutional structure plays in determining regulatory outcomes. These competing theories are then examined—tested to the extent possible—in the context of a particular set of cases that have been flowing into the DOC in recent years. These cases make up the ongoing disputes over trade in lumber and logs—the "timber trade wars"— that have been raging between the United States and Canada for a decade (see Kalt 1988). As of 1992, the United States had imposed CVDs on Canadian softwood lumber imports on the grounds that the Canadians provide publicly owned trees to loggers at subsidized prices, and that Canadian log export restraints (LERs) subsidize the prices that Canadian sawmills pay for raw logs.

In order to get leverage on the concept of "institutions," this research focuses on the role that a particular legal institution—legal precedent—plays in determining the subgame successes and failures of contending parties as they tussle over such matters as the applicability of CVD law, the definition of the relevant product and geographic markets affected by allegedly countervailable foreign subsidies, the measurement of the magnitude of alleged subsidies, and the attendant size of a CVD. Legal precedent is treated as a costly "entry" barrier that litigants face when trying to exert political influence. Resources are expended by competing parties to defend or break down precedents in a stochastic process of "take your best shot (via legal argument) and hope you hit the bull's-eye." What arguments work and why?

Section 5.2 discusses alternative theories of the political economy of the administrative process of economic policy making, focusing on "capture theory" and "neo-institutionalist" explanations for the role of legal proceedings before the DOC's ITA. Section 5.3 then provides background on the issues and stakes in the U.S.-Canada lumber dispute. Section 5.4 discusses the testing methodology and specific hypotheses regarding the determinants of successful pleadings before the ITA. This section also sets out the specific arguments regarding a set of 14 key issues disputed by the contending parties in their arguments to the ITA. Section 5.5 implements the empirical tests, making use of newly developed methods for determining the informational content of small sample, dichotomous "cases." Section 5.6 summarizes findings and pursues ramifications.

5.2   Competing Theories of the Role of Institutions in Political Economy

5.2.1   Capture Theory and the New Institutionalism

At some risk of caricature, economic theories of rational political economy (or what used to be called the "economic theory of regulation") are currently pulling scholars into two broad camps: Capture Theory (CT) and the New Institutionalism (NI). Under the former, it is argued that political outcomes can be predicted and explained by a combination of two primary economic factors: (1) the differential stakes that contending parties have in a particular law or regulation, that is, where the rents are, and (2) the differential costs of effective political organization that contending rent-seeking interest groups confront as a result of standard Olsonian forces of free riding.[1] Within this framework, regulatory outcomes and processes are "captured" by successful interest groups who wield the most effective political influence, where "influence" is usually measured by either votes delivered to politicians or votes plus campaign contributions delivered to politicians.

The New Institutionalism does not deny that the two primary factors underlying CT are indeed important (if not strictly "primary") but adds a third fundamental explanatory factor to efforts to understand political outcomes. This factor is the institutional context—laws, procedures, precedents, regulations, voting rules, and so forth—that forms the playing field upon which contending rent seekers meet. NI lays claim to every bit as much economic rationality in the modeling of political actors as does CT but argues that institutional structure constitutes binding constraints, or at least conditioning costs, that limit the range of actors' investments in political outcomes and hence play determinative roles in political outcomes.[2] Thus, to understand why, for example, the United States moved in 1992 to impose tariffs on imports of Canadian lumber, and why the tariff structure and rates are what they are, NI asserts it is necessary to understand the formal institutional setting through which the U.S.-Canada lumber dispute has been mediated.

A fundamental divergence between CT and NI arises over the issue of the endogeneity (and speed of endogeneity) of political institutions. CT tends to view institutions as ephemeral: political actors have the ability to change political institutions, and if a capturing interest group needs an institution changed in order to garner wealth through political influence, support-seeking political actors will change that institution. NI, on the other hand, views political institutions as more exogenous: certainly they can be changed, but in any particular case (say, of regulatory agency behavior), it is costly to change institutions and such costs make institutions "sticky." This stickiness reflects rational commitment on the part of agents (e.g., Congress) to a governmental structure that can substitute for perfect monitoring by principals (i.e., voters and interest groups), but which is therefore imperfect and open to inertia, principal-agent–subagent slack, ideological considerations, and so forth.

In a nutshell, it is CT that argues, for example: "It doesn't matter who is president or if we reform Congress; policies will be driven by the underlying economic interests of effectively organized interest groups." NI responds: "Those interest groups have to work through an institutional context that can-

---

1. The classic statements here are from the Chicago School: Stigler (1971), Peltzman (1976), and Becker (1983).
2. See, e.g., North (1990), Bates (1988), and the writings of the "rational political economists."

not be changed overnight and will make them more or less powerful in influencing the president or Congress or an administrative agency."

As these theories play out in investigation of a particular class of political actions, such as decisions of the ITA and the ITC regarding trade protection for U.S. lumber interests, they carry testably different implications. According to CT, institutions such as legal proceedings are "Stiglerian theater": the real game is being played out behind the scenes of the hearing rooms by interest groups and support-maximizing politicians. Legal rulings and such matters as precedent may be a language by which the game is explained or justified after the fact to appease the press and the public but is not determinative of outcomes. NI would hold, however, that such institutions as precedent, standards of evidence, and burdens of proof *matter*: agency decision makers and the judges cannot simply ignore precedent, evidence, or procedure, no matter how much political clout the beseeching interest group has. If a group does not have a good argument by which to satisfy or overcome precedent, or meet its evidentiary burden, it runs a substantial risk of losing before the agencies and the courts.

5.2.2   Research Design

These descriptions of CT and NI present them as sharply distinct, alternative hypotheses. As in many contexts where the demands of research are to isolate testable differences in hypotheses, however, the differences here are drawn too starkly. The added ingredient of NI—the determinative role of institutional structure—is not at odds with the rational, choice-theoretic underpinnings of CT, and CT defenders might agree that in any particular instance of economic policy making, institutions can matter. The link is suggested above: the principal-agent problem readily generates institutional structure as a constraint on agents that parties (such as members of the Congress) rationally adopt when they are captured every bit as much as implied by CT, but can only imperfectly monitor how well their agents (such as the regulatory agencies) are doing at the kind of constituent support maximization that underlies CT.[3]

Recognizing these intersections of CT and NI, the tests proposed here must be thought of more modestly than "testing CT versus NI." Rather, the objective of this study is to see whether the added ingredient of NI—the institutional structure of the legal proceedings by which CVD decisions are made in the United States—adds significantly to our understanding of the political economy of the particular case of the U.S.-Canada lumber dispute.

The discussion of sections 5.1 and 5.2.1 suggests the outlines of a research design by which to understand whether and how the quasi-judicial litigatory process of CVD law administration influences the success or failure of requests for protection. Specifically, the research results reported below attempt to sys-

---

3. The nature of such support maximization is worked out for the case of no principal-agent slack by, e.g., Peltzman (1976) and Becker (1983).

tematically examine a moderate-sized sample of actual legal arguments made before the ITA in the U.S.-Canada lumber dispute in order to test whether success in making an argument can be systematically explained as a function of determinants of the severity of the beseeching party's precedential burden or other contextual aspects of the legal proceedings (per NI theory). Or, alternatively, is success or failure unrelated to apparent precedential burdens and institutional context of the legal proceedings (per CT theory)?

The testing of NI against CT in the case at hand begins with identification of salient attributes of the CVD legal proceeding before the ITA and then tests whether variation in those attributes across a range of issues argued before the ITA provides explanation for variation in ITA decisions—where "variation in ITA decisions" refers to whether the "winner" in a particular argument is the pro-CVD party (U.S. lumber interests) or the anti-CVD party (the Canadian parties). Under U.S. law (conditioned by various trade acts and U.S. participation in the General Agreement on Tariffs and Trade [GATT]), parties seeking to establish tariff protection for U.S. industries under the rules governing CVDs do so by initiating a legal petition before the ITA. The ITA's core responsibilities in CVD proceedings are to determine whether, in fact, the targeted foreign government is engaging in a countervailable subsidization of its home industry and, if so, by how much (commonly measured as the net reduction in cost realized by the subsidized sector). On a separate legal track, the ITC has the responsibility of determining whether the U.S. industry of interest has been injured as a result of the asserted countervailable subsidy. Should a party prevail at the ITA and the ITC, CVDs are then normally imposed unless blocked by the president under oversight executive powers reserved to the office under U.S. law.

Upon acceptance of a CVD petition for consideration, legal proceedings are launched whereby the ITA first gathers information regarding the nature (e.g., legal origin, method of payment, and level of production) and extent (e.g., magnitude and coverage within and across industries) of any purported subsidy by a foreign government. Interested parties typically include the U.S. industries which compete with the allegedly subsidized foreign industries, the affected foreign industries, and the foreign government.[4] The ITA itself can be a party to the dispute by self-initiating CVD inquiries. Although the particular vehicles of participation can depend on legal criteria of standing, interested parties typically have the ability to participate in the formal ITA proceedings, providing information and legal and substantive argument through the written submissions, provision of data, and oral statements of expert witnesses, industry participants, and legal counsel. Following a round of initial submission and consideration, the ITA issues a preliminary determination to which parties with

---

4. Interestingly, U.S. consuming interests are typically absent from formal ITA proceedings—in keeping with the predictions of CT that the very wide dispersal of their interests and low per capita stakes leave them unable to overcome Olsonian free-rider problems and become a cohesive interest group.

standing can reply. Following replies and further consideration, the ITA then typically issues a final determination. As a result of the free trade agreement between Canada and the United States, final determinations in CVD proceedings such as the lumber dispute are referred for appeal and review to a five-member binational panel.

I wish to focus here on the final determination phase of CVD proceedings, wherein the ITA of the DOC makes its key rulings and sets forth and imposes specific duties. To this point in CVD proceedings, the ITA is the key adjudicator of parties' disputes, with its procedural, policy, and evidentiary standards codified in law and precedent. In most cases, the key decisions leading to imposition of protective tariffs on behalf of domestic industries are made at this level; a doctrine of "deference to the agency" makes it very difficult for an appealing party to overturn the ITA's findings, particularly on matters of factual evidence.

The doctrine of legal precedent sits at the institutional heart of ITA (and other regulatory agency) legal proceedings. When prior rulings of the agency or appellate bodies overseeing the agency have established particular procedural, policy, or evidentiary standards, such standards play central roles in determining the burdens and natures of proof that a party must satisfy in order to justifiably prevail in an argument. Precedent (and the doctrines of legislative intent and due process on which it is based) thus conditions the ability of a party to win an argument. Where precedent has established a high burden of proof for a party, for example, the likelihood of prevailing declines. Where precedent has created a strong legal principle, securing a ruling contrary to that principle is less likely.

Within the framework of NI, precedent can be represented as exerting two kinds of influences on the outcome of regulatory policy making. First, for a given precedent, a party seeking a ruling contrary to that precedent should require particularly strong arguments. "Strong" here is contextual, and "should" means "if NI is adding to our understanding of the outcome of the policy process." If the precedent, for example, concerns evidentiary thresholds (which can range from a standard of a "more than a mere scintilla" of the evidence to "beyond a reasonable doubt"), the party to whom precedent assigns the burden of proof should require more clear-cut, fewer controvertible facts which fit that theory, and/or clearer exposition, in order to win the argument at issue as the height of the burden increases.

Second, precedents themselves can vary in strength. U.S. administrative law changes over time. Congress modifies underlying legislation; appellate bodies clarify or modify previous rulings; administrative agencies exercise latent discretion; and so on. Experience in the administrative law process, however, indicates inertia and variation in the mutability of various precedents. Within NI, precedents should be "stronger"—that is, harder for an opposing party to overcome or easier for a supporting party to uphold—the longer and more frequently they have withstood previous challenges and been reaffirmed by appropriate authorities, and the more clear is the underlying legislative intent and/ or directive.

In short, relative to CT, NI predicts that:

NI-1. For a given precedent, variation in the ability of a party to overcome that precedent or meet the burden of that precedent should be positively related to the strength of that party's arguments.

NI-2. Variation in the ability to overcome precedents or meet the burdens of precedents should be positively related to variation in the strength of relevant precedents.

With the kinds of definitions of "strength" discussed above (and elaborated below), these two hypotheses form the testable difference between CT and NI in the context at hand.

Under strict CT, variation in the success or failure of a party's arguments should not depend on contextual attributes of the institutions of precedent. Rather, variation in the success of arguments ought to be related to the stakes of the contending parties:

CT-1. The decision maker should be more likely to award a victory to an argument, the larger the stakes of the beseeching party, independent of the strength of the party's arguments and the strength of the precedent at issue.[5]

In the proceeding under examination, on any given issue it is the case that the magnitude of one party's gain is (to a first approximation) also the opponent's loss; stakes are generally of equal but opposite sign from the contending parties' perspectives. Across issues, however, stakes differ in their magnitude. An issue such as the very existence of a countervailable subsidy is an all-or-nothing matter, while disputes over measurement of marginal adjustments to a purported subsidy put less at stake for the contending parties. Within the kind of "equalize support at the margin" version of CT developed by Peltzman (1976) and Becker (1983), support-seeking principals (and their agents) faced with support-offering constituents of unequal political clout should secure support from disparate parties by arriving at regulatory decisions that differentially favor the more influential party but do not cut the less influential party completely out.[6] This perspective on argument CT-1 is implemented below.

---

5. Much of the research that is focused on CT (as well as NI) is directed at variations in the ability of potentially affected interest groups to organize and exert influence. In the present context, the hurdle of organization has already been overcome; the parties are already in the hearing room exerting whatever influence they have.

6. This is the litigation analog to the optimizing equilibrium demonstrated by Peltzman (1976), wherein the support-maximizing decision maker equates the marginal support gained from a decision favorable to group A to the marginal support lost as a result from group B.

These competing hypotheses, NT-1 and NT-2 versus CT-1, about how the ITA legal process works form the core of the analysis undertaken here. An illustration is helpful to explain the framework. The U.S. lumber industry has long argued that the Canadian federal and provincial governments provide the rights to cut trees ("stumpage" rights) at below-market prices to Canadian loggers *and* that this constitutes a countervailable subsidy to lumber production in Canada. Economists testifying on behalf of the Canadians (e.g., William Nordhaus of Yale University) and economists researching the matter independently (e.g., myself)[7] have argued that the evidence *and* the theory indicate that to the extent Canadian stumpage may be below market, the consequence is merely an inframarginal transfer of Ricardian and Hotelling rent to loggers. The supply of logs and hence lumber is left unchanged. U.S. lumber producers, therefore, face no incremental competitive pressure from Canadian lumber producers and are not harmed by Canadian stumpage policy.

This argument has held little or no sway before the ITA or the ITC. It appears to be misunderstood and dismissed as irrelevant theorizing by university economists. Such appearances, however, do not justify any general conclusions as to how the quasi-judicial CVD process operates or as to which arguments take hold and which do not. In order to draw generalizable conclusions in this regard, systematic evidence must be garnered from a framework which isolates alternative determinants of what makes one argument take hold while another falls on deaf ears.

Below I identify a set of central, stakes-bearing issues that have been adjudicated by the ITA in the latest round of the U.S.-Canada trade dispute. These issues can be categorized according to who—the U.S. petitioners or the Canadians—has won each of them as of the ITA's final determination, reached in May 1992. This creates a dichotomous winner-loser variable by which to gauge the outcome of the legal proceedings. For each of the arguments in the data set, I then code the stakes at issue in the argument for their magnitude and code the argument of the winning party for its consistency with precedent, its analytic or theoretical straightforwardness, the strength of the winner's evidence, and the ease of exposition entailed by the winner's argument (these concepts are given more delineation below).

The objective is to create a data set that can be analyzed under the pseudoregression Boolean techniques pioneered by Ragin (1987). These techniques permit dichotomous data sets representing panels of cases to be reduced to their logical meaning in terms of necessary and sufficient conditions in a manner that continuous variable econometric techniques, familiar to most economists and political scientists, are unable to do. If the cross-case tests for the two central hypotheses, NI-1 and NI-2, listed above are borne out, the results will be consistent with an NI view of the regulatory process. If there is no

---

7. See Kalt (1988). This research was undertaken and published prior to any engagement with any party to the lumber dispute.

coherent pattern to the explanatory factors except the stakes at issue, the results will be most consistent with CT theory (per CT-1).[8]

5.3   "Lumber III": History and Issues

The United States and Canada have been engaged in a long-running dispute over softwood lumber imports from Canada into the United States. These imports compete directly with lumber supplies produced in the United States, with sawmillers—in the Pacific Northwest region of Washington, Oregon, Idaho, and British Columbia most notably—going head to head for sales in North America and the Far East. In both the United States and Canada, the public sector owns vast forest resources that are provided to private sector loggers at fees known as "stumpage." As noted, certain U.S. milling interests have long complained that they pay market value for stumpage under auction procedures used in U.S. public sector sales while Canadian formula-based stumpage is below market. Moreover, allege the U.S. interests, provincial and federal restraints on log exports restrict the ability of foreign buyers to purchase logs in Canada for export and cause the prices paid for Canadian logs by Canadian sawmillers to be lower than they otherwise would be.[9] Both alleged below-market stumpage and depression of log prices below free trade levels are asserted to constitute countervailable subsidies to Canadian lumber producers.

5.3.1   Lumber I, II, and III

The history of the timber trade wars between the United States and Canada is summarized in table 5.1. The first round of the timber trade war—"Lumber I"—was commenced by a CVD investigation of Canadian stumpage launched by the DOC in 1982. Lumber I ended with a final negative determination by the DOC in 1983, with the DOC finding that stumpage rights were allocated in a way that failed to satisfy the technical legal criterion of "specificity" (which requires that a subsidy be provided to a specific enterprise or industry, or group of enterprises or industries, in order for such a subsidy to be countervailable).

Lumber II arose in 1986 in response to a petition for investigation by the Coalition for Fair Lumber Imports (CFLI), a trade organization and lobbying group representing (predominantly) small and medium-sized U.S. sawmill companies. The CFLI again sought to countervail the Canadian stumpage system. The DOC found on preliminary determination that the Canadian stumpage system was both "specific" (in the sense described above) and "preferential" (i.e., it "distorted" the marketplace for lumber by affecting the supply schedule of Canadian lumber). DOC set the CVD rate for Canadian lumber imports at 14.5 percent ad valorem. The Lumber II CVD was effectively pre-

---

8. A third theory, contractarianism (per the Buchanan tradition), might predict that the "truth will out" and that the correctness (absence of ambiguity) of an argument would be the only or the dominant explainer.

9. Ironically, the United States has LERs of its own.

Table 5.1   History of CVD Actions in the Timber Trade Wars between the United States and Canada

Case	Allegation	U.S. DOC Decision	CVD on Lumber Imports	Resolution
Lumber I 1982–83	Canada subsidizes mills with below-market stumpage	Stumpage subsidy is not "specific"	Zero	No further action
Lumber II 1986	Canada subsidizes mills with below-market stumpage	Stumpage subsidy is "specific" and distortive	14.50% ad valorem	Canada retaliates; memorandum of understanding replaces U.S. CVD with 15% Canadian export tax
Lumber III 1992–94	Canada subsidizes mills with below-market stumpage and log export controls	Stumpage and export controls are "specific" and distortive	11.54% ad valorem	Binational panel overrules DOC; appeals underwa

empted, however, when escalating retaliatory threats by the Canadians compelled the United States and Canada to enter into a memorandum of understanding (MOU). The Lumber II MOU obligated Canada to impose a 15 percent fee on softwood lumber exports to the United States.[10]

In 1991, Canada and a number of its provinces concluded that the MOU had been satisfied by various reforms in Canadian stumpage pricing procedures. Accordingly, they lifted the 15 percent export fee. The DOC's ITA immediately launched Lumber III, an investigation into the possibility that Canadian stumpage continued to constitute a countervailable subsidy. At the invitation of the ITA, the CFLI filed submissions arguing that Canada's LERs also constitute a countervailable subsidy by Canada to its lumber producers. Various Canadian parties, led by the various provinces' forestry ministries, in turn intervened to plead their case as to why neither the stumpage system nor LERs constituted countervailable subsidies. The ITA found on preliminary determination in March 1992 that both Canada's stumpage system and its LERs were countervailable and set a CVD at 14.48 percent for lumber imports into the United States from all of Canada except the (volumetrically insignificant) Atlantic provinces. Following rounds of written and oral submissions by the CFLI and the various Canadian provincial governments, the ITA issued its final determination in May 1992.

On final determination in Lumber III, the ITA found both Canadian stumpage and the LERs to be countervailable and set an ad valorem CVD of 6.51 percent for all Canadian lumber imported into the United States from Alberta, British Columbia, Ontario, and Quebec. This CVD was a mixture of asserted

10. See Kalt (1988) for a discussion and calculation of the international welfare effects of Lumber II.

stumpage and LER countervailable subsidy findings, with all affected provinces found to have stumpage subsidies. Only British Columbia was found to have subsidies emanating from LERs, and reflecting the geography and heterogeneous forest types of British Columbia, the asserted LER subsidy applied only with respect to logs produced along its coastal regions. Following the final determination, Lumber III went before a binational panel (established pursuant to the new free trade agreement between Canada and the United States) for review and remand. The panel remanded the final determination back to the ITA for reconsideration and supplementation on a number of legal and evidentiary issues. The ITA then issued a determination on remand, raising the CVD to 11.54 percent, with the increase coming primarily from the ITA's conclusion that the entire province of British Columbia constituted an integrated relevant log market and was thereby subject to the asserted LER subsidy. In late 1993, the binational panel rejected the ITA's determination on remand (potentially voiding any CVD), basing its rejection of the ITA's findings primarily on the grounds that it had not been shown that stumpage and the LERs were specific in the sense described above. The ITA immediately launched an appeal of this threat to its authority. This "extraordinary challenge" to the binational panel's decisions, however, was rejected in mid-1994. This leaves the Canadian interests the ultimate victors in Lumber III (pending a potential further round of appeals), notwithstanding their notable lack of success before the key administrative agency—the ITA.

5.3.2   The Parties and Their Stakes

The magnitude of the CVDs arrived at by the DOC in Lumber II and III may suggest that the stakes in the lumber dispute are small. However, duties on the order of 5–15 percent translate into hundreds of millions of dollars annually. Lumber II, for example, concerned only stumpage, yet it has been estimated that its CVD would have produced (i.e., but for the MOU) tariff revenues of more than $340 million per year for the United States and net gains for U.S. lumber producers of more than $400 million per year (see Kalt 1988). In the case of Lumber III, the stakes are summarized in table 5.2. The ITA's final determination estimates that the CVD would offset subsidies totaling close to $400 million per year, with that much revenue to be collected by the U.S. government through import duties.

The U.S. interests seeking tariff protection in the lumber disputes were successful in doing so before the ITA in Lumber II and III, but unsuccessful in Lumber I (table 5.1). This pattern of differential success—failure to secure protection in the early 1980s, followed by favorable ITA decisions in the late 1980s and early 1990s—does not appear to be explained by a change in either the organizational capabilities of tariff-seeking interest groups in the United States or the impact of Canadian lumber imports in the U.S. marketplace. The tariff-seeking interests throughout Lumber I, II, and III have consisted of medium-sized and smaller U.S. logging and milling operations organized as

Table 5.2   ITA Estimates of Countervailable Subsidies: Final Determination
                   (million dollars per year)

Province	Stumpage	Log Export Restraints	Total
Alberta	5.1	0	5.1
British Columbia	145.7	205.2	350.9
Manitoba	0	0	0
Northwest/Yukon	0	0	0
Ontario	34.3	0	34.3
Quebec	0.1	0	0.1
Saskatchewan	0	0	0
Total	185.2	205.2	390.4

the CFLI, joined with force by at least one of the very large U.S. operators (Georgia Pacific Corporation), and orchestrated by a U.S. law firm renowned for lobbying and legal efforts on behalf of protection-seeking parties. The legal strategies, efforts and expense of these interests do not show perceptible change over Lumber I, II, and III.

By the same token, it cannot be argued readily that Lumber I can be distinguished from Lumber II and III on the basis that Canadian lumber imports constituted more of a threat to the U.S. industry after Lumber I in 1982. Although a number of studies have found that the prospects of success in seeking tariff protection in the United States rise when a domestic industry experiences high and rising competition from imports (see, e.g., Baldwin 1984), such trends are not obvious in the case of Canadian or B.C. lumber shipments to the United States (table 5.3). The demand for lumber is driven to a very significant degree by housing starts and other construction needs. As shown in table 5.3, U.S. lumber demand, consumption, and sawmill industry employment were declining in the period leading up to the Lumber I decision (arguably reflecting the economywide recession of 1980–82) but were recovering strongly leading up to the Lumber II decision at the end of 1986. Preceding initiation of Lumber III in 1992, U.S. sawmill employment and consumption were weakening, but the level and share of Canadian and B.C. lumber imports do not appear to make those imports the culprit (table 5.3). Rather, weak macroeconomic conditions and tightening environmental restrictions were impinging on the domestic lumber sector.

In fact, two arguably causal factors stand out as changing between the failure of U.S. interests to secure CVD protection in Lumber I and their successes before the ITA in Lumber II and III. First, between Lumber I and Lumber II, legal precedent regarding the definition of when a foreign nation's asserted subsidies are specific was evolving in unrelated cases toward a lower hurdle for protection-seeking parties. Second, the tightening of environmental restrictions on logging in the United States—particularly in the early 1990s follow-

Table 5.3   Economic Conditions in North American Wood Fiber Trade

Year	U.S. Housing Starts (million) (1)	U.S. Softwood Lumber Consumption (billion board feet) (2)	Softwood Lumber Imports from Canada (billion board feet) (3)	Canadian Share of U.S. Consumption (%) (4)	Softwood Lumber Imports from British Columbia (billion board feet) (5)	B.C. Share of U.S. Consumption (%) (6)	U.S. Sawmill Employment (7)	U.S. Sawmill Average Hourly Earnings ($) (8)
1980	1.3	35.4	9.5	27	n.a.	n.a.	175,000	6.36
1981	1.1	33.6	9.1	27	n.a.	n.a.	161,000	6.80
1982	1.1	33	9.1	28	n.a.	n.a.	132,000	7.66
1983	1.7	42	11.9	28	7.2	17.0	143,000	7.86
1984	1.8	44.9	13.2	29	7.6	17.0	143,000	8.08
1985	1.8	45.9	14.5	32	8.3	18.0	136,000	8.22
1986	1.8	47.8	14.1	29	7.8	16.4	145,000	8.57
1987	1.6	50.4	14.6	29	9.2	18.2	148,000	8.45
1988	1.5	48.7	13.7	28	9.2	18.9	152,000	8.75
1989	1.4	47.7	13.5	28	8.9	18.0	144,000	8.94
1990	1.2	45.3	12.4	27	7.4	16.1	139,000	9.23
1991	1.0	42.5	11.7	28	7.1	16.7	130,000	9.33

Sources: Cols. (1)–(5) U.S. Department of Commerce, International Trade Administration, *In the Matter of Certain Softwood Lumber Imports* (Washington, D.C., 1986, 1992), selected filings; cols. (6) and (7) U.S. Department of Commerce, *U.S. Industrial Outlook, Wood Products* (Washington, D.C.: Government Printing Office, 1988, 1994).

ing the listing of the northern spotted owl as an endangered species—placed congressional delegations in logging states in a particular bind. Under pressure from environmental interests to back plans for protecting the northern spotted owl and other environmental amenities, elected officials sought countervailing measures that would allow them to appear supportive of the interests of the logging industry. Attacking Canadian imports provided such a measure. While explaining the success of Lumber II and III relative to Lumber I is outside the purpose of this study, these factors stand out as plausible explanations.

As indicated by table 5.2, there are hundreds of millions of tariff dollars at stake in the timber trade wars, with concomitant stakes in terms of producer rents and consumer surplus (see also Kalt 1988). These stakes clearly stand behind the doggedness of the CFLI over the last decade of legal and political action. Interestingly, as summarized in table 5.4, the coalition has consisted largely of the smaller U.S. sawmills. A number of larger U.S.-based operators, such as Weyerhauser, in fact, have been expanding their investments in Canada. This apparently has tended to cool any enthusiasm for CVD action against Canadian lumber imports. While the direct effect of a CVD action on the profitability of large U.S.-based, but internationalized, producers is still likely to be positive on net, the potential for lingering negative political and regulatory ramifications in Canada seems to induce such producers to lie low in the proceedings before the ITA. The notable support for CVD action by Georgia Pacific Corporation is consistent with this reading, as this corporation is not significantly invested in Canada. Table 5.4 also notes that the U.S. government has been an active supporter of CVD action against Canadian lumber imports. This has been especially evident in Lumber III, where the ITA itself initiated the CVD action and consistently has advocated protection for the U.S. industry.

Lumber consumer interests on both sides of the border have largely been inactive in the lumber dispute. If and to the extent that U.S. tariffs on Canadian lumber shipments to the United States would tend to keep such lumber at home, Canadian consumers could benefit from resulting reductions in domestic Canadian lumber prices. On the other hand, U.S. consumers tend to be harmed by lumber import duties, as the tariffs raise U.S. prices. Notwithstanding these impacts, the basic argument of CT appears to rule: free-rider problems thwart organized political action by large groups with diffuse stakes. When informed, for example, by the organized Canadian milling interests of the potential deleterious effects on U.S. consumers arising under a U.S. CVD action against Canadian lumber, U.S. consumer groups with some organization in place (such as home builders' associations) acknowledge their interest but lend only token opposition to the CVD action. Similarly, U.S. loggers (who stand to benefit from duties on lumber made from Canadian logs) and Canadian loggers (who stand to lose) have generally recognized their interests but have been inactive politically and in the legal arena at the DOC.

The organized and active opposition to CVD action against Canadian lumber consistently has come from Canadian sawmills and the Canadian govern-

Table 5.4   **Economic Stakes and Affected Interests in the Timber Trade Wars between the United States and Canada**

	Supported	Inactive	Opposed
Winners	Georgia Pacific Corp. Small U.S. mills U.S. government (ITA in Lumber III)	Other large U.S. mills U.S. loggers Canadian consumers	
Losers		U.S. consumers Canadian loggers	Canadian mills Canadian government

ment. In particular, participation in the legal proceedings has been led and financed by the provincial forestry ministries and, to a lesser extent, the federal government of Canada. The Canadian mill operators have cooperated for the most part with their governmental agents, providing information and testimony. The direction of the financial stakes of the Canadian mills is straightforward to perceive, and their interests in influencing the role and forcefulness of the various Canadian governmental agents follow. At both the provincial and federal levels, however, these agents see broader support at home for their active opposition to U.S. CVD actions. Specifically, U.S. CVD actions against Canadian stumpage and log export policies are widely interpreted in the Canadian public as assaults on Canada's sovereignty in the area of natural resource policy. This clearly bolsters the governments' active efforts in opposing imposition of U.S. duties, as evidenced by the highly visible and vociferous retaliatory response of the Canadians in Lumber II.

5.4   Framework for Boolean Representation of the Legal Arguments in Lumber III

The legal proceedings engendered by Lumber III have undoubtedly increased the demand for logs in the world—by increasing the demand for paper. Hundreds of thousands of pages of legal briefs, official rulings, expert reports, hearing transcripts, correspondence, and data reporting have been produced and reproduced as the parties have argued their respective positions. In the course of the proceeding, a multitude of arguments has been put forth and debated. These arguments range from the legal and technical to the substantive and factual. Among the many arguments afoot, however, the focus of the proceedings in Lumber III has ended up on a modest number of key matters. I now turn to a discussion of these for purposes of arriving at Boolean codings of their NI-relevant and CT-relevant attributes—precedential status, analytic straightforwardness, evidentiary strength, expositional hurdles, stakes, and so forth. I begin with an introduction to the applicable Boolean pseudoregression techniques.

5.4.1   Boolean Logic and Pseudo-Regression Techniques

Following the framework of section 5.2, we would like to see if and to what extent the success of an argument made in the legal context of the ITA's CVD procedures depends on such variables as the strength of the argument's analytic underpinnings, the strength of the precedent it encounters, the quality of the evidence in its favor, the stakes riding on it, and so forth. Such an analysis encounters significant methodological difficulties. Not the least of these is the creation of a metric by which to measure otherwise vague concepts such as the "strength" of precedent or the "quality" of evidence. For social science researchers accustomed to continuous and naturally metered data (a good thing) and training that emphasizes the ideal of large sample sizes leading to quantitative measures of confidence (a good thing, but only one quadrant of the philosophy of scientific method), measurement in a context of qualitative "cases" is commonly a dead end for production of usable research results. Indeed, in the legal context, questions such as "Why did that party win its case?" are typically relegated to discursive case studies, to be published in law journals.

Pioneering (and prize-winning) methodological developments hold some promise for enabling the scientific researcher to isolate the usable information contained in comparative and qualitative case studies. These methods of "Boolean analysis" have been given modern social science impetus by (especially) Charles C. Ragin and rely on the rules of logic and Boolean mathematics to parse the useful information contained in such contexts (Ragin 1987). Notwithstanding unsettled questions regarding the epistemological relationship of these methods to more familiar methods of classical and Bayesian statistics, these methods do provide rigorous insight into the information content of otherwise qualitative cases.

The Boolean analysis undertaken here relies on the rules of logic to isolate qualitative causes of a dichotomous outcome. At its core, Boolean analysis relies on logic of the following form to reach conclusions regarding the explanatory role of alternative postulated factors: suppose two causes, A and B, are postulated as explanations of an event, Y. A and B occur in various combinations of "presence" and/or "absence," and sometimes Y occurs. In an otherwise well-specified model of causation that identifies A and B as possible causes, if A is always present when Y occurs, but Y occurs with B present and with B absent, B can logically be eliminated as a necessary ingredient in the causation of Y. If the researcher can specify explanatory factors and determine their presence or absence across multiple instances of Y and not-Y, scientific information is gained through Boolean (presence/absence) logic of this form.

Boolean analysis proceeds by coding an outcome of interest for yes/no (0/1) results. In the case at hand, for example, it is possible to examine the various arguments in Lumber III and determine objectively whether the CFLI (or, alternatively, the Canadian parties) won or lost a particular dispute. Possible explanatory factors in determining when an outcome (e.g., Win) occurs are then coded (0/1) for their presence or absence in each observed instance in which an outcome occurs. (This "measurement" of "right-hand side" variables is the more difficult problem and is taken up below.) The resulting coding can be represented by a Boolean summary (or truth) table of the kind in table 5.5.

In this summary, Boolean analysis would code the outcome Y in the first case (row) as $Y = aB$. The second case would be coded as $Y = AB$. Multiplication in Boolean analysis is read as "and," while addition is read as "or." Thus, we can say that $Y = aB + AB$; that is, Y occurs when either a and B are present together or A and B are present together. If this is a well-specified model of the causation of Y, the result that $Y = aB + AB$ can be further reduced by factoring to $Y = B(a + A) = B$. In other words, B is a necessary and sufficient condition to cause Y, and it does not matter whether A is present or not.

The expression from the illustration to the effect that $Y = B$ is a "prime implicant." Prime implicants indicate necessary and sufficient conditions in the following way:

$Y =$ B   B is both necessary and sufficient.

$Y =$ $A + B$ A and B are each sufficient but not necessary.

$Y =$ AB   Both A and B are necessary but not sufficient.

$Y = A(B+C)$ A is necessary but not sufficient.

Note that Boolean analysis of dichotomous factors is a form of "pseudoregression." This derives from the fact that, when two states, a and A, are both present when Y occurs and other factors are constant across the relevant observations (i.e., B is present along with a and A), there is clearly a collinearity problem—Y occurs with both A and not-A. Just as with standard multiple regression techniques, the Boolean analysis assigns a coefficient of 0 to the A/a factor because no causation can be attributed to it. Similarly, as with standard regression techniques, the validity of results from Boolean analysis depends on the outside-the-data specification that the researcher brings to the evidence. Specification bias can plague Boolean analysis just as it plagues

Table 5.5	**Hypothetical Boolean Summary Table (uppercase = presence; lowercase = absence)**		
	Outcome	Factor (A or a)	Factor (B or b)
	Y	a	B
	Y	A	B
	y	a	b

more familiar statistical approaches to isolating the effects of individual independent explanatory factors. Such bias could arise in the illustration if, for example, there is an omitted factor, C, such that the accurate prime implicant is Y = aB + AB + AC. In this circumstance, rejection of A as a factor in explaining Y would be erroneous: A plays an explanatory role when it occurs along with C.

For researchers accustomed to large-sample, continuous variable analyses and hypothesis testing, the most obvious disadvantage of Boolean analysis is the absence of quantitative measures of confidence in expressed results. At the same time, however, Boolean analysis utilizes the rules of logical contradiction to arrive at epistemologically valuable conclusions.[11] Indeed, when problems of specification bias are not present, the ability of Boolean analysis to yield statements regarding necessary and sufficient conditions represents an advantage over more familiar quantitative techniques (which focus primarily upon the marginal contributions of multiple variables).

As noted above, the coding of "left-hand side" variables in a case such as ITA's Lumber III final determination is largely objective and straightforward. It entails identifying the "winner" of a particular argument in the proceeding, as this is indicated in the actual ITA decision. Determining the presence or absence of particular possible explanatory factors that might explain an argument's success or failure, on the other hand, requires more judgment, and intensive reading of the appropriate legal records. Such investigation has required me to make certain qualitative assessments regarding, for example, the straightforwardness of the economic theory of natural resource rent, but is bolstered by the fact that the final determinations enunciated by the ITA frequently provide direct discussion of such matters and the direction of influence on its findings. These yield the key right-hand side variables necessary for completion of an actual version of the hypothetical Boolean summary table. The resulting variables and their expected influences (or "signs"), according to the ITA (by both direct assertion and argument passim) and bolstered by the reasoning from the NI interpretation of legal proceedings discussed above, are:

1. *Precedent:* Having precedent on one's side increases the likelihood of winning an argument (see discussion above). In the Boolean analysis which follows, this factor is referred to as P/p.

2. *Straightforward theory:* Having a straightforward theory (e.g., an economic explanation or theory) improves the likelihood of winning an argument. Apparently, having to resort to complicated or exotic theories to make one's case reduces credibility (where "complicated," "exotic," etc., refer, in part, to

---

11. Not to get too Kantian about the matter, but in so doing it might be argued that Boolean techniques in some circumstances can produce results that are more reliable than familiar quantitative methods *provided the problem of specification bias is not present.* Of course, this qualifier regarding specification bias is equally applicable to the familiar techniques of quantitative analysis. See, e.g., Leamer (1978).

being outside the familiar modes of reasoning of the ITA). Examples discussed below include the concepts of general equilibrium and natural resource rent, which modify familiar supply-demand reasoning. In the Boolean analysis which follows, this factor is referred to as T/t.

3. *Evidence:* All else equal, having the preponderance of evidence on one's side increases the likelihood of winning an argument. In the Boolean analysis which follows, this factor is referred to as E/e.

4. *Ease of exposition:* All else equal, the likelihood of winning an argument increases with the ease with which it can be communicated. This is sometimes related to, but is not the same as, having a straightforward theory. An example from below is the "law of one price," which is relatively easy to express as the intersection of a supply and a demand curve, but which is quite complicated to explain in application to real-world factual contexts (owing to the introduction of considerations of the law's underlying preconditions related to transactions costs, quality differentials, cross-elasticities, and the like). In the Boolean analysis which follows, this factor is referred to as X/x.

In addition to these factors, CT suggests that the stakes riding on an argument can influence the likelihood of winning. In general, the ITA could not be expected to refer to this since the justice it administers is "blind." Nevertheless,

5. *Stakes:* Assuming CT, the likelihood of the winning argument being made by the more influential party increases with the stakes at issue in the argument. In the Boolean analysis which follows, this factor is referred to as S/s.

5.4.2   The Arguments in Lumber III

I now turn to coding the foregoing factors for a set of 14 actual and salient arguments that parties have contended over in Lumber III. The arguments and the results of the coding are set forth in table 5.6. The table also indicates the winning party in each argument as reflected in the ITA's final determination. Recalling that the Lumber III investigation was initiated by the DOC, the proceeding has presented a recurring difficulty in distinguishing between the DOC's role as advocate and its role as adjudicator. Indeed, this has led to formal claims of bias on the part of the Canadian parties.[12] The resulting ambiguity is reflected in the "DOC/CFLI" designation of winner as applicable in table 5.6. For each of the issues that follow, the 0/1 codings shown in table 5.6 are derived from the written record of the Lumber III proceeding. A brief summary of each issue is provided here.

1. *Rent theory:* As discussed above, the economics of natural resource harvesting have played an important role in the Canadian response to allegations that the Canadian stumpage system subsidizes the production of lumber by

---

12. The primary claim arises as a result of the fact that ITA has employed a former spokesperson for CFLI in the Lumber III investigation.

Table 5.6 Boolean Summary of the Attributes of Observed Winning Arguments in the U.S.-Canada Lumber Dispute (affirmative = 1; otherwise = 0)

Issue	Winner	Precedent Favors Winner (P = 1; p = 0)	Large Stakes (S = 1; s = 0)	Applicable Theory Straightforward (T = 1; t = 0)	Evidence Favors Winner (E = 1; e = 0)	Winner Ease of Exposition (X = 1; x = 0)
Rent theory	DOC/CFLI	0	1	0	0	1
LER as subsidy	DOC/CFLI	0	1	0	0	0
Market distortion	DOC/CFLI	0	1	1	0	1
LER price change	Canadians	1	0	1	1	1
General equilibrium effects: existence	Canadians	1	0	1	0	0
General equilibrium effects: measurement	DOC/CFLI	0	1	0	0	0
Causation tests	Canadians	1	1	0	1	1
Other provinces	DOC/CFLI	0	0	0	0	1
Law of one price	Canadians	1	1	0	0	0
Relevant market/1	Canadians	0	1	0	0	1
Relevant market/2	DOC/CFLI	1	0	0	0	1
Export prep. costs	DOC/CFLI	1	0	0	0	1
Transport costs	Canadians	1	0	1	1	1
Company exclusions	Canadians	1	0	1	1	1

Canadian millers. Obviously, the stakes here are very large (see table 5.1); if the Canadians were to prevail in demonstrating that the effects of below-market stumpage were entirely inframarginal, the stumpage CVD would be insupportable. Moreover, the only concerted evidence to test the inframarginality of Canadian stumpage pricing was that developed by Nordhaus on behalf of the Canadian parties. The economic theory of rent, however, is neither straightforward nor easily communicated. There apparently is not strong precedent one way or the other as to the applicability or legitimacy of rent theory in CVD proceedings.

2. *LER as subsidy:* "Border measures" such as LERs have had an unsettled history in the administration of U.S. CVD law. Prior to a single ruling in 1990, border measures had been held to be noncountervailable. This placed the DOC/CFLI at a precedential disadvantage in its arguments for the countervailing of Canada's LERs. In fact, the DOC had to go so far as to argue that "administrative agencies, however, are authorized to depart from a long-standing and consistent practice . . . [and] the Department concludes that the [pre-1990 case] determinations finding border measures in general to be *per se* noncountervailable pursuant to U.S. law were wrongly decided."[13] Clearly, the stakes were all or nothing, and the DOC/CFLI was compelled to labor hard to muster what evidence it could in its favor (eventually appealing to its interpretation of congressional intent). Exposition by the eventual winner, DOC/CFLI, was similarly impeded; and the theory as to why border measures are or ought to be countervailable is not straightforward—at either the ITA or in the broader context of GATT and trade—as they confront difficult issues of national sovereignty and measurement.

3. *Market distortion:* In some prior proceedings, the DOC had indicated that CVDs are justified only when another country's alleged subsidies to domestic processors distort the results of the marketplace in an inefficient direction. In the case at hand, Canadian LERs may, in fact, improve world resource allocation. Evidence is consistent with the conclusion that U.S. LERs and Japanese barriers to trade in lumber (of which Japan is nevertheless a major importer) artificially prop up (especially) Japanese demand for Canadian logs. Canada's LERs counteract this distortive effect.

4. *LER price change:* In the initial stages of the Lumber III proceeding, the CFLI, in particular, maintained that the asserted subsidy realized by B.C. sawmills as a result of LERs should be measured as the difference between a measured foreign price of logs and a measured Canadian domestic price of logs. Precedent, however, seems to support the view that a countervailable sub-

---

13. Note that I do not intend to be asserting the rightness or wrongness of the positions taken by the parties on this or any other matter listed here. Rather, as this instance indicates, relative to many other issues in the proceeding, the DOC was having to argue very hard in order to make its precedential points; i.e., the precedential burden in practice did not favor its arguments. The quoted passage is from U.S. Department of Commerce, International Trade Administration (1992, 176–77).

sidy must be measured by the difference between the price that Canadian millers would pay for logs absent the LERs and the price they presently pay. Because of general equilibrium effects when a border measure is imposed on an intermediate product (see, e.g., Wiseman and Sedjo 1981) and the large-country position of Canada in wood fiber trade, it would generally be expected that foreign log prices would come down toward Canadian domestic prices in the absence of LERs—making the CFLI measurement contrary to precedent.

5. *General equilibrium effects—their existence:* As noted, economic theory (and evidence in Lumber III) indicates that the context of Canadian LERs makes it highly likely that general equilibrium effects (between log markets and lumber markets) play significant roles in determining log prices. Although the measurement of the quantitative differences between partial and general equilibrium prices for logs absent Canadian LERs is complicated in theory and difficult to demonstrate and explain, the existence of general equilibrium effects is relatively straightforward and easy to communicate (e.g., "The LERs may not affect total log demand in British Columbia; they may only affect where the Japanese have the logs that they buy milled.")

6. *General equilibrium effects—their measurement:* See item 5 above. Both the theory of the proper structure of a model able to capture general equilibrium effects and the implementation of such a model for the purpose of measuring the no-LER price of Canadian logs is complicated and difficult to describe in the context of the ITA's legal proceedings (see, e.g., Wiseman and Sedjo 1981; Moschini and Meilke 1992). Based on what evidence is available, the magnitude of the stakes is likely to be perceived as large by the ITA.

7. *Causation tests:* Because border measures are indirect in their potential effects, the Canadian LERs' effects on Canadian millers' costs are not directly observable (as they would be if, say, subsidies were paid in cash to millers). Nevertheless, the ITA is under a burden to demonstrate a "direct and discernable" impact of the LERs on Canadian sawmillers' costs. In the previous border measure case of 1990 (noted above), the ITA employed regression analyses of the differences between foreign and domestic prices to meet its burden. Notwithstanding the resulting precedential implications and the all-or-nothing stakes, the ITA in Lumber III eschewed its previous approach (and evidence generated therefrom).

8. *Other provinces:* Although other provinces besides British Columbia are subject to LERs, they are relatively minor participants in the marketplace for wood fiber. Moreover, both straightforward theory and accompanying evidence seem to indicate that LERs in the other provinces are not generally economically binding (e.g., some are net importers of logs themselves). The implications are bolstered by the "direct and discernable" standard noted above, and by the ease of exposition.

9. *Law of one price:* In lieu of hypothesis tests and statistical measurement of the magnitude of price effects attendant to LERs, the ITA relies on a partial equilibrium spreadsheet model that utilizes elasticities of supply and demand for an aggregated foreign-log–only sector and a Canadian-log–only sector to

calculate a unique price at which foreign and B.C. log prices would be equated in the absence of Canadian LERs. This approach is justified by what DOC/CFLI refers to as the "universally accepted Law of One Price," and despite considerable evidence that the conditions required for the law to hold in the strong form adopted by the ITA do not apply even within "free trade" regions (such as western Washington). Without the law, however, the DOC/CFLI would run the risk of having no mechanism for identifying and calculating an asserted subsidy. In its favor, the DOC/CFLI have ease of exposition when compared to the Canadians' need to turn to more complicated theories that presumably sound like quibblings about qualifications to the law (see above).

10. *Relevant market/1:* As noted above, the ITA's final determination in Lumber III found that logs in the interior of British Columbia were not in the same relevant market as the rich forestlands of the coastal region (as a result of species heterogeneity, limited cross-elasticities of demand, and high transport costs). The Canadian's case for this conclusion was built up from detailed evidence and extensive discussion of theory and evidence. In their favor, the "direct and discernable" burden faced by the DOC/CFLI created a favorable precedential for the Canadian view: the ITA's spreadsheet model used to identify and measure a subsidy to coastal B.C. log prices was built only for the coastal region. The stakes surrounding the treatment of the interior of the province are large; upon including the interior in its eventual remand determination, ITA raised the calculated value of the countervailable LER subsidy from the figure shown in table 5.1 to more than $450 million per year.

11. *Relevant market/2:* The exclusion of interior logs from the subsidy calculation under the final determination represents the only identifiable case in which the Canadian interests have prevailed before the ITA on an argument with large stakes. While the ITA's eventual reversal in its remand determination is outside of the "final determination" framework on which I am primarily focused, it is included in table 5.6 and discussed below.

12. *Export preparation costs:* In general, precedent recognizes that it is appropriate that any comparison between foreign and domestic log prices for purposes of identifying and measuring an asserted countervailable subsidy be adjusted for intervening costs and quality differences that would sustain cross-border price differences even in the absence of LERs (see the next argument below). Through a complicated and hard (for the Canadians) to explain and measure process of sorting logs for export, certain costs are borne that arguably require accounting for in the ITA's calculation of asserted subsidies. Nevertheless, the incremental stakes in the issue do not appear to be overwhelming, and the ITA can rely on the precedent of "deference to the agency's expertise" in ignoring export preparation costs in its calculations.

13. *Transport costs:* In light of the precedent mentioned above, the Canadian parties have been successful in arguing that transport costs should be deducted from foreign-derived log prices in any attempt under the LER analysis to arrive at log prices netted back to domestic B.C. markets. The resulting adjustments are relatively minor.

14. *Company exclusions:* Under CVD precedent and law, individual companies can be exempted from a CVD if they can be shown to be outside the affected sector or do not use the particular item (B.C. logs, in this case) that is allegedly being subsidized. Such exclusions are not quantitatively important, and the Canadian parties have generally been successful in proving up particular companies for exclusion.

5.5   Results

Having constructed table 5.6 from considerations of the foregoing form, it now provides the basis for a Boolean analysis of the determinants of successful arguments before the ITA. I proceed by converting the indicated 0/1 designations to the uppercase/lowercase notation indicated above and in the table, and then factoring the resulting expressions into prime implicants. Thus, for example, the first case (rent theory) in table 5.6 becomes

$$\text{DOC/CFLI Win} = p\text{SteX},$$

while the second case (LER as subsidy) becomes

$$\text{DOC/CFLI Win} = p\text{Stex}.$$

In words, the first case says that the DOC/CFLI won the argument under conditions in which precedent was not particularly in its favor *and* the stakes were large *and* the applicable theory was complicated *and* available evidence did not favor the DOC/CFLI *and* the DOC/CFLI found it relatively easy to exposit its argument against the Canadian position. Phrased this way, it is clear why individual case studies have such a difficult time yielding clear results; with so many "ands," isolating why the DOC/CFLI won the rent theory issue is not possible. But this points to the potential value of the full Boolean analysis.

Upon fully factoring table 5.6, the resulting prime implicant for designation of a winning argument is

$$\text{Win} = p\text{St} + \text{PsX}(t\text{E} + \text{Te}).$$

This is the complete summary of table 5.6, and reflects the process of logical reduction described above.[14] In words, the prime implicant for Win says: A winning argument before the ITA has either precedent running against it (p) and a complicated theory (t) but large stakes (S); or it has precedent in its favor (P), low stakes (s), and easy exposition (X), and either a combination of a complicated theory (t) but strongly supportive evidence (E) or a simple theory (T) albeit weak evidence (e).

At first impression, some of these results may appear contradictory or difficult to interpret. For example, the first term in the prime implicant (pSt) says

14. The case of relevant market/1 is treated as an aberration or outlier for the reasons noted above.

that a winning argument has precedent running against it and weak evidence behind it but large stakes. This result should not be interpreted to mean that this combination makes for a winning argument, or a higher likelihood of a winning argument than, say, a combination of pST (which has a simple theory on its side, when compared to pSt). Rather, the Boolean implicant must be interpreted as merely saying that, when the analysis removes all logical redundancies from table 5.6, it is left with pSt as the logically minimum conditions observed when a win arises despite a lack of supportive precedent. The cases under investigation are insufficiently rich to distinguish further, via Boolean logic alone, between p, S, and t as determinants of Win. In this regard, the power of the Boolean analysis here parallels the common situation found in many multivariate quantitative analyses which lack sufficient data to overcome collinearity among explanatory factors.

Closer inspection of the process of factoring and reduction that produces the prime implicant for Win above reveals that the cases in table 5.6 that produce the first term (pSt) in Win are entirely cases in which DOC/CFLI is the winning party. Similarly, the cases which produce the second term in Win (i.e., PsX-(tE + Te)) are entirely cases in which the Canadians are the winners of the argument. From this observation comes the key findings of this study:

DOC/CFLI Wins = pSt   and   Canadians Win = PsX(tE + Te).

Just as in the case of familiar large sample, continuous variable regression methods, the researcher may come to the Boolean analysis of the table 5.6 data with supportable prior beliefs concerning such matters as the permissible signs of the effects of independent variables, the proper structural form of specification, and, of course, the basic specification of explanatory factors to be included in the analysis. In so doing, the collinearity present in the data (i.e., in the logical reduction here to pSt, but no further) may be overcome to some extent, allowing more information to be drawn from the data (Leamer 1978). Thus, consider the above expression for DOC/CFLI Wins. The p in pSt represents the absence of supporting precedent for the position taken by the winning party. It is only reasonably interpreted (through the kinds of prior considerations set forth above) as an impediment to winning an argument. The same interpretation applies to t—the absence of a straightforward theory behind the position taken on the winner's argument.

In short, p and t impede the ability of the DOC/CFLI to win an argument. Yet, when the stakes are large (S), the DOC/CFLI wins anyway. We cannot quite say that no matter which institutional factors (i.e., p, t, x, and/or e) run against the DOC/CFLI, the group wins when the stakes are large; the sample of issues in table 5.6 does not include cases in which DOC/CFLI wins or loses with large S and x and/or e running against it. Nevertheless, it can be said that in the cases available, none occur in which institutional aspects of ITA proceedings block a DOC/CFLI win if the stakes in the matter are large.

This last observation *is* the prediction of CT. It says, contrary to NI, that in at least the cases represented here, no evidence is found that large stakes will not permit the influential, capturing party from overwhelming institutional blockades such as the absence of supportive precedent or the absence of an uncomplicated theory for one's argument. Having weighed in heavily in prior research against straightforward CT and in favor of NI (e.g., Kalt and Zupan 1984, 1990), I am surprised by these findings. They could not have been deduced by ruminating on the various instances of ITA decision making. The Boolean analysis has permitted the isolation of the informational content—what can and cannot be said—that is contained in the case materials of table 5.6.

NI is not wholly rejected, however. While DOC/CFLI has succeeded in Lumber III in securing the ITA's support for tariff protection against Canadian forest products, the Canadian parties have won some arguments along the way. In so doing, they have tempered the level of protection successfully sought before the ITA by the DOC/CFLI. As noted above, the second term in Win arises from cases in which the Canadian parties prevail in their legal arguments before the ITA, and the Canadian parties win arguments when PsX(tE + Te). Imposing on this expression the priors that neither complicated theories (t) nor weak evidence (e) assist the Canadians in winning an argument, the prime implicant for Canadians Win reduces to[15]

$$\text{Canadians Win} = PsX(tE + Te) = PsX(E + T).$$

This result says that, within the sample of cases encompassed by table 5.6, if the Canadians are to win arguments before the ITA, they require not only issues for which the stakes are small (s), but also institutional help in the form of supportive precedent (P), easy exposition (X), and either strong evidence (E) or a straightforward theory (T). Apparently, the Canadians do not need to have everything in their favor (i.e., PsXET) to win an argument before the ITA. Yet, even when the issue is a matter with small stakes, they need a considerable array of institutional factors on their side in order to win (i.e., P, X, and E or T).

5.6   Summary

For more than a decade, the United States and Canada have been engaged in a rancorous dispute over trade in softwood lumber. Through three successive rounds of administrative litigation before the DOC, the U.S. sawmill industry has sought to have CVDs imposed on Canadian lumber imports. The U.S. interests argue that Canada subsidizes its sawmills by providing timber from

---

15. This imposition of priors seems to be pushing the Boolean analysis farther than that set forth by Ragin (1987). Doing so here is based on the logical deduction that, given the model specification (in which the explanatory variables are taken to be fully described by S/s, P/p, T/t, E/e, and X/x), the only alternative treatment of the term in parentheses in Canadians Win yields PsXET. That is, the Canadian parties have both E and T going for them. This could only be a stronger position for the Canadians than the observed Canadians Win = PsX(tE + eT). Such strength of argument is not necessary for the Canadians to win.

public forests at below-market prices, and (in Lumber III) by restricting exports of Canadian logs.

The trade war over lumber is waged to a significant extent in the hearing rooms of the DOC. This study has examined whether, and to what extent, the institutional framework—the legal rules, standards, and precedents—of CVD law influences the fate of the contending parties. Two alternative theories of political economy have been tested, capture theory and the new institutionalism. CT deemphasizes the role of institutional settings of the kind at work here: the outcomes of political action are determined by the stakes and organization of rent-seeking parties, and the quasi-judicial regulatory proceedings of the DOC are mere Stiglerian theater. NI, on the other hand, posits that the structure and form of such proceedings are conditioning constraints, with the capacity to significantly influence the outcome of rent-seeking battles. Applying pseudoregression Boolean analysis to the actual legal issues argued before the DOC, I find more support for CT than for NI—at least in so far as particular institutions such as legal precedent and evidentiary burden are concerned. Even when the institutional aspects of ITA proceedings run against its interests, the protection-seeking DOC/CFLI prevails in its arguments when the stakes are large. Even when the stakes in an issue are small, the Canadians are only successful when the array of institutional aspects of ITA proceedings run overwhelmingly in their favor.

It should be stressed that the results regarding the role of institutions in conditioning policy outcomes only applies to the quasi-judicial setting of the ITA. The case can be made that, viewed in the large, the relevant U.S. institutions do matter in the NI sense to the making of trade policy, even as applied to the case of lumber. The ITA is only one step in a gauntlet of institutions that a protection-seeking party must traverse in order to succeed. Indeed, in Lumber III, the layers of post-ITA appeal have thus far produced wins for the Canadians. Perhaps this is what should be expected in a political system of checks and balances. CT may have won a battle at the ITA, but NI may yet win the war.

References

Baldwin, R. E. 1984. Trade policies in developed countries. In *Handbook of international economics,* vol. 1, ed. R. W. Jones and P. B. Kenen, chap. 12. New York: North-Holland.

Bates, R. 1988. Contra-contractarianism: Some thoughts on the new institutionalism. *Politics and Society* 16 (June/Summer): 387–401.

Becker, G. 1983. A theory of competition among pressure groups for political influence. *Quarterly Journal of Economics* 98 (August): 371–400.

Kalt, J. P. 1988. The political economy of protectionism: Tariffs and retaliation in the timber industry. In *Trade policy issues and empirical analysis,* ed. R. Baldwin. Chicago: University of Chicago Press.

Kalt, J. P., and M. A. Zupan. 1984. Capture and ideology in the economic theory of
politics. *American Economic Review* 74 (June): 279–300.
———. 1990. The ideological behavior of legislators: Rational on-the-job consumption
or just a residual? *Journal of Law and Economics* 33, no. 1 (August): 103–31.
Leamer, E. E. 1978. *Specification searches: Ad hoc inference with non-experimental
data.* New York: Wiley.
Moschini, G., and K. D. Meilke. 1992. Production subsidy and countervailing duties in
vertically related markets: The hog-pork case between Canada and the U.S. *American
Journal of Agricultural Economics* 74, no. 4 (November): 951–61.
North, D. 1990. *Institutions, institutional change, and economic performance.* Cam-
bridge: Cambridge University Press.
Peltzman, S. 1976. Toward a more general theory of regulation. *Journal of Law and
Economics* 19, no. 2 (August): 211–40.
Ragin, Charles C. 1987. *The comparative method.* Berkeley and Los Angeles: Univer-
sity of California Press.
Stigler, G. 1971. The economic theory of regulation. *Bell Journal of Economics* 2
(Spring): 3–21.
U.S. Department of Commerce. International Trade Administration. 1992. *Final coun-
tervailing duty determination: Certain softwood lumber products from Canada.*
Washington, D.C.: U.S. Department of Commerce, May 15.
Wiseman, C. A., and R. Sedjo. 1981. Effects of an export embargo on related goods:
Logs and lumber. *American Journal of Agricultural Economics* 63, no. 3 (August):
423–29.

Comment   Geoffrey Carliner

Do trade institutions matter in the outcome of trade policy?[1] Not much, according to the evidence presented in several of the papers in this volume. Several of the U.S. industries studied here have shown great creativity in finding
new ways to protect their markets from imports. The auto industry, or at least
one of its firms, obtained loan guarantees from the federal government and
then secured "voluntary" export restraints from the Japanese even though normal trade institutions turned down their request for protection under section
201 of the trade law. The semiconductor industry received U.S. and Japanese
government assurances that its market share in Japan would be 20 percent, a
remedy completely outside normal trade rules. The textile and apparel industries have received special treatment under the Multi-Fiber Arrangement for
years. Agriculture negotiated a new program of export subsidies during the
1980s. And the lumber industry persuaded existing trade institutions to change
their view of Canadian stumpage procedures, and therefore to grant U.S. producers protection from Canadian imports in 1986 and 1991 but not in 1982.

Geoffrey Carliner is executive director of the National Bureau of Economic Research.
1. The information in this comment comes from participants on both sides of this trade dispute,
all of whom wish to remain anonymous.

All this evidence strongly suggests that trade institutions are malleable and relatively sensitive to changes in political pressures.

The economic conditions of the U.S. lumber industry do not seem to explain why it failed to receive protection in 1982 but did gain the help of the Commerce Department and the International Trade Commission in 1986 and again in 1992. As figure 5C.1 indicates, employment in logging camps and sawmills was unusually low in 1982 but not in 1986 or 1992. Lumber production in 1986 and 1992 also did not dip dramatically. Residential housing accounts for about 70 percent of U.S. lumber consumption (nonresidential construction takes 15 percent, and other uses such as shipping pallets account for the remaining 15 percent). Yet housing starts were strong in 1986 but weak in 1982 and 1991. The import protection which the lumber industry obtained in 1986 clearly was not the result of depressed conditions.

In no year did lumber users strongly oppose the protection from imports which the lumber industry sought. The residential construction industry is well represented by the National Association of Home Builders (NAHB), whose members are construction contractors. The NAHB estimated that the Canadian

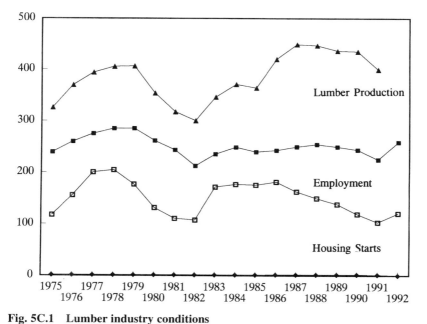

Fig. 5C.1   Lumber industry conditions
Source: Housing starts (tens of thousands of starts)—*Economic Report of the President* (Washington, D.C.: Government Printing Office, 1994), 330; employment in SIC industries 241 and 242 (thousand production workers) and lumber production (hundred thousand board feet)—U.S. Department of Commerce, Bureau of the Census, *Statistical Abstract of the United States* (Washington, D.C.: Government Printing Office, various years).

export tax imposed in 1986 would increase the price of lumber by only 2 percent, or a few hundred dollars per house. Since NAHB members do not have to worry about competition from imported housing, they could afford to ignore a small increase in lumber prices, unlike downstream users in industries which export their products or which compete with imports.

Moreover, the NAHB needed to concentrate its political efforts in 1986 on fighting to save the deductibility of mortgage interest. If the Tax Reform Act of 1986 had eliminated this provision, construction contractors would have suffered far more serious declines in demand than if Canada imposed an export tax on lumber. Therefore, although the NAHB did offer mild opposition to the lumber industry's petition, it saved its serious fire for the tax bill.

As Kalt's econometric evidence suggests, the story of the U.S.-Canada lumber dispute is consistent with capture theory. In 1981 the U.S. lumber industry had not captured U.S. trade institutions and therefore lost its case for protection. By 1986, with help from Congress, and again in 1991, it had solidified its friendship with the relevant agencies and had their full support in obtaining protection from Canadian imports. By 1991 this friendship was so strong that the Commerce Department took the unusual step of initiating a section 301 petition. This creative step by Commerce suggests how responsive institutions can be under political pressure.

But now there is a new institution which may prove more resistant to U.S. political pressure. The U.S.-Canada Free Trade Agreement created bilateral panels of experts to review all trade disputes. These experts are chosen by both sides and are supposed to be familiar with trade law and conditions in the industry requesting protection. Domestic U.S. institutions which are subject to capture by U.S. interests no longer have the final say.

As this is being written (March 1994), one of these panels is considering whether Canada's unilateral lifting of the export tax should be allowed.[2] It will be interesting to see whether this new institution does in fact insulate international trade from political pressures. It will also be interesting to see in a few years whether domestic U.S. industries learn how to exert pressure on these new institutions, the way they learned during the 1980s to exercise their political power on domestic U.S. trade institutions.

2. See table 5.1 of Kalt's paper for the history of the lumber dispute.

6   The Political Economy of U.S. Export Subsidies for Wheat

Bruce L. Gardner

U.S. agricultural commodities are predominantly exported rather than imported, but border price distortions for the exported commodities nonetheless exist, in the form of export subsidies. This paper investigates the economics and politics of export subsidies for the commodity where these subsidies are most important, wheat, and focuses on the Export Enhancement Program initiated in 1985.

6.1   Background: Agricultural Price Support Programs

Systematic programs to support agricultural commodity prices date from the initial New Deal legislation of 1933. Wheat was one of the original "basic" commodities supported (the others were cotton, corn, hogs, rice, tobacco, and milk).[1] Wheat continues to be one of the most heavily supported commodities. Table 6.1 shows estimates of transfers to producers of wheat and other commodities during 1984–87, our period of primary concern. Wheat fares well, with $3.25 billion in estimated net gains (producers' surplus) annually, 48 percent of the market value of wheat.

The means of support have been predominantly domestic market interventions—government purchases, supply controls, payments to producers—but border measures have inevitably been required to maintain U.S. prices above

Bruce L. Gardner is a professor in the Department of Agricultural and Resource Economics at the University of Maryland.

Helpful comments on this chapter were received from Robert Chambers, Thomas Grennes, Howard Leathers, Erik Lichtenberg, David Orden, Larry Salathe, and Daniel Sumner, as well as participants in the NBER conference at which this chapter was first presented.

1. Rye, flax, barley, grain sorghum, cattle, peanuts, and sugar (beets and cane) were added in 1934. The only important commodities excluded were poultry and eggs, soybeans, forage crops, fruits, and vegetables. A useful, detailed discussion of agricultural policy in the 1930s is Benedict (1953).

291

Table 6.1   Estimated Annual Gains from Commodity Programs, 1984–87

Commodity	Number of Producers (thousands) (1)	Producers' Gains (million $) (2)	Market Value of Crop (million $) (3)	Protection Rate (2) ÷ (3)
Wheat	352	3,250	6,770	.48
Corn	627	4,200	16,550	.25
Soybeans	442	410	10,520	.04
Rice	12	460	870	.53
Cotton	43	680	3,580	.19
Tobacco	137	360	2,310	.16
Sugar crops	9	610	1,670	.36
Peanuts	19	820	1,080	.76

Sources: (1) U.S. Department of Commerce, Bureau of the Census, *U.S. Census of Agriculture, 1987*, vol. 1, part 51 (Washington, D.C.: Government Printing Office, 1987) (2) Lin and Gardner (1988); (3) U.S. Department of Agriculture, (USDA), *Agricultural Statistics, 1992* (Washington, D.C., 1992).

corresponding world market levels. Commodities imported into the United States—sugar, citrus juices, dairy products, wool, meats—are protected by means of tariffs or quantitative restrictions on imports. But a substantially greater volume of U.S. agricultural output is exported (fig. 6.1), causing greater difficulty for domestic price support.

Attempts have been made to explain the economic and political forces that result in agricultural price supports generally, and the political economy of differences between the support provided for different commodities. Explanations have focused on political factors such as the long tenure of mostly rural Southern committee chairmen in Congress, the fact that rural areas are more than proportionally represented in the Senate, and general sympathy for farm people among the nonfarm population (see Benedict 1953; Hardin 1968; Bonnen and Browne 1989; Rapp 1988).

In Gardner (1987), I attempt to explain differences between commodities in the level of support granted. There is not clear evidence that having either a small or large number of producers or being geographically concentrated or dispersed makes much difference in the degree of protection. But it helps a commodity's political prospects significantly to be an imported product and to have experienced a recent price decline. And it harms a product's prospects to be highly elastic in both supply or demand (making it difficult for either production controls or subsidies to transfer a large amount to producers without generating relatively large deadweight losses). Nonetheless, most of the commodity-to-commodity variation in protection remains unexplained. Further progress in understanding U.S. agricultural protection may well require more detailed investigation of particular commodity policies.

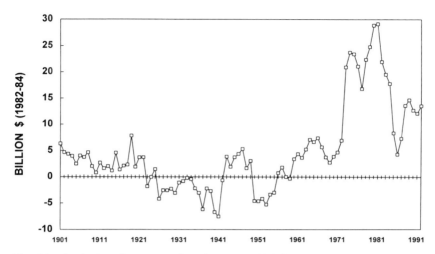

Fig. 6.1   Agricultural exports minus imports (1982–84 dollars)
Source: USDA, *Agricultural Statistics* (Washington, D.C., various years).

6.1.1   Wheat Trade and the Wheat Program

Immediately following World War II wheat exports became a large component of the demand for U.S. wheat (fig. 6.2). In 1950, 35 percent of production was exported, and over half the crop has been exported in 1980–93. At the same time, wheat prices have been seen by producers as generally too low throughout the postwar period. These concerns have been politically potent enough to maintain Depression-era wheat program mechanisms in place to the present. The new element in the 1950s was the importance of the export market, and the problems and opportunities this posed for the wheat price support program.

The traditional means of price support is a governmental agreement, through its Commodity Credit Corporation (CCC), to buy wheat at the support price. This program periodically led to governmental acquisition of large stocks which were costly to store and for which markets did not exist at the support price level. Three main policy instruments have been on the agenda for solving the surplus commodity problem: subsidizing sales abroad, implementing acreage reduction programs, and permitting market prices to fall while compensating producers with "deficiency" payments when the market price falls below a legislated target price.

In post–World War II wheat policy, subsidized sales abroad were the first approach tried. Continued foreign donations of wheat were a natural follow-up to the Marshall Plan. They were systematized in the Agricultural Trade and Development Act of 1954 (known as P.L. 480 and, as reformulated in the 1960s, Food for Peace). At the same time U.S. commercial wheat exports were

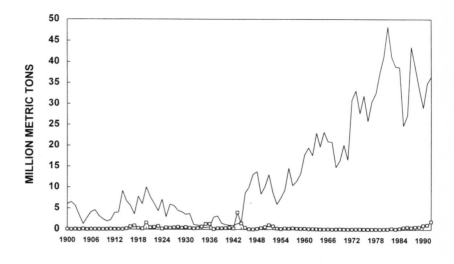

— EXPORTS —o— IMPORTS

Fig. 6.2   Wheat trade
Source: USDA, *Agricultural Statistics* (Washington, D.C., various years).

subsidized in the framework of the International Wheat Agreement, under general authority given the secretary of agriculture in the 1930s. The subsidy ranged from 5 to 30 percent of the price of wheat, depending on world and U.S. market conditions in each year. The Agricultural Adjustment Act of 1933 (section 22) gave the president authority, strengthened in the Agricultural Act of 1948, to impose import quotas if imports threatened the effectiveness of any price support program.[2]

In the mid-1950s it became apparent that food aid and subsidized commercial exports were insufficient to dispose of U.S. wheat surpluses. Acreage allotments, a feature of the 1930s programs, were reintroduced in 1954 and reduced planted acreage by about 18 million acres (from 79 million in 1953 to an average of 61 million in 1954–56). Each producer had to stay under the farm's allotment in order to be eligible for price support loans. In 1956 the Soil Bank program was introduced. It paid wheat growers about $20 per acre (roughly market rental rates) to idle an average of 12 million more acres (20 percent of preprogram acreage) in 1956–58.

In 1964 the approach of letting price supports fall, with compensating payments to producers, was introduced. The support price was cut essentially to

2. Small quantities of wheat imports were grandfathered in by a lower limit of the wheat import quota at 50 percent of the quantity imported in a base period determined by the president. The wheat imports shown in fig. 6.2 are from Canada. Section 22 quotas were suspended by executive order in 1974, but a recent increase in U.S. imports of Canadian wheat has led to calls for their reimposition and a one-year tariff rate quota in 1994–95.

the world market-clearing level, with the idea of reducing CCC stocks and the need for export subsidies. At the same time, payments were made to guarantee higher farmer receipts for that fraction of the wheat crop sold domestically. Each producer received a "domestic allotment" for purposes of calculating this payment.

Acreage idling, payments, and export subsidies all remained in place until the commodity boom that erupted with the large Soviet wheat purchases of July 1972. During 1973–76 market prices were well above support levels. The conflation of Soviet purchases, the oil shock, income growth in food-importing countries, and accelerating U.S. inflation convinced many that a watershed had been crossed that meant an end to the era of agricultural surpluses. Acreage reduction programs were abandoned and farmers were encouraged, in the secretary of agriculture's phrase, to plant fencerow to fencerow. The Nixon administration went so far as to replace export subsidies by quantitative limitations on exports to Eastern Europe and the Soviet Union in 1974–76.

By late 1976 the boom mentality had begun to fade, for wheat before any other major crop. In October 1976 President Ford, at the urging of Senator Dole and others, raised the CCC loan rate for wheat from $1.37 to $2.25 per bushel. President Carter was confronted within a year of taking office by a tractorcade, led by wheat growers, that resulted in legislation that resurrected the traditional wheat policy instruments. However, sustained intervention on the pre-1972 scale did not reappear until the mid-1980s. See table 6.2 for a summary of indicators.

6.2   Origins of the Export Enhancement Program

Agriculture in general faced severe economic problems in the early 1980s. The problems are apparent in the data on farm income and the farm sector's balance sheet. Real farm income (including government assistance) in 1980–84 averaged about half its level in 1971, before the commodity boom (fig. 6.3). The USDA's estimate of farm equity, the value of farm assets minus liabilities, declined from $1.14 trillion (1987 dollars) on January 1, 1979, to one-half of that value, $0.6 trillion, on January 1, 1985.

With respect to wheat growers more specifically there are no data on income or equity value, but an indication that is particularly useful in political terms can be obtained from state-level statistics. Kansas and North Dakota are the two most important wheat states, the centers of the winter and spring wheat growing areas, respectively. Together they account for about 30 percent of U.S. wheat acreage. Within these states, 46 percent of Kansas cropland and 45 percent of North Dakota cropland is planted to wheat. In both states, real farm equity declined sharply after 1979 (fig. 6.4), at about the same rate as in the nation as a whole. Figure 6.5 shows the real price of cropland in Kansas, North Dakota, and the United States, again all declining sharply.

These indicators are sufficient (but perhaps not necessary) conditions to ex-

Table 6.2   Wheat Policy Instruments, 1960–90

Crop Year	Government Inventory (million bushels)	Government Payments	Acreage Diversion (million acres)
1960	·1,280	0	0
1961	1,134	0	10.2
1962	1,111	286	10.7
1963	839	243	7.1
1964	646	443	5.1
1965	343	509	7.1
1966	132	681	8.2
1967	102	727	0
1968	163	746	0
1969	301	856	11.0
1970	378	871	15.7
1971	380	886	13.5
1972	155	859	20.1
1973	19	478	7.3
1974	1	102	0
1975	0	51	0
1976	0	143	0
1977	390	1,157	0
1978	454	719	9.6
1979	448	72	8.2
1980	560	228	0
1981	750	635	0
1982	1,253	489	5.8
1983	799	1,080	30.0
1984	1,032	1,556	18.4
1985	1,198	2,208	18.8
1986	1,462	3,673	21.0
1987	750	3,290	28.1[a]
1988	477	1,686	29.6[a]
1989	267	724	18.4[a]
1990	177	2,420	17.8[a]
1991	202	2,245	26.0[a]
1992	178	1,370	17.9[a]

Source: USDA, Agricultural Stabilization and Conservation Service, "Wheat: Summary of 1993 Support Program and Related Information" (Washington, D.C., November 1993).

[a]Includes wheat base placed in the Conservation Reserve Program under 10-year contracts (10.6 million acres in 1992).

plain cries of economic pain from the wheat growers. The wheat program as revised in the Agriculture and Food Act of 1981 involved considerable government efforts to assist wheat producers. The price paid to farmers for wheat placed in government ownership was increased to $4.00 per bushel for the 1982 crop. It had been only $1.37 up to 1975. U.S. wheat acreage planted expanded 45 percent, from 59 million acres in 1973 to 86 million acres in 1982, and the USDA increased its wheat stocks to over a billion bushels in

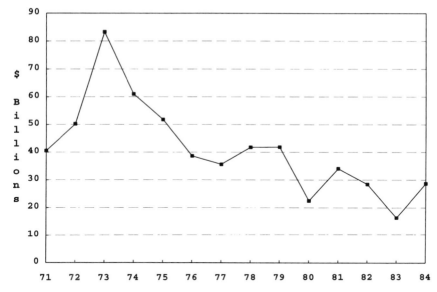

Fig. 6.3   Farm income (1987 dollars)
Sources: USDA, Economic Research Service, *National Financial Summary* (Washington, D.C., 1992); USDA, Economic Research Service, *Economic Indicators of the Farm Sector* (Washington, D.C., 1993).

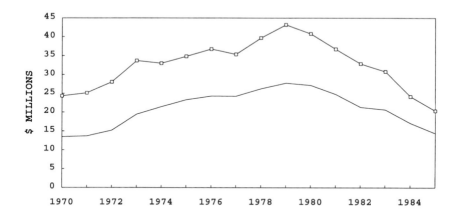

–□–KANSAS EQUITY ——NORTH DAKOTA EQUITY

Fig. 6.4   Farm equity: assets minus liabilities (1987 dollars)
Sources: USDA, Economic Research Service, *National Financial Summary* (Washington, D.C., 1992); USDA, Economic Research Service, *Economic Indicators of the Farm Sector* (Washington, D.C., 1993).

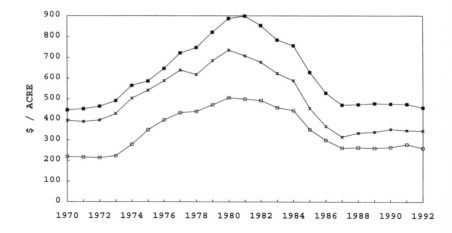

─■─U.S. LAND ─✳─KANSAS ─◻─NORTH DAKOTA

Fig. 6.5   Cropland prices (1987 dollars)
Sources: USDA, Economic Research Service, *National Financial Summary* (Washington, D.C., 1992); USDA, Economic Research Service, *Economic Indicators of the Farm Sector* (Washington, D.C., 1993).

1982, the highest level since the early 1960s. In reaction, the payment in kind (PIK) program was introduced and idled 30 million acres of wheat base in 1983, the largest supply control effort ever. In 1984, direct payments to wheat growers rose to exceed $1.5 billion. Yet none of these measures was capable of stemming the decline in income and equity values through 1985.

6.2.1   Underlying Economic Situation

The supply-demand situation is sketched in figure 6.6. Production in 1985 is shown as the vertical line S_{1985}. While well above mid-1970s levels, production in 1985 was only slightly higher than the 2.38 billion bushels of 1980.[3] The notable change in market conditions is on the demand side, where 2.3 billion bushels cleared the market at $3.99 a bushel in 1980, while 1.96 billion bushels sold for only $3.08 (nominal) in 1985. The demand curves sketched show the magnitude of demand reduction that occurred, and the separate demand function shown for U.S. exports indicates that reduction in demand is accounted for entirely by a decline in the foreign demand for U.S. wheat. Exports declined by 40 percent despite lower U.S. prices in 1985 than in 1980.

3. Although a point is plotted at the market price of $3.08 and 2.42 billion bushels on S_{1985}, this is not a point on a supply curve in the usual sense. The market price is not the incentive price for production because producers also receive deficiency payments and because producers held 18.8 million acres of wheat land idle in order to qualify for deficiency payments. The underlying market supply curves for 1985 is somewhere to the right of S_{1985} for prices above $3.

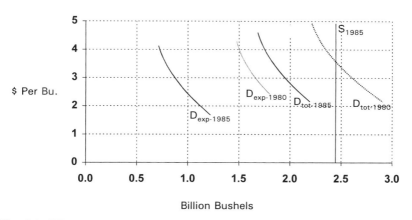

Fig. 6.6   Wheat supply and demand

Several econometric investigations were undertaken in the early 1980s to explain U.S. wheat exports (e.g., Gallagher et al. 1981; Sharples 1982; USDA 1986). Other studies have been conducted since that time, but the ones cited indicate the informational basis for policy decisions in 1985. Two factors received most of the blame for the decline in export demand: the strong dollar and the agricultural policies of the European Community. Between 1980 and 1985 the dollar rose 17 percent against the Canadian dollar and more than doubled against the French franc, the principal alternative sources of wheat in world trade. The overall trade-weighted value of the U.S. dollar rose about 60 percent. An exchange rate weighted by wheat export market shares rose 50 percent over this period (Dutton and Grennes 1985). This means that the apparent fall of 25 percent in the dollar price of wheat between 1980 and 1985 was actually a rise of about that much relative to competing sellers in terms of the buyers' currencies.

EC policies in this period were a continuation of those in effect since the 1960s under the Common Agricultural Policy (CAP) of the European Community. Wheat prices received by producers in the European Community have averaged about double the U.S. farm price. The main means of protection is a variable import levy, a tariff adjusted weekly to make up the difference between world prices and the protected ("threshold") price level in the European Community. In 1985 the levy varied between 57 and 140 ECUs ($64 and $175) per metric ton, 40 to 110 percent of the world (Rotterdam) average price. This mechanism provides EC farmers with a price that is not only high but also stable.

Behind this protective wall EC wheat production expanded steadily, despite a limited land area. Between 1969–71 and 1989–91 the wheat area of Western Europe (including 4.0 million hectares outside the European Community in 1970 but now in) increased from 17.1 to 17.6 million hectares, a little over half the U.S. wheat area. Yield per hectare, however, increased more sharply, from 2.7 to 5.1 metric tons per hectare, a rate of growth of over 3 percent annually. Over this period U.S. wheat yields grew at a rate of about 0.5 percent annually. By 1989–91 U.S. yields were a little less than half of European yields. EC yields grew not so much through genetic improvements as through increasing and increasingly sophisticated use of chemical fertilizers and pesticides. EC production methods have been tried in humid areas of the United States and have doubled yields there, but are too costly to be profitable at U.S. wheat prices.

The result in trade is that the European Community moved from self-sufficiency in wheat in 1970 to being a net exporter of about 25 percent of its production in the mid-1980s, making it the second-largest wheat exporter in the world. These exports are accomplished in the face of EC internal prices well above world trading prices by means of export subsidies. These subsidies in the mid-1980s were $80–$100 per metric ton of wheat, bringing the EC price from $230–$250 internally to a $140–$160 world level (Rotterdam basis) and costing the EC budget $1.0–$1.5 billion annually in 1980–85.

Between 1979–81 and 1984–86, EC annual wheat exports increased about 5.5 million metric tons. This amounts to 200 million bushels, one-third of the U.S. wheat export decline between 1980 and 1985.

Overall, it appears plausible (from the perspective of 1994 as well as that of 1985) that the combination of the high value of the dollar and EC subsidies accounted for much and quite possibly all of the decline in U.S. wheat export demand during the early 1980s. With an elasticity of foreign demand for U.S. wheat of −1.5, a 25 percent real price increase would reduce U.S. wheat exports by about 500 million bushels. Together with the 200 million bushel EC export gain being shared proportionally by export losses of the United States and other wheat exporters, one can explain a decline of about 600 million bushels, which is the entire 1980–1985 actual loss.

Another factor that received much attention in 1981–85 was the role of U.S. wheat policy, particularly the high prices paid for grain entering the Farmer-Owned Reserve and acreage controls, especially the reduction of 16.5 million acres of wheat harvested that occurred in 1983 under the PIK program. Under this program U.S. wheat production fell by 350 million bushels in 1983, a reduction of 13 percent from 1982. This would be expected to cause a reduction in U.S. wheat exports; but at the same time Farmer-Owned Reserve stocks were reduced by 450 million bushels—the payment in kind was in the form of CCC stocks. So it is not clear that the PIK program reduced exports (or propped up world prices to the benefit of the European Community). But it is clear that the combination of high loan rates and supply management during 1981–85 held wheat prices (U.S. and world) above the levels to which they would otherwise have fallen. Since the 25 percent rise in the value of the dollar could have been offset by a 25 percent fall in the U.S. wheat price, it is an oversimplification to point to the value of the dollar but not U.S. price supports as a cause of the wheat export slump.

6.2.2   Political Situation in 1980–85

The economic problems of administering the wheat program involved not only export demand but also CCC stock accumulation as demand fell and serious financial difficulties of farmers, stemming largely from borrowing heavily at high interest rates to buy land at the high prices of 1979–81. So it is not obvious that wheat growers would have concentrated on the export market as the principal source of their problems or export subsidies as a plausible remedy. Nonetheless, there was a heavy emphasis on wheat export issues by all the interested groups: farmers, agribusiness, economic analysts, the USDA, and Congress. The main political decision points are listed in table 6.3.

In 1983 the Reagan administration, at the urging of Secretary of Agriculture John Block, after debate settled only at the cabinet level, accepted the idea of ad hoc subsidized exports of CCC-owned wheat to targeted North African markets where EC wheat was being sold with the help of their export subsidies. This was intended to serve the dual purpose of reducing excessive stock levels and smiting the European Community. This venture was a substantial political success, affording an opportunity to attack the European Community, please farmers, and hold off congressional pressure for more sweeping programs. The impetus was thus established that led eventually to the full-fledged Export Enhancement Program (EEP).

In Congress, the idea of legislation to target in-kind export subsidies at the European Community did not prevail when first seriously considered in 1983. The principal reason given by opponents was the worry that such legislation would trigger a trade war in which the European Community would increase their subsidies and perhaps withdraw previously negotiated concessions such

Table 6.3	Events in the Political History of the EEP
1983	Reagan administration cabinet, responding to wheat grower requests to USDA, authorizes the use of CCC stocks to subsidize certain wheat exports.
April–May 1985	In an agreement between the Reagan administration and Senate Agriculture Committee bipartisan leadership, the EEP is formally established and publicly announced as an ongoing in-kind export subsidy, with $2 billion in CCC stocks to be used for this purpose.
October–December 1985	The EEP is incorporated in the 1985 Farm Act.
October 1990	The EEP is reauthorized by Congress and supplemented by a "GATT trigger" that reinforces and expands EEP in the event no GATT agreement is reached.
December 1993	GATT agreement is reached which requires reduction in EEP and in the European Community's export subsidies.

as their duty-free binding on U.S. oilseed products and feed grain substitutes. In addition, the secretary of agriculture already possessed sufficient authorities for ad hoc export subsidies as needed for surplus management or strategic purposes.

Two years later, as the 1985 farm bill deliberations began, the situation was different in two respects: farm groups had refined their general support for export promotion to more concrete proposals, and U.S. wheat exports had declined still further while the European Community's grew. In this situation the administration's desire to continue ad hoc subsidization without binding legislation was no longer politically tenable.

Congressional Debate

A detailed investigation of the political positions and arguments concerning the EEP is helped greatly by the focus of all parties on the 1985 farm bill as the venue for debate. Existing legislation, governing target prices and acreage reduction programs, in the Agriculture and Food Act of 1981 expired with the 1985 crops. Because of economic problems of the farm sector and dissatisfaction with existing programs, many sought substantial changes in the existing legislation.

Both the House and Senate agriculture committees conducted extensive hearings in preparation for the 1985 farm bill. The Senate committee, controlled by Republicans and chaired by Jesse Helms of North Carolina, appeared particularly interested in a fundamental review of agricultural policy (although tobacco policy was excluded). In 1983 Chairman Helms wrote to some 300 industry and academic people, asking for comments and suggestions for the 1985 legislation. A selection of the responses was published by the committee (U.S. Congress, Senate 1984). In late 1984 and early 1985 both the House and Senate committees held hearings at various locations in the country and in Washington, D.C., at which academic experts as well as interested parties responded to requests for suggestions to revamp the commodity programs (U.S. Congress, Senate 1985c).

Two issues of program structure emerged for the grain programs (beyond the overriding general issue of the budget for these programs). The first was whether to support farmers' returns by means of further acreage controls coupled with increased market price support via CCC loan rates, or to let support levels follow market prices and support farm income through deficiency payments. The second was what steps to take to promote increased exports of U.S. commodities.

Producer groups were divided on the first issue, with the National Farm Organization, the National Farmers Union, and the National Grange arguing for high loan rates and stringent production controls, and the (much larger) American Farm Bureau Federation arguing for fewer controls and market-oriented loan levels. The National Association of Wheat Growers (NAWG) took a middle position of marginal changes in the existing wheat program.

The Reagan administration, in its proposed Agricultural Adjustment Act of

1985, took the Farm Bureau position on phasing out acreage controls but went significantly further in the market-oriented direction by calling for much lower target prices than any of the farm groups wanted. The administration's wheat provisions were outlined on March 7, 1985, as:

> Loan rates are based on 75 percent of national average prices received by farmers in the immediately preceding three years.
>
> Target prices are based in 1986 on 100 percent of national average prices received by producers during the immediately preceding three years; this percentage would drop 5 percent each year until it reaches 75 percent for the 1991 and succeeding crops.
>
> An acreage reduction will be required of program participants at the following levels: 15 percent—1986 crop year; 10 percent—1987; 5 percent—1988 crop year; 1989 and thereafter, the authority for acreage reduction would be eliminated. (U.S. Congress, Senate 1985c, part 1, 403)

The administration largely prevailed on loan rates (where they took essentially the Farm Bureau position) but lost on target prices and on phasing out acreage controls. The implied target price cuts led members of the congressional committees to label the administration's bill "dead on arrival."

With respect to export promotion, the administration wanted to maintain discretionary authority to negotiate with trading partners to remove barriers to U.S. exports, and to continue export credit programs and food aid programs. But there were no explicit export subsidies proposed. In Congress and among agricultural interest groups, however, sentiments were quite different. The successful use of CCC stocks to pay farmers for idling additional land in the 1983 PIK program prompted several commodity groups to adopt the label for an "export PIK" program in which CCC stocks would be used to subsidize exports. The domestic PIK resulted in additional wheat on the market in the United States, partly offsetting the price-increasing effect of acreage idling. An export PIK, it was argued, would remove commodities that were overhanging the U.S. market and hence drive up U.S. prices. In February 1983, the NAWG and the Nebraska Wheat Strike Force had testified before the Senate Agriculture Committee in favor of this general approach. Unlike the case of acreage controls, the American Farm Bureau also supported the export PIK idea, providing a united front among farm groups.[4]

In 1985, the wheat growers, principally through NAWG and U.S. Wheat Associates, the growers' market development arm, had been arriving at their position through many months of meetings. The wheat growers' focus on international marketing traditionally had to deal with a "prairie populist" isolationist impulse that emphasized supply management and higher prices in the domestic market. These sentiments had been fatally discredited for a majority of wheat growers by the prosperity brought by the export boom and sales to the

---

4. Statements of Ron Delano, president of American Farm Bureau, Don Leslie, president of NAWG, and Frank Johannsen, Nebraska Wheat Strike Force (U.S. Congress, Senate 1983, 28, 40–44).

Soviets in the 1970s. The populist impulse for an antigovernment position was satisfied by the wheat growers' vociferous objection to controls on export sales to Eastern Europe and the Soviet Union in 1974–76 and 1980.

As the 1985 farm bill debate began, NAWG backed a "marketing loan" approach, under which producers could repay their CCC loans at the local market price of wheat and reclaim the wheat for sale. This essentially would establish a general (domestic and export) subsidy. However, the wheat growers also supported the EEP in written testimony for the Senate Agriculture Committee in 1984 (Schwensen 1984). The EEP approach was easy to assimilate to export promotion proposals NAWG already had made.[5]

On the agribusiness side, the grain-exporting companies of course supported export subsidies, with caveats about maintaining the companies' autonomy in negotiating sales. Even bakers and grain millers, who might have opposed the subsidized export of their raw material, did not object. The American Bakers Association's president did not take a position on the subject, and the Millers National Association testified in favor.[6] One reason is that the first major shot fired in the export subsidy dispute with the European Community had been an arrangement negotiated under existing authorities of the secretary of agriculture in which 30 million bushels of CCC wheat was given free of charge to flour mills who then sold 1 million tons of flour (requiring about 50 million bushels of wheat) to Egypt, at a price low enough to capture that market from the European Community. This "largest flour sale in history" won the hearts of the millers. A second reason is that subsidies paid in kind out of existing stocks would place additional wheat on the market and would not raise the domestic price of wheat as a cash export subsidy would.

Executive Branch Action

Senator Dole took the lead in organizing a series of meetings in spring 1985 to get the Reagan administration to establish a targeted export subsidy program focused on grains, especially wheat. Representatives of NAWG as well as other farm groups attended these meetings in Dole's office. In May 1985, the administration (represented by the Office of Management and Budget [OMB] and USDA) and the Senate leadership (principally Dole and Senator Zorinsky) agreed to implement under existing authorities[7] an EEP.

5. Among many interesting arguments of the wheat growers, one was that the Reagan administration "has a double standard bordering on hypocrisy. They advocate but close off export markets by placing protectionist measures against steel, textiles, and other products they need to send to us to gain foreign exchange" (U.S. Congress, Senate 1985a, 42). This is one of the very few instances in the thousands of pages of testimony on the 1985 farm bill in which farmers rehearsed elements of their traditional free trade line. Nonetheless, the wheat growers practical thrust was for export (and domestic) subsidies.

6. Statement of Roy M. Henwood, president of Millers National Association (U.S. Congress, Senate 1983, 257–59); statement of Robert Wager, president of American Bakers Association (U.S. Congress, House 1985a, part 5, 82–84).

7. Authorities of the secretary of agriculture as chief executive officer of the CCC under the CCC Charter Act of 1936.

In particular, the EEP was given the breath of life by the conjunction of interests represented by three individuals: Senator Zorinsky's strong desire, as the ranking Democrat on the Agriculture Committee and representative of Nebraska, for a substantial export subsidy program; David Stockman's need for Democratic votes on key economic legislation; and Senator Dole's brokering savvy, with interests in supporting both the administration (as majority leader) and Kansas wheat growers. Stockman agreed the administration would implement an export subsidy program, in exchange for Zorinsky's vote on the budget resolution containing the Reagan administration's fiscal proposals, with the subsidies to take the form of unwanted CCC surplus commodities with a zero budget score.

The agreed-upon program committed $2 billion worth of CCC-owned commodities to be made available as a bonus to U.S. exporters to expand sales of U.S. agricultural commodities in targeted markets. The objectives stated were to increase U.S. farm exports and to encourage trading partners to begin serious negotiations on agricultural trade problems.[8]

Guidelines for the EEP, established by the Economic Policy Council of the White House, were that each subsidized sale should meet the following criteria: (1) additionality, that is, net increase in export sales caused by the subsidized sale; (2) targeting to displace competing exporters who are subsidizing their sales; (3) a net gain to the U.S. economy; and (4) budget neutrality. Each proposed EEP initiative was to be tested against these criteria by an interdepartmental committee chaired by the U.S. trade representative and USDA, but also having representatives of the OMB, Council of Economic Advisors (CEA), Treasury, State, Labor, Commerce, and National Security Council (NSC). It was never publicly stated how the "net gain to the U.S. economy" and "budget neutrality" criteria were to be defined and measured. Participants in the process indicated that criterion 3 was not a factor in interagency debate, although 1, 2, and 4 were.[9]

Despite the creation of the EEP through executive branch action, farm and commodity groups were so strongly in favor of an export subsidy program that Congress wished to exercise authority and claim authorship of the EEP by establishing it in the 1985 farm legislation. The key general issue[10] was whether to target export subsidies to counter competitors' subsidies or to subsidize exports more broadly. The House Agriculture Committee took the broad view that subsidies in kind would boost exports by "countering the effects of

8. Recall that the EEP was announced in the months leading up to the Ponte del Este meeting which launched the Uruguay Round of General Agreement on Tariffs and Trade (GATT) negotiations.
9. In November 1989, USDA published revised guidelines in the *Federal Register* which emphasized the trade policy objectives of challenging competitors who subsidize exports and encouraging negotiations in the Uruguay Round (see Ackerman and Smith 1990, 6–7).
10. "General" meaning basic principles of design. Committee deliberations devoted more time to specific issues of interest to members (e.g., how much white wheat from Washington in the program) than to any general issue.

foreign subsidies in international markets; compensating for the high value of the dollar; [and] alleviating the cost of transportation[11] of U.S. agricultural goods" (U.S. Congress, House 1985b, 71). This led the House to support a broad, untargeted export subsidy program called BICEP—Bonus Incentive Commodity Export Program—apparently to highlight the application of governmental muscle to agricultural exports.

Legislative Action

The Food Security Act (FSA) as finally enacted in December 1985 reflected the Senate's closer ties to the administration by codifying the EEP essentially as the administration had established it six months earlier. The main issues, as often in enabling legislation, were what the executive branch "shall" (be required to) do and "may" (has discretionary authority to) do. The 1985 act required the secretary of agriculture to provide CCC commodities at no cost to "United States exporters, users, and processors and foreign purchasers" and required that a total of $2 billion in CCC commodities be used for this purpose during the three fiscal years ending September 30, 1988. The purposes which the subsidized exports were to serve are even more broadly stated than in the House bill: in addition to combating other countries' subsidies and the high value of the dollar, export subsidies may be used to offset "the adverse effects of U.S. agricultural price support levels that are temporarily above the export prices offered by overseas competitors in export markets" (U.S. Code 99 Stat. 1483).

In addition, the act authorized the unlimited use of cross-subsidization, that is, the use of one CCC commodity to subsidize the export of another. This was politically important because many commodity interests, including processed products and products which did not have price support programs, prevailed upon the agriculture committees for support. Egg producers and pork producers, for example, testified that they needed assistance in competing with EC export subsidies. But no CCC stocks of these commodities existed. The legislation shared EEP benefits across commodities by permitting CCC wheat stocks to be used to subsidize egg or pork EEP exports, for example.[12]

The 1985 act thus established the authority for either narrowly targeted or broad-based export subsidies, and mandated $2 billion in spending on the pro-

11. Transportation costs are a quantitatively small but highly politically charged issue in U.S. export promotion programs. "Cargo preference," a requirement that food aid be shipped on U.S. vessels, has been an issue in EEP, export credit, and sales to the Soviets. Cargo preference has not been required for EEP shipments.

12. The EEP is not as barter based as this discussion might suggest. Exporters never received actual tons of CCC grain as a subsidy, but rather certificates entitling them to grain at any time up to an expiration date six months from the date of issue. A market quickly emerged in which these certificates could be sold at only a small discount from the market value of the grain. Since exporters could take their transactions costs into account in their bids, the subsidy in kind is very close to the equivalent of a cash subsidy. And when available CCC stocks ran out in 1991, the program was smoothly converted to one where certificates are redeemable for cash.

gram over three years.[13] The EEP was not subject to discipline in the annual appropriations process because the Appropriations Committees provide generally open-ended funding for the CCC to achieve its price support mandates. The committees do not control how the CCC uses its acquired commodity stocks. Congress could have brought budgetary disciplines to bear by scoring EEP costs in Budget Committee proceedings. However, Congress agreed with the OMB on zero scoring for EEP. The principal argument was that CCC commodities cost so much to store that it was worth about as much to give them away as to keep them. In addition, to the extent that increased exports increased the U.S. market price, deficiency payments for wheat and other target price commodities would be reduced.

The EEP in a Broader Political Context

The EEP came into being with very little opposition between February and December 1985. Why was the way so clear? The natural opponents of an export subsidy are U.S. domestic wheat buyers and foreign wheat producers. In the case of EEP U.S. millers were diverted by their participation in subsidized flour exports and by the release of CCC stocks to pay the subsidies, as discussed earlier. The bakers and broader consumer groups were relatively weak participants, and their participation in the 1985 farm bill debate was focused on opposition to acreage controls and on limiting budgetary outlays. The latter point was the dominant item of contention throughout 1985.

The 1985 farm bill was debated in the culminating period of the "farm crisis" and at the same time the bill known as Gramm-Rudman-Hollings (GRH)[14] was being developed. Just before the congressional farm bill debate began, in February 1985, President Reagan vetoed a farm bailout bill that would have forgiven billions of dollars of farm debt and made new subsidized and guaranteed loans to farmers in trouble. The administration's proposal, in its Agricultural Adjustment Act of 1985, to go still further and cut benefits that farmers were already receiving caused this aspect of the bill to be labeled, correctly, as "dead on arrival" by congressional Democrats.

While the testimony on export promotion was proceeding as described earlier, much more contentious and widely reported hearings were being held on the broad problems of agriculture. *Newsweek* had a five-page story featuring an Iowa State agricultural economist's estimate that 12 percent of U.S. farmers would go out of business in 1985 and 30 percent were "sliding toward insol-

---

13. In the context of budgetary pressures, authorized spending for this period (FY 1985–88) was amended to a reduced minimum of $1 billion and a maximum of $1.5 billion in 1986. However, the actual value of bonuses for this three-year period turned out to be $2.2 billion. After the $1.5 billion ceiling was reached, in mid-1987, USDA announced that EEP bonuses would continue under the CCC Charter Act under which the EEP was originally established (see Ackerman and Smith 1990, 5, for more detail on authorization and spending under EEP).

14. Enacted as the Balanced Budget and Emergency Deficit Control Act of 1985, to become effective in early 1986.

vency" (*Newsweek,* February 18, 1985, 52). At a special hearing staged by congressional Democrats (no Republicans attended) three famous actresses of the day (Jane Fonda, Jessica Lange, and Sissy Spacek) appeared, each of whom had starred in movies featuring heroic struggles of farmers against economic adversity and insensitive bureaucrats. The actresses "decried the farm policies of the Reagan administration as uncaring and insensitive to rural America's anguish" (*Washington Post,* May 7, 1985).[15]

In this context it was probably not reasonable to expect national consumer groups to adopt positions in support of cuts in farm support, and none did.

The role of outside experts on the economics of agriculture is more difficult to explain. Many such experts submitted testimony on many aspects of farm programs. In 1984, 12 economists made written contributions to the Senate Agriculture Committee's trade policy compendium (U.S. Congress, Senate 1984b). Of these, none proposed export subsidies, and the three that addressed the issue directly all raised objections to the idea (Johnson 1984; O'Rourke 1984; Sharples 1984). In the 1985 hearings also, no economists supported the EEP. This may be in part due to a lack of opportunity, since the EEP was not spelled out in a form that testifying economists could react to before it was introduced as a nonlegislated fait accompli in May 1985. But even if economists did not object formally to the EEP, it was clear from their general comments on trade policy that they would have opposed it because of concern about igniting a subsidy war and because of low expected benefits to farmers per dollar of cost to consumers and taxpayers.

Another source of independent testimony was the statements of five former secretaries of agriculture—Orville Freeman (Kennedy), Clifford Hardin (Nixon), Earl Butz (Nixon/Ford), John Knebel (Ford), and Bob Bergland (Carter) (U.S. Senate 1984b). Their comments focused on trade issues and supported various measures to stimulate exports. But none advocated direct export subsidies.

During October–December 1985 the farm bill assumed its final form. The House passed its version on October 8, the Senate on November 22, and the Conference Committee reached agreement on a bill which achieved final passage on December 18. This period was marked by sharp debate. The anti–farm-support side was almost entirely a matter of budgetary exposure, the endgame issue turning on whether target prices should be frozen for one year (administration) or four years (congressional Democrats) before declining. The ultimate compromise was a two-year freeze followed by modest cuts. The wheat target price was kept at $4.38 in 1986 and 1987, then cut in steps to $4.00 by

---

15. This was the only 1985 agricultural hearing to run on all three prime-time network newscasts. The *Post* quoted one actress as saying "the solid core of our agriculture is threatened," and further quoted: " 'It is heartbreaking to witness their anguish as they watch their lives being stripped away,' Lange said of farmers as she choked back tears." The *Post* played the story on page 1, but it was page 1 of the "Style" section under the headline, "The Farm Act." This deflated the impact somewhat.

1990.[16] Because the debate focused almost exclusively on budgetary issues, for wheat and other commodities (notably dairy), the EEP received little legislative attention.

The overall compromise achieved was of the highly pragmatic type in which legislators like Congressman Foley and Senator Dole worked from a middle ground outward to obtain a majority. Both the most ardent profarmer voices and most ardent budget cutters opposed the bill. The vote for final passage was 325–96 in the House and 55–38 in the Senate. Both the chairman of the Senate Agriculture Committee, Jesse Helms (N.C.), and the ranking Democrat, Ed Zorinsky (Nebr.), voted against the bill, for opposite reasons. President Reagan signed the bill into law on December 23, 1985.

In summary, the EEP was enacted in 1985 because wheat growers and exporters asked for it and no interest group opposed it, except economists in general terms. Because the pressure to assist agriculture was strong, and was countered only by budgetary pressures, the OMB finding that the EEP would be budget neutral ensured its supporters of an easy political victory.[17]

6.2.3   Related Export Assistance

In addition to the EEP, wheat exports continue to be promoted by:

- Food assistance, through P.L. 480 and related programs, under which about 3 million tons of wheat are shipped each year under generous credit terms that amount on average to a substantial subsidy on limited quantities in country-to-country agreements.
- Export credit, with guaranteed repayment to lenders by the U.S. Treasury if the foreign borrower defaults. The interest rate is a commercial rate negotiated by borrower and lender, typically just above the LIBOR (London Interbank Offer Rate), a rate available only because of the guarantee. The U.S. government has had to absorb substantial losses from loans to Iraq, and the possibility of big losses on credits to Russia.
- The Targeted Export Assistance program, introduced in the 1985 act, provides matching funds for private sector initiatives to promote agricultural exports. This program was reformulated as the Market Promotion Program in the 1990 Farm Act, and its budget has been reduced from over $300 million

---

16. While there were no immediate budgetary savings through target price cuts, it was known by the time of Conference Committee action that GRH provisions would require a reduction in deficiency payments for FY 1986 (the first crop year of the new bill, for which winter wheat was already planted). In the event, farmers had their payments reduced by 4.3 percent in FY 1986. The wheat target price remained at $4.00 through 1993 and continues at that level through 1995.

17. Congress' own budget agency, the Congressional Budget Office (CBO), has not accepted the budget neutrality argument. Indeed CBO has in recent years called attention to the EEP as a potential area for budgetary savings, estimating most recently a $4.2 billion saving in FY 1995–99 if the baseline EEP spending of $5.0 billion over this period were eliminated (U.S. Congress, Congressional Budget Office 1994, 218). Their clinching argument against the budget neutrality of EEP is the following: Whatever price effects could be achieved by EEP could also be achieved at lower budget cost using ARPs. With both EEP and ARPs the subject of annual policy determination, one should not hold the ARP constant when evaluating the EEP.

authorized in 1985 to about $100 million for FY 1994. About 10 percent of the program's expenditures have been used to promote grains and grain products with $50 million spent in 1986–89 (Ackerman and Smith 1990, 39).

Farm and agribusiness groups have consistently supported these programs. Groups interested in international development—mainly nonprofit foundations and charitable organizations—have questioned the negative impact of food aid on food production in the recipient countries. But these groups have also supported food aid in times of famine or emergency. Other international interests have promoted food assistance for geopolitical reasons, notably to Russia, Egypt, and Pakistan. There has been no sustained political opposition to these programs, except as part of generic budget cutting.

An illustration of how these programs work in tandem is afforded by recent wheat sales to the former Soviet Union (FSU). In FY 1992, roughly coinciding with President Yeltsen's first year as leader of Russia, the United States exported 8.7 million metric tons of wheat to the FSU. Market receipts for the wheat were $1.022 billion, or $117 per ton. Russia and the other former republics could not afford to pay hard currency for this wheat. The wheat was sold through a combination of government-guaranteed commercial credit, EEP subsidies, and food aid programs. Credit of $810 million was allocated to the FSU for wheat and wheat product purchases in late 1991. EEP bonuses of $350 million were paid on 8.4 million tons of wheat in FY 1992 ($41.50 per ton on average). The credit program, called GSM-102, involves short-term credit, up to three years, with a repayment schedule beginning in the first year. By November 1992 Russia's repayments were sufficiently in arrears to trigger its suspension from the program. However, in FY 1993 a more liberal credit program for Russia was established under the Food for Progress authorities of USDA. This credit is financed directly from the U.S. government rather than through commercial banks and has a longer repayment period and lower than commercial interest rates. Credit is even granted, using CCC funds, for freight and handling costs. In addition, 700,000 tons of feed wheat have been donated to the FSU. (For further details, see USDA 1993, 39–45.) Overall, while the EEP subsidy on U.S. wheat exports to the FSU amounts to about 30 percent of the U.S. Gulf price, the package altogether amounts to a much larger export subsidy.

The main political pressures in these subsidies have come from representatives and senators whose wheat growers have been concerned that credit has not been allocated quickly enough to keep wheat moving. Fiscal cautions have also been raised and have restrained FY 1993 and 1994 wheat sales to the FSU.

6.3   Consequences and Evaluation of the Program

Questions were being raised about the effectiveness of the EEP even before its legislative enactment. The administration announced its first EEP initiatives in May 1985. By October only two sales had been made, 500,000 tons of wheat and 175,000 tons of wheat flour to Egypt. The administration in May had appointed an advisory committee on the EEP, consisting primarily of commodity group and agribusiness representatives. In August, the committee's representatives from the National Corn Growers and U.S. Wheat Associates, joined by four other committee members, issued a press release saying they were "disappointed and frustrated over the lack of any concrete results from the EEP" (National Corn Growers Association 1985). In October and November the House Committee on Agriculture's Subcommittee on Department Operations, Research, and Foreign Agriculture held hearings to review complaints about EEP administration.

The substance of the commodity group complaints was that the EEP was being carried out in too restrictive a manner. In particular, the groups argued that wheat sales to the Soviets fell under the EEP criteria listed earlier. The European Community had since 1980 expanded its subsidized wheat exports to the Soviet Union substantially, yet USDA had not approved an EEP initiative for U.S. wheat sales to the Soviet Union. The Soviets were switching wheat purchases from the United States to the European Community, even though that meant not honoring their purchase agreements with the United States under a previously negotiated long-term grain sales agreement. The hearings made clear, however, that even if USDA were willing to accede to the Soviets' ploy to acquire previously agreed upon shipments at a lower price, potential exporters of nonagricultural products to the USSR would not accept the subsidizing of wheat sales to the USSR while other holds on U.S.-Soviet economic arrangements were in place as part of the political struggle for freer emigration from the USSR (U.S. Congress, House 1986). It was not clear, however, which particular export industries Congress was hearing from on this point.

Apart from being subject to such political constraints, the procedures for implementing EEP were far from clear. There were (and are) two main steps: administration approval of an EEP initiative and USDA's acceptance of exporters' bids for bonuses under the initiative. Approval of an initiative is done by the EEP interagency committee described earlier, after a proposal by USDA, based on the criteria of additionality, targeting, cost effectiveness, and budget neutrality.[18] For example, one of the first initiatives approved was for the sale of 1 million tons of wheat to Algeria. With the initiative in place, a U.S. exporting firm can attempt to arrange a sale with an importing firm (or government agency) in Algeria. If the exporting firm cannot meet the price offered by competing exporters, in this case the European Community, it will apply to USDA for a "bonus" of commodity certificates equal in value to the amount needed to make up the difference between the cost of U.S. wheat delivered to Algeria and the price negotiated to make the sale. USDA assesses U.S., EC,

18. The outside EEP advisory committee understood there to be two additional criteria: coincidence with overall U.S. trade policy and approval by the interagency committee (U.S. Congress, House 1986, 88).

and Algerian market conditions and either approves or disapproves the deal. If the transaction is approved, the firm receives the certificate requested and ships the wheat.

This mechanism is quite different from the approach used for wheat export subsidies by the European Community, or by the United States in its pre-1972 program, of periodically announcing a dollar value of the subsidy, say $35 per ton, and then letting any firms who export U.S. wheat collect that amount on the exported quantities. The approach raises questions of how USDA can determine, for each proposed sale, what the competitors' price is. Wouldn't the competitors' price itself be affected by EEP? And, is there sufficient incentive for U.S. commercial exporters to obtain the highest possible market price?

USDA Under Secretary Amstutz testified on the new EEP mechanism as follows:

> Program implementation, in terms of mechanics such as tendering and contractual arrangements, has remained flexible. Procedures have varied from country to country to accommodate the individual buying systems of the importing nations involved in the program.
>
> The bonus is to be sufficient to allow our commodities to be competitive, but it is not intended to undercut the world market price. In other words, the program is designed to ensure that sales made under it are at commercial, not concessional, prices.
>
> To ensure that we are meeting these competitive and commercial objectives, a price review process has been developed. The process calls for a review of the level of both the bonus and the sale price. This is to assure not only that the bonus paid to exporters is not too high, but also that the sale price, relative to subsidized foreign competition, is not too low.
>
> In the price review we determine the cost of delivering the U.S. commodity to the foreign buyer and the price at which the same commodity can be delivered to the same destination by subsidized foreign competitors.
>
> The difference between the two—the amount by which the competition can under-price us—is used in determining the acceptable bonus.
>
> Currently, an exporter is required to post a performance security with CCC before CCC will consider the exporter's offer. Once an offer is accepted, the exporter reserves bonus commodities from CCC inventories. After shipment, the exporter must furnish proof of export to request delivery of the bonus commodity. After the exported goods arrive in the destination country, USDA releases the performance security posted by the exporters. (U.S. Congress, House 1986, 142)

Neither this nor other statements of USDA have answered questions about U.S. exporters' incentives and pricing behavior under the EEP. But these were not issues of concern to Congress in 1985 (or later). The main objection of House Agriculture Committee members to the EEP was their desire for a program that would subsidize most or all wheat exports, not just a subset of targeted markets. Two main concerns were raised about the operation of the EEP: first, it would antagonize traditional buyers of U.S. commodities who did not receive the subsidized price, hence possibly driving them to other suppliers, and second, it would drive down the prices received by nonsubsidizing competitors like Argentina and Australia. At the House hearings, several commodity groups raised the first concern, and the General Accounting Office (GAO) the second.

6.3.1   Economic Analysis of EEP

While economists' analyses did not play a role in the 1985 legislative process, analytical work was available that did not make the EEP attractive. The standard argument (e.g., in Dixit and Norman 1980) that, for purposes of domestic income redistribution, a domestic distortion is always preferable to a border distortion should apply to agricultural export subsidies undertaken for the purpose of farm income support. The question addressed in agricultural economists' analyses is whether there are second-best or other special characteristics of the world wheat situation that make targeted, in-kind export subsidies more attractive.

General (untargeted) Export Subsidy

Consider the effect of a subsidy in the 1985 U.S. wheat market. Using elasticities of -2.1 for the short-run demand for U.S. wheat exports and -0.2 for U.S. domestic demand (consistent with USDA analysis at the time), the 1985 crop situation is shown in figure 6.7. Of the 2,400 million bushels produced, 900 million bushels were exported and 1,050 were consumed domestically, leaving 450 million bushels added to CCC stocks at the farm-level supported price of $3.10.[19] Despite the inelastic demand for domestic use, CCC activity creates perfectly elastic demand at the market support price (not the target price).

Suppose we introduce an export subsidy, *s*, of $0.40 per bushel ($15 per ton). This drives down the world price of wheat by $15 per ton and increases the demand for U.S. wheat by about 300 million bushels. The U.S. domestic price remains unchanged because of the CCC loan program. If the price were to rise above the supported level, wheat would not go into the CCC program; but there is too much wheat to clear the market at any price above the support level. CCC loan availability creates a perfectly elastic demand at the support price level, so the total demand for wheat, in the absence of the export subsidy, is D_T. Introducing the export subsidy shifts total demand to D_T'. Wheat is exported rather than going into stocks.

The gains and losses to the United States are as follows. Domestic consumers and producers are unaffected, since the U.S. price remains the same. Budgetary outlays are *s* times the quantity exported, here $0.40 × 1.2 billion bushels = $480 million annually. But there is a budgetary saving from not having to

---

19. The legislated support price was $3.30, but this translated to an average farm-level price of $3.10 in the 1985–86 marketing year.

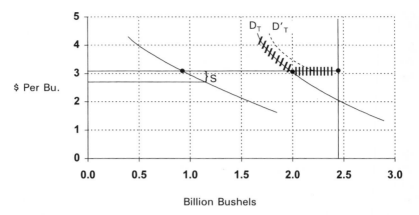

Fig. 6.7   Wheat export subsidy

pay CCC loans of $3.10 × 300 million bushels, or $930 million. This implies a net budgetary saving of $450 million in the current fiscal year. However, current-year flow accounting (although it is what drives budget scoring) does not take into account the value of the wheat the government owns. There is no agreed-upon valuation of CCC stocks, or even an agreed-upon method for determining their value. The principal necessary calculations are (discounted) expected storage costs over the period the grain will be held, and the expected value of the grain when sold. Assuming three years of storage costs and eventual sale at roughly the loan rate (acquisition price), the present value of $930 million spent on CCC wheat is about half its cost, or $465 million. So the net government costs are (480 − 465 =) $15 million.

According to the analysis so far, farmers do not gain from the export subsidy. However, this also occurs only because the diagram shows only the current year, in which wheat acreage and input decisions are fixed by wheat program provisions. Under the wheat program the supply function is changed in more complicated ways than is the demand side of the market. Producers receive a deficiency payment that they know will make up the difference between the target price ($4.38 in 1985) and the U.S. average price in the five-month peak marketing season (June–October). So they should make planting decisions, in the preceding autumn for winter wheat and spring for spring wheat, based on the target price, not the expected market price. However, in order to qualify for deficiency payments farmers had to stay within their acreage base and hold idle 20 percent of base acreage. Therefore, the incentive price for growing wheat is considerably less than the target price. For 1985 I have estimated that the average producer's incentive price was about $3.75 per bushel as compared to the $4.38 target price (Gardner 1991). Moreover, producers are limited in their ability to respond to the incentive price. They cannot expand acreage as already mentioned. They can expand output by using more fertilizer or other inputs, but deficiency payments provide no incentive for this because payments are made on a fixed (since 1981) yield base which is assigned to each producer. A final complication is that, principally because of land-idling requirements, some farmers choose not to participate. For them the incentive price is the market price.

In calculating farmers' gains from an export subsidy, these considerations come into play through the annual determination of the acreage reduction percentage (ARP). The reason the ARP was as high as 20 percent in 1985 (and 27.5 percent in 1986 and 1987) is the large prior CCC stock accumulation. The 450 million bushels added to stocks from the 1985 crop was piled on top of the 1.4 billion already accumulated. If 300 million bushels could have been exported instead of being added to stocks, the ARP could have been reduced accordingly. At the U.S. average yield of about 35 bushels per acre, 8.5 million acres could have been planted that had been held idle. At a net rental value of wheat land of $40 per acre, the gain to wheat producers would be $340 million.

The results of the two ways of accommodating a general wheat export subsidy under 1985 conditions are summarized in table 6.4.

Given the existence of excessive CCC wheat stocks or ARPs, an export subsidy program has quite small costs. However, an option with still smaller costs would be to have a domestic consumption subsidy also. In figure 6.7, if s were paid on all consumption the budget cost of the subsidy would be offset, except for a small triangle, by gains to U.S. consumers.[20] An alternative, better policy would be to pay a larger subsidy on domestic consumption than on exports (or even taxing exports). This avoids using U.S. Treasury funds to provide lower-cost consumption abroad.

Special Features of EEP

The EEP differs from a general export subsidy in three key respects: *targeting* of particular importing countries to receive subsidies, *limiting the quantity* of wheat eligible to each targeted country, and *payment in kind* of the subsidy in the form of CCC stocks.

Targeting and quantity limitation are attractive because they reduce budgetary outlays for subsidies and because they do not undercut the prices of our nonsubsidizing competitors, notably Argentina and Australia. At least that is

---

20. In fig. 6.7, this is achieved at a price of $2.00 per bushel. As compared to the $3.10 price, this policy would add $1.10 × 2.4 billion = $2.64 billion of budget outlays, partly offset by consumer gains of roughly $430 million and net CCC stock savings of $700 million (assuming CCC stocks valued at half the support price) or $510 million in producer gains if ARPs are reduced and stock buildup maintained. In either case the net cost of the policy is over $1.5 billion (mainly because of the bonanza given to foreign consumers). In fact, the 1985 marketing loan proposal of the wheat growers would have generated this kind of result. Because of its potential budget costs (which depend crucially on the elasticity of total demand for wheat) this proposal was a nonstarter in the 1985 congressional debate.

Table 6.4   **Results of Alternative Implementations of a $0.40 Wheat Export Subsidy under Mid-1980s Market Conditions (million dollars)**

Effect	Policy 1[a]	Policy 2[b]
Budget cost of subsidy	−480	−480
Budget savings on CCC stocks	465	0
Overall budget effect	−15	−480
Farm income effect	0	+340
Welfare gain	−15	−140

[a]Policy 1: Give a $0.40 export subsidy, holding ARP constant and reducing CCC stocks by 300 million bushels.
[b]Policy 2: Give a $0.40 export subsidy, holding CCC stocks constant and reducing ARP by 8.5 million acres.

the thought. We pay the subsidy of s to reduce the price of, say, one-third of U.S. wheat exports while continuing to sell the rest at unsubsidized world price.

The question with respect to country targeting is whether the policy is capable of creating the price wedge s between the targeted and nontargeted wheat-importing countries. Transportation and other transactions costs between these countries suggests there would not be fully price-equalizing arbitrage. But there is also the problem of redirection of the competitors' wheat exports. If the United States sends wheat to Algeria, replacing EC wheat, then the European Community sends the wheat that otherwise would have gone to Algeria to Iran, say. But despite the multichannel nature of world wheat trade there are possibilities of U.S. export subsidies changing the spatial price pattern, and some economists have developed arguments on how the United States could exploit differing elasticities of demand for U.S. wheat to profit from targeted subsidies as a form of price discrimination (Dutton 1990). However, the knowledge base on these elasticities and arbitrage possibilities is essentially nil, and these studies have no detectable connection with the actual administration of the EEP, or with what the wheat producers had in mind.

The quantity limitation raises other problems. As the wheat growers noted in their criticism of the first EEP sales to Egypt, once the sales were complete the European Community reentered the market and sold at the pre-EEP prices. It appears that the price at the margin is the nonsubsidized price, so there is no reason for the EEP recipients to consume more wheat with the EEP in place than without it. But if no country consumes more wheat because of the EEP, the market-clearing price will remain unchanged, as will U.S. and other countries' exports. EC exports and prices remain unchanged, and the United States will have done nothing to force the European Community to increase their export subsidies, hence driving them to the GATT bargaining table. We have simply transferred funds from U.S. taxpayers to Egyptian buyers (probably the government) on an intramarginal quantity of wheat imports. However, there are complications.

First, it is not clear that the U.S. EEP quantities are so limited as make sales intramarginal in the targeted countries. Second, payment in kind makes a real difference, even though subsidies are given to wheat exporters in the form of generic certificates that are transferable and can be used against any CCC-owned commodity. Even if exporters cash out their certificates, the buyer of them must redeem them for CCC commodities before their expiration date, so that wheat will inevitably be redeemed.[21] This was important in 1985 because the CCC by law could not dispose of its stocks until market prices rose well above their current or likely attainable levels.[22] Therefore, the EEP provided a way to place on the market commodities that otherwise would have been sequestered. In this way the EEP tended to place general downward pressure on world wheat prices, by increasing marketed supplies. Chambers and Paarlberg (1991) argue that this effect could have caused the EEP to generate a net loss to the United States. However, if CCC stock reductions trade off with equivalent ARP changes, the supply-increasing feature of the EEP subsidy can always be neutralized.

6.3.2   Assessment of EEP Operations

It seems impossible to predict much about the consequences of EEP on the basis of a general economic analysis of it. How then are the criteria to be met for EEP sales—additionality, net economic gain, and budget neutrality—to be assessed against the program's operations? Turning first to the data for 1985–92, statistics of EEP shipments are shown in table 6.5. After a slow start, EEP exports reached 26.6 million metric tons in FY 1988, about half of all U.S. wheat exports.[23] The average subsidy reached $38 per ton in 1987. A price wedge this large on substantial quantities would be expected to make a noticeable difference in world trade flows and prices.

"Additionality"

As an initial step in assessing the effectiveness of targeted export subsidies under EEP, several economists have attempted estimates of additionality—the net increase in U.S. wheat exports caused by each ton of EEP-assisted shipments. If one simply regresses wheat exports on EEP tonnage using the data of table 6.5 for 1986–92, the result indicates that each ton of EEP sales generates 0.8 ton of exports. This means only 20 percent of the EEP sale replaces

21. Indeed, by the end of 1991 all available CCC commodities had been distributed to holders of certificates or otherwise sold.
22. The 1985 and 1990 farm acts made it easier to dispose of these stocks after 1985.
23. Reporting of fiscal-year EEP data and crop-year total export data creates possible confusion. Fiscal years are October to September, and wheat crop years are June to May. Fiscal years are referred to by the calendar year in which they end, and crop years by the calendar year in which they begin.

Table 6.5   **EEP Wheat Sales and Bonuses**

Fiscal Year	EEP Sales (million metric tons)	Total EEP Bonus (milion $)	Average EEP Bonus ($ per million tons)	Total U.S. Exports[a] (million metric tons)	EEP Share[b] (%)
1985	.5	11	21.84	28.0	2
1986	4.8	126	26.20	20.7	23
1987	14.1	541	38.33	28.1	50
1988	26.6	819	30.83	40.6	66
1989	16.0	288	18.05	37.6	43
1990	14.3	241	16.84	33.2	43
1991	17.7	767	43.18	26.7	67
1992	19.7	813	41.14	34.3	58
1993	21.6	1,281	33.82	–	–

Sources: Ackerman and Smith (1990); Ackerman (1993, private communication).

[a]Fiscal-year exports, which differ from crop-year data used elsewhere in this paper. Constructed from USDA monthly export statistics.

[b]EEP tonnage as percentage of total export tonnage.

commercial exports that would have been made anyway; that is, "additionality" is 80 percent. However, if we include the three years immediately preceding the EEP, thus incorporating a before-EEP and after-EEP contrast in the data, the result indicates additionality of zero. These results together indicate that a simple annual regression cannot provide a believable estimate of additionality.

The approach taken in the literature is to build a supply-demand model of the world wheat market and simulate the effects of the EEP. To do this one has to model not only supply and demand equations in the countries involved, both the targeted markets and nontargeted ones, but also the trade linkages between them and the policy instruments that influence wheat trade. Moreover, some policy instruments abroad should be treated as endogenous since they may respond to EEP. Brooks, Devadoss, and Meyers (1990) argue that analyses that take policies other than the U.S. EEP as given miss a key element, at least as far as Canada is concerned. Canada's wheat export policy is not explicitly rule driven; wheat is priced for export on an ad hoc basis by decisions of the Canadian Wheat Board, which has a monopoly on exports. The board has announced it has a special program to counter U.S. EEP sales but has not revealed details, nor the prices received for Canadian wheat in the EEP-targeted markets. Australia has a similar wheat export monopoly.

Given the difficulties of specifying a simulation model that one can have confidence in for the purposes at hand, it is perhaps heartening that the range of additionality estimates is not large. Brooks et al. estimate that a ton of EEP exports added 8 to 13 percent of a ton to total exports in 1986–88. Ackerman and Smith (1990, 12) summarize five USDA Economic Research Service studies whose estimates of additionality range from 2 to 30 percent.

Additionality has become important in EEP policy because the budget neutrality of the program depends on additionality. In the earlier calculations involving a general export subsidy additionality depended only on the elasticity of foreign demand for U.S. wheat. Matters are more complicated with the targeted EEP. Until the end of FY 1991, subsidies in the form of CCC stocks made budget neutrality easy to justify because of the high costs of carrying these stocks.[24] Since November 1991, when the CCC exhausted its available stocks and introduced cash subsidies, the budget neutrality of EEP depends upon the program's ability to increase the U.S. price of wheat and thus reduce deficiency payments.

The way EEP increases the U.S. price is by increasing the total demand for U.S. wheat. USDA has been using a wheat simulation model in which each million ton increase in wheat exports generates an increase of $0.10 per bushel in the U.S. farm price of wheat. The assumption that the CCC support level sets the market price is no longer appropriate since after 1985 the support level has been reduced and has always been substantially below the market price of wheat. Each $0.10 rise in the price of wheat reduces deficiency payments by $174 million. Empirical studies suggest additionality of 10 to 30 percent. Therefore an EEP of 20 million tons adds 2 to 6 million tons to U.S. export demand. With a $40 per ton bonus level, the budget outlays for the EEP are $800 million annually (recent levels). The 2 to 6 million ton increase in exports causes the wheat price to rise $0.20 to $0.60 per bushel and hence deficiency payments to decline $350 to $1050 million annually. Thus, if the high end of additionality pertains, which is what USDA assumes, deficiency payments fall by more than the cost of EEP bonuses and the EEP is budget neutral or better.

Farm Income and Consumer Welfare Effects

The main losses from the EEP accrue to domestic buyers of U.S. wheat. The exact incidence on the buyers' side—among farmers who feed wheat, millers, bakers, retailers, and final consumers—has not been estimated. Because domestic final demand for foods containing wheat is quite inelastic, domestic consumption of these products is unlikely to change appreciably because of the EEP, and in fact domestic use has been quite stable over time despite large changes in wheat prices. It is therefore unlikely that the EEP reduced the demand for, and thus the returns earned by processors, distributors, or other middlemen. Certainly the evidence in the political debate is consistent with this conclusion. Millers and bakers who took public positions favored the EEP (usually because they had export as well as domestic interests).

Farm use of wheat in feeding ranges from 5 to 20 percent of U.S. production. Wheat feeding is highly concentrated in the late summer months after

24. CCC costs of holding grain are much higher than commercial storage rental rates plus the opportunity cost of funds tied up, which sum to about $0.40 per bushel annually. Stocks are "rotated" (old wheat replaced with new) and relocated periodically. GAO estimates it costs the CCC over $1.00 per bushel per year (25–30 percent of the price) to hold wheat.

winter wheat is harvested but before the fall corn harvest, especially when year-end stocks of feed grains are low and old-crop prices high. Generally, livestock producers who use this wheat have very good substitutes in other feeds, so that feed use practically disappears in high-price years. If the EEP drives up the U.S. price of wheat 10 percent ($0.35 per bushel), and if livestock prices do not rise so that livestock producers absorb the feed cost increase, the expected cost of the EEP to the livestock industry is about $100 million annually. To the extent meat prices rise, the cost is shifted to consumers. The remainder of the cost of higher wheat prices is absorbed by consumers of bread, breakfast cereals, bakery products, and other food items containing wheat.

USDA's economic analysis, which is the basis for OMB's budget work on EEP, uses a model which provides estimates of farm income gains and consumer costs of EEP. The model estimates that an increase of $0.10 per bushel in the price of wheat raises farm income by $60 million and reduces consumers' surplus by $120 million (Salathe 1991). The consumer cost estimate assumes farm price increases for all domestically used wheat are passed on to consumers without any change in the farm-to-consumer markup or profits in the wheat-processing industry. The farm income increase is only about one-fourth of the rise in the market value of the wheat crop because three-fourths of wheat production is protected by deficiency payments which decline cent for cent as the market price rises.[25]

The overall domestic welfare effect of the EEP can be estimated by summing the budget, consumer, and producer changes if we assume the farm income change is a change in economic rents (i.e., farmland and farm operator labor taken as fixed in supply). For the range of additionality of 0.1 to 0.3, the EEP at its average recent size of about 20 million tons and cost of $800 million annually generates the results shown in table 6.6. While an optimistic assumption of additionality permits EEP to achieve the objective of budget neutrality, no assumption permits the program to achieve its cost effectiveness objective of providing a benefit to the U.S. economy.[26] It is possible, however, under optimistic additionality assumptions, that the EEP is not an extremely inefficient mechanism for transferring income to farmers. With 0.3 additionality,

25. This assumes the price rise occurs in the five-month peak marketing season. In the 1990 Farm Act, in any case, the calculation of deficiency payments was changed to a full-year basis after 1993. Since the full-year price averages $0.10 per bushel above the five-month price, and the payment will be determined by the maximum of the full-year price or the five-month price plus $0.10, this change was scored as a budget saving (about $120 million a year) in the 1990 Budget Reconciliation Act negotiations.

26. If such calculations are to be used in budget planning, one should also consider the ARP as an alternative policy instrument. This is not a counterfactual exercise in the way invoking a lump-sum transfer as an alternative policy would be. The ARP is in fact adjusted annually. The CBO has argued that it would be preferable to reduce wheat acreage rather than grow wheat and subsidize its export. Assuming 0.3 additionality, the same deficiency payment, farm income, and consumer costs as in the right-hand column of table 6.6 could be achieved with a paid land division program that would cost about $400 million (for 8 million acres) instead of the $800 million EEP subsidy cost.

Table 6.6   **Economic Gains from the EEP (million dollars annually)**

	Additionality	
Gain	0.1	0.3
Cost of EEP subsidies	−800	−800
Deficiency payment reduction	350	1,050
Subtotal: budgetary gain	−450	250
Crop producers' income gain	120	360
Gain of wheat buyers (consumers and livestock feeders)	−240	−720
Total U.S. gain[a]	−570	−110

[a]Assumes set-aside acreage (ARP) held constant.

table 6.6 says it costs the U.S. economy a net (deadweight) loss of $110 million to transfer $360 million to wheat growers.

International Effects

Political discussion of the EEP from its inception emphasized the effects abroad as well as domestic effects in the United States. The Bush administration in 1989 and Congress in its reauthorization of EEP in 1990 focused even more sharply on the foreign effects. The Food, Agriculture, Conservation and Trade (FACT) Act of 1990, which authorizes the EEP at a level of not less than $500 million annually and explicitly authorizes cash as well as in-kind subsidies, gives the only purpose of the EEP as being "to discourage unfair trade practices" (U.S. Congress, House 1990, 335). The context for this focus was the continued expansion of EC subsidized exports and EC intransigence on agriculture in the Uruguay Round, then scheduled for completion in December 1990. The Omnibus Budget Reconciliation Act, enacted in October 1990 along with the FACT Act, contained a "GATT trigger" which required spending $1 billion annually on EEP if no Uruguay Round agreement had been reached by June 30, 1992. Since no agreement had been reached at that time, EEP spending has proceeded at about the $1 billion rate.[27]

The international effects of the EEP are impossible to estimate with precision. Uncertainties about effects on other countries' exports and on world prices are even greater than in estimates of U.S. export additionality. The intention of targeted EEP subsidies is to displace EC subsidized exports and increase the cost of EC export subsidies, yet not displace the exports of nonsubsi-

27. The wheat EEP activity shown in table 6.2 accounts for most of U.S. agricultural export subsidies, but EEP bonuses have also been paid for exports of feedgrains, vegetable oil, rice, eggs, frozen poultry, and dairy cattle. In FY 1992, total EEP bonuses were $966 million, of which $838 million were for wheat and wheat flour.

dizing exporters. If perfectly realized, the result would be no change in worldwide wheat imports, no change in (nonsubsidized) world wheat prices, but a rise in the U.S. wheat price and wheat exports, and a fall EC wheat exports achieved by increased stocks and reduced acreage in the European Community.

In fact, the European Community would be expected to respond by reducing acreage, as they have done, but also by countering EEP subsidies with increased subsidies of their own, thus retaining part of the market. This competition would be likely to remove the intramarginal nature of the subsidized price in importing countries and reduce the price of all wheat in these contested markets. Therefore, total wheat imports in these countries should increase. The best markets in which to observe the consequences of the subsidy war are the North African wheat importers (Egypt, Algeria, Morocco, Tunesia, and Libya), traditional buyers of French wheat and flour which were the first and largest EEP targets (except Libya) and whose imports account for about 15 percent of world wheat trade. Aggregate wheat imports in these countries have increased since 1985. Indications are that North African buyers—principally government-related enterprises with substantial market power locally—have filled their needs via tenders and bargaining which results in all suppliers— the European Community, the United States, Canada, Australia, and (in Libya) Argentina—selling for comparable prices (Ackerman 1993; Parker 1990). So the nonsubsidizing suppliers are being harmed as well: the Canadian and Australian wheat boards have to subsidize their sales in these markets also.

A question can also be raised about the program's capability of separating targeted and nontargeted countries. Why would nontargeted countries keep buying at nonsubsidized prices? Even if reexports from, say, Morocco to Korea are ruled out by transportation costs, Australian exports could easily be redirected from North Africa to Korea if the price were higher in Korea. So we should expect to see wheat prices falling worldwide, except inside the United States and European Community. Other countries' wheat exports should be replaced by U.S. and EC wheat in importing countries where the United States and European Community compete, while competing exporters should increase their market share in countries where the United States and European Community do not offer subsidies. Such shifts have in fact occurred, but nonetheless the United States has retained the ability to export about half its wheat without EEP subsidies (although most of this has credit subsidies or is shipped in the P.L. 480 food assistance programs). Notably, Japan continues to buy about 3 to 5 million metric tons of U.S. wheat annually (10–15 percent of U.S. exports) at nonsubsidized prices.[28]

28. Taking Japan as an importer with inelastic demand while other importers have relatively elastic demand and exporters inelastic supply, we have an approximation (if other exporters cooperate) of the situation shown by Dutton (1990) to create the possibility of targeted export subsidies being a second-best mechanism for exporters to exercise monopoly power. This result would show up empirically as an increase in the U.S. price of wheat for a given level of imports (as U.S. wheat

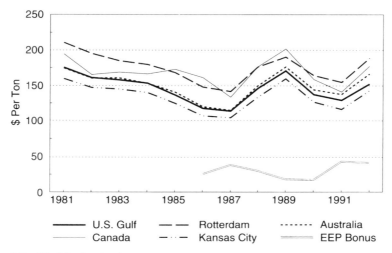

Fig. 6.8   World wheat prices
Source: USDA, Economic Research Service, *Wheat Yearbook* (Washington, D.C., February 1994).

Data on wheat border prices in several countries are shown in figure 6.8. The EEP, if effective, should have increased the U.S. price, from which the subsidy is subtracted and transportation added to obtain the importing buyer's price. And, if the EEP affected other countries' prices it should have reduced them. Comparing two U.S. prices (Kansas City and U.S. Gulf) with Canada, Australia, and Rotterdam prices, no such pattern is apparent. Of course, the price levels everywhere are determined more by world crop conditions, U.S. ARPs, and macroeconomic factors than by the EEP. But none of these factors would place a wedge between U.S. and other exporters' wheat prices in the way the EEP might do. Yet, to take a long-term comparison, the difference between the U.S. Kansas City price and the Argentine, Canadian, Rotterdam, and Australian prices are largely the same in 1984 with no EEP and in 1992 with an average EEP bonus of $40 per ton. Indeed, if there is a difference it is that the U.S. prices *fell* relative to the foreign prices.

The data are more consistent with the hypothesis that the EEP drove down the price of wheat in the targeted importing countries, with all the competing exporters who remained in those markets offering matching subsidies, while prices in the remaining markets were mutually determined by spatial market forces which are basically the same as with no EEP. If this is true, the economic effects of the EEP are at the low end of the ranges given in table 6.3, perhaps even lower.

The price relationship most crucial to the essentially null-effect interpreta-

---

is reallocated from elastic-demand to inelastic-demand markets). Empirical evidence that this has occurred is lacking.

tion of EEP effects is that between the United States and Canada. If the EEP were to place a $30 to $50 wedge between U.S. and Canadian prices for a period of eight years there would be tremendous pressure to export Canadian wheat to the United States. In fact, such pressure in the past has led to the imposition of import quotas under the section 22 authorities described earlier. But section 22 import quotas were removed by executive order in 1974 and have never been reinstated.

In 1992 and 1993 there has at last occurred a surge of wheat imports from Canada, about 2 million tons each year. This is a quadrupling of such imports compared to the 1980–90 average. Yet as a percentage of either Canadian or U.S. wheat exports, the amounts are quite small (refer back to fig. 6.2). It is noteworthy also that much of these imports are of durum wheat, a type used primarily in making pasta, and grown in the United States predominantly in North Dakota and in Canada just across the border. The price of durum wheat moves rather independently of other wheats.

The U.S. International Trade Commission (USITC) investigated the Canadian exports of durum wheat to the United States in response to congressional requests. Their report (USITC 1990) attributes these exports in part to the EEP driving down the price of durum wheat in the markets to which Canada has traditionally been exporting this product. Since the ITC report, durum imports from Canada have increased substantially, from about 0.2 million metric tons annually to 0.7 million tons in 1992–93. U.S. durum exports have continued at about 1.5 million tons annually during this period, with the majority receiving EEP subsidies in the range of $25–$50 per ton. In 1992, U.S. durum exports under EEP were 0.9 million tons, with an average bonus of $42.50 per ton (Alston and Carter 1993). This would appear a clear case of the EEP creating a wedge between U.S. and Canadian prices, so that durum wheat going out through the front door (to North Africa and South America) comes back in through Canada. The picture is complicated, however, by the facts that U.S. durum wheat in 1992 had declined in price since 1989, sold at a lower price than average wheat in the U.S., and that U.S. durum wheat acreage and production declined in 1992 by roughly the amount of the increased Canadian shipments to the United States. The NAWG has cited the data of table 6.7 as showing a lack of correlation between U.S. durum exports under EEP and Canadian wheat exports to the United States.

The economic analysis carries political freight because if the imports are attributable to autonomous Canadian policies rather than being caused by the EEP, the case is better for imposing section 22 import quotas. The case to be made is that Canadian exports interfere with the operation of the U.S. wheat program. These imports can be argued to have increased the cost of the program by driving up deficiency payments slightly, but whether this argument is legally sufficient remains to be determined. In the course of the NAFTA debate, the Clinton administration promised another inquiry into the matter, which the ITC subsequently undertook. In July 1994, the ITC found that wheat

Table 6.7   **Data on Wheat Trade between Canada and the United States (thousand metric tons)**

Crop Year (July–June)	U.S. EEP Sales of Durum Wheat (worldwide)	Canadian Durum Exports to the United States	All Canadian Wheat Exports to the United States
1985–86	50	0	280
1986–87	1,122	59	417
1987–88	942	177	320
1988–89	187	191	285
1989–90	700	173	379
1990–91	990	330	547
1991–92	673	393	858
1992–93	895	420	1,320

Source: National Association of Wheat Growers (1993, private communication).

imports from Canada were increasing the cost of the U.S. wheat program but disagreed on the amount and made no recommendation for a remedy. In August the United States and Canada reached a one-year agreement under which Canadian wheat would be subject to a $50 per ton tariff for quantities above about two-thirds of 1993–94 import levels. The political context for this protection was the Clinton administration's effort to obtain the Democratic wheat-state senators' support for the Uruguay Round GATT agreement.

6.4 Political Response to the EEP

In 1990 the legislation authorizing the EEP (and other farm programs) expired and was reconsidered in a comprehensive set of hearings (U.S. Congress, House 1991; U.S. Congress, Senate 1991). This provided a convenient opportunity for interest groups to express second thoughts and suggested modifications of the EEP. The NAWG, as well as representatives of other commodities using the program, were totally supportive of continuation of the EEP without substantial change. Concerns that had been expressed in the 1985 House hearings about targeting as opposed to a generally available subsidy disappeared. Grain users might have been expected to be more critical, but more of them supported EEP in 1990 than had in 1985. The American Bakers Association, the Biscuit and Cracker Manufacturers' Association, and the North American Export Grain association all testified in favor of continuing the program.

Grain exporters asked for changes in the procedures by which export bonuses are awarded, which would give the companies greater flexibility in making deals with importers (U.S. Congress, Senate 1991, part 13). This however was the one area where concerns had been expressed by nonfarm and some farm groups—that the program was too friendly to exporting companies and that these companies rather than farmers were profiting from the program. This concern persists to the present, as exemplified in the recent *New York Times* series on "Tainted Trade," the first installment of which was headlined on page 1: "Abuses Plague Programs to Help Exports of Agricultural Products" (*New York Times,* October 10, 1993). None of the particular abuses cited—and substantively there were not many—involved the wheat EEP program.[29] In addition, economists have continued to assert, based on arguments and analysis discussed earlier, that the EEP generated few benefits to farmers for its costs.

Because of firm support from commodity and agribusiness groups, and weak opposition, the EEP emerged unchanged in structure and strengthened in budget in the 1990 Farm Act. EEP spending was far higher in FY 1991–93 than in any previous three-year period (table 6.5). The solid political support was attributable not so much to particular export achievements of the EEP, but to farmers' general satisfaction with the recovery of farm income from mid-1980s lows and the role of the commodity programs in that recovery. CCC wheat inventories had been sold off, deficiency payments protected producers from low prices in 1986, the export market had recovered with the dollar's decline from its 1985 high, and reduced output boosted wheat prices back to 1980–81 level in 1989 and 1990. Farm interests in the 1990 farm bill debate were devoted mainly to attempting to forestall the budget cuts of about $2 billion annually that the Bush administration was calling for. The EEP was thus seen as a piece of a set of programs that was working. Beyond general satisfaction with the situation,[30] a principal threat to U.S. grain producers was seen to be EC subsidized exports. The EEP was seen as particularly valuable in this situation, with the Uruguay Round languishing.

Opposition to EEP was mitigated because farm bill reformers focused on other policies. The only organized reform effort, by a coalition of conservative Republicans and urban Democrats in the House of Representatives, brought to the floor of the House amendments to reduce or eliminate the sugar, wool, and honey programs and eliminate deficiency payments to farms with over a million dollars in sales or to farmers who earned more than $100,000 from off-farm sources. These amendments all failed. These had more apparent popular appeal than an anti-EEP amendment would have; this helps explain why none was offered.

A second important factor mitigating opposition to EEP was its being scored as budget neutral. The reforms that were successful in the 1990 Farm Act, most notably the introduction of a 15 percent reduction in deficiency payments by making 15 percent of each producer's base acreage ineligible for payments,

29. The two main abuses were tobacco export assistance (not under EEP) that subsidized exports by U.S. tobacco companies of foreign-grown leaf and corruption (Iraq allegedly using credit meant for grain import to buy arms) in the sale of rice to Iraq in the period leading up to the invasion of Kuwait in 1990.

30. It may be thought that farmers' positive attitude is being overstated in view of the complaints of many farm witnesses and the gloomleading of many Agriculture Committee members. Evidence that this was aimed at forestalling cuts rather than changing programs is the absence of major proposed changes in the 1990 debate. Recall too that President Bush won the farm vote in 1992 (see Cook, Art, and Evans 1991).

was driven by the budget reconciliation agreement to cut $13 billion from farm program spending over the five fiscal years 1992–96. The $1 billion annual spending on EEP would have been a prime target for cuts if the program had not been scored as budget neutral by OMB.

After passage of the 1990 Farm Act the EEP became politically still stronger. In 1993–94 EEP sales were extended to Mexico. The GATT triggers locked a minimum of $1 billion annually for EEP bonuses. The Canadian government has objected to this program on several occasions. When President Bush was planning his visit to Australia in 1991, the White House found to their surprise that the lead item for discussion between the heads of state, in the Australian view, was U.S. wheat exports under the EEP.

The desired route to demise of the EEP would be implementation of the Uruguay Round GATT agreement. In agriculture the agreement requires multilateral phase-down of export subsidies, including the EEP. In the end, this agreement could be considered a success in the same vein as President Reagan's arms buildup in promoting nuclear weapons agreements with the USSR. Even without the Uruguay Round, it is noteworthy that the European Community has in 1991–94 introduced significant reforms of the CAP, including acreage set-aside and other measures to reduce outlays on their export subsidies. The strength of U.S. willingness to spend on EEP quite likely had a role in encouraging these reforms, though how important a factor is unclear.[31]

6.5 Conclusions

A summary of interest group positions on the EEP, and how they fared, is shown in table 6.8. The most active group, wheat producers, were substantial economic gainers from the program. Wheat-exporting businesses were less active but were also supportive of EEP, and were winners. Other agricultural producers, notably feed grains, gained by obtaining a piece of the EEP action and also supported the program. The losing groups—domestic grain processors and consumers—did not visibly oppose the program.

The most striking feature of the political economy of the EEP is how little impact standard economic arguments have had. Economists have produced many analyses showing that the program, even as a second-best measure, gen-

31. What is the U.S. gain from CAP reform? Although it is even more conjectural than the earlier calculations, CAP reform along the lines being implemented could well reduce EC wheat exports by 3 to 4 million tons annually and raise the U.S. market price by $0.20 to $0.30 per bushel. The resulting gain for U.S. producers would be $120 to $180 million annually, and the gains to taxpayers would be $350 to $520 million (because of less deficiency payments). U.S. consumers would lose $240 to $360 million. The overall net gain to the United States, equal roughly to the price increase times wheat exports, would be $230 to $350 million.

Suppose the EEP accelerated CAP reform by five years. Then the EEP generated $1.1 to $1.8 billion for the United States. The overall U.S. cost of the EEP in 1990–92 was about $350 million annually, or about $2 billion for 1986–93. These calculations are of course crude, but they indicate that it is quite difficult to obtain any net U.S. gain from EEP as a strategic investment, even under the assumption that it successfully induced policy changes in the European Community.

Table 6.8   **Interest Groups' Positions on the EEP in the 1985 Congressional Debate**

	Support			
	Most Active	Least Active	Inactive or Neutral	Opposed
Winners				
Wheat producers	X			
Wheat exporters		X		
Rice, feed grains, and other EEP-eligible farmers	X			
Custom wheat harvesters and input supplies			X	
Mixed or no effect				
General farm organizations	X			
Millers[a]		X		
Losers				
Consumer groups			X	
Livestock producers		X	X	
Bakers			X	
Public-interest watchdogs[b]			X	X

[a]Millers were not all losers because subsidies are paid for some flour as well as wheat exports.
[b]Principally op-ed columnists and other authors.

erates a net loss to the U.S. economy, although some have muddied the waters by showing that a precisely calibrated system of country-specific export subsidy rates could be welfare increasing if the United States has varying degrees of monopoly power in different wheat import markets (e.g., Abbott, Paarlberg, and Sharples 1987). The lack of clout of the overall U.S. welfare argument is not surprising given the prevalence of government activity that generates deadweight losses in order to redistribute income.

It is perhaps more surprising that fact-based analyses that argued farmers as well as the rest of the economy would be better off under alternative policies did not cut more ice politically (e.g., Paarlberg 1988). It seems clear in retrospect that for such an argument to be effective it has to be accepted by farmers themselves as well as by disinterested observers. The agriculture committees take their cue first and foremost from farmers, and if farmers are united, only very strong opposition can be effective.

In order for wheat growers to abandon EEP, they would have to be shown how they could be made just as well off with alternative policies that are politically feasible. The option of cutting acreage with an increased ARP causes farm income to be lower for a given price of wheat because of the opportunity cost of idled acres. Political feasibility also means avoiding the one nonfarm source of strong opposition, objection to increased budget outlays. This rules out the standard approach that economists offer, nondistorting or less distorting transfer payments. With acreage and yield bases fixed, and farmers free to plant alternative program crops without affecting their payments, increasing the wheat target price would provide payments not far from being a nondistorting transfer (apart from the marginal cost of raising government funds). But budgetary pressure makes this a nonstarter.

The biggest losers from the EEP are buyers of wheat, with losses of $250 to $600 million per year according to estimates presented earlier, with recent world price data suggesting the lower end of the range is more likely. But no buyers of wheat—millers, bakers, livestock producers, or consumers of retail products containing wheat—have raised politically significant objections to the program. Agribusiness interests probably did not bear any losses. Livestock feeders' costs have not been substantial, and a feeling of solidarity together with logrolling keeps them from opposing the program.[32] Consumer costs are only about $1 to $3 per year per person; and the general public remains generally supportive of farmers according to polls.

In short, the EEP has proved a political winner because: wheat producers see a benefit from it; wheat producers have a unified view on the issue, and they have effective channels of influence through the congressional agriculture committees; wheat buyers have not opposed the program; the program has been accepted as budget neutral.

There are two points of vulnerability for the EEP in the near future. The first is in the budgetary arena. Budget-neutrality arguments are becoming less plausible now that CCC stocks are no longer used as bonuses, and apparent effects on U.S. prices are small. FY 1995 agricultural appropriations, enacted in September 1994, contain a $200 million reduction in EEP that has been scored as a budget savings. The second point is that the GATT agreement in agriculture requires a reduction of the EEP. This places EEP reform as part of a policy package that would make U.S. farmers as well as nonfarmers better off than at present.

References

Abbott, P. C., R. L. Paarlberg, and J. A. Sharples. 1987. Targeted agricultural export subsidies and social welfare. *American Journal of Agricultural Economics* 69:723–32.

Ackerman, Karen Z. 1993. The Moroccan wheat market. In *Wheat situation,* WAS-303, 22–25. Washington, D.C.: USDA, Economic Research Service.

Ackerman, Karen Z., and Mark E. Smith. 1990. Agricultural export programs. Staff Report no. AGES 9033. Washington, D.C.: USDA, Economic Research Service.

Alston, Julian M., and C. A. Carter. 1993. Effects of farm programs on gains from

---

32. Livestock producers do not have price support programs, but logrolling can occur because cattle feedlots get lower-priced feeder calves when grazing costs are lower, so cattle interests need crop producers' support on keeping federal grazing fees low; and poultry products have been exported under EEP using CCC grain as a source of bonuses, so the poultry industry has an interest in the EEP.

Canada-U.S. wheat trade. Paper presented at Canadian Agricultural Economics meetings, July 12–14, Edmondton.

Benedict, Murray R. 1953. *Farm policies of the United States, 1790–1950.* New York: Twentieth Century Fund.

Bonnen, James, and W. P. Browne. 1989. Why is agricultural policy so difficult to reform? In *The political economy of U.S. agriculture,* ed. Carol Kramer, 7–33. Washington, D.C.: Resources for the Future.

Brooks, H. G., S. Devadoss, and W. H. Meyers. 1990. The impact of the EEP on the world wheat market. *American Journal of Agricultural Economics* 38:253–77.

Chambers, Robert G., and P. L. Paarlberg. 1991. Are more exports always better? Comparing cash and in-kind export subsidies. *American Journal of Agricultural Economics* 73:142–54.

Cook, Kenneth A., Andrew B. Art, and Molly C. Evans. 1991. Bush defeats Clinton! An analysis of 1992 election results in farming-dependent counties. Washington, D.C.: Center for Resource Economics.

Dixit, A. K., and V. Norman. 1980. *Theory of international trade.* Welwyn: Nisbet/ Cambridge University Press.

Dutton, John. 1990. Targeted export subsidies as an exercise of monopoly power. *Canadian Journal of Economics* 23:705–10.

Dutton, John, and Thomas Grennes. 1985. Measurement of exchange rates appropriate for international trade. Economic Research Report no. 51. Department of Economics, North Carolina State University.

Gallagher, Paul, M. Lancaster, M. Bredahl, and T. Ryan. 1981. The U.S. wheat economy in an international setting. Technical Bulletin no. 1644. Washington, D.C.: USDA, Economic Research Service.

Gardner, Bruce L. 1987. Causes of U.S. farm commodity programs. *Journal of Political Economy* 95:290–310.

———. 1991. Agricultural policies: United States. In *Agricultural protectionism,* ed. F. H. Sanderson, 19–63. Washington, D.C.: Resources for the Future.

Hardin, Charles M. 1968. Farm politics and the separation of powers. In *Readings in agricultural policy,* ed. R. J. Hildreth, 69–77. Lincoln: University of Nebraska Press.

Johnson, D. Gale. 1984. Agriculture and U.S. trade policy. In *Trade policy perspectives,* U.S. Congress, Senate, 157–68. Washington, D.C.: Government Printing Office, December.

Lin, William, and Bruce Gardner. 1988. Aggregate effects of commodity programs. Washington, D.C.: USDA, Economic Research Service. Mimeograph.

National Corn Growers Association. 1985. News Release. Washington D.C.: National Corn Growers Association, August 15.

O'Rourke, Desmond A. 1984. Taking account of competitive realities. In *Trade policy perspectives,* U.S. Congress, Senate, 119–23. Washington, D.C.: Government Printing Office, December.

Paarlberg, Robert L. 1988. *Fixing farm trade,* Cambridge, Mass.: Ballinger.

Parker, John B. 1990. U.S.-EC competition in North Africa wheat market. In *Wheat situation,* WAS-290, 36–38. Washington, D.C.: USDA, Economic Research Service.

Rapp, David. 1988. *How the U.S. got into agriculture, and why it can't get out.* Washington, D.C.: Congressional Quarterly, Inc.

Salathe, Larry. 1991. Budget neutrality of EEP. Washington, D.C.: USDA, Economic Analysis Staff, November. Mimeograph.

Schwensen, Carl. 1984. The United States—A major wheat producer and exporter. In *Farm policy perspectives: Setting the stage for 1985 agricultural legislation,* U.S. Congress, Senate, 24–31. Washington, D.C.: Government Printing Office, April.

Sharples, Jerry A. 1982. The short-run elasticity of demand for U.S. wheat exports.

Staff Report no. AGES 8200406. Washington, D.C.: USDA, Economic Research Service, April.

————. 1984. Are export subsidies the answer to U.S. grain surpluses? In *Trade policy perspectives,* U.S. Congress, Senate, 176–86. Washington, D.C.: Government Printing Office, December.

U.S. Congress. Congressional Budget Office. 1994. Reducing the deficit: Spending and revenue options. Report to House and Senate Budget Committees. Washington, D.C.: Congressional Budget Office, March.

U.S. Congress. House. Committee on Agriculture. 1985a. *General Farm Bill of 1985: Hearings March–May.* 99th Cong., 1st sess., pts. 1 and 5. Washington, D.C.: Government Printing Office.

————. 1985b. *Report to accompany H.R. 2100: Food Security Act of 1985.* 99th Cong., 1st sess., H. Rept. 99–271, pt. 1. Washington, D.C.: Government Printing Office, September 13.

————. 1986. *Review of the EEP: Hearings October–November 1985.* 99th Cong., 1st sess., H. Rept. 99–16. Washington, D.C.: Government Printing Office.

————. 1990. *Conference report to accompany S. 2830.* 101st Cong., 1st sess. H. Rept. 101–916. Washington, D.C.: Government Printing Office, October 22.

————. 1991. *Formulation of the 1990 Farm Bill.* 101st Cong., 1st sess., pts. 1–14. Washington, D.C.: Government Printing Office.

U.S. Congress. Senate. Committee on Agriculture, Nutrition, and Forestry. 1983. *Agricultural export trade.* 98th Cong., 1st sess., S. Hrg. 98–70. Washington, D.C.: Government Printing Office, February.

————. 1984a. *Farm policy perspectives: Setting the stage for 1985 agricultural legislation.* Washington, D.C.: Government Printing Office, April.

————. 1984b. *Trade policy perspectives.* Washington, D.C.: Government Printing Office, December.

————. 1985a. *Examining the competitive position of U.S. agriculture.* 99th Cong., 1st sess., S. Hrg. 99–57. Washington, D.C.: Government Printing Office, February 7.

————. 1985b. *Framework and analysis for agricultural policy in 1985.* 99th Cong., 1st sess., S. Hrg. 99–55. Washington, D.C.: Government Printing Office, March.

————. 1985c. *Reauthorization of the Agriculture and Food Act of 1981.* 99th Cong., 1st sess., S. Hrg. 99–115, pts. 1 and 2. Washington, D.C.: Government Printing Office, March–April.

————. 1991. *Preparation for the 1990 Farm Bill.* 101st Cong., 1st sess., pts. 1–15. Washington, D.C.: Government Printing Office.

USDA (U.S. Department of Agriculture). 1986. Embargoes, surplus disposal, and U.S. agriculture. Agricultural Economic Report no. 564. Washington, D.C.: USDA, Economic Research Service, December.

————. 1993. Former USSR. RS-93–1. Washington, D.C.: USDA, Economic Research Service, May .

U.S. General Accounting Office. 1994. Wheat support: The impact of target prices versus export subsidies. Report to Congress, GAO/RCED-94–79. Washington, D.C.: U.S. General Accounting Office, June.

USITC (U.S. International Trade Commission). 1990. Durum wheat: Conditions of competition between the U.S. and Canadian industries. USITC Publication no. 2274. Washington, D.C.: U.S. International Trade Commission, June.

Comment   Robert Paarlberg

Gardner's paper on the Export Enhancement Program (EEP) is exceptionally strong, by far the best work that has yet been done on this topic. What interested me most was his questioning how such a costly and ineffective policy could remain politically popular for so long. Several years ago I wrote a brief article of my own entitled, "The Mysterious Popularity of EEP" (Paarlberg 1990). Gardner's analysis is thorough and careful on the evolution and the consequences of EEP, but to some extent it only deepens the mystery as to the program's popularity.

One key to the program's survival, Gardner shows, was its scoring by the Office of Management and Budget (OMB) as "budget neutral." Several larger questions arise from this scoring which might deserve more analysis.

First, what explains the fact that the deficit hawks at OMB were sooner willing than the Congressional Budget Office (CBO) to designate EEP as budget neutral, despite evidence from inside the U.S. Department of Agriculture (USDA) itself that the additionality gained by EEP was only about one-third the amount needed to claim budget neutrality?[1] More important, why did OMB hold on to this unrealistic claim even after surplus stocks were gone and the program was cashed out in 1991? My own suspicion is that OMB was taking an indulgent view of EEP in part because of its own original role in creating the EEP, in 1985. OMB was reluctant to punish EEP because OMB, under David Stockman's leadership, had been the original midwife of the program. In this regard, EEP may not be the only program instrument that plays a prominent role in U.S. agricultural policy because of the influence and indulgence of OMB. Acreage reduction programs (ARPs) also tend to be championed by OMB, despite the long-term damage they do to the competitiveness of U.S. agricultural exports, and to the economic health of rural America.

A second question also arises from EEP's budget-neutral scoring. How is it that measures like budget neutrality have come to be more important, in the agricultural policy debate, than measures such as cost effectiveness in contributing to national welfare, or even to farmer income? The EEP, as Gardner shows, is a terribly inefficient way to support farm income in the United States. Like most export subsidies, its primary effect is to transfer welfare to foreign customers (who get the wheat they normally would have been buying at a lower than normal cost). If the purpose of the program is to boost farm prices in the United States by removing wheat from the market, it would actually be cheaper for taxpayers to remove that wheat by purchasing it and burning it, rather than trying to create additional sales abroad with subsidies that tend to be immedi-

Robert Paarlberg is professor of political science at Wellesley College and associate at the Harvard University Center for International Affairs.

1. Kenneth W. Bailey estimated only 0.1 additionality during the early years of the program (Bailey 1989).

ately offset by similar subsidies from competitors such as the European Community.

In the policy debate in Washington, however, the only important standard for measuring EEP has seemed to be its short-term budget cost *compared to current policy*. In areas like agriculture where current policy is costly and ineffective, this is not strict enough a standard. Under these circumstances, praising the EEP for budget neutrality is a bit like praising someone for having switched from gambling away his paycheck to drinking away his paycheck, because his behavior change was "paycheck neutral."

Another area I might look into more deeply is the alleged contribution made by EEP to Common Agricultural Policy (CAP) reforms, and to the recent completion of the Uruguay Round of the General Agreement on Tariffs and Trade (GATT) negotiations. Gardner makes an interesting calculation, that even if EEP advanced CAP reform by five years, its overall cost to the U.S. economy still exceeded the benefit. I would go farther, since there is no convincing evidence that EEP was key to CAP reform. The Australian Bureau of Agriculture and Resource Economics estimated several years ago that EEP was only increasing the budget cost of the CAP in Europe by about 1.5 percent. It takes courage to argue that this small straw played any role in breaking the camel's back. In some ways, EEP was on balance unhelpful in the Uruguay Round since it antagonized our allies there (Australia and Canada) much more than it punished the European Community. True, the United States in the end traded away a 21 percent reduction in EEP for a 21 percent subsidized export volume reduction in the European Community, but this came after the European Community had already embraced its MacSharry Plan reform, which would have made likely a significant volume reduction in any case, with or without a GATT agreement. Moreover, it is not yet clear how the modified Blair House agreement on export subsidies will function. There is some danger that as the use of direct export subsidies declines, the use of export credits, credit guarantees, blended credits, market promotion, barter, and "food aid" will expand.

There is also a danger that the Uruguay Round outcome will help, in the end, to keep the EEP in place indefinitely. Farm groups will argue that "we bargained hard" for an allowable level of export subsidies, and to provide anything less will be "unilateral disarmament." The GATT ceiling on export subsidies, in other words, could start to become a floor.

What might it take, in the end, to prompt a termination of EEP? Most of my own predictions, until now, have been wrong. I originally thought the program would end after the 1988 summer drought, which eliminated U.S. surplus stocks of wheat, and hence ended the "surplus disposal" justification for the program. EEP remained in place, however, because farm groups said they needed it as a "bargaining chip" in the Uruguay Round. They claimed they wanted EEP to get a better GATT, but in fact they were using the negotiations in GATT to hold on to a bigger EEP.

I next thought the program would end in 1992, when stock shortages actually forced the CCC to stop providing "bonus" wheat flour to the domestic school lunch program. I could not imagine there would be support for continuing to subsidize consumers in Russia and Egypt at a time when poor consumers in the United States were being denied. Several months later, however, President Bush expanded the program, part of an election-year play to wheat-state political leaders.

I then concluded that the program probably would not end until it became clear that scandalously large subsidies were going to foreign governments with which the United States had major diplomatic differences. This, after all, was how an earlier U.S. wheat export subsidy policy was ended, following the "great grain robbery" sale to the Soviet Union in 1972. In early 1994, however, even this hypothesis proved unfounded, when USDA offered a record-high $65 per ton subsidy to the government of China, at precisely the same moment that China was being targeted by other U.S. government agencies with economic sanctions, for various human rights transgressions. Not even this sale was sufficient to discredit the program.

So it is that the mystery of EEP's popularity deepens.

References

Bailey, Kenneth W. 1989. An analysis of the Export Enhancement Program for wheat. Paper presented at the summer meetings of the American Agricultural Economics Association, Baton Rouge.

Paarlberg, Robert L. 1990. The mysterious popularity of EEP. *Choices,* no. 2: 14–17.

7 Agricultural Interest Groups and the North American Free Trade Agreement

David Orden

During 1993 a shrill public debate over the North American Free Trade Agreement (NAFTA) took place in the United States. The idea of negotiating one or more bilateral free trade agreements (FTAs) had initially been raised by the Reagan administration in the early 1980s. The dual intent of proposing these agreements was to lower barriers to trade with important U.S. economic partners and to build pressure for multilateral reforms under the General Agreement on Tariffs and Trade (GATT). After a delay of several years, an Israel-U.S. agreement developed relatively quickly and was approved by Congress in May 1985. The multilateral Uruguay Round GATT negotiations were launched subsequently (September 1986), and a bilateral agreement with Canada was approved in September 1988.

Mexico proposed developing a FTA with the United States in May 1990. The GATT negotiations were stalled, but entering into a bilateral trade agreement with Mexico was more controversial than the previous agreements with Israel and Canada. Nevertheless, the United States embraced negotiations, which were expanded to include Canada in 1991. A trilateral agreement was reached in August 1992 and was signed by the three heads of state in December.

With the change in administration early in 1993, newly elected President Clinton sought supplementary (side) agreements to clarify and strengthen the original provisions of NAFTA with respect to environmental protection, labor

David Orden is associate professor of agricultural and applied economics at Virginia Polytechnic Institute and State University.

The author thanks Barbara Craig, Carol Goodloe, and Anne Krueger and other participants in the NBER's conference on the political economy of trade protection for helpful comments on an earlier version of this paper. He is also indebted to the many parties to the NAFTA debate who shared their insights in interviews and other correspondence, and to Nicole Fatseas, Laura Zepp, and the staff of the Senate Committee on Agriculture, Nutrition and Forestry for their assistance.

rights, and mechanisms to protect domestic producers from unanticipated import surges. Negotiations for these side-agreements were completed in August. Still facing substantial domestic opposition to NAFTA, the Clinton administration then launched an intense campaign for passage of the implementing legislation. It won a crucial and surprisingly large come-from-behind victory with a majority of Republican support when the House of Representatives approved the bill on November 17 by a 234–200 vote. This decision set the stage for concluding efforts on the multilateral GATT negotiations in December 1993, and NAFTA took effect January 1, 1994.

This paper focuses on the attempts of U.S. agricultural interest groups to influence the outcomes of both the negotiations for NAFTA and the congressional debate over its implementing legislation. The objectives of the analysis are to investigate the goals and strategies of different interest groups and to evaluate the success of their efforts either to have NAFTA create expanded export opportunities or to limit the scope of the agreement in order to retain existing protection. Agricultural issues have loomed large in world trade discussions since the inception of the Uruguay Round GATT negotiations, and Canada and Mexico are important agricultural trade partners of the United States; they account jointly for more than one-fourth of U.S. agricultural imports and one-sixth of U.S. agricultural exports. For these reasons, the agricultural provisions of NAFTA became an important component of the agreement. Moreover, agricultural interests ultimately played a crucial role in the coalition that supported the NAFTA implementing legislation.

More specifically, the agricultural commodity groups became aligned as supporters of trade liberalization under NAFTA or as proponents of limits on the scope of the agreement based on their particular interests in trade with Mexico and Canada and their perceptions of NAFTA's broader implications. Early in the negotiations, the various groups confronted a high-level decision by Mexico and the United States to include all agricultural products under provisions for long-run liberalization. The U.S. agricultural groups supporting trade liberalization had some influence on this decision, but it was more widely attributed to willingness of Mexico to remove trade barriers from its politically sensitive and historically highly protected corn sector.

Under the negotiated agreement announced in August 1992, all licenses and quotas restricting Mexico-U.S. agricultural trade were to be converted to tariffs in January 1994. These and other tariffs were also to be completely phased out over adjustment periods of up to 15 years. Canada had resisted such full coverage of the agricultural provisions of NAFTA, and the U.S. agricultural groups and others favoring liberalized trade had not been able to extract Canadian concessions. Instead, it had been agreed that pending modification by an Uruguay Round GATT agreement, the less comprehensive Canada-U.S. FTA, which left nontariff barriers intact for dairy, poultry, and other sectors, would remain in effect for bilateral Canada-U.S. trade. Mexico and Canada had negotiated a similar agreement.

Because NAFTA promised to liberalize U.S. agricultural trade with Mexico, the agreement as negotiated received support in the United States from market-oriented general-membership farm organizations and from most export-oriented producers of grains, oilseeds, livestock, and some horticultural products. The dairy and cotton sectors, although protected by U.S. import quotas, joined the NAFTA supporters when it became apparent that Mexico had little capacity to produce competitive imports and strong rules of origin were adopted.

The NAFTA negotiations and the August 1992 agreement were opposed by farm groups favoring restrictive supply controls to raise domestic prices, wheat producers seeking leverage on Canadian export subsidy issues, and protected sugar, peanut, and citrus and other winter fruit and vegetable producers objecting to specific transition-period provisions. The presidential election in November 1992 appeared to open renewed opportunities for influence by these groups, but the side-agreements negotiated by the new Clinton administration were limited in scope. Dissatisfied with these results, the producer groups opposed to various NAFTA provisions sought further accommodations in the subsequent legislative debate. Willingness to withdraw their opposition in exchange for specific concessions gave them substantial bargaining power relative to organized labor and others committed to the defeat of the NAFTA implementing legislation.

As the heavily contested congressional vote approached in November 1993, critical support for the implementing legislation from agricultural interest groups (or at least the withdrawal of their active opposition) came at the expense of some weakening of the original agreement and other related costs. Concessions made to agricultural interests protected U.S. sugar from Mexican competition, provided some transition-period protection to winter fruits and vegetables, and ensnared the United States in disputes about Canadian exports of wheat and peanut butter. While the long-run provisions for agricultural trade liberalization remained intact, with the final concessions NAFTA results in essentially no reform of entrenched domestic agricultural support programs in the United States (or Canada) during the lengthy tariff phase-out periods. Thus, those interests favoring more open trade can only be judged partially successful in their efforts and, likewise, the NAFTA process only partially successful in expanding international market opportunities, at least for the next 10 to 15 years.

To develop these themes, this paper is organized as follows. Section 7.1 provides a brief description of U.S. agricultural production, trade, and price support policies as a basis for evaluating the stakes of various interest groups in NAFTA. Section 7.2 examines the initial positions of the agricultural interest groups and their strategies for influencing the negotiations. Next, the provisions of the negotiated agreement are summarized and public and private sector assessments of these provisions are reviewed. The focus then turns to the side-agreements negotiated by the Clinton administration, the activities of the various agricultural interest groups during the congressional debate over the implementing legislation, and the final concessions and guarantees offered to obtain support for the legislation from agricultural interests. The concluding section addresses some issues raised by the NAFTA outcomes for agriculture.

7.1 Diversity within Agriculture

From an aggregate perspective, agriculture represents less than 3 percent of national output. Even so, agricultural production is diffused among many diverse sectors. Descriptive statistics about production, aggregate trade, and bilateral trade with Canada and Mexico at the outset of the NAFTA negotiations (1989–91 averages) are presented for the major groups of commodities in table 7.1.

Grains and oilseeds accounted for one-fifth of the value of U.S. production of agricultural commodities and their direct products during 1989–91. Grains and oilseeds are generally exported crops, with one-fourth of the value of production sold in world markets and the percentage as high as 60 to 75 percent for wheat and rice. Imports of grains and oilseeds are minimal but imports from Canada comprised over one-third of their value, and essentially all of the value of imported wheat, barley, and soybeans.

Livestock and poultry products accounted for another one-fifth of the value of domestic agricultural production during 1989–91. The United States has maintained some quantitative meat import restrictions, and trade has been less important for livestock and poultry products than for grains and oilseeds. The value of imports and the value of exports of livestock and poultry products were less than 5 percent, respectively, of the value of domestic production. Of this trade, Canada produced over 35 percent of U.S. import value and Mexico another 10 percent. Canada and Mexico each accounted for over 15 percent of the value of U.S. exports.

A third group of commodities important in the context of NAFTA are those for which the United States has traditionally imposed import quotas under section 22 of the Agricultural Adjustment Act of 1935 and its extensions. The section 22 legislation authorized trade restrictions when imports "render ineffective or materially interfere with" domestic supply control and price support programs of the U.S. Department of Agriculture (USDA). Dairy products, cotton, and peanuts are among the commodities for which there have been section 22 quotas. Imports of these commodities have been restricted to less than 2 percent of domestic production. Exports of dairy products were also less than 2 percent of domestic production at the beginning of the NAFTA negotiations, but exports accounted for more than 40 percent of U.S. cotton and 15 percent of the value of peanut production.[1] Mexico received over one-third of the U.S.

1. Dairy products are priced above world levels in domestic markets and are exported with subsidies, while the price support mechanisms for cotton facilitate exports at most times despite

Table 7.1   U.S. Production and Trade of Agricultural Products, 1989–91 Averages

| | | U.S. Imports | | | | | | U.S. Exports | | | | | |
| | | Total | | Canada | | Mexico | | Total | | Canada | | Mexico | |
Commodity	Production[a]	Amount[a]	Percentage of Total Production	Amount[a]	Percentage of Total Imports	Amount[a]	Percentage of Total Imports	Amount[a]	Percentage of Total Production	Amount[a]	Percentage of Total Exports	Amount[a]	Percentage of Total Exports
Grains and oilseeds	86,633	1,669	1.93	646	38.71	45	2.70	20,993	24.23	595	2.83	1,445	6.88
Livestock and poultry	85,520	3,510	4.10	1,245	35.47	358	10.20	2,974	3.48	505	16.98	476	16.01
Section 22 commodities													
Dairy products	43,932	808	1.84	15	1.86	<.05	<.05	324	.74	18	5.55	123	37.96
Cotton	4,627	4	.09	<.05	1.25	.70	17.50	1,856	40.11	67	3.61	50	2.69
Peanuts	1,260	11	.87	4	36.37	<.05	<.05	209	16.59	40	19.14	7	3.35
Sugar	4,574	669	14.63	14	2.09	13	1.94	183	4.00	25	13.66	82	44.81
Sugar-containing products	53,203	1,325	2.49	357	26.94	73	5.51	1,643	3.09	447	27.20	115	7.00
Horticultural													
Vegetables[b]	18,540	1,270	6.85	170	13.39	343	27.00	1,468	7.92	481	32.77	100	6.81
Winter vegetables	1,290	563	43.64	11	1.95	523	92.89	127	9.84	121	95.27	3	2.36
Citrus juices	1,154	482	41.76	1	<.05	66	13.69	203	17.59	79	38.92	<.05	<.05
Other fruits[c]	9,279	2,315	24.95	62	2.68	300	12.96	1,883	20.29	559	29.69	43	2.28
Subtotal	310,012	12,626	4.07	2,525	20.00	1,722	13.64	31,863	10.28	2,937	9.22	2,444	7.67
Other[d]	83,539	14,131	16.91	1,768	12.51	768	5.43	9,536	11.40	1,213	12.72	331	3.47
Total	393,551	26,757	6.80	4,293	16.04	2,490	9.30	41,399	10.52	4,150	10.02	2,775	6.70

Source: U.S. International Trade Commission (USITC 1993).

[a]In million dollars.

[b]Excludes winter vegetables.

[c]Includes citrus other than juices.

[d]Remaining categories (e.g., fish, wood, alcoholic beverages, cut flowers).

dairy exports and provided one-sixth of the U.S. cotton imports. Canada provided almost one-third of the U.S. imports of peanuts and peanut products.

Historically, section 22 quotas on imports of sugar and sugar-containing products were also used to protect U.S. producers and give preferential treatment to selected foreign suppliers. Domestic production of cane and beet sugar has increased since 1980 under the most recent trade restrictions. High domestic sugar prices have also contributed to use of high-fructose corn sweeteners increasing from less than one-fourth of total caloric sweetener consumption in 1979–81 to almost one-half in 1989–91.

The U.S. sugar import quotas were challenged by Australia in 1989 under GATT rules because domestic supply controls were not in effect at that time.[2] To settle the GATT dispute, the import quotas were replaced by a two-tier tariff regime. Under the two-tier tariffs, a limited quantity of imports, known as a tariff-rate quota (TRQ), enters under a low rate ($0.01/lb). Potential additional imports carry an over-quota tariff of more than 80 percent ($0.18/lb).

While in principle the two-tier sugar tariff regime allows access to the U.S. market in response to world market conditions, the over-quota tariffs have been prohibitive and the TRQ and two-tier tariffs have had trade restrictive effects similar to the previous quota system. To protect domestic producers, sugar imports have been reduced from over 3 million metric tons (MMT) in 1980 to less than 2 MMT—just under 15 percent of domestic production—during 1989–91. Mexico provided only a small fraction of U.S. imports of sugar and sugar-containing products. Canada provided over one-fourth of the sugar-containing products that were imported.

A final group of agricultural commodities is composed of horticultural products. The bulk of domestic production is of vegetables for which imports or exports accounts for less than 10 percent of production value. Trade is more important for seasonal winter vegetables. For these commodities, imports were over 40 percent and exports were almost 10 percent of the value of domestic production during 1989–91. Over 90 percent of the imports came from Mexico, and over 90 percent of the exports went to Canada. Trade is also relatively important for citrus and other winter fruits. Citrus imports are primarily frozen concentrated orange juice from Brazil that competes with production in Florida. Citrus exports are mostly fresh products from California, with Canada an important export market. California fruit and vegetable producers and processors have also integrated their operations into Mexico to a greater extent than their Florida counterparts. Thus, the horticultural sector is characterized by divergent commodity, seasonal, and regional interests.

---

the section 22 quotas. Peanut exports arise from a two-tier pricing scheme that allows sales at lower world price levels of U.S. peanuts beyond a quantity produced for the domestic market.

2. Domestic production quotas were assigned in 1993 for the first time since Cuban sugar imports were proscribed after Fidel Castro took power in 1959.

Table 7.2   Number of Farms and Distribution of Production by Value of Farm Sales

| | | Value of Farm Sales | | | | | |
| | | Less than $50,000 | | $50,000 to $500,000 | | More than $500,000 | |
Commodity	Number of Farms	Percentage of Farms	Percentage of Production	Percentage of Farms	Percentage of Production	Percentage of Farms	Percentage of Production
Grains and oilseeds	407,503	61.14	15.08	37.80	74.18	.75	10.73
Livestock and poultry							
Beef cattle excluding feedlots	626,366	89.67	26.53	9.76	44.00	.56	29.45
Beef cattle feedlots	65,888	73.98	2.37	20.98	12.49	5.03	85.14
Hogs	93,256	57.52	9.94	40.64	69.82	1.83	20.24
Poultry and eggs	36,410	17.62	.46	65.36	37.17	12.70	62.36
Section 22 commodities							
Dairy	131,542	28.94	5.57	67.53	64.83	3.51	29.59
Cotton	22,841	32.72	4.04	63.08	71.46	4.19	24.49
Sugar[a]	107,791	83.93	10.86	14.87	49.04	1.19	40.10
Horticultural							
Vegetables and melons	23,375	68.62	4.98	26.35	28.95	5.02	66.06
Fruits and tree nuts	89,369	74.76	9.93	22.21	39.10	3.03	51.26
Other	275,226	84.45	17.22	15.26	58.44	2.72	24.23
Total	1,879,567	72.94	10.84	25.43	50.86	1.62	38.29

Source: U.S. Department of Commerce, Bureau of the Census, *Census of Agriculture* (Washington, D.C.: Government Printing Office, 1987).

[a]Includes sugarcane and sugar beets but also field crops other than grains and oilseeds for which there have not been any section 22 restrictions.

7.1.1   Farm Numbers

Some characteristics of the different production sectors are summarized in table 7.2. Grains and oilseeds were produced on over 400,000 farms and beef cattle on over 625,000 farms and ranches. There were over 130,000 dairy farms, and just over 100,000 farms produced sugar or field crops other than grains and oilseeds. Less than 100,000 farms fattened cattle on feedlots, raised hogs, or produced fruits and tree nuts, respectively, while less than 50,000 farms produced poultry and eggs, cotton, or vegetables and melons.

Of the units counted as farms, almost three-fourths had gross sales of under $50,000 and provided less than full-time employment for a farm operator. This type of farm produced less than 10 percent of the total value of output except in the cases of grains and oilseeds, beef cattle (excluding feedlots), and sugar and other field crops. In contrast, less than 2 percent of all farms had sales of $500,000 and above. The farms in this sales class produced from 40 to 90 percent of the beef cattle on feedlots, poultry and eggs, sugar and other field crops, vegetables and melons, and fruits and tree nuts.

7.1.2   Levels of Support and Protection

There are differences among the sectors in terms of the level of support provided through domestic farm programs and the protection provided by trade policies. Producer subsidy equivalents (PSEs), shown in the first two columns of table 7.3, estimate the percentage of farm income derived from a wide range of policy interventions, including price policies, direct payments, trade barriers, and insurance, credit, tax, and other input and processing subsidies. Annual PSEs have been calculated by the Organisation for Economic Co-operation and Development (OECD) and USDA since the early 1980s. These estimates have been utilized as a basis for comparing agricultural policies among countries during negotiations of the GATT Uruguay Round, the Canada-U.S. FTA, and NAFTA.

The levels of protection provided to various commodities by tariffs and other border policies are also reported in table 7.3. The tariff rates in effect at the beginning of the NAFTA negotiations are shown in the third column. Estimates of the differences between domestic and world prices induced by tariffs and quantitative border restrictions are shown in the fourth column.

The PSEs and protection measures in table 7.3 show that U.S. policy interventions provide high levels of support for some export crops as well as for the commodities protected historically by import quotas. Support for export crops is provided primarily through acreage-reduction-based supply restrictions, direct payments to producers that supplement market returns, and floor prices ("loan rates") at which farmers can place their output in storage and receive a loan from the government. Wheat producers also benefit particularly from export subsidies. The PSEs have been higher for wheat, barley, and rice than for corn, oats, sorghum, and soybeans. Tariff levels are relatively low for all of the grains, reflecting the policies of domestic market prices near world levels and

Table 7.3 **Support and Protection Levels among Commodities**

Commodity	Producer Subsidy Equivalents (% of domestic prices) 1982–91	1991	Border Protection (% of international prices) 1991 Tariffs[a]	Tariff Equivalents[b]
Grains and oilseeds				
Barley	36	50.8	<2.5	3.0
Corn	28	16.8	0.6	2.0
Oats	10	14.9	0.0	0.0
Rice	47	39.7	6.5	8.0
Sorghum	31	18.4	7.0	7.0
Wheat	40	53.6	3.7	6.0
Durum wheat	–	–	4.1	6.0
Soybeans	8	16.5	0.0	0.0
Meal	–	–	<5.0	<5.0
Oil	–	–	22.5	22.5
Other edible oils	–	–	18.5	18.5
Livestock and poultry				
Beef and veal	8	7.0	<5.0	31.1
Pork	6	5.9	<5.0	2.0
Poultry	9	7.3	<15.0	16.3
Section 22 commodities				
Dairy	49	40.5		
Butter	–	–	<15.0	95.7
Cheese	–	–	<20.0	69.5
Nonfat dry milk	–	–	<5.6	83.1
Cotton	–	–	<5.0	26.0
Peanuts	–	–		
Shelled	–	–	16.1	186.1
Unshelled	–	–	5.8	123.1
Peanut butter	–	–	<5.0	126.0
Sugar	60	52.5	TRQ[c]	83.7
Sugar-containing products	–	–	Various	120.3
Horticultural				
Orange juice (frozen concentrate)	–	–	25.0–30.0	25.0–30.0
Fruits and vegetables	–	–		
Cucumbers	–	–	20.0–30.0	20.0–30.0
Melons	–	–	10.0–20.0	10.0–20.0
Onions	–	–	5.0–10.0	5.0–10.0
Peppers	–	–	5.0–10.0	5.0–10.0
Tomatoes	–	–	5.0–10.0	5.0–10.0

Sources: PSEs are from USDA (1994); 1991 tariffs are from USDA (1992a); estimates of tariff equivalents of border protection are from Sanderson (1994) except for dairy products, cotton, and shelled and unshelled peanuts, which are from USDA (1992b).

Note: (–) Not available.

[a]Many tariffs are expressed at fixed rates, so ad valorem estimates vary with commodity prices.

[b]Estimated differences between domestic and world prices induced by various border restrictions.

[c]Tariff-rate quota (limited imports at low duty and prohibitive tariff for additional quantities).

support through direct payments.

For the import-quota or TRQ-protected commodities dairy, peanuts, and sugar, large distortions favoring domestic producers have been created by the import restrictions, as shown by the estimated tariff equivalents of these barriers. Cotton producers, while protected by section 22 quotas, also receive direct payments, and U.S. prices are usually near world levels.

In contrast to the section 22 commodities or the principal grains and oilseeds, fruits and vegetables have not been subject to import quotas, and producers have received few direct support payments (PSEs are not available for fruits and vegetables). In general, producers of fruits and vegetables receive relatively low levels of protection from tariffs, but there are a few exceptions. The support and protection levels have also been relatively low for livestock and poultry. The estimated tariff equivalent for beef (31.1 percent) suggests that meat import restrictions have had more effect than indicated by the estimated PSEs but have been less severe than for the section 22 commodities.

The policy interventions in U.S. agriculture and the levels of support and protection provided to different commodities are the cumulative result of convoluted economic and political forces. In an empirical assessment, Gardner (1987), for example, found that support (measured similarly to the PSEs by the producer price gains resulting from farm programs) increased systematically across commodities when elasticities of supply and demand were low, a larger share of output was imported or exported, and the lagged level of total farm income declined relative to nonfarm income. Given these determinants of support, factors that facilitated political organization by a sector also were significant. There was a nonlinear relationship between the number of producers of a commodity and the level of support obtained, with less support of commodities for which there were either fewer or greater numbers of producers. Support also increased with the size of the average unit and with the geographic concentration of production and stability of its location over time.

Observations based on tables 7.1–7.3 corroborate several of Gardner's hypotheses and suggest a few others (see also Swinnen and van der Zee 1993, and the references therein). Most commodities produced domestically are protected from import competition. Among the exported commodities, levels of support are positively correlated with the degree of export dependence, although the direction of causality remains open to question. The high levels of support obtained by wheat and barley producers may be explained by the lack of alternative production opportunities (inelastic supply) in the dryer parts of the midwestern grain belt where these commodities are produced. Grains generally receive more support than oilseeds even though they are often grown on the same farms. This is a historical consequence of the origins of the support programs in the Depression-era policies of the New Deal when soybeans were not grown as a livestock feed on a commercial basis.

Among the factors affecting the relative demands for support and protection, the levels of intervention are higher for the moderate number of farms producing grains or dairy than for either the large number of farms producing beef cattle or the relatively small number producing cattle on feedlots, poultry and eggs, cotton, or vegetables and melons. The extent of processing associated with the products from a sector also might be hypothesized to be related to the levels of support and protection. But dairy, sugar, and peanuts obtain high levels of protection and soybeans and beef cattle relatively low levels of support even though the products from each of these sectors requires substantial processing.

7.2   Interest Group Approaches to the Negotiations

Agricultural interests are represented both by general-membership organizations and by numerous commodity-based associations. The approaches of these various groups to the NAFTA negotiations were affected by specific aspects of bilateral trade with Mexico and Canada and the levels of support and protection received by producers, described above, and by their perceptions of NAFTA's relationship to other bilateral and multilateral trade agreements. A chronology of relevant events is shown in table 7.4.

When the Mexico-U.S. free trade negotiations were jointly announced, Mexico's President Carlos Salinas de Gortari and President Bush articulated a

Table 7.4   **Chronology of NAFTA**

Early 1980s	Free trade agreements with Israel, Canada, and Mexico contemplated by the Reagan administration
May 1985	Israel-U.S. Free Trade Agreement approved by Congress
September 1986	Ministerial declaration launched the Uruguay Round GATT negotiations
September 1988	Canada-U.S. Free Trade Agreement approved by Congress
April 1989	Midterm agreement reached for Uruguay Round negotiations on agriculture
June 1990	President Bush and President Salinas issued a joint statement in support of negotiating a bilateral free trade agreement
May 1991	Canada officially joined the trade negotiations with Mexico and the United States
June 1991	NAFTA negotiations initiated
August 1992	NAFTA negotiations concluded
September 1992	President Bush announced to Congress his intent to sign the agreement
October 1992	Presidential candidate Clinton announced his support for NAFTA if supplemental (side) agreements were negotiated to address issues of the environment, labor, and import surges
December 1992	Leaders of Canada, Mexico, and the United States signed NAFTA in their respective capitals
March 1993	Negotiations on side-agreements initiated
August 1993	Negotiations on side-agreements concluded
September 1993	President Clinton signed the side-agreements and began an intense campaign for passage of the implementing legislation
November 1993	NAFTA legislation approved by Congress
December 1993	Uruguay Round GATT negotiations concluded
January 1994	NAFTA went into effect

broad mandate for reducing trade barriers and supporting Mexican reforms in agriculture and other sectors. In particular, bilateral trade had been affected by the high levels of protection that Mexican agriculture had received in the mid-1980s: PSEs had averaged 47.6 percent among 14 major commodities (USDA 1994). Under reforms initiated by the administration of President Salinas, the average Mexican PSE had declined to 19.9 percent by 1990. Concurrently, the value of U.S. agricultural exports to Mexico increased from $1.2 billion to $2.5 billion.

The growth of agricultural exports stimulated commodity group interest in the United States in further development of trade opportunities. Even so, and despite the reforms initiated by the Salinas administration, the high levels of protection traditionally provided to many commodities in both countries created considerable uncertainty about the extent to which agriculture would be included under the mandate for Mexico-U.S. trade liberalization.

The uncertainty about agriculture increased when Canada joined Mexico and the United States in seeking a trilateral agreement. Nontariff agricultural trade barriers had not been addressed in the previous Canada-U.S. FTA (see, e.g., Miner 1993). Import restrictions were retained by Canada to protect its dairy and poultry sectors, which benefited in 1991 from PSEs of 67.0 and 35.0 percent, respectively, and by the United States for dairy, cotton, peanuts, and sugar. Although both the Canadian and the U.S. wheat producers sought agreements to bar unfair domestic and export subsidies, because of differences in their support and marketing systems finding mutually acceptable definitions remained elusive for these highly subsidized and export-dependent competitors. Canada retained import licensing authority for grains unless U.S. PSEs fell below Canadian levels, and little progress was made on mutual commitments to develop rules governing subsidies. Both countries retained the right to reintroduce either quotas or tariffs on grains if "imports increase significantly as a result of a substantial change in either Party's support programs."

There was also uncertainty with respect to NAFTA's agricultural provisions because the negotiations took place against the backdrop of as yet undetermined outcomes of the multilateral GATT negotiations. The United States had originally proposed a comprehensive "zero option" in GATT calling for the elimination of essentially all trade-distorting border measures and domestic support payments by its members. The zero-option proposal had proved untenable by the midterm GATT review in 1988. By the beginning of the NAFTA negotiations, the GATT discussions were focused on more restricted provisions for capping domestic support levels, partial reduction of export subsidies, and tariffication of import quotas, licenses, and other nontariff restrictions on trade. The nontariff restrictions were to be replaced by minimal market access provided by TRQs and high initial over-quota tariff levels, as in the case of U.S. sugar imports, with the over-quota tariffs subject to only modest reductions over time.

Faced with all this uncertainty about likely outcomes, the various agricultural interest groups took active roles in seeking to shape the NAFTA negotiations. They became aligned along two broad positions: those favoring their inclusion under provisions for agricultural trade liberalization and those favoring limits on the scope of the agreement with retention of some of the traditional trade restrictions. The basic positions of a selected subset of the most active agricultural and agriprocessing industry groups are shown in table 7.5.

7.2.1   Proponents of Liberalization

The American Farm Bureau Federation (AFBF) is the largest of the general-membership organizations and is oriented toward competitive markets. At the outset of the NAFTA negotiations, the AFBF commissioned a study of the potential impacts on domestic agriculture of reduced trade barriers with Mexico. This study showed generally positive effects and provided the basis for the AFBF's approach to the negotiations. Although the study was criticized by some farm groups for minimizing the potential impacts on sectors that might face increased import competition, the AFBF concluded it would support comprehensive liberalization that included even the most politically sensitive import-competing commodities. The AFBF sought an active role in the negotiations, based partly on a view that it had not been vocal enough during negotiations for the Canada-U.S. FTA.

Table 7.5   **Selected Agricultural Interest Groups**

Favoring Liberalization	Favoring Limits to the Agreement
American Farm Bureau Federation (AFBF)	National Farmers' Union (NFU)
National Grange	American Corn Growers Association (ACGA)
American Soybean Association	National Association of Wheat Growers
National Corn Growers Association (NCGA)	(NAWG)
U.S. Feed Grains Council	National Peanut Council of America
National Cattlemen's Association (NCA)	Southwest Peanut Growers
National Pork Producers Council	Florida Sugar Cane League
National Milk Producers Federation (NMPF)	U.S. Beet Sugar Association
Agribusiness Council, Inc.	Florida Citrus Mutual
Sweetener Users Association (SUA)	Florida Fruit and Vegetable Association
Food Marketing Institute	Western Growers
	United Food and Commercial Workers, AFL-CIO

Note: Representatives of the 22 groups listed were interviewed about their NAFTA position and activities during August–October 1993. The classification shown is based on the author's judgments from the content of the interviews and does not necessarily represent the legal or otherwise official positions of the groups. Interviewees were selected from a sample of 37 farm groups and 15 processing industry groups with representatives in the Washington, D.C., area. In addition, representatives of Florida Citrus Mutual and the Florida Fruit and Vegetable Association were interviewed at their state offices. The initial sample of groups was identified from the membership of USTR's Agricultural Policy Advisory Committee and 10 agricultural technical advisory committees and from respondents to a survey about NAFTA sent to 300 groups and individuals by the Senate Committee on Agriculture, Nutrition and Forestry.

Many of the grain and oilseed commodity associations joined the AFBF in support for eliminating trade barriers under NAFTA. For these commodities, the 1987–90 export trend was interpreted to imply that reduced protection and increased income growth in Mexico would provide market opportunities. In particular, increased exports of U.S. corn and other feed grains were expected if Mexico further reduced its traditional support programs and trade restrictions. The National Corn Growers Association (NCGA), the largest organization of corn producers and processors (with about 25,000 members), became an active supporter of NAFTA. The NCGA sought maximum opening of the Mexican market. It requested an initial TRQ for corn of 3.5 MMT, which was considered a level "tough for Mexico to grant." The NCGA expected further gains in derived demand for corn from a growing Mexican market for U.S. livestock products.

Livestock producers concurred in anticipating gains from liberalized trade with Mexico. The approach toward the negotiations of the National Cattlemen's Association (NCA) was representative of their efforts. The NCA was interested in expanding foreign market access and cited as a successful precedent the 1988 bilateral agreement to replace Japanese beef quotas with TRQs and declining over-quota tariff levels. Mexico did not have import quotas on beef when the NAFTA negotiations were initiated, but there was uncertainty about continued openness of the border and the levels at which tariffs on livestock products would be set.

The corn growers and cattlemen, among others, were actively engaged in the NAFTA negotiations. The NCGA had extensive discussions of goals and strategy in meetings of their voting delegates, stayed in close contact with the senior negotiators, and kept their supporters in Congress informed about the process. The NCGA was represented on the Grains and Feed Technical Advisory Committee of the United States trade representative (USTR), one of 10 agricultural technical advisory committees (ATACs) established as part of USTR's private sector advisory structure by the Trade Act of 1974.[3] The NCA worked closely with the broader Meat Industry Trade Policy Council and was represented on USTR's Livestock and Livestock Products Technical Advisory Committee, its multicommodity Agricultural Policy Advisory Committee, and its president's Advisory Committee on Trade Policy and Negotiations (ACTPN). Representatives of the NCA concluded that they had ample opportunities to influence the outcome of the negotiations through regular interaction with USDA and USTR and through Congress.

---

3. The presidentially appointed private sector advisory system is arranged in three tiers: the president's Advisory Committee on Trade Policy and Negotiations; seven policy advisory committees (Services, Investment, and Intergovernmental, managed solely by USTR, and Industry, Agriculture, Labor, and Defense, managed jointly with other agencies); and more than 30 technical, sectoral, and functional advisory committees. The 10 agricultural technical advisory committees (ATACs) address cotton, dairy products, fruits and vegetables, grains and feed, livestock and livestock products, oilseed and products, poultry and eggs, processed foods, sweeteners, and tobacco.

Support for an agreement to liberalize agricultural trade also came from representatives of many processing and supply industries. Typical of the industry organizations was the Sweetener Users Association (SUA), sponsored by 16 major food processors. While recognizing that the sweetener users had little influence on the agricultural committees of Congress, an SUA representative and two other user-industry representatives served on USTR's Sweeteners Technical Advisory Committee. Other processing industries were represented on commodity-specific technical advisory committees (oilseeds, dairy, and cotton) and on the separate Processed Foods Technical Advisory Committee.

Representatives of the dairy industry were also marginally among the supporters of eliminating trade barriers with Mexico and Canada. Although protected by import quotas, the dairy industry had initiated a broad lobbying effort to obtain legislative authority for industry-funded export subsidies—called their "self-help" legislation. Industry statements suggested this was viewed as a means to reduce domestic supply and obtain higher domestic prices by exploiting an inelastic domestic demand (Barr 1993). Since Mexico produced few import-competing dairy products and accounted for a large fraction of U.S. dairy exports, as shown in table 7.1, greater market access under NAFTA was consistent with the industry's overall initiative. The industry also believed that it could be competitive in Canada if dairy trade restrictions were eliminated.

Throughout the NAFTA negotiations, a coalition of dairy cooperatives, represented by the National Milk Producers Federation (NMPF), remained noncommittal but not opposed to NAFTA. While supporting expanded export opportunities, the NMPF argued against tariffication of U.S. section 22 dairy quotas, especially if Canada maintained its import barriers. The NMPF was represented on the Dairy Technical Advisory Committee and worked closely with USDA and USTR at the staff and policy levels to develop strong rules of origin in the event U.S. quotas for Mexico were eliminated on a bilateral basis. Representatives of NMPF also "wrote the obligatory letters" and participated in congressional hearings. Otherwise, they spent "almost no time on the Hill" because they felt the congressional agricultural committees were less interested in dairy issues than issues concerning peanuts and sugar.

7.2.2 Proponents of Limits on the Agreement

Among the groups that were opposed to the NAFTA negotiations or sought limits on the scope of any agreement, the National Farmers Union (NFU), a general organization with membership concentrated in the upper midwestern states, and several other small general-membership organizations had long argued for policies to raise prices for farm products through restrictive supply management. Because of NFU's support of supply management rather than export-based market expansion, its representatives viewed themselves as "not being allowed at the table" and, likewise, as not having been interested in negotiating details of a trade agreement. The NFU, which claims to represent the traditional family farmer against agribusiness interests, sought intensive congressional involvement, arguing that the Congress would "give the left out entities a chance to have their say."

The NFU view of the negotiations was shared by the American Corn Growers Association (ACGA). The ACGA, with 10,000 members, also seeks higher domestic corn prices through restrictive supply management. It traced its origins to a split with the NCGA over endorsing lower corn loan rates in 1985 as a means to increase international competitiveness.[4] The ACGA opposed NAFTA and was not interested in participating in the negotiations for specific provisions.

Wheat producers also took a contentious approach toward NAFTA. They raised concerns that U.S. competitiveness was being adversely affected by nontransparency of the pricing policies of the Canadian Wheat Board—the exclusive agent for Canadian wheat exports—and by eastbound grain transportation subsidies in Canada. These were among the issues left unresolved under the Canada-U.S. FTA. The U.S. producers argued that increased Canadian exports of wheat into the United States and Mexico after 1988 (capturing of a large share of the Mexican wheat market) were the result of Canadian export subsidies. The Canadian producers counterargued that their export shipments resulted from the price differentials and U.S. shipment patterns resulting from the United States' own wheat export enhancement (subsidy) program.

To address their concerns, the National Association of Wheat Growers (NAWG) sought elimination of Canadian subsidies and imposition of import restrictions (wheat had been subject to section 22 quotas that were allowed to lapse in 1974 when world wheat prices and U.S. exports rose sharply). The wheat producers, unlike the NFU and ACGA, actively engaged in the NAFTA negotiating process to press their case. The NAWG kept its members "highly informed" of its objectives, participated in hearings of the agricultural committees of Congress, worked through contacts at USDA and USTR, and brought what its representatives termed "collaborative input from Congress" to bear on the negotiators. A NAWG representative served on USTR's Grains and Feed Technical Advisory Committee but viewed the committee as having little influence.

Limits on the access to U.S. markets provided by NAFTA were also sought by representatives of the cane and beet sugar industries and the commodities protected by import quotas. These sectors shared two concerns at the outset of the negotiations: that elimination of the trade restrictions with Mexico would create potential competition from Mexican producers, and that it would set a precedent for further weakening of protective quota restrictions either in subse-

---

4. With the high value of the U.S. dollar in the mid-1980s, world corn prices were resting on the U.S. loan rate and U.S. exports had declined markedly. Lowering the loan rate under these circumstances lowered domestic market prices, to which the ACGA objected, but also reduced the quantities going into storage and increased exports.

quent negotiations or by subjecting the remaining restrictions to legal challenge (Gillon 1992).

With their mutual concerns, a strong coalition might be expected to have developed among the protected sectors. However, the views of the dairy industry were tempered by its recognition of the limited competition and potential export opportunities that NAFTA might create, as described above. Cotton producers and processors, represented by the National Cotton Council of America (NCCA), also tempered their position. They recognized that expanded export opportunities might arise if a North American free trade area for textiles and apparel was associated with strong rules of origin for the fiber content of the final products—industry perceptions that mirrored the argument made against the trade diversionary effects of such rules of origin by Krueger (1993).

The moderated views of the dairy and cotton producers (assuming there were strong rules of origin) left producers of peanuts and sugar as the most strident proponents of limits on NAFTA's market access provisions. Although Mexico was a net peanut importer, the U.S. producers expressed intense opposition to possible import competition, partly on the basis of ostensible concern about illegal transshipments through Mexico of non-NAFTA peanuts from the Caribbean and elsewhere if quotas were removed on a bilateral basis. The peanut producers, represented primarily by nine state organizations, pressed their case through USTR's Oilseed and Products Technical Advisory Committee and through Congress. The producers argued that their concerns were exacerbated because consideration of NAFTA came after several years of what they termed "extreme uncertainty" about the effects a GATT agreement could have on the peanut support program by increasing foreign access to their domestic market.

The sugar sector's similar view of liberalized trade under NAFTA as a threat to their interests came in response to an initial Mexican request for access to the U.S. market of a sugar TRQ of 1.5 MMT—more than the combined TRQs of all other countries. The U.S. producers claimed they had been assured by the Bush administration that the traditional pattern of trade—with Mexico a net importer of sugar—would not be disrupted by NAFTA. In this context, they viewed the Mexican access request as a "shot out of the barrel." This volume of exports was considered possible if Mexican production and refining were modernized and if a shift in relative prices between corn and sugar resulted in the use of corn sweeteners in the Mexican soft drink industry.

The sugar producers took a strong stand in defense of their protected domestic market during the NAFTA negotiations. They opposed any trade liberalization that would put pressure on the U.S. sugar support program. Illustrative of their potent avenues of influence was the appointment to USTR's Agricultural Policy Advisory Committee of the executive vice-president of the Florida Sugar Cane League, representing one of the major sugar-producing states. This appointment came after intensive pressure on the Bush administration by members of Congress.

Representatives of some commodities in the horticultural sector also expressed strong reservations about trade liberalization with Mexico. The USTR's Fruits and Vegetables Technical Advisory Committee became a forum for discussing the positions of the diverse interest groups within this sector. An early statement in September 1990 cited concerns about increased import competition and called for adequate transition periods for tariff reductions (Fruits and Vegetables Agricultural Technical Advisory Committee 1990). It noted that price-based tariff snapbacks to protect Canadian farmers against import surges that depressed domestic prices had been included in the Canada-U.S. FTA and called for similar provisions in NAFTA to protect U.S. farmers. Florida vegetable producers also sought exemptions from the agreement until disparities in environmental and labor conditions were eliminated, a stance not supported by the producers and processors in California.

Florida citrus producers, represented on USTR's Processed Foods Technical Advisory Committee, were one of the most active groups to oppose NAFTA, arguing they would be "one of the losers" from an agreement with Mexico. The Florida citrus producers initially proposed that orange juice be excluded from the agreement for 20 years. Their proposal would have maintained existing protection for the productive life of the extensive new plantings that took place in southern Florida after severe freezes in the 1980s.

With the import-competing Florida producers of citrus and other winter fruits and vegetables joining the sugar sector in opposition to NAFTA, a strong coalition emerged to press the case of Florida agriculture. These interests developed a unified position with other agricultural groups. The Florida Farm Bureau and the Florida Cattlemen's Association joined the coalition, and both eventually broke ranks with their national organizations' support for NAFTA. The state commissioner of agriculture became an active proponent of the Florida concerns, and the producers received endorsements from the state legislature and elsewhere. Together, the agricultural groups exerted a powerful influence on Florida's large congressional delegation, whose cooperation they judged to be "superb."

7.2.3   Measuring the Activity Levels

Both proponents of liberalization of agricultural trade and proponents of limits on the scope of the agreement were actively engaged in asserting their positions during the NAFTA negotiations. Avenues for influence ranged from individual contacts with USDA and USTR at the staff and policy levels, to participation in USTR's 10 ATACs and its Agricultural Policy Advisory Committee, to intervention by members of the agricultural committees of Congress or other individual members, to direct interactions with the president. Specific groups were often engaged in the process through a variety of channels, but a reasonable generalization is that groups that found the broad outline of the negotiations amenable to their interests were able to work closely with the negotiators and their technical staffs, while groups opposed to the general direction of the negotiations sought redress through Congress.

One quantitative indicator of the levels of interest in NAFTA among the various agricultural sectors comes from the information about the agreement provided by publications aimed at their different constituents. A summary of articles about NAFTA in 30 general and commodity-specific agricultural magazines is presented in table 7.6. The sample period covers the original negotiations, the change in administration after the 1992 elections, and the initial discussions of the side-agreements negotiated by the Clinton administration.

Using the average number of articles about NAFTA per issue of a magazine as a measure of intensity of attention, the highest average was found for the magazines in the sugar sector (1.08), followed by grains and oilseeds (0.80), and horticulture (0.48). General farm magazines and the magazines in the dairy and peanut sectors show somewhat lower averages (<0.30), and the lowest average (0.11) was found for livestock and poultry publications.

Based on a qualitative content assessment, the articles were also classified

Table 7.6   **Coverage of NAFTA during the Negotiations: Selected Sample of Farm Magazines**

	Number of:				Type of Article			
			Articles on	Articles per		Factual	Analysis or Opinion	
Category	Magazines	Issues	NAFTA	Issue	News		Supportive	Opposed
General	7	193	52	0.27	16	19	10	7
Grains and oilseeds	3	108	87	0.80	38	12	27	10
Livestock and poultry	6	184	21	0.11	4	2	14	1
Dairy	2	49	14	0.28	8	3	3	0
Peanuts	3	56	15	0.27	7	3	0	5
Sugar	2	26	28	1.08	9	6	1	12
Horticulture	7	185	88	0.48	21	16	26	25
Total	30	801	305		103	61	81	60

Note: Selection was based on a search at the National Agricultural Library and the Carroll M. Newman Library at Virginia Polytechnic Institute and State University. The subset of magazines included in the review are (1) general: *Farm Journal, Kiplinger's Agricultural Letters, Ohio Farmer, Progressive Farmer, Southeast Farm Press, Successful Farmer, Top Producer;* (2) grains and oilseeds: *Feedstuffs, Soybean Digest, Wheat Grower;* (3) livestock and poultry: *Drover's Journal, Inside Beef Today, Meat and Poultry, Pigs Monthly, Sheep Breeder Highlights, World Poultry;* (4) dairy: *Dairymen's Digest, Hoard's Dairymen;* (5) peanuts: *Peanut Farmer, Peanut Grower, Virginia-Carolina Peanut News;* (6) sugar: *Cane Press, Sugar Beet Grower;* (7) horticulture: *American Fruit Grower, American Vegetable Grower, California Grower, California Tomato Grower, Citrus and Vegetable Magazine, Spudletter, Virginia Fruit.* The sample period is generally August 1990 to May 1993, but in 11 cases a somewhat shorter sample was dictated by availability.

as being either reports of news or presentations of analysis or opinion. The latter articles were divided among those that presented factual material without either explicit support or opposition to the agreement, those that were supportive of the agreement, and those in which opposition was expressed. Magazines in the sugar sector not only showed the highest intensity level but the articles were primarily expressions of opposition. Articles in the grains and oilseeds and horticulture magazines were split more evenly among news reports, analysis, and differing opinions. Largely factual coverage of NAFTA was presented in the general farm magazines, while articles in the small sample of dairy and peanut magazines were evenly divided between news and analysis or opinion, with a generally supportive position in the dairy magazines and opposition in the peanut magazines.

A second quantitative measure of the involvement of the various interest groups in the NAFTA negotiations is provided by their testimony before congressional committees. There were 13 hearings at which agricultural groups were represented during the negotiations for the initial-agreement and the subsequent side-agreements (three each by committees or subcommittees on agriculture, energy, and commerce, and ways and means, and one each by foreign affairs, public works, small business, and education and labor).

Testimony at the various hearings reflected the diverse views of the general-membership and commodity-specific agricultural groups. Of 20 appearances by general-membership organizations, the AFBF and NFU were represented three times each, with remaining testimonies from a variety of other groups. Supporters of trade liberalization from the grains and oilseeds sector testified 12 times, the NAWG had three opportunities to raise its concerns about Canadian policies, and the ACGA testified once against the agreement. Livestock and poultry producers testified four times in support of the agreement. Dairy and cotton groups were also represented four times each, and peanut interests testified two times. Sugar producers testified eight times, while the industrial sweetener users testified only once. The horticultural sector was represented in 44 testimonies. The Florida coalition was represented six times by vegetable groups, four times by the state commissioner of agriculture, and twice by the citrus association. California and other western and Mexican horticultural groups were represented 26 times in the hearings.

A third basis for assessing the levels of activity among the various agricultural interest groups comes from informal observations of the negotiators and commodity group representatives. One key negotiator indicated that despite the efforts of the AFBF and other supporters, there was not a forceful lobby for comprehensive trade liberalization during the negotiations. Negotiators on both sides frequently cited keeping defensive domestic interests "on board" as their most difficult task, and many participants in the process acknowledged that established interests that feared losses were better organized than the potential beneficiaries of greater international trade. As one observer put it, "there was no *white* corn growers association ready to claim the benefits of expanded export opportunities into Mexico," or, as several participants noted, nothing motivated a commodity group like "getting its ox gored."

7.3   Agricultural Provisions of NAFTA

Against the backdrop of the various producer interests, high-level negotiators for Mexico and the United States agreed in February 1992 that all agricultural products would be included in the long-run provisions for trade liberalization. The U.S. agricultural groups may have exerted some influence on this decision, but informally the U.S. negotiators attributed it largely to the willingness of Mexico to include its politically sensitive corn sector, leaving little room for other exclusions. Canada continued to object to full coverage of the agricultural provisions, and the U.S. farm groups and others favoring liberalized trade were unable to exert sufficient influence for their negotiators to extract Canadian concessions. Instead, the negotiators agreed that pending modification by a GATT agreement, the Canada-U.S. FTA was to remain in effect for bilateral Canada-U.S. agricultural trade and a similar bilateral agreement on agricultural tariffs and market access would be developed between Mexico and Canada.

Agreements on the provisions of NAFTA were announced by the negotiating parties in August 1992. For Mexico and the United States, the agricultural tariff and market access provisions called for all quotas and licenses to be converted to TRQs upon enactment. For imports above the TRQs, over-quota tariffs were set to provide initial protection equivalent to the previous nontariff measures. The over-quota tariffs were to be completely phased out over adjustment periods of 10 or, in some cases, 15 years. Almost 21 percent of the value of pre-NAFTA trade received this type of adjustment mechanism. An additional 23 percent of the value of pre-NAFTA trade was subject to straightforward phasing out of tariffs over 5 to 15 years, while about 56 percent of the value of bilateral trade occurring under the pre-NAFTA restrictions already was, or was scheduled under NAFTA to immediately become, duty free.

In addition to its market access and tariff provisions, NAFTA addressed issues concerning grades and standards and sanitary and phytosanitary regulations related to human, animal, and plant health. Trade restrictions arising in these areas had traditionally been problematic, and the agreement enunciated principles intended to reduce these sources of friction. The principles included that grades and standards be applied on a nondiscriminatory basis. Each country also retained the right to maintain its own health and safety standards as long as they were "scientifically based and administered in a forthright and expeditious manner." Detailed dispute settlement procedures were established in an effort to provide a forum for resolution of conflicts among the parties.

While placing no restrictions on domestic support levels, the long-run NAFTA provisions for agriculture accomplished on a bilateral basis the basic objective with respect to trade barriers of the initial U.S. zero-option GATT proposal. This was a notable achievement in comparison to previous bilateral efforts to liberalize trade of agricultural products, which had not addressed quantitative restrictions, or the then-pending Uruguay Round GATT negotiations, in which tariffication of quotas and licenses was being considered with only minimal requirements for market access and reduction of the levels of over-quota tariffs over time. The NAFTA result led Hufbauer and Schott (1993) to conclude, for example, that there was "laudable progress in the liberalization of farm trade barriers." In their widely cited evaluation, they assigned an "A" grade to the outcomes of the negotiations for agriculture, one of the four highest grades assigned among 18 aspects of the agreement. Similarly, a key U.S. agricultural negotiator expressed the exuberant view that NAFTA would create "the freest trade in agricultural products between any two countries." Other anecdotal evidence also supports a sense of accomplishment among the negotiators.

One cannot be as sanguine about the short-run NAFTA provisions for agriculture. For the commodities protected by import quotas or licenses, market access under the initial TRQs was based on 1989–91 trade levels. Quantities receiving market access under the TRQs were scheduled to increase at only a 3 percent annual compound rate. Over-quota tariffs provided high levels of protection against additional imports in the short and medium run. Proposed initial Mexican over-quota tariffs were 215 percent for corn and 260 percent for chicken, for example, while proposed U.S. over-quota tariffs were 70 percent for cheeses and 123 percent for shelled peanuts. Corn, dry edible beans, milk powder, and peanuts were considered particularly sensitive commodities and received 15-year adjustment periods for phase-out of the over-quota tariffs.

More complex protective TRQ transition mechanisms were negotiated for sugar. Mexico agreed to raise its external sugar tariff to the U.S. over-quota level by the seventh year of the agreement. Mexican access to the U.S. sugar market was restricted by a TRQ of 25,000 metric tons during this period, with the over-quota tariff between Mexico and the United States phased out over 15 years. Mexico gained increased low-duty access to the U.S. market after seven years if it became a surplus sugar region based on domestic production and consumption, with unlimited access for its surpluses if it became a surplus producer for two consecutive years. The negotiators did not address the question of whether the United States would maintain its aggregate global TRQ for sugar, in which case any Mexican surpluses would divert trade from other foreign suppliers, or whether U.S. commitments to other countries would be honored, in which case the Mexican surpluses would put downward pressure on U.S. production and prices.

A complex TRQ was also negotiated for frozen concentrated orange juice, which had been subject previously only to tariff barriers. The within-quota imports were assessed a tariff of one-half the most-favored-nation (MFN) level. The over-quota tariffs were set initially at MFN rates, then declined linearly by 15 percent during the first six years, remained constant for four years, and were phased out over an additional five years.

Two additional adjustment mechanisms were included in the negotiated agreement to address other concerns of the U.S. producers of horticultural products. First, tariffs on cucumbers, asparagus, broccoli, melons, dried onions, and garlic were phased out over 15 years instead of 10 years. Second, a mechanism named a special safeguard was applied to seasonal U.S. imports of tomatoes, peppers, onions, eggplants, squash, and watermelons. The special safeguard commodities were to have TRQs with 10-year periods of adjustment, but the over-quota tariffs were held at MFN levels during the adjustment period, then eliminated in one step at the end.

A final adjustment mechanism was provided by the emergency action provisions of the agreement. During the transition periods, a tariff reduction could be suspended and the MFN tariff rate reestablished for up to four years if imports were found to have become, or to threaten to become, a substantial cause of serious injury to a domestic industry. The investigating authority for emergency action decisions for the United States was the International Trade Commission (ITC). Emergency actions were limited to a single application for any commodity during the transition period. After the transition period had expired, such actions could only be applied with the consent of, and compensation to, the other party.

From these brief descriptions of the transition mechanisms for agricultural trade, the influence of various producer groups on the negotiations is evident. Within the framework of long-run liberalization of trade with Mexico, likely gainers among U.S. producers confronted the lengthy adjustment mechanisms included to protect Mexican farmers. Import-competing U.S. commodities were provided with similar adjustment protection. Given these provisions, the end-constraint of complete tariff elimination is crucial to the assertion that NAFTA accomplished long-run bilateral trade liberalization for agriculture.

7.4   Estimated Effects of the Agricultural Provisions

Several quantitative estimates have been made of the long-run effects of NAFTA on Mexico-U.S. agricultural trade. The range of these estimates is illustrated in table 7.7. The results from a model developed by Grennes and Krissoff (1993) with support from USDA are compared to composite assessments underlying the preliminary (September 1992) and revised (March 1993) reports from the secretary of agriculture's Office of Economics. The latter assessments were frequently used by the Bush and Clinton administrations in congressional testimony and elsewhere.

Grennes and Krissoff developed a 29-commodity, three-region (Mexico, United States, and rest of world) partial equilibrium model using the Armington assumption that commodities from different regions are close but im-

Table 7.7   **Estimates of NAFTA's Long-Run Effects on Mexico-U.S. Agricultural Trade (million dollars)**

Commodity	Static Model (Grennes-Krissoff)		Composite Estimates (USDA)	
	U.S. Imports	U.S. Exports	U.S. Imports	U.S. Exports
Grains and oilseeds	2	430	0	–
Corn	0	219	0	280
Other coarse grains	0	123	0	–
Wheat	0	2	0	40
Soybeans (includes meal and oil)	0	34	0	220
Other oilseeds (includes meal and oil)	2	48	0	–
Livestock and poultry	56	48	293	1,508
Cattle	56	18	266	879
Beef	0	6	2	139
Pork	0	9	–	440
Poultry	0	15	–	50
Section 22 commodities	–	–	–	–
Dairy	0	2	–	138
Cotton	0	1	–	–
Peanuts	–	–	–	1
Sugar	0	0	–	–
Horticultural	0	0	198	–
Orange juice (frozen concentrate)	45	0	22	–
Fruits and vegetables	58	0	176	163
Melons	11	0	28	–
Cucumbers	9	0	9	–
Onions	7	0	18	–
Peppers	5	0	13	–
Tomatoes	26	0	17	–
Other	–	–	91	–
Other Products	3	3	202	273
Total	164	485	693	2,623

Sources: Grennes and Krissoff (1993); USDA (1993); private communication with the authors and USDA's Office of Economics.

Note: (–) Not available.

perfect substitutes. An equilibrium solution estimated under the assumption that agricultural trade barriers between Mexico and the United States were eliminated was compared to the equilibrium solution obtained incorporating price differentials equivalent to the tariffs and nontariff barriers in 1988. Thus, Grennes and Krissoff estimated the long-run impact of NAFTA on annual trade flows with technology and national incomes implicitly held constant.

Consistent with the basic comparative advantages reflected in the pre-NAFTA trade flows, the Grennes-Krissoff model showed an increase in U.S.

grain, oilseed, and livestock exports to Mexico under NAFTA, while Mexico increased its exports of horticultural products and live cattle. Agricultural exports from the United States to Mexico increased by $485 million annually and agricultural imports from Mexico by $164 million. Grennes and Krissoff pointed out that appreciation of the U.S. dollar relative to the Mexican peso could reverse the estimated net trade effects, and Grennes (1993) noted that the discounted value of the gains from trade were reduced substantially by the long transition periods involved.

In terms of adjustments within each country, the production and price of corn in Mexico were estimated to decline by 7.3 and 15.9 percent, respectively, in the Grennes-Krissoff model, with proportional impacts on other coarse grains. The impacts on U.S. grain and oilseed production and prices were positive but negligible. Effects on the livestock sector were also relatively larger in Mexico than in the United States. Grennes and Krissoff did not model a shift from sugar to corn sweeteners in the Mexican soft drink industry; thus, they found essentially no change in Mexico-U.S. sugar trade. For the horticultural products included in their model, Mexican production expanded while U.S. production and prices fell. No horticultural product experienced a production or price decrease of more than 2 percent.

The results from the Grennes-Krissoff model suggest moderate overall benefits of NAFTA for U.S. agricultural producers. The reports by USDA's Office of Economics asserted a more positive view of NAFTA's potential beneficial impacts. The analysis for these reports was based on a variety of USDA model outcomes and analysts' judgments. It also incorporated estimated demand effects resulting from a projected increase in annual economic growth in Mexico of 0.5 percent of GDP due to NAFTA.

The final Office of Economics report concluded that U.S. agricultural exports to Mexico were likely to be more than $2.5 billion higher annually with NAFTA by the end of the 15-year adjustment period—an increase five times the level estimated by Grennes and Krissoff—while imports of agricultural products from Mexico would increase by $500 to $600 million. The difference between the export estimates by the Office of Economics and Grennes-Krissoff is attributable mostly to greater exports of income-responsive livestock and poultry ($1,508 million compared to $48 million), with somewhat greater exports of grains and oilseeds, dairy products, and fruits and vegetables. The Office of Economics estimated greater U.S. imports of cattle, horticultural commodities, and other products.

Among the commodities protected by U.S. import quotas, the Office of Economics concluded that exports of milk powder to Mexico were expected "to grow by about 20,000 metric tons by the end of the 15-year transition period," while Mexican exports of dairy products to the United States were unlikely to increase. The Office of Economics concluded that U.S. exports of both raw cotton and the cotton equivalent of textiles and apparel would increase under

NAFTA, and that the United States would "enhance its role as a major supplier of peanuts to Mexico," with"little reason to expect Mexico to become a significant supplier of peanuts."

The reports by the Office of Economics also downplayed the possibility of adverse impacts of NAFTA on domestic producers of sugar and winter fruits and vegetables. Specific estimates of the value of increased imports were not published, but the final report concluded for sugar that it was "uncertain to what extent Mexico might achieve a net production surplus" and that "any net production surplus would likely develop gradually because of . . . the constraints to switching to corn sweeteners in the Mexican soft drink industry." For winter fruits and vegetables, the Office of Economics concluded that any price effects would be moderated by the 10- and 15-year adjustment periods and the special safeguards. The potential increased competition for citrus was acknowledged with the qualifier that the effects on the U.S. industry were "expected to be small" (U.S. imports "about 3–4 percent higher with NAFTA" and U.S. prices "slightly lower").

7.5 Interest Group Assessments of the Agreement

The USTR's Agricultural Policy Advisory Committee (1992) and 10 ATACs (1992) completed their legislatively mandated assessments of NAFTA in September 1992. The Agricultural Policy Advisory Committee generally reflected the position of the AFBF, concluding that it "believes that the proposed NAFTA provides long-term net export growth opportunities for U.S. agriculture and is in the economic interest of the United States."

The commodity groups that had supported bilateral trade liberalization under the agreement were also mostly satisfied with the results of the negotiations. In their ATAC report, the feed grain representatives stated that their market access objectives "had been met." The oilseed producers and processors noted that the agreement "will afford the U.S. industry with a comparative advantage in the Mexican market over imports from competing suppliers in South America, Europe and elsewhere." Livestock (and poultry and egg) producers concluded that the negotiations were generally successful but called attention to the "glaring differences in state and national veterinary service infrastructure." They noted the need for "animal health programs to be in place in Mexico that will protect the livestock industries of both countries." Subsequently, the livestock producers expressed renewed concerns when Mexico imposed new tariffs of 15 to 25 percent on livestock and meat products in November 1992. The NCA saw NAFTA as an opportunity to remove these tariffs and the threat of future tariffs.

Support for the negotiated agricultural provisions of NAFTA was also expressed by many food-processing industries. Representatives of the industrial sweetener users expressed appreciation for "the manner in which the trade negotiators have endeavored to keep us informed of the details of these complex negotiations" and strongly supported the agreement. The Processed Foods Technical Advisory Committee (except citrus) also supported the agreement but pointed out that its acceptance of tariffication of section 22 quotas under NAFTA was "based solely on the status of production/consumption considerations in the three countries." Similarly, the Dairy Technical Advisory Committee, while noting that the dairy sector opposed tariffication of section 22 quotas, concluded that the TRQs and rules-of-origin provisions were "sufficient to prevent disruptive levels of dairy imports" and that U.S. dairy producers would benefit if they were able to take advantage of the export opportunities NAFTA created.

In contrast to these expressions of support for NAFTA (even with technical reservations), many of the agricultural groups that had sought limits on the agreement were not satisfied with the negotiated outcomes. The NFU continued to express broad opposition to the agreement, and wheat producers expressed dissatisfaction that their concerns about Canadian Wheat Board pricing and grain transportation subsidies were not addressed. The NAWG acknowledged that there had been a lot of access to the negotiating process but concluded that "whether you get what you want is another question." Their ATAC representative viewed the Republican administration as unresponsive. Foreshadowing the bargaining that would occur during the congressional debate to follow, he recommended that the "important matters (concerning Canada) be addressed in the implementing legislation."

The import-quota-protected sectors other than dairy also continued to express opposition to NAFTA. Cotton producers noted their opposition to elimination of section 22 quotas and argued that there were "no reliable estimates of how traditional cropping patterns will be affected by provisions of the NAFTA." Cotton processors, in contrast, endorsed the agreement but not "expansion of NAFTA to include other countries."

Peanut producers and shellers remained more unified in their opposition to the agreement. They called attention to Canada's exclusion of "sensitive products" and concluded that "the U.S. government should have insisted on the same provisions for U.S. Section 22 commodities." The Washington representative of many of the state peanut organizations faulted the U.S. negotiators for not attaining this outcome but gave credit to Congressman de la Garza, chairman of the House Committee on Agriculture, for "taking care" of peanut concerns for tough rules of origin "as late as the last day of the negotiations."

Sugar producers also remained unified in their opposition to the outcome of the NAFTA negotiations. They accused the administration of being out to "get sugar" and objected that the negotiations proceeded "in great haste and unprecedented secrecy." Twisting the effects of high domestic sugar prices to their own ends, their representatives argued that the sugar sector had gone through a difficult rationalization to, as they put it, "modernize the domestic industry." They argued that it would be "unfair" for U.S. producers to bear the burden of adjustment if lower Mexican corn prices and higher sugar prices resulted in similar "modernization" in Mexico (use of high-fructose corn sweeteners in the soft drink industry) and consequent sugar surpluses and exports. The sugar producers asserted that they had "no hand" in the provisions that were included in the negotiated agreement and called for two fundamental modifications. First, they argued that the Mexican surplus status be calculated "not just on the basis of sugar, but on caloric sweeteners, including corn sweeteners." Second, they argued that Mexican access to the U.S. market "be capped at a growing TRQ" for the full 15-year adjustment period even if Mexico became a surplus producer for two consecutive years. Representatives of the producers on the sweeteners ATAC also raised concerns about whether NAFTA would be extended to other countries. Although not mentioned specifically, these countries potentially included Cuba with its annual sugar surpluses in excess of 5 MMT.

Finally, the horticultural sector, like the cotton industry, held mixed views about the negotiated agreement. Winter fruit and vegetable producers in Florida continued to oppose NAFTA. The Florida producers felt they had pursued all of the avenues open to participating in the negotiations and viewed their access to the negotiators as good throughout most of the process. In the end, however, like the sugar producers, they concluded that the Bush administration had "failed to honor its commitment to Congress to provide protection for the most sensitive products." The Florida producers suggested again that some winter fruits and vegetables be excluded from the agreement. At a minimum, they argued that the tariff phase-out periods be extended to 20 years for sensitive commodities, with more commodities included in the category subject to the longest transition.

Reactions of other horticultural producers illustrated the diversity of interests within this sector. California producers generally expressed less opposition to the agreement than producers in Florida. The U.S. wine industry, in particular, was dissatisfied with the phase-out periods for Mexican tariffs being too long. Together with potato producers, who had similar concerns, the wine industry concluded it could not support the agreement unless more favorable access to the Mexican market were obtained.

7.5.1   Survey by the Senate Committee

To complement USTR's advisory committee reports and other expressions of the views of producers and other interested parties, Senators Leahy and Lugar, chairman and ranking member of the Senate Committee on Agriculture, Nutrition and Forestry, conducted a survey of opinions about NAFTA. As had been done for previous important policy decisions, the survey was mailed to 300 groups and individuals identified by the committee staff as having an interest in the issues. By June 1993, 124 responses were received. The relatively low response rate may suggest that the survey was not considered an effective means to express an opinion to Congress by many interest groups. Nevertheless, the responses provide a broad overview of the positions of the various agricultural interests.

Based on a qualitative analysis of the responses (e.g., stated position, strength of the language, number of caveats), 24 provided strong support for the agreement, 51 provided support, 21 were opposed, 9 were strongly opposed, and 19 took no position.[5] Among the general-membership organizations, positions remained divided. Several government and public agencies submitted letters (with opposition from Florida and support from Arizona, California, and Texas), and the embassies of five Caribbean countries submitted an unsolicited letter of opposition because of potential reductions of their sugar TRQs. Grain and oilseed producers and some livestock groups were supportive of the agreement, but others had reservations or had not taken a position. The dairy and cotton respondents were divided between supporters and those not having a position, while peanut and sugar producers expressed their strong opposition. Respondents among horticultural interests again reflected diverse views, with opposition expressed by the coalition of Florida producers. Food processors and suppliers and the forestry industry overwhelmingly supported NAFTA, while the United Food and Commercial Workers, AFL-CIO, expressed organized labor's opposition, citing particularly its concern that NAFTA might cause meat-packing jobs to move from the United States to Mexico.

One interesting aspect of the letters received by the Senate committee is that supporters tended to identify fewer specifics than opponents. There were an average of 3.86 and 5.47 comments per letter from those providing strong support or support, respectively, compared to 7.41 and 7.88 from those opposed and strongly opposed. Supporters also tended to be less focused on their perceptions of benefits than opponents were on their concerns. Among respondents providing strong support, an average of almost 80 percent of the comments were expressions of benefits. This share dropped to 46 percent among respondents providing support. In contrast, essentially all of the comments of respondents expressing opposition or strong opposition were objections to the agreement.

To summarize the positions of agricultural interest groups at the conclusion of the NAFTA negotiations, there was widespread support for the agreement among the AFBF and other market-oriented general-membership farm organizations, from most export-oriented producer groups for grains, oilseeds, livestock, and some horticultural products, from many food processors and suppliers, and, among the sectors protected by import quotas, within the dairy and cotton industries. Opposition was expressed by general-membership organizations such as the NFU that favor domestic supply controls and labor unions. Wheat producers withheld support in an effort to obtain leverage on Canadian export issues, while producers and processors of peanuts, sugar, winter vege-

---

5. The classification of the responses is based on analysis of their content by the author and does not represent the view of the Senate committee or its staff. A summary of the individual survey responses is available on request.

tables, and citrus and other winter fruits expressed opposition to specific provisions of the agreement.

7.6 Side-Agreements and Implementing Legislation

After the November 1992 elections, the Clinton administration followed through on its campaign pledge not to reopen negotiations on the original NAFTA text but to negotiate supplemental (side) agreements with respect to the environment, labor, and import surges. The administration worked closely with a coalition of private organizations during the negotiations for the environmental side-agreement and won the endorsement of NAFTA by seven of the principal groups. The negotiations on the labor side-agreement were less ambitious than the negotiations on the environment and did not satisfy the concerns of organized labor nor its principal supporters in Congress. The AFL-CIO had essentially indicated it would oppose NAFTA regardless of the outcome of the side-negotiations and subsequently declared its continued intent to defeat the NAFTA implementing legislation in the House of Representatives.

The side-agreement on import surges provided an opportunity to address the concerns of the various agricultural producer interests. The sugar producers, in particular, had found a receptive audience in the new administration. One key Capitol Hill staff person expressed the view that the Bush administration had done poorly on the initial agreement for agriculture, especially for sugar. This concern was quickly recognized by the designated USTR, Mickey Kantor. As early as his January 1993 preconfirmation hearings, he pointed out that the side-agreement on import surges would "affect agriculture and particularly be protective, we hope, of the sugar industry, if such a surge should take place" (U.S. Congress, Senate 1993).

Despite this expressed interest in providing strengthened protection, the side-agreement negotiated by the Clinton administration only established a consultative process to consider issues related to the original NAFTA emergency action provisions. While this process could expedite subsequent consideration of industry injury claims, the side-agreement did not address the types of changes sought in other initial provisions of NAFTA by the agricultural producer groups.

As the negotiations for the three side-agreements carried into the late summer of 1993, the Clinton administration withheld active support for NAFTA pending their conclusion. Internal debate continued within the administration over the level of priority to place on the passage of NAFTA. In the meantime, between the signing of the initial agreement in December 1992 and completion of the side-agreements in August 1993, increased opposition to NAFTA was articulated by individuals and groups that included some of the Democratic leadership of Congress, the AFL-CIO, third-party presidential aspirant Ross Perot, some environmental, civil rights, and consumer groups, and conservatives such as Pat Buchanan and others.

A setback for supporters of NAFTA came on June 30 when a federal district judge ruled that its implementation required an environmental impact statement. This ruling could have indefinitely delayed consideration of the agreement by Congress.

A subsequent low point for NAFTA supporters came after the congressional recess in August. Many members of Congress were bombarded by the vocal opposition to NAFTA by Ross Perot's backers and others within their districts. Crucial Republican support for the agreement seemed to be slipping. One high-ranking member of the White House NAFTA task force observed that the Perot people had done to Republican support for NAFTA what organized labor had done to the support among Democrats.

In this setting, President Clinton used the September 13, 1993, signing ceremony for the side-agreements to launch an intense campaign for implementation of the agreement. The ruling that NAFTA required an environmental impact statement was overturned on September 24 by a unanimous decision of the U.S. Court of Appeals. The Clinton administration then proceeded with efforts to build a broad public case for the benefits of NAFTA and to pursue the necessary votes in Congress "one or two and five or ten at a time." Agricultural interest groups played a role in each of these strategies.

7.6.1   Ag for NAFTA and the Citizens Trade Campaign

When it became apparent that NAFTA was in trouble in Congress, several of the agricultural groups began to consider ways of making a more visible show of support. Their perception early in the summer was that agriculture was viewed as divided on NAFTA, not as an industry that would benefit. Five groups—the AFBF, the NCGA, the NCA, the National Pork Producers Council, and Farmland Industries—formed an umbrella support organization called "Ag for NAFTA." Membership was open to any agricultural group willing to add its name with no financial or other commitments required. Ag for NAFTA lent its support to the broader proagreement coalition USA*NAFTA but remained separate in its financing, organizing, and activities.

The perception of the Ag for NAFTA organizers was that the Clinton administration was "hungry for support" since there was little grass-roots effort developing in favor of the agreement. Ag for NAFTA brought 150 farm representatives to Washington at the end of July and sponsored a variety of publicity activities. The staff person responsible for spearheading Ag for NAFTA expressed the view that these activities (including press conferences at the House of Representatives and with USTR Mickey Kantor) had "completely turned around perceptions of agriculture's views" despite receiving limited coverage. He rated their success on this initial objective as "excellent." By September, Ag for NAFTA had 140 affiliated organizations.

The next objective of Ag for NAFTA was to reassure members of Congress that they had a base of support if they voted for the agreement. One hundred and seventy members were targeted for attention. The tactic was simply to try to insure that these members heard from their constituents in support of NAFTA at town meetings, office visits, and through the mail.

A third activity of Ag for NAFTA was to build grass-roots support for the agreement among their constituents. The organizers felt members of their own groups had been "bombarded with the opposition position" and viewed it as crucial to counter some of the opposition statements and dispel misconceptions among farmers. Supporters were encouraged to write to their newspapers, participate in radio talk shows, and take other steps to promote knowledge of the benefits of the agreement for agriculture.

Much general commentary has been directed at the total levels of expenditures by various parties in their efforts to affect the NAFTA negotiations and congressional debate (see, e.g., Grayson 1993; Lewis and Ebrahim 1993). In the context of the millions of dollars of apparent expenditures, the scale of the Ag for NAFTA activities was modest. The key organizer devoted about one-half of his time to NAFTA and another staff person about one-fourth of her time. Ag for NAFTA had an initial budget of about $10,000. The respective member organizations paid the travel expenses of participants in Ag for NAFTA activities, and its final budget for publicity, advertising, and other expenses was less than $100,000.

In addition to the efforts of Ag for NAFTA, the AFBF and many of the specific commodity associations also devoted staff and resources to support passage of the NAFTA implementing legislation. Again, a typical commitment involved the assignment of one or two staff persons to preparation of informational materials and efforts to mobilize the membership to support the agreement and convey their support to the public and Congress. The representatives of these organizations widely acknowledged that their efforts would only be successful if President Clinton was fully committed.

Opponents of NAFTA also continued to mobilize around the implementing legislation. The NFU made defeat of NAFTA one of its top priorities. It was a founding member of the Citizens Trade Campaign (CTC), the umbrella group that led the opposition efforts, and provided the CTC with office space and other services. The NFU argued that supporters of NAFTA had not done the grass-roots organizing necessary to succeed and launched grass-roots efforts of its own and in conjunction with the CTC. While not formally aligned with Ross Perot, representatives of the NFU believed he had changed the media dynamics and reduced the prospects for passage of the implementing legislation.

7.6.2   Wheat Opposition

Continuing their break with the other export-oriented commodity groups, wheat producers held their support for NAFTA hostage to resolution of the price transparency and transportation subsidy issues with Canada. Their representatives viewed these as issues on which they would "never give up." In exchange for their support for NAFTA, the wheat producers asked the administration to take action under the emergency provisions of section 22. The emergency provisions permit the secretary of agriculture to recommend immediate quotas or tariffs rather than wait for an ITC investigation and ruling. The wheat producers resisted prodding to join the coalition of NAFTA supporters unless their contentions toward Canada were addressed. A representative of the NAWG viewed as its trump card an ability to "provide a level of comfort to members on the fence who want to vote for NAFTA but need political cover." He expected "a lot of hard bargaining" before the implementing legislation was approved.

7.6.3   Division among the Import-Quota and TRQ-Protected Commodities

The import-quota and TRQ-protected commodities pursued the different approaches to the implementing legislation suggested by the particular circumstances of each sector. Consistent with the dairy ATAC report, the NMPF adopted a position of support for the agreement during summer 1993. Representatives of the NMPF met with Mickey Kantor to point out that it was the first section 22 group to endorse a trade agreement. They asked for his support in return for their "self-help" legislation and on favorable levels of dairy market access in the GATT Uruguay Round. The NMPF also sought support for its view that the provisions of the Canada-U.S. FTA that eliminated agricultural tariffs would apply retroactively to dairy products if Canada were to tariffy its quantitative dairy trade barriers under a GATT agreement. Such an interpretation of the language and intent of the Canada-U.S. agreement had been consistently opposed by Canadian milk producers and the Canadian negotiators.

The NCCA also endorsed NAFTA in October 1993 rather than hold out for final concessions. The producer members of the council continued to express reservations about the agreement but agreed not to oppose the processors' consensus in its favor. The NCCA made it clear, however, that it did not support the provisions of the pending GATT agreement with respect to cotton.

While dairy and cotton interests moved toward support of NAFTA, peanut producers remained opposed. Some state organizations (in particular, Georgia) were very active in opposition. Other state organizations took a less active role because they did not want to alienate Congressman de la Garza after his efforts on their behalf. The Washington lobbyist for the producers pressed ahead with efforts to influence the implementing legislation, and the producer groups kept pressure on the members of Congress from districts where they had strength. The peanut producers indicated that the intensity of their final opposition to NAFTA would depend on the assurances provided in the implementing legislation in terms of blocking transshipments, quality control, and other issues affecting access to their protected market.

Sugar industry groups were also united on opposition to NAFTA. The sugar producers made strong efforts to obtain their two modifications of the initial agreement: inclusion of corn sweeteners in determining the balance of production and consumption affecting Mexican access to the U.S. sugar market and a ceiling on Mexico's access for the full 15-year adjustment period. The sugar producers lobbied USDA and USTR and pressed their case through the Senate sweeteners caucus. A letter of support for the producers signed by 34 senators was given to the secretary of agriculture just prior to his consultations with the Mexican government in late August, together with separate letters of support from Senators Conrad and Dole, a letter of concern signed by ambassadors from 16 Caribbean Basin Initiative countries, and the transcript of a public meeting intended to show that the Mexican sugar industry had advised its government that it did not object to the U.S. producers' recommendations. The sugar producers were satisfied that the secretary and the USTR understood their concerns and were sympathetic to them. Nevertheless, they committed to "go hell bent to defeat NAFTA" if the agreement was not revised. On September 27, they pledged up to $500,000 to a campaign of opposition, indicating that their opposition would be withdrawn if their specific concerns were addressed.

The demands of the sugar sector brought into focus the competing interests of different commodity groups within U.S. agriculture and the relative strength of the Mexican and U.S. negotiating positions. The NCGA indicated that if the sugar provisions could be modified without changing the negotiated corn TRQ (2.5 MMT, compared to the 3.5 MMT the producers had sought initially), then they would not object, even though the modification would reduce the likelihood of additional demand being created by a shift to corn sweeteners in the Mexican soft drink industry. The corn growers indicated they would oppose modifying the initial sugar agreement if it involved lowering the negotiated corn TRQ.

The sugar issues were even tougher on the Mexican side. Mexico was going to give up its traditional and politically sensitive protection for corn under NAFTA and sought access to the U.S. sugar market as a potential opportunity for some of its agricultural producers. While Mexican consumer well-being would be improved by lower corn prices, more than offsetting the loss to producers, sugar prices for consumers were to rise under NAFTA if Mexico fulfilled its pledge to raise tariffs on non-NAFTA countries to the U.S. over-quota level. The opportunity to sell some of its sugar in the protected U.S. market would offset part of the cost to Mexico of adjusting to U.S. sugar policies. The Mexican negotiators had worked hard for concessions on sugar, although, as indicated in the sweeteners ATAC report and elsewhere, most participants in the negotiations agreed that the Bush administration had not resisted provisions that might put pressure on the U.S. sugar program. In any case, Mexico did not consent to modifying the sugar provisions of the initial August 1992 agreement until it became critical to do so near the end of the U.S. congressional deliberations.

7.6.4   The Florida Coalition

Working along commodity lines as well as through the unified position among agricultural groups within the state, the Florida coalition pressed further for accommodation of the concerns of sugar, winter vegetables, and citrus and other winter fruits. The fruit and vegetable producers continued to seek longer tariff phase-out periods for more commodities and price-based import surge safeguard mechanisms. They also continued to express concern about the effects on their competitiveness of disparities in environmental and labor regulations. A key citrus representative described their particular goal as "a safeguard whereby if Mexico sells below a breakeven price for Florida producers, then the tariff will snap back in place." Characterizing this as a "permanent" system, he argued for a tariff equal to the differences in costs of production between Florida and Mexico. This was the type of barrier to trade popularized under the name of a "social tariff" by Ross Perot in his highly visible anti-NAFTA campaign (Perot and Choate 1993).

The coalition of Florida agricultural producers remained central to the NAFTA debate by working closely with the state's congressional delegation. Throughout the congressional deliberations about NAFTA legislation, almost the entire Florida delegation of 10 Democrats and 13 Republicans remained on record as opposed to the agreement.

7.7 End-Game Concessions

As the November 17 vote on the NAFTA implementing legislation approached, the administration continued to struggle to assemble a supportive coalition. Leaders of the opposition, including Congressmen Richard Gephardt and David Bonior, the majority leader and second-ranking member of the Democratic congressional leadership, claimed to be closing in on the votes needed to defeat the legislation. Organized labor, the CTC, Ross Perot, and others pressed their opposition in public forums and congressional lobbying.

With the fate of the agreement uncertain in the House of Representatives, the agricultural commodity groups were positioned to play a significant role in the bargaining to win support for the implementing legislation. Unlike organized labor and other opponents publicly committed to defeat of the agreement in its entirety, most of the agricultural commodity groups had expressed opposition only to specific aspects of the agreement. Moreover, between the Florida delegation and the sugar, peanut, and wheat interests, a large number of congressional votes rested at least in part on satisfying the concerns of the agricultural producers.

The end game exploded into public view in early November. Concessions obtained for agriculture in the last two weeks of the debate are summarized in table 7.8.

7.7.1 Initial Letters and Concessions

An initial November 3 letter from the USTR to Mexico's secretary of commerce addressed concerns of the wine industry (Office of the U.S. Trade Representative 1993). The letter indicated that the United States would seek mu-

Table 7.8   Final NAFTA Concessions and Assurances to Agricultural Interests

Item	Concession
Wine/brandy	U.S. to seek mutual agreement to accelerated tariff reductions
Sugar	Consumption of corn sweeteners included in the determination of net production surplus
	Mexican TRQ capped at 250,000 metric tons for the seventh through fourteenth years of the agreement
Citrus	MFN rate of duty on imports from Mexico in excess of 70 million gallons annually through 2002 (90 million gallons during 2003–07) if the price of fresh concentrated orange juice drops below an average based on the preceding five years for five consecutive days.
	GATT tariffs cuts on fresh and processed citrus products limited to 15 percent
	Non-NAFTA citrus juices to be reclassified as perishable commodities to expedite injury claims
	Citrus products not to receive additional special status under GSP or CBI
Fruits and vegetables	Early-warning import surge mechanism
	GATT tariffs cuts limited to 15 percent on tomatoes, peppers, lettuce, cucumbers, celery, and sweet corn
	Sensitive products not to receive additional special status under GSP or CBI
	Postponement of decertification of methyl bromide for use as a soil fumigant until 2000
	Funding for soil and postharvest fumigant research; completion and funding for U.S. Horticultural Research Station, Fort Pierce, Florida
	Doubled purchases of fresh tomatoes and new purchases of sweet corn for school lunch programs
	Trade representative assurance of effective price-based and volume-based tariff snapback provisions for fresh tomatoes and peppers
Wheat	End-use certificates to prevent subsidized reexport of Canadian wheat and barley
	Bilateral consultations to address transportation subsidies and Canadian Wheat Board pricing practices and an ITC investigation of whether imports interfere with the domestic wheat program within 60 days unless the consultations were successful
Peanuts	Bilateral consultations to address the increase in imports of peanut butter/paste from Canada and an ITC instigation of whether imports interfere with the domestic peanut program within 60 days unless the consultations were successful
	Secretary of agriculture assurance to work vigorously to limit the volume of imports from Canada
Transshipment	Commissioner of customs assurance of at least 10 investigations and 350 positions, including 100 new hires, to enforce rules of origin

tual agreement to accelerated tariff reductions for wine and brandy (as well as flat glass, home appliances, and bedding components).

A second and more significant letter confirmed the trade representative's understanding that the two parties had agreed that substitution of corn syrup for sugar could "result in effects not intended by either Party" and that subsequently they had reached an agreement that consumption of corn syrup would be included in the determination of "net production surplus." The letter also indicated an agreement had been reached that, notwithstanding previous provisions, the ceiling for Mexican sugar sales in the United States under NAFTA would be 250,000 metric tons for the seventh through fourteenth years. In short, Mexico had conceded to the demands of the U.S. sugar producers. Subsequently, the sugar industry indicated it would withdraw its opposition to NAFTA. At least a dozen votes in the House of Representatives were expected to be influenced to support the implementing legislation by the decisions of the sugar associations.

A third letter between the U.S. and Mexican negotiators addressed the issue of a price-based safeguard for citrus. The letter specified that the countries had agreed that if the U.S. price of fresh concentrated orange juice dropped below an average based on the preceding five years for five consecutive days, then the United States could apply the prevailing MFN rate of duty on imports from Mexico in excess of 70 million gallons annually through 2002 and in excess of 90 million gallons annually during 2003–07. This change provided only a modest modification of the original citrus provisions, nothing like the social tariff protection that had been called for by some representatives of the industry.

In addition to this modest change in the provisions of NAFTA, the citrus producers had bargained for other concessions from the administration. The board of directors of Florida Citrus Mutual voted to withdraw their opposition to the agreement on November 10. They announced that the association had won three additional concessions: that tariffs on all forms of fresh and processed citrus products would not be cut more than 15 percent under the pending Uruguay Round GATT agreement, that non-NAFTA citrus juices would be reclassified as perishable commodities under U.S. law (expediting future injury claims by the industry), and that no foreign citrus products would receive additional special status under the Generalized System of Preferences (GSP) or the Caribbean Basin Initiative (CBI).

As the anti-NAFTA Florida coalition collapsed and momentum was gained for passage of the implementing legislation by Congress, the other Florida fruit and vegetable producers also sought accommodation with the administration. Their representatives were not offered modifications of the agreement that required the concurrence of Mexico. Instead, they were offered a range of administrative concessions in exchange for helping deliver support for NAFTA from the Florida congressional delegation. These concessions included the use of an early-warning import surge mechanism and limits for certain commodities with respect to GATT, the GSP, and the CBI similar to those offered for citrus. They also included an environmentally controversial postponement of decertification of methyl bromide for use as a soil fumigant until 2000 and funding for research intended to "insure that Florida agriculture would continue to have access to commercially viable technologies" for soil treatment and postharvest fumigation (including funding for a particular horticultural research station). Finally, the administration agreed to increase purchases of fresh tomatoes and sweet corn for school lunch programs. Based on these concessions, the board of directors of the Florida Fruit and Vegetable Association announced they had voted to withdraw its opposition to NAFTA on November 11.

7.7.2   The Final Days

With less than a week before the scheduled congressional vote and with leaders of the opposition still claiming they would defeat NAFTA in the House of Representatives, the administration and its supporters could not relax their efforts to obtain passage of the implementing legislation. The Ag for NAFTA coalition sponsored a "fly-in" that brought 50 to 60 leaders of various member organizations to Washington for a final round of lobbying on behalf of the agreement. They contributed to the decisions of a number of undecided representatives, but the real action was with the groups that had been or remained opposed.

The wheat producers engaged in tense late-deal bargaining. They had been able to insert into the implementing legislation a provision for end-use certificates for wheat and barley intended to counteract their use by Canada and insure that Canadian products did not receive U.S. export subsidies. However, the producers' earlier hopes for emergency section 22 import quotas were scuttled when, by several accounts, the administration determined that the wheat growers could not influence many congressional votes. The wheat producers were told "emphatically" that the administration would not take emergency section 22 action. However, the president agreed to accommodate the producers by asking the ITC to initiate a section 22 investigation in 60 days to determine whether imports from Canada were interfering with the wheat support programs of the Department of Agriculture. The ITC investigation would be undertaken unless there were successful bilateral negotiations to address Canadian policies, including "transportation subsidies and Canadian Wheat Board pricing practices." A letter from the president to this effect was sent to the ITC and several individual congressmen on November 15. The next day, less than 36 hours before the scheduled vote in the House of Representatives, the NAWG announced it would "now work for congressional approval of NAFTA."

Partly on the basis of the wheat concessions, five congressmen, including two counted by the Associated Press as leaning against the agreement and two counted as undecided, announced their support for the implementing legislation. One of these representatives, Congressman English, was also concerned about illegal transshipment of peanuts and beef through Mexico. To address the opposition of the peanut producers and Congressman English's concerns, the president committed the administration to bilateral consultations on imports of peanut butter from Canada and to a second ITC investigation within 60 days if necessary. The secretary of agriculture assured one congressman that he would "work vigorously . . . to limit the volume of Canadian exports of peanut butter and paste, which would include your suggestion of a cap at 1 percent of U.S. domestic consumption." Congressman English, who resigned shortly after the NAFTA vote to accept an appointment as head of the National Rural Electric Cooperative Association, was also assured by the commissioner of customs that there would be "at least ten visits to agricultural processing sites in Mexico" and that "350 positions, including 100 newly hired employees" would be assigned to enforcement of the NAFTA rules of origin.

Final critical decisions were made by the Florida congressional delegation. It scheduled a closed-door meeting on Tuesday, November 16. An Associated Press poll had counted only five of the 23 members of the delegation as supporting or leaning toward supporting the agreement the previous day, so a large number of votes were at stake. Some of the Florida agricultural producer groups, and many of the individual producers, disagreed with the decisions of Florida Citrus Mutual and the Florida Fruit and Vegetable Association to withdraw their opposition. Moreover, the case against NAFTA had been made on numerous grounds in Florida. Not all of the state's congressional representatives seemed convinced that the accommodations offered to agriculture were sufficient for them to support the agreement.

A pivotal senior member of the Florida delegation was Representative Tom Lewis who served on the House Committee on Agriculture. To provide Congressman Lewis with assurance about his concerns required an additional letter from Mickey Kantor specifying that NAFTA contained "effective price and volume-based snapback provisions to deal with increased imports of fresh tomatoes and peppers." The next day, Congressman Lewis and 12 other members of the delegation voted with the administration. The NAFTA implementing legislation passed in the House of Representatives by a 234–200 majority.

7.7.3   Unconfirmed Deals

In addition to the confirmed concessions and assurances and the votes that went with them, there were rumors in the press of more insidious deal making. One rumor was that the administration would back away from its intention to raise grazing fees on federal lands from $1.86 to $4.28 per animal unit in exchange for support for NAFTA from 10 western congressmen. The Interior Department denied such a connection (*Wall Street Journal* 1993b), but the administration subsequently partially backed down and proposed raising the grazing fees to $3.96 over three years.

It was also rumored that the $0.75 per pack increase in the cigarette tax proposed to finance health care reform might be scaled back in exchange for support for NAFTA. The administration denied such a deal but two North Carolina Democrats, Charles Rose and Steve Neal, who had previously been opposed or leaning toward opposition ended up voting in favor of the implementing legislation after several meetings with House Ways and Means Committee Chairman Dan Rostenkowski. Congressman Neal denied his vote on NAFTA had anything to do with the tobacco tax, and Congressman Rose, while vague, acknowledged that the president had not promised him anything (*Wall Street Journal* 1993a). The $0.75 tax was subsequently included in the president's proposed 1995 budget.

In the context of these rumors of possible deal making on issues not directly related to trade, it is of interest that one possible deal never seemed to be under consideration. Concurrent with the NAFTA debate, the administration was engaged in court-ordered discussions with Florida sugar and fruit and vegetable producers seeking an out-of-court settlement on a program to restore the Everglades. At issue were how to purge agricultural runoff of phosphorous and other chemicals and who would pay the costs of such efforts. The producers had agreed to take some land out of production to create filtration marshes, but the talks broke down in December 1993 over their demands for strong assurances on the limits of their future obligations. Despite the importance of the Florida delegation in the NAFTA debate, there was no linkage of the NAFTA vote to this environmental negotiation.[6]

7.8   Conclusions from the NAFTA Outcomes

In drawing inferences about the political economy of trade protection on the basis of the participation of various agricultural groups in the NAFTA negotiations and the congressional debate over its implementing legislation, a crucial issue is the extent to which the process provided a mechanism for overcoming established protection among agricultural sectors and expanding international markets. The NAFTA outcomes highlight the dual character of international negotiations that Putman (1988) has referred to as a simultaneous two-level game. At one level, a framework has to be established for a mutually acceptable international agreement. At a second level, any such agreement must be ratified within the domestic political processes of the negotiating partners.

In the case of NAFTA, President Salinas and President Bush articulated support for comprehensive liberalization of trade between Mexico and the United States. The high-level decision to include all agricultural products under provisions for long-run trade liberalization was endorsed by the Mexican side, within a relatively autocratic decision-making structure, and by some U.S. agricultural interests.

The decision to achieve liberalization of agricultural trade in the long run accomplished bilaterally one of the goals of the original U.S. zero-option GATT proposal and established a strong objective for the NAFTA negotiations, especially compared to the relatively weak provisions for agriculture in previous trade agreements and the significant weakening of the zero option in

---

6. There was some discussion within the sugar industry of linking the two issues, but it was concluded that it would be infeasible to do so.

the final Uruguay Round GATT agreement.[7] For this reason, the provisions for agriculture negotiated between Mexico and the United States may deserve the "A" grade received from Hufbauer and Schott (1993) in their NAFTA evaluation. However, Canada resisted participating in an agreement of such broad scope for agriculture. Those interests in the negotiations that favored trade liberalization lacked sufficient influence to force Canadian concessions. Instead, they had to settle for extension of the less-comprehensive bilateral agricultural market access provisions of the previous Canada-U.S. FTA and a similar agreement between Mexico and Canada.

Once the broad direction of the NAFTA negotiations was set, the domestic political process provided multiple points of access for interest groups in the United States to influence specific provisions of the agreement. The politically palatable but conflicting principles that expanded export opportunities were desirable but that imports should not cause too much disruption of domestic industries guided the negotiations toward the tariffication of quantitative import restrictions, with limited initial TRQs, high initial over-quota tariffs, and long transition periods for expanding market access and reducing tariff levels. Agricultural producer groups were faced with either seeking concessions related to the parameters of the adjustment mechanisms or simply opposing the agreement. Few of the agricultural groups chose outright opposition. Rather, they acquiesced to the Bush and, subsequently, Clinton administrations' support for the long-term objectives of the agreement but sought modifications of specific adjustment provisions.

From the efforts made on NAFTA by interest groups within agriculture and more widely, it is apparent that both groups that anticipated gains and those trying to avoid expected losses were involved in the decision-making process. At the risk of oversimplification, the stakes for various agricultural interest groups and the levels of their participation in the process are summarized in table 7.9. Rational behavior might be hypothesized to result in all groups falling on the main diagonal of the table, with their positions and activity levels correlated with the likely economic impacts.

To a large extent, agricultural interest group responses to NAFTA were consistent with its estimated economic impacts. The signs of these impacts, together with various nonquantified related issues (particularly extension of

---

7. The final GATT agreement replaced quantitative restrictions (including all U.S. section 22 quotas) with TRQs and high over-quota tariffs on a multilateral basis. However, the GATT agreement only requires minimal market access of 5 percent of consumption under TRQs and reductions of over-quota tariffs by an average of 36 percent (15 percent minimum) after six years. The effectiveness of the over-quota tariff cuts on improving market access will depend on the levels from which the cuts are made, and there is a strong possibility that the tariff equivalents of many quantitative restrictions were inflated. The final GATT agreement also places some limits on domestic support payments, unless they are decoupled from production levels, and constrains export subsidies. The U.S. implementing legislation stipulates that sugar imports from Mexico will be included in, not additional to, its global TRQ commitment.

Table 7.9   **Summary of the Economic Stakes and the Activities of Interest Groups**

	Activity Level			
Economic Stakes	Strong Support	Support	Opposition	Strong Opposition
Positive	Corn Livestock			
Modestly positive	Processing industries	Feed grains Oilseeds Dairy Cotton		Wheat
Modestly negative				Sugar Peanuts Florida fruits and vegetables

NAFTA to other countries), rather than the magnitude of the direct impacts often seemed important determinants of interest group behavior. Accounting for some of the related issues brings a closer correlation of the economic interests of some of the groups and their roles in the NAFTA process than is initially evident.

Given the different responses to NAFTA among agricultural interest groups, questions arise concerning the avenues of influence they utilized to affect the negotiated agreement or obtain subsequent concessions. A wide range of options were available, and groups generally participated in the process in a variety of ways. A reasonable generalization is that groups that found the broad outline of the negotiations amenable to their interests were able to work closely with the negotiators and their technical staffs, and some path toward liberalized trade was achieved. Interest groups objecting to the general direction of the negotiations sought redress through Congress.

Too much can be made, however, of the choice by interest groups among avenues of influence on purely institutional grounds. Despite the broad commitment to the trade agreement by both the Bush and Clinton administrations, receptivity to the interests of specific groups changed after the 1992 election. In particular, support for the sugar program is usually identified with the Democratic party, and the tension between sugar producer groups and the trade negotiators during the Bush administration is not disputed by participants in the process. The Clinton administration signaled very early that it was more receptive to the concerns of the sugar sector, and this receptivity was reflected in the executive branch. Likewise, wheat producers did not expect much support from the executive branch when a Republican administration was in power. Thus, even with bipartisan support for NAFTA, there was a partisan aspect to the avenues that were effective for specific commodity groups.

More generally, there is a widespread supposition that interest groups likely to benefit from expanded export opportunities have difficulty becoming as organized on their own behalf as interests likely to face increased competition (with reference to agriculture, see, e.g., McCalla 1993). This supposition is confirmed by various aspects of the agricultural interest groups' activities on NAFTA. These aspects include the relative attention to NAFTA in different agricultural magazines, the frequency of congressional testimonies by supporters and opponents, the observations of participants on the degree to which potential losses motivated commodity group involvement, the intensity of the opponents' responses to the survey by the Senate Committee on Agriculture, Nutrition and Forestry, the resources committed to the debate over the implementing legislation by various producer groups, and the ability of the various groups to mobilize their supporters.

Another set of questions related to the activities of specific interest groups pertains to unanimity of the sectors seeking liberalization or protection. In the case of NAFTA, the strongest coalition to emerge naturally was the geographic coalition in Florida. The key members of the coalition were sugar, winter vegetables, and citrus and other winter fruits. The Florida coalition had a strong presence during the negotiations and legislative deliberations, but its unanimity broke down in the final days of the congressional debate. Sugar was the most protected of the commodities in the coalition. Florida sugar producers, acting in unison with the sugar industry in other parts of the country, were able to strike their own deal with the Clinton administration and obtain substantial concessions. The other Florida commodities receive less protection than sugar. The producers of these commodities had no similar natural allies elsewhere and were less successful in their bargaining. Thus, the Florida coalition was only partially helpful in obtaining concessions for its member groups.

Some other coalitions that might have emerged during the NAFTA process were not evident among either export-oriented or import-competing interests. Notwithstanding the efforts of Ag for NAFTA, the divisions among the general-membership farm organizations precluded a united approach for the likely exporters. Among the grains, wheat had idiosyncratic issues that affected its approach to the negotiations and even some corn growers opposed the agreement. Among the import-competing commodities, the specifics of NAFTA looked favorable to the dairy and cotton sectors but not to the peanut and sugar sectors. Issue can be taken with the analyses of particular commodity groups, as in the case, for example, of USDA's Office of Economics with the opposition expressed by peanut producers, but the point remains that the interest group perceptions precluded formation of coalitions. Issues extending beyond NAFTA were particularly important in this regard. The dairy sector apparently anticipated better medium-term opportunities in world markets (or simply more success in obtaining export subsidies) than the peanut or sugar sectors, which face numerous pressures for greater foreign access to their domestic markets.

A second aspect to the unanimity issues concerns groups other than producers that might benefit from trade or be harmed by protection. The sugar producers were opposed by the industrial sweetener users, but as in many previous policy decisions, the sweetener users were not very effective. Other processing and supply industries also supported NAFTA. The Food Marketing Institute and others among these industries argued that the agreement would benefit consumers through lower prices. The general public did not express a strong position in terms of consumer prices but was heard from in terms of environmental issues, labor issues, and overall political support for NAFTA. The proportion of the public favoring the agreement increased as the congressional vote approached but remained less than 50 percent by most late polls.

A reason for some optimism in this context is that the final efforts to win support for NAFTA were successful. A bipartisan coalition, of which agricultural interests were only a small part, was marshalled to make the case for the agreement. The broad challenge to its leadership by the AFL-CIO, Ross Perot, and others was defeated. Thus, the danger that the United States would turn conspicuously inward on an important economic and foreign policy decision was held at bay in a post–Cold War setting. In this regard, the disadvantages NAFTA created for Japan and the Europeans were unfortunately often touted as an argument. This theme undermines efforts to liberalize trade on a multilateral basis, quite to the contrary of the intent of the original consideration of bilateral agreements in the early 1980s.

For agriculture, despite the apparent inability of the export-oriented interests to become as well organized in their own behalf as the import-competing interests, and despite the grueling congressional NAFTA debate and the associated bargaining and concessions, the original provisions of NAFTA that eliminate trade barriers between Mexico and the United States in the long run remain largely intact. A careful examination also suggests that many of the concessions and assurances offered to U.S. agricultural interest groups to secure votes for the implementing legislation weaken the original NAFTA transition period provisions only marginally. Other acknowledged concessions to the interest groups are also relatively minor.

This said, the notion that a trade agreement can serve as a channel for reform of entrenched domestic U.S. agricultural programs fared poorly under NAFTA. Among the protected commodities, dairy and cotton came to support the agreement only when strong rules of origin were adopted and the absence of any threat to their domestic markets became apparent. They conceded nothing generally about the protection they receive. Peanut producers fought hard against the agreement and battled in the end for concessions to sustain their protection.

More egregious than the dairy and peanut provisions of the agreement, among its trade-distorting effects NAFTA initially created a common sugar market between Mexico and the United States from which both Mexican and U.S. producers were potentially going to benefit at the expense of consumers and excluded producers. The subsequent concessions to U.S. sugar interests, which helped deliver over a dozen congressional votes, exacerbated the initial distortion by essentially stealing from the Mexican producers some of their potential market opportunity while enhancing the potential demand facing U.S. producers. It was an impressive show of strength by the U.S. sugar industry. The concessions obtained gutted the agreement for freer bilateral trade, albeit within a protected common market, for at least the next 15 years. They also raise the question of whether the agreement to allow unrestricted trade in sugar between Mexico and the United States after 15 years is ultimately credible.

The differences in the NAFTA outcomes between Mexico and Canada are also telling. The U.S. producer groups were most successful with respect to Mexico, which agreed to open itself to much more competition from U.S. agricultural products than did the United States to competition from Mexican products. Reducing trade barriers is good policy for Mexico overall, but Mexican agricultural producer groups that might have supported a stronger agreement in terms of their own export opportunities had limited ability to influence the negotiations. Nor was there much countervailing power to the pressure of import-protected U.S. agricultural producers for concessions. To insure NAFTA's approval, the U.S. government succeeded in pressing these concessions on the Mexican government.

It remains uncertain exactly how Mexico will fulfill its NAFTA commitments on agriculture. Facilitating trade liberalization with transfer payments to its affected producers as part of the reform of its domestic agricultural policy may result in the anticipated increase in trade. But in light of the political rebellion launched in the southern state of Chiapas on the day NAFTA went into effect, and the subsequent assassination of the presidential candidate of the Institutional Revolutionary Party (PRI) in March 1994, it also remains possible that Mexico will utilize its support policies to stimulate its domestic agriculture. No limits were set on domestic support levels under NAFTA and, while the GATT agreement subsequently imposed some constraints, such a policy reversal could dampen U.S. export prospects compared to the expectations of some producer groups.[8]

With Canada, the story is different. Throughout the NAFTA process, import-competing Canadian agricultural producers were more effective in defending their established protection than the Mexican producers. Canada's participation in the agreement was largely ignored in the United States except by a few special interests. But to insure passage of the NAFTA implementing legislation, the Clinton administration made unilateral promises to several U.S. agricultural commodity groups about their perceived grievances over imports

---

8. Alma Guillermoprieto (1994) relates the story of a July 1994 preelection campaign rally at which President Salinas distributed the first of close to four million checks providing direct income subsidies to campesinos. "And what are you going to do with the money?" Salinas asked rhetorically. "Buy a tractor? Very good! Buy fertilizer? Excellent!"

from Canada. Thus, one outcome of the process was that it prolonged disputes between the United States and Canada over wheat, peanut butter, and other products.

Given the focus on Mexico in the public NAFTA debate, the unresolved issues with Canada were a surprising outcome. Subsequent to NAFTA's enactment, the United States offered to settle the agricultural trade disputes with Canada by adopting bilateral free trade in agricultural products. This offer was declined, and the United States then imposed a TRQ on peanut butter under the GATT agreement. This satisfied the domestic producer interests, and they withdrew their request for an ITC investigation. For wheat, GATT ruled out establishing a permanent TRQ. The ITC issued a divided report (USITC 1994) on whether trade barriers were warranted under section 22 provisions that were, in any event, scheduled to expire when GATT took effect. After intense negotiations, Canada then agreed to temporary bilateral trade restrictions. On both counts, post-NAFTA agricultural trade between the United States and Canada ends up more laden with barriers than before.

On a somewhat different theme, the bargaining power agricultural groups held toward the end of the NAFTA debate is striking. The agricultural interest groups positioned themselves to bargain for concessions because they sought modifications of specific provisions but did not explicitly oppose the entire agreement. The concerns of the Florida coalition, sugar, peanuts, or wheat mattered to the outcome of close to 30 congressional votes.

The question that arises is why other groups did not do more to put themselves in such a position. The concessions made to agriculture toward the end of the debate were not the only concessions offered by the Clinton administration. One wonders, for example, why the AFL-CIO did not approach the president with concerns about specific industries and to seek additional transition-period protection in these areas in exchange for delivering their support for the agreement. One can imagine a very different coalition having been put together to pass the implementing legislation in such circumstances. Agricultural interests could have found themselves irrelevant to the congressional vote and the sugar and wheat producers sent away to make their case in another context. Curiously, one doubts these parties to last-minute concessions were the intended beneficiaries of organized labor's political efforts.

Consideration of possible alternative coalitions in support of NAFTA also raises the question of whether one-by-one bilateral negotiations offer any realistic hope for reducing agricultural or other trade barriers on an extensive (eventually global) basis. Though free trade zones are proliferating, the lesson from NAFTA seems discouraging. For each agreement one can imagine the various specific interest groups lining up in different arrays. Favoring trade liberalization when it is to their advantage, these interest groups lobby equally strongly for benefits that come from introducing policy distortions rather than removing them. On these shifting sands, negotiating multiple FTAs and building coalitions in their support looks like it leads to drudging trench warfare.

For agriculture, in particular, attaining freer trade with Mexico under NAFTA accomplished only a small percentage of the goals sought eventually through GATT. Progress to be sure, but at such a rate as perhaps to be negligible unless the agreement with Mexico becomes a prototype for multilateral trade liberalization in the long run. This is the outcome that protected agricultural interests claim to fear but so far have avoided.

References

Agricultural Policy Advisory Committee. 1992. *Report on the North American Free Trade Agreement.* Washington, D.C.: Office of the U.S. Trade Representative.
ATACs (Agricultural Technical Advisory Committees). 1992. *Reports on the North American Free Trade Agreement.* Washington, D.C.: Office of the U.S. Trade Representative.
Barr, James C. 1993. Testimony on the Dairy Budget Reconciliation and Self-Help Initiative Act of 1993 before the Subcommittee on Livestock, Committee on Agriculture, U.S. House of Representatives. Arlington, Va.: National Milk Producers Federation.
Fruits and Vegetables Agricultural Technical Advisory Committee. 1990. Statement on issues in the NAFTA negotiations. Washington, D.C.: Office of the U.S. Trade Representative.
Gardner, Bruce L. 1987. Causes of U.S. farm commodity programs. *Journal of Political Economy* 95:290–310.
Gillon, William A. 1992. Letter to Jules Katz, deputy U.S. trade representative. Washington, D.C.: National Cotton Council of America.
Grayson, George W. 1993. *The North American Free Trade Agreement.* Headliner Series no. 299. New York: Foreign Policy Association.
Grennes, Thomas. 1993. Toward a more open agriculture in North America. In *Assessing NAFTA: A trinational analysis,* ed. Steven Globerman and Michael Walker. Vancouver, B.C.: Fraser Institute.
Grennes, Thomas, and Barry Krissoff. 1993. Agricultural trade in a North American Free Trade Agreement. *World Economy* 16:483–502.
Guillermoprieto, Alma. 1994. The only way to win? *New Yorker,* August 15, 32–37.
Hufbauer, Gary Clyde, and Jeffrey J. Schott. 1993. *NAFTA: An assessment.* Washington, D.C.: Institute for International Economics.
Krueger, Anne. 1993. Free trade agreements as protectionist devices: Rules of origin. NBER Working Paper no. 4352. Cambridge, Mass.: National Bureau of Economic Research.
Lewis, Charles, and Margaret Ebrahim. 1993. Can Mexico and big business USA buy NAFTA? *Nation,* 826–39.
McCalla, Alex F. 1993. Agricultural trade liberalization: The ever elusive grail. *American Journal of Agricultural Economics* 75:1102–12.
Miner, William M. 1993. Agricultural trade under the klieg lights: Domestic pressures and bilateral frictions. Ottawa: Carleton University, Center for Trade Policy and Law.
Office of the U.S. Trade Representative. 1993. Letters from administration officials prepared in connection with the NAFTA debate. Transmitted to the Senate Committee on Finance. Washington, D.C.: Office of the U.S. Trade Representative.

Perot, Ross H., and Pat Choate. 1993. *Save your job, save our country: Why NAFTA must be stopped—now!* New York: Hyperion.

Putman, Robert D. 1988. Diplomacy and domestic politics: The logic of two-level games. *International Organization* 42:427–60.

Sanderson, Fred H. 1994. The GATT agreement on agriculture. Washington, D.C.: National Center for Food and Agricultural Policy.

Swinnen, Jo, and Frans A. van der Zee. 1993. The political economy of agricultural policies: A survey. *European Review of Agricultural Economics* 25:261–90.

U.S. Congress. House. 1993. *North American Free Trade Agreement, Supplemental agreements and additional documents.* 103d Cong., 1st sess., H. Doc. 103–160. Washington, D.C.: Government Printing Office.

U.S. Congress. Senate. Committee on Finance. 1993. *Hearings on the anticipated nomination of Mickey Kantor, U.S. trade representative designate.* 103d Cong., 1st sess., S. Hrg. 103–12. Washington, D.C.: Government Printing Office.

USDA (U.S. Department of Agriculture). 1992a. NAFTA side-by-side tariff schedule. Washington, D.C.: USDA, Foreign Agricultural Service.

———. 1992b. North American Free Trade Agreement: U.S. nontariff barrier offer. Washington, D.C.: USDA, Foreign Agricultural Service.

———. 1993. *Effects of the North American Free Trade Agreement on U.S. agricultural commodities.* Washington, D.C.: USDA, Office of Economics, March.

———. 1994. *Estimates of producer subsidy equivalents and consumer subsidy equivalents: Government intervention in agriculture, 1982–1992.* Statistical Bulletin no. 913. Washington, D.C.: USDA, Economic Research Service.

USITC (U.S. International Trade Commission). 1993. *Potential impact on the U.S. economy and selected industries of the North American Free-Trade Agreement.* USITC Publication no. 2596. Washington, D.C.: U.S. International Trade Commission.

———. 1994. *Wheat, wheat flour and semolina.* USITC Publication no. 2794. Washington, D.C.: U.S. International Trade Commission.

Wall Street Journal. 1993a. Anatomy of a victory: "Deals" and sense of Clinton's commitment clinched NAFTA. November 19.

———. 1993b. White House hopes to trade changes in grazing-fee plan for NAFTA support. November 10.

Comment   Robert Paarlberg

David Orden has done a clean and careful job of reconstructing the U.S. side of the agricultural component of the North American Free Trade Agreement (NAFTA). I am in strong agreement with most of his judgments, especially near the end of the paper, but there are some shades of difference along the way.

Orden starts by implying that the agricultural component of NAFTA was a victory for free trade, perhaps more so than the Uruguay Round, because NAFTA successfully embraced the original Uruguay Round concept of phasing out all border protection. I would suggest toning down this assertion. In its

Robert Paarlberg is professor of political science at Wellesley College and associate at the Harvard University Center for International Affairs.

agricultural component, NAFTA did significantly liberalize some important import-competing sectors on the Mexican side (especially corn), but it did nothing to eliminate some important existing distortions on the U.S. side. In corn markets, while Mexican growers will lose their tariffs and import licenses, U.S. growers will not lose their target prices and deficiency payments (a domestic measure which nonetheless functions in part like an export subsidy). In corn markets, this was unilateral disarmament for Mexico.

And most conspicuously, NAFTA did not significantly liberalize U.S. sugar policy. Instead, it just extended the highly illiberal pricing regime created by that policy to sugar producers in Mexico (by raising Mexico's tariffs to the over-quota U.S. level). U.S. sugar growers complained about this because of fears that the eventual result in Mexico would be a replay of what had already happened in the United States: a replacement of sugar in beverages by high-fructose corn sweeteners, freeing up sugar for export to the United States. Orden accurately describes these details when his analysis gets to the case of sugar, but he never quite qualifies the earlier assertion that NAFTA was a victory for nondistorting free trade.

A larger concern, however, is with the process lessons that can and cannot be drawn from this case. If the dependent variable is policy liberalization, then there is probably more to be learned on the Mexican side of NAFTA than on the U.S. side. And on the Mexican side, I suspect most of the liberalization that occurred came neither from the bargaining dynamic of the NAFTA negotiation, nor from an internal dynamic of interest group representation within Mexico. Mexico was able to liberalize agriculture because the Mexican government is an authoritarian one-party presidential state. Even before the NAFTA agreement, President Salinas (and his mostly nonaccountable technocratic advisers) had decided to shift Mexican agriculture out of low-value maize production and into higher-value fruit and vegetable crops. Salinas was able to do this without much concern about opposition, within the system, from Mexico's own corn producers because the Mexican government operates top down rather than bottom up (a surprising expression of opposition came later from outside of the political system, with the January 1, 1994, Zapatista uprising).

Probably the most useful process lesson drawn by Orden at the U.S. end is his observation that agricultural interest groups gained influence for the paradoxical reason that they were neither for the agreement in principle, nor opposed in principle, a stance which made them worth courting with side-payments. The ability of farm groups to pursue commodity-specific side-payments in this fashion, outside of the confines of the normal farm bill process, deserves more attention. Sugar producers set the standard in 1981 when they held up that year's budget process for a revived domestic sugar program. Orden's paper shows how wheat growers were able to use the NAFTA vote on Mexico to gain additional concessions in their running trade disputes with Canada. And the paper by Bruce Gardner in this volume (chap. 6) shows how one or two wheat-state senators were able to use a 1985 Senate budget resolution vote to get a $2 billion Export Enhancement Program.

The political lesson would seem to be an almost impossible one to apply: liberal-minded presidents should do their best to avoid large, make-or-break, *close* votes in Congress. In winning such votes, the president can easily end up giving away more than he gains.

8 Differences in the Uses and Effects of Antidumping Law across Import Sources

Robert W. Staiger and Frank A. Wolak

8.1 Introduction

Given the success with which tariff reductions have been negotiated during the postwar period, it is not surprising that the rules which govern the exceptions from the negotiated tariff bindings have replaced the tariff bindings themselves as the central focus of international cooperation in trade policy. In 1947, the principal task confronting the contracting parties of the General Agreement on Tariffs and Trade (GATT) was the reciprocal lowering of high statutory trade barriers in place at that time. Today, in contrast, the heart of international trade policy negotiation consists of such issues as the conditions under which countries can reimpose temporary "safeguard" protection, the rules under which one country can impose a countervailing duty on another's subsidized exports, and procedures for settling disputes concerning the interpretation of these and other trade rules as they arise.

Nowhere is this change in emphasis more apparent than in the rising friction associated with antidumping law. Accusations that foreign firms are "dumping" products onto the domestic market and the belief that dumping is injurious to the domestic industry are by no means new.[1] Almost 80 years ago, such

Robert W. Staiger is associate professor of economics at the University of Wisconsin-Madison and a research associate of the National Bureau of Economic Research. Frank A. Wolak is associate professor of economics at Stanford University and a research associate of the National Bureau of Economic Research.

The authors thank Kala Krishna and participants at the NBER conference for helpful comments. They also gratefully acknowledge financial support from the National Science Foundation. Very able research assistance was provided by Phil Levy, Paul Liu, and Kerry Pannell. The authors are grateful to Azita Amjadi for providing them with access to her compilation of data on antidumping petitions.

1. Dumping is defined as exporting products to the domestic market at export prices "below fair value," i.e., either below the prices of comparable products for sale in the domestic market of the exporting country or below costs of production.

accusations and beliefs led the United States to adopt its first antidumping legislation, as contained in sections 800–801 of the Revenue Act of 1916. But while the original intent of the law was to protect U.S. firms from the "unfair competition" implied by the alleged dumping practices of the highly cartelized and heavily protected German industries of the period (see Viner 1966, 242), antidumping law today seems to elicit a much broader usage.[2]

With the use and abuse of antidumping law now regularly a central concern of both multilateral and bilateral trade negotiations, it is especially important to have as full an understanding as possible of the impact of existing antidumping laws on the free flow of trade, and of the uses to which antidumping law is put in practice. In this regard, several researchers have challenged the view that antidumping law restricts trade only when antidumping duties are actually imposed, arguing that the threat or even the mere possibility of duties can also affect import flows. We explore in this paper the differences across import sources in the uses and effects of antidumping law, accounting for both direct as well as possible indirect effects on imports and domestic import-competing output.

In an earlier paper (Staiger and Wolak 1994a) we studied three possible channels through which these indirect effects might arise that when combined with the direct effects of duties capture most of the trade effects of antidumping law. We referred to these three nonduty effects as the "investigation effect," the "suspension effect," and the "withdrawal effect." The first refers to the trade distortions associated with ongoing antidumping investigations, the second to the effects of "suspension agreements" (under which investigations are suspended in exchange for a promise by foreign firms to stop dumping), and the third to the effects of petitions that are withdrawn prior to a final determination. Our empirical findings, which reflected data on the timing and outcome of every antidumping investigation that covered a manufacturing industry product in the United States during the 1980–85 period, indicated that the investigation and suspension effects are substantial. Specifically, we found that suspension agreements lead to trade restrictions similar in magnitude to what would have been expected if antidumping duties were imposed instead. The effect of a typical antidumping investigation is to reduce imports during the period of investigation by roughly half the reduction that could be expected if antidumping duties had been imposed from the beginning of the investigation. We found little evidence to support a significant withdrawal effect.

Our focus on the broader trade effects of antidumping law also allowed us to consider the possibility that different firms might file antidumping petitions for different reasons. In particular, we found evidence of two distinct filing strategies that appeared to coexist in the data, and we referred to firms as "out-

---

2. This broadening usage was in part facilitated by explicit changes in U.S. antidumping law. For example, under the original U.S. law, predatory intent had to be shown to establish a finding of dumping. However, the Revenue Act of 1921 dropped the intent requirement.

come filers" or "process filers" depending on which strategy they appeared to be using. Outcome filers are firms that file antidumping petitions in anticipation of obtaining a finding of dumping and the relief that comes with it (either antidumping duties or a settlement agreement). Process filers are firms that file antidumping petitions, not to obtain a dumping finding, but rather to obtain the effects that arise solely from the investigation process itself. Our estimates suggested that while outcome filers are by far the dominant users of antidumping law, process filing was the likely strategy used by between 3 and 4 percent of the industries in our sample.

In the present paper we continue this line of research by looking for evidence of differences in the use and impacts of U.S. antidumping law as it is applied to imports from different trading partners. As we discuss in the next section, whether an antidumping petition is initiated for process or for outcome should depend not only on the characteristics of the domestic industry but also on the characteristics of the exporting country or countries against which the petition is filed. In our earlier work we allowed for the possibility that filing strategies might differ across U.S. industries, but we required firms in a given industry to pursue a common filing strategy against foreign imports, regardless of the country of origin. In this paper we allow the filing strategies of firms to be different for different import sources, but we impose the restriction that firms in all U.S. industries pursue the same overall filing strategy. Thus, we consider the possibility that U.S. firms may be outcome filers against imports from some countries and process filers against others.

Using this method of analysis we are able to quantify significant differences in filing strategies used by U.S. industries against five sets of trading partner countries. We are also able to quantify the extent of import and domestic output distortions due to the various stages of the suit resolution process for each of these five sets of trading partners. Finally, we are able to distinguish between regions exporting to the United States that are primarily targets of process filings by U.S. industries, as well as those regions that are primarily targets of outcome filings by U.S. industries.

We argue that the countries most likely to be the targets of process filings in the United States during our 1980–85 sample period are those whose export production over this period is predominantly destined for the U.S. market and accounts for a relatively large and stable U.S. market share. These characteristics point to Canada and Mexico as countries against which process filing by U.S. firms is likely to occur. Analyzing the filing behavior against imports from Canada and Mexico as well as against imports from four other regional groupings, we find evidence in the filing behavior and in the nature of the trade impacts which accompany filing to suggest that Canada and Mexico were indeed the most likely targets of antidumping petitions filed under the process filing strategy during our sample period. The regions against which the filing strategy of U.S. firms and the nature of the associated trade impacts seems most consistent with our outcome filing view of antidumping suit activity are the countries of Western Europe and the region composed of Japan and the newly industrialized countries (NICs) of East Asia.

The rest of the paper proceeds as follows. The next section briefly describes our motivation for including investigation, suspension, and withdrawal effects with the duty effects when quantifying the impact of antidumping law on imports and domestic output. It then describes the different investigation effects expected under outcome and process filing strategies. We also discuss in this section why some countries are more likely to be the target of process filing by U.S. firms than others. This discussion motivates the regional grouping of U.S. imports that we employ to carry out our empirical analysis. Section 8.3 then describes our data and model for estimation and presents the results. Section 8.4 concludes with an interpretation of our findings.

8.2   U.S. Antidumping Law

In this section we motivate why we believe it is important to consider the effects of suspension agreements, withdrawn petitions, and the investigation process itself, in addition to the effects of duty imposition, when quantifying the impacts of antidumping law on imports and domestic output. We also describe the different investigation effects on imports and domestic output that would be expected to arise under outcome and process filing. We then describe domestic filing behavior under these two filing strategies.[3] Finally, we discuss why some countries are more likely to be the target of process filing by U.S. firms than others.

We begin by making several observations concerning the practice of antidumping law in the United States which may be helpful to keep in mind. First, there are two findings necessary for a determination of dumping: (1) sales of imports at less than fair value (LTFV) and (2) material injury to the domestic industry due to these imports. One government agency is assigned to each of these determinations—the International Trade Commission (ITC) determines injury to the domestic industry and the Commerce Department's International Trade Administration (ITA) makes the LTFV determination. A second point to bear in mind is that for each of these decisions there is a preliminary and final decision made by each agency. The statutory time allotted for the entire investigation ranges from 10 months to 14 months under special circumstances. Finally, except in "critical circumstances" (a condition described more fully below but in practice rarely met), a final determination of dumping will bring the retroactive imposition of antidumping duties on all imports of the relevant products which entered the United States on or after the date of the preliminary LTFV finding, provided that the preliminary LTFV finding was affirmative (as it was for 93 percent of the products whose investigations made it to this stage of the investigation process during the 1980–85 period). With these general

---

3. A more detailed discussion of these points is contained in Staiger and Wolak (1994a).

points in mind we now turn to a discussion of the various potential trade-distorting effects of antidumping law.

8.2.1   The Trade Effects of Antidumping Law

A simple view of the trade effects of antidumping law would hold that trade flows are only affected by antidumping law when a petition is filed, dumping is found, and antidumping duties are imposed. Were this indeed the case, one could get a fairly complete understanding of the trade effects of antidumping law by examining those instances where antidumping duties were actually imposed. However, there are a number of reasons to believe that this simple view is inadequate, that many of the effects of antidumping law are indirect and subtle, and that a narrow focus on antidumping duties alone would overlook important nonduty channels through which antidumping law could act. We now describe three nonduty effects which, we believe, when combined with the effects of duties, capture a major component of the possible trade effects of antidumping law.[4]

Investigation Effect

First, it is often claimed (see, e.g., Dale 1980, 85–86; U.S. Congress, House 1978, 12, 278) that imports are restricted during the period over which an antidumping investigation is ongoing. As described more fully in Staiger and Wolak (1994a), there are two broad hypotheses concerning the reasons for and nature of this investigation effect. We refer to these two hypotheses as the "outcome filer" hypothesis and the "process filer" hypothesis. According to the outcome filer hypothesis, the investigation effect reflects actions taken by domestic importers and/or foreign exporters in anticipation of the duties that would be imposed in the event of a final affirmative dumping determination and that would be assessed retroactively back to the date of an affirmative preliminary LTFV determination. That is, as noted above, an affirmative preliminary LTFV determination carries with it the liability of duty assessment for all imports entering thereafter if a final affirmative dumping determination is made subsequently. Consequently, a preliminary finding of LTFV sales would be expected under this hypothesis to lead to a sharp drop in imports, with these trade-restricting effects lasting for the remainder of the investigation

---

4. There is a growing empirical literature concerned with the determinants and the duty and nonduty effects of antidumping law. See, e.g., Finger (1981), Hernander and Schwartz (1984), Salvatore (1987), Hartigan, Kamma, and Perry (1989), Messerlin (1989, 1990), Lichtenberg and Tan (1990), Harrison (1991), Prusa (1991), and Staiger and Wolak (1994a, 1994b). The two papers closest in spirit to our work here and in Staiger and Wolak (1994a) are Lichtenberg and Tan (1990) and Harrison (1991). However, unlike the present paper, neither Lichtenberg and Tan nor Harrison attempts to distinguish among the phases of the investigation process, nor does either paper attempt to account exhaustively for the various postinvestigation outcomes. Also, neither paper attempts to explore the possibility that the use and effects of antidumping law are source-country specific. See Staiger and Wolak (1994a) for a more detailed comparison of our work with these papers.

period, as long as the petition was perceived as having a reasonable chance of ending in a final dumping determination. In fact, this kind of investigation effect figures prominently in many press accounts of ongoing antidumping actions. For example, in reference to a U.S. antidumping petition brought by the National Knitwear and Sportswear Association against sweater producers in Hong Kong, South Korea, and Taiwan, the *New York Times* (1990) observes: "The [preliminary dumping] margins were announced as retailers are about to place orders for delivery next fall. Some industry officials said prospects of higher prices, or just the uncertainty over what the new price levels would be, could cause some retailers to switch to domestic suppliers."

In addition to a drop in imports coming with an affirmative preliminary LTFV determination, the outcome filer hypothesis carries with it two additional implications. First, in light of the possibility of an affirmative preliminary LTFV determination and subsequent falloff in import flows, imports might, if anything, be expected to rise somewhat during the first months of the investigation in anticipation of this effect. In fact, evidently anticipating this possibility, U.S. law provides for an assessment of "critical circumstances" under which duties can be imposed retroactively to the date of filing if the filing of a petition brings with it a significant import surge. For this reason, we would expect any import increase associated with the early stages of an investigation under the outcome filer hypothesis to be small. Second, under the outcome filer hypothesis, any petitions filed without regard to measures important for the final dumping determination would be unlikely to exhibit strong investigation effects, since this hypothesis presumes a significant probability of a final dumping determination and consequent duty imposition. It is for this reason that we refer to this hypothesis as the outcome filer hypothesis: the strength of the investigation effect under this hypothesis reflects the fear of retroactive duty imposition in the event of an affirmative final determination at the end of the investigation process and therefore ought to reflect the likelihood that the final outcome will be a finding of dumping.

It is also possible that there are investigation effects that do *not* reflect a significant probability of retroactive duty imposition at the end of the investigation process but reflect rather the effects of the investigation process itself. This embodies the process filer hypothesis. In an earlier paper (Staiger and Wolak 1991), we presented a model in which domestic firms make strategic use of the ongoing antidumping investigation of the pricing and sales practices of foreign firms to prevent the occurrence of price wars which might otherwise be triggered by periods of slack demand and low capacity utilization. Our theory suggests that domestic firms may value the competition-dampening effects of an ongoing antidumping investigation for its own sake and may file such petitions when capacity utilization is low with no expectation that they would actually result in duties or other remedies.

Specifically, we showed in Staiger and Wolak (1991) how access to antidumping law in the domestic country can lead to the filing of antidumping petitions by the domestic industry when capacity utilization is sufficiently low, and to less aggressive pricing by foreign firms and greater market share for domestic firms—and in fact to a fall in imports and a rise in domestic output—during the period of investigation as a result. This occurs despite the fact that antidumping duties are never actually imposed and were never expected to be imposed. That is, the entire investigation effect of antidumping law under this interpretation comes in the form of a threat to "punish" foreign firms with a duty if they should "misbehave" and price too aggressively. Such a threat is made credible by filing the petition; because it is credible, the threatened duties need never materialize. In Staiger and Wolak (1994a), we referred to such filers as process filers and noted that (1) the act of filing ought to have an immediate trade-dampening effect which lasts for the duration of the investigation, distinguishing the investigation effects under process filers from those under outcome filers, and (2) process filers ought to file antidumping petitions on the basis of low capacity utilization and little else, and in particular should not be concerned with measures important for the final determination of dumping, thus distinguishing the filing behavior of process filers from that of outcome filers.

Suspension Effect

Turning to the suspension effect, a second way in which antidumping law may restrict trade through nonduty channels is through the effects of "suspension agreements," under which antidumping investigations are suspended by the Commerce Department in exchange for an explicit agreement by foreign firms named in the antidumping petition to eliminate sales in the U.S. market at less than "fair value." Since the intent of a suspension agreement is to provide a nonduty alternative by which previous dumping activities can be halted, it would be surprising if there were not a suspension effect in the data. A prominent example involving such a suspension agreement (though not falling in our sample period) was the 1986 U.S.-Japan Semiconductor Trade Arrangement.

Withdrawal Effect

Finally, a third way in which antidumping law may restrict trade through nonduty channels concerns the withdrawal effect.[5] That is, the imposition of antidumping duties or the negotiation of a suspension agreement need not be the only outcomes of an antidumping petition for which postinvestigation relief from imports is secured. In this regard, Prusa (1992) has argued that petitions which are withdrawn by the domestic industry before a final determination can have as restrictive an impact on subsequent trade flows as would be the case if a final determination of dumping had been made and duties imposed.

---

5. In addition, a number of papers, e.g., Anderson (1992), Staiger and Wolak (1992), and Prusa (1988), have suggested that the mere existence of antidumping law can have trade effects even in periods when no petition is filed.

Essentially, Prusa argues that domestic firms can use the threat of antidumping duties, together with the protection from domestic antitrust laws afforded when an antidumping proceeding is in progress, to bargain with foreign firms over domestic market share, and that the antidumping petition is withdrawn by the domestic industry if and when a sufficiently attractive bargain is struck.[6]

8.2.2 The Targets of Process Filers

Focusing on the three nonduty effects described above, together with the duty effect of antidumping law, in Staiger and Wolak (1994a) we found evidence of substantial investigation effects, and of the trade restrictiveness of suspension agreements, but found no evidence that withdrawn petitions had lasting trade-restricting effects. We also found some evidence for the coexistence of outcome and process filers in our data. However, we did not allow the filing strategy pursued by a domestic industry to differ by the identity of the country whose firms were named in the petition. Nor did we allow the trade effects of these petitions to vary systematically with the identity of the country against whose firms the petition was filed. In the next section we will present an extended framework which allows us to detect differences in filing strategies and in the impacts of antidumping law across the target countries named in the petition. However, before doing this we discuss why certain countries may be more likely targets of the process filing strategy than others.

The logic of our process filing strategy is that domestic firms use the antidumping investigation process to reduce the temptation of foreign firms to cut prices during periods of low capacity utilization. For this strategy to be sensible for domestic firms to pursue over our sample period, several conditions must be met in the country (countries) against which this filing strategy is being used. First, the firms exporting from each country named in the antidumping petition should account for a significant share of the relevant U.S. market, since otherwise the threat posed by these firms to the profitability of U.S. firms in the event of a breakdown in price discipline is likely to be small. Second, the U.S. market share captured by the firms exporting from these countries should be relatively stable over the sample period, since otherwise the premise of an orderly pricing arrangement, whose breakdown during periods of falling capacity utilization can be avoided through the competition-dampening effects of antidumping investigations, would be in doubt. Third, exporters from these countries should be relatively dependent on the U.S. market for their sales, since otherwise demand shifts in the U.S. market which lead to falling capacity utilization of U.S. firms might not lead to a significant fall

---

6. Agreements between foreign firms and domestic petitioners are permitted under the Noerr-Pennington doctrine which provides exemption from prosecution under U.S. antitrust law. Direct conversations between domestic and foreign firms concerning prices or quantities would not be protected, so settlements are typically negotiated through the Commerce Department (Horlick 1989). See Prusa (1992) for a detailed analysis of this exemption and its implications for the effects of antidumping law.

in capacity utilization rates for the foreign exporters (and therefore would not give rise to a significant temptation on the part of foreign exporters to cut prices in the U.S. market).

With these three criteria in mind, we note first that the five largest non–oil-exporting trading partners of the United States in 1980 by import values were Canada (16 percent of total U.S. imports), Japan (13 percent of total U.S. imports), Mexico (5 percent of total U.S. imports), Germany (5 percent of total U.S. imports), and the United Kingdom (4 percent of total U.S. imports), with a number of countries then clustered, each at just under 2 percent of total U.S. imports (International Monetary Fund 1987). Of these five biggest import-source countries for the United States, the growth in U.S. imports from Japan over the 1980–85 period was three times the growth in total U.S. imports over this period, and nearly twice as fast as the growth in U.S. imports over this period from the country with the next fastest import growth (Germany). Of the remaining four countries with high and relatively stable shares of the U.S. market over this period, 65 percent of Mexico's worldwide exports went to the U.S. market in 1980 and 61 percent of Canada's exports did, while the United Kingdom and Germany exported 10 and 6 percent of their worldwide exports, respectively, to the U.S. market (Japan exported 24 percent of its worldwide exports to the U.S. market). On this basis, we expect that Canada and Mexico would be the most likely targets of process filings from U.S. firms over our sample period because they represent two countries whose export production over this period is predominantly destined for the U.S. market and accounts for a relatively large and stable U.S. market share.

8.3   The Uses and Impacts of Antidumping Law

To investigate whether the filing strategies pursued by domestic firms and the impacts of the ensuing investigation process on the flow of imports and domestic output vary systematically with the identity of the country whose firms are named in the petition, we must first describe our choice of regional groupings and the data sources used for all of the empirical work presented in this paper. We then describe our econometric framework, which extends that of Staiger and Wolak (1994a). Finally, we estimate a model of industry-level antidumping suit filings and of the import and output effects associated with the various phases and potential outcomes of the investigation process. We assess the degree to which our findings differ systematically as a function of the identity of the countries whose firms are targeted by the investigation.

8.3.1   Regional Groupings

To select the different exporting regions used in our analysis we attempted to balance several concerns. On the one hand, we had to keep the number of regions from getting too large, lest the estimation of the model become unmanageable. But at the same time, we also felt that similar economies should be grouped together. We settled on five regions: Canada and Mexico, as the region representing the most likely target of process filings, and four other regions. Our desire to group similar economies together led us to put all of the planned economies of Eastern Europe along with the former Soviet Union together as a single exporting region. We call this region the planned economy region. This desire also led us to group together all of the countries of Western Europe. In those cases in which we did not have a sufficient number of filings from a single country we grouped countries according to their location. This led us to group Japan in with the NICs of South Korea, Taiwan, Singapore, and Hong Kong. Our fifth region is a residual of all of the other countries. Further disaggregation of this region into smaller regions along geographic lines did not lead to statistically significantly different results for these subregions, so we retained this level of aggregation.

8.3.2   Data Sources

The source of data for the industry-level economic magnitudes is the National Bureau of Economic Research *Trade Data File* (see Abowd 1990 for a detailed description of this data set). This data set contains annual data for the period 1958–85 on the value of domestic shipments, imports, and exports for 450 U.S. manufacturing industries by four-digit 1972 Standard Industry Code (SIC). It also contains information on such industry-level economic aggregates as the level of employment and the size of the capital stock, as well as an industry-level output price deflator. The source for the filing dates for all antidumping petitions and the dates and outcomes of all the subsequent stages of the investigation process, as well as the identity of the countries whose firms are named in the investigation, is the National Technical Information Service's *Trade Action Monitoring System (TAMS) Pending Investigation Report*. This publication is produced by the Commerce Department on a monthly basis and tracks all petitions having to do with the 1974 Trade Act, such as petitions for escape clause relief, antidumping duties, countervailing duties, and remedies for unfair practices in import trade. Each month it lists the current disposition of each petition until its final determination. When an antidumping petition is filed, the petition must allege dumping of specific imported products. For purposes of the investigation, the ITC must then link the products under investigation to product codes of the *Tariff Schedules of the United States* (TSUS). Consequently, the TAMS data set records for each petition the TSUS codes for the products which are allegedly being dumped, the country or countries from which these imports came, and the petition's disposition in the current month.

We explicitly account for filing at the TSUS product code level in our econometric model of the suit-filing process and in our model of the impacts of antidumping suits on imports and domestic output flows. However, since our economic data is available at the four-digit 1972 SIC industry level, we must have a concordance between the TSUS codes and the four-digit 1972 SICs to assign antidumping suits to SIC industries. We obtain a year-by-year concordance between TSUS product codes and the four-digit 1972 SIC codes from the Commerce Department's Foreign Trade Division's *Imports Extract Master Concordance.* This concordance allows us to assign each TSUS product covered by an antidumping petition to a four-digit SIC industry. Because TSUS codes are based on traded products and SIC code assignments are based on a firm's principal productive activities, several SIC industries do not have any TSUS code associated with them over our sample. Consequently, a necessary requirement for an SIC industry to appear in our data set is that it contains at least one TSUS code product for each year during our sample. Only four industries were deleted from the sample because they had no TSUS code in them for only a portion of the sample time period. Most of the industries omitted had no TSUS codes in them for all years. This concordance procedure left a total of 338 industries for our time period of 1980–85.

Our empirical work focuses on 1980–85 because significant changes in the structure of U.S. antidumping law were made in the Trade Agreement Act of 1979. Modifications of this act were made by the Trade and Tariff Act of 1984, but none of these are directly relevant to the issues we consider in our research.

8.3.3   Econometric Model

There are several aspects of the economic environment we are modeling that our econometric model should capture. These involve the joint determination of the decision to file a petition with the level of imports and domestic output in an industry, as well as a number of specific characteristics of the petition-filing process and of the impacts of filings on the level of imports and domestic output. We begin with a brief discussion of these modeling issues and then present the econometric model which we estimate.

First, the decision to file an antidumping petition is likely to be determined jointly with the level of imports and domestic output in the industry. As such, filing, import, and output equations should be estimated jointly, allowing for the possibility of various correlations across equations. We allow for contemporaneous correlation between the level of imports and domestic output and the decision to file an antidumping suit against any of our five importing regions by the presence of an unobservable industry characteristic which affects the conditional mean of each of these variables. Our econometric model also allows for the existence of contemporaneous correlations among imports, domestic output, and the filing rates, as well as correlations over time among these seven variables.

Second, in attempting to understand the filing strategies used by firms, and to ask whether these strategies differ systematically with the identity of the countries whose firms are targeted by the petitions, there are several characteristics which we need to capture in our econometric model. Of primary importance is the fact, as mentioned above, that antidumping suits are filed at the TSUS code level although all of our economic data is at the four-digit SIC level. Consequently, we must construct a model which allows us to recover information about the TSUS-level filing process using SIC-level economic data as regressors for the filing rate process. The number of filings in a given TSUS code is a nonnegative discrete-valued random variable that is zero for most time periods, but in the periods in which it is nonzero, it can take on large values. We select a discrete distribution for the TSUS-level number of antidumping suit filings which allows for this "contagion" property. In addition, to match the industry-level aggregation of our import and domestic output data, we need a distribution for TSUS-level filings which can be aggregated to the four-digit SIC level in a straightforward manner.

Third, to measure the impacts of various stages of the antidumping investigation process on the flow of imports and domestic output, and to ask whether these impacts differ systematically with the identity of the countries involved, several characteristics of the investigation process must be accounted for. First, a single antidumping investigation can straddle more than a single year, while each of the various stages of the process last only a fraction of a year. In addition, at the level of multilateral imports several antidumping investigations or outcomes can be simultaneously active in a single TSUS code because of filings against the same product imported from different countries. These characteristics present a problem because, as mentioned above, our data on imports and domestic output are only available on an annual basis at the four-digit SIC level and our import data is not broken down by source country. Consequently, we must specify a model which will allow us to recover the TSUS-level impacts on the flows of imports and on domestic output from stages of the investigation process which may run over adjacent years or for a fraction of a year, accounting for the possibility of multiple filings from the same TSUS code, using data which is time aggregated to annual magnitudes and cross-sectionally aggregated to the four-digit SIC industry level, and with import data which is only available at a multilateral level. Our TSUS-level, within-year flow model provides a framework for us to recover within-year country-specific effects from annual multilateral import and domestic output levels using indexes of country-specific suit activity in that year.

Our SIC-level model of the filing rate process and the impacts of the investigation process can be interpreted without reference to the underlying TSUS-level processes. However, our bottom-up approach, starting with a TSUS-level model which has not been time aggregated to the annual magnitudes nor aggregated across country to multilateral magnitudes, specifies an econometric model at the level of time, country, and product aggregation at which the true underlying processes are occurring. It is then aggregated across time, product, and country to an industry-level model. This modeling strategy allows the recovery of both TSUS- and industry-level impacts because the industry-level model is obtained from the explicit aggregation of the TSUS-level model. In addition, the strategy makes explicit the restrictions imposed on the TSUS-level and region-level models which are implied by estimating an industry-level model.

We now describe the details of our econometric model of suit-filing behavior and its impacts on the level of imports and domestic output. Let f_{grit} be the number of antidumping suits filed in industry i against good g from region r in period t, where $g = 1, \ldots, G_{it}, t = 1, \ldots, T, r = 1, \ldots, R$, and $i = 1, \ldots, N$. In the present case $R = 5$, $T = 6$, and $N = 338$. Because antidumping suits are filed at the TSUS code level, for the purposes of this paper a good is defined to be a TSUS product code.

Let λ_{grit} denote the rate at which suits are filed in industry i against good g from region r in period t. We assume that the distribution of f_{grit} given λ_{grit} is Poisson ($P(\lambda)$) with parameter $\lambda = \lambda_{grit}$. We denote this fact using the notation

(1) $$f_{grit} \mid \lambda_{grit} \sim P(\lambda_{grit}).$$

These assumptions are consistent with f_{grit} being a Poisson point process for the time interval t to $t + 1$, which we will call time period t.

We further assume that λ_{grit} possesses a gamma distribution $\Gamma(\mu_{rit}, \sigma_r)$, where $\mu_{rit} = \exp(X'_{it}\gamma_r + \delta_r\theta_i)$. The vector X_{it} contains the observable characteristics of industry i as of the beginning of time t which affect its filing rate; the vector γ_r and the scalars σ_r and δ_r are parameters to be estimated.[7] The variable θ_i is the unobservable characteristic of industry i which affects the mean filing rate for that industry, and δ_r is the parameter which denotes the impact θ_i has on the filing rate against region r. We assume that θ_i is independently and identically distributed across industries and remains constant over time. Using our above notation we have

(2) $$\lambda_{grit} \mid \{X_{it}, \theta_i\} \sim \Gamma(\exp(X'_{it}\gamma_r + \delta_r\theta_i), \sigma_r).$$

Assumption (2) implies that each product class from region r within industry i and in time period t has a different mean rate of filing (λ_{grit}), although all of these filing rates are drawn from the same gamma distribution.

Combining assumptions (1) and (2), we have

(3) $$f_{grit} \mid \{X_{it}, \theta_i\} \sim P(\lambda_{grit}) \, O_{\lambda_{grit}} \, \Gamma(\exp(X'_{it}\gamma_r + \delta_r\theta_i), \sigma_r),$$

where $O_{\lambda_{grit}}$ denotes compounding or mixing the parameter λ_{grit} of the Poisson distribution with a gamma distribution $\Gamma(\exp(X'_{it}\gamma_r + \delta_r\theta_i), \sigma_r)$. Results from Johnson and Kotz (1969, chap. 5) imply that f_{grit} has a negative binomial distribution with parameters σ_r and $\mu_{rit} = \exp(X'_{it}\gamma_r + \delta_r\theta_i)$. We abbreviate this as $f_{grit} \sim NB(\sigma_r, \mu_{rit})$. This discrete density takes the following form:

(4) $$\text{pr}[f_{grit} = k] = \binom{\sigma_r + k - 1}{\sigma_r - 1}(\mu^f_{rit})^k(1 + \mu^f_{rit})^{-(\sigma_r + k)}.$$

The mean of f_{grit} is $\sigma_r\mu_{rit}$. We assume that conditional on θ_i, f_{grit} is independent of f_{hqjs} so long as any one of the four subscript indexes differ.

---

7. In Staiger and Wolak (1994a), we constrained all r-subscripted variables to be equal across all regions.

Our data generation process captures the following logic. In each period t, λ_{grit}, the filing rate against product class g imported from region r in industry i, is drawn from a $\Gamma(\exp(X'_{it}\gamma_r + \delta_r\theta_i), \sigma_r)$ distribution. Conditional on this draw of λ_{grit} and the value of θ_i, the actual filing behavior against an individual product class from region r evolves according to a Poisson process with rate λ_{grit}. For each regional import source, this compound distribution model allows for differences in filing rates across product classes within an industry. At the same time, for each regional import source, the model imposes the restriction that the filing rates against imports for all product classes within an industry have the same expectation. From our estimation procedure we can recover estimates of the parameters of both the distribution $\Gamma(\exp(X'_{it}\gamma_r + \delta_r\theta_i), \sigma_r)$ and the filing Poisson process conditional on the realized value of λ_{grit}.

The filing of an antidumping suit is a rare event, but when it occurs there tends to be clustering in the number of filings. Within the context of our econometric model we can think of this clustering of suits as caused by the positive skewness in the gamma distribution for λ_{grit}, so that most realizations of the rate of the Poisson process are very small. However, a large realization occurs very rarely, which in turn implies a large number of observed filings. In addition, the unobserved heterogeneity across industries represented by θ_i allows for a much larger (or smaller) level of filing activity from a given industry than is predicted by its observable characteristics. Both the stochastic nature of the mean filing rate and the impact of unobservable industry-level heterogeneity θ_i on the filing rate allow for a substantial amount of variability in the TSUS-level filing rates across industries.

To compute f_{rit}, the total number of suits filed within industry i against region r during period t, we sum f_{grit} from $g = 1$ to G_{it}, the total number of TSUS product codes within industry i in period t. This summation yields

$$(5) \qquad f_{rit} = \sum_{g=1}^{G_{it}} f_{grit}.$$

This industry-level annual amount of filing activity against region r is the observable dependent variable used to estimate the parameters γ_r and σ_r and the across-industry distribution of heterogeneity $f(\theta)$.

To construct the conditional density of f_{rit} given θ_i, we utilize the fact that the sum of two independent NB(α, β) random variables is NB$(2\alpha, \beta)$. This implies that f_{rit} possesses a negative binomial distribution with parameters $G_{it}\sigma_r$ and $\mu_{rit} = \exp(X'_{it}\gamma_r + \delta_r\theta_i)$, conditional on the value of θ_i. Consequently, the conditional distribution of f_{rit} given θ_i is

$$(6) \qquad \mathrm{pr}[f_{rit} \mid \theta_i] = \frac{\Gamma(G_{it}\sigma_r + f_{rit})}{\Gamma(f_{rit} + 1)\,\Gamma(G_{it}\sigma_r)}\exp(f_{rit}(X'_{it}\gamma_r + \delta_r\theta_i))$$

$$\times\ (1 + \exp(X'_{it}\gamma_r + \delta_r\theta_i))^{-(G_{it}\sigma_r + f_{rit})},$$

where $\Gamma(\alpha)$ is the gamma function

$$\Gamma(\alpha) = \int_{0}^{\infty} t^{\alpha - 1} e^{-t} dt.$$

We have also made use of the relationship $\Gamma(\alpha + 1) = \alpha!$. The joint density function of $f_i = (f_{1i}, f_{2i}, \ldots, f_{Ri})$, where $f_{ri} = (f_{1980,i}, f_{1981,i}, \ldots, f_{1985,i})'$, is

(7) $$\text{pr}[f_i \mid \theta_i] = \prod_{r=1}^{R} \prod_{t=1980}^{1985} \text{pr}[f_{rit} \mid \theta_i],$$

where $\text{pr}[f_{rit} \mid \theta_i]$ is defined in equation (6). Henceforth let $t = 1, \ldots, T = 6$ denote the years 1980–85. The structure of equation (7) accounts for several aspects of our underlying data generation process. First, it allows for contemporaneous correlation across regions in the filing rates for a given industry. Second, it allows for correlation over time in filing rates both for a given region and across regions. Finally, it accounts for the discrete, nonnegative support and extreme positive skewness in the density of filings for each region.

We now turn to our model of the impact of antidumping investigation activity and outcomes on industry-level imports and output which is linked to the model of filing activity through the unobserved industry heterogeneity θ_i. As discussed above, because we are attempting to measure the within-year effects of the stages and various outcomes of the antidumping investigation process from annual magnitudes, we first specify a model for the rate of imports of product class g in industry i from region j within any given year t which incorporates how each of the stages and outcomes of the investigation process affects this rate. We then aggregate this regional import rate equation over regions to obtain the (multilateral) import rate equation. Specifying an analogous equation for the rate of domestic output, we then aggregate these two within-year flow equations to obtain the annual level of imports and domestic output by product class. This aggregation process produces indexes of annual suit activity consistent with our model of import and domestic output flows. Aggregating these TSUS-level annual-level equations over all products in each four-digit SIC industry yields industry-level equations which can be estimated using our industry-level data.

Specifically, let IMP_{gjit} denote the level of imports from region j for product class g in industry i in time period t. Let OUT_{git} denote the level of output produced domestically in product class g in industry i in time period t.

Our within-year model of the impacts of suit activity assumes that for any year t and industry i, the following linear differential equations characterize the instantaneous annual rate of change in the quantity of imports from region j and domestic output at the TSUS code level:

(8r) $$\frac{d\,\text{IMP}_{gjit}}{ds} = \beta_j^m \theta_i + \xi_{jt}^m + \sum_r \sum_k \beta_{jrk}^m I_{grit}^k(s) + e_{gjit}(m),$$

$$(9) \qquad \frac{d\text{OUT}_{git}}{ds} = \beta^o \theta_i + \xi^o_t + \sum_r \sum_k \beta^o_{rk} I^k_{grit}(s) + e_{git}(o),$$

where β^m_j and β^o are coefficients quantifying the impact of the unobservable industry heterogeneity on the rate of change of imports from region j and industry i and of output in industry i for all time, ξ^m_t and ξ^o_t are fixed time effects for the two rates of change for year t, and $\sum_z$ denotes a summation over the range of the index z. The count variables $I^k_{grit}(s)$ ($k = $ OGP, OGPLFV, OGSUS, OGWD, and OGD) count, respectively, the number of currently ongoing antidumping petitions (OGP), ongoing affirmative preliminary LTFV determinations (OGPLFV), ongoing suspension agreements (OGSUS), ongoing withdrawn petitions (OGWD), and ongoing antidumping duties (OGD) for all $s \in [t, t + 1)$ against product class g from region r in industry i and time period t. Hence, equation ($8r$) allows for the possibility that suit activity k against region r can affect import flows from region j (as measured by β^m_{jrk}). The variables $e_{gjit}(m)$ and $e_{git}(o)$ are independent identically distributed shocks to the rate of imports from region r and output for product class g in industry i during period t.

We now aggregate the regional import rate equation ($8r$) over the $R = 5$ regions to obtain the (multilateral) import rate equation (8) analogous to the output rate equation (9):

$$(8) \qquad \frac{d\text{IMP}_{git}}{ds} = \beta^m \theta_i + \xi^m_t + \sum_r \sum_k \beta^m_{rk} I^k_{grit}(s) + e_{git}(m) ,$$

where $\text{IMP}_{git} = \sum_j \text{IMP}_{gjit}$, $\beta^m = \sum_j \beta^m_j$, $\xi^m_t = \sum_j \xi^m_{jt}$, $\beta^m_{rk} = \sum_j \beta^m_{jrk}$, and $e_{git}(m) = \sum_j e_{gjit}(m)$. The coefficients β^l_{rk}, ($l = o, m$) quantify the impact of a one-unit change in region r's count variables $I^k_{grit}(s)$ on the annual rate of (multilateral) imports and domestic output for good g in industry i during time period t. We assume that the disturbance vector $e_{git} = (e_{git}(m), e_{git}(o))'$ possesses a bivariate normal distribution with mean zero and covariance matrix Σ. We assume that e_{git} is independent and identically distributed across goods and industries and over time.

To clarify how the workings of antidumping law affect the quantity of imports and domestic output in our model, consider the following example. Suppose that no antidumping investigation or action is currently in effect on imports from product class g in industry i during year t. In this case the rate of imports in product class g in industry i is

$$(10) \qquad \frac{d\text{IMP}_{git}}{ds} = \beta^m \theta_i + \xi^m_t + e_{git}(m).$$

Suppose now that an antidumping investigation is initiated some time during period t on imports in this product class from region r. The variable $I^{\text{OGP}}_{grit}(s)$ will then take on the value 1 for all $s \in [t, t + 1)$ such that the antidumping investigation is currently active. Consequently, the rate of imports will increase by the value of $\beta^m_{r,\text{OGP}}$ because an investigation is currently ongoing against goods of that product class from region r. Should another petition be filed against imports within this product class from somewhere else in region r during the same time interval, then $I^{\text{OGP}}_{grit}(s)$ will take on the value 2 for as long as both sets of investigations are ongoing; it will return to the value of 1 when a single investigation is again active, and 0 when no investigations are active. Each of the other count variables behaves in a similar manner.

Continuing with the derivation of our TSUS-level import and output equations, we integrate equations (8) and (9) with respect to s from t to $t + 1$ to obtain

$$(11) \qquad \text{IMP}_{git} = \beta^m \theta_i + \xi^m_t + \sum_r \sum_k \beta^m_{rk} k_{grit} + e_{git}(m),$$

$$(12) \qquad \text{OUT}_{git} = \beta^o \theta_i + \xi^o_t + \sum_r \sum_k \beta^o_{rk} k_{grit} + e_{git}(o),$$

where

$$k_{grit} = \int_t^{t+1} I^k_{grit}(s) \, ds.$$

In order to compute industry-level import and output equations from these product-level equations, we must aggregate over all of the product classes g within industry i in period t. Summing over all g yields

$$(13) \qquad \text{IMP}_{it} = \beta^m \theta_i G_{it} + \xi^m_t G_{it} + \sum_r \sum_k \beta^m_{rk} k_{rit} + \eta_{it}(m),$$

$$(14) \qquad \text{OUT}_{it} = \beta^o \theta_i G_{it} + \xi^o_t G_{it} + \sum_r \sum_k \beta^o_{rk} k_{rit} + \eta_{it}(o),$$

where

$$\text{IMP}_{it} = \sum_{g=1}^{G_{it}} \text{IMP}_{git}, \quad \text{OUT}_{it} = \sum_{g=1}^{G_{it}} \text{OUT}_{git},$$

$$k_{rit} = \sum_{g=1}^{G_{it}} k_{grit}, \quad \eta_{it}(l) = \sum_{g=1}^{G_{it}} e_{git}(l),$$

for $l = m, o$. This aggregation procedure implies that $\eta_{it} = (\eta_{it}(m), \eta_{it}(o))'$ is $N(0, G_{it}\Sigma)$ so that η_{it} is heteroskedastic conditional on G_{it}. Dividing equations (13) and (14) by G_{it} yields a model more amenable to estimation. This form of the model is analogous to the conventional fixed time effects, random individual effects panel-data model. The model is

$$(15) \qquad \text{IMP}_{it}/G_{it} = \mu^m_{it} + \eta_{it}(m)/G_{it}, \quad \text{OUT}_{it}/G_{it} = \mu^o_{it} + \eta_{it}(o)/G_{it},$$

where

$$(16) \qquad \mu^m_{it} = \beta^m \theta_i + \xi^m_t + \sum_r \sum_k \beta^m_{rk} k_{rit}/G_{it},$$

$$\mu_{it}^o = \beta^o \theta_i + \xi_t^o + \sum_r \sum_k \beta_{rk}^o k_{rit}/G_{it}.$$

The variables μ_{it}^m and μ_{it}^o are the conditional means of the normalized annual imports and output from industry i in period t. Each of the normalized count variables now can be interpreted as a measure of the intensity of suit activity. The normalized error vector η_{it}/G_{it} is still heteroskedastic because of the distribution for η_{it} given above. Consequently, we apply the appropriate weighting scheme in the construction of the likelihood function.

Using our distributional assumptions we can construct the joint density of $\text{IMP}_i^* = (\text{IMP}_{i1}/G_{i1}, \ldots, \text{IMP}_{iT}/G_{iT})'$ and $\text{OUT}_i^* = (\text{OUT}_{i1}/G_{i1}, \ldots, \text{OUT}_{iT}/G_{iT})'$ conditional on θ_i as follows. Conditional on the value of θ_i, the joint density of the two-dimensional vector $(\text{IMP}_{it}/G_{it}, \text{OUT}_{it}/G_{it})'$ is

(17)
$$\phi(\text{IMP}_{it}/G_{it}, \text{OUT}_{it}/G_{it} \mid \theta_i) =$$
$$\frac{1}{2\pi} \mid G_{it}^{-1}\Sigma \mid^{-1/2} \exp\left(-1/2(v_{it}'(G_{it}^{-1}\Sigma)^{-1}v_{it})\right),$$

where $v_{it} = ((\text{IMP}_{it}/G_{it} - \mu_{it}^m), (\text{OUT}_{it}/G_{it} - \mu_{it}^o))'$. This implies that the joint density of $(\text{IMP}_i^*, \text{OUT}_i^*)'$ conditional on θ_i is

(18)
$$h(\text{IMP}_i^*, \text{OUT}_i^* \mid \theta_i) = \prod_{t=1}^{T} \phi(\text{IMP}_{it}/G_{it}, \text{OUT}_{it}/G_{it} \mid \theta_i).$$

Combining this joint density with the joint density of regional filings over the sample period yields the following joint density of filings against the five regions, output, and imports over our sample period conditional on θ_i:

(19)
$$g(f_i, \text{IMP}_i^*, \text{OUT}_i^* \mid \theta_i) = h(\text{IMP}_i^*, \text{OUT}_i^* \mid \theta_i)\, \text{pr}(f_i \mid \theta_i).$$

To complete the construction of the unconditional joint density of filings, output, and imports over our sample period for any industry we must integrate this conditional density with respect to the density of θ. We choose a discrete factor approximation to this unknown density. Recent Monte Carlo work by Mroz and Guilkey (1991) has found these discrete factor structures are able to model a wide variety of potential unobserved heterogeneity distributions. For many models involving discrete and continuous endogenous variables, the parameters of the conditional distribution of interest estimated from these models were found to dominate those obtained from the maximum likelihood estimator in terms of mean squared error loss for sample sizes considered. Integrating with respect to this discrete density of θ, (π_h, θ_h) for $h = 1, \ldots, H$, where H is the number of points of support of the discrete density and π_h the probability associated with the point of support θ_h, yields

(20)
$$p(f_i, \text{IMP}_i^*, \text{OUT}_i^*) = \sum_{h=1}^{H} \pi_h g(f_i, \text{IMP}_i^*, \text{OUT}_i^* \mid \theta_h).$$

In our empirical work, we found that choosing $H = 3$ was sufficient to adequately estimate $f(\theta)$. We found that for larger values of H the parameters of the conditional mean function for the five filing variables and the imports and domestic output equations did not change appreciably.[8] Taking the logarithm of $p(f_i, \text{IMP}_i^*, \text{OUT}_i^*)$ and summing from $i = 1$ to N yields the log-likelihood function for our model.

Before presenting the estimates of the parameters of the joint density of these seven variables we must first discuss the variables entering X_{it}, the vector of observable industry characteristics shifting the conditional mean of the filing rate of industry i and time period t. Because we wish to allow for the possibility that firms pursue the outcome filing strategy against some regions and the process filing strategy against others, we include in X_{it} variables suggested by both filing strategies. Note that the absence of an r subscript on the vector X_{it} reflects the restriction that regional filing rates do not depend on the characteristics of the regions. Our lack of data at the regional level necessitated this restriction.

Our main objective in selecting outcome filer variables for inclusion in X_{it} follows from the logic that if a variable is used to determine injury in an antidumping suit proceeding and industries are aware of this, then these variables should be predictors of future dumping suit activity (under the outcome filing strategy). Although the domestic industry must concern itself with the establishment of injury, a LTFV determination is also necessary for dumping to be found. Moreover, the margin by which the Commerce Department finds that final sales to the domestic market are made at less than fair value determines the magnitude of the antidumping duties that the petitioning industry can expect. Nevertheless, the Commerce Department's final LTFV margin is extremely unpredictable, and there are biases inherent in the process used to determine its level which favor finding a positive margin.[9] For these reasons, we hypothesize that firms pursuing the outcome filing strategy file primarily based on the observable industry characteristics that determine injury and allow for a sufficiently rich stochastic structure for our model to account for unobservable differences in filing behavior across industries.

A major indicator of injury to the petitioning firms is the import penetration ratio $\text{IMPEN}_{it} = \text{IMP}_{it}/(\text{IMP}_{it} + \text{OUT}_{it})$. A large value of IMPEN is indicative of a large foreign presence in the domestic market, which may be injurious to the domestic firms. A second variable which is used to assess injury is the domestic firm's capacity utilization rate, which we represent at the industry level by $\text{CAPU}_{it} = \text{OUT}_{it}/\text{CAP}_{it}$ (where OUT_{it} is real shipments and CAP_{it} is real capital stock). We compute OUT_{it} as the nominal value of annual ship-

---

8. This result is consistent with the Monte Carlo evidence in Mroz and Guilkey (1991), who found small values of H were sufficient to adequately capture variability due to θ.

9. This uncertainty is due in part to the different methodologies, sometimes for a single suit, that can be used to determine this margin. Boltuck and Litan (1991) contains several papers which discuss the large amount of uncertainty inherent in the dumping margin determination process. In addition, a conclusion which is fairly consistent throughout most of the papers in this volume is that there are strong biases in the process toward finding a positive dumping margin. The papers by Francois, by Palmeter, by Anspacher, and by Boltuck, Francois, and Kaplan in the Boltuck and Litan (1991) volume are particularly persuasive in this regard.

ments divided by the industry-specific shipments price index. All real magnitudes are in 1972 dollars. We include $IMPEN_{i,t-1}$ and $CAPU_{i,t-1}$ in X_{it} because they are both predetermined as of the beginning of year t. We also include time fixed effects in X_{it} to account for any trends in filing activity not accounted for by changes in observable or unobservable industry characteristics.

We also include several additional variables to account for the fact that the magnitude of IMPEN and CAPU necessary to find harmful dumping may vary with the size and the structure of the domestic industry. We measure the size of an industry by EMP_{it}, aggregate employment for industry i in period t, and expect that a given level of IMPEN and CAPU is more likely to be associated with a finding of injury the larger the size of the industry. We attempt to proxy for the (vertical) structure of an industry by value added per dollar of output in the industry, $VADD_{it}/OUT_{it}$, and expect that a given level of IMPEN and CAPU is more likely to be associated with a finding of injury to the domestic industry the lower is VADD/OUT, that is, the farther downstream the domestic industry is located and thus the smaller the share of primary factor payments in total industry cost and the more sensitive those factor payments will be to industry price changes. The final control variable we include is the percentage of all workers in the industry that are unionized, UNION. We hypothesize that this variable captures the ability of the industry to organize and file antidumping petitions against foreign competitors. Because these variables are predetermined at the beginning of year t, lagged values of VADD/OUT, EMP, and UNION (their values for period $t - 1$) are included in X_{it}.

As we have noted above, under the process filing strategy we would expect filing to be related to CAPU and little else and, in particular, not to be related to other measures important for the final determination of dumping (IMPEN, EMP, and VADD/OUT). As with outcome filing, we also hypothesize that UNION captures the ability of the industry to organize and file antidumping petitions against foreign competitors under the process filing strategy.

Table 8.1 contains the sample means and standard errors for all of the variables used in our analysis. The most striking aspect of the table is the large standard deviation of all filing and suit resolution process variables. In addition, the sample skewness of these variables is also very large and positive. These properties are indicative of the extreme rare event nature of antidumping suit activity and underscore the importance of specifying a statistical model which accounts for these characteristics of the economic environment. As mentioned above, all dollar magnitudes are in real 1972 dollars.

8.3.4 Results

Tables 8.2–8.6 present estimates of the parameters of the filing rate equation for our five importing regions. We first will discuss these results and then turn to a discussion of our import and output equations.

To interpret the results in tables 8.2–8.6, recall that under our assumptions

Table 8.1   **Means and Standard Errors of Variables: 2040 Year-Industry Observations ($i = 1, \ldots, N = 338$ industries and $t = 1, \ldots, T = 6$ years)**

Variable	Definition	Mean	Standard Error
f_{it}^{Japan}	Total filings from Japan and NICs	0.231	2.454
f_{it}^{Europe}	Total filings from Europe	0.249	4.021
f_{it}^{Planned}	Total filings from planned economies	0.078	1.694
f_{it}^{CANMEX}	Total filings from Canada or Mexico	0.062	1.455
f_{it}^{Other}	Total filings from other countries	0.280	6.157
G_{it}	Total TSUS codes	33.63	131.86
IMP_{it}	Real imports in 10^6 1972 dollars	289.55	1147.98
OUT_{it}	Real output in 10^6 1972 dollars	2174.03	4152.99
$\text{EMP}_{i, t-1}$	Industry-level employment $\times 10^3$	41.97	62.37
$\text{VADD}_{i, t-1}/\text{OUT}_{i, t-1}$	Value added per dollar of real output	0.483	0.133
$\text{CAPU}_{i, t-1}$	Capacity utilization rate	2.856	1.929
$\text{IMPEN}_{i, t-1}$	Import penetration ratio	0.109	0.140
$\text{UNION}_{i, t-1}$	Percentage of workers unionized	12.25	28.98
$\text{OGP}_{it}^{\text{Japan}}$	Ongoing antidumping petition against Japan and NICs	0.164	1.649
$\text{OGPLFV}_{it}^{\text{Japan}}$	Ongoing preliminary LTFV determination against Japan and NICs	0.055	0.603
$\text{OGSUS}_{it}^{\text{Japan}}$	Ongoing suspension against Japan and NICs	0.00[a]	0.00[a]
$\text{OGWD}_{it}^{\text{Japan}}$	Ongoing withdrawal against Japan NICs	0.020	0.595
$\text{OGD}_{it}^{\text{Japan}}$	Ongoing duties against Japan and NICs	0.170	2.231
$\text{OGP}_{it}^{\text{Europe}}$	Ongoing antidumping petition against Europe	0.131	2.238
$\text{OGPLFV}_{it}^{\text{Europe}}$	Ongoing preliminary LTFV determination against Europe	0.033	0.871
$\text{OGSUS}_{it}^{\text{Europe}}$	Ongoing suspension against Europe	0.065	1.488
$\text{OGWD}_{it}^{\text{Europe}}$	Ongoing withdrawal against Europe	0.354	6.971

(continued)

Table 8.1   (continued)

Variable	Definition	Mean	Standard Error
OGD_{it}^{Europe}	Ongoing duties against Europe	0.065	1.347
$OGP_{it}^{Planned}$	Ongoing antidumping petition against planned economies	0.043	1.074
$OGPLFV_{it}^{Planned}$	Ongoing preliminary LTFV determination against planned economies	0.014	0.269
$OGSUS_{it}^{Planned}$	Ongoing suspension against planned economies	0.027	0.495
$OGWD_{it}^{Planned}$	Ongoing withdrawal against planned economies	0.017	0.773
$OGD_{it}^{Planned}$	Ongoing duties against planned economies	0.002	0.044
OGP_{it}^{CANMEX}	Ongoing antidumping petition against Canada or Mexico	0.038	0.997
$OGPLFV_{it}^{CANMEX}$	Ongoing preliminary LTFV determination against Canada or Mexico	0.012	0.412
$OGSUS_{it}^{CANMEX}$	Ongoing suspension against Canada or Mexico	0.003	0.077
$OGWD_{it}^{CANMEX}$	Ongoing withdrawal against Canada or Mexico	0.013	0.581
OGD_{it}^{CANMEX}	Ongoing duties against Canada or Mexico	0.008	0.277
OGP_{it}^{Other}	Ongoing antidumping petition against other	0.165	3.563
$OGPLFV_{it}^{Other}$	Ongoing preliminary LTFV determination against other	0.045	1.146
$OGSUS_{it}^{Other}$	Ongoing suspension against other	0.080	1.810
$OGWD_{it}^{Other}$	Ongoing withdrawal against other	0.149	4.178
OGD_{it}^{Other}	Ongoing duties against other	0.052	0.951

[a]No suspension agreements with Japan or the NICs were made during our sample time period.

Table 8.2 **Filing Rate Equation Estimates for Japan and NICs ($N = 338$ industries for $T = 6$ years)**

Variable	Coefficient Estimate	Standard Error
Constant	-2.807	1.153
$\text{IMPEN}_{i,t-1}$	5.523	1.580
$\text{CAPU}_{i,t-1}$	-0.188	0.121
$\text{EMP}_{i,t-1}$	0.0079	0.0024
$\text{VADD}_{i,t-1}/\text{OUT}_{i,t-1}$	1.165	2.335
$\text{UNION}_{i,t-1}$	0.061	0.018
$\sigma \times 10^4$	4.970	0.858
YEAR81	1.036	0.821
YEAR82	1.136	0.851
YEAR83	2.039	0.813
YEAR84	1.359	0.824
YEAR85	1.671	0.749

Note: NICs = Taiwan, Singapore, South Korea, and Hong Kong.

Table 8.3 **Filing Rate Equation Estimates for Western Europe ($N = 338$ industries for $T = 6$ years)**

Variable	Coefficient Estimate	Standard Error
Constant	-5.386	1.871
$\text{IMPEN}_{i,t-1}$	3.939	1.963
$\text{CAPU}_{i,t-1}$	-0.298	0.121
$\text{EMP}_{i,t-1}$	0.0028	0.0032
$\text{VADD}_{i,t-1}/\text{OUT}_{i,t-1}$	3.859	2.528
$\text{UNION}_{i,t-1}$	0.119	0.023
$\sigma \times 10^4$	6.023	1.185
YEAR81	-1.897	1.192
YEAR82	-0.819	0.937
YEAR83	2.229	0.796
YEAR84	0.431	0.815
YEAR85	1.759	0.786

Table 8.4 **Filing Rate Equation Estimates for Planned Economies of Eastern Europe ($N = 338$ industries for $T = 6$ years)**

Variable	Coefficient Estimate	Standard Error
Constant	-8.948	3.915
$\text{IMPEN}_{i,t-1}$	-5.572	5.948
$\text{CAPU}_{i,t-1}$	-0.280	0.345
$\text{EMP}_{i,t-1}$	0.0041	0.0072
$\text{VADD}_{i,t-1}/\text{OUT}_{i,t-1}$	4.515	5.406
$\text{UNION}_{i,t-1}$	0.203	0.060
$\sigma \times 10^4$	3.705	1.383
YEAR81	-1.993	1.705
YEAR82	-1.512	2.406
YEAR83	-2.998	2.700
YEAR84	0.387	1.856
YEAR85	2.447	1.716

Table 8.5   **Filing Rate Equation Estimates for Canada or Mexico ($N = 338$ industries for $T = 6$ years)**

Variable	Coefficient Estimate	Standard Error
Constant	−3.508	2.051
IMPEN$_{i,t-1}$	0.176	0.652
CAPU$_{i,t-1}$	−0.487	0.145
EMP$_{i,t-1}$	−0.0047	0.0032
VADD$_{i,t-1}$/OUT$_{i,t-1}$	1.824	2.510
UNION$_{i,t-1}$	0.142	0.029
$\sigma \times 10^4$	3.492	1.254
YEAR81	−3.335	0.643
YEAR82	−1.067	0.652
YEAR83	2.012	1.112
YEAR84	−1.028	0.580
YEAR85	−0.839	0.652

Table 8.6   **Filing Rate Equation Estimates for All Other Countries ($N = 338$ industries for $T = 6$ years)**

Variable	Coefficient Estimate	Standard Error
Constant	−1.991	2.216
IMPEN$_{i,t-1}$	−9.127	4.650
CAPU$_{i,t-1}$	−0.456	0.178
EMP$_{i,t-1}$	−0.0068	0.0052
VADD$_{i,t-1}$/OUT$_{i,t-1}$	−2.283	3.206
UNION$_{i,t-1}$	0.074	0.022
$\sigma \times 10^4$	5.132	1.324
YEAR81	−0.022	1.717
YEAR82	4.860	1.371
YEAR83	2.121	1.325
YEAR84	2.875	1.324
YEAR85	4.229	1.293

the mean of the filing rate against region r in industry i for period t is $E(f_{rit}) = \exp(X'_{it}\gamma_r + \delta_r\theta_i)\sigma_r$. Taking the natural logarithm of both sides of $E(f_{rit})$ yields

$$\ln[E(f_{rit})] = X'_{it}\gamma_r + \delta_r\theta_i + \ln(\sigma_r).$$

Consequently, each element of γ_r can be interpreted as the percentage increase in the mean number of filings against region r as a result of a one-unit change in the associated element of X_{it}. This result allows us to make unitless comparisons of elements of γ_r across regions.

Before discussing differences across the tables in parameter estimates we describe our test of whether these differences are statistically significant. We tested whether all of the elements of γ_r (besides the constant term and time dummies) were equal across the five regions. This involves imposing 20 equality constraints in moving from the null model with five coefficients on

(IMPEN, CAPU, EMP, VADD/OUT, and UNION) to 25 coefficients (five variables and five regions) in the unrestricted model. Under both the null and alternative hypotheses we allow the σ_r and time dummies and constant terms to differ across regions. The value of the likelihood ratio statistic for this test is 124.19, which is significantly larger than the 0.01 critical value from a χ^2_{20} random variable of 37.57. Hence there is strong evidence of significant differences in filing behavior across the five regions.

The general conclusion to emerge from a comparison of results across these tables is that for filing behavior against the European region and the Japan/NICs region, the outcome filing strategy seems the most plausible, while filing behavior against the Canada/Mexico region yields results most consistent with the use of a process filing strategy. For filings against Europe and Japan and the NICs, the coefficient on IMPEN is precisely estimated and of the expected sign, something not shared by the estimation results for any other regional grouping. In addition, the estimated coefficients on CAPU for the European region and on EMP for the Japan/NICs region, additional variables which are important to the ITC's final injury determination, are also estimated with precision and of the expected sign. This is consistent with our outcome filer hypothesis. In contrast, for filings against the Canada/Mexico region, only CAPU is a strong predictor of filing activity, both in terms of its relative magnitude and statistical precision. The other variables important for the ITC's final injury determination lack predictive power for filing behavior against this region. This is consistent with our process filer view. For the planned economies and for our residual other region, it is difficult to argue if the data is at all informative as to which of the two strategies is more likely.

Perhaps the most strikingly uniform result across all of the regions is the dramatic predictive power of UNION. For all importing regions, a higher percentage of unionized workers in an industry predicts a significantly higher number of filings against that region. This presumably reflects the general importance of overcoming the free-rider problem associated with bearing the cost of bringing an antidumping petition forward.

Comparing the Japan/NICs results to the Europe results yields several conclusions. First, CAPU appears to be both an economically and statistically more important predictor of filing activity against Europe than against Japan/NICs. Second, the opposite conclusion holds for IMPEN when comparing the two regions.

Tables 8.7 and 8.8 present our import and domestic output equation results which yield estimates of the parameters of the conditional mean functions given in equation (16) which are used to assess the impact of the investigation process itself and of the outcome of the investigation on the flow of both imports and domestic output.

We make a number of observations. First, the investigation effects implied by the coefficient estimates for $\beta^m_{r,\text{OGP}}$ and $\beta^m_{r,\text{OGPLFV}}$ in table 8.7 and for $\beta^o_{r,\text{OGP}}$ and $\beta^o_{r,\text{OGPLFV}}$ in table 8.8 are consistent with our findings regarding the filing

Table 8.7   **Import Equation Estimates ($N = 338$ industries for $T = 6$ years)**

Variable	Coefficient Estimate	Standard Error
OGP_{it}^{Japan}/G_{it}	41.95	30.52
$OGPLFV_{it}^{Japan}/G_{it}$	−80.11	35.83
$OGSUS_{it}^{Japan}/G_{it}$	0.0	0.0
$OGWD_{it}^{Japan}/G_{it}$	−33.79	55.02
OGD_{it}^{Japan}/G_{it}	−39.19	18.47
OGP_{it}^{Europe}/G_{it}	11.70	12.28
$OGPLFV_{it}^{Europe}/G_{it}$	−51.37	24.48
$OGSUS_{it}^{Europe}/G_{it}$	−36.59	19.28
$OGWD_{it}^{Europe}/G_{it}$	−7.48	16.62
OGD_{it}^{Europe}/G_{it}	−13.65	6.38
$OGP_{it}^{Planned}/G_{it}$	−59.22	60.51
$OGPLFV_{it}^{Planned}/G_{it}$	77.88	103.45
$OGSUS_{it}^{Planned}/G_{it}$	49.31	22.43
$OGWD_{it}^{Planned}/G_{it}$	−45.91	60.38
$OGD_{it}^{Planned}/G_{it}$	−11.10	3.14
OGP_{it}^{CANMEX}/G_{it}	−42.05	20.11
$OGPLFV_{it}^{CANMEX}/G_{it}$	−69.59	119.63
$OGSUS_{it}^{CANMEX}/G_{it}$	−156.73	186.89
$OGWD_{it}^{CANMEX}/G_{it}$	18.41	35.54
OGD_{it}^{CANMEX}/G_{it}	−25.56	11.34
OGP_{it}^{Other}/G_{it}	−77.86	100.34
$OGPLFV_{it}^{Other}/G_{it}$	87.88	98.13
$OGSUS_{it}^{Other}/G_{it}$	−3.80	14.50
$OGWD_{it}^{Other}/G_{it}$	−8.12	22.17
OGD_{it}^{Other}/G_{it}	−18.02	11.24
Constant	11.64	1.45
YEAR81	−0.74	2.03
YEAR82	0.50	2.23
YEAR83	2.05	2.40
YEAR84	6.12	2.96
YEAR85	7.97	3.26

strategies across regions noted above. In particular, the filing of a petition against firms in Europe or the Japan/NICs region leads to a rise in the rate of imports up until an affirmative preliminary LTFV determination, at which point the rate of imports falls precipitously and remains low until the conclusion of the investigation. These investigation effects are consistent with the outcome filer hypothesis. In contrast, the filing of a petition against firms in the Mexico/Canada region leads to an immediate fall in the rate of imports, which remains low until the conclusion of the investigation. These investigation effects are consistent with the process filer hypothesis. As was true with the filing equation results, the investigation effects implied by the planned

Table 8.8   **Output Equation Estimates ($N = 338$ industries for $T = 6$ years)**

Variable	Coefficient Estimate	Standard Error
$\mathrm{OGP}_{it}^{\mathrm{Japan}}/G_{it}$	29.92	50.49
$\mathrm{OGPLFV}_{it}^{\mathrm{Japan}}/G_{it}$	25.24	16.81
$\mathrm{OGSUS}_{it}^{\mathrm{Japan}}/G_{it}$	0.0	0.0
$\mathrm{OGWD}_{it}^{\mathrm{Japan}}/G_{it}$	8.58	8.51
$\mathrm{OGD}_{it}^{\mathrm{Japan}}/G_{it}$	9.47	21.24
$\mathrm{OGP}_{it}^{\mathrm{Europe}}/G_{it}$	−27.10	39.61
$\mathrm{OGPLFV}_{it}^{\mathrm{Europe}}/G_{it}$	25.54	16.48
$\mathrm{OGSUS}_{it}^{\mathrm{Europe}}/G_{it}$	−99.83	176.60
$\mathrm{OGWD}_{it}^{\mathrm{Europe}}/G_{it}$	−20.59	50.81
$\mathrm{OGD}_{it}^{\mathrm{Europe}}/G_{it}$	27.05	12.11
$\mathrm{OGP}_{it}^{\mathrm{Planned}}/G_{it}$	17.92	22.89
$\mathrm{OGPLFV}_{it}^{\mathrm{Planned}}/G_{it}$	68.81	125.40
$\mathrm{OGSUS}_{it}^{\mathrm{Planned}}/G_{it}$	51.48	24.18
$\mathrm{OGWD}_{it}^{\mathrm{Planned}}/G_{it}$	−44.48	51.28
$\mathrm{OGD}_{it}^{\mathrm{Planned}}/G_{it}$	8.14	4.01
$\mathrm{OGP}_{it}^{\mathrm{CANMEX}}/G_{it}$	38.17	21.17
$\mathrm{OGPLFV}_{it}^{\mathrm{CANMEX}}/G_{it}$	−85.01	190.89
$\mathrm{OGSUS}_{it}^{\mathrm{CANMEX}}/G_{it}$	−44.50	76.83
$\mathrm{OGWD}_{it}^{\mathrm{CANMEX}}/G_{it}$	24.48	57.01
$\mathrm{OGD}_{it}^{\mathrm{CANMEX}}/G_{it}$	12.19	10.31
$\mathrm{OGP}_{it}^{\mathrm{Other}}/G_{it}$	29.07	45.06
$\mathrm{OGPLFV}_{it}^{\mathrm{Other}}/G_{it}$	−69.70	172.29
$\mathrm{OGSUS}_{it}^{\mathrm{Other}}/G_{it}$	71.53	145.04
$\mathrm{OGWD}_{it}^{\mathrm{Other}}/G_{it}$	−98.43	194.73
$\mathrm{OGD}_{it}^{\mathrm{Other}}/G_{it}$	15.41	17.92
Constant	285.49	10.31
YEAR81	−8.59	18.39
YEAR82	−16.17	18.45
YEAR83	−14.33	18.43
YEAR84	4.05	18.41
YEAR85	4.45	18.53

economy and the residual other regions are inconclusive with regard to the implied filing strategy. The results from the output equation estimation reinforce these conclusions, although the parameters are estimated less precisely.

As for the differing effects of investigation outcomes on postinvestigation imports and domestic output, our parameter estimates imply that the imposition of antidumping duties against any region strongly reduces imports of the products involved, while the response of domestic import-competing output is positive but less precisely estimated. Petitions against a region which are subsequently withdrawn appear to have no lasting effects on imports or domestic output, confirming our earlier findings (Staiger and Wolak 1994a). Finally, the paucity of suspension agreements in our sample makes it difficult to assess regional differences (the Japan/NICs region, e.g., did not negotiate any suspension agreements with the United States during our sample period), but to the extent that the estimates are informative they suggest that only suspension agreements with Europe are successful in restricting imports of the products involved. This, of course, does not necessarily imply that suspension agreements with other regions do not reduce bilateral imports from those regions, but only that such agreements are not effective in reducing the overall imports of the relevant product into the U.S. market.

8.4 Conclusion

Our cross-country analysis of the determinants and impacts of antidumping suits has revealed a substantial amount of heterogeneity between the different trading regions. At the most basic level these results show that although there is a large stochastic component, antidumping suit filings are predictable events using observable industry magnitudes. Against Western Europe and Japan and the NICs, the use of antidumping law appears to be consistent with the view that firms file in expectation of obtaining relief via antidumping duties or suspension agreements—outcome filers in our nomenclature. This is suggested by the pattern of filing against these regions, which appears to reflect a concern for meeting the injury requirements necessary to secure a finding of dumping, as well as by the import and domestic output responses to filing and the various phases of the suit resolution process. But we have also argued that a distinctive filing strategy against Canada and Mexico would be expected on *a priori* grounds and, in particular, that Canada and Mexico are the most likely targets of process filing by U.S. firms over our sample period because their export production is predominantly destined for the U.S. market and accounts for a relatively high and stable U.S. market share. In line with these a priori views, we find evidence in the use of antidumping law against Mexico and Canada that is consistent with our process filer logic, where firms file primarily to obtain the protection afforded during the investigation process itself. This is supported by the pattern of filing against these countries, which appears to be driven primarily by the level of capacity utilization but unrelated to other observable measures of injury, as well as by the import and domestic output responses to filing and the various phases of the suit resolution process.

Finally, we can use our coefficient estimates in table 8.7 to provide a rough idea of the magnitudes of all the trade-distorting effects, by region and by type of effect, that are associated with the use of antidumping law during our sample period. We compute the total sample distortions to U.S. imports from the investigation process associated with petitions against region r as follows:

$$D_{INVr}^m = \sum_i \sum_t \beta_{1r}^m OGP_{rit} + \beta_{2r}^m OGPLFV_{rit}.$$

The total sample distortions to U.S. imports from the postinvestigation effects due to petitions against region r are computed as follows:

$$D^m_{\text{END}r} = \sum_i \sum_t \beta^m_{3r} \, \text{OGSUS}_{rit} + \beta^m_{5r} \, \text{OGD}_{rit}.$$

We exclude the effects of withdrawn petitions because the coefficients associated with OGWD_{rit} in the import equation are never statistically different from zero. We then compute IMPTOT, defined as the sum of multilateral imports over all industries and years in our sample, and express $D^m_{\text{INV}r}$ and $D^m_{\text{END}r}$ as a percentage of IMPTOT.

For our sample of industries and for the six years of available data, the total amount of U.S. import reductions from all investigation effects against Western Europe amounts to approximately -0.05 percent of total U.S. imports over the sample period, while the total distortion attributable to postinvestigation effects against Western Europe is -1.14 percent of total imports over the sample period. For Japan and the NICs, the distortions to U.S. imports from investigation and postinvestigation effects from petitions against this region amount to 0.87 and -2.31 percent, respectively, of total U.S. imports.[10] For both these regions, the major import distortions associated with the use of antidumping law are attributable to postinvestigation effects. For Mexico and Canada, on the other hand, the relative importance of investigation and postinvestigation effects is reversed: the distortions to U.S. imports associated with investigation and postinvestigation effects of petitions against Mexico and Canada are -0.84 and -0.25 percent, respectively, of total U.S. imports. This conforms to our findings that U.S. firms appear to be outcome filers against Europe and Japan and the NICs, and hence the main import restrictions come with the explicit remedies provided by the law (duties or suspension agreements), while U.S. firms appear to be process filers against Mexico and Canada, and hence the main import restrictions come from the investigation effects.

A final implication of our process filer/outcome filer distinction is that the frequency with which outcome filers ought to secure duties should be substantially higher than for process filers. To investigate this hypothesis we computed the sum of OGD_{rit} in Mexico and Canada for all industries and all six years in our sample, and then divided this sum by the sum of f_{rit} for all industries and all six years for the same region. This ratio gives the per-suit level of duty activity against Mexico and Canada, the region against which U.S. firms appear to be process filers. We then repeated this calculation for Europe and Japan and the NICs, treating this as the aggregate region against which U.S. firms appear to be outcome filers. Dividing the "outcome filer ratio" by the

---

10. The positive boost to U.S. imports associated with investigation effects of petitions against Japan and the NICs reflects the fact that the effect of filing on imports is positive and relatively large and the effect of an affirmative preliminary LTFV determination, while negative, does not persist long enough to reverse this cumulative positive effect.

"process filer ratio" yields 3.73, suggesting that in our sample, a product-level antidumping petition is 3.73 times more likely to end in duties when it is filed against firms in Europe, Japan, or a NIC versus firms from Canada or Mexico. This result is consistent with the view that suits against Canada and Mexico are filed less for the eventual protection provided by duties than are suits against Europe and Japan and the NICs.

References

Abowd, John M. 1990. The NBER immigration, trade, and labor markets data files. NBER Working Paper no. 3351. Cambridge, Mass.: National Bureau of Economic Research.

Anderson, James E. 1992. Domino dumping, I: Competitive exporters. *American Economic Review* 82 (March): 65–83.

Boltuck, R., and R. E. Litan, eds. 1991. *Down in the dumps: Administration of the unfair trade laws.* Washington, D.C.: Brookings Institution.

Dale, Richard. 1980. *Anti-dumping law in a liberal trade order.* New York: St. Martin's.

Finger, J. M. 1981. The industry-country incidence of "less than fair value" cases in U.S. import trade. *Quarterly Review of Economics and Business* 21 (Summer): 260–79.

Harrison, Ann. 1991. The new trade protection: Price effects of anti-dumping and countervailing measures in the United States. World Bank working paper. Washington, D.C.: World Bank, April.

Hartigan, J., S. Kamma, and P. Perry. 1989. The injury determination, category and the value of relief from dumping. *Review of Economics and Statistics* 71 (February): 183–86.

Hernander, M., and J. B. Schwartz. 1984. An empirical test of the impact of the threat of U.S. trade policy: The case of antidumping duties. *Southern Economic Journal* 51 (July): 59–79.

Horlick, Gary. 1989. Private communication.

International Monetary Fund. 1987. *Direction of trade statistics yearbook.* Washington, D.C.: International Monetary Fund.

Johnson, N. L., and S. Kotz. 1969. *Distributions in statistics: Discrete distributions.* New York: Wiley.

Lichtenberg, F., and H. Tan. 1990. An industry level analysis of import relief petitions filed by U.S. manufacturers, 1958–85. Manuscript.

Messerlin, Patrick A. 1989. The EC antidumping regulations: A first economic appraisal, 1980–85. *Weltwirtschaftliches Archiv* 125(3): 563–87.

———. 1990. Anti-dumping regulations or pro-cartel law? The EC chemical cases. *World Economy* (December): 465–92.

Mroz, Tom, and D. Guilkey. 1991. Discrete factor approximations for use in simultaneous equations models with both continuous and discrete endogenous variables. Department of Economics, University of North Carolina.

New York Times. 1990. Imported sweaters face duty. April 24, C1.

Prusa, Thomas J. 1988. Pricing behavior without settlements. In *International trade policies, incentives, and firm behavior.* Ph.D. dissertation, Stanford University.

———. 1991. The selection of antidumping cases for ITC determination. In *Empirical studies in commercial policy,* ed. R. E. Baldwin. Chicago: University of Chicago Press.

————. 1992. Why are so many antidumping petitions withdrawn? *Journal of International Economics* 33 (August): 1–20.

Salvatore, D. 1987. Import penetration, exchange rates and protection in the United States. *Journal of Policy Modeling* 9 (Spring): 125–41.

Staiger, Robert W., and Frank A. Wolak. 1991. Strategic use of antidumping law to enforce tacit international collusion. Manuscript.

————. 1992. The effect of antidumping law in the presence of foreign monopoly. *Journal of International Economics* 32 (May): 265–87.

————. 1994b. The trade effects of antidumping law: theory and evidence. In *Analytical and negotiating issues in the global trading system,* ed. Alan Deardorff and Robert Stern, 231–61. Ann Arbor: University of Michigan Press.

————. 1994a. Measuring industry specific protection: Antidumping in the United States. *Brookings Papers on Economic Activity: Microeconomics,* 51–118.

U.S. Congress. House. Committee on Ways and Means. Subcommittee on Trade. 1978. *Administration's comprehensive program for the steel industry.* 95th Cong., 2d sess. Washington, D.C.: Government Printing Office.

Viner, Jacob. 1966. *Dumping: A problem in international trade.* New York: Kelley.

Comment   Kala Krishna

This is a really nice paper, both for the interesting econometric methodology used, as well as for the questions asked. In previous work, Staiger and Wolak empirically examined the determinants of suit filing and the trade impacts of U.S. antidumping law. Here, they build on that work to try and see whether there are differences in "the uses and effects of U.S. antidumping law on imports and domestic output across the major regions exporting to the United States." The overall topic is of considerable importance for policy as previous work has shown that filing itself, as well as settlement, and not just winning the case, has effects on prices and imports in the market. This suggests that antidumping petitions may actually be used to support tacit collusion as argued by Prusa (1991, 1992).

My comments are divided into three parts. In the first part, I argue that there seems to be a problem in one of the key features of this paper, namely, an attempt to distinguish between what the authors call "outcome" and "process" filers. In the second, I make some suggestions for extensions which may or may not be feasible. And in the third, I make some suggestions for organization and presentation. I shall say little about the econometrics: it is always easy to point out that the specification rules out interactive effects of a particular kind, and I leave these criticisms to the reader. Rather, I shall try and focus on what might be conceptual or organizational issues and possible extensions.

Kala Krishna is professor of economics at Pennsylvania State University and a research associate of the National Bureau of Economic Research.

One of the key features of this paper, in contrast to its precursors, is that it attempts to show that suits are filed for different reasons on different groups of importers. The five groups are (1) Canada and Mexico, (2) Europe, (3) Japan and the NICs, (4) planned economies, and (5) other countries. At the heart of their analysis is a distinction between what they call "outcome filers" (firms for which the prospect of an antidumping duty is an important ingredient in the decision to file) and "process filers" (firms for which filing is driven largely by a desire to secure the trade restricting effects of the investigation process itself). There is, however, a bit of a problem with this aspect of the paper.

First, trying to infer the motivation of filers—what is going on in their heads—from the outcome is always difficult. The reasons for filing could easily be the same, but the outcome different, if the countries themselves differ. U.S. law provides for an assessment of "critical circumstances" under which duties can be retroactively imposed to the date of filing if filing brings with it a surge of imports. Given this, it could be that one country or group of countries behaves differently because its importers are risk averse and cannot afford to take the chance of retroactive duties, and not because of a difference in the kinds of suits filed. However, in all fairness I should also point out that there are other pieces of the puzzle which the authors also consider in their arguments.

Second, there are likely to be mixed motives in any filing, and a priori, I for one would not expect to be able to separate them based on the kind of data that is likely to be available. Case studies and interviews might help here, but I can see very little else that might.

Third, it is commonly understood that antidumping suits filed in steel were of a very different form than those elsewhere. The attempt to flood the system with petitions by this industry commonly hypothesized might suggest taking steel cases out of the data and looking at them separately.

Fourth, if Europe and Japan attract outcome filers as suggested, then these suits should be stronger intrinsically than those against the other countries. Is this reflected in the settlement and determination data? A by-product should also be that for stronger suits, as the probability of antidumping duties is higher, imports should fall more after a preliminary positive finding than for weaker suits. However, in the import equations, the coefficient on the OGPLFV variable is negative in all but the planned economies case, though it is not significant for the other country group.

Moving on to the second part of my comments, possible suggestions for extensions, a different cut at the data might be to look at what happens in the cases where there is a negative preliminary finding. Are there any such cases? Do the different groups of countries look different?

Another question that might be worth pursuing is whether there has been a change in recent years in the way that antidumping suits have been used. There is a perception that in recent years such suits have been increasingly used to implicitly restrict imports and that nuisance suits are on the increase. Is there any evidence of such a change in regime?

Finally, some simple presentation changes could help improve the readability of the paper. First, it is always nice to see some rough data cuts which, without any sophisticated econometrics, might help motivate the main thrust of the paper: that suits against Europe and Japan look different than those on other countries. Are the settlement rates higher? Are the positive finding rates higher? Are the dumping margins evaluated higher?

Second, the regressions could be better presented. To make it easier to compare against countries, the results on the same variable across countries could be put on one row, with the level of significance given for ease of comparison.

Third, the model itself should be relegated to an appendix and a quick summary left in the text. It is hard to plough through it to get to the results.

To conclude, the paper has many things to recommend it. The questions it asks are important and thought provoking, as well as cleanly analyzed. I look forward to seeing more on this important issue in the future.

References

Prusa, Thomas J. 1991. The selection of antidumping cases for ITC determination. In *Empirical studies in commercial policy,* ed. R. E. Baldwin. Chicago: University of Chicago Press.
————. 1992. Why are so many antidumping petitions withdrawn? *Journal of International Economics* 33 (August): 1–20.

Comment   Anne E. Brunsdale and Keith B. Anderson

The most interesting contribution of this paper and of an earlier one by the same authors (Staiger and Wolak 1994) is their estimates of the effects antidumping investigations and orders have on the quantity of imports. The authors examine not only the effect of antidumping orders—the end result of a "successful" petition—but also how imports are affected at various stages in the investigational process. They find that imports are significantly reduced once the Department of Commerce finds that the price of the subject imports is too low. (In the jargon of antidumping law, the subject imports are found to be sold at less than fair value (LTFV).) In some cases the decline in imports comes even sooner—as soon as the investigational process is triggered by the filing of a petition. Completion of the investigation and the entry of a final antidumping order generally leads to no additional decline in imports.[1]

Anne E. Brunsdale is a former chairman of the U.S. International Trade Commission, where Keith B. Anderson served as her senior economic advisor.
    1. The authors also look at the effect of the suspension of an investigation as the result of an agreement being reached with the foreign producers and the effect of the withdrawal of a petition prior to final action. The authors also examine the effects of antidumping orders and investigations

These results should not be surprising to those who are familiar with the arcane and convoluted process involved in establishing antidumping duties. However, it is useful to have empirical evidence to support our intuition. Under the statutory scheme, once the Commerce Department finds that imports are being sold at an unfairly low price, importers must begin posting bonds equal to the estimated dumping margin. (The importer's ultimate liability is determined by an *ex post* comparison of the price actually paid and what the Commerce Department determines to be the fair value of those imports.)[2] Provided the U.S. International Trade Commission (USITC or ITC) finds material injury, nothing really changes when the final order goes into place. Bonds covering estimated dumping margins are still required, and the importer's ultimate liability remains indeterminate until an *ex post* review is conducted.[3] Therefore, it is not surprising that the effects prior to the final order are similar to those afterward.[4]

While these findings are useful and consistent with our expectations, we are concerned that Staiger and Wolak seem to have assumed that every dumping investigation has the same effect on the dollar value of imports and domestic production.[5] The effect of a dumping case is assumed to be independent of the size of the industry, the unfair imports' share of the total sales in the industry, and the degree to which the prices charged are below fair levels—the size of the dumping margin. Simple economic theory suggests that these assumptions cannot be correct. Effects should be greater in larger industries and in industries where the unfair imports account for a larger percentage of total sales. Similarly, the effect should be greater where the difference between the actual price of the imports and their "fair" level is relatively high.[6]

---

on domestic production. In general, the estimates of these effects are much less robust than the effect on imports.

2. In general, fair value is the price charged in the country where the imported product is produced, the price in some third country, or the total cost of producing the product, including statutorily mandated minimum levels for profits and overhead expenses. (For a general discussion of the details of U.S. antidumping practice, see Horlick [1989].)

3. In fact, reviews are not always conducted. If no interested party requests a review covering imports during a period of time, the importer's final liability is simply set equal to the estimated dumping duty.

There is one minor difference between the importer's ultimate liability before a final dumping order is entered and its liability after the order is entered. Prior to the publication of the final dumping order, the importer's maximum liability is the level of the bond paid. After the order is in place, this is no longer true. If the Commerce Department ultimately determines that the margin of dumping is greater than the bond that has been posted, the importer is required to make up the difference. During either period, if the ultimate margin is less than the bond, the difference is refunded.

4. Similarly, an investigation can only be stopped by means of a suspension agreement if the foreign producers agree to raise their prices to completely eliminate their unfairly low prices. Thus, it is not surprising that Staiger and Wolak find that a suspension agreement has the same effect as a final order.

5. Technically, the assumption is that the effect per tariff classification covered by the investigation is a constant.

6. In addition, the effect will depend on the degree to which the imports and the domestic product are substitutes, the elasticity of demand for the product, and the elasticity of domestic supply.

That the effects of antidumping cases on imports and domestic shipments differ substantially from case to case can be seen by looking at the eight cases examined by Anderson (1993b) in a study of the welfare effects of antidumping actions. In these cases, we estimate that the antidumping process on average caused imports to decline by approximately $31 million per year and domestic production to increase by about $28 million per year.[7] However, there were very large differences from case to case. In chrome-plated lug nuts from the People's Republic of China, the antidumping investigation and order decreased imports by only an estimated $200,000 per year and increased the value of domestic shipments by only about $100,000. At the other extreme, the antidumping investigation and order involving portland cement and cement clinker from Mexico decreased imports by approximately $145 million and increased the value of domestic shipments by approximately $165 million.[8]

In addition to estimating the effects of dumping investigations, Staiger and Wolak seek to test two alternative models of why antidumping petitions are filed. In the first model, the petitioner—an "outcome filer"—is hypothesized to be truly interested in the long-term reduction in imports that will result from a final antidumping order. The second model hypothesizes that some petitioners—"process filers"—merely want to obtain the temporary benefits that will arise while the investigation is underway. These petitioners supposedly do not care much whether they get an affirmative final injury determination, just that they get an affirmative preliminary injury determination and an affirmative LTFV determination so that duties will be collected for a few months. They only care about temporary benefits because they and foreign producers have, at least tacitly, a market-sharing agreement which is threatened by a temporary downturn in demand and resulting excess capacity. The filing of a dumping petition will, the authors hypothesize, persuade the foreign producers to keep to the agreement and not engage in active price competition.

While the notion that firms may use the antidumping process to limit competition has a certain appeal and is not new,[9] Staiger and Wolak's model suffers from a misunderstanding of exactly how the administrative process works at the ITC. One area of misunderstanding is the authors' belief that the commission's preliminary determinations are based on the information contained in the petition and that the commission does not have information on a number of factors, such as employment and import penetration, that will be considered in

7. These estimates are based on standard partial equilibrium analysis using the elasticities and other parameter values discussed in Anderson (1993b). The domestic production change figures are based on the midpoints of the estimated ranges of values for the individual cases reported there. The level of imports after the antidumping process has had its effect, and therefore the change in imports resulting from the process, is estimated from the reported tariff revenue effects and knowledge of the size of the antidumping duty and of any existing regular duty.

8. We note that these estimates are for the entire case, while Staiger and Wolak examine the effects per included tariff classification. This however does not alter our point. Since there were three harmonized tariff categories affected by cement and one in the case of chrome-plated lug nuts, the effects per import category are several hundred times greater in the case of cement than in lug nuts.

9. The same argument has been made in Messerlin (1990).

a final investigation. This is not correct. Prior to a preliminary determination, the ITC staff conducts its own investigation of the subject imports and the condition of the domestic industry. In addition, the staff holds a public hearing where both petitioners and respondents have an opportunity to make arguments and provide information, and both parties have the opportunity to submit briefs arguing their case. While the information available at the time of a preliminary determination is not as complete as is available at the time of a final determination, the same types of data are available and are the result of an independent investigation by ITC staff, not a simple reliance on the information contained in the petition.

A second misunderstanding relates to the use of data on industry performance during the period between the filing of a petition and the time of the final ITC injury determination. Staiger and Wolak hypothesize that foreign producers will not compete aggressively during the pendency of an antidumping investigation since a less aggressive stance during this period should reduce the likelihood that the domestic industry will be found to be materially injured. While the logic of this argument is impeccable, it has not gone unnoticed by ITC commissioners. As a result, the commission is very reluctant to place much weight on evidence relating to the period after a petition is filed. Indeed, the reluctance is sometimes carried too far. In a 1991 case involving fresh Atlantic salmon from Norway, the majority of the commission found injury even though salmon imports from Norway had declined precipitously since the filing of the petition as a result of changes in exchange rates, not as a result of any action taken by the Norwegian producers.[10]

If the process-filer theory has shortcomings, how does one explain the difference in results found between cases involving Western European and major Asian countries and those involving other countries? Why does the level of imports increase when a petition is filed against imports from Western Europe or Japan and the Asian NICs but decline when a petition is filed against imports from other countries? Staiger and Wolak see this as evidence that their outcome-filer model explains cases filed against Europe and Japan and the NICs, while the process-filer model explains cases against the developing countries. However, it seems to us that the result may have more to do with the ability to control the timing of shipments than with the strategy behind the filing. If an imported good is coming from one of the major developed countries, controlling when the shipment is received is likely to be easier than when the good is being produced in a country with less-developed manufacturing, communications, and transportation systems. (While this may be becoming less true today, recall that the authors' data covers the period from 1980 to 1985.) As a result, importers may be hesitant to place orders for shipments

10. Cf. the dissenting views of Acting Chairman Anne E. Brunsdale (USITC 1991, 33–35) with the views of the commission (USITC 1991, 17). ("We have given less weight to the recent decline in imports in 1990 because it appears to be largely the result of the filing of the petition and/or the imposition of provisional antidumping and countervailing duties.")

from such countries after a petition is filed for fear that the order will not arrive until after the preliminary decision and that they will therefore be liable for dumping duties of an unknown magnitude.[11]

In conclusion, in spite of some methodological concerns, the most interesting finding of the two papers by Staiger and Wolak is the empirical confirmation that the effect of an antidumping order occurs no later than the Commerce Department's preliminary LTFV determination. There is no additional effect from the entry of an antidumping order at the end of the investigational process. There appear to be more significant problems with the authors' attempt to model and test the reasons firms choose to seek antidumping orders.

References

Anderson, Keith B. 1993a. Agency discretion or statutory direction: Decision making at the U.S. International Trade Commission. *Journal of Law and Economics* 36 (October): 915–35.

———. 1993b. Antidumping laws in the United States: Use and welfare consequences. *Journal of World Trade* 27 (April): 99–117.

Horlick, Gary N. 1989. The United States antidumping system. In *Antidumping law and practice: A comparative study,* ed. John H. Jackson and Edwin A. Vermulst, 99–166. Ann Arbor: University of Michigan Press.

Kaplan, Seth T. 1991. Injury and causation in USITC antidumping determinations: Five recent approaches. In *Policy implications of antidumping measures,* ed. P. K. M. Tharakan, 143–73. New York: North-Holland.

Messerlin, Patrick. 1990. Antidumping regulations or pro-cartel law? The EC chemical cases. *World Economy* 13 (December): 465–92.

Staiger, Robert W., and Frank A. Wolak. 1994. Measuring industry specific protection: Antidumping in the United States. *Brookings Papers on Economic Activity: Microeconomics,* 51–118.

USITC (U.S. International Trade Commission). 1991. Fresh and chilled Atlantic salmon from Norway, Invs. Nos. 701-TA-302 (final) and 731-TA-454 (final). USITC Publication no. 2371. Washington, D.C.: U.S. International Trade Commission, April.

---

11. The authors, of course, also find differences in the determinants of petition filing depending on the country from which the product is coming. In terms of that equation, the support for the process-filer model appears to turn on the absence of a significant relationship between filings and import penetration for countries other than the major developed countries. Import penetration is included in the filing equation because it is presumably an important determinant of ITC decision making. However, both our understanding of the analysis employed by most ITC commissioners during the late 1980s and early 1990s and available empirical evidence suggest that this is not the case. (For a discussion of the analytic methods used by different ITC commissioners, see Kaplan [1991]. An empirical indication that import penetration is not an important determinant of commission decisions is found in Anderson [1993a].)

9   Conclusions

Anne O. Krueger

In an ideal world, the political process would either automatically lead to, or be constrained in order to result in, an outcome that achieved political goals in an economically efficient, or low-cost, fashion. But that does not always seem to happen.[1]

If it was desirable to support the U.S. semiconductor industry in 1986, there were a number of ways in which support could have been provided that would not have adversely affected U.S. computer makers, could have avoided yielding extra profits for Japanese producers, would not have induced the entry of Korean firms into the market, and would not have resulted in a European protest against the violation of the General Agreement on Tariffs and Trade (GATT) by the bilateral deal with the Japanese.

If income support of wheat farmers is deemed a legitimate objective of policy, the Export Enhancement Program is surely an economically inefficient way to achieve that support. Similar arguments could be made about textile and apparel protection (where the poor are clearly adversely affected by higher clothing prices and where the "rents" on import restrictions go to foreign producers), sugar support in the North American Free Trade Agreement (NAFTA), and protection of steel. *If* assistance to the auto and steel industries was deemed desirable, lower-cost economic means could have been found regardless of the objective. If it was income of the workers, estimates of the costs of protection per job are so high as to indicate that the American people could have paid auto- and steelworkers more than twice their wages and yet been better off than they were with the voluntary export restraints (VERs). If the objective

Anne O. Krueger is professor of economics at Stanford University and a research associate of the National Bureau of Economic Research.

1. See Becker (1983) for a model of political economy in which wealth transfers are achieved in cost-minimizing ways, and the introduction for a fuller discussion.

was to help the industry, questions arise as to why VERs were the instrument, when profits of firms in the industry in countries with VERs resulted.

In the case of lumber, Kalt argues that the Canadian pricing system had no economic impact and that the entire objective was to increase the profits of the domestic lumber industry. In that instance, the fundamental question is whether increasing the profits of the loggers would be deemed a legitimate objective of policy. If so, a direct income transfer financed by taxes would achieve the same goal at a lower economic cost (but the very suggestion probably puts the lie to any argument that the lumber producers could gain political support in an open process).

If the purpose of administered protection is to avoid predatory pricing, as appears on the surface, why do Staiger and Wolak find that administration of the same law has significantly different protective impacts on different countries (in chap. 8 of this volume) and industries (in their earlier research)?

Even from these few cases, it is evident that there is not an ideal world. There are clearly political costs to economically low cost solutions. Understanding why the process of protection works as it does must therefore become important as a step toward improved analysis of economic policy, and perhaps even finding ways in which the economic costs of protection can be reduced.

The experiences with protectionist pressure and protection in the seven industries reported on here, along with the cross-sectional evidence gleaned from ITA-ITC cases, are highly suggestive of a number of hypotheses. In this concluding chapter, some of the themes that seem to emerge from a comparison of the results of the individual studies are outlined. As noted in the introduction, these analyses supplement existing research results analyzing the structure of protection by exploring the ways in which protection was sought and conferred. This examination of the "processes" by which protection is obtained is richly suggestive of interesting avenues for further research.

From the perspective of political economy, there are eight themes/insights that emerge from analysis of the individual studies which supplement the political economy of protection literature discussed in the introduction. These are first briefly set forth here. Then, the key aspects of the individual studies that are pertinent for these eight propositions are reviewed. Then each of the eight is considered in greater detail.

A first question concerns the extent to which current trade policy is in U.S. national interests. Several individual studies suggest that it is not. Second, one of the recurring themes from the individual studies centers on the role of ideas in shaping the political process, constraining both protection seekers and those granting protection in both the mechanisms sought and granted and the level of protection.

Somewhat related to the role of ideas is a third issue: the economic determinants of "political strength" as a factor influencing the forum or forums in which protection is sought. A fourth phenomenon worthy of note focuses on the role of institutions. The particular institutional mechanisms administering trade policy were deemed significant by several authors in affecting and/or constraining political outcomes.

A fifth issue is the extent to which individual actors are rational in seeking and/or attempting to thwart protection. In this regard, an intriguing question arises from some of the studies as to how much protection helps the protected. Sixth, yet another set of findings relates to the importance of industry unanimity in obtaining protection. Several of the authors noted this prerequisite for protection; questions as to why unanimity should be essential may shed further light on the process of protection seeking.

Seventh, some interesting insights into the role of lobbying and organization emerge from the individual studies. While this might be interpreted as an aspect of the role of institutions, it seems to be sufficiently important to warrant discussion in its own right. Finally, the history of earlier protection received by an industry does appear to "matter" in interesting ways, in the sense that once there is protection, the threshold barrier for keeping it seems to be lower than that for obtaining it in the first place.

Each of these themes is discussed in turn below. First, however, it is worthwhile to review the individual studies, noting the major points at which salient insights emerge that are particularly useful in the evaluation of these eight issues.

9.1   Findings from Individual Studies

No brief summary of the results of the individual studies can possibly do them justice: indeed, one of the points of the NBER project was to go beyond quantitative generalizations about protection, and to examine the details of the process of seeking, obtaining, and keeping protection. The purpose here is to highlight those findings from the studies that inform the eight hypotheses/generalizations that are discussed below.[2]

9.1.1   Automobiles

The auto industry began seeking protection in the 1970s after there had been a "regime change," in the words of Nelson, as the Big Three U.S. automakers were challenged by foreign, and especially Japanese, producers.

Until the early 1980s, however, there was less than unanimity among the Big Three: Chrysler received its loan in the late 1970s, and General Motors still believed that it could compete without protection. When unanimity in seeking protection was achieved, strong congressional pressure for action emerged. The arguments made in support of protection included the "need" for a U.S.

---

2. See the introduction for a brief description of the characteristics of each industry which led to their inclusion in the project.

industry, the unfair nature of foreign competition, and an appeal for support of the industry's employees who would lose their jobs should the industry contract.

The executive branch still opposed protection but finally entered into a VER agreement with Japan for fear that otherwise the measures taken by Congress would be even more restrictive. Thus, the fact that VERs were employed does not prove that the administration was in the forefront of those seeking more protection: the Reagan administration claimed to have moved to forestall congressional action.

There are several findings of great interest. First, Nelson notes that the International Trade Commission (ITC) had already turned down any resort to administered protection on the ground that the industry's difficulties were not primarily the result of imports: instead it was the domestic recession that had reduced demand. And, interestingly, in the first years of the VER, it was not binding: Japanese auto producers actually shipped fewer cars than they had agreed to.

With the upturn, however, the VER on automobiles did become binding. It is estimated that the additional cost to American consumers per car was on the order of $1,000–$2,000. Translated into "jobs saved," a best estimate is that the cost was around $100,000 per job—more than four times the average wage in the industry!

Perhaps the most surprising findings arising from the auto study center on the effects of protection on the industry. It seems clear that VERs on Japanese automobiles did not achieve the results the automakers apparently hoped for: when the VER did become binding, it resulted in higher profits for Japanese companies (thus strengthening their competitive position) and also in increased imports from other countries. Nelson's analysis demonstrates convincingly that the turnaround for U.S. automakers was a result of competition, and not of protection per se. Interestingly, that turnaround involved the reduction in employment in the industry that advocates of protection said they sought to avoid.

9.1.2   Steel

Like automobiles, the steel industry had been highly concentrated. A few large U.S. companies had been preeminent in the world steel market. As foreign competition increased, those companies were unaccustomed to responding to competitive challenges from other sources of supply. In consequence, they sought relief through protection, like automakers appealing to the "unfair" nature of foreign competition, the "need" for a strong U.S. industry, and the plight of those steelworkers who would lose their jobs as the industry contracted.

The steel industry sought administered protection, especially through countervailing duties in response to foreign subsidies. It became a master of the process of filing for protection in order to induce the U.S. executive branch to take other protective measures. In 1982, for example, more than 200 petitions were filed before the U.S. administration negotiated a VER with major foreign suppliers.

Interestingly, it is not evident whether the various protectionist measures imposed on steel imports did in fact help the domestic industry. In Moore's analysis, the emergence of minimills was speeded up by the higher price of steel that resulted from protection: instead of losing share to imports, Big Steel lost share to the minimills.

An important aspect of the industry's weakened ability to obtain protection originated from the development of a new technology—associated with the smaller scale and less geographically concentrated minimill. That resulted in greatly reduced cohesion within the industry in seeking protection. In addition, some steel users became active opponents of steel protection—the only case cited in which a user group became active in the protection-seeking process. Caterpillar Tractor organized opposition to continued protection for steel in the late 1980s. This is a clear-cut case in which the "indirect" effects of protection are important, and the only instance in the project studies in which using industries became at all significant as opponents of protection.[3]

A final aspect of the experience with steel concerns the way in which it sought protection. When the steel industry was still cohesive in seeking protection, it used the administered trade processes, antidumping and countervailing duties, as an instrument to induce the executive branch to take action, filing as many as 200 antidumping and countervailing duty complaints simultaneously!

The experience with steel also demonstrates the effectiveness of a well-organized and cohesive industry effort in lobbying for (or in the case of steel users, against) an outcome.

9.1.3 Semiconductors

The U.S. semiconductor industry was dominant, with a very high share of the world market, until the 1970s. Then, Japanese producers began increasing their production and market share, particularly in the memory chip segment of the market.

The semiconductor industry first sought protection in the early 1980s, but it was not successful until the mid-1980s, when in fact, a large part of its difficulties were due to cyclical factors in the computer industry. The industry is a much smaller employer than auto- and steelmaking but is generally regarded

---

3. At the Washington conference held on the results of the project in September 1994, several participants supported, and provided further evidence from their personal experience to strengthen, the general conclusion that using industries are highly reluctant to oppose supplier industries' requests for protection. One member of the audience reported that, at one point when the House Ways and Means Committee was seeking testimony as to the adverse effects of protection, most users refused to testify even when approached. It is not clear whether this response is cultural, or instead results from a reluctance to antagonize suppliers, or exists for other reasons.

as a "high-tech" industry, contrasted with the older steel and auto industries. Arguments for protection were centered on the widely perceived importance to the United States of having a high-tech industry. Semiconductors were viewed as a linchpin, a key input for other new high-tech industries.

The semiconductor industry represents another instance in which administered trade processes were used to induce the American and Japanese governments to agree on a VER rather than permit the administered protection process to reach its conclusion.[4] It also represents another instance in which a number of questions may be raised as to whether the protection that resulted helped the U.S. industry since by the time relief was provided virtually all U.S. firms had exited that segment (memory chips) of the industry. Furthermore, profits were increased for existing Japanese firms, enabling them to invest in the next generation of chips that much sooner. Third-party effects were also important as Korean firms were attracted into the industry by the higher world prices, and Japanese firms located plants within the United States to avoid U.S. protection.

Another significant feature of the semiconductor experience is the impact of protection on the computer industry in the United States, which was inactive at the time the agreement was reached but began vigorously opposing those features of the agreement that left American assemblers paying higher prices than their foreign competitors. Some computer producers actually moved their production offshore in response to protection!

Although opposition of downstream users of semiconductors proved important in eventually limiting the extent of protection, the semiconductor negotiations also raise significant questions as to the extent to which U.S. trade policy can be driven by the interests of one or a few firms. As Irwin notes, at one point, the position of the U.S. trade representative (USTR) was identical with that of one firm (Micron), and the industry held virtual veto power over negotiated agreements.

9.1.4 Textiles and Apparel

The very fact that the textile and apparel industry has been protected since the mid-1950s raises questions about the efficacy of protection as an instrument to achieve the goals desired by the industry. Employment was declining before the industry received protection; when it did receive protection, new plants opened in the South and plants in New England closed in any event. One analysis even suggests that protection accelerated the rate at which the industry relocated to the South (see Isard 1973).

One interesting aspect of the evolution of protection for textiles and apparel is that protectionist pressures first originated in New England, where woolen mills were predominant. However, once protection was achieved, New Eng-

---

4. The marginal costs of producing a semiconductor are very low, which means that proof that sales were "below cost" would be more difficult to establish in that industry than in many others.

land textile mills in any event were closing down, and the industry expanded in the South.

The evolution of protection of the industry also attests to the extent to which an instrument, once in place, tends to become more complex over time as more and more groups attempt to seize it for their own purposes. American protection for textiles and clothing started with a focus on one country (Japan) and one commodity (cotton textiles—on the rationale that the U.S. cotton program prejudiced the American industry). By the 1980s, there were over 100 different commodity categories subject to quota, and over 60 countries subject to quota!

The Multi-Fiber Arrangement (MFA) is scheduled to be phased out under the Uruguay Round agreement over a 10-year period. That this may happen attests to the role of institutions in affecting political outcomes: except in the context of negotiations over many trade issues, it is doubtful whether such a plan could have been approved.

Another aspect of institutions is also prominent in the MFA case. That is, Finger and Harrison point to the coherence of the industry's organization and lobbying activities: they attribute some of the restrictiveness of the MFA, as well as its perpetuation, to that effectiveness.

9.1.5 Lumber

As Kalt demonstrates, Canadian policy toward lumber results in intramarginal transfers, but economic analysis demonstrates fairly convincingly that it does not affect exports to the United States. That experience, in turn, raises some interesting issues as to the sorts of ideas and arguments that are effective in winning support for protection.

Despite the failure of economic analysis to support the case, the U.S. industry has been able to appeal to the administered protection process to achieve protection that, in that instance, Kalt judges to be of substantial benefit to the industry by raising the U.S. price of lumber.

In evaluating the arguments that are effective in achieving a ruling favorable to the industry seeking protection, Kalt finds that the political influence of the participants is a significant factor in determining the outcome: that is, when the potential gains from winning are significant and the group seeking protection is politically influential, protection is more likely to follow from the process. It may be noted that, by "politically influential," Kalt means that the lumber interests were concentrated (and important enough) in some key states, especially in the Pacific Northwest, that they could bring pressure to bear on behalf of their industry. It may be significant that alternative approaches to seeking protection (such as resort to Congress), which were threatened by large industries, were not a factor for the lumber interests.

As in the case of the MFA, however, institutions may turn out to be important in the longer run and may constrain protection: the U.S.-Canada binational panel established to adjudicate disputes under the free trade agreement overturned the latest rulings in favor of U.S. lumber producers. This is an instance in which a broad-based trade agreement (such as NAFTA) enabled at least some particular interests to receive less favorable treatment than when they were able to isolate their case from that of other industries.

9.1.6 Wheat

The wheat Export Enhancement Program (EEP) was established in the early 1980s to subsidize wheat exports at a time when farm incomes were low and wheat producers (among other farm groups) were pressuring for government assistance. One reason they were able to obtain the EEP was the promise that the funds available to subsidize exports would be used to finance a variety of agricultural commodity exports: in reality, however, virtually all of the funds have been devoted to wheat.

The economic benefits to wheat growers of the program are small relative to the cost of the subsidies, and the question is why, in the absence of a strong rationale, these subsidies have persisted since their initial introduction.

Gardner points to the unity between the farmers and agribusiness as a key factor in achieving continuing support for EEP. Notably, also, domestic wheat users have not opposed the program. The fact that EEP supporters are well organized and effective in their political representation has been important. It is also significant that the program was originally scored to be budget neutral (because of the existence of large government stocks), which enabled Congress to support the program without budgetary consequences. Finally, it is an instance of the advantages to a group of "having" a protectionist measure in place: it is very doubtful whether an EEP could have been enacted in 1991 if it had not already existed. But the threshold for its removal was far above the threshold level of support required for its initiation.

9.1.7 Agriculture in NAFTA

Whereas the EEP affects only one group of farmers, negotiations over NAFTA potentially affected many groups. Analysis of the positions of various farm groups, and the determinants of the degree to which groups received benefits under NAFTA, is therefore informative as to the relative strength of different groups.

Perhaps the most significant result to emerge from an analysis of the factors influencing the outcome for different agricultural commodities of the NAFTA agreement is the importance of the early decision, in the interests of broader negotiations, that at the end of a (fairly long) transition period all agricultural protection between the United States and Mexico would be removed. That decision, in an important way, set the agenda and determined the context in which various agricultural groups could attempt to influence the outcome: they could slow down the process but could not stop it.

A second significant result from analysis of the determinants of NAFTA is the extent to which those who were able to remain "moderate" in their opposition (compared, say, to organized labor) and were willing to offer specific modifications or to accept other deals until the final moments before the NAFTA accord was to reach Congress were able to extract relatively large gains (in terms of their narrowly defined self-interest) in return for their support. Sugar producers were most successful because of their influence with a sizeable number of members of Congress. Wheat producers and others were less successful in this regard.

9.1.8   Antidumping and Countervailing Duty Decisions

Staiger and Wolak, instead of focusing on the evolution of protection in an industry, address the question of how industries use the antidumping and countervailing duty (administered protection) processes to deter imports. They assess the indirect protective effects of administered protection, noting that the very threat of filing complaints against foreign exporters may serve as protection for a domestic industry. They had earlier demonstrated that these indirect effects were substantial when suspension agreements were reached (instead of the imposition of antidumping duties); the reduction in imports was about the same as when antidumping duties were imposed. Similarly, even during the period of investigation, before any findings are reached, imports are reduced by roughly half the amount that is estimated would have occurred had antidumping duties been imposed immediately.

They had also detected two strategies used by American firms in resorting to administered protection. On one hand, there were "outcome filers," who registered their complaints in the hope of obtaining antidumping or countervailing duties. On the other hand, there were "process filers," whose intent was to obtain the protection inherent in the investigation process (and possibly in a suspension agreement).

In their work for this project, Staiger and Wolak carried the analysis further, asking whether the effects of administered protection are different depending on the country of origin of imports. They found significant differences in strategies followed by the same industry against imports from different countries, thus demonstrating still further the extent to which U.S. import-competing producers recognize the uses of administered protection processes, as well as other avenues, in protecting themselves from import competition.

9.2   Hypotheses Emerging from the Individual Studies

On the basis of these conclusions, and other evidence, presented in the individual studies, supplemented by that available elsewhere in the literature, a number of interesting political economy hypotheses emerge. These were mentioned at the outset of this chapter. Here, each is spelled out in turn.

9.2.1   Does Current Trade Law Reflect U.S. Interests?

Economists who have analyzed U.S. protectionist policies have tended to ground their analyses in arguments based on economic efficiency. Clearly, in almost all instances of protection, economic efficiency is not enhanced by protection, and that has been taken as a basis for analysis.[5] But it has generally been taken for granted that protection served recognized political ends.

There are serious grounds for questioning whether protection, and the processes that generate it as illustrated by these studies, in fact is in the national interest even in political, if not in economic, ways.

First of all, there are powerful grounds for arguing that the United States is so important in the international economy that its actions significantly affect the actions undertaken by its trading partners. To the extent that the United States is protectionist, the temptation for politicians in other countries to succumb to protectionist pressures is larger, and that redounds on U.S. exporters.

In the mid-1990s, other countries were adopting "unfair trading" laws patterned after U.S. law covering countervailing duties and antidumping.[6] To the extent that these laws have the same sorts of protective effects as does American administered protection as demonstrated by Staiger and Wolak, the increased protectionism in the rest of the world must be weighed against any perceived benefits from administered protection processes.

The United States clearly has a systemic interest in an open international trading system that far outweighs the benefits (if any) that can be achieved from individual affirmative findings in administered protection cases, the imposition of VERs, and other protective measures. Even if protection through any of these channels could be shown unequivocally to benefit the American economy, questions could still be raised about the total effect when repercussions on foreign countries are taken into account.

Quite aside from that overarching concern, however, there are grounds for concern about the impact of protection that are not recognized in political debates about trade policy and in the criteria used in U.S. trade law for determining whether protection is warranted. A first and obvious omission, long noted by economists, is that the interests of final consumers are not represented. In political debates, this is no doubt a reflection of the organization costs among large numbers of individuals, each of whom has a small amount to gain if a particular product's price is lower.

However, even more surprising is the fact that under U.S. trade law, the ITC is not empowered to take consumer interests into account in its findings with respect to administered protection. Moreover, the ITC is not even permitted to

5. See, e.g., the estimates of economic costs of protection in Hufbauer and Elliott (1994).

6. There are a number of criticisms that can be made of U.S. trade laws, in addition to those made here. Chief among them are: (1) the law is administered in ways which provide protection even during the period when litigation is proceeding—the Staiger-Wolak finding; (2) the procedures for construction of costs, and other aspects of administrative procedures, can result in findings of "selling below cost" even when the foreign firm is not so doing; and (3) there are circumstances in which foreign firms can be found guilty of practices that, if adopted by an American firm, would be legal. See the essays in Boltuck and Litan (1991) and Finger, Nelson, and Hall (1982).

consider the impact of protection on *other American industries,* including users of the product.[7] Thus, even if economists could convincingly show that the effect of protection on other American industries (because, e.g., of a loss of competitiveness vis-à-vis imports) was quantitatively more harmful than the benefits to the prospectively protected industry,[8] that would not constitute admissible evidence to reject protection.

It should be noted that the failure to consider the "general equilibrium" consequences of protection is a characteristic of political debates on protection, as well. Debates over protection for steel and for machine tools come to mind as particularly telling examples in which the products are purchased primarily by other producers and increased prices inevitably raise their cost structure. But the experience with semiconductors—in which producers of personal computers discovered that they would be at a significant disadvantage vis-à-vis their foreign competitors—also vividly illustrates the point.

Even when users are not concentrated in a few industries, the effects on other industries of raising costs can be significant.[9] Yet in all these instances, the political process treats protection to the industry seeking it as something that can be accomplished without harmful effects on any other sectors of the American economy. Not only is protection itself an economic act of discriminating against the many in favor of the few, but the criteria used politically and administratively for awarding protection are biased in that direction. While it might be the case that, for example, society deems the benefits of protection to apparel to exceed the costs, a procedure (or rules of political discourse) that at least permitted these costs to be taken into account would be far preferable to present practices.

There is yet another theme that emerges from consideration of the individual studies. That is, in many instances (most notably steel, automobiles, and semiconductors) protection was sought by industries experiencing difficulties because of a cyclical downturn. Periods of recession are certainly times when politicians are more receptive to political pressures for protection. Yet, protection once in place is not removed once the recession has ended. In that sense, protection is conferred in response to cyclical difficulties but is inappropriate as it is a longer-term response.

7. There is the question, of course, as to why users do not oppose the imposition of protection on their inputs. As seen in Moore's analysis of steel, they can so oppose (if the protection sought is through VERs, but not if it is through the ITC), but it seems to require a fairly major stake in the outcome to induce the necessary organization. The steel case was highly unusual, however. As seen in Irwin's study of semiconductors (and earlier in the case of steel), users are generally silent when protection for their input is proposed.

8. It is assumed here that the benefits of protection to the protected industry are positive. As indicated above, however, even this assumption is suspect.

9. Net effects of protection have been evaluated in static general equilibrium models by Goldin, Knudsen, and van der Mensbrugghe (1993), Nguyen, Perroni, and Wigle (1993), and Lewis, Robinson, and Wang (1994).

9.2.2   The Role of Ideas in Determining Protection

It is certainly evident from the individual studies that lobbying and special interest groups play an important role in determining protection. However, there are also interesting questions as to the role of ideas. Clearly, to the extent that popular opinion sees protection as "giving in to special interests," it becomes more costly for politicians to confer protection. The extent to which popular opinion is on the side of protection or free trade clearly matters both in determining whether protection is given and in its height. This was seen clearly in the NAFTA debate when public opinion was crucial to the outcome and favorable opinion ratings rose steadily as the congressional showdown approached.

Kalt addresses this issue by asking which arguments were effective in the Canadian lumber disputes. He notes that arguments that could be simply put were effective, whereas more complex arguments (e.g., that Canadian pricing was intramarginal and therefore did not affect the supply going to the United States) were less effective.

More generally, it is interesting that the "need" for an industry (steel, automobiles, and semiconductors) is put forth as a rationale both for old, established traditional industries and for the new high-tech industries. This need presupposes something about how the industry will evolve in the absence of protection, but since reasons for the need are not clearly spelled out, it can apparently apply to any industry.

In like vein, appeals to "fairness" and "equity" are frequently the basis on which appeals for protection are couched. It may certainly be questioned whether special treatment for a firm or industry in adversity due to import competition is more deserved than favorable treatment for one in which technological change accounts for its plight. Nonetheless, it is of interest that the fairness and equity arguments are made with respect to industries perceiving their difficulties originating in imports far more frequently than they are made with respect to industries feeling the pressures of competing technologies.

In both steel and automobiles, public support for protection has been sought partly through an emotional appeal about the fate of the workers who will lose their jobs. Interestingly, many lost their jobs in any event, and no distinction is drawn between postponing job loss one year and the permanent maintenance of a job. Clearly, the distinction is important both for ascertaining the costs of protection and for the degree to which the public may be willing to support the industry: if, in fact, all protection does is to postpone the date at which workers will lose their jobs by a short period of time, the argument for protection (as contrasted with adjustment assistance) is surely weakened. The gains from freeing up trade may be less transitory as industries find world markets in which they are competitive. These distinctions do not seem to have been drawn in debates about protection.

In the case of textiles and apparel, the argument made for protection is based almost entirely on an appeal for sympathy with the plight of workers in those industries, although it is not at all evident that they have been the greatest beneficiaries (contrasted with profits of firms in the industries) of protection. To a degree, this has been buttressed by allegations that competition from "cheap foreign labor" is unfair, despite the insights from economics that comparative advantage rests largely in relative cost differences for different factors of production in relation to productivity levels. Interestingly, Finger and Harrison point to the effective organization and lobbying of the industry as factors in determining its success in obtaining protection: clearly, the industry was more concerned with profitability than with employment. The arguments made publicly in support of protection are quite clearly somewhat distinct from the reasons for seeking it. Finally, wheat farmers—like most farm groups—appealed to the misfortunes of the family farm and the desirability of maintaining "viable" family farms.

For lumber and the agricultural interests that "won" in the NAFTA agreement, efforts to receive protection have been largely kept away from public scrutiny: lobbying, good organization, and effective positioning relative to issues appear to have been more important.

Yet another example of the role of ideas in determining protection arises from administered protection. The fact that predatory pricing can be shown by economists to constitute a "valid" case for protection serves as the basis for instituting antidumping and countervailing duty legislation and procedures. But, once these procedures are put in place, validated by this idea, they are then seized for protectionist purposes, as demonstrated by Staiger and Wolak, as well as by some of the other studies.

It may also be noted that the appeal to "fair" trading practices has been used repeatedly as protection (and export support) has been sought. This was certainly true in the semiconductor agreement, and in wheat export subsidies (where the European practices were held up as a rationale for those measures). Clearly, the idea that "opening up others' markets" accords with fair trade has been important in legitimating the appeal for protection in these cases.[10]

From all of this, it seems clear that the public arguments made for protection are whichever seem to be most likely to gain public support given the situation of the industry: desirability of maintaining high-tech competence (and, to a lesser extent, unfairness of foreign competition) for semiconductors; jobs for unskilled workers in textiles and apparel; jobs, the unfairness of foreign competition, and the need for the industry in the case of steel and automobiles; preservation of a reasonable income on the family farm and an appeal to the unfairness of European subsidies in the case of wheat (and much else in agriculture). Whether protection is granted because of public sympathy with these arguments, because of public perceptions of the industry's difficulty, or because of behind-the-scenes lobbying tactics is an open question.

10. See the excellent essay on this topic by Irwin (1994).

On even casual examination, it seems evident that there is no economic activity for which effective lobbyists cannot find an ad hoc argument on one or more of these bases. A number of interesting questions therefore arise. Given that decisions for protection are often significantly influenced by the ways in which effective lobbying groups approach trade officials and politicians, why do these organizations and lobbies even bother with the public argument? What role does public support, as garnered through the dissemination of these relatively simplistic appeals, play in determining the ability of the politicians to grant protection? Clearly, it must matter or lobbying organizations would neglect the public relations efforts involved in disseminating their appeals.

In this regard, an interesting question concerns the degree to which changing ideas regarding protection may affect the extent of protection. Certainly, international trade theory in the 1980s was augmented by consideration of models of imperfect competition, under which it could be shown that some type of intervention might be economically preferable to laissez faire.[11] How perceptions of this change in ideas have affected protectionist outcomes is an important question.

Finally, why cannot the case for free trade, and the costs of protection, be made more effectively? Is this an example writ large of Kalt's finding that arguments must be simple to be effective? Or, is it the "free rider" principle yet again? A problem with accepting the latter perspective arises insofar as significant user groups have not objected to protection that will raise their costs.[12] The case is certainly made more effectively in broad international agreements (when export interests can support broad-based reciprocal liberalization) than in circumstances in which specific industries hold sway.

Assessing the role of economic ideas as constraints on, or enabling mechanisms for, politicians' decisions is clearly difficult. Nonetheless, it is at least a plausible hypothesis that understanding how these simple ideas are formed in the public mind plays a role in circumscribing the political process of protection seeking and granting.

9.2.3 The Role of Political Strength

For economists, some of the important lessons emerge from conclusions regarding the determinants of protection. The Staiger-Wolak findings, the analysis of decisions regarding lumber, the determinants of influence in affecting NAFTA, and, indeed, all the other studies point strongly to the influence of political strength (generally unrelated to considerations of static or dynamic

---

11. For policy purposes, the literature is far more ambiguous than its interpretation: while intervention may be called for, it might be an export or import subsidy, as well as an import duty. But in popular discussion, the imperfect competition literature has been interpreted to sanction protectionist measures.

12. It is often alleged that protection exists because producer interests are stronger than consumer interests (which are more diffuse). A difficulty with this argument is that export interests (which should surely support free trade) are at least as concentrated as import-competing interests.

efficiency and even to income distribution arguments often heard) as a major determinant of protection. This appears to be so even for the administered protection processes, which are in theory governed by legal considerations set out in law.[13]

From the perspective of politicians and policymakers, this conclusion is hardly surprising. From the viewpoint of the public interest, however, it raises significant questions as to the feasibility of devising institutions or mechanisms that can differentiate between those seeking protection out of narrow self-interest and those for whom industrial protection might be warranted because of the sorts of considerations to which the "new trade theory" points. For economists concerned with framing policy, therefore, questions as to the capacity of the political process to be constrained in ways that enable trade policy to respond to broader interests must be addressed. That leads immediately to another phenomenon that recurred in the various studies.

9.2.4   The Role of Institutions as Constraints

It is not enough to conclude that protection was granted in certain instances. One can also ask why the level of protection granted was not higher, why protection was not there before, why protection is sometimes phased out, and why some industries are not protected while others are.

Orden notes that the context for the pulling and tugging for special treatment in the NAFTA agreement among agricultural representatives was constrained by the initial ground rules: all agricultural protection between Mexico and the United States was to be phased out—the only question was how long it would take.[14]

Likewise, the Uruguay Round agreement schedules the phasing out of the MFA. This probably could not have been achieved as a stand-alone policy. However, in the context of the overall negotiations, it was accepted despite political resistance, albeit over a fairly long time frame with end loading so that most of the bite is postponed.

In the case of wheat, the fact that the EEP was declared budget neutral was critical to its initial implementation and continuation. The argument that it was budget neutral was based on the fact that the overall farm bill provides for price supports for wheat: to the extent that wheat is exported, the cost of purchasing and storing wheat diminishes. When the 1995 farm bill is considered, questions will arise concerning this budget neutrality, and hence the future of EEP may be doubtful: again, an institutional constraint of some importance.

---

13. But the law itself permits the ITC only to consider factors *within the industry* in determining outcomes: from the viewpoint of economic theory, evaluation should surely take into account the effects on the American economy as a whole, and not simply on the industry receiving protection.

14. In the final dealing, several significant changes were made. For example, high-fructose corn syrup was to be counted against Mexico's eligibility to export to the United States—a huge increase in the implicit protection to American producers. However, the basic constraint remained present, even if occasionally marginally bent.

It seems clear that trade policy made on a one-off basis toward individual sectors is much more susceptible and sensitive to pressures from the interest groups seeking protection. The role of institutions may well be to devise mechanisms that force the political process to recognize the trade-offs and economic costs of protection on an across-the-board basis.[15] Further research on the role of the GATT, other institutional constraints, and how they may be designed to achieve outcomes generally agreed to be in the public interest is clearly warranted.

9.2.5   Does Protection Help the Protected Industry?

There has been protection for textiles and apparel since the mid-1950s. The first such measure was termed the Short Term Arrangement and covered only imports from Japan. Protection has increased over the years, both by increased coverage of the MFA to other countries and products, as already noted, and through more "bite" in the individual quotas. Despite that, the industry has chronically complained that protection was "inadequate" and did not "help enough." Increasing restrictiveness, especially in the late 1980s, has not stemmed protests from the industry. Moreover, some of those who initially sought protection (New England textile producers, e.g.) quite clearly lost from it (since cotton, primarily produced in the South, was covered while wool, made in New England, was not).

Protection for automobiles (also in the form of VERs) does not appear to have reversed the fortunes of the U.S. automobile industry: Nelson concludes that competition was the important stimulant.[16] The same questions can be raised about the semiconductor agreement, although industry representatives believe that they were assisted by the agreement. For steel, a technological change—the emergence of the minimills—seems to have been important in affecting the industry:[17]it is questionable how much the old integrated mills benefited from VERs on steel imports.

In agriculture, Gardner believes that the EEP arguably did little for wheat growers and certainly did less than their enthusiastic support for the program suggests they believed that it would. Sugar producers have lost half of the caloric sweetener market to corn syrup as a result of their high domestic price.

To be sure, in these instances, there may have been a timing issue involved: protected domestic producers often obtain substantial short-term rents. In some cases, too, the timing of protection may have facilitated adjustment. For example, the automobile protection may have provided breathing space (once the

---

15. Of course, both sides must be willing to do this, as Orden's contrast of the NAFTA agricultural outcomes with Mexico and Canada highlight.

16. See Scherer (1992, 188–89). Scherer notes that firms in general react more "passively" to foreign competition when trade barriers are in place and, because of that, have less satisfactory performance.

17. There also appears to be a role of ideas here: the opposition of minimills to protection is based partly on support for free trade.

VERs became binding) for the U.S. industry to lower costs.[18] For Big Steel, higher prices may have relieved pain in the short run, even though they also made minimills more profitable and thus encouraged their more rapid expansion. For semiconductors, the temporary reprieve may have been valuable,[19] despite the longer-term consequences.[20] If that is so, it would imply that protection can help an industry as a short-term palliative, but at the cost of the industry's fortunes in the longer run.

Among the protected industries studied in the NBER project, then, there is only one instance in which the author believes that U.S. producers unequivocally benefited: lumber. Ironically, he also believes that the Canadian pricing policies to which the producers had objected had arguably not changed supply, so that protection in fact raised the price in the United States and domestic producers gained.[21] In all the other cases, it cannot be persuasively argued that the protection accorded an industry was important in turning its fortunes around or in benefiting it over the longer term.[22]

This raises important questions about the efficacy of protectionist trade policies, even in assisting the industries that seek protection. To the extent that trade barriers give producers false assurances, they may indeed be counterproductive from the industry's perspective in the long run.

9.2.6 There Will Be Protection When the Industry Is Unanimous

Perhaps the most intriguing finding arising from the studies and also from discussions with policymakers concerns the reluctance of using industries to oppose protection, and the general belief that protection will be granted when the industry is unanimous in supporting it.[23]

The most effective defense against protection would appear to be a division within the industry. The most vivid example of this among the NBER cases is steel, for which prospects of protection diminished substantially after the owners of minimills opposed it. For semiconductors as well, industry unanimity

18. In fact, however, the U.S. industry does not appear to have undergone its effective productivity improvement program until the late 1980s when the reality of permanent foreign competitive pressures became clear.

19. The antidumping finding only really helped two firms: Micron and Texas Instruments; by the time it came into effect, no one else was producing. Even then, of course, gains had to be offset against the costs to user industries (the computer assembly industry moved offshore) and the entry of third parties, notably Koreans.

20. It is possible, of course, that the rents collected by Japanese producers may have led to their failure to pursue an increased market share. To that extent, the agreement may have been valuable in the longer term.

21. Even then, it must be recognized that in the longer term, builders would substitute other materials for lumber, thus reducing the size of the industry.

22. The NAFTA agreement is only now going into effect, and therefore the question of the benefits to different agricultural groups cannot be fully addressed. Preliminary data indicate an increase in trade, with U.S. agricultural exporters among those gaining.

23. This regularity was noted by several of the "witnesses" when participants in the projects met with policymakers in Washington, D.C., in July 1993. The same point has been made by Milner (1988).

was not achieved prior to the mid-1980s: until that time, the industry's efforts to obtain protection had failed. In NAFTA, commodity divisions (among grains) and regional divisions (among fruits and vegetables) limited the effectiveness of some sectors in the NAFTA negotiations; sugar was unanimous and successful in retaining protection. Evidence from other sources and all analysts' accounts point to the same conclusion.

This raises a number of interesting, and unanswered, questions. Why, for example, did the auto industry—a major steel user and itself in difficulty—not oppose steel VERs in the early 1980s? Why did it take until the late 1980s for producers of agricultural machinery finally to oppose continued protection for steel, as William Lane's commentary documents? And, to cite another example, why do apparel makers side *with* textile manufacturers in seeking protection when, as using industries, their interests in textile protection would appear to diverge?[24]

When policymakers were queried in this regard at the project meeting in Washington, responses generally focused on a "gentleman's agreement," or understanding, that each industry would not protest others' protection, but rather seek its own (implicitly, unopposed). If such is the case, questions arise as to how such tacit understandings came about. If there are not such implicit understandings, the puzzle remains as to why opposition is not more frequently voiced.

9.2.7   Good Lobbying and Organization Do Matter

Short-term economic interests generally determine the side on which various interest groups fall in pressuring for or against protection. However, some groups are better organized, or more readily organized, than others. The correlation between the magnitude of economic interests and the effectiveness of organized lobbying efforts does not appear strong. Some groups that might benefit from protection (or its removal) do not appear well organized, while others are extremely effective.

Finger and Harrison point to the well-organized efforts of the textile and apparel groups as a key factor in their achieving as much protection as they in fact receive. Moore's chapter and Lane's discussion show the importance of effective organization and lobbying in seeking and maintaining (and opposing) protection.[25]

Protection for the semiconductor industry appears to have been another in-

---

24. Here, of course, a possible answer might be that the two industries together form a more effective lobby that can achieve more than either could separately, and that the joint gains exceed the potential if each goes it alone. Similar issues arise in agriculture, where the sectors have to weigh their mutual versus specific interests. In NAFTA, corn growers did not object to sugar provisions that would reduce the likelihood of Mexico using corn sweeteners but drew the line if a sugar deal affected the direct access to the Mexican market they had negotiated.

25. The needed degree of effectiveness is clearly greater for achieving initial protection than for perpetuating it. Even when protection is perpetuated, however, it can be restrictive to varying

stance in which a well-organized industry group was crucial to the achievement of protection. Once opposition from users (the personal computer assemblers, who had to compete with foreign assemblers) formed, the degree to which the industry could sustain protection diminished.

In this regard, however, perhaps the most interesting and telling cases among the studies are those concerning agriculture: maneuvering regarding the timetable for reduced protection to agriculture under Mexican entry into NAFTA was heavily influenced by the pressures that different producer groups were able to bring to bear. Likewise, the wheat growers were able to organize to achieve the EEP in ways that other farm groups apparently were not.

What determines whether a particular organization is effective ex ante (as opposed to the ex post observation that it achieved its purpose) is a difficult question. The steel and auto industries were highly concentrated; textiles and apparel are widespread and diffuse; there are a large number of wheat farmers; there are few sugar producers. Yet all of these are "effective" in achieving protection.

One hypothesis is that individuals, and organizational history, do matter in determining organizational effectiveness. If so, there are elements of "accident," entrepreneurship, or "fortune" in affecting levels of protection. Understanding why organizations are effective is important, however, not only to understand why some are more successful than others but also because such insights may point to institutional designs and other mechanisms that would constrain trade policy to function less in response to individual industries and more in response to across-the-board considerations than it apparently does under existing arrangements.

9.2.8   Past Protection Matters

The evidence from these studies, and elsewhere, strongly suggests that the existence of a protectionist instrument—VER, EEP, sugar quota, or whatever—in the past strongly increases the ease with which protection may be obtained today. Stated otherwise, the expected level of protection in the future is higher, for the same industry characteristics: (1) if the industry received protection in the past and (2) the higher protection was in the past.

Clearly, each round of MFA negotiations started with the preceding level as a base: much of the industry's lobbying efforts were directed to achieving heightened protection. Likewise, Gardner points to the ease with which the wheat growers were enabled to achieve a renewal of EEP, contrasted with the initial barrier to obtaining it. A semiconductor agreement with Japan in 1991 was far easier to obtain because there had been one in 1986. The history of protection for steel in the 1970s made it easier for the industry to persuade the U.S. administration to negotiate again.

---

degrees. A more effective lobby will, presumably, achieve greater restrictiveness than a less effective one.

9.3 An Agenda for Further Research

Protectionism, and the pressures that lead to it, is much better understood than it was several decades ago. Focus in the studies contained in this volume has been on the determinants and evolution of protection in individual industries. In some of those industries—notably automobiles and steel—protection once obtained was nonetheless subsequently lost. It is not clear that protectionist pressures are, overall, winning, but it is certainly the case that better understanding of the institutions and mechanisms which permit across-the-board considerations to decide protection, rather than case-by-case decisions, may yield better decision making in the future than has occurred in the past.

Each of these eight key findings is really a tentative hypothesis and an agenda for future research. Better understanding would be desirable in and of itself but would also be useful to inform the policy process.

Some issues—such as the reasons for unwillingness of users to oppose protection for their suppliers—may require multidisciplinary research. Others bring in questions from the new institutional economics. Nonetheless, taken together, they form a challenging agenda for further exploration into the political economy of U.S. trade policy and protection.

It seems likely that there are also interrelationships among the eight hypotheses. Ideas may influence politicians and also affect the way in which constraints affect activities. Industry unanimity may be desirable in part because the general ideas of economists regarding economically efficient policies have not sufficiently pervaded the body politic. And, if the hypothesis that protection provides little, if any, long-term benefit to most industries is correct, further research probing that hypothesis could significantly affect the degree of protection seeking.

Further understanding of those interrelationships, however, probably must await advances in understanding of each of them individually. It is to be hoped that the readers of this volume will be inspired to pursue these, and other investigations, in the hope that in the future U.S. trade policy determination can be more adequately understood.

What does emerge clearly from the studies in this volume, as well as earlier work on protection, is that the processes and mechanisms by which protection forms and levels are determined bring about results that are often very costly. Questions concerning the efficacy of protection in directly improving an industry's fortunes become even more pressing when it is recognized that the indirect negative effects are not adequately taken into account. Conversely, the economic costs of failing to examine indirect effects of protection loom larger if questions arise concerning the sign and magnitude of direct effects.

When consideration is further given to the proposition that using industries that may be harmed by protection are reluctant to protest, economic efficiency may be further diminished when a unanimous industry seeks protection as a perceived means of alleviating its problems. When effective organization and political clout is then important in determining outcomes, there is a further delinking of economic efficiency from the granting of protection.

Add to these considerations concerns as to the fairness of the administered protection laws, and it seems clear that considerable further analysis is called for as to the degree to which current U.S. trade policy achieves objectives that are in the interest of the American people and economic efficiency.

References

Becker, Gary S. 1983. A theory of competition among pressure groups for political influence. *Quarterly Journal of Economics* 98 (3): 371–400.

Boltuck, Richard, and Robert E. Litan, eds. 1991. *Down in the dumps: Administration of the unfair trade laws.* Washington, D.C.: Brookings Institution.

Finger, M., H. K. Hall, and D. Nelson. 1982. The political economy of administered protection. *American Economic Review* 72 (3): 452–66.

Goldin, I., O. Knudsen, and D. van der Mensbrugghe. 1993. Trade liberalization: Global economic implications. Washington, D.C., and Paris: World Bank and Organisation for Economic Co-operation and Development.

Hufbauer, Gary C., and Kimberley Elliott. 1994. *Measuring the costs of protection in the United States.* Washington, D.C.: Institute for International Economics.

Irwin, Douglas A. 1994. *Managed trade: The case against import targets.* Washington, D.C.: American Enterprise Institute.

Isard, Peter. 1973. Employment impacts of textile imports and investment: A vintage-capital model. *American Economic Review* 63 (3): 402–16.

Lewis, Jeffrey D., S. Robinson, and Z. Wang. 1994. Beyond the Uruguay Round: The implications of an Asian free trade area. Washington, D.C.: World Bank.

Milner, Helen. 1988. *Resisting protectionism: Global industries and the politics of international trade.* Princeton, N.J.: Princeton University Press.

Nguyen, T. T., C. Perroni, and R. M. Wigle. 1993. An evaluation of the draft final act of the Uruguay Round. *Economic Journal* 103: 1540–58.

Scherer, F. M. 1992. *International high-technology competition.* Cambridge: Harvard University Press.

Contributors

Keith B. Anderson
Bureau of Economics
Federal Trade Commission
Washington, DC 20580

Robert E. Baldwin
Department of Economics
Social Science Building 6462
University of Wisconsin-Madison
1180 Observatory Drive
Madison, WI 53706

Randi Boorstein
Federal Trade Commission
6th and Pennsylvania Avenue NW
Room 5628
Washington, DC 20580

Anne E. Brunsdale
412 Independence Avenue SE
Washington, DC 20003

Geoffrey Carliner
NBER
1050 Massachusetts Avenue
Cambridge, MA 02138

Richard N. Cooper
Department of Economics
Harvard University
Center for International Affairs
Cambridge, MA 02138

I. M. Destler
School of Public Affairs
University of Maryland
College Park, MD 20742

Andrew R. Dick
Department of Economics
University of California, Los Angeles
405 Hilgard Avenue
Los Angeles, CA 90024

J. Michael Finger
The World Bank
Room R2–015
1818 H Street NW
Washington, DC 20433

Bruce L. Gardner
Department of Agricultural and Resource
   Economics
University of Maryland
College Park, MD 20742

Ann Harrison
Graduate School of Business
Columbia University
Office 615 Uris Hall
New York, NY 10027

Douglas A. Irwin
Graduate School of Business
University of Chicago
1101 East 58th Street
Chicago, IL 60637

Joseph P. Kalt
Kennedy School of Government
79 JFK Street
Harvard University
Cambridge, MA 02138

Kala Krishna
Department of Economics
Pennsylvania State University
State College, PA 16802

Anne O. Krueger
Department of Economics
Stanford University
Stanford, CA 94305

William C. Lane
Caterpillar, Inc.
818 Connecticut Avenue NW
Suite 600
Washington, DC 20006

James R. Markusen
Department of Economics
University of Colorado
Boulder, CO 80309

Michael O. Moore
Department of Economics
George Washington University
Washington, DC 20052

Michael H. Moskow
Federal Reserve Bank of Chicago
230 South LaSalle Street
Chicago, IL 60604

Douglas R. Nelson
Department of Economics
Tilton Hall
Tulane University
New Orleans, LA 70118

David Orden
Virginia Polytechnic Institute and State
    University
Department of Agricultural and Applied
    Economics
Hutcheson Hall
Blacksburg, VA 24061

Robert Paarlberg
Department of Political Science
Wellesley College
Wellesley, MA 02181

Robert W. Staiger
Department of Economics
University of Wisconsin-Madison
1180 Observatory Drive
Madison, WI 53706

Frank A. Wolak
Department of Economics
Stanford University
Stanford, CA 94305

Name Index

Abbott, P. C., 328
Abernathy, W., 150, 171, 172f
Abowd, John, 223f, 226f, 227f, 233, 394
Ackerman, Karen Z., 305n9, 310, 318, 322
Adams, Walter, 74, 78n1, 92, 133n1, 162n42, 175n65
Aggarwal, Vinod K., 211–12, 217, 218, 219
Alston, Julian M., 324
American Iron and Steel Institute (AISI), 78, 110–11
Anderson, James E., 391n5
Anderson, Keith B., 89n16, 419, 421n11
Art, Andrew B., 326n30
Askew, Reuben, 137

Bailey, Kenneth W., 332n1
Baker, James, 37, 143
Baldrige, Malcolm, 103
Baldwin, Richard E., 27
Baldwin, Robert E., 67, 198, 199
Ball, George W., 220
Barnett, Donald F., 78, 80
Barr, James C., 349
Bates, R., 263n2
Baucus, Max, 183
Bauer, Raymond A., 246, 250
Bauge, Kenneth L., 205, 206, 211
Becker, Gary S., 263n1, 264n3, 267, 423n1
Benedict, J. G., 228
Benedict, Murray R., 291n1, 292
Bentsen, Lloyd, 139
Bergsten, C. Fred, 60, 147n19
Berliner, D., 145

Berndt, E., 162n42
Bhagwati, Jagdish, 37n33, 157n33
Bieber, Owen, 165, 184
Block, John, 301
Blomqvist, A., 174n64
Boltuck, Richard, 89–90n17, 403n9, 432n6
Bonior, David, 369
Bonnen, James, 292
Bork, Robert H., 167
Boyle, S., 162n42
Brandis, R. Buford, 209, 210, 212, 213, 215n22, 221, 222
Branson, W., 147n19
Bresnahan, T., 151n26, 162n42
Brock, J., 133n1, 162n42, 175n65
Brock, William, 3, 32, 34, 41, 103, 144
Brooks, H. G., 318
Browne, W. P., 292
Brunsdale, Anne, 48
Bryan, M., 152n28
Bush, George, 108–9, 112, 118, 374

Campbell, J., 159n36
Carlson, R., 174n64
Carter, C. A., 324
Caves, R. E., 199
Chamberlain, G., 241n29
Chambers, Robert G., 317
Chiang, J., 162n42
Choate, Pat, 369
Citrin, D., 147n20
Clark, K., 150
Clifton, E., 147n20

447

Subject Index

AAA. *See* Agricultural Adjustment Act, 1933 (AAA)

Acreage reduction programs (ARPs), 294–95, 323, 332

AD. *See* Antidumping

Additionality, 317–21

Administered protection: congressional mechanisms for, 200, 207; costs of pursuing, 87–88; defined, 2n4; executive discretion, 197; in 1930s legislation, 201–6; sought by U.S. auto industry, 134–46; used by U.S. textile industry, 198, 248. *See also* Antidumping laws; Countervailing duties (CVDs)

AFBF. *See* American Farm Bureau Federation (AFBF)

Agreements, multilateral: Kennedy administration negotiation of textile, 220–22; Short Term and Long Term Arrangements on Cotton Textiles, 214–18; steel industry, 115–16, 131–32

Agricultural Adjustment Act, 1933 (AAA): import quotas under section 22 amendment (1935), 338–40; interest group support for section 22 import quotas, 367–68; interpretations of section 22 amendment (1935), 209–10, 294; provisions related to tariffs in, 206; U.S. textile industry use of (1959, 1961), 212–13, 248

Agricultural sector: economic performance at beginning of NAFTA negotiations, 338–45; economic problems (1980s), 295–301; interest group positions in

NAFTA debates, 345–55, 360–69; NAFTA debate concessions to, 369–74; NAFTA provisions for, 355–60, 375–81; NAFTA-related concessions to, 369–72; predicted benefits from NAFTA trade, 357–60

Agricultural Trade and Development Act, 1954 (P.L. 480), 293, 309

Agriculture Act (1948), 294

Agriculture Act (1956): amended section 204 provisions related to MFA, 218–19; section 204 amendment to limit textile imports (1962), 250–51; section 204 presidential power to limit textile imports, 209

Agriculture and Food Act (1981), 296, 298, 302

American Corn Growers Association (ACGA), 350, 354

American Cotton Manufacturers Institute (ACMI), 249

American Electronics Association (AEA), 23–24, 43

American Farm Bureau Federation (AFBF), 347–48, 354, 360, 365–66

American Textile Manufacturers Institute (ATMI), 249, 255, 257–59

Antidumping actions: complaint of U.S. semiconductor industry (1985), 44–45; Japanese response to U.S. (1985), 45; against South Korean semiconductor industry, 60–61; U.S. semiconductor industry (1985), 44–46

Antidumping laws: econometric model of uses